PROPERTY TAX IN ASIA

PROPERTY TAX IN ASIA

Policy and Practice

Edited by

William McCluskey, Roy Bahl, and Riël Franzsen

Cambridge, Massachusetts

ISBN: 978-1-55844-423-2 (paper)
ISBN: 978-1-55844-426-3 (epub)
Library of Congress Control Number: 2022941513

Composed in Janson by Westchester Publishing Services in Danbury, Connecticut.
Printed and bound by Books International in Dulles, Virginia.
♲ The paper is acid-free, FSC certified, 30 percent post-consumer recycled fiber.

MANUFACTURED IN THE UNITED STATES OF AMERICA

Contents

List of Illustrations, Tables, and Boxes   ix

Foreword   xv
SALLY WALLACE

Preface   xvii

PART 1 Comparative Analysis

1   **Context and Comparative Analysis**   3
    ROY BAHL, WILLIAM MCCLUSKEY, RIËL FRANZSEN,
    AND WENJING LI

2   **Current Policies and Practices**   19
    ROY BAHL, WILLIAM MCCLUSKEY, AND RIËL FRANZSEN

3   **Lessons Learned and Prospects for Reform**   89
    ROY BAHL, WILLIAM MCCLUSKEY, AND RIËL FRANZSEN

PART 2 Case Studies

4   **China: An Evolving Property Tax**   109
    ZHI LIU

5   Hong Kong: A Well-Administered Property
    Tax System   139
    MIMI BROWN

6   India: A Macro View of the Property
    Tax System and Insights into Delhi's System   172
    OM PRAKASH MATHUR

7   Indonesia: Devolution of the Property Tax   199
    RIATU MARIATUL QIBTHIYYAH

8   Japan: Challenges to a Mature Property Tax System   225
    ANDREW DEWIT

9   Republic of Korea: A Unique Two-Tier System of Land and
    Property Taxation   268
    YOUNGHOON RO

10 Malaysia: Property and Land Taxes in a
    Federal System   299
    DZURLLKANIAN ZULKARNAIN DAUD AND
    SALFARINA SAMSUDIN

11 Pakistan: Rebuilding the Tax Base   321
    RAJUL AWASTHI

12 Philippines: Policy, Administration, and
    Revenue Mobilization   351
    NIÑO RAYMOND B. ALVINA

13 Singapore: A Policy Strategy for Land and
    Property Taxation   399
    LAY CHENG JASMINE LIM AND NIGEL WOODS

14 Taiwan: Implementation of a Split-Rate Property Tax   425
    TZU-CHIN LIN AND WEN-CHIEH WU

15 Thailand: A Reform of the Property Tax   445
    DUANGMANEE LAOVAKUL

16 Vietnam: A Property Tax System in Transition   472
    TRUONG BA TUAN

List of Contributors   507

Index   511

About the Lincoln Institute of Land Policy   531

Illustrations, Tables, and Boxes

Figure 1.1   Relationship Between Income Levels and Effective Property
              Tax Rates   13
Figure 4.1   Local General Budgetary Revenues and Land Concession
              Revenues, 2001–2019   120
Figure 4.2   China's Land-Based Finance Mechanism   121
Figure 4.3   Chinese National Real Land Price Index, 35 Markets,
              Constant   123
Figure 7.1   Policies and Regulations on Property Tax in Indonesia   200
Figure 7.2   Property Tax Revenues by Type (as % of total property taxes)   203
Box Figure 7.1 DKI Jakarta Realized and Target Revenues from Urban
              and Rural Property Taxes   207
Figure 7.3   Administration of Urban and Rural Property Taxes   213
Figure 7.4   Administration of Property Transfer Tax   214
Figure 7.5   Percentage of Arrears Collection by Central Government,
              2010–2014   216
Figure 7.6   Ratio of Urban and Rural Property Tax Arrears to Revenues,
              2015–2018   217
Figure 8.1   Ratio of National and Subnational Taxes, FY 2017   226
Figure 8.2   Principal Municipal Tax Revenues, FY 2017   227
Figure 8.3   Japan's Three Tiers of Government   230
Figure 9.1   Classification of Property-Related Taxes in Korea   270
Figure 9.2   Property and Land (Real Estate) Tax as Percentage of
              Total Tax Revenue for Selected OECD Jurisdictions   271
Figure 9.3   Recurrent Taxes on Real Estate   271
Figure 9.4   Housing Market Trends in Seoul and Korea: Housing
              Composite Price Index (November 2017 = 100)   280
Figure 10.1   Application Process for Exemption from or Reduction
              of Property Tax   308

Figure 12.1 Composition of Annual Regular Income of LGUs, FY 2020   383
Figure 12.2 Share of Local Tax Revenue Sources, 1972–2020   384
Figure 12.3 Real Property Tax to GDP Ratio, 1972–2020   384
Figure 13.1 Housing Stock, 2000–2020   406
Figure 13.2 Number of Properties and Property Tax Revenue
Collected, 2010–2019   414
Figure 13.3 Inland Revenue Authority of Singapore Organizational
Structure   417

Table 1.1   Property Tax Revenues and Key Data in Asian Jurisdictions   6
Table 1.2   Average Levels of Property Taxation in Asia and Other Regions   11
Table 1.3   Multiple Regression Analysis of the Determinants of
Variations in Property Tax Revenues   15
Table 2.1   Recurrent Property Taxes and Tax Bases, by Jurisdiction   23
Table 2.2   Vacant Land and Underused Properties   35
Table 2.3   Application of Automated Mass Valuation   41
Table 2.4   Frequency of Revaluations   45
Table 2.5   Objection and Appeal Systems   51
Table 2.6   Responsibility for Valuation   53
Table 2.7   Property Transfer Taxes and Other Fees and Charges on Land   62
Table 2.8   Features Affecting Distribution of Property Tax Burdens   74
Table 2.9   Features Affecting Land Use and Property Markets   80
Table 3.1   Projected City Growth from 2018 and 2030   94
Table 3.2   Revenue Division Between Recurrent and All Other Property
and Land Tax Revenues   98
Table 4.1   Government Revenues, 2019 (RMB trillion)   111
Table 4.2   Tax Revenues by Year, 1995–2019   112
Table 4.3   Revenues from Five Taxes on Real Estate Properties,
2013–2019 (RMB billion)   115
Table 4.4   Individual Tax Revenues, 2013–2018 (RMB billion)   125
Table 4.5   Property Tax Experiments in Shanghai and Chongqing   128
Table 5.1   Valuation List: Distribution of Assessments and Ratable
Values by Category as of April 1, 2020   149
Table 5.2   Proposals, Objections, and Appeals, 2015/2016–2019/2020   152
Table 5.3   Arrears Amount as a Percentage of Annual Demands   158
Table 5.4   Ad Valorem Duty for First-Time Home Buyers   161
Table 5.5   General Revaluation Results   164
Table 5.6   Rates Concessions Since 2014/2015   165
Table 5.7   Number of Rating Assessments and Rates Contributions to
Government Operating Revenue and GDP   167
Table 5.8   Property Tax Contributions to Government Operating
Revenue Compared with Capital Revenues from Sales of
Government Land (HKD million)   169
Table 6.1   Tax Revenues Across Governmental Tiers as % of Total
Revenues   176

Table 6.2	Structure of Municipal Revenues	176
Table 6.3	Fiscal Role of Property Taxes, FY 2017–2018	180
Table 6.4	Interstate Variation in Property Tax Revenues	182
Table 6.5	Demographic, Economic, and Fiscal Profile of Delhi	184
Table 6.6	Obligatory and Discretionary Taxes: Local Governments in Delhi	186
Table 6.7	Delhi's Property Tax Revenues, FY 2015–2016	190
Table 6.8	Stamp Duties of All States	192
Table 6.9	NCT of Delhi Revenues from Stamp Duty	193
Table 6.10	Local (Urban) Government Revenues from Stamp Duty	194
Table 7.1	Property Tax Revenues by Type (selected measures)	202
Table 7.2	Property Taxes in DKI Jakarta Province (selected measures)	204
Table 8.1	Municipal Fragmentation in Japan and OECD Member States, 2018	232
Table 8.2	Real GDP and Property Tax Revenues, 2008–2018	233
Table 8.3	FAT Revenues and Expenditures, 2008–2017	234
Table 8.4	Japan FAT Categories and Revenue, 2008–2018 (JPY trillion)	236
Table 8.5	Total Value of FAT Exemptions, by Category, 2015	237
Table 8.6	FAT Characteristics, FY 2018	238
Table 8.7	FAT Rates by Municipal Population, 2018	239
Table 8.8	CPT Characteristics, FY 2018	240
Table 8.9	CPT Rates, FY 2015	240
Table 8.10	Distribution of Lands, 2012	242
Table 8.11	Special Measures for Tokyo Residential Land, FY 2019	247
Table 8.12	Tokyo's Property Tax Revenues, 2008–2018	254
Table 8.13	Tokyo's CPT Revenues, 2008–2018	255
Table 9.1	General Aggregate Land Taxation Rate of Local Property Tax (KRW thousand)	273
Table 9.2	Special Aggregate Land Taxation Rate of Local Property Tax (KRW thousand)	273
Table 9.3	Fixed-Rate Taxation on Land under Local Property Tax	274
Table 9.4	Local Property Tax Rate on Houses	274
Table 9.5	Local Resource and Public Facility Tax (KRW thousand)	275
Table 9.6	Assessment Ratios for Local Property Tax and Gross Real Estate Tax (GRET)	277
Table 9.7	General Aggregate Land Taxation Rate of GRET (KRW thousand)	281
Table 9.8	Special Aggregate Land Taxation Rate of GRET (KRW thousand)	282
Table 9.9	GRET Housing Taxation Rate, Fewer Than Three Houses (KRW thousand)	282
Table 9.10	GRET Housing Taxation Rate, Ownership of Three or More Houses (KRW thousand)	282
Table 9.11	Decomposition of Total Property Taxes in Local and Central Levies	284

Table 9.12 Property Transfer Tax Rates for Housing and Land (%)   286
Table 9.13 Revenue Performance of Property and Land Taxes   289
Table 9.14 Seoul Metropolitan Government Local Tax Revenue
            Budget, 2018 and 2019   290
Table 9.15 Tax Collection by Local Governments and Sources, 2017
            (KRW 100 million)   291
Table 10.1 Local Governments in Malaysia   300
Table 10.2 Basic Features of Land and Property Taxes   302
Table 10.3 Stamp Duty for Real Estate Transactions, 2020   303
Table 10.4 Real Property Gains Tax Rates, 2020   304
Table 10.5 Quit Rent Rates for Residential, Commercial, and Industrial
            Land in Kuala Lumpur   304
Table 10.6 Property Tax Bases Adopted by Local Governments   306
Table 10.7 Property Tax Rates Imposed by Local Governments   307
Table 10.8 Taxable Properties in Kuala Lumpur   311
Table 10.9 Property Tax Rate Imposed by Kuala Lumpur City Council   312
Table 10.10 Annual Value, Revenue, and Capping for the Revaluation
            of January 1, 2014   313
Table 10.11 Property Tax Revenue in Kuala Lumpur   313
Table 10.12 Total Property Tax Revenue and Arrears, 2016–2018   314
Table 10.13 Tax Exemption by Category, 2018   314
Table 10.14 Property Transfer Tax as Percentage of Total Government
            Tax and GDP, 2019   315
Table 10.15 Property Transfer Taxes as Percentage of GDP in Kuala
            Lumpur, 2019   315
Table 11.1 Provincial Economy and Disparity, 2017   322
Table 11.2 Provincial Own-Tax Revenue as % of Total Revenue,
            2019–2020   323
Table 11.3 Overview of Federal and Provincial Property-Related Taxes   326
Table 11.4 Provincial Tax Revenue Totals   329
Table 11.5 Provincial Property Tax Revenues   330
Table 11.6 Punjab's Residential Property Valuation Assessment
            Table for Urban Immoveable Property Tax (UIPT), July 1, 2021   331
Table 11.7 Punjab's Commercial Property Valuation Assessment
            Table for Urban Immoveable Property Tax (UIPT), July 1, 2021   332
Table 11.8 Property Transfer Taxes   341
Table 12.1 Key Taxing Powers by Level of Government   352
Table 12.2 Growth of Internal Revenue Allotment of LGUs, 2018–2020   353
Table 12.3 Share of LGUs' Annual Regular Income (ARI) and
            Internal Revenue Allotment (IRA)   354
Table 12.4 Share of LGUs' Locally Sourced Revenues (LSR) to
            Annual Regular Income (ARI)   354
Table 12.5 Individual Local Taxes as % of Total Local Income   356
Table 12.6 Accrual, Payment, and Sharing Arrangements of Local
            Property-Related Taxes   358

Table 12.7   Real Property Tax Assessment Levels on Land and Machinery   359
Table 12.8   Schedule of Assessment Levels for Buildings and Other
             Structures   360
Table 12.9   LGU Compliance in Property Revaluation, 2010–2020   374
Table 12.10 Property Tax Revenue from Real Property Units (RPUs)
             of Metro Manila Cities, FY 2018   377
Table 12.11 LGU Collection of Recurrent Property Taxes   379
Table 12.12 LGUs' Fiscal Performance Pre- and Post-LGC of 1991   381
Table 12.13 Real Property Tax and Special Education Fund Profile,
             FY 2016–2018   382
Table 12.14 Overall Performance of Local Property-Related Taxes   385
Table 12.15 Overall Performance of National Property-Related Taxes   386
Table 13.1   Principal Laws and Statutory Boards Governing
             Real Estate   403
Table 13.2   Fiscal Position for FY 2017–2019   404
Table 13.3   Household Tenancy   406
Table 13.4   Stamp Duty Income, 2017–2019   409
Table 13.5   Stamp Duty Income from Private Residential Properties,
             2017–2019   410
Table 13.6   Tax Rates for Non-Owner- and Owner-Occupied Residential
             Properties   413
Table 13.7   Breakdown of Property Tax, 2010 and 2019   415
Table 14.1   Land Value Tax Rates 2019   427
Table 14.2   Building Tax Rates, Since 2014   428
Table 14.3   Land Value Increment Tax Rates   429
Table 14.4   Integrated Real Estate Income Tax Rates   430
Table 14.5   Components of Property Tax Revenues   432
Table 14.6   Property Holding Tax Revenues for Major Metropolitan
             Cities, 2020   433
Table 14.7   Property Taxes Relative to Total Local Government
             Tax Revenue in Taipei City, 2020   433
Table 14.8   Major Property Taxes in Taipei City (as % of property
             tax revenue)   434
Table 15.1   Local Governments   447
Table 15.2   Local-Government (LG) Revenue Structure (%), 2011–2020   448
Table 15.3   Sources of Local-Government Revenue   450
Table 15.4   Building and Land Tax Revenue as a Percentage of GDP,
             All Tax Revenue, and Local-Government Revenue, 2012–2019   456
Table 15.5   Local Development Tax Revenue as a Percentage of GDP,
             All Tax Revenue, and Local-Government Revenue, 2012–2019   457
Table 15.6   Property and Land Tax Revenue as a Percentage of GDP,
             Local-Government Revenue, and All Tax Revenue, 2012–2020   458
Table 15.7   Land and Building Tax Rates per Usage   463
Table 15.8   Revenue from Property-Related Taxes and Fees, Selected
             Budget Years   467

Table 16.1   Government Revenue from Selected Taxes (as % of
                   nominal GDP)   475
Table 16.2   Government Tax Revenue Mix in Vietnam (% of total)   475
Table 16.3   Nonagricultural Land Use Tax Rates   481
Table 16.4   Hanoi's Revenue and Nonagricultural Land Use Tax, 2016   482
Table 16.5   Land- and Property-Related Revenue   488
Table 16.6   Land- and Property-Related Revenue by Item
                   (% nominal GDP)   490
Table 16.7   Structure of Land- and Property-Related Revenue
                   (% of total)   490

Box 1.1   Data Used for the Comparative Analysis   9
Box 2.1   The Property Tax Revenue Identity   21
Box 2.2   Statutory Tax Rates and Effective Tax Rates   31
Box 2.3   Is the Property Tax Burden Distributed Equitably in
                 Low- and Middle-Income Jurisdictions?   73
Box 4.1   Recent Perspectives on the Need for a Property Tax   127
Box 5.1   Valuation Professionals' Education and Training   143
Box 5.2   The Lands Tribunal   151
Box 5.3   Customer-Centric Service Delivery   157
Box 6.1   Data Sources   173
Box 6.2   Politics and Public Response   189
Box 6.3   Database on Delhi Properties   191
Box 6.4   The (Un)Willingness to Tax   195
Box 7.1   Property Taxation in DKI Jakarta Province   206
Box 8.1   Japan's Intergovernmental System   230
Box 8.2   Property Tax Assessment   242
Box 8.3   Collaboration on Assessment and Data Accuracy   258
Box 9.1   Korean Governance   269
Box 10.1   Example of Calculation of Tax   309
Box 10.2   Property Tax Reforms   318
Box 11.1   Tax Administration in Pakistan   323
Box 11.2   Property Tax Exemptions in Punjab   333
Box 11.3   UIPT Property Tax Exemptions in Sindh   336
Box 13.1   The Cost of Property Tax Administration   418
Box 16.1   Development of Land Price Frame and Land Price Table   480

Foreword

It is no secret that the property tax is one of the most efficient taxes that governments can use to generate the revenue needed to meet the demands of their citizenry. Also, it is no secret that, in many nation-states and jurisdictions, the property tax has not met expectations as a robust revenue producer, leading some to ask, Why have a property tax?

Property Tax in Asia: Policy and Practice offers insights and lessons regarding the practice of property taxation in a diverse set of jurisdictions from one of the most economically, politically, and environmentally consequential regions of the world. Chapter by chapter, jurisdiction by jurisdiction, the authors describe their experiences with what has worked and what hasn't worked, and they outline options for reform. Whether viewing the property tax as a benefits tax, a tax to affect development, or a pure wealth tax, academics, policy makers, international agencies, and practitioners can derive from this volume solid reasons why the property tax should have an influential seat at the public finance table and practical methods on how to fulfill its promise.

The landscape of the property tax has changed markedly over the last several decades. Rapid urbanization and globalization of our economies have increased demand for property in some areas (particularly cities), leading to substantial increases in property tax capacity. The increase in value of real property worldwide swamps the growth of other components of wealth. Countries that give up on the property tax as a way to generate revenue to provide public goods, affect externalities, and address equity will find it difficult to secure public finance through other taxes. Most income and consumption tax systems cannot capture the rapidly rising value of property in their tax bases. Other wealth taxes, such as estate tax and gift tax, rarely produce sufficient revenue. The property tax remains the most important component of the public finances of any region and must do its job as well as possible.

This examination investigates underdeveloped property tax systems and highly developed systems in Asia, an area where technological advancement is high and economic activity, in general, is robust. Careful case studies of 13 jurisdictions illuminate much of the infrastructure and capacity needed to get to that highly developed stage. Even within jurisdictions, the authors note stark differences in infrastructure between major cities and rural areas. However, success in some places—such as the territories of Japan, Korea, and Singapore and some cities in China and Indonesia—demonstrates the potential for these successful examples to proffer technical assistance to others in their region in pursuing a robust property tax. Making widespread use of geographic information systems (GIS), for example, reduces the start-up cost of technology and shores up property appraisal and, potentially, collection. Currently, no resource provides this rich detail by jurisdiction.

Another gift of this volume is its analysis of the determinants of success of the property tax and of the effects of the policy infrastructure (rates, bases, progressivity, exemptions) and technical infrastructure (cadastre, GIS, appraisal techniques) on revenues. Furthermore, readers have the opportunity to dig into the outliers in these analyses. The data that identify these characteristics are not readily available, and many students of property tax don't have time to go hunting for it. The introductory chapters in part 1 and the case studies in part 2 provide much of the data we need to do a new, up-to-date analysis of the determinants of property tax success, which we might measure as the relative level of revenue.

The editors of this volume and its authors have taught much of the world, including me, the importance of tax policy, tax administration, and tax institutions. They once again take us out of our textbooks and the world of "first best" to understand how property taxes work; why they do and don't work; and what we can do as researchers, policy makers, and practitioners to make the property tax live up to its potential. The thoughtful case studies furnish many aha moments, often summarized at a chapter's end, where we can see how that case study's system could move forward—or how obstacles have been overcome. The volume is an important addition to the land and property tax work of the authors and the Lincoln Institute of Land Policy and will be a go-to resource for many who are interested in the future of this important source of revenue.

Sally Wallace
Dean and Professor of Economics
Andrew Young School of Policy Studies
Georgia State University

Preface

This book grew out of a long-standing and continuing engagement with the Lincoln Institute of Land Policy, based in Cambridge, Massachusetts, and a leading global think tank on land policy and property taxation. In the first two decades of this century, the Lincoln Institute has published comparative property tax analyses of Europe (Brown and Hepworth 2002), Latin America (De Cesare 2016), the British Commonwealth of Nations (Franzsen and McCluskey 2005), and most recently, Africa (Franzsen and McCluskey 2017). After the volume on property taxation in Africa was completed, Asia was the next logical target for investigation. Asia offers interesting lessons for improving the practice of land and property taxation, such as research suggesting that Asian countries in general have a low tax effort relative to their capacity to tax.

We needed to develop an analysis that would represent approximately 50 countries on a continent with different levels of economic development; data that were often incomparable; and vast differences in geography, demography, political structure, language, and cultural history. We selected 13 jurisdictions to analyze because of their use of property tax, innovative administration, use of technology, and in several cases, their long history with land and property taxation. These jurisdictions are in East Asia (China, Hong Kong, Japan, the Republic of Korea, and Taiwan), Southeast Asia (Indonesia, Malaysia, the Philippines, Singapore, Thailand, and Vietnam), and South Asia (India and Pakistan). Collectively, they are home to more than 3.7 billion people. Our case studies of these 13 nations found that methods to modernize the property tax vary widely among them, including how they capture its advantages as a revenue-raising measure and make it an instrument for rationalizing land use policy and promoting social equity. Property tax revenues seem to lag rising land values and business growth while the needs of infra-structure are growing.

The goal of this book is to provide a central source for authoritative data on land and property tax in Asia and a reference volume for those who design and administer property and land taxes and for those who monitor and evaluate them. We hope this work will become a valuable resource for organizations advising on tax policy reform and implementation, such as the International Monetary Fund, the World Bank, and regional development banks. We believe it will be useful to international donor and aid agencies, national ministries of finance and local governments with responsibility for property tax policy, regional and national research and policy institutes, and scholars of public finance and public administration.

We express our gratitude to the board and staff of the Lincoln Institute of Land Policy, especially George "Mac" McCarthy (president and CEO), Joan Youngman (senior fellow and chair of Valuation and Taxation, and Semida Munteanu (associate director of Valuation and Land Markets), who provided continual support and encouragement. We also thank the world-leading experts on land and property taxation who critically reviewed the work in progress: Dr. Peadar Davis, Professor Roy Kelly, Dr. Frances Plimmer, Professor Jay Rosengard, Professor Enid Slack, and Professor Lawrence Walters. We also thank Professor Sally Wallace, dean of the Andrew Young School of Policy Studies at Georgia State University for writing the foreword.

References

Brown, P. K., and M. A. Hepworth. 2002. "A Study of European Land Tax Systems." Working paper. Cambridge, MA: Lincoln Institute of Land Policy.

De Cesare, C. M., ed. 2016. *Sistemas del impuesto predial en América Latina y el Caribe* [Property tax systems in Latin America and the Caribbean]. Cambridge, MA: Lincoln Institute of Land Policy.

Franzsen, R. C. D., and W. J. McCluskey. 2005. "An Exploratory Overview of Property Taxation in the Commonwealth of Nations." Working paper. Cambridge, MA: Lincoln Institute of Land Policy.

Franzsen, R., and W. McCluskey, eds. 2017. *Property Tax in Africa: Status, Challenges, and Prospects*. Cambridge, MA: Lincoln Institute of Land Policy.

PART 1

Comparative Analysis

1

Context and Comparative Analysis

ROY BAHL, WILLIAM MCCLUSKEY, RIËL FRANZSEN,
AND WENJING LI

The 2020s could see more emphasis on land and property taxation in Asia. Certainly, the timing and the setting are right: Jurisdictions in South and East Asia are rapidly urbanizing, land values have risen, and demand for better public infrastructure and poverty alleviation in cities has increased. The coronavirus pandemic has left many Asian jurisdictions struggling with higher debt and deficits and facing pressure to find new ways to support budget expenditures. Some jurisdictions in the region have overcome the constraints to adopting modern property tax practices and could be role models for transforming property taxation into a stronger revenue-raising instrument for other jurisdictions.

Property taxation is not new to Asia. China has some of the oldest examples of property and land taxes, the Philippine version has been emerging since 1901, and the property tax laws in Hong Kong (a special administrative region, or SAR, of China) were in place in 1845. Some Asian jurisdictions have modernized their property taxes to keep in step with their economic growth, but others have allowed their property taxes to fall into disrepair. This analysis aims to show how to make good practices better and how to put weak practices on a path to improvement.

Scope of Study

This book addresses three questions:

- Why has land and property taxation not emerged as a more important revenue source in East, Southeast, and South Asia?

- Is there likely to be fiscal space[1] to increase the level of property taxation during the next decade?

- What types of reforms are most likely to advance property taxation as a revenue instrument?

Part 1 of this book attempts to answer these questions. In doing this, we try to strike a balance between using international comparisons and in-depth studies of specific jurisdictions and territories. The case study analyses in part 2 give detailed accounts of property tax practices and outcomes in 13 jurisdictions (countries or administrative regions).

This chapter provides an overview of the jurisdictions chosen for in-depth analysis and examines the extent to which they represent South and East Asia. It also presents a statistical analysis of the determinants of regional variations in property tax revenues and compares property tax performance in Asia with the rest of the world, which helps explain why some jurisdictions and regions use property and land taxes more than others.

Chapter 2 compares best practices with current practices in these jurisdictions. Detail is provided on tax base and rate features, valuation, administration, transfer taxes, and equity and allocative effects. This allows a deeper analysis of the problems with implementing property tax policy than that underlying the reform proposals often offer.

Chapter 3 gives some answers to the three questions posed and lays out the prospects for property tax reform according to what was learned from this study of Asian property taxation. It can guide policy makers looking to translate these lessons into a reform strategy that increases revenues.

Overview of the 13 Case Studies

The sheer size of Asia entailed limiting the analysis to 13 jurisdictions in East and South Asia. They are not meant to be a representative sample in the statistical sense. To compare richer jurisdictions that apply more modern approaches with ones at earlier stages of economic development, the following were purposely included:

- All the largest economies in South and East Asia.

- All jurisdictions with readily available data and recurrent property tax revenues that were reported to be equivalent to about 1 percent or more of GDP (gross domestic product).

- Low- and middle-income jurisdictions with available, adequate data and where the property tax was already established by 2020.

Table 1.1 shows data for the thirteen jurisdictions studied and for five other jurisdictions in East and South Asia.

The 13 jurisdictions show significant variation in per capita income (GDP). Five have per capita GDP greater than USD 20,000 and six have GDP of less than USD 10,000. Population sizes and degrees of urbanization also vary greatly. Some have centralized forms of revenue mobilization and do not make much room for local-government revenue autonomy (e.g., Korea and China), whereas others have embraced features of fiscal federalism (e.g., India, Pakistan, the Philippines, and Malaysia). China and Vietnam do not allow private ownership of land and so rely more heavily on taxing user rights. Most have long experience with property taxation (e.g., Hong Kong and the Philippines), one has more recently adopted a new system (Thailand), and another has undergone significant structural changes (Singapore). The sample may not be fully representative in all dimensions of socioeconomic structure, but it does appear to offer a good cross section of the Asian experience with land and property taxation.

What Is a Property Tax?

The variable of most interest in this empirical analysis is the amount of revenue raised from property taxation. Most Western jurisdictions use *property tax* to refer to an annual tax on the value of property, but this study uses a broader definition that includes all taxes related to the transfer of ownership or user rights, all taxes on registration of property, and all taxes designed for betterment or land value capture (see box 1.1). As discussed later, transfer tax revenues exceed annual property tax revenues in many of the jurisdictions studied. Part 1 separates discussion of the annual property tax from discussion of the more broadly defined *total property taxes*.

In this study, land and property taxes are defined in accordance with the *Government Finance Statistics Manual*, the flagship compilation by the International Monetary Fund (IMF) of comparative international fiscal data: "Taxes payable on the use, ownership, or transfer of wealth" (IMF 2014, 93). This view of taxes on land and property encompasses not only

Table 1.1 Property Tax Revenues and Key Data in Asian Jurisdictions

Jurisdiction[1]	Year[2]	Property Tax Revenue (% of GDP)[3]	Recurrent Property Tax Revenue (% of GDP)[4]	GDP per Capita (in current USD)[5]	Total Population (millions)[5]	Urban Population (% of total population)[5]
Afghanistan	2017	0.00	0.00	519.90	36.3	25.3
Bhutan	2018	0.00	0.00	3,243.50	0.8	40.9
China	2018	2.00	0.67	9,976.70	1,392.7	59.2
Hong Kong SAR, China	2018	4.53	0.96	48,542.70	7.5	100.0
India	2018	0.61	0.15	1,996.90	1,352.6	34.0
Indonesia	2019	0.42	0.28	4,135.20	270.6	56.0
Japan	2018	2.56	1.89	39,159.40	126.5	91.6
Korea, Rep.	2018	3.30	1.23	33,422.90	51.6	81.5
Lao, PDR (Laos)	2018	0.12	0.12	2,542.50	7.1	35.0
Malaysia	2018	No data	No data	11,377.70	31.5	76.0
Mongolia	2018	0.44	0.44	4,135.00	3.2	68.4
Nepal	2017	0.01	No data	1,048.50	27.6	19.3

Pakistan	2018	No data	0.13	1,482.20	212.2	36.7
Philippines	2018	0.81	0.35	3,252.10	106.7	46.9
Singapore	2018	1.70	0.92	66,679.00	5.6	100.0
Taiwan, China	2018	1.43	0.93	25,026.00	23.6	79.6
Thailand	2018	0.23	0.23	7,296.90	69.4	49.9
Vietnam	2018	3.87	0.03	2,566.40	95.5	35.9

Sources: IMF (2020, 2021); OECD (2021a); World Bank (2021); and the case studies in part 2 of this book.

[1] The 13 jurisdictions in boldface are analyzed in part 2.

[2] Data are for the latest year available between 2016 and 2019.

[3] Data for China, Hong Kong SAR, China, India, Indonesia, the Philippines, Singapore, Taiwan, China, and Vietnam are from part 2 case studies; data for other jurisdictions are from IMF (2020).

[4] Data for Hong Kong SAR, India, Indonesia, Pakistan, Taiwan, and Vietnam are from part 2 case studies; data for Afghanistan, China, Japan, Republic of Korea (South Korea), Mongolia, Singapore, and Thailand are from IMF (2021); and data for Bhutan, Lao PDR, and the Philippines are from OECD (2021a).

[5] Data are from World Bank (2021).

the recurrent tax on the value of land and improvements but also the taxes on property transfers (e.g., stamp duties, transfer taxes, and registration taxes). If personal property such as cars, boats, or machinery and equipment is part of a jurisdiction's tax base, this is also included. For jurisdictions that capture data on betterment charges, development charges, and other forms of value capture, these are also counted as property taxes. In jurisdictions where all land is government owned, several forms of land and property taxes are charged. These include rents on leased properties and taxes on the right to use the land or to exchange the right to use the land. All these are defined as land and property taxes and are in the definition used here.

In many cases, data are not fully reported in the IMF's government finance statistics (GFS) framework, possibly because of lack of definitional clarity or because of data-gathering issues. If data for a jurisdiction are not available, IMF's World Revenue Longitudinal Data (WoRLD) dataset sometimes imported data from the Organization for Economic Cooperation and Development (OECD). If the WoRLD data set seemed incomplete or was at odds with the case studies, we used the respective government estimates of property tax revenues. In doing this, we tried to stay within the definitional boundaries set by the international agencies (OECD 2021b), but we recognize that these data might not be fully consistent with the WoRLD dataset. These data adjustments are described in more detail in box 1.1.

International Comparisons

Nearly all jurisdictions and dependent territories in Asia have some form of taxation tied to land and property, but these taxes do not make a major contribution to government revenues. On average, total property tax revenues account for about 1.3 percent of GDP for the 17 jurisdictions in East, Southeast, and South Asia for which comparable data are available, versus 3.4 percent in North America (table 1.2). The comparable numbers for recurrent property taxes are 0.45 percent and 2.94 percent, respectively. These disparities suggest a missed opportunity for Asian jurisdictions to mobilize additional revenues.

What Explains the Variations Among Jurisdictions and Territories?

As shown in table 1.2, average property tax revenues as a percentage of GDP in East, Southeast, and South Asia exceed the average for all 130 jurisdictions reported by the IMF. But there is a great deal of variation across the regions and even within Asia. This suggests that the explanation for differences goes well beyond location.

Box 1.1 Data Used for the Comparative Analysis

Ideally, all taxes on real property would be included in this comparison of property tax revenue mobilization in Asia with that in the rest of the world, irrespective of how the tax is levied. The comparisons would include all recurrent taxes on real property–whether the tax base is rental value, capital value, or area–and all one-time levies on property transfers, including capital gains taxes on real property sales. In jurisdictions where land is government owned, the definition would include annual taxes on user rights such as rents and the transfer of user rights. Unfortunately, no such data set exists.

Two data sources are available. The IMF's GFS framework and the OECD's Global Revenue Statistics Database are the most comprehensive databases (OECD 2021a, b). We decided on the GFS as reported in the WoRLD dataset because the coverage is greater (189 jurisdictions) and because some jurisdiction statistics in the WoRLD database are the same as those from the OECD. We augmented the database in four ways.

- Data were not available in the WoRLD or GFS series for some of our 13 jurisdictions. After study of the property tax classifications in GFS, we decided that the data reported in the case studies of Taiwan, India, and Vietnam in part 2 would be suitable.

- The Hong Kong data in WoRLD appear to understate property transfer tax revenue and recurrent property tax revenue. We have substituted Hong Kong data from the case study for the WoRLD entries.

- The main data source for recurrent property tax revenues is the GFS data set from the IMF. We have adjusted this data set by substituting the missing values with those in OECD's Global Revenue Statistics Database if available. As a result, the recurrent property tax revenues for 91 jurisdictions are from IMF's GFS data set and for 44 jurisdictions are from OECD's Global Revenue Statistics Database. We carry out robustness tests on both the adjusted and the unadjusted samples.

- Finally, we note that there is ample opportunity for a misstatement of data on transfer taxes. In fact, there are significant differences in the data reported for China, Singapore, the Philippines, and Indonesia case studies and that reported in WoRLD. We have substituted the jurisdiction case study data for that reported by WoRLD.

We are more confident in the adjusted data set for recurrent property tax revenues than for total property tax revenues because there was a closer match between the case study and the GFS data. The following table presents the comparisons.

Box Data Table 1

Jurisdiction	WoRLD Set PT/Y (year)	GFS Data RPT/Y (year)	Case Study Data PT/Y (year)	Case Study Data RPT/Y (year)
China	1.48 (2017)	0.67 (2018)	2.00 (2018)	0.58 (2018)
Hong Kong SAR, China	0.96 (2017)	0.73 (2017)	4.53 (2018)	0.96 (2018)
India	–	–	–	0.15 (2018)
Indonesia	0.35 (2018)	0.35 (2018)	0.42 (2019)	0.28 (2019)
Japan	2.56 (2018)	1.89 (2018)	2.69 (2018)	1.96 (2018)
Korea, Rep.	3.30 (2018)	1.23 (2018)	3.30 (2017)	1.10 (2017)
Malaysia	–	–	–	–
Pakistan	–	–	–	0.13 (2018)
Philippines	0.48 (2018)	0.35 (2018)	0.81 (2018)	0.38 (2018)
Singapore	0.92 (2018)	0.92 (2018)	1.70 (2018)	0.90 (2018)
Taiwan	–	–	1.43 (2018)	0.93 (2018)
Thailand	0.23 (2018)	0.23 (2018)	0.21 (2018)	0.21 (2018)
Vietnam	–	0.03 (2018)	3.87 (2018)	0.03 (2018)

Note: PT/Y (year) = total property tax as a percentage of GDP in a given year; RPT/Y = recurrent property tax as a percentage of GDP in a given year.

Table 1.2 Average Levels of Property Taxation in Asia and Other Regions[1]

Jurisdiction	Property Tax Revenue (% of GDP)[2]	Recurrent Property Tax Revenue (% of GDP)[3]	Per Capita GDP (current USD)[4]	Population (millions)[4]	Number of Jurisdictions[5]
All jurisdictions	0.95	0.58	19,393.18	46.17	130/137/218
Europe and Central Asia	1.30	0.84	32,170.92	18.79	44/48/58
Latin America and Caribbean	0.66	0.52	10,263.50	23.61	27/26/42
Middle East and North Africa	0.80	0.41	19,133.07	26.09	9/8/21
North America	3.42	2.94	54,759.16	181.95	2/2/3
Sub-Saharan Africa	0.21	0.19	3,463.73	16.38	23/24/48
South Asia and East Asia–Pacific[6]	1.18	0.42	17,012.05	129.67	25/29/46
East, Southeast, and South Asia[7]	**1.31**	**0.45**	**17,770.95**	**192.45**	**17/19/26**

Sources: IMF (2020, 2021); OECD (2021a); World Bank (2021); and supplemented by data from part 2.

[1] "Other regions" as defined by the World Bank.

[2] Data are for the latest year available between 2016 and 2018 except for the Philippines (2019) from IMF (2020) and supplemented by data from part 2.

[3] Data are for the latest year available between 2016 and 2018 (except for Indonesia data in 2019) from IMF (2021), supplemented by data from OECD (2021a) and from part 2.

[4] The year is the same as for recurrent property tax in percentage of GDP.

[5] The leftmost number represents jurisdictions whose property taxes in percentage of GDP is available in the constructed data set described in note 2. The middle number represents jurisdictions whose recurrent property taxes in percentage of GDP is available in the constructed data set described in note 3. The rightmost number represents total jurisdictions in each region defined by the World Bank.

[6] A combination of region groups of "East Asia and Pacific" and "South Asia" defined by the World Bank.

[7] A subset of jurisdictions in the South Asia and East Asia–Pacific group are excluded because adequate comparative recurrent property tax data are not readily available: Bangladesh, Brunei Darussalam, Cambodia, Democratic People's Republic of Korea (North Korea), Malaysia, Nepal, and Sri Lanka.

One approach to understanding this variation is to statistically link the level of property tax revenues to individual jurisdiction characteristics. Property tax revenue performance is determined by three factors: the size and structure of the tax base (taxable capacity), external factors related to the socioeconomic structure of the jurisdiction, and the discretionary actions taken to capture property tax revenues from this base (tax effort). The multiple regression analysis carried out here takes into account the taxable base and the external factors. The remainder of the variation can be attributed to differences in property tax effort and to random variations. The regression results help explain why some governments use the property tax more intensively than others.

Regression Model

The dependent variable in this regression analysis is property tax revenue, standardized as a percentage of GDP. This is a measure of the effective rate of property tax and is a reasonable and widely used basis for comparing property tax revenues across regions. Two definitions of the dependent variable are specified in this study. First, we follow the practice used in most comparative studies of property taxation and define the dependent variable to include only recurrent property tax revenues as a percentage of GDP (RPT/Y) (Norregaard 2013). Second, we analyze total property tax revenues as a percentage of GDP (PT/Y), which includes both recurrent revenue and one-time levies such as property transfer taxes.

The determinants of property tax revenue levels in this analysis are measured by six independent variables. Typically, jurisdictions with a higher per capita GDP (Y/P) have a stronger base for property taxation. All other things being equal, higher income levels will lead to a higher-value housing stock and will be supported by a larger and more advanced commercial and industrial sector; in addition, the jurisdiction or territory will likely have a more formal and active property market, which may stimulate a larger volume of property transfers. Higher-income jurisdictions are more likely to have adopted a fiscal decentralization strategy for financing subnational governments, and the property tax is well suited for local-government taxation (Bahl and Bird 2018; Martinez-Vazquez 2015). Figure 1.1 shows the relationship between income levels and effective property tax rates.

The degree of urbanization (U) in a jurisdiction or territory signals a stronger property tax base. In many ways, land and property taxes are urban taxes, and property tax collections concentrate in the larger urban centers. About 38 percent of Philippine national property tax collections are raised in the metro Manila cities of Manila City, Quezon

Figure 1.1 Relationship Between Income Levels and Effective Property Tax Rates

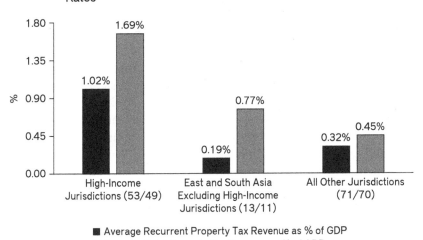

Sources: IMF (2020, 2021); OECD (2021a); World Bank (2020); and supplemented by data from part 2 case studies.

Note: The numbers below each group of jurisdictions are the numbers of jurisdictions with data on recurrent property tax (number on the left) versus total property tax (number on the right).

City, and Makati; Jakarta accounts for about 43 percent of total Indonesian property tax collections; and Bangkok and Pattaya City collect 40 percent of Thailand's national property taxes. We also test the hypothesis that jurisdictions with larger populations will raise more from property taxation.

Rural land is typically subject to annual property taxes and taxes on land use transfers and property ownership transfers. The rural sector, particularly agricultural property, often receives preferential treatment in rate, valuation, or exemption levels. We measure variations in the potential for taxing rural land using the share of arable land (AL) of the total land and expect a positive effect on per capita property tax revenues.

The more effectively the government implements its policies, the more likely it is to realize the potential of the property tax base. The World Bank's indexes of government effectiveness include the rule of law—that is, perceptions of the extent to which people have confidence in and abide by the rules of society, including the quality of contract enforcement, property rights, the police, and the courts (Kaufman, Kraay, and Mastruzzi 2010). We include this index of rule of law (RL) as an independent variable.

The size of a jurisdiction should also be related to the level of property taxation because of the expected greater numbers of local governments and the expected greater degree of fiscal decentralization. We control for this effect by including population size (TP) as an independent variable.

Finally, as noted previously, jurisdictions with a tradition of highly centralized governance are less likely to have devolved significant revenue autonomy to subnational units of government. The absence of property tax competition among local governments and the presence of stronger enforcement by central governments and more government involvement in land management may lead to higher levels of property taxation and thus may impose heavier effective tax rates on land and land transfers. We include a dummy variable (Trans) to identify transition jurisdictions, which are those defined as such by the United Nations (former Soviet Union jurisdictions, jurisdictions of the former Yugoslavia, mainland China, and Vietnam).

Results

This multiple regression analysis explores two questions: How much of the wide disparity in property tax revenue performance can be explained with these six variables? Which of the six are statistically significant determinants?

The regression models presented here explain nearly half the variation across jurisdictions in both measures of the dependent variable. Although these models do provide useful information about patterns of revenue mobilization, they also suggest that about half the variation cannot be explained. This suggests that tax effort, the willingness to tax, is a major part of the story.

Table 1.3 presents the results for three specifications of this model for each dependent variable.

The results for the recurrent property tax (RPT/Y) in models I–III show that property tax revenues are significantly higher in jurisdictions with a higher per capita GDP[2] and a higher rate of urbanization. This result squares with expectations and with the findings of earlier work. Different specifications lead to the same conclusion about the strong influence of income and urbanization on the effective property tax rate but also show that, ceteris paribus, revenues tend to be higher in transition jurisdictions. Neither the arable land nor the rule of law variable was significant, the former perhaps because of the property tax preferences given to the agricultural sector and the latter arguably because of its high correlation with national income levels. The total population of a jurisdiction was not a significant determinant. This model explains 47 to 50 percent of the

Table 1.3 Multiple Regression Analysis of the Determinants of Variations in Property Tax Revenues

Variables	Dependent Variable: ln RPT/Y			Dependent Variable: ln PT/Y		
	Model I	Model II	Model III	Model IV	Model V	Model VI
ln Y/P	0.5418***	0.5564***	0.5659***	0.2303	0.5996***	0.1748
	(0.1807)	(0.0975)	(0.0970)	(0.1833)	(0.1124)	(0.1845)
ln U	0.8535**	0.8296**	0.7517**	0.9525**	0.8284**	1.1704***
	(0.3800)	(0.3329)	(0.3290)	(0.3724)	(0.3532)	(0.3649)
ln AL	0.0319	0.0914		0.0875	0.2304**	0.1609
	(0.1012)	(0.0888)		(0.1049)	(0.1002)	(0.1011)
ln TP	0.0445			0.1409**		
	(0.0617)			(0.0637)		
ln RL	0.2516			2.0149***		1.9214***
	(0.6331)			(0.6441)		(0.6529)
Trans	0.5651**		0.5724**	0.6043*		0.5419*
	(0.2695)		(0.2591)	(0.3219)		(0.3258)
Constant	-10.6559***	-9.7247***	-9.4021***	-11.6495***	-10.2287***	-9.8329***
	(1.3379)	(1.0819)	(1.0252)	(1.3531)	(1.1094)	(1.0927)
Observations	112	114	115	127	128	127
Adj. R-squared	0.4804	0.4597	0.4613	0.4711	0.4193	0.4541

Note: RPT/Y = recurrent property tax as a percentage of GDP in a given year; PT/Y = total property tax as a percentage of GDP in a given year; Y/P = GDP per capita in a given year; U = urbanization; AL = arable land; TP = total population; RL = rule of law; Trans = transition jurisdictions. Models are estimated by the ordinary least squares method on cross section data for the latest year during 2016–2018 for which data are available. Data are expressed in logarithms. Panel data were not used because many years were missing. Standard errors are in parentheses.

*** p < .01, ** p < .05, * p < .1

variation in recurrent property tax revenue levels, suggesting that much of the variation is due to lower levels of tax effort.

When the dependent variable is specified as total property tax revenues (PT/Y) and includes property transfer taxes, the results are similar in that higher levels of revenue are associated with higher levels of income and urbanization. In table 1.3, the results for total property tax revenues and recurrent property tax revenues are not strictly comparable because the sample size for total property tax revenues is significantly reduced owing to lack of data. Higher revenue being associated with higher income and urbanization is consistent with the hypothesis that the level of annual property tax revenues is driven by the economy of cities. Interestingly, the arable land variable is significant, suggesting a significantly greater role for land use changes in revenue mobilization. Moreover, these results show that, for a given level of income and urbanization, transition jurisdictions raise more revenue from land and property taxes.

The results of this statistical analysis are helpful in thinking about the future of property taxation and property tax reform. They are consistent with a conclusion that this tax is now structured to suit higher-income jurisdictions with more developed business and residential infrastructures. In effect, it is an urban tax on the value of land and improvements of the residential and commercial or industrial sectors in urban areas and, to a lesser extent, a tax on land in rural areas.

Often missed in the analysis of the determinants of property tax revenue performance is recognition that the part of the tax levied on transfers of ownership and land use is a large share of property tax revenues in many jurisdictions. Because transfer taxes are often imposed by a higher level of government than are recurrent property taxes, their effective tax rate may be higher and their enforcement better than that of recurrent property taxes.

Implications

These results are consistent with three general directions for reform:

- Only about half the interregional variation in the revenue productivity of property tax is explained by these models. As we argue in the next two chapters, much of the rest is due to an unwillingness to raise effective tax rates. Political leaders know what to do to produce more revenue from the property tax; they just do not want to do it. Consistent with this finding, the chapters in part 2 lay out reform programs that would require discretionary actions, such as building databases that assist in identifying properties, increasing nominal tax rates, reducing exemptions and preferential treatment, updating valuations, and seeking stronger enforcement. These problems and options are explored in chapters 2 and 3.

- The property tax revenue base is heavily concentrated in cities, and the property tax structure should be rethought so as to give urban governments more incentive to increase effective tax rates. This might include more discretion to use development charges and land value capture approaches and possibly even reductions in intergovernmental transfers to cities.

- The reliance on one-time versus annual property taxes is of some concern in Asian jurisdictions. But the concerns can be turned into advantages by a better merging of policies and administration of the recurrent property tax and property transfer taxes. This is further discussed in chapters 2 and 3.

Notes

1. Fiscal space refers to the ability of a government budget to expand so that government resources are sustainably sufficient to fund a desired purpose. Fiscal space depends on tax capacity, or the size and structure of the tax base.

2. Because these are log-log form regressions, the coefficients are interpreted as elasticities. For example, when a jurisdiction's income elasticity is 0.5564 and we assume a 1% property tax revenue share of GDP, a 10% higher level of per capita GDP indicates that the jurisdiction's property tax share of GDP would rise from 1% to $1\% + (10 \times 0.5564\%) = 1.05564\%$.

References

Bahl, R., and R. M. Bird. 2018. *Fiscal Decentralization and Local Finance in Developing Countries*. Cheltenham, UK: Edward Elgar.

IMF (International Monetary Fund). 2014. *Government Finance Statistics Manual*. Washington, DC: IMF.

———. 2020. World Revenue Longitudinal Data. https://data.imf.org/?sk=77413F1D-1525-450A-A23A-47AEED40FE78.

———. 2021. Government Finance Statistics. https://data.imf.org/?sk=a0867067-d23c-4ebc-ad23-d3b015045405.

Kaufman, D., A. Kraay, and M. Mastruzzi. 2010. The Worldwide Governance Indicators: Methodology and Analytical Issues. https//papers.ssrn.com/sol3/papers.cfm?abstract_id+1682130.

Martinez-Vazquez, J. 2015. "Tax Assignments at the Regional and Local Levels." In *Handbook of Multilevel Finance*, ed. E. Ahmad and G. Brosio, 358–388. Cheltenham, UK: Edward Elgar.

Norregaard, J. 2013. "Taxing Immovable Property: Revenue Potential and Implementation Challenges." Working paper WP/13/129. Washington, DC: IMF.

OECD (Organization for Economic Cooperation and Development). 2021a. Global Revenue Statistics Database. https://stats.oecd.org/.

———. 2021b. "The OECD Classification of Taxes and Interpretative Guide." In *Revenue Statistics*. Paris: OECD.

World Bank. 2021. World Development Indicators. https://datatopics.worldbank.org /world-development-indicators/.

2

Current Policies and Practices

ROY BAHL, WILLIAM MCCLUSKEY, AND RIËL FRANZSEN

Asian jurisdictions tax real property in many different ways: some tax ownership and some land use; some tax land and some land and buildings; and some have no property tax. These broad differences in what they tax lead to important differences in how they tax real property: how they value property, what they do not tax, and how they go about their collections.

Each chapter in part 2 examines an individual jurisdiction. This chapter compares practices in all 13 jurisdictions with good practices in property taxation to suggest the best way forward. It begins with a review and analysis of how these jurisdictions have structured their property tax bases and rates to mobilize revenues. Most have gone to great lengths to reduce the burden on property taxpayers. The chapter then describes the development of the fiscal cadastre—those factors required for implementation of a property tax system. Here, valuation, billing, collection, and enforcement are compared and discussed in some detail. We also take up the subject of taxes on property transfers and discuss why this has long been a missing link in achieving the goals of better property taxation. The chapter closes with a discussion of how jurisdictions and territories in Asia have attempted to use land and property taxes to influence the distribution of tax burdens and the efficiency of land use.

This chapter draws heavily from the case studies in part 2 of this book.

Recurrent Land and Property Tax Structures

Recurrent property taxes should not penalize those who use property in different ways. Special features that narrow the tax base, such as exemptions or preferential rates, should have well-justified equity or resource-allocation objectives or be prompted by administrative considerations. The tax rate should be set at a level that will raise a targeted amount of revenue, and the approach to property valuation should be in step with the legal base of the tax. Administration should be efficient, keep costs reasonable, and be transparent. Collections of tax liabilities should be strictly enforced. The tax laws should be understandable, the structure should be as simple as possible, and the results should be regularly reported to the public.

In the real world, however, property tax structures always miss these norms, and in some jurisdictions, they miss them by a lot. In part, this is because the taxation of land and property is complex, the political economy has led to some unfortunate tax structure choices, and management practices have been lax. Of course, bad practices can be fixed, but as our case studies show, some fixes have been less effective than others, especially in poorer jurisdictions.

Property taxation in Asia is heavily influenced by traditions and laws regarding property rights and by land use, land tenure, topography, and government structure. Jurisdictions' efforts to reform their property tax are constrained by tight budgets, limited resource capacity, and low taxpayer morale. In general, the richer jurisdictions have more success than the poorer ones.

What Determines Revenue Mobilization?

To evaluate the likely impacts of property tax reform, we view the property tax as a system. The government levying the tax often controls four parts of the property tax system: the statutory tax rate, exemptions and preferential treatments, assessments, and collections.[1] These four components are linked, and all must be considered when evaluating the revenue impact of any single discretionary change in the tax system. Box 2.1 presents a systematic approach for examining the relationship between discretionary changes in property tax structure and property tax revenue.

Tax Base

The recurrent property tax is a family of levies on the holdings of real property or on user rights to real property. It is levied on some measure of value, or in some cases, on physical area. Value-based approaches are generally considered better than area-based approaches, in part because

---

Box 2.1 The Property Tax Revenue Identity

Property tax analysts use a simple identity to explain and estimate the impact of discretionary changes in property tax structure and administration on the level of property tax revenues (Bahl and Linn 1992, 102; Kelly, White, and Anand 2020):

$$PT/GDP = (PT/PTL)\,(PTL/TAV)\,(TAV/AV)\,(AV/MV)\,(MV/GDP),$$

where

    PT = property tax revenue collections

    GDP = gross domestic product

    PTL = property tax liability

    TAV = taxable assessed value

    AV = total assessed value

    MV = market value of real property.

The first term on the right-hand side of the identity is the collection rate, the second is the statutory tax rate, the third is the percentage of assessed value of property that is taxable, and the fourth is the rate at which the market value of property is assessed. These are the variables over which many jurisdictions have some degree of control in their efforts to influence revenue yield. The fifth term is the magnitude of the market value of real property, which is usually assumed to be constant in the short run. This identity can be used to simulate the revenue impacts of property tax policy or administrative changes made by governments. All the discretionary measures are important in estimating the revenue impact of changing any one of these. For example, revaluation may affect the assessment ratio (AV/MV), but the revenue impact will be substantially lessened if the collection rate or the statutory rate is low.

---

the value of a property better reflects the benefits received from the services it finances (Bahl and Bird 2018; Franzsen and McCluskey 2017; Kelly 2014; Kelly, White, and Anand 2020; McCluskey, Bell, and Lim 2010). Property values are driven by supply and demand, by the capitalization of the value of local infrastructure (such as roads, sewers, storm-water drainage, and street lighting), and by the benefits from local-government services (such as public schools, fire stations, police stations, and parks). A value-driven approach also provides the potential for a buoyant tax base (i.e., tax revenue moves up or down with GDP), whereas area-based systems tend to be static unless regularly adjusted with value-approximation coefficients.

Area-based systems can have great benefits in property tax regimes because they can be imposed in jurisdictions where there is only a fledgling property market, and they can get around the shortage of qualified valuers because limited individual valuation is required. In effect, each property is assigned to a value zone, and each value zone is assigned a tax rate. Revenues grow by changing the zone that properties are assigned to, by changing the tax rate, or by receiving new properties on the tax roll. In fact, area-based systems have long been used, especially in rural areas and in transition jurisdictions (Bahl and Bird 2018; Bing, Connelly, and Bell 2009; Rao 2008).

The jurisdictions analyzed in part 2 use value-based systems and assess either the annual rental value (the amount a tenant and landlord could agree on in an open market) or the capital value (the amount a willing buyer and seller could agree on). More than one recurrent property tax is in force in Korea, and Malaysia has more than one tax base option to choose from. Moreover, within any one jurisdiction, different types of property may be treated differently in terms of how they are assessed. For example, urban property may be value based, but rural property may be assessed according to land area. The range of tax-base choices made by the 13 jurisdictions covered in part 2 of this book include (1) capital value of land and improvements, valued as a unit (Japan, Malaysia, and Thailand); (2) capital value of land and improvements valued separately (Indonesia, Korea, Philippines, Taiwan, and Thailand); (3) annual rental value (Hong Kong, Malaysia, Pakistan, and Singapore); (4) land value (Taiwan, Thailand, and Vietnam); (5) building value (Taiwan and Pakistan); and size of the property (China, Malaysia, and India).

Table 2.1 describes the diversity of the tax bases by providing more information about what is taxed in each of the 13 case study jurisdictions.

In the first years of the 2000s, some Indian cities, including Delhi, replaced their annual rental value systems[2] with unit-area value systems, which are based on the physical area of the property. This was a pragmatic alternative meant to compensate for the lack of good data on market values.[3] However, the factors used to convert physical-area measurements to a property tax liability must be reviewed and adjusted periodically if revenues from an area-based system are to be buoyant and the distribution of property tax burdens is to remain fair (Ahmad, Brosio, and Jiménez 2019). Such adjustments to the base have not taken place in all the Indian cities that have implemented a unit-area value system. In Delhi, for example, taxable property values have not been adjusted for more than a decade.

In addition to deciding whether to tax value or area, governments can broaden or narrow their tax base by treating land and improvements differently, introducing a separate wealth tax on real property, or singling out

Table 2.1 Recurrent Property Taxes and Tax Bases, by Jurisdiction

Jurisdiction	Taxpayer	Recurrent Tax	Tax Base	Comment
China	User	Urban and township land use tax	Land area in commercial use	Private residential use is excluded.
	Owner of building	Real estate tax	Housing and buildings used for commercial ypurposes	Private residential use is excluded.
Hong Kong	Occupier	Rates*	Annual rental value	Valuations are based on rental records and other data and use computer-assisted mass appraisal.
	Owner	Property tax on rented properties	Annual rental value	
India (Delhi)	Owner	Rates*	Unit-area value in Delhi	Until 2004, annual rental values were used as tax base.
Indonesia	Owner	Urban and rural land and building tax	Capital value of land and buildings	Both forms of recurrent property taxes were devolved to local governments in 2011.
		Property tax on forests, plantations, and mining operations	Capital value of land and buildings	
Japan	Owner	Fixed asset tax	Assessed value	
		City planning tax	Assessed value	Only 647 of 1,719 municipalities (about 38%) levy this tax.
Korea	Owner	Local property tax	Capital value of land and improvements	
	Owner	Gross real estate tax	Capital value of total nationwide real estate holdings	This is a central tax, but revenue is shared among local governments.

(continued)

Table 2.1 Recurrent Property Taxes and Tax Bases, by Jurisdiction (*continued*)

Jurisdiction	Taxpayer	Recurrent Tax	Tax Base	Comment
Malaysia	Owner or tenant	Quit rent	Fixed amount per square meter	Tax differentiates on the basis of location and property use (residential, industrial, or commercial); it also varies by state.
	Owner	Property tax	Annual rental value or improved value	Only 20 local authorities use improved value; 134 use annual value.
Pakistan	Owner	Urban immovable property tax	Annual value	Provincial laws govern the tax.
Philippines	Owner	Real property tax	Assessed value	
	Owner	Special education tax	Assessed value	
	Owner	Idle land tax	Assessed value	Tax is viewed by many as a land policy tool as much as a revenue source.
Singapore	Owner	Property tax	Annual rental value	Tax is payable by owner.
Taiwan	Owner	Land value tax	Capital value of the land	Tax is based on all holdings within a local jurisdiction.
	Owner	Building tax	Capital value of the building	Up to three buildings by an owner are entitled to a preferential rate for owner occupancy.
	Owner	Idle land tax	Land value	Idle land is vacant plots or where building value is less than 10% of land value.
Thailand	Owner	Land and building tax	Capital value of land and buildings	A new property tax regime was put in place in January 2020 and is still in a transition period.
Vietnam	Owner	Nonagricultural land use tax	Land price indexes	Tax rates depend on use. About 75% of residential taxpayers are exempt.
		Agricultural land use tax	Land area	Different tax rates apply to different land categories.

Source: Case studies in part 2 of this book.

* *Rates* refers to the local property tax in former Commonwealth jurisdictions and regions.

certain types of property for special treatment. Each of these base enhancements is directed at a particular objective. But some could have less desirable impacts and could lead to more complication of the recurrent property tax and to higher administrative costs.

There has long been worldwide interest in taxing land more heavily than improvements in order to better capture the efficiency gains from taxing an immobile factor at a higher rate. The rationale for using a land value tax or a split-rate tax with a lower rate on buildings than land—as in Taiwan—is in step with the goals of encouraging property development (Dye and England 2009; Franzsen 2009; Netzer 1998; Youngman 2016). William Vickrey, a Nobel laureate in economics, stated, "The property tax is, economically speaking, a combination of one of the worst taxes—that part levied on real estate improvements . . . and one of the best taxes—the tax on land or site value" (Dye and England 2009, 3). To realize the benefits of this strategy, the tax rate differential must be great enough to induce enough new development to offset the economic costs of implementing the split-rate system. The cost of valuation is high because credible and defensible values must be determined for both the land and the building components (Franzsen and McCluskey 2013).

A split-rate system is only one approach to taxing land more heavily than buildings. Under Vietnam's recurrent property tax system, only the land is taxed. The situation is similar in China with respect to residential properties. In contrast, Pakistan levies a higher tax on buildings (covered areas) than land, implying a disincentive for development. In Japan, property taxes on buildings raise about 10 percent more revenue than do taxes on land.

In one sense, all recurrent property tax systems are a tax on wealth. But some Asian jurisdictions have carried this one step further. Korea's annual gross real estate tax, levied by the central government, uses a property owner's total countrywide real estate holdings to arrive at a tax liability. The stated purpose of the tax is to deconcentrate the distribution of land ownership, but it covers only about 2 percent of real estate landholders. Vietnam's nonagricultural land tax also applies to a taxpayer's separate landholdings, and Taiwan requires the aggregation of all landholdings in the local jurisdiction before the progressive rate structure is applied. Other jurisdictions have tried to tax real property wealth by imposing separate taxes on high-value holdings. In 2014, Pakistan's Punjab Province introduced an additional one-time tax on luxury residential property; and Indonesia imposed a one-time sales tax of 20 percent on luxury houses, apartments, and condominiums worth more than INR 30 billion (about USD 2.1 million).

Certain types of property have been singled out for special treatment under the recurrent property tax. Vacant or underused land is often a target, with a goal of either gaining revenue or encouraging better land use (Taiwan and the Philippines are examples). But the tax is often not levied at a high enough rate to matter, and moreover, the administration can be problematic. Another example of special treatment is extending the tax base to assets other than land and buildings. For example, in Japan, Hong Kong, Thailand, and the Philippines, certain types of plant and machinery are included. With the exception of Japan, these types of property taxes do not generate much revenue.

Tax Relief

A major contributor to the low revenue productivity of the property tax in Asia is tax relief programs. This is surprising in light of the low amount of revenues raised from property taxes, especially in the low-income jurisdictions of Asia. Depending on the program, the tax relief is often justified as protecting low-income families, encouraging home ownership, encouraging better land use patterns, or stimulating economic development (Bahl and Bird 2018, chap. 6). But the property tax is wildly unpopular with voters, leading to tax relief enhancement proposals from politicians seeking votes or even bending to powerful lobbies (Rosengard 2012). Whatever the reason, studies of property tax reform usually call for scrutiny of tax relief programs and for a full accounting of the resulting tax expenditures (ADB 2020; Kelly, White, and Anand 2020).

Tax relief programs are part of every jurisdiction's system and not easily dislodged once in place. The benefits of tax relief are not often compared with their costs, and in fact, most jurisdictions do not even monitor their effects, much less track the amount of tax revenue given up.[4] Still, Asian jurisdictions continue to give tax relief in many ways. Sometimes this is highly visible to taxpayers, such as a reduction in the tax rate for preferred properties or an outright exemption. In other cases, it is almost invisible to taxpayers because it is hidden in complicated valuation rules.

Exclusions, Exemptions, and Thresholds

Every property tax system provides exclusions and exemptions. The accepted practice in most jurisdictions is full exemption from property tax for places used for public worship or charitable purposes and for most government purposes. Others can be more controversial, particularly when they are costly to government revenue budgets. To be sure, some are well meant, such as recognition of the positive externalities generated by some exempt properties (Kelly 2014). However, many others are traceable to political rationales.

Value thresholds are a simple way to provide relief for low-income families and to lighten administrative workloads. The danger is that the threshold may be set so high that it excludes much of the tax base. The threshold of Korea's tax on land wealth is so high that it excludes a large share of real estate owners, and so it cannot easily succeed with its objective of deconcentrating the ownership of land. Thailand's new tax regime also uses a high tax threshold to exempt most owner-occupied properties from the tax base, making it regressive and greatly limiting its revenue productivity. On the other hand, high thresholds can be consistent with government policy. By establishing a high exemption level, Singapore effectively excludes most owner-occupiers living in subsidized public housing—consistent with the country's policy of taxing wealth and encouraging owner occupancy. It should also be noted that the management of thresholds can require maintenance, and in particular, revaluations usually require a periodic reset.

Some Asian jurisdictions track their use of exemptions, presumably to control revenue loss. In Hong Kong, for instance, properties are closely monitored to confirm their exempt status. In 2018, less than 2 percent of total assessments on the valuation list were exempt from rates payment. In Vietnam, the revenue forgone from exemptions from the nonagricultural land use tax was estimated to account for 10 to 11 percent of total revenue collected from 2012 to 2016. In most jurisdictions, however, the cost of property tax relief is not tracked.

Rate Capping, Rebates, and Discounts

Rate capping, revenue capping, and phase-in provisions provide tax relief when sticker shock causes problems—for example, with the introduction of a new valuation roll. Japan moderated increases in tax burdens in cities and metropolitan areas by capping the increase in assessed values. In Malaysia, the revaluation in 2014 was accompanied by a cap on the tax increase. The Hong Kong region has introduced a rates concession scheme to cushion the short-term impact of increases in property tax payments while preserving the long-term fairness and integrity of its rating system. Thailand's new property tax law provides for soft transition measures, phasing in the new tax over a three-year period.

A rebate or partial exemption of property tax liability is a further option for granting relief. Some rebates are given in consideration of poor public services, such as Hong Kong providing tax reductions for properties with unfiltered or no water supply. In other cases, tax rebates have been used to encourage socially desirable actions. For example, to increase the supply of more durable residential construction or to remodel homes for elderly residents, Japan offers a tax rebate of 50 percent over five years for qualifying houses. In Vietnam, certain types of land and categories of tax-payers are eligible for a 50 percent tax reduction for investment projects in regions experiencing socioeconomic difficulties. In Hong Kong, the Rating Ordinance provides for one-time rebates and concessions in times of economic difficulty, such as in 2003 when Hong Kong was affected by the outbreak of SARS (severe acute respiratory syndrome).

Discounts for early payment lower tax burdens and also provide bene-fits to the taxing government. In Punjab, Pakistan, taxpayers who pay the full amount of tax before a specified date are entitled to a 5 percent dis-count. The law in the Philippines allows for advance payment incentives of up to 20 percent.

Valuation and Assessment Adjustments

Tax relief in Asia is also given by applying different valuation methods to different types of property or by reducing the assessed values of certain types of properties. Formal fractional assessments are not uncommon. For example, in Khyber Pakhtunkhwa, Pakistan, offices of the local and fed-eral governments, nongovernmental organizations, private commercial organizations, guesthouses, hostels, and banks are taxed at only 20 percent of the assessed annual rental value. Korea and the Philippines also take this route. Hong Kong (and many other jurisdictions) deducts a statutory percentage from (gross) rental value to determine net annual value.

Tax Deferrals and Amnesties

Tax deferrals are a practical way to address the asset-rich, cash-poor dilemma—a phenomenon often encountered with retired residential property owners. This occurs when property values and property taxes rise faster than incomes. Careful design of such relief programs is impor-tant; if too many taxpayers qualify for deferral, government cash flow may see a significant, negative impact. Moreover, properly managed tax deferral schemes require a certain level of administrative machinery, which imposes a cost. Deferrals are especially problematic in jurisdic-tions with rapidly aging populations, such as Japan.

Amnesties can provide significant one-time revenue collections of back taxes, but they also have significant drawbacks. Drawing delin-quents back into the system with an amnesty does not guarantee that they will remain in the system; moreover, compliance by other taxpay-ers may fall. Multiple amnesties may create a disincentive for compli-ance when they lead to an expectation of future forgiveness of taxes, penalties, or interest.

In the Philippines, 56 local governments in highly urbanized regions with high-value real properties granted amnesties to taxpayers in the first two decades of this century. These amnesty programs yielded an estimated aggregate revenue of about USD 564.5 million, or about half the average annual national property tax revenues raised in the Philippines in 2014–2018.

Special Cases of Tax Relief

Three special cases of tax relief are worth noting because of their importance and widespread use. These are the exemption of government property, the preferential treatment of owner-occupied property, and special provisions for property taxation during the COVID-19 pandemic.

EXEMPTION OF GOVERNMENT-OWNED PROPERTY

The tax exemption of government-owned property is often fixed in the central property tax laws. As a result, most jurisdictions do not tax properties that are dedicated to government use. Korean law exempts real estate owned by the government and lands used for public utilities, whereas in the Philippines properties owned by any level of government, and registered cooperatives, are exempt.

Exempting property owned (or used) by higher levels of government can be especially burdensome for the underlying local governments. This is surely the case in capital cities (McCluskey and Franzsen 2013; McCluskey, Franzsen, and Bahl 2017b), where government-owned real estate may constitute a significant part of the potential local tax base. Moreover, these properties require municipal services and benefit from local infrastructure, and if exempt, they force reliance on cross subsidies or other revenue sources.

PREFERENTIAL TREATMENT OF OWNER-OCCUPIED RESIDENTIAL PROPERTY

Most Asian jurisdictions extend preferential treatment to owner-occupied residential properties under the recurrent property tax (Bird and Slack 2004; Kelly 2014; McCluskey, Franzsen, and Bahl 2017b). This happens in China, Malaysia, Taiwan, Thailand, and the Philippines (where lower rates are used in combination with lower assessment levels).

The international experience, generally, and the experience in most of the jurisdictions studied here, is that preferential treatment of owner-occupiers can lead to a large reduction of the tax base. As an extreme example, China excludes all residential properties from the real estate tax—although these properties appear to be formally included in the tax base. In Vietnam, certain residential land within regions with extreme socioeconomic difficulties and land that is used by poor households are exempt. In India and Pakistan, lower tax rates apply to primary residences. The tendency to apply lower rates for owner occupancy generally might be ascribed to political reasons. In Thailand, it was seen as almost a necessary condition for passing the new property tax law in 2020.

SPECIAL CORONAVIRUS PANDEMIC RELIEF

The fiscal impact of the coronavirus pandemic is considerable. One estimate places the resulting GDP decline at about 4 percent and for the emerging economies an increase in fiscal deficits equivalent to 2.8 percent of GDP (Oxford Economics and ITIC 2020). The International Monetary Fund (IMF 2021) estimates that bringing debt back to pre-COVID-19 levels will require significant increases in the primary surplus—that is, tax increases.

Governments across Asia, like those elsewhere, have attempted to cushion the impacts with ad hoc and formal measures. The property tax has been one of the fiscal instruments used. One form of property tax relief has been to defer property tax payments and waive penalties. In Indonesia, the city of Jakarta decided not to increase the property tax for the year 2020 and continued previous policies of forgiving administrative fines for late payments. In the Philippines, local governments may reduce the real property tax partially or fully after a calamity. Local assessors are also mandated by law to reassess real properties if sudden inflation or deflation of property values occurs or in any abnormal circumstances. In Taiwan, businesses that closed, such as restaurants and hotels, are entitled to a preferential housing tax rate.

Asian jurisdictions will be challenged to put their preexisting fiscal administrative arrangements back in place once the pandemic is under control (IMF 2020). The tax compliance machinery in governments, as well as in many businesses, is in disarray; borrowing rules have been bent; and earmarked funds have been raided. The property tax will be particularly difficult to restore as temporary preferential treatments are rescinded and the issue of establishing a new valuation roll is taken up. In many places, it will be a long road back.

Statutory Tax Rates

The most straightforward way to provide property tax relief is to reduce the statutory tax rate (see box 2.2). It is easy enough to structure and to target particular kinds of property. In Asia, rate differentiations are based on the location of a property (China and the Philippines), value (Indonesia), use (Malaysia and Vietnam), nature of occupation (whether owned or tenanted; e.g., India), or a combination of these factors and size (Pakistan). There also are drawbacks. Rate increases are the most visible discretionary

BOX 2.2 STATUTORY TAX RATES AND EFFECTIVE TAX RATES

It is important to distinguish between the *statutory tax rate* (also called the nominal rate) and the *effective tax rate*. The former, a legal concept, refers to the tax rate specified in the law to be applied to the taxable base. The effective tax rate is an economic concept, and it must be calculated. The numerator is the total amount of property tax collected against current-year liability; and the denominator may be GDP, for a national effective rate, or the market value of the property, for a local effective rate. The effective tax rate reflects the combined revenue impact of the statutory rate structure, the collection rate, the accuracy of assessments, and preferential treatments. See also the discussion in box 2.1 and Kelly, White, and Anand (2020, 168–169).

Example

Property market value	**$1,000,000**
Assessed value	$900,000
Statutory tax rate	**1.5%**
Initial tax amount	$13,500
10% rebate	$1,350
Tax amount	$12,150
Effective tax rate	**1.215%** (= $12,150 ÷ $1,000,000)

This example highlights only the effect of a lower assessed value and tax relief. Kelly, White, and Anand (2020, 168–169) provide further actual and illustrative examples.

change and can serve as a flash point for taxpayer discontent. Later, we use the information from the 13 case studies as a context for discussing four critical questions related to rate setting and design.

How Are Statutory Tax Rates Determined?

The main determinants of statutory tax rates are the size of the taxable base, the revenue required for the budget, the availability of other revenue sources, government policy priorities, and politics. In theory, statutory rates may change every year, depending on any or all of these factors, but in practice, they do not change frequently. Political leaders shun tax rate increases, particularly if they are large one-time increases; and often would prefer changing fractional assessments, changing the exemption list, or even revaluing part of the property tax base.

Who Sets Rates?

In Asian jurisdictions, there are all sorts of arrangements for determining tax rates. In some fiscally decentralized jurisdictions, locally elected councils set tax rates. This is the case in Malaysia. However, in much of Asia, setting rates tends to be a responsibility of the central government because most property taxes are central-government levies (or state or provincial levies). For example, in Korea, both the local property tax and the gross real estate tax are legislated centrally, with only minor rate adjustment power left to local governments. The situation is similar in Taiwan.

But limited rate-setting autonomy at the local-government level does not mean that subnational governments have no control over rate structures and revenues. For example, the minimum and maximum rates for the urban and township land use tax in China are set centrally on the basis of city size and occupied land area. Local governments, however, determine the exact rates on the basis of local needs and affordability. In federal systems, recurrent property taxes may be devolved or retained by the state or provincial governments (as in India and Pakistan, respectively). Malaysia's property tax is levied under state government law, yet rates are determined locally. Even in jurisdictions where the tax rate may be set at the local-government level, a higher level of government may stipulate maxima and minima or simply a standard rate (Japan, Philippines, Thailand, and Indonesia).

What Are the Options for Rate Structure and Design?

Tax rate structures differ widely across Asia. This is because they have evolved over time in response to different pressures for relief, special preferences, social engineering, and revenues. A central issue in Asia is whether complicated rate structures are worth the difficulties that they bring to administering the property tax.

TAX RATES

Some jurisdictions apply a uniform tax rate countrywide to certain types of properties. Because Hong Kong annually revalues all taxable properties, its uniform 5 percent tax rate on annual rental value has stayed in place since 1999. Singapore also revalues annually, and its uniform 10 percent rate for nonresidential property has remained unchanged since 2001. The appeal of a uniform rate tax is its simplicity, the ease of making discretionary adjustments, and that revenue increases are mostly tied to tax-base increases. In Indonesia, local governments may set the rate structure within a national maximum of 0.3 percent. The annual rental value and therefore the statutory tax rates can differ within and among provinces in Pakistan.

A number of Asian jurisdictions use a progressive rate schedule, meaning that the statutory rate increases as the assessed property value increases. The general idea is that those with more real property wealth ought to be taxed at a higher rate, and the degree of rate progression is always a subjective decision.[5] Although some higher-income jurisdictions (Korea and Taiwan) impose progressive rate structures, they are more common in the lower-income jurisdictions. A distinguishing feature of a progressive rate schedule is that revenue increases are driven by both growth in assessed values and bracket creep.[6]

A problem with progressive tax rate structures is that they complicate the property tax. Korea uses a number of different progressive rate structures for its local property tax. For commercial building sites, progressive rates range from 0.2 percent to 0.4 percent. For so-called speculative land, the range is slightly higher: 0.2 percent to 0.5 percent. For other types of land, different uniform tax rates are applied to specific use categories. Korea's wealth tax (its annual gross real estate tax) is also subject to a progressive rate structure, but it is especially difficult to administer because an owner's property values are aggregated countrywide, and the tax is sensitive to nonuniform assessment practices.

In Vietnam, the progressive rate structure with respect to residential land use was implemented to curb speculation and to ensure more efficient land use. The recurrent tax rates on land are so low, however, that they are unlikely to affect taxpayer behavior. In 2018, taxpayers in Vietnam paid only about an average USD 4.30 per year in recurrent property taxes, about the same amount as a takeaway meal.[7] In Taiwan, the upper rate bracket boundaries were set so high that they affected few taxpayers.

Some jurisdictions have set floor or ceiling, or both, rates for the property tax. Japan abolished maximum rates in 2004 and now sets a standard rate of 1.4 percent for its fixed asset tax. Municipalities that choose to use a lower rate will receive less in intergovernmental transfers. Although more than 90 percent of municipalities apply the standard rate, almost 9 percent apply a higher rate. The highest rate as of 2020 is 1.8 percent—still well below the previous maximum rate, which was 2.1 percent. For the city planning tax, there is a maximum rate of 0.3 percent, but about half the municipalities use a lower rate.

Despite decentralizing the administration of tax on land and buildings to local governments, Indonesia's central government still determines the maximum tax rate. Policy changes since 2014 allow local rate setting, but the locally determined tax rate may not exceed the maximum rate of 0.3 percent. Some local governments apply a flat rate; however, others apply multiple or graduated tax rates. In the Philippines, provincial governments can impose a basic tax rate up to a maximum of 1 percent, but the maximum rate for cities is 2 percent. Only 18 percent of cities apply the maximum rate, likely because they have other lucrative sources of revenue, whereas 95 percent of provinces use the maximum rates, suggesting that this ceiling rate could be raised.

The important feature of this approach to rate setting is that it allows some autonomy for setting rates at the local-government level, even while allowing the central government to more or less control the overall level of rates. Interestingly, these case studies show that even when they are given authority to set higher rates, local governments do not always take advantage of this discretion.

SINGLE VERSUS MULTIPLE OR DIFFERENTIAL RATES

A single tax rate that applies to all property types (land and buildings) or all use categories is uncommon in Asia. As is the trend elsewhere around the world, differential tax rates are increasingly used as a tool to incentivize taxpayer behavior or to promote equity. One hardly ever finds the sort of simple, flat-rate structure that most public finance scholars recommend. In most systems, the local-government tax base and tax rate regimes are jointly determined by central government, with policy makers often more concerned with keeping their constituents happy than getting the local policy mix right (Bahl and Bird 2018). Tax rates in Asia are differentiated on the basis of several factors.[8]

Differential rates have been considered in Hong Kong. Those who oppose this proposal tend to focus on issues around inequity, increased cost of doing business for commercial and industrial property owners, and the potential of causing hardship to certain sectors, such as small and medium enterprises. The taxation rating system in Hong Kong is simple in that it is based on annual rental values and applies a single rate percentage to all properties irrespective of use, location, and so on. The arguments for differential rates are that the system is well established and understood by ratepayers and the property leasing market is active with abundant rental evidence. Moreover, the existing rating system is progressive because it is ad valorem—that is, the higher the ratable value of a property, the higher the amount of rates payable, and the higher value ostensibly reflects an ability to pay (RVDSAR 2021).

The Tax Treatment of Underused Land and Property

Governments sometimes impose higher effective tax rates on the owners of vacant or idle land, unoccupied buildings, or underused property (Bahl and Bird 2018; McCluskey, Franzsen, and Bahl 2017b). The rationale is to provide an incentive for development of land parcels for which the municipality makes available services and infrastructure (Grote, Nersesyan, and Franzsen 2019).

Good examples of this practice can be found in jurisdictions outside Asia. For example, in the capital city of South Africa, Pretoria, the 2018–2019 tax rate on vacant plots was 3.65 times higher than the tax rate for developed residential properties, and in Johannesburg it was 4 times higher. Seoul, Korea, and Windhoek, Namibia, follow a different approach. Vacant land parcels in new township developments are taxed at standard rates for a specified number of years. Thereafter, the tax rate is increased if the parcels remain undeveloped (Grote, Nersesyan, and Franzsen 2019). Vietnam follows a similar approach. As shown in table 2.2, global practices vary widely.

As Haas and Kopanyi (2017, 13) point out, defining what constitutes vacant or unused land may be challenging in fast-growing cities in both industrial and developing jurisdictions. Since 2015, the law in Japan specifically allows land on which an uninhabited dwelling stands to be declared

Table 2.2 Vacant Land and Underused Properties

Tax Treatment of Vacant or Unoccupied Properties	City Examples
Excluded or exempted	**Bangkok**; Cairo; **Karachi**
Exemption on application for unoccupied buildings	Accra; Dar es Salaam
Vacant land taxed at lower rates than occupied land	**Kuala Lumpur** (commercial)
Vacant and unoccupied property taxed at standard tax rate	**Jakarta**; Kingston; Nairobi; São Paulo
Vacant and unoccupied property taxed at higher rate	**Bangalore; Kuala Lumpur** (residential)
Vacant and unoccupied property taxed at significantly higher rate	Belo Horizonte; Bogotá; Buenos Aires; Cape Town; Gaborone; Johannesburg; **Manila**; Mexico City; Porto Alegre; Seattle; **Seoul**; Tshwane; Washington, DC; Windhoek

Sources: Adapted from Haas and Kopanyi 2017; McCluskey and Franzsen 2013; and information from part 2 chapters. Boldface indicates cities in case studies.

vacant land—resulting in a sixfold increase in the fixed asset tax. China's urban and township land use tax is levied on land use in cities and towns to encourage more efficient use of urban land. Thailand increases the tax rate for vacant land every three years until a maximum of 3 percent is reached. Provinces and cities in the Philippines are authorized to impose an additional tax on idle lands, but in 2015, only 15 percent of the provinces and 30 percent of the cities imposed the idle land tax, and only two provinces and nineteen cities were able to collect it.

Higher taxes may not be very effective in bringing underused properties into development. Forcing owners to develop or sell requires a tax rate that is high enough to influence behavior. But often the tax rates applied to vacant or idle urban (or rural) land are low and are applied to very conservative estimates of assessed value, and therefore the tax burden on owners is insignificant. The result is that the tax does not encourage development or redevelopment of the land, and it may perpetuate land hoarding by speculators, almost without penalty. For example, in its 2020 tax reform, Thailand established a ceiling rate for vacant land of 3 percent, but land prices have been increasing at a 7 percent rate. Another example is Kuala Lumpur, Malaysia's capital city, which applies a lower tax rate for vacant commercial land, but for vacant residential land the rate is slightly higher than for occupied residential land (see table 2.2).

Valuation and Fiscal Cadastre Management

The key to having a good property tax is having a good valuation practice. This involves assigning values to all properties according to the law and keeping them current by regularly testing the accuracy of the estimates, reporting the results to taxpayers, and having in place a fair system for objections. A good valuation practice will shy away from complicated preferential treatments of properties. A good valuation system is difficult to implement, because it requires determining values and keeping them current, managing a huge database, dealing with objections, bringing new properties onto the roll, coordinating with other agencies, and more. And the valuation process must live with some constraints that are not easily resolved in the short run. Most of the poorer jurisdictions in Asia have inadequate data for accurate valuation, a shortage of qualified valuers, a land market that is not functioning well, and political leadership that often does not see a good valuation practice to be in its interest.

No country measures up fully to the standards of a good valuation system, but some of the higher-income jurisdictions of Asia (Hong Kong,

Singapore, Japan, and Korea) come close. The experience in the lower-income jurisdictions has not been good (Thailand, Philippines, Indonesia, India, and Pakistan). The norms outlined here are further from their reach, and revenue mobilization will continue to be stuck at a low level unless some long-standing problems with the valuation of real property are resolved. The assessment ratios reported in the part 2 case studies are low. Most reviews of the practice in low- and middle-income jurisdictions place the ratio of assessed value to market value below 50 percent (Bahl and Bird 2018; De Cesare 2012; Kelly, White, and Anand 2020). China, Vietnam, and Malaysia have property tax regimes or valuation systems that are still emerging.

Valuation Methods

The value of a property is normally determined on the basis of market value or current-use value (Kelly, White, and Anand 2020; Kitchen 2013). Market value assumes that all possible uses are taken into account in determining highest and best use and that legal regulations and building restrictions have been taken into account. Current-use value represents a market value that reflects only the present use of the property (Bird and Slack 2007; McCluskey and Franzsen 2013). The two bases differ when the current use is not the highest and best use—for example, agricultural land that would have a higher market value if it were developed for residential or commercial purposes. Often the property tax legislation will specify the value standard, such as market value, assuming highest and best use or assuming current-use value. The use of annual rental value as the basis often implies that it is the market rent that must be estimated but on the basis of current use. Therefore, if the property has a higher-value use, this potential is ignored, as is done in Hong Kong (RVDSAR 2021). Such differences can have important implications for property tax burdens.

To maximize fairness and transparency in a property tax system, assessments should be based on the market value of property, and legislation should support this principle. In Hong Kong, the property tax base is the estimated annual rental value in the open market. In Japan, it is the assessed market value. In a dynamic economy, property values constantly change. Values in one area may increase and decrease in another. Only a system based on market value will capture such changes in the distribution of property-related wealth. Jurisdictions with a high level of administrative capability and technical skills that can implement annual revaluations include Hong Kong, Japan, Korea, and Singapore.

The reason for a valuation for property tax purposes is to accurately estimate the market value of the real estate asset. The valuation process involves the combination of sound judgment and application of appropriate valuation methodologies. Still, the resulting valuation is, at best, an opinion of value that may or may not be accurate given that it depends on availability of relevant data and the valuer's skills. Interestingly, in Hong Kong there is no statutory requirement to use any particular method of valuation in arriving at the ratable value of a property. It depends primarily on the availability of rental evidence.

All this said, the standard of market value is not widely adopted for all categories of real property. For example, buildings are typically valued using depreciated reproduction costs in Japan, Korea, the Philippines, and Thailand. This approach is followed for buildings because accurate data on market transactions are scarce. Also, it is more straightforward for national or provincial government to develop uniform cost schedules for buildings to be applied by local government. For land valuation, market transactions, if available, are normally used. Assessment values in Hong Kong and Malaysia are determined directly using market rental evidence. The main problem with basing assessments on market value data is the absence of accurate estimates of market values. For the richer jurisdictions in Asia, some of the reported market values for rents and capital values would seem to be trustworthy, but for the lower-income jurisdictions these data may be inaccurate and not a good basis for assessment. This issue is discussed at length later.

The three usual methods of determining the market value of a property are the comparable sales or rentals approach, the cost approach, and the income capitalization approach (Franzsen and McCluskey 2013). All are used in Asia. The comparable sales approach compares the subject property against other similar properties that have recently been sold or leased. This method is typically used for the valuation of land, single-family residences, condominiums, and other types of property that exhibit a high degree of similarity and for which a ready sales or rental market exists. Hong Kong, Singapore, and Malaysia all apply this approach for residential, retail, and office properties. Value is determined for the whole property, land and buildings together.

The cost approach establishes value on the basis of the current cost of producing or replacing the existing building and then reflecting the actual condition of the building through a depreciation allowance. The principle behind this technique is that the market value of an asset should not exceed the cost of obtaining a substitute asset of comparable features and functionality. In other words, replacement cost is the greatest amount that a buyer would pay for a specific asset. Typically, if land and buildings are valued separately, the land component is valued using the comparable sales method and buildings are valued using the cost method. The cost method uses building costs as a proxy for value. This approach is usually taken if there are few open market sales. There is a trend toward using this method of assessing the value of buildings as is done in the Philippines, Indonesia, Korea, and Taiwan. In Japan, the fixed asset tax assessment for buildings is based on the assessment of replacement costs and other factors (i.e., not directly related to market value). Thailand, under its 2020 property tax reforms, now values buildings on the basis of nationally determined building cost schedules.

The income capitalization approach, often simply called the income approach, values commercial and investment properties (such as office and retail buildings). This method capitalizes an income stream into a present value that can be considered the market value. It relies on information on market sales to determine the capitalization rate and on sufficient rental transactions. The method applies the market-derived yields to the annual income or rental stream to determine the market value. The most common types of properties valued by this method include hotels, resort properties, cinemas, theaters, and sports stadiums. It is widely used in Asia— for example, by Hong Kong, Malaysia, and Singapore.

Automated Mass Valuation

The scale of the property tax valuation task is immense. Most jurisdictions include hundreds of thousands if not millions of properties to be valued or revalued, often all at the same time. One solution is to do mass valuations, which are quite different from one-by-one single-property valuations (IAAO 2010). That is not to say that case-by-case valuations are not undertaken alongside mass valuation; however, they tend to be applied to particular property types, such as airports, high-end hotels, resort properties, ports and harbors, and specialized industrial properties. According to Almy (2013), the driving force behind the development of mass valuation methods has been the need to improve the valuation efficiency of the immovable property tax. Ultimately, the scale of the valuation— number of properties—has led to the widespread use of technology and automation (IAAO 2018; Kok, Koponen, and Martinez-Barbosa 2017).

Mass valuation is generally considered to mean the valuation of homogeneous property types at the same valuation date by applying statistical methodologies (Eckert 1990). The objective is to replicate the market within which real estate is traded (Fibbens 1995; Wang and Li 2019). Traditional and mass valuation use essentially the same methods, but mass valuation uses statistical models (IAAO 2017). In Hong Kong, for example, the majority of residential units, offices, and factories are valued by rental comparison, which makes extensive use of automated valuation techniques by a computer-assisted mass appraisal (CAMA) system.[9] To enhance the accuracy of the regression models, Hong Kong's Rating and Valuation Department uses an automated program to update the valuation characteristics.

Table 2.3 illustrates the use of mass valuation and geographic information systems (GIS) across the jurisdictions covered in this analysis. Hong Kong and Korea are examples of advanced application of mass valuation. Malaysia and the Philippines are establishing mass valuation techniques, but responsibility for valuation in these two jurisdictions is at the municipal level and progress has been slow. In Taiwan, despite the demonstrated capability of advanced automated valuation models in constructing property price indexes, these technologies have not been used. However, GIS technology is widely employed in various aspects of valuation—for example, displaying valuation results to the members of valuation committees.

When revaluations based on market values are done frequently (yearly, every second year, or even every third year), it is impossible to manually revalue every property. In its Standard on Mass Appraisal, the International Association of Assessing Officers (IAAO) considers annual assessment to be an integral component of a market value system, but it states, "Annual assessment does not necessarily mean, however, that each property must be re-examined each year. Instead, models can be recalibrated, or market adjustment factors derived from ratio studies or other market analyses applied based on criteria such as property type, location, size, and age" (IAAO 2017, 10). Annual revaluations conducted in Hong Kong, Singapore, and Korea are made possible by mass valuation techniques.

The mass valuation system in Korea values some 30 million land parcels annually. A sample of 450,000 parcels are designated as standard parcels and are then appraised by professional fee appraisers and the Korea Real Estate Board. These official values of standard parcels become benchmark values within value zones, or geographic areas of similar property types having broadly similar values. This benchmark value is applied to all individual land parcels within a zone and then adjusted by using estimated coefficients of factors affecting the unit price of land. A parcel's size, location, shape, usage, proximity to amenities, and other characteristics are collected, and the observed difference of these attributes from those of the standard parcels are measured and multiplied by the estimated coefficients derived from multiple regression models. Japan uses a similar approach in identifying standard parcels having a road frontage for the valuation of residential land.

Table 2.3 Application of Automated Mass Valuation

Jurisdiction	Use of Automated Valuation Methods	Use of GIS	Comment
China	Several cities have been developing mass valuation approaches in readiness for any property tax implementation. See Davis et al. 2020.	Several property tax projects have involved the use of GIS-based valuation modeling.	If China introduces a recurrent property tax, mass valuation and GIS-based techniques are expected to be extensively used.
Hong Kong	Multiple regression analysis is used for revaluations.	GIS is fully integrated into the property valuation methodology, particularly for commercial property.	Indexation can be used to update values for commercial property.
India (Delhi)	The unit-area method uses a fairly straightforward ward formula, and the method is used in several cities. Reassessments in Delhi have not taken place for several years.	GIS in urban municipalities is becoming more widespread.	GIS is now used to assist with the administration of the property tax, determining the tax base, and facilitating collection.
Indonesia	Under disrepair following devolution in 2001 and decentralization of the property tax in 2011, but some automated mass appraisal approaches were applied.	Central government had developed a GIS-based mass valuation system.	The GIS-based mass valuation system fell into disrepair following devolution in 2001, but some of the larger cities have been developing their own solutions.
Japan	Over 40,000 reference properties are appraised, and values are imputed to zones within the country.	GIS has been progressively integrated to support valuation.	
Korea	Mass valuation market-based models are widely used.	GIS is an integral part of the valuation exercise.	The country has a unified land value system. Buildings are valued using the cost methodology.

(continued)

Table 2.3 Application of Automated Mass Valuation (*continued*)

Jurisdiction	Use of Automated Valuation Methods	Use of GIS	Comment
Malaysia	CAMA is not widely used by local-government valuation departments. Capacity of staff is an issue.	Valuation departments make limited use of GIS.	Only the larger local governments (e.g., Kuala Lumpur) use CAMA and GIS.
Pakistan	Given the formulaic approach to assessment, the process is fully automated across the provinces.	GIS is integrated into the property tax system only in Punjab.	GIS captures the tax base and helps coordinate billing and collection activities.
Philippines	Some local-government areas use mass appraisal approaches.	No significant progress has been made in integrating GIS.	A mass appraisal manual has been developed, but the use by assessor departments of mass valuation approaches has been limited.
Singapore	The city applies regression analysis to determine average rental values.	GIS is fully integrated into the property tax system.	
Taiwan	Automated valuation and advanced regression approaches are not used to determine land value.	GIS is used in the administration of the land value process.	GIS is widely used in cities to indicate the spatial value of land. A commission is now studying the possibility of CAMA use.
Thailand	Automated approaches to analyze the price of land are used, but regression models are not widely used.	The Ministry of Land uses GIS in building their land parcel registry.	Buildings are valued using nationally announced building costs.
Vietnam	No mass valuation system is being used. Valuation is based on land price tables that list estimated prices per square meter for land.	No application of GIS is made within the property tax system.	The Ministry of Natural Resources and Environment is running pilot projects with technical assistance from the Korea Real Estate Board that use mass valuation and GIS. No broad-based recurrent property tax system is in place.

Source: Case studies in part 2 of this book.

None of this is to say that CAMA systems are fault-free. The use of a regression analysis alone tells us that the goal is to estimate an average value for all properties with certain characteristics. The actual observed values for properties will fall around this regression average, and so there will be differentials between actual and estimated values for most properties. A second problem is that the cost of annually repopulating the data system every year can be quite large. A third is that CAMA is not very transparent—that is, an individual taxpayer may not understand how taxable property value was determined.

There have been significant advances in the use of artificial intelligence and machine learning approaches (IPTI 2021; McCluskey et al. 2012). Research conducted by the International Property Tax Institute (IPTI 2021) concluded that although existing mass appraisal tools can be highly effective and produce excellent performance results, artificial intelligence offers another viable tool that, used properly, can efficiently produce equally—or, arguably, more—accurate valuations than can mass appraisals for many jurisdictions.[10]

Frequency of Revaluations

For the property tax to be fair and equitable, the underlying valuations should be regularly revised to reflect changes in market value. In dynamic real estate markets, revaluations provide fairness and revenue buoyancy (IAAO 2020; Walters 2011). Legislation may specify the frequency of revaluations, but they may be delayed, postponed, or canceled, as has been the case in India, Indonesia, Malaysia, and Pakistan. Kuala Lumpur undertook a revaluation in 2014 following a gap of 22 years. The timing of general revaluations in Hong Kong is not specified in the Rating Ordinance, but since 1988 general revaluations in Hong Kong have been conducted annually. According to the IAAO, all properties should be revalued at least every four to six years (IAAO 2020). Frequent revaluations maintain the legitimacy of the tax and reduce the risk of sudden valuation shocks and of significant shifts in tax burdens (Bird and Slack 2004). In a value-based system in which property market values change over time, a shorter revaluation cycle is preferable.

In the Philippines, all provinces and cities are mandated to update and revise real property assessments and classifications every three years. Since about 1990, compliance has been generally poor, and many provinces and cities use dated valuation rolls. Still, there are no penalties under the law for noncompliance with the three-year rule, and no administrative sanctions or incentives for compliance have been introduced. Land values in Thailand before the 2020 property tax reform had not been revised for 30 years. In

Taiwan, land values are updated every two years, and building values are updated every three years. Even so, certain buildings in Taiwan have assessed values that are badly outdated.

Annual revaluations, which have the benefit of keeping property tax values current, are relatively rare internationally. Jurisdictions that have dynamic or volatile property markets tend to use them (Hong Kong and Korea). Table 2.4 shows the frequency of reassessment across systems, some as often as annually but most ranging from three to ten years. The main reasons for the infrequency of revaluations are (1) political inertia due to a perception that increased values will lead to tax increases; (2) the lack of financial resources to undertake property inspections and build the necessary databases; (3) the high cost of acquiring new software programs and automated valuation tools, including GIS, to support revaluation; and (4) skill shortages and technical capacity gaps limiting the ability to conduct revaluations.

The costs of revaluation can be high even though technology and automated approaches can reduce these. The cost benefit of annual revaluations should be carefully considered. Although legislation may specify the period of revaluation cycles, many jurisdictions (Indonesia, Malaysia, Pakistan, and Philippines) have difficulty adhering to the law.

An alternative to revaluation of the tax roll is indexing (for example, by the consumer price index or rate of inflation). This is relatively uncommon in Asia. Indexing all properties by the same factor fails to capture the differential rates at which individual properties change in value, but giving up some fairness may be a small price to pay if there are insufficient resources to regularly conduct revaluations (Bird and Slack 2004; Kitchen 2013). In Hong Kong, indexation is considered appropriate if new ratable values are to be generated or adjusted in bulk and on a uniform basis. Indexing the assessment base (between infrequent reassessments) to keep up with inflation has been discussed in Pakistan, where valuation tables for land and buildings are used (Bahl, Cyan, and Wallace 2015). It has also been recommended that India make a more frequent adjustment to the coefficients used in the calibrated area system (Rao 2008).

Property Data for Valuation Purposes

Valuation and assessment are data driven and will likely become more so in the future. But recording the particulars of every parcel in a country and managing the data flow to support valuation is a daunting task. In many Asian jurisdictions, the volume of information generated by new technology appears to be outrunning the resources available to use it. Major data challenges are (1) getting enough accurate estimates of the market

Table 2.4 Frequency of Revaluations

Jurisdiction	Revaluation Frequency	Comment
China	–	No national, broad-based property tax yet exists.
Hong Kong	Annual	Annual revaluations have been conducted since 1988. There are about 2.5 million assessments and 1.85 million residential properties.
India (Delhi)	Every three years	Delhi's move to the unit-area value system effectively removes the need for revaluation. However, benchmark base values should be revised every third year. Indexation of the base values can be done, but has not. Assessments in some large cities are outdated.
Indonesia	Every three years	Municipalities have some autonomy as to the frequency of revaluations. Most local governments have not revalued according to the three-year cycle recommended in the law.
Japan	Every three years	Revaluations are generally updated according to this cycle.
Korea	Annual	About 30 million properties are revalued annually. Values are pre-scribed nationally for local-government use. The values of land and buildings are announced annually.
Malaysia	Every five years	The frequency is specified in legisla-tion but few local governments meet this schedule. Kuala Lumpur's last revaluation was 2014; the previous one was in 1999.
Pakistan	The valuation tables according to legislation are to be revised every ten years by provincial tax departments.	The valuation tables in Sindh are very outdated. In Punjab the tables were updated in 2014. Recommendations have been made to apply an index in the years between revaluations.
Philippines	Every three years	The majority of local governments are unable to meet the three-year cycle.

(*continued*)

Table 2.4 Frequency of Revaluations (*continued*)

Jurisdiction	Revaluation Frequency	Comment
Singapore	Annual	To revalue 1.53 million assessments annually, extensive use of automated valuation methods is made.
Taiwan	Land values are reassessed every two years. Building costs and adjustment factors are reviewed every three years.	No value coordination occurs because land values and building values are assessed separately and at different intervals. Updating of building values tends to lag changes in market construction costs.
Thailand	Every four years	The national government announces new appraisal values on a four-year cycle. A new tax roll was available for 2020, but the previous roll was extended during the transition to the new tax regime.
Vietnam	Every five years	The national government establishes the land price framework within which the provincial people's committee develops land price tables.

Source: Case studies in part 2 of this book.

value of property; (2) managing interagency data flows; (3) handling the large amount of data necessary to support the property tax administration; and (4) assessing the potential of "big data."

Ensuring Ample, High-Quality Data on Property Transactions

Accurate and timely data on real property transactions (both sales and rentals) are key information for a market value–based property tax (Bahl and Bird 2018; Kelly 2014; Walters 2011). However, the quantity and quality of transaction data is problematic. Without an adequate number of sales or rents by property type across all locations, inferences cannot be made about the total population of properties. If buyers and sellers are dishonest in declaring the sale price and underdeclarations are not policed, data will be inaccurate. This is a long-standing and worldwide problem (Alm, Annez, and Modi 2006; Bahl 2004; Franzsen 2020).

Underdeclaration of sales prices is driven by high property transfer tax rates, perceived low probabilities of being detected, and a weak penalty system.

In Indonesia and the Philippines, for example, sales data are available from the declaration required for the levy of the transfer tax, which also is a local tax. The question is whether the assessing governments can use this declared, but suspect, data to assist in revaluations.

In most lower-income jurisdictions in Asia, the declared transaction price is accepted even when suspect. The Philippines attempted to deal with underdeclaration by developing official land values according to location. These values were to be updated every three years, but this rarely happened. In Indonesia, the declared transaction prices are used for transfer taxes unless they are lower than the government-estimated value of the property. But the government-estimated value is itself understated by about 50 percent.

Sharing Property-Related Information Across Agencies

In addition to problems with the quality of and quantity of data, there are issues with the flow of information to the valuation authority. The valuation authority is often not a direct recipient of market price information (McCluskey, Franzsen, and Bahl 2017a), because the transactions are recorded within a different government organization. For example, in Malaysia, the property transfer tax (known as stamp duty) is a federal tax and is administered by national government valuers. However, the land information system containing ownership data at the state level is neither integrated nor linked with property data held by local authorities. Property registration is under the state authority, and any change of ownership on the title is not directly shared with the local government. A similar situation holds in Thailand. This is a significant problem for the administration of a value-based property tax. Solutions to such problems could be as easy as the government entities signing and honoring a memorandum of understanding to allow data sharing. But in practice, the political economy and sometimes the law make the solution much more difficult.

Managing Huge Amounts of Data

Property tax administrations must handle a huge information flow. For example, if 500,000 properties are on the valuation roll and each property has 15 characteristics, the database system must hold 7.5 million bits of information. In addition, property tax systems often require that specific categories of property be valued—for example, Japan's fixed asset tax allows municipalities to levy tax on land, structures, and depreciable assets (construction equipment, machinery, factory equipment, and other assets).

In Hong Kong, the Rating and Valuation Department has been able to track and annually refresh the details of about 382,000 rental records, comprising about 228,000 domestic and 154,000 nondomestic properties. These rental details provide core evidence for valuations carried out by the department. In the 2019/2020 valuation list, this information was used to value 2.1 million residential property assessments and 410,000 commercial assessments.

Local governments in Thailand have the responsibility to survey all properties in their jurisdictions manually and to calculate the land and building tax liability of each owner. In Japan, there are almost 41 million registered owners of land and some 42 million owners of buildings in the tax cadastre (as of fiscal year 2018). In Malaysia, legislation empowers the local authority to enter any property to inspect it. In addition, the law also empowers the local authority to require the owners or occupiers of any property to furnish information on the size of the property, situation, quality, use, and rent necessary for the preparation of the valuation list.

The administrative costs of property taxation in Korea come mainly from the massive data-handling requirements required for annual reassessment. Approximately 30 million taxable objects (land and housing units) are listed in the property tax roll, and at least 25 percent of them need to be updated annually for the changes to their ownership and physical characteristics.

Harnessing New Technology to Manage Big Data

Administrations are collecting an ever-increasing amount of property-related data from traditional sources but also from digital sources such as orthoimagery, digital payments, electronic invoicing, and connected devices such as point-of-sale solutions—handheld credit-card payment machines used by revenue collectors. Many administrations are expanding their data collection capabilities even further into new areas such as aerial imagery, and the use of unmanned aerial vehicles (drones) has created an exponential source of spatial data in places like Hong Kong and Korea. Satellite imagery has been very successfully used in Punjab, Pakistan, to identify land and buildings. Jakarta, Indonesia, has also been using drones to track property changes.

To address the rapid influx of information, more and more administrations are looking to modernize their big data capabilities. Big data is a field that systematically analyzes, extracts information from, or otherwise deals with data sets that are too large or complex for traditional data-processing application software to handle (Kok, Koponen, and Martinez-Barbosa 2017; Marr 2015). This includes integrating data from multiple sources such as own-source data, taxpayer-declared information, third-party data (land registry), information collected by utility companies, and aerial and satellite imagery.

Successful data-management strategies focus on the desired outcome of the valuation administration, resources required for implementation, and the right balance of data security and transparency. Having a clear strategy helps valuation administrations assess their data collection processes in terms of data quality (data cleansing), data management, storage options (traditional versus cloud), the need to build representative data sets, data modeling output, active searches for and integration of new data sources (internal or external, structured or unstructured), and the application of effective data analytics.

Establishing effective data analytics processes requires a blend of technical skills, including mastery of statistical techniques, geospatial tools, and deep data analysis. For valuers and data modelers, the emphasis is moving toward data mining, machine-learning tools, and artificial intelligence–based solutions (PricewaterhouseCoopers 2022). The ultimate objective is the delivery of high-quality valuations that meet quality control metrics and standards while providing understandable values.

Higher-income jurisdictions in Asia are making considerable progress in establishing data analytics. Progress has been slower in the lower-income jurisdictions, in part because of their resource and capacity limitations in absorbing new technology. In the meantime, a simplification of property tax structures could be a useful policy program.

Objections and Appeals

Property tax legislation should include objection and appeal processes to allow property owners to challenge their valuations. International best practice (IAAO 2014) suggests that taxpayers want a process from start to finish that is quick, cheap, simple, proportionate, stress-free, rigorous, and authoritative. Even though quick and cheap, and rigorous and authoritative are not likely to be achieved by an appeals process, best practice appears to embody (1) independence from those whose decisions are being reviewed; (2) timeliness and proportionality; (3) an initial informal hearing to attempt resolution of the matter in dispute; (4) comprehensive, nontechnical information about the process; (5) nonadversarial hearings that are not too legalistic; (6) consistent and comprehensible decisions; and (7) good value to the taxpayer (Kitchen 2013; McCluskey, Franzsen, and Bahl 2017b; Plimmer 2013).

Appeals should provide an opportunity for property owners to be heard, and if appropriate, to meet with the valuation agency (McCluskey and Franzsen 2013). In the case of valuation disputes, an objection or appeal system should make possible opportunities for informal meetings with the valuation agency and for formal process meetings before independent bodies are involved in the dispute resolution. Key components of any valuation appeal system are reliance on clearly written procedures, a well-developed public relations program for notification, and avoidance of actions that might suggest discrimination in the way objections are treated and resolved (Plimmer 2013).

Asian jurisdictions differ in their approaches to the objection and appeal process (table 2.5). Generally speaking, value-based property tax systems have transparent objection and appeal processes. However, where property values are prescribed by national, provincial, or local government, the rights to object are severely limited. The cases in point are cities in India under the unit-area property tax and Punjab and Sindh Provinces in Pakistan, where valuation tables are developed at the province level. In both India and Pakistan, objections can be made only against inaccuracies in the size of the land or building or whether it is owner occupied or rented. Because the valuation tables are prescribed, there is no real opportunity to object to the values. This is also true in Vietnam, where land price frameworks and land price tables are prescribed by the national and provincial governments.

Responsibility for Valuation

Assigning responsibility for valuation is a key decision, because valuation is arguably the most difficult aspect of administering a property tax. The best approach will be to use some combination of central government, provincial or local government, and the private sector, depending on the comparative advantage of each (Kelly, White, and Anand 2020; Kitchen 2013; Walters 2011). The division of valuation functions should follow those comparative advantages. A specialized central-government agency may be best equipped to undertake valuations nationally. Also, the setting of valuation standards, practices, and procedures might be more efficiently done at the center because it permits efficiency advantages of scale and technical expertise to be captured.

But centralized valuation administrations have some disadvantages: (1) the scale of the valuations can overwhelm the administration; (2) higher-level governments might have little incentive to make extra effort to improve revenue collections for local governments; (3) there can be greater political influence at the national level, which can affect frequency of revaluations; (4) centralized valuation activities can lead to a disconnect with local real estate dynamics; and (5) the local property tax regime might be different from that at the central level.

In Korea, the determination of property values is the responsibility of a designated government-run assessment agency, the Korea Real Estate Board. This board is governed by appointed officials of the Ministry of Land, Infrastructure, and Transportation.

Table 2.5 Objection and Appeal Systems

Jurisdiction	Objection and Appeal Process
China	None; no annual broad-based property tax exists.
Hong Kong	Objection to commissioner of Rating and Valuation. Further appeal to the Lands Tribunal and then on points of law to the Court of Appeal.
India	With the expansion of self-assessment, the concept of appeals has been diluted, although the municipal corporation can audit taxpayer returns, which can result in appeals from the taxpayer.
Indonesia	Objections to the land value and building value can be made to the valuation department of the municipality.
Japan	Objections are made to the local municipality.
Korea	Objections can be made against the individual assessments on both land and buildings. The Korea Real Estate Board handles all appeals.
Malaysia	Taxpayers can object to their assessed value or to correct clerical errors. Objections are made to the municipality that prepared the valuation.
Pakistan	Because the property tax is based on prescribed tables, taxpayers have no opportunity to appeal the assessed value.
Philippines	The first appeal is to the assessor. A further appeal can be made to the local board of assessment appeals and from there to the Central Board of Assessment Appeals.
Singapore	Objections are made to the chief assessor. Objectors dissatisfied with the result may, within 30 days, appeal to the Valuation Review Board. Further appeal goes to the High Court.
Taiwan	Valuation disputes are heard by the expert committees. A further appeal can then be made to the administrative courts.
Thailand	If taxpayers believe their assessment to be inaccurate, they can appeal to the local authorities, who have one month to determine the appeal. If dissatisfied, taxpayers can then make a further, final appeal to the civil court.
Vietnam	National government establishes a land price framework that is then used by the provinces to determine land price tables used for the land tax. Using established prices, owners declare the characteristics of their land and calculate the tax due. Essentially no objection is allowed to the prescribed land value per square meter.

Source: Case studies in part 2 of this book.

In Thailand, the national Treasury Department establishes schedules of land prices and building costs, which are then applied by local government in determining individual assessments. Under the Property Appraisal Act, the nationally determined appraisal values must reflect the uses and types of properties and be in accordance with appraisal and economic principles, particularly the market value of the property. This approach separates the valuation of land and buildings, whereby the price of the latter varies with the type of construction. The approach used by the government is to determine the value of buildings and condominiums according to a set nationwide values per square meter. A depreciation allowance is established on the basis of type of construction material. Both land prices and building costs are reviewed and adjusted at four-year intervals.

Valuations in Taiwan are conducted by higher-level government assessors. Before values can be adopted, the assessors must submit their values along with supporting evidence to an expert committee. This committee has the authority to make changes to the submitted valuations.

An advantage of having valuations conducted by a local administration is familiarity with the local property market. However, valuations by local government may suffer from a lack of technical valuation capacity and inadequate investment in valuation systems and tools. But all local governments in a country are not alike, and larger urban areas may have the capacity for better property tax administration. A major problem with the devolution of responsibility for the property tax in Indonesia is the differing capacity in local governments. One view is that the most effective valuation administrative strategy is to share administrative responsibilities on the basis of comparative advantage (Kitchen 2013). In 1996, the Local Tax Act in Korea was amended to prohibit local governments from maintaining their own land valuation systems; they were required to apply a certain percentage of the publicly declared value estimated by national government as their taxable land and housing value. Of course, the setting is also important in determining the proper division of administrative responsibility—for example, high-income regions will find decentralization more feasible than low-income areas.

Table 2.6 summarizes the responsibility for valuation in the relevant jurisdictions.

Fractional Assessments

Fractional assessment fixes assessments of different types of property at different percentages of estimated full market value (IAAO 2011). In effect, it allows certain types of properties to be taxed at a lower effective rate than other properties (Bird and Slack 2004). The classifications are often

Table 2.6 Responsibility for Valuation

Jurisdiction	Tier of Government	Valuation Responsibility
China	–	Not yet formally decided, but it is likely to be municipal administrations if a recurrent property tax is implemented.
Hong Kong	Central	Rating and Valuation Department.
India (Delhi)	Local	Municipal corporations, Municipal Valuation Committees.
Indonesia	Local; provincial for Jakarta	Devolution of property tax administration began in 2011 when municipalities and city governments began taking over from central government.
Japan	Local	Private-sector valuers, tasked by municipalities.
Korea	Central	Government-run assessment agency, the Korea Real Estate Board.
Malaysia	Local	Department of Valuation and Property Services.
Pakistan	Provincial	Excise and Taxation Department.
Philippines	Provincial and city	Provincial assessment departments; local assessment departments.
Singapore	Central	Inland Revenue Authority.
Taiwan	Central	Land values are determined by the local land administration department and building values by the revenue service department. Each set of valuations is reviewed and approved by separate expert committees.
Thailand	Central	The Ministry of Finance establishes national land prices and average building costs, which provincial assessment committees may adjust.
Vietnam	Central and provincial	Central government establishes base value ranges for provinces. Provincial people's committees then apply these base values to the districts.

Source: Case studies in part 2 of this book.

based on current use; for example, agriculture is generally given a preferential assessment rate. It may fall to the valuer to classify each property in order to apply the proper fractional assessment.

The practice of fractional valuation varies from country to country. Formerly, local governments in Korea were empowered to set the assessment ratio. However, a presidential decree has now set a nationally uniform fractional assessment ratio for residential property at 60 percent and 70 percent for land and commercial buildings. In addition, differential statutory tax rates are imposed on commercial and residential buildings.

In Japan the standard fixed asset tax rate for land is about 70 percent of the public valuation. For agricultural land, the assessment ratio is 45 percent of the public valuation. The Philippines assesses residential property at 20 percent and commercial property at 50 percent.

Some might see classification of properties for assessment purposes as violating the economic principles of value-based (ad valorem) taxation because properties tend to be taxed at more or less favored percentages of value, on the basis of political rather than objective considerations. Classification also adds a layer of complexity. A system with three classes of property and assessment fractions ranging from 10 percent to 50 percent of market value may not be too difficult for taxpayers to understand. Some systems, however, may have 10 or more classes and fractions ranging from 5 percent to 60 percent of market value. Property classification can violate the transparency standard by creating a less open system in which assessment equity errors are easier to hide and more difficult to discover.

Self-Assessment

There are three versions of self-assessment. Under the first version, the taxpayer declares the characteristics of her property, such as size, number of rooms, and age. The valuation authority then vets and approves them. The second version is the declaration of value or factors determining value. Taxpayers may complete a self-assessment form that asks the location of their property, the type and area of the building and land, and the use (residential, commercial, industrial, etc.). Taxpayers can then calculate the assessed value of their property from schedules provided by the taxing jurisdiction. On the basis of this valuation, an automated routine calculates the tax liability (e.g., in India, Vietnam).[11] In a third version, the property owner self-declares the value.

Before Thailand's reforms that began in 2017 and culminated in 2020, property tax was based on self-declaration. In the newly reformed system, the Treasury Department will undertake the valuations. Taiwan had a self-declaration system in place for several years, but it failed badly because taxpayers did not report truthfully. In the Philippines any person owning real property or having a legal interest in it is required to file with the local assessor a sworn statement that describes the property in detail and declares its true value. This must be done once every three years, coinciding with the mandated period of revaluation of property values at the local level. This is a useful practice when transaction data are unavailable to support market value determination.

The two main advantages of self-assessment and mandatory data reporting are that (1) large amounts of data can be collected over a relatively short period (as opposed to the time it would take the property tax administration to make in-the-field inspections); and (2) administrative costs are reduced because the obligation is moved from the government to the taxpayer. The main disadvantages relate to the potential lack of accuracy and uniformity in the data reported, and the likelihood that taxpayers will not be honest in their reporting.

Administration of the Property Tax

Jurisdictions strive for full coverage of all taxable properties, a near 100 percent collection rate, and low compliance costs for taxpayers. Of course, no country achieves this, but some come very close. Property tax administrative efficiency is generally better in Asia's high-income jurisdictions (Hong Kong, Japan, Korea, Singapore, and Taiwan) than the middle- and lower-income jurisdictions (India, Indonesia, Malaysia, Pakistan, Philippines, Thailand, and Vietnam), as evidenced by the higher collection rates in the former group. By 2018, rates arrears in Hong Kong stood at less than 0.5 percent of annual rates demanded. In 2017, collection of the fixed asset tax and city planning tax in Japan were, respectively, 99.3 percent and 99.4 percent of taxes due. Also in 2017, the recurrent property tax collection rate was 97 percent in Korea, 95 percent in Singapore, and 96 percent in Taiwan. (China has not yet introduced a recurrent property tax.)

Data on collection rates for some lower-income jurisdictions are not readily available, but indications from the case studies in part 2 are that they are well below those reported for the higher-income jurisdictions. For example, the property tax collection rates reported for the Philippines and Indonesia are 65 percent and 80 percent, respectively, and in Indonesia the level of arrears is equivalent to about 25 percent of property tax revenues. Although collection levels vary among Pakistan's provinces, the average is reported to be between 50 and 60 percent. These estimates correspond with the collection rate estimates reported for developing jurisdictions of between 30 and 60 percent (Bahl and Bird 2018; Kelly 2014; Kelly, White, and Anand 2020; Mohanty 2014). With reference to a Finance Commission of India Report of 2009, Mohanty (2014) reports a collection efficiency rate of only 37 percent for Indian cities.

The discussion that follows sheds some light on the reasons for the weak administration of property taxation in the poorer jurisdictions of Asia. It covers several issues related to the property tax: supervision and control of the billing and collection processes, payment options, enforcement and recovery of arrears, and communication with taxpayers. In nearly all facets of property tax administration, property tax practices appear to be more cost effective in jurisdictions that have reached a higher level of economic development.

Supervision and Control

Not surprisingly, administrative processes and procedures and taxpayer support are better developed in the high-income jurisdictions (Hong Kong, Japan, and Singapore). In Hong Kong, the Rating and Valuation Department provides a one-stop service to ratepayers, who can opt to receive one consolidated bill covering all their properties. The printing and enveloping of rates demands are outsourced to a private contractor, and the delivery of tax bills is outsourced to the Hongkong Post (the government's postal services department). The Rating and Valuation Department has been making service improvements and innovations—for example, combining demands for rates and government rent to ratepayers with multiple properties. Although the responsibilities are contracted out, the department remains accountable for the outsourced tasks. The control of the property tax administration is similarly efficient in Singapore and Japan.

Control of property tax administration is more difficult in the poorer Asian jurisdictions. In the Philippines, provincial and city governments have wide-ranging responsibilities that must be coordinated. Implementing an effective property tax requires involvement of local tax authorities and, thus, coordination and collaboration among all the relevant ministries and between levels of government. This is not easy to achieve in practice. They have the authority to decide on the property values and tax rates, and they provide relief for property owners and taxpayers, impose interest and penalties, apply discounts, and enforce tax collection measures within their jurisdictions. The assessor is important in the first three phases (property identification, appraisal, and assessment) and in records management, and the local treasurer oversees tax collection and enforcement. Coordination can be difficult. In Vietnam, the Ministry of Finance, the Ministry of Construction, and the Ministry of Natural Resources and Environment all provide information for administering property taxation. This fragmentation likely results in gaps and duplication of effort. Implementing the property tax effectively also requires the involvement of local tax authorities, and thus calls for coordination and collaboration among all the relevant ministries and between levels of government.

Billing, Payment, and Compliance Costs

For many lower-income Asian jurisdictions, compliance rates for the property tax remain high (Kelly 2014). Where compliance costs have come down, collection rates are higher. The collection problem in low-income jurisdictions does not appear to be affordability, because the effective tax rate is often very low and because most jurisdictions offer flexible payment options. For example, the real property tax in the Philippines may be paid in a lump sum or in four equal installments without any interest.

The failure to deliver notice of taxes due can be a problem, especially in jurisdictions with many small governments. Again drawing on the experience in the Philippines, some local-government units (LGUs) previously sent bills by courier services, but the present practice is to post notices on real property tax payment deadlines in public places. Although all nonagricultural land taxpayers in Vietnam are on the tax roll and assessed, payment notifications are sent to only about 25 percent of taxpayers, those whose tax due exceeds the cost of billing.

Payment Options

Technology has significantly reduced the compliance (time) costs of paying property taxes in the richer jurisdictions of Asia (RVDSAR 2021). In 2017–2018, 36 percent of rates payments in Hong Kong were made by electronic means. Payments were made through bank autopay, payment by phone services, ATMs, the Internet, and postal service or in person at one of the 121 post offices or 1,400 convenience stores. In Japan, options for payment include ordinary banks and postal banks; most convenience stores; the Pay-easy network, which allows payment via the Internet or ATMs; registered bank transfer; and credit card. Similarly, in Taiwan, taxpayers can pay at ATMs, banks, or shops or via debit order, electronic funds transfer, or the Taiwan pay system. Singapore piloted digital property tax bills in 2017 with text messages (SMS notification). Acting on taxpayers' positive response, government dispatched nearly 1 million e-PT bills in 2018.

The local governments in the low-income jurisdictions of Asia are at an earlier stage of using electronic modes of property tax payment, although progress is noticeable. Several payment options are available in the Philippines, though these differ among LGUs. Satellite collection offices are commonly set up and operated directly by city or municipal treasury officers during the collection period. Some LGUs allow electronic payment, using credit and debit cards; others have mobile or off-site payment facilities. Government financial institutions where LGUs maintain their accounts can also be used. In Pakistan's Punjab Province, payment by mobile phone is also possible; and in Jakarta, Indonesia, payments can be made at ATMs.

Collection of the nonagricultural land use tax in Vietnam may be outsourced to a collection agency through a fee-based contract with the local tax authorities. Fees range from 5 percent (Hanoi and Ho Chi Minh City) to 8 percent in the mountainous provinces in the northern region and the provinces in the Central Highlands. However, not many agencies accept these contracts because the nonagricultural land use tax yields little revenue, making the collection fee very small.

Enforcement and Recovery of Arrears

Finding delinquent taxpayers and recovering arrears are important components of any property tax system. Hard administrative measures (such as interest and penalties) and legal measures (such as tax liens, debt recovery through the courts, and forced sales) are available in most jurisdictions. But so are soft measures (better communications, naming and shaming). To the extent there is a pattern in Asia, it is that higher-income jurisdictions are willing to enforce with hard measures, and lower-income jurisdictions tend to be more hesitant.

In Hong Kong, rates not paid by the due date may be subject to a surcharge of 5 percent and a further 10 percent if still unpaid after six months. Rates are recoverable as a debt to the government. For arrears not exceeding about USD 6,450, cases are heard in the Small Claims Tribunal; the District Court handles larger amounts. If rates remain outstanding after the court's judgment, the commissioner of Rating and Valuation may prohibit any transfer of the property until rates are paid. The law in Hong Kong is silent on further stringent measures such as allowing distress and sale of goods.

Indonesia, Japan, Pakistan, and the Philippines charge interest on late payments. In Japan, the interest amounts to 2.6 percent for the first month of arrears, but increases to 8.9 percent in the second month. In practice, these interest rates align with the prime lending rate. Malaysia follows detailed steps in the case of delinquency, issuing forms one after the other. In both Japan and Malaysia, authorities may seize the assets of a delinquent taxpayer and sell them in a public auction.

Taiwan heavily penalizes arrears. A penalty fee of 1 percent for every two days in arrears and forced execution of penalties (e.g., seizure of bank accounts) by the courts is possible after only thirty days. In Thailand, taxpayers may face penalties of 10 to 40 percent of the total amount of the unpaid tax and a further 1 percent interest on the total amount of the unpaid tax per month. If taxpayers refuse to pay their taxes without cause, they must pay a fine and in some cases can be jailed.

The Philippines places a lien for unpaid property taxes on the subject property, which is superior to all liens, charges, or encumbrances, that will be extinguished only when the tax and all the related interests and expenses are paid. City and municipal treasurers must apply payments of real property taxes to prior years' debt first, including interest and penalties. Only after settlement of these liabilities will payment cover the current year's liabilities. In Singapore, outstanding property tax also constitutes a tax lien (first charge) against delinquent properties, and as a last resort, these properties may be seized and sold. This is also the case in Thailand.

Although penalties for nonpayment seem to be in place, detailed evidence on enforcement results is not readily available. It remains unclear as to whether the probability of detection or the enforcement of penalties are effective deterrents.

Communication with Taxpayers

Property tax policy and administration ought to be transparent. This begins with good communication with taxpayers. Taxpayers need to know why their tax bill is what it is and why their neighbors pay more or less than they do. It is important that they understand proposals to increase tax bills. All this can play an important role in enhancing compliance and lowering resistance to property taxation.

Hong Kong's Rating and Valuation Department prides itself on its transparency of property and market information, operational efficiency, and good communications with taxpayers. An online property information platform integrates more than 2.5 million records held by the department and the Land Registry. Billings and payments, viewing of accounts, changes to payers' details, searches for ratable values in new valuation lists, and signing and submission of specified forms can all be done online. A 24-hour call center responds to telephone inquiries on all aspects of services, and the user-friendly website is updated regularly.

In Japan, most municipalities encourage taxpayers to pay their property taxes by providing notice of assessment and by explaining the purposes of property taxation. If taxpayers cannot make a required tax payment, municipal authorities seem quite willing to negotiate a suitable arrangement (such as deferral of payment or reduction of the burden for taxpayers who qualify for hardship relief) as alternatives to seizing and disposing a taxpayer's assets. The Tokyo Metropolitan Government has detailed web pages explaining the property and land tax assessment and payment systems.

Malaysia experienced a somewhat surprising administrative regression. Its online system, created in 2004, was supposed to provide online services for the public to interact electronically with local authorities. The system allows the public to review license and rental accounts, lodge complaints, and make payments. But many customers apparently prefer direct over-the-counter service. In 2019, only 14 local authorities were using the on-line service, compared with 64 local authorities in 2012.

In 2013 and 2014, the Philippines resorted to naming and shaming as part of the Department of Finance's Tax Watch campaign to increase transparency on the payment of national and local taxes and to encourage people to be tax compliant. Provinces and cities were profiled and ranked according to the age of their schedule of fair market value, and the public was informed of revenues forgone by LGUs for not revising the property values. The goal was to inform the public of the noncompliance of some LGUs and to recognize those that were following the legal mandates in updating property valuations. The response by councils was an increase in total real property tax revenues in 2015 and 2016.

Taxes on Property Transfers

Property tax usually refers to the recurrent annual tax on land or build-ings. If property transfer taxes are even included in the discussion, they are treated as separate taxes and their connections to the recurrent prop-erty tax often are ignored. This is probably because transfer taxes are lev-ied only when transactions occur, they are often levied by central govern-ment, and their rate and base changes are often centered on correcting overheated housing markets. But there are good reasons to view the prop-erty transfer tax as part of the overall property tax regime and to look for ways to harmonize its structure and administration with recurrent prop-erty taxes.

The annual property tax and property transfer taxes have essentially the same base (the value of property or the user right), liability for pay-ment of both is with the (past and present) owners,[12] both may be an impor-tant source for local-government revenues, and they are linked, however imperfectly, by their assessments. Moreover, transfer taxes often are struc-tured to enhance vertical and horizontal equity in the taxpaying population and to affect patterns of land use and land ownership. Recurrent property taxes take on these same objectives.

For several reasons, real estate transfer taxes have found their way into tax systems, and their staying power has been great (Alm, Annez, and Modi 2004; Bahl 2004; Franzsen 2020). First, it is an easy tax handle because buyers and sellers in many jurisdictions want a legal record of ownership and therefore will voluntarily comply (Bird and Slack 2014, 117). Second, it can be collected with ease, because the title or deed registration system is the audit mechanism to ensure compliance (Franzsen 2020). Third, the distribution of the tax burden may be progressive, especially in jurisdictions where value thresholds (Indonesia) or progressive rates (China, Korea, and Malaysia) apply. Fourth, a property transfer tax might reach that part of the taxable capacity (real property wealth) that is not captured by most other taxes. Finally, governments use property transfer taxes to cool down an overheated investment market in real property.

In some Asian jurisdictions, the property transfer tax yields significant revenue, equivalent to a large share of the recurrent property tax. This is also the case in the European Union, where, in 2015, revenue raised from property transfer taxes was larger than that raised from recurrent taxes in nine of the twenty-eight member states (Brzeski, Románová, and Franzsen 2019).

The Practice in Asia

All the jurisdictions covered in part 2 levy some form of tax or charge on property transfers. The taxpayers are both individuals and companies. Systems range from a single tax on property transfers (India, Japan, and Malaysia) to complex systems that collect multiple taxes when properties or property rights are transferred (China, Pakistan, Philippines, Taiwan, Thailand, and Vietnam). The practice is more advanced in some jurisdictions (Hong Kong and Singapore), and in others it is more rudimentary (India and Pakistan). Graduated tax rates are applied in China, Korea, Pakistan, Singapore, and Taiwan, which further complicates the administration. Singapore and Korea use separate surcharges on the basic rate of the transfer tax (table 2.7).

Tax Structure

The base of the property transfer tax is the market value of the property (or user right) transferred or the sales price of the property or the profits derived from the transfer. In some jurisdictions, the de facto tax base has become the declared price of the transaction, and in others it can be an

Table 2.7 Property Transfer Taxes and Other Fees and Charges on Land

Jurisdiction	Tax Type	Taxpayer	Tax Base	Tax Rate/Fee	Revenue	Comment
China	Deed tax	Buyer	Transfer of user right for lands and buildings	3%–5% of the purchase price	Local	Rates are preferential or exclude residential properties.
	Land appreciation tax	Buyer	Net income from the transfer of user rights	30%–60%, based on net income	Local	A progressive scale applies.
	Stamp tax	Buyer		0.05%	Local	
Hong Kong	Ad valorem stamp duty for first-time buyers	Buyer		Progressive scale up to 4.25%	Central	Hong Kong permanent residents who are buying their first homes or switching homes pay this tax.
	Special stamp duty	Seller		20%; 15%; 10%	Central	Applies from October 27, 2012, on residential property, and rate depends on how long property was held.
	Buyer's stamp duty	Buyer		15%	Central	Applies from October 27, 2012, on residential property except for permanent residents buying property for themselves.
India (Delhi)	Stamp duty	Buyer	Selling price or market value	Different rates in different states; Delhi surcharge rate is 5%	State and local	Revenues are shared with cities in some states.
	Registration fee	Buyer		1% (Delhi)	State	
Indonesia	Acquisition tax	Buyer	Based on the value of the transaction	5% of the sales price as ceiling	Local	Tax-free value threshold of IDR 80,000.
	Property transfer tax	Seller	Based on the value of the transaction	2.5%	Central	On sales price or locally assessed value, whichever is higher.

Country	Tax	Payer	Tax base	Level	Notes
Japan	Real property acquisition tax	Buyer	4% standard rate; 3% for land and residences	Prefectures	Same value base as fixed asset tax, not purchase price; value thresholds apply for land and buildings.
Korea	Acquisition tax	Buyer	1%–4% of purchase price	Local	Higher, progressive rate structures are applied to higher-value properties.
	Surtax for rural development		0%–0.2% of purchase price		
	Education surtax		0.06%–0.4% of purchase price		
			Declared price or the "standard market price fixed by Govt.		
Malaysia	Stamp duty	Buyer	1%–4% (sliding scale)	Central	As of 2019, 4% above MYR 1 million; also a capital gains tax.
Pakistan	Stamp duty	Buyer	3%	Provincial	
			Capital value as determined by the district council		
	Capital value tax	Buyer	2%	Provincial	
	Registration fee	Buyer	Up to 1%	Local	
			Same as stamp duty		
			Same as stamp duty		
	Withholding tax	Buyer and seller	2% (buyer); 1% (seller)	Federal	Payable when value of property is greater than PKR 4 million.
			Advance on other taxes due on property sales		
Philippines	Local transfer tax	Seller	0.5% (provinces); 0.75% (cities)	Local	
			Fair market value of the property		
	Document stamp tax		1.50%	Central	Administered by the Bureau of Internal Revenue.
			Sales price of the property		
	Capital gains tax	Seller	6%	Central	
			Fair market value of the property		

(continued)

Table 2.7 Property Transfer Taxes and Other Fees and Charges on Land (*continued*)

Jurisdiction	Tax Type	Taxpayer	Tax Base	Tax Rate/Fee	Revenue	Comment
Singapore	Buyer's stamp duty	Buyer		1%–3% nonresidential; 1%–4% residential	Central	Differentiates by use.
	Seller's stamp duty	Seller		12%; 8%; 4%	Central	Resales year 1; year 2; year 3.
	Additional buyer's stamp duty	Buyer		12%–30%	Central	Only on second homes and residential investment property.
Taiwan	Deeds tax	Buyer	Sales value of buildings	6%	Central	In most cases, the base is the same as for the building tax.
	Stamp duty	Buyer	Sum of the bases of land value increment tax and deeds tax	0.1%	Central	
	Land value increment tax	Seller	Capital gain on land sale	Progressive rate schedule	Local	Relatively few taxpayers in the top bracket.
	Integrated real estate income tax	Seller	Capital gain on building sale	Progressive rate schedule	Central	Levied jointly with land value increment tax.
Thailand	Transfer fee	Buyer		2%	Local	Department of Lands collects and remits; often split between the parties.
	Stamp duty	Seller		0.5%	Local	Payable only if business tax is not payable.
	Special business tax	Seller		3.3%	Central and local	0.3% (i.e., 10% on the 3%) is a municipal tax.
	Withholding tax	Seller		Individuals: progressive rates from 5% to 35%; legal persons: 1%	Central	

Vietnam	Registration charge	Buyer	The higher of the declared sales price and the value in the land price table	0.5%	Local	The transfer value is determined on the basis of the land price table and housing price as stipulated by the provincial people's committee.
	Land use levy collected when land user rights are assigned by the government	Buyer	Government-estimated land prices or competitive auctions	Rate is based on land use, land area, and land prices	Local	The transfer value is determined on the basis of the land price table as stipulated by the provincial people's committee. Improvements are not included in the tax base.
	Land rental payment	Household, business, and organization	Land price tables or auction	Rate is based on land use, land area, and land prices		The rent is paid annually or prepaid in full for the whole duration of the lease term.

Source: Case studies in part 2 of this book.

Note: This table excludes value-added taxes and goods and services taxes on real property transactions.

adjusted declared price (as described later). A basic exemption from taxation of these transfers may be given, and a special rate may be imposed for certain types of transfers. For example, Singapore taxes second homes at a higher rate and taxes properties held for shorter periods at higher rates, and Taiwan and Korea impose a different rate structure depending on the number of houses owned. A separate regime is always in place for inherited properties.

One might expect that the legal structures of property transfer taxes and recurrent property taxes would overlap considerably. After all, they are both value-based taxes on real property. But with a few exceptions, there is not much overlap. When transfer taxes are levied against the declared value of the property exchange and the transfer tax rate structures are independently determined, the transfer tax can be very different from the recurrent property tax in a country. Sometimes the two taxes are imposed by two different levels of government.

Statutory Tax Rates

The level and structure of statutory tax rates differs widely among Asian jurisdictions. Among those that tax the total sales value of the transfer, it ranges from a 0.5 percent registration charge in Vietnam to 10 percent or more in Pakistan. The wide range of tax rates has several explanations. The tax might be set high to affect property sales, as in Korea, where the top rate in its progressive acquisition tax rate structure has fluctuated between 2.7 percent and 4.6 percent as the government has tried to cool down the housing market. Or the transfer tax rate may be set high to compensate for an expected underdeclaration of the sales base, as it might be in India and Pakistan.

Transfer tax rate structures can be complicated. For example, in Thailand, transfer fees are levied at 2.5 percent of the appraised value of the property being transferred, but if the seller is a company, the tax rate is 1 percent of the registered sale price or appraised value, whichever is higher. If the seller is a person and not a corporation, the withholding tax is calculated according to a progressive rate schedule based on the appraised value of the property. In the Philippines, tax rates differ between provinces and cities. Furthermore, some LGUs use zonal values as the basis of this tax, rather than the fair market value stipulated by law. Vietnam replaced the transfer tax on land use right with a capital gains tax, but it still collects a 2 percent tax if the capital gain cannot be accurately determined. Taiwan's tax increment levy imposes marginal rates ranging from 20 percent to 40 percent, but few taxpayers are in the top-rate bracket.

Administration

In Indonesia, the property transfer tax was enacted as a central-government tax but in 2011 was decentralized to the local level. In Japan, the prefectures levy the real property acquisition tax. In some jurisdictions, the transfer tax (or taxes) are levied and collected centrally, and in others, it involves tax sharing or even outright local-government administration. Either way, however, it can be a significant source of revenue for subnational governments. In India, stamp duty revenues are shared between the state government and large local (urban) bodies in some states; in others, municipal corporations levy a surcharge on the stamp duty collected by the state. Stamp duty and registration fee accruing to local governments in Delhi, India, account for 16 percent of the total revenues and are equivalent to about 70 percent of total recurrent property tax receipts.[13]

Valuation

Several different approaches are taken to value property transfers. Transfer taxes in many low- and middle-income Asian jurisdictions take the form of sales taxes, with the tax base self-declared and sometimes accepted without adequate verification. In jurisdictions where underreporting of values is likely to go undetected or unpunished and where the property transfer tax is levied at high nominal rates, property owners have a significant incentive to understate taxable value (Bahl 2004; McCluskey, Franzsen, and Bahl 2017b; Norregaard 2013). This leads to a revenue loss and, in some jurisdictions, also weakens the database that is necessary for objective assessment of the recurrent property tax (Bahl and Bird 2018).

Underdeclaration is a major issue for property transfer tax administration, and in many jurisdictions its resolution is not satisfactory. In some jurisdictions there is a provision for reassessment by a higher-level authority if the declared values are thought to be too low. In some cases, it is explicitly stated that the taxable value is that declared by the taxpayer, unless it is lower than an existing government-determined value for the property (Malaysia and the Philippines). But this becomes a vicious circle because the government value may itself have been partially determined by the underdeclared property transfer tax sales amount.

At the other end of the spectrum, in higher-income jurisdictions in Asia, third-party data are available to establish something closer to true market value for transferred properties. In Hong Kong, the large case load referred by the Stamp Office to the commissioner of Rating and Valuation for examination and valuation necessitates the use of CAMA techniques. Multiple regression analyses are applied to scrutinize the stated consideration submitted by taxpayers in property sales transactions for stamp duty purposes. In 2017–2018, 8.6 percent of the valuations received were for transactions with no or inadequate consideration.

Preferential and Punitive Treatment

Some of the problems with property transfer taxes parallel those of recurrent property taxes. Jurisdictions build complicated rate structures, preferential assessments, and base exclusions into the system with the intention of influencing choices and affecting the allocation of resources. These distortions may or may not be consistent with the discretionary choices made for the recurrent property tax. The same may be true for the vertical equity features built into the property transfer tax. There are many examples of this in the case studies here.

Some transfer tax systems provide for tax rate differentiation on the basis of use, mostly between residential and nonresidential property (e.g., China, Hong Kong, Malaysia, and Singapore). Additional relief is granted for smaller residential units. In Hong Kong, steep increases in property values after 2010 prompted the government to intervene. First, stamp duties were added to address the considerable rise in property values. Second, different tax rates were applied—depending on whether the buyer is a Hong Kong permanent resident or a company and whether the property is residential or nonresidential. Similarly, Singapore provides relief by applying a sliding scale (of 1–3 percent) to residential property acquisitions, and it also introduced an additional stamp duty on buyers of second homes or of residential investment property. In both Hong Kong and Singapore, stamp duties have been added for resales that occur within three years in an attempt to curb speculation in the residential property market.

In China, the farmland occupancy tax, which is akin to a development charge, is a one-time charge levied at differential rates (based on the area occupied) on entities and individuals who construct improvements on arable land to be used for nonagricultural purposes. The Chinese land appreciation tax (also a one-time charge) is structured more to deter property speculation than to raise revenues for local governments. Its progressive tax rates apply at four levels, rising from 30 percent to 60 percent. The incremental value is the total income from the property transfer minus the costs paid by the transferor for the land use rights, land development and structure construction, and tax payments related to the transfer.

Indonesia and Japan tax property transfers above a threshold value. Although the standard tax rate in Japan is 4 percent, the rate for land and residential buildings has temporarily been reduced to 3 percent. Various tax rates—ranging from 1 to 4 percent—are applied for the acquisition tax in Korea, depending on the type of property.

Impacts

Property transfer taxes have many features that must be taken into account in evaluating their effectiveness as a local-government revenue source. Some of these are offsets against the strengths of the recurrent property tax, and some are reinforcing.

As shown in the case studies in part 2, transfer taxes can be revenue productive, as in Hong Kong, Singapore, and Korea. Moreover, they are characterized by a high rate of voluntary compliance. In low-income jurisdictions, the ratio of transfer tax to recurrent tax revenue is less impressive. In the former socialist economies (China and Vietnam), where land is owned by the government, an effective, broad-based system of recurrent property taxation does not exist, and most revenue is derived from transfers of user rights, land use levy, and land rental. Because land is owned by the nation-state, there is not the same problem with determining values.[14]

A disadvantage is that property transfer tax revenues are prone to volatility, responding sharply to business and housing market cycles. This is, for example, evident in India where a slowdown in the property market was reflected in a declining percentage of the share of stamp duty receipts in the total revenues of the Delhi government. This volatility in the revenue flow is a negative factor from the vantage of local governments, which deliver essential services but have only limited borrowing power. However, it should be noted that in many instances property transfer tax revenue is already shared with local governments and they have been living with this volatility.

The property transfer tax imposes a cost on property transactions, thereby reducing the volume of formal transactions and slowing the development of the real estate market. Higher transfer taxes are levied to address growing housing prices. The recurrent property tax, in contrast, shows a stable pattern of revenue growth, which is in step with what is needed to deliver essential services.

The transfer tax and the recurrent property tax share a major problem. The base of both taxes is compromised by underdeclaration of transaction values for the former and undervaluation of land and property for the latter. The result is that neither tax reaches its revenue potential, particularly in the lower-income jurisdictions where assessment rates and tax morale are often low.

Finally, some jurisdictions impose multiple levels and layers of property transfer taxes (e.g., the Philippines), which can significantly raise the overall effective tax rate on some transferred properties. This may yield cascading taxes that further increase the risk of tax evasion behavior (Wallace 2018). Other nontax transaction fees associated with property transfers include registration fees, notary fees, and estate agent fees. These third-party fees sometimes include the value-added tax (Franzsen 2020).

Capital Gains Taxes

Some of the 13 jurisdictions under study here have at some point introduced a form of capital gains tax.[15] That is, the tax base is the difference between the gross income realized from selling the property (or the user right) and the total of the original purchase price, the total of the tax payments made at the time of transfer, and other allowable costs. In some jurisdictions, a separate capital gains tax is imposed on real property transfers under the national income tax.

The actual practice varies from jurisdiction to jurisdiction. Malaysia's real property gains tax is the sole tax on capital gains. It is imposed primarily to control property speculation, rather than to tax unearned increments in land values or to increase the supply of land for development. In India, the capital gains tax is levied and collected under the Income Tax Act by the central government. The act provides that long-term capital gains arising from transfer of a residential property may be exempted from income tax if the capital gain is used to acquire or construct another residential home within a specified period. In Pakistan, the capital gains tax is a federal tax payable by the seller on any capital gain realized, at a tax rate of 10 percent if realized within one year, 7.5 percent if sold during the second year and 5 percent if sold during the third year. These gains are calculated according to the fair market value, which is based on the Federal Bureau of Revenue's valuation tables rather than actual contractual prices.

Taiwan's version of a capital gains tax is different in that the original purchase price is approximated by a percentage of assessed value as determined by higher-level government valuers. The tax liability for both land value increment tax and integrated real estate income tax under a property sale is with the seller. Acquisitions and transfers of user rights in Vietnam are taxed or charged in several ways. The most revenue productive is a land use levy on the assignment of property rights by government. Land leases and rentals may be assessed as a one-time or an annual charge and yield a significant amount of revenue. There is also an income tax on real estate transfers by individuals and corporations. The tax for individuals is based on the realized sales price of the asset; for corporations, on capital gains.

Should Transfer Taxes and Recurrent Property Taxes Be Part of the Same System?

Transfer taxes and recurrent property taxes could be brought closer together by administering them jointly and by harmonizing their rate and base structures. The present system of policy and administrative separation in many Asian jurisdictions has led to two parallel property tax systems that do not always reinforce one another. Together, they generate significant revenues, but they can pursue different equity outcomes with their rate and base features, and they both have features that can affect land use.

A reform program to make land and property taxation a more productive instrument of public policy might be the following: First, convert the present transfer tax to something like a capital gains tax. With a capital gains tax, at least the buyer has an interest in declaring the true market value, because underdeclaration will deflate the property's base cost when sold. This self-checking feature should effect a more accurate self-declaration of sales prices, thereby improving the database for recurrent property tax valuation (Bahl and Wallace 2010). However, capital gains taxes impose administrative burdens, especially in establishing the basis for the tax, developing an index for inflationary increases, and adjusting for qualifying investments in real property (Wallace 2018). The richer jurisdictions in Asia have dealt with these issues, but the poorer ones would need to start with a simplified version.

Second, the governance issue surrounding transfer taxes might be resolved by defining a basic and a surtax, with the former being part of the recurrent property tax and the latter under the control of the unit of government charged with macroeconomic policy. However, all revenues raised would be recurrent property tax revenues. The new transfer tax would be administered jointly with the recurrent property tax. Under this arrangement, and with appropriate penalties for underdeclaration and an effective valuation monitoring system in place, the transfer tax can be designed such that voluntary disclosure of the actual price or market value is less likely to be undermined. In addition, introducing a value-threshold exemption (Indonesia) or a tax rate of 0 percent below a specified value threshold (as is done in South Africa) could be methods of achieving this objective. A realistic value threshold, especially if coupled with a zero rate and effective monitoring, should not discourage the transfer of properties below the threshold value and could make it easier for first-time buyers to enter the formal property market.

Equity and Allocative Effects

Reforms of the recurrent property tax structure are mostly driven by revenue considerations. But most property tax systems include features that are designed to influence the distribution of tax burdens and to support land use policies. These nonrevenue objectives are important because they can be instrumental in gaining more acceptability for the property tax and possibly promote sustained and more fair economic growth. The basic approach to addressing equity and land use issues is typically spelled out in the property and land tax laws, but economic development has given rise to special issues that also have been addressed.

Sometimes reforms are championed by social engineers who have good intentions about making tax burdens more equitable, making land use patterns more beneficial to society, or even cooling down an overheated property market. Other times the reasons are more nefarious. Sometimes reforms are based on hard evidence about the potential impacts, and sometimes they are not.

As the preceding sections of this chapter make clear, Asian property taxation systems differ from country to country, and there is no single common practice. Even the reforms are undertaken in different ways, often using a combination of rate and base structure and valuation to address the same question. Some skeptics might argue that this shotgun approach is likely to make the system more complicated and more costly to administer. Others say it is the only way to achieve the objective sought. The fact is that property tax structures change over time and in piecemeal ways as reformers attempt to make them more equitable and more friendly to good land use patterns.

Equity

A good property tax spreads the burden across taxpayers in ways that are in step with social norms in the country. Jurisdictions differ on how they state this objective, but its essence is usually that the tax will not bear heavily on low-income households and sometimes even that higher-income households will be singled out to bear more of the burden (see box 2.3). Two kinds of equity are discussed here. Vertical equity refers to the property tax burden rising with income level. Horizontal equity refers to the property tax falling equally on persons and businesses who are in the same circumstances. For a good discussion of equity in property taxation, see Youngman (2016, chap. 2). As shown in part 2, some jurisdictions have introduced progressive features, which indicates a concern for vertical equity. However, these reforms have not always led to a more progressive distribution of property tax burdens. In fact, in numerous cases jurisdictions have introduced progressive rates and simultaneously introduced regressive owner-occupier exemptions.

Some examples of the measures taken by Asian jurisdictions to make land and property taxes more horizontally and vertically equitable are outlined in table 2.8. But because empirical research on the distribution of property tax burdens is scarce, we can make only subjective judgments about the possible intent of the specific interventions summarized in the table. Note that the table explores only the *marginal effects of single actions* and not the offsetting (or reinforcing) effects of other elements of the property tax structure—for example, it does not address the possibility that the marginal effects of a progressive rate structure may be more than offset by exemption policies and assessment practices (see boxes 2.1 and 2.2). Neither does the table recognize the possibility that those who design these equity packages rely on notional evidence about what makes a property tax more equitable.

Box 2.3 Is the Property Tax Burden Distributed Equitably in Low- and Middle-Income Jurisdictions?

Equitable distribution has been a focus of research, especially with respect to higher-income jurisdictions and regions where the tax is levied at a higher effective rate. The general conclusion of the theoretical research, which admittedly makes some very simplifying assumptions, is that the property tax is borne by owners of capital and tends to be progressive (Zodrow 2006). The theoretical model of property tax incidence has also been studied for the special case of low- and middle-income jurisdictions, and here the conclusion of progressivity is less easy to reach, particularly because of assumptions that property taxes are national and about the supply and mobility of capital (Bahl and Linn 1992, chap. 5). Moreover, none of the theoretical models address the implications of the very different rate and base provisions that jurisdictions (or local governments in those jurisdictions) introduce to make the property tax more progressive. But the plethora of progressive rates, exemptions, and thresholds that favor low-income families and preferential assessment practices have convinced many that the property tax is progressive in its distribution of burdens (Birdsall and Gupta 2018). The view here is that the best way to understand the distribution of tax burdens is on a jurisdiction-by-jurisdiction approach. This is, sadly, not often attempted (Alleyne, Alm, Bahl, and Wallace 2007).

Table 2.8 Features Affecting Distribution of Property Tax Burdens

Jurisdiction	Structural Feature	Intended Marginal Impact	Comment
China	Higher tax rates for commercial and industrial property	Progressive	Most property tax revenues come from transfers of land user rights.
	Tax preferences for first-time home buyers	Progressive	
Hong Kong	Threshold exemption level	Progressive	Less than 2% of all assessments are exempt.
	Progressive statutory rates, additional stamp duties, with some exemption for first-time home buyers	Progressive	Levied to control speculation.
India	No revaluation of unit-area value system since 2005; no indexation has been allowed	Regressive	Less than one-fourth of properties are in the taxpaying population.
Indonesia	Threshold exemption level	Progressive	The threshold exemption is not rigidly enforced.
	Property transfer tax	Progressive	Declared value of the transaction is most often the base.
Japan	Indexed valuation adjustments	Correct outdated assessments	
	Threshold tax liability	Progressive	Residential land is assessed at one-third of full assessed value.
	Classified property assessment ratios	Progressive	

Korea	Graduated rate schedule under all three types of property taxes	Progressive	
	Wealth tax on total holdings of property, levied with a progressive rate schedule	Progressive, but burdens some taxpayers; also a high property value threshold introduces a regressive element	Wealth tax liability is concentrated in higher-income brackets, but only a small proportion of landowners are covered.
	Fractional assessments	Progressive	Differential assessment rates by use of property.
Malaysia (Kuala Lumpur)	Higher tax rates on commercial and industrial property	Progressive	
	Lower rate on low-income apartments	Progressive	
Pakistan	Preferential treatment of owner-occupiers vs. renters	Regressive	
	Tax on luxury housing	Progressive	
	Capital gains tax	Progressive	
	Threshold exemption based on lot size	Progressive	2% of landowners own 30% of the land.
Philippines	Properties below a minimum threshold value are exempt from taxation	Progressive	
	Sectoral assessment ratios	Progressive	Residential ratio is 20% and commercial-industrial is 50%.

(continued)

Table 2.8 Features Affecting Distribution of Property Tax Burdens (*continued*)

Jurisdiction	Structural Feature	Intended Marginal Impact	Comment
	Property tax surcharge earmarked for social housing	Progressive	
	Discretionary relief can be granted by the president or the local council	Varies by case	Special relief is granted to some companies or under tax holidays.
Singapore	Minimum value exemption	Progressive	20% of owners of subsidized housing pay no tax; property tax from subsidized housing is only 2.8% of total. .
	Lower tax rates on subsidized housing	Progressive	Punitive rates of property tax and stamp duties.
	Progressive tax rate schedule	Progressive	
Taiwan	Higher tax rates on land than improvements, and a progressive rate structure	Progressive (% of income paid in taxes rises as income rises)	Small proportion of taxpayers are in highest rate bracket.
	Land tax base is total holdings of land in the jurisdiction by each owner	Discourage concentration of land ownership	Effective tax rates may be very low.
	Capital gains (land value increment tax) rate structure is progressive	Progressive	

Thailand	Threshold exemption level	Regressive	Threshold exemptions are very high, and many higher-income owners are exempt from tax.
	Higher tax rates for commercial and industrial property	Progressive	
	Graduated rate schedule	Progressive	
Vietnam	Base for recurrent, nonagricultural tax is total (national) landholdings by each individual or company	Progressive	
	Extensive preferential treatments for land taxes	Unclear	About 75% of exemptions are for vacant land.
	Tax rates are graduated above a standard land area threshold	Progressive	
	Threshold for payment of annual recurrent property tax exempts about 75% of households	Progressive; reduce administrative costs	Threshold is set by law at about half the actual tax burden.

Source: Case studies in part 2 of this book.

Asian property tax systems use different approaches to lower the tax burden on low-income households. Most adopt a threshold housing value (or a threshold tax liability or even a threshold space level) below which no property tax is charged (Hong Kong, Singapore, and the Philippines). Malaysia gives a preferentially lower tax rate to low-income flats. Another approach is to tax higher residential property values at higher rates, such as might result from a graduated rate structure, a luxury house tax rate as in Pakistan, a wealth tax on all landholdings as in Korea and Vietnam, or the imposition of a land value increment tax as in Taiwan. The most common approach is to impose a graduated rate schedule, but here the results depend on how taxpayers are distributed among the rate brackets. For example, the Taiwan case study shows that less than 1 percent of taxpayers are in the highest tax bracket, thereby limiting the overall progressivity.

Another general approach to addressing equity in land and property taxation is to group taxpayers according to the classification given to their properties and to tax each class of property differently. Many systems assume that commercial and industrial property have more taxpaying capacity and assign them higher burdens (and lower burdens on the agricultural and residential sectors because they are deemed to have a lower taxpaying capacity).[16] This is done in some jurisdictions with differential tax rates (Malaysia) and in others with differential assessment ratios (Philippines).[17] The flaw in this approach is that it ignores the shifting of tax burdens. For example, depending on market conditions, the burden of a higher property tax on commerce or industry might be shifted forward to consumers, shifted backward to labor, or borne by the owners of the business. A better approach would be to adopt a uniform assessment ratio, as is done in Hong Kong, and to let the difference in the value of the property be the guideline for capacity to pay.

Finally, there is the burden of property transfer taxes, stamp duties, and capital gains taxes. These are generally imposed on all transfers of property, whether made by individuals or corporations. The subject of who bears the burden of such taxes is complex. The general presumption is that such taxes are capitalized into the value of the asset being transferred and that the burden is distributed, depending on market conditions, between buyer and seller. To the extent that land and asset ownership is concentrated at the high end of the income distribution, the burden of the tax is progressive.

Land Policy and Land Use

Interest in land policy has been heightened by the accelerating pace of urbanization and the growing need for infrastructure. Clearly, Hong

Kong and Singapore are good examples of addressing and providing solutions for land scarcity through vertical development above- and belowground. Many Asian governments, therefore, use land and property taxes as a component of their ongoing programs to help control and direct land use and land markets. Some of these land and property tax interventions are summarized in table 2.9. We can flag governments' intentions for these policy measures, but we cannot address the more important question of the impact of these policies. This knowledge is bedeviled by the absence of a strong body of research in almost all jurisdictions.

Asian jurisdictions are using land and property taxes to achieve land policy objectives to address nonrevenue issues. China and Vietnam are concerned about the implications of urban growth for farmland preservation, Hong Kong and Singapore harmonize tax policy and land use policy, Malaysia differentiates its property tax regime within Kuala Lumpur according to the degree of urbanization, and Indonesia and Japan encourage certain kinds of investment in land and property. The social engineers in these jurisdictions have been as active in using property taxes to support land policies as they have been in introducing equity policies.

Four objectives seem to have guided the practice. The first is to encourage better uses of land. Taiwan has established a split-rate tax system with a heavier rate on land than improvements, following Henry George's ([1879] 1958) long-lived maxims about land taxes.[18] Hong Kong has proposed a new tax on open land. Vietnam, Taiwan, and the Philippines also have taxes on open land (but these taxes are underused and not all have worked well). Japan has introduced property tax incentives to encourage more efficient use of land and to produce higher-quality housing.

The second objective is to discourage and control land speculation. Urbanization in Asia has led in several areas to boom-and-bust cycles in property prices, and tax policy has been used to control speculation. China, Hong Kong, Korea, and Singapore have all used capital gains and property transfer taxes to smooth prices in real estate markets.

The third is to establish more transparent property markets. Some jurisdictions (for example, Singapore, Hong Kong, Japan, and Taiwan) have succeeded. Others still need to manage data flows, establish clear ownership records, and improve compliance.

The fourth is to establish innovative financing schemes to improve services or amenities and therefore the efficient use of the land. Singapore has had success with development charges. Other attempts include property tax revenues earmarked for social housing in the Philippines and Japan's

Table 2.9 Features Affecting Land Use and Property Markets

Jurisdiction	Structural Feature	Intended Marginal Impact	Comment
China	Tax on farmland buildings not in agriculture use (no tax is imposed on rural buildings)	Preserve farmland	Prices for urban land are driven up by limited supply available for commercial and residential uses.
	Transfer tax on appreciation of land use value	Discourage speculation	Levied at progressive rate.
	Land concession revenue	Fund local infrastructure	
Hong Kong	Vacant unused land is untaxed	Reduce efficiency of land use	Vacant property surtax has been proposed.
	Additional stamp duty on transactions	Reduce speculation	Levied at progressive rate.
Indonesia	Lower property transfer tax rate for real estate investment trusts	Encourage investment in real estate	Property transfer rate is 5%, preferential rate is 1%.
Japan	Special property tax on floor space and number of employees in cities	Compensate for pressures of urbanization	Smaller businesses are exempt.
	Implement strategies to improve ownership records	Enable better land management	
	Incentivized assessment policies	Promote better lot size choices, better-quality housing	
	Tax reduction for newly built homes	Encourage new residential housing	50% property tax reduction for first three years.

Country/City	Instrument	Objective	Notes
	Vacant land tax	Stimulate removal of unused properties	Increases assessment level sixfold.
	Tax burden adjustment mechanisms	Control speculation	Adjust taxable values to reflect property price increases.
	Higher taxes on unused farmland	Preserve farmland	
Korea	Urban areas taxed more heavily	Reflect benefits from better public services	Special property tax sur-rate of 0.14% for cities.
	Wealth tax levied on total national landholdings	Control land speculation; reduce the concentration of land and housing ownership	Levied only on a small fraction of the population.
	Undervaluation	Provide an incentive to hold properties off the market	
Malaysia	Real property capital gains tax	Control speculation	Top rate is 30%.
Kuala Lumpur	Lower tax rate on vacant properties	Reduce incentive for development	
Kuala Lumpur	Higher tax rates in central locations	Reflect access to services and amenities with a surcharge	
Philippines	Tax on idle lands	Improve efficiency of land use	Rarely used.
	Betterment levies	Capture value for infrastructure finance	Rarely used.
Singapore	Additional stamp duty	Discourage land banking	Higher taxes on rented properties to encourage owner occupancy.
	Development charge on land use changes	Capture value	

(continued)

Table 2.9 Features Affecting Land Use and Property Markets (*continued*)

Jurisdiction	Structural Feature	Intended Marginal Impact	Comment
Taiwan	Split-rate property tax system with a higher rate on land	Reduce penalty on investing in improvements, improve efficiency of land use	
	Land value increment tax	Discourage speculation; return unearned increment to the public	Tax rates range from 20% to 40%.
	Tax on idle land	Improve efficiency of land use; discourage speculation	Idle land tax is rarely used.
	Land tax base is total holding of land in the taxing jurisdiction	Break up concentration of land ownership; discourage speculation	
Thailand	Outdated valuation roll still in effect	Encourage holding unproductive land	New property tax regime was introduced in 2020.
	Higher tax rate on vacant land	Encourage more efficient land use	Land prices are rising faster than the penalty rate.
	Low tax rates and low coverage of tax base	Discourage more efficient land use and encourages speculation	
Vietnam	Higher tax rates for vacant land	Improve efficiency of land use	Effective property tax rates are very low.
	Transfer tax on user rights to land does not include improvements	Encourage more intensive land use	
	Penalty rates for underused and larger landholdings	Discourage speculation; encourage earlier development of properties	

Source: Case studies in part 2 of this book.

business occupancy tax, which offsets the costs of urbanization (McCarthy 2021).[19] Much more could be done with value capture, which is still rarely used in Asia (Smolka 2013). Many Asian jurisdictions use their land and property tax regime for better land use, and for value capture, but these methods have not yet gained wide acceptance in the region.

Notes

1. To simplify the presentation, we do not explicitly include the coverage of the tax base in this equation.

2. The annual rental value system was introduced by the British during colonial times and is still in effect in other jurisdictions in Asia, such as Hong Kong, Malaysia, Pakistan, and Singapore.

3. It also, arguably, bypasses rent control ordinances when assessing taxable property values. For a discussion of the unit-area value system in India, see Rao (2008).

4. Tracking the revenue cost of tax relief is difficult. It would involve measuring revenues from the tax against a hypothetical counterfactual system with no tax relief measures. We know of no country that does this, though some do attempt to measure the tax expenditures for selected relief programs.

5. The idea of a progressive statutory rate structure being a fair way to tax property ownership has complicating issues. For a good discussion, see Youngman (2016, 25–27).

6. In some countries and jurisdictions, these progressive rate structures are set up as slabs (property value groupings) with marginal tax rates, and in others they increase average tax rates with the total value of the property.

7. In Vietnam, the cost of a Big Mac in 2021 was about USD 3. Have it with fries and a drink and this claim might be about right (Szmigiera 2021).

8. These factors include (1) type of subnational government—e.g., province or city (Philippines); (2) urban or rural location (Korea and Malaysia); (3) property type—i.e., land or buildings or both (Taiwan); (4) property use—e.g., residential or commercial (Malaysia and Thailand); (5) classes of property within use categories, such as retail or office (India); (6) value (Indonesia); (7) property size (China, Pakistan, and Vietnam); (8) population size (China); and (9) occupancy (Pakistan and Thailand).

9. The International Association of Assessing Officers (IAAO 2014) defines an automated valuation model as a computer program for property valuation that analyzes data using an automated process such as multiple regression. Computer-assisted mass appraisal is an integrated system for valuing property. The system typically has modules such as property data (textual), spatial data, and transaction data and statistical models that use multiple regression techniques, geographic weighted regression, and boosted regression trees.

10. IPTI (2021) defines artificial intelligence (AI) as machine learning (ML) designed to predict an outcome or provide an estimate of value, e.g., most probably sales price.

11. The taxpayer calculates only assessed value using the valuation and rate schedules provided in the self-assessment forms.

12. Legal liability for payment of the transfer tax may rest with the buyer or with the seller or it may be split between them. In most systems covered in this book, the legal responsibility is with the transferee (China, Japan, Korea, Malaysia, Pakistan, and Vietnam). However, when evaluating the burden of transfer taxes, it is not important who bears legal liability for making the tax payment. Where the final burden rests, i.e., the *incidence* of the tax, is important.

13. In Delhi, India, stamp duty rates differ by gender: 6 percent for males and 4 percent for females.

14. Under the Constitution of China, urban land is owned by the state, and rural land by the village collectives. The amended Land Administration Law of 2020 gave village collectives more control over the sale of their user rights.

15. The definition of property transfer taxes used here is the recurrent and nonrecurrent taxes on the use, ownership or transfer of properties. Sometimes, OECD, IMF and countries make different decisions about how to classify taxes. For example, OECD (2021, pp 166) notes that a transfer tax on immovable property that is based on profits made from the sale is classified as a capital gains income tax and not as a property tax.

16. This assigning of different burdens to commercial and industrial property and to agricultural and residential sectors might also be done to protect revenues, because the compliance rate might be higher in the commercial and industrial sectors.

17. Properties might be classified in other ways, for other purposes. For example, owner-occupiers are often given preferential treatment (Pakistan), presumably to encourage owner occupancy.

18. The 19th-century social philosopher Henry George argued for a land tax and had a significant influence on thinking about how property tax systems should be shaped. See Netzer (1998) and Franzsen (2009).

19. According to McCarthy (2021, 3), "The World Bank estimates that more than US$90 trillion in new infrastructure will be needed by 2030 to prepare cities for 2 billion new inhabitants, primarily in sprawling metropolises in low-income countries."

References

ADB (Asian Development Bank). 2020. *Mapping Property Tax Reform in Southeast Asia.* Manila: Asian Development Bank.

Ahmad, E., G. Brosio, and J. P. Jiménez. 2019. "Options for Retooling Property Taxation in Latin America." Paper presented at the eighth Jornadas Iberoamericanas de Financiación Local, Mexico (October 1–2).

Alleyne, D., J. Alm, R. Bahl, and S. Wallace. 2007. "Tax Burden in Jamaica." Jamaica Tax Reform Project, Working paper 9. Atlanta: Andrew Young School of Policy Studies, Georgia State University.

Alm, J., P. Annez, and A. Modi. 2004. "Stamp Duty in Indian States: A Case for Reform." World Bank Policy Research Paper 3413. Washington, DC: World Bank.

Almy, R. 2013. *Property Tax Regimes in Europe.* Nairobi, Kenya: United Nations Human Settlements Program.

Bahl, R. 2004. "Property Transfer Tax and Stamp Duty." ISP Working paper 04-27. Atlanta: Andrew Young School of Policy Studies, Georgia State University.

Bahl, R., and R. M. Bird. 2018. *Fiscal Decentralization and Local Finance in Developing Countries.* Cheltenham, UK: Edward Elgar.

Bahl, R., M. Cyan, and S. Wallace. 2015. "The Potential of Provincial Taxation." In *The Role of Taxation in Pakistan's Economic Revival*, ed. J. Martinez-Vazquez and M. Cyan, chap. 8. Oxford: Oxford University Press.

Bahl, R. W., and J. F. Linn. 1992. *Urban Public Finance in Developing Countries.* New York: Oxford University Press.

Bahl, R., and S. Wallace. 2010. "A New Paradigm for Property Taxation in Developing Countries." In *Rethinking the Conventional Wisdom About the Property Tax*, ed. R. Bahl, J. Martinez-Vazquez, J. Youngman, 165–201. Cambridge, MA: Lincoln Institute of Land Policy.

Bing, Y., K. Connelly, and M. E. Bell. 2009. "A Compendium of Countries with an Area Based Property Tax." Working paper WP09BY1. Cambridge, MA: Lincoln Institute of Land Policy.

Bird, R. M., and E. Slack, eds. 2004. *International Handbook of Land and Property Taxation.* Cheltenham, UK: Edward Elgar.

Bird, R. M., and E. Slack. 2007. "Taxing Land and Property in Emerging Economies: Raising Revenue . . . and More?" In *Land Policies and Their Outcomes,* ed. G. K. Ingram and Y.-H. Hong. Cambridge, MA: Lincoln Institute of Land Policy.

Birdsall, N., and S. Gupta. 2018. "On the Equity-Friendly Property Tax: Time for Developing Countries to Invest?" CGD Blog, Washington, DC: Center for Global Development.

Brzeski, J., A. Románová, and R. Franzsen. 2019. "The Evolution of Property Taxes in Post-Socialist Countries in Central and Eastern Europe." Working paper WP-19-01. Pretoria, South Africa: African Tax Institute, University of Pretoria.

Davis, P., P. Bidanset, M. McCord, and M. Cusack. 2020. "Nationwide Mass Appraisal Modeling in China: Feasibility Analysis for Scalability Given Ad Valorem Property Tax Reform." Working paper WP20PD1. Cambridge, MA: Lincoln Institute of Land Policy.

De Cesare, C. 2012. "Improving the Performance of the Property Tax in Latin America." Policy focus report. Cambridge, MA: Lincoln Institute of Land Policy.

Dye, R., and R. England. 2009. "The Principles and Promise of Land Value Taxation." In *Land Value Taxation: Theory, Evidence, and Practice,* ed. R. Dye and R. England, 3–10. Cambridge, MA: Lincoln Institute of Land Policy.

Eckert, J. K. 1990. *Property Appraisal and Assessment Administration.* Chicago: International Association of Assessing Officers.

Fibbens, M. 1995. "Australian Rating and Taxing: Mass Appraisal Practice." *Journal of Property Tax Assessment and Administration* 1 (3): 61–77.

Franzsen, R. C. D. 2009. "International Experience." In *Land Value Taxation,* ed. R. Dye and R. England, 27–47. Cambridge, MA: Lincoln Institute of Land Policy.

Franzsen, R. C. D. 2020. "A Review of Property Transfer Taxes in Africa." In *Rethinking Land Reform in Africa: New Ideas, Opportunities, and Challenges,* 112–131. Abidjan, Ivory Coast: African Development Bank.

Franzsen, R., and W. J. McCluskey. 2013. "Value-Based Approaches to Property Taxation." In *A Primer on Property Tax: Administration and Policy,* ed. W. J. McCluskey, G. C. Cornia, and L. C. Walters, 41–68. Oxford: Wiley-Blackwell.

Franzsen, R., and W. McCluskey. 2017. Introduction to *Property Tax in Africa: Status, Challenges, and Prospects,* ed. R. C. D. Franzsen and W. J. McCluskey, 3–28. Cambridge, MA: Lincoln Institute of Land Policy.

George, H. (1879) 1958. *Progress and Poverty.* Reprint, New York: Robert Schalkenbach Foundation.

Grote, M., N. Nersesyan, and R. Franzsen. 2019. "Republic of Armenia: Growth-Friendly Rebalancing of Taxes." International Monetary Fund Technical Assistance Report. https://www.elibrary.imf.org/view/journals/002/2019/031/article-A001-en.xml.

Haas, A. R. N., and M. Kopanyi. 2017. "Taxation of Vacant Urban Land: From Theory to Practice." IGC Policy Note. London: International Growth Center (July 2017).

IAAO (International Association of Assessing Officers). 2010. *Standard on Automated Valuation Methods.* Kansas City, MO: IAAO.

———. 2011. *Standard on the Mass Appraisal of Real Property.* Kansas City, MO: IAAO.

———. 2014. *Standard on Assessment Appeals.* Kansas City, MO: IAAO.

———. 2017. "Standard on Mass Appraisal of Real Property." Kansas City, MO: IAAO. https://www.iaao.org/media/standards/StandardOnMassAppraisal.pdf (July).

———. 2018. *Standard on Automated Valuation Models.* Kansas City, MO: IAAO.

———. 2020. *Standard on Property Tax Policy.* Kansas City, MO: IAAO.

IMF (International Monetary Fund). 2020. "World Revenue Longitudinal Data." https://data.imf.org/?sk=77413F1D-1525-450A-A23A-47AEED40FE78.

———. 2021. *Fiscal Monitor: Strengthening the Credibility of Public Finances.* Washington, DC: IMF (October).

IPTI (International Property Tax Institute). 2021. "The Potential of Artificial Intelligence in Property Assessment." White paper. Toronto: IPTI.

Kelly, R. 2014. "Implementing Sustainable Property Tax Reform in Developing Countries." In *Taxation and Development: The Weakest Link? Essays in Honor of Roy Bahl,* ed. R. M. Bird and J. Martinez-Vazquez, 326–363. Cheltenham, UK: Edward Elgar.

Kelly, R., R. White, and A. Anand. 2020. *Property Tax Diagnostic Manual.* Washington, DC: World Bank.

Kitchen, H. 2013. "Property Tax: A Situation Analysis and Overview." In *A Primer on Property Tax: Administration and Policy,* ed. W. J. McCluskey, G. C. Cornia, and L. C. Walters, 1–40. Oxford: Wiley-Blackwell.

Kok, N., E.-L. Koponen, C. A. Martinez-Barbosa. 2017. "Big Data in Real Estate? From Manual Appraisal to Automated Valuation." *Journal of Portfolio Management* 43 (6): 202–211.

Marr, B. 2015. *Big Data: Using SMART Big Data Analytics and Metrics to Make Better Decisions and Improve Performance.* Sussex, UK: John Wiley and Sons.

McCarthy, G. W. 2021. "We Need to Get Infrastructure Right. The Stakes Couldn't Be Higher." President's Message. *Land Lines* 33 (4): 4–6.).

McCluskey, W., M. Bell, and L. J. Lim. 2010. "Rental Value Versus Capital Value: Alternative Bases for the Property Tax." In *Rethinking the Conventional Wisdom About the Property Tax,* ed. R. Bahl, J. Martinez-Vazquez, and J. Youngman, 119–157. Cambridge, MA: Lincoln Institute of Land Policy.

McCluskey, W. J., M. McCord, P. T. Davis, D. McIlhatton, and M. Haran. 2012. "The Potential of Artificial Neural Networks in Mass Appraisal: The Case Revisited." *Journal of Financial Management of Property and Construction* 17 (3): 274–292.

McCluskey, W. J., and R. C. D. Franzsen. 2013. "Property Taxes in Metropolitan Cities." In *Financing Metropolitan Governments in Developing Countries,* ed. R. W. Bahl, J. F. Linn, and D. L. Wetzel, 159–182. Cambridge MA: Lincoln Institute of Land Policy.

McCluskey, W., R. Franzsen, and R. Bahl. 2017a. "Challenges, Prospects and Recommendations." In *Property Tax in Africa: Status, Challenges and Prospects*, ed. R. C. D. Franzsen and W. J. McCluskey, 551–592. Cambridge, MA: Lincoln Institute of Land Policy.

McCluskey, W., R. Franzsen, and R. Bahl. 2017b. "Policy and Practice." In *Property Tax in Africa: Status, Challenges and Prospects*, ed. R. C. D. Franzsen and W. J. McCluskey, 29–104. Cambridge, MA: Lincoln Institute of Land Policy.

Mohanty, P. K. 2014. *Cities and Public Policy: An Urban Agenda for India:* New Delhi: Sage Publications

Netzer, D., ed. 1998. *Land Value Taxation: Can It and Will It Work Today?* Cambridge, MA: Lincoln Institute of Land Policy.

Norregaard, J. 2013. "Taxing Immovable Property: Revenue Potential and Implementation Challenges." Working paper WP/13/129. Washington, DC: International Monetary Fund.

OECD (Organization for Economic Cooperation and Development). 2021. *Revenue Statistics in Asia and the Pacific 2021: Emerging Challenges for the Asia-Pacific Region in the COVID-19 Era.* Paris: OECD. https://doi.org/10.1787/ed374457-en.

Oxford Economics and ITIC. 2020. "Coronavirus: Fiscal Challenges for Emerging Markets." *Tax Notes*, September 4, 2020.

Plimmer, F. 2013. "Legal Issues in Property Tax Administration." In *A Primer on Property Tax: Administration and Policy*, ed. W. J. McCluskey, G. C. Cornia, and L. C. Walters, 187–205. Oxford: Wiley-Blackwell.

PricewaterhouseCoopers. 2022. https://www.pwc.com/us/en/services/consulting/analytics/artificial-intelligence.html (Accessed on 8 April 2022).

Rao, U. A. V. 2008. "Is Area-Based Assessment an Alternative, an Intermediate step, or an Impediment to Value-Based Taxation in India?" In *Making the Property Tax Work: Experiences in Developing and Transitional Countries*, ed. R. Bahl, J. Martinez-Vazquez, and J. Youngman, 241–267. Cambridge, MA: Lincoln Institute of Land Policy.

Rosengard, J. K. 2012. "The Tax Everyone Loves to Hate: Principles of Property Tax Reform." Cambridge, MA: Harvard Kennedy School.

RVDSAR (Rating and Valuation Department, Hong Kong Special Administrative Region). 2021. "Property Rates in Hong Kong: Assessment, Collection and Administration." Hong Kong: RVDSAR.

Smolka, M. 2013. *Implementing Value Capture in Latin America: Policies and Tools for Urban Development.* Cambridge. MA: Lincoln Institute of Land Policy.

Szmigiera, M. 2021. "Global Price of a Big Mac as of July 2021, by Country." Statista .com. https://www.statista.com/statistics/274326/big-mac-index-global-prices-for -a-big-mac/.

Wallace, S. 2018. "Property Transfer Taxes." Working paper WP-18-02. Pretoria, South Africa: African Tax Institute, University of Pretoria.

Walters, L. 2011. "Land and Property Tax: A Policy Guide." Nairobi: United Nations Human Settlements Program.

Wang, D., and V. J. Li. 2019. "Mass Appraisal Models of Real Estate in the 21st Century: A Systematic Literature Review." *Sustainability* 11 (24): 7006. https://doi.org/10.3390 /su11247006.

Youngman, J. M. 2016. *A Good Tax: Legal and Policy Issues for the Property Tax in the United States*. Cambridge, MA: Lincoln Institute of Land Policy.

Zodrow, G. 2006. "Reflections on the New View and Benefit View of the Property Tax." In *Property Taxation and Local Government Finance*, ed. W. Oates, 79–111. Cambridge, MA: Lincoln Institute of Land Policy.

3

Lessons Learned and Prospects for Reform

ROY BAHL, WILLIAM MCCLUSKEY, AND RIËL FRANZSEN

Chapter 1 of this book poses three questions:

- Why has land and property taxation not become a stronger source of funding for governments in Asia?

- Could the land and property base generate a significantly greater flow of revenue?

- What reforms could produce such an outcome?

To answer these questions, we begin with two general observations. The first is that asking about *Asia* paints with too broad a brush. Property and land taxes in the five higher-income jurisdictions studied here (Hong Kong, Japan, Korea, Singapore, and Taiwan) have performed well. These jurisdictions have embraced new technologies and have shaped their rate and base structures to fit their economic and social goals. Although problems remain, all are in positions to increase revenue mobilization from the property tax.

China and Vietnam have not yet committed to adopt a broad-based, revenue-productive annual property tax regime, yet they raise revenues from land and property taxes that are near or above the level of their middle-income cohort. Both jurisdictions, however, have the decision about a broad-based annual tax on their policy agendas.

Five other jurisdictions (India, Indonesia, Pakistan, the Philippines, and Thailand) fall in the low-performing category. Although there is room for improvement across all Asia, these lower-income jurisdictions face the most binding constraints, including a technology and management infrastructure too weak to support an efficient property tax system and the inability to overcome political opposition to taxing property wealth. It is not yet clear whether these jurisdictions will restructure their land and property tax systems to increase revenue mobilization.

The second general observation draws a distinction between more revenue-productive property taxation and better property taxation. Better property taxation could result from reforms to make the tax more fair, more efficiently run, and less politically driven. This could be done by rolling back exemptions, bringing all eligible properties into the net, improving collection rates, and improving the equity of valuation. The additional revenues raised from better taxation could be rolled into lower statutory rates, thereby making the reform package revenue neutral. Thus, better property taxation can lead to a more efficient revenue growth path, whereas generating more revenue from current rate and base structures would amplify the distortions and inefficiencies that are now in place.

Constraints on Property Tax Revenue Mobilization

Every property tax system is different, and roadblocks to better revenue performance must be studied on a case-by-case basis. As Kelly, White, and Anand (2020, 14, 89) put it, the answers are almost always "situation-specific." That said, the case studies in part 2 identify several constraints to revenue growth shared by lower-income jurisdictions in South and Southeast Asia. Perhaps the most important constraint is the one they cannot address in the short run—their low-income status. Their capacity to raise property taxes will remain low until the base they collect from is larger. Compared with higher-income jurisdictions, the informal sector of their economies is relatively large, they are more rural, small-scale agriculture is widespread, the aggregate value of real property is low, and so on (World Bank 2006). For example, Indonesia and the Philippines have farther to reach to gain a particular revenue target than do Korea and Singapore. Even if low-income jurisdictions can modernize the structure and management of their property tax systems, property tax revenues will remain low.

Another way to look at the issue is to assess the potential of low-income jurisdictions to mobilize higher revenue levels from their property taxes, under existing conditions. If defining *potential* as the revenue yield from a broader tax base, better valuation, and more efficient administration, clearly their revenue has room to grow. The problems and constraints to reaching revenue potential in the lower-income jurisdictions in Asia involve the following:

THE TAX BASES ARE NARROW

Generating high revenue yield requires high statutory tax rates. Exemptions and preferential treatments are rarely tracked, but qualitative analysis suggests that they significantly lower revenues. In addition, properties are assessed at values lower than market levels, and collection rates in many jurisdictions are low. In the higher-income jurisdictions of Asia, by contrast, these tax expenditures are monitored and appear to be better controlled.

REVENUE ELASTICITY IS LOW

In lower-income jurisdictions, most of the automatic growth in revenues comes from wider coverage of the tax and from new construction. As a consequence, property tax revenue growth cannot keep pace with GDP growth. Revenue growth from discretionary changes comes from revaluations and reassessments at a higher percentage of market value, but most lower-income jurisdictions have been slow to make these changes. And when they do, much of the new revenue often is given back as a transition benefit to make the new tax roll acceptable. The higher-income jurisdictions in Asia tend to revalue more frequently, some annually. The ratio of property tax revenues to GDP in 24 Asian and Pacific jurisdictions has remained constant over 2010–2019 (OECD 2021, 69).

ANNUAL LAND AND PROPERTY TAXES ARE EXPENSIVE TO IMPLEMENT

New technologies and the training for them may not be affordable (or may not be a high priority) in some low-income jurisdictions, especially considering the relatively low amount of revenue likely to be realized. But not embracing new technologies also has a cost. The failure to modernize administration of the property tax translates to only a 32 percent coverage of properties in Indonesia and about 30 percent in India (where a formal count of properties in a jurisdiction is not even required). In Thailand, where a new property tax regime was put in place in 2020, the seemingly impossible task of documenting and valuing every piece of property still lies ahead. Malaysian valuations are more than 10 years out of date and are held back by a predominantly manual system.

OTHER TAXES ARE FAVORED OVER THE PROPERTY TAX

Other taxes are more easily administered and more revenue productive and impose less visible burdens on taxpayers. Local political leaders prefer, for example, revenue from business taxes or intergovernmental transfers paid from central government taxes because they can be promoted as having someone else pay for local services. In the Philippines, the largest inter-governmental transfer in the fiscal system now accounts for two-thirds of local-government revenues, and the property tax share is only about 13 percent.

Property tax administration is difficult

The players involved in identifying and valuing properties, collecting the tax, and managing the data lack coordination. In the Philippines, 20 different government agencies have some responsibility for valuation. In Indonesia, the data management system is not coordinated even among the different agencies that administer the property tax. And in Vietnam there is weak coordination of data sharing. Taiwan's split-rate property tax (different rates on land than buildings) is administered by two different departments that do not coordinate closely. Even high-income jurisdictions can face challenges in organizing data, as evidenced by the issues surrounding Japan's property ownership records. But in most of the higher-income jurisdictions of Asia, this tends to be less of a problem.

Governments and taxpayers are unwilling to make changes

The property tax has many vocal enemies and few champions. Arguably, the greatest constraint to increased property taxation among the lower-income jurisdictions of Asia is the unwillingness of political leaders and some voters to accept the discretionary changes necessary to make property taxes more effective revenue instruments. The tax can seem unfair to homeowners because it is paid annually on an asset that does not produce a cash flow, because its base is defined subjectively, and because they think (probably correctly) that all property tax reform does is tax them more heavily. Taxpayers do not like it because they are reminded annually about the amount they pay and politicians dislike it because they equate higher property tax burdens with fewer votes (Ahmad, Brosio, and Jiménez 2019; Bahl and Bird 2018). It almost always draws the ire of powerful interest groups such as the agricultural sector and developers. Attempts at revaluation in Delhi, India, are regularly rejected by the local councils. In Vietnam, a proposed broad-based property tax was turned back because of strong resistance from interest groups. In Thailand, a new property tax regime was legislated only after significant revenue-losing concessions were made to objectors.

External Factors

Urbanization is driving up land and property values, technology advances are making property tax administration more efficient, and fiscal decentralization is increasing the demand for local-government taxes. Asian governments could take advantage of these trends to improve the budgetary importance of their land and property taxes (UN-Habitat 2020).

URBANIZATION INCREASES REVENUE POTENTIAL

Asia already has more megacities—metropolitan areas with 10 million people or more—than any other continent[1] and is riding a wave of urbanization (table 3.1, and see chapter 1, table 1). Between 2000 and 2025, an estimated 1.1 billion people will have migrated into Asian urban areas. The agglomeration benefits of urbanization and more advanced infrastructure and education systems will bring higher productivity and earnings (Glaeser and Joshi-Ghani 2015). To improve their infrastructures, cities will have to raise government revenues. Increasing urban property values, more demand for public services, a large concentration of population and economic activity—all bode well for the prospects of increased revenues from property and land taxation (Bahl 2018; Bryan, Glaeser, and Tsivanidis 2021; Collier 2017).

In many ways, land and property taxes *are* urban taxes. About 40 percent of all property taxes in India are collected in Mumbai, 42 percent of Thailand's are from Bangkok, 43 percent of Indonesia's are from Jakarta, and 27 percent of Malaysia's are from Kuala Lumpur. The square-meter value of residential land in Tokyo is nearly six times the national average, and commercial and industrial land is valued at sixteen times the national average.

Capturing the fiscal space generated by urbanization will not be easy or automatic. For example, assessment ratios in Vietnam's larger cities are as low as 30–50 percent. Hanoi, Vietnam's capital and second-largest city, has experienced rapid urbanization but collects very little from recurrent property tax—only about USD 2 per capita from its nonagricultural land use tax in 2016. In Taiwan, where the six largest cities account for more than 80 percent of revenue collections, assessment ratios were last updated in 2018. India is home to some of the world's largest cities yet has one of the weakest property tax regimes, due in part to intergovernmental fiscal tensions. India's 28 state governments determine the fiscal space for the more than 4,000 urban local governments by defining local tax policies, including the choice of tax rates and the determination of whom to include or exclude from payment of taxes. Some would argue that state governments in India have not set the stage for increased property taxation in big cities (Mohanty 2014; Pethe 2013). In Japan, policy makers have yet to fully address the problem of land and property ownership.

Table 3.1 Projected City Growth from 2018 and 2030

Jurisdiction	2018			2030		
	No. Cities, Population 1–5 Million	No. Cities, Population 5–10 Million	No. Cities, Population 10 Million+	No. Cities, Population 1–5 Million	No. Cities, Population 5–10 Million	No. Cities, Population 10 million+
China	105	13	6	146	19	8
Hong Kong	0	1	0	0	1	0
India	52	4	5	62	2	7
Indonesia	13	0	1	18	0	1
Japan	4	2	2	4	2	2
Korea	9	1	0	9	0	1
Malaysia	0	1	0	1	1	0
Pakistan	8	0	2	9	0	2
Philippines	1	0	1	4	0	1
Singapore	0	1	0	0	1	0
Taiwan	0	5	0	0	5	0
Thailand	3	0	1	3	0	1
Vietnam	4	1	0	4	1	1
Total	**199**	**29**	**18**	**260**	**32**	**24**

Source: United Nations (2018).

Technology is here

Technology is already strengthening administration of land and property taxes in low- and middle-income jurisdictions, and their ability to absorb these innovations is improving. Computer-assisted mass appraisal keeps valuation rolls more current; geographic information systems (GIS) better identify properties, which increases property tax coverage; and database management links the agencies that administer the tax. Hong Kong and Singapore, at one end of the spectrum, administer state-of-the-art systems that generate high rates of compliance. At the other end, lower-income jurisdictions of Asia have remained burdened with more primitive and partially manual systems.

To reform their property tax systems, several cities in India digitized property tax data and developed a GIS-based mapping of properties to ensure that all properties were captured in the database. Some cities were not covered by a GIS; their property tax data was made compatible so that it could be easily integrated into the database in the future. "The reform was built around an information and communication technology system. This system provided the cities with web-based platforms for effective administration and taxpayer interface, including e-filing and e-payment. The . . . technology provided the potential . . . [for] improving outcomes by strengthening property identification, automating aspects of valuation, improving data management, and reducing the scope for rent-seeking" (Kelly, White, and Anand 2020, 132).

Zanzibar offers an interesting solution to a property tax regime that was "largely ineffective, with low tax base coverage and incomplete implementation of the property tax legislation, leading to poor collections. . . . The reform strategy has centered on building a fiscal cadastre (tax base) with the use of drone technology." . . . The creation of the fiscal cadastre [resulted in spatially identifying] some 500,000 building footprints across Zanzibar's two islands . . . using drone technology. . . . Of these buildings, individual property information on 13,232 buildings was collected through field data collection and on-the-ground inspections. This was a notable achievement given that the current property tax system under the 1934 Ordinance had only 1,370 buildings on the tax roll" (Kelly, White, and Anand 2020, 146).

Property taxes are an important revenue source in fiscally decentralized jurisdictions

The property tax usually meets the important criterion that the boundaries of its benefits and burdens roughly correspond (Bahl and Bird 2018). One econometric analysis consistent with the hypothesis that the intensity of use of the property tax is driven significantly by the jurisdiction's degree of expenditure decentralization is in Bahl and Martinez-Vazquez (2008). Central governments in a postpandemic world are likely to expect more local-government revenue mobilization and may grade local governments according to their property tax effort.

Indonesia devolved the administration of the property tax to local government in 2011. The objective was to give greater autonomy to local government and an incentive to more efficiently collect revenues. Thailand reformed property tax administration by giving local government more responsibilities in collecting building information data and assessing land and buildings on the basis of values supplied by its treasury department.

Most jurisdictions that have decentralized their fiscal system have concentrated on assigning expenditure responsibilities to subnational governments. The assignment of revenue-raising powers, especially in low-income jurisdictions, has been more limited (Bahl and Martinez-Vazquez 2008). Where property taxing powers have been devolved (the Philippines and Indonesia), there has been a wide disparity in the ability to value and collect the tax.

Some jurisdictions, notably China, Vietnam, Korea, and Japan, have given local governments relatively little fiscal autonomy and arguably have dampened some of the accountability gains that property taxation might have offered. Yet even in these places, effective property tax rates are relatively high, possibly because of stronger enforcement and/or because of heavy reliance on transfer taxes.

Reform Directions

Urbanization and a growing value base suggest that there is significant room for property tax revenue increases. But assigning a target level of revenue to this potential requires a detailed jurisdiction study of exemptions, preferential tax treatments, assessment rates, and collection rates. One of the few studies that attempted to estimate the revenue potential of property taxes (for Pakistan) found that even an increase to 0.5 percent of GDP would involve major administrative and policy reforms (McCluskey and McCord 2021).

There are four ways to increase property tax revenues in poor jurisdictions in Asia: integrating all (or most) land and property taxation into a single system, implementing specific policies to hit higher revenue targets, better managing property taxes, and upgrading technology. Each of these reform options will find advocates and detractors, and buy-in will be hard to attain.

Develop a Property and Land Tax Strategy

Most jurisdictions do not have a comprehensive strategy guiding property tax reform—or at least, not a written strategy they consult. Rather, they opportunistically identify discretionary changes in their tax structure, and their reform choices are heavily influenced by the contemporary political economy. Past performance should be an important contributor to this process, but in fact, many jurisdictions do not even monitor their property tax systems very well.

There are exceptions. Singapore and Hong Kong know where property taxation fits in their overall tax regime. In Singapore, a key national economic and social goal is to provide adequate and affordable housing for all citizens and to encourage owner occupancy. This goal has been achieved in part by keeping the annual cost of housing down and by limiting acquisition and holding costs for low- and middle-income homeowners. Hong Kong has used its ample reserves and land leases to maintain its position as a city with a relatively low property tax. In both jurisdictions, the ratio of recurrent property tax revenue to GDP is less than 1 percent, lower than the roughly 1.4 percent international average for high-income jurisdictions. The property tax is well managed in both jurisdictions, and its outcomes are transparent. If the current revenue mobilization strategy holds, these two cities are not likely to significantly increase revenues from the annual property tax, even though both have the capacity to do so. Both jurisdictions raise more revenue from taxes on property transfers than from recurrent property taxes (table 3.2).

By contrast, most of the lower-income jurisdictions covered in this book do not have a long-term strategy for improving their recurrent property tax system or, as we argue later, for moving toward an improved property transfer tax system. Some, however, have been debating this. For example, policy makers in China and Vietnam are concerned whether property taxes on land use transactions and land leases can be sustained at present levels. The Chinese government has for some time been in internal discussions about the possibility of introducing an annual property tax, and some of the same issues have been considered in two (failed) reform proposals in Vietnam.

Take a Comprehensive Approach to Reform

The reforms described in the 13 case studies are a mixture of structural and administrative changes. For the lower-income jurisdictions, the reform agendas are extensive and could take years. For example, restructuring bases and raising rates, rethinking and reducing exemptions, increasing coverage of the base, updating valuations, and improving

Table 3.2 Revenue Division Between Recurrent and All Other Property and Land Tax Revenues

Jurisdiction	Year	Revenues from Recurrent Property and Land Taxes (%)	Nonrecurrent Revenues from Other Property and Land Taxes (%)
China	2016	45	55
Hong Kong	2016	28	72
India	2017	31	69
Indonesia	2017	46	54
Japan	2017	82	18
Korea	2017	75	25
Malaysia	n/d	n/d	n/d
Pakistan	2017	16	~84
Philippines	2018	49	51
Singapore	2017	48	~52
Taiwan	2017	67	33
Thailand	2013	21	79
Vietnam	2017	1	99

Source: Case studies in part 2 of this book.

compliance are on nearly every reform list. As pointed out in chapter 2 (see box 2.1), revenue outcomes from the property tax depend on all the components of the reform working in the same direction. For example, an updated valuation roll means relatively little if only 50 percent of tax liabilities are collected, and a 100 percent collection rate generates little revenue if the statutory tax rate is very low, and so on. The bottom line here is that a productive and sustainable property tax reform has five legs—tax base, valuation, tax rates, collections, and continuous system management—and all must be part of the reform if revenues are to be increased and sustained.[2] Especially for the low-performing jurisdictions, this is a big hurdle to overcome, politically, institutionally, and even technically.

Clarify the Different Roles of Statutory Rates and Valuation

Valuation is the way that government defines its tax base, in terms of ability to pay or benefits received. The tax will be fair in such a system if all properties are assessed on the same basis. The statutory rates are determined as part of the political process, usually on the basis of revenue needs and on equity objectives in the case of progressive revenue structures. But too often governments in Asia do not keep these roles separate and use fractional assessments and other preferential valuation policy as part of the tax rate structure. Property taxation in these jurisdictions would be better served by keeping the valuation and rate setting components separate.

Eliminate Unnecessary Tax Preferences

Almost all the property tax systems studied here are complicated and cluttered with tax relief programs and interventions to promote or discourage certain activities. Most reformers argue that the property tax base should be expanded by removing exemptions and preferential assessments that are not achieving their objectives and those that are no longer needed (Kelly 2014). Policy makers and students of the property tax have noted this and have urged a review to clean out the tax relief package. But few have adopted this strategy, and in fact, most jurisdictions do not even track the revenue cost of these programs.

The recommendations here are to make property tax preferences more transparent and to evaluate their effectiveness. This involves doing four things. First, restructure the intergovernmental transfer system to penalize improper property tax exemptions or substandard tax rates, as is done in Japan. Second, make an annual inventory of all exemptions and preferential treatments and identify the revenue cost of each. Third, for all future exemptions and preferential treatments, require that each be accompanied by a fiscal note that identifies revenue costs and each be reevaluated periodically as a condition of being revoted. Fourth, make this information widely available to the public.

All thresholds set for the taxation of real property should be evaluated according to their revenue costs and their benefits. This analysis will shed light on the important question of how much tax base is being given away with high thresholds.

To be sure, there are no immutable laws about who deserves property tax preferences, but there is a need for the public to understand who is benefiting from these tax structure arrangements and how much could be gained by making them less liberal.

Simplify the Tax Structure

Property tax structures are usually complicated. Different statutory rate structures apply to different uses of property, and different assessment ratios apply to different sectors of the economy. On top of this, different valuation approaches are used for different types of property. Special features abound. The situation becomes even more confused when jurisdictions impose several different property taxes.

A careful review of the tax structure may show that much of its complication is unnecessary because the effective rates are set so low that the complications have little effect. They make the tax more costly to administer and hard for taxpayers to understand. If taxpayers do not understand a rule, they will possibly not be willing to comply with it and might be generally more resistant to property taxation.

Rationalize the Use of Property Transfer Taxes

The property transfer tax has significant revenue potential. However, in many jurisdictions it is not considered part of the general property tax regime. Integrating the recurrent property tax and the property transfer tax might unlock the revenue potential of land and property tax. This might be done in several ways (Bahl and Bird 2018; Franzsen 2020; McCluskey, Franzsen, and Bahl 2017; Wallace 2018). Jurisdictions could build transfer taxes into their property tax revenue strategies. The impacts of transfer taxes on housing markets should be harmonized with those of the other components of the recurrent property tax system—for example, the rates of holdings taxes. The transfer taxes and recurrent property taxes could be jointly administered so as to improve the valuation accuracy of both (Bahl, Cyan, and Wallace 2011). The way this might be done is to levy a base rate for revenue purposes and an additional surrate to address housing market issues. Finally, the reform path would replace the property transfer tax with a tax on capital gains on the transfer of immovable property. Although some administrative obstacles to implementation of a capital gains tax exist, the problems are no more difficult to resolve than those that prevent the present sales tax on transfers from working. Some parts of Asia (e.g., China, Korea, Malaysia, and Taiwan) already have some experience with capital gains taxes on real property transfers.

Improve Valuation

Possibly the most binding constraint on increased property tax revenue in lower-income Asian jurisdictions is the undervaluation of property. The property tax base is usually set as a market value, but the actual valuation is almost always much lower. If the assessment ratio is 50 percent, as has been roughly estimated by past researchers, only about half the property tax revenue potential is captured and sometimes is reduced even further by fractional assessment practices. In the higher-income jurisdictions of

Asia, the valuation rates are much higher, in part because property transfers are usually reported at market levels.

An important step toward moving assessment ratios closer to market levels in the low-income jurisdictions is to force accurate declarations of real property sales prices. This can be done with four actions. First, levy and vigorously enforce a heavy penalty on the underdeclaration of sales values. Second, employ a specific cadre of valuers to check the declared sales values against market levels. Third, require a match between the taxable values used for the property transfer tax and the recurrent property tax. With such a system in place and properly monitored, the revenue potential of both taxes could be increased. Fourth, the valuations of properties for transfer tax purposes and for recurrent property tax purposes should be harmonized or even merged. The use of accurately declared property values could make computer-assisted mass appraisal systems work more effectively and support market value assessments.

Improve Voluntary Compliance with the Property Tax

The high-income jurisdictions of Asia have almost full voluntary compliance with the property tax. Individuals and companies tend to pay amounts due in a timely fashion. But in the lower-income jurisdictions of Asia, collection rates are much lower, and consequently, revenue loss and rates of arrears are greater in some jurisdictions. Possible reasons for lower rates of compliance in the low-income jurisdictions in Asia are that compliance costs are too high, enforcement is not aggressive enough, and the social contract between governments and voters is inadequate.

At first glance, high compliance cost does not appear to be the problem, because all jurisdictions seem to have lowered the cost of compliance, and collections have moved toward urban areas, where electronic means of payment are more likely to be used. High rates of delinquency, however, suggest inadequate fear of penalties. Records on the application of penalties are not readily available, but many low-income jurisdictions are reticent to use aggressive enforcement measures. Also, some taxpayers may perceive no obligation to pay property taxes because the government has not provided adequate public services.

The reform strategy here is straightforward. The government must vigorously enforce the tax by applying the penalties that are in place for nonpayers and pressing for collections of arrears. Taxpayers need to believe they will be detected and penalized if they are delinquent. Fixing the social contract is a more difficult matter, but it begins with transparency in the management and outcomes of the property tax law.

Simplify and Improve Public Management

Fiscal management is a problem in many low-income jurisdictions, and in almost every jurisdiction there are calls for consolidation of duplicative government activities. Perhaps nowhere is this more evident than for the recurrent property tax and the property transfer tax. The case studies in part 2 of this book provide specific examples, such as the Philippines' 20 different agencies responsible for some aspect of valuation; Indonesia's six property taxes, each administered by a different agency; and in other jurisdictions, ownership records that are not regularly transmitted to valuation offices on a timely basis and duplicative tasks and overlapping assignments. The consolidation of responsibility for property tax management is long overdue and should be high on the agenda in many low- and middle-income jurisdictions.

Harness the Power of Information Technology

Efficient administration of the property tax requires use of information technology (IT). The days of manual administration with paper-based record keeping should be relegated to history. The handling of large volumes of data on many thousands of individual properties requires relational databases. An administrative system with digital data directly contributes to greater taxpayer confidence (McCluskey et al. 2018). Few would dispute that IT presents many advantages for both taxpayers and administration departments, including enhanced electronic services and payment options. These service enhancements make the process of paying taxes and fees simpler, faster, and easier to understand, thereby making compliance easier and more efficient (McCluskey et al. 2018).

The majority of the jurisdictions included in this book have integrated IT within the management of the property tax. More specifically, data on the valuation rolls are integrated with ownership and occupancy information. Generation of property tax bills monthly or annually requires a huge effort that can be effectively undertaken only by software solutions. Collection-led strategies (Kelly 2014) can achieve greater efficiency if the billing system is automated. There are good examples of cashless payments made through the banking system or via numerous payment points (such as shops, post offices, and ATMs).

Jurisdictions have improved their revenue administration by incorporating IT-based solutions, but automation of valuation and data collection activities lags in some places. Data collection still relies on manual interventions in Indonesia, Malaysia, Philippines, Thailand, and Vietnam, although the situation is improving. For example, Indonesia (Jakarta) uses unmanned aerial vehicles (drones) to capture imagery and spatial data, and municipalities in Malaysia and the Philippines are gradually developing their own GIS-based applications.

There is significant scope for greater reliance on automated valuation, but development of such techniques remains a challenge in some jurisdictions. Hong Kong and Korea are clear world leaders, having developed advanced mass valuation solutions that have given them the capacity to conduct annual revaluations. Vietnam has been exploring (with the technical assistance of the Korea Real Estate Board) the development of GIS-based approaches for land valuation. Where the property tax is administered by local government, the capacity to develop mass valuation techniques moves at a slower and rather fragmented pace (Indonesia, Malaysia, and Philippines). Much depends on higher-level governments taking the lead and providing technical training, as has been seen in the Philippines. In Malaysia, the university sector has led the way in developing mass valuation systems that are being used by local government.

Many areas now recognize that all aspects of property tax administration need to be reengineered to reduce costs and improve revenue collection. Collaboration and sharing of best practices are growing, evidenced by the Korea Real Estate Board sharing expertise with Vietnam. China has also been benefiting from the technical experience that its Hong Kong Special Administrative Region has developed over the last 100 years with its property tax.

Donor agencies such as the World Bank and Asian Development Bank have been supporting reform projects. India, Indonesia, Pakistan, the Philippines, and Thailand have taken advantage of these technical assistance programs, and many of these projects are still in progress.

Conclusion

The higher-income jurisdictions of Asia have budgetary space to increase revenue mobilization from their modern, well-structured property tax systems. These systems accurately assess land and property according to value. If urbanization in Asia continues to drive up land and housing prices, these jurisdictions are in a position to realize budgetary benefits.

The property tax systems of China and Vietnam are in transition. Both have property and land tax regimes that tax transfers of user rights, but neither has adopted a broad-based annual property tax. In these jurisdictions, it is questionable whether one-time taxes and charges on land use rights will be a sustainable revenue source.

In some lower-income jurisdictions in Asia, revenues from recurrent property taxes are well below 1 percent of GDP. The cause is often piecemeal reforms over a long period, leading to narrow tax bases, undervaluation, poor compliance, and an unwillingness to take on the tough reforms needed. The jurisdictions that can reform their property tax system to have a more fair and efficient base will see increased revenues.

An often-overlooked reform of property taxation in lower-income jurisdictions is the reform of property transfer taxes. Properly administered and properly integrated with recurrent property taxes, they could lead to significantly greater overall property tax revenue.

Notes

1. The United Nations reports 20 megacities in Asia as of 2018, plus another 28 cities with 5–10 million and 250 cities with 1–5 million. By 2030, these totals are expected to grow to 27, 34, and 330, respectively (United Nations 2018).

2. For a more formal discussion of this argument, see Bahl and Bird (2018, 245–247, 270–274) and Kelly, White, and Anand (2020).

References

Ahmad, E., G. Brosio, and J. P. Jiménez. 2019. "Options for Retooling Property Taxation in Latin America." Paper presented at the eighth Jornadas Iberoamericanas de Financiación Local, Mexico (October 1–2).

Bahl, R. 2018. "Metropolitan City Finances in the Asia and Pacific Region: Issues, Problems and Reform Options." In *Tax Policy for Sustainable Development in Asia and the Pacific*, ed. T. Subhanij, S. Banerjee, and Z. Jian, 25–70. United Nations Publication ST/ESCAP/2806. Bangkok: United Nations Economic Social and Economic Commission for Asia and the Pacific.

Bahl, R., and R. M. Bird. 2018. *Fiscal Decentralization and Local Finance in Developing Countries.* Cheltenham, UK: Edward Elgar.

Bahl, R., M. Cyan, and S. Wallace. 2011. "Challenges to Intergovernmental Fiscal Relations in Pakistan: The Revenue Assignment Dimension." In *Decentralization in Developing Countries*, ed. J. Martinez-Vazquez and F. Vaillancourt, 131–154. Cheltenham, UK: Edward Elgar.

Bahl, R., and J. Martinez-Vazquez. 2008. "The Property Tax in Developing Countries: Current Practice and Prospects." In *Making the Property Tax Work: Experiences in Developing and Transitional Countries*, ed. R. Bahl, J. Martinez-Vazquez, and J. Youngman, 35–57. Cambridge, MA: Lincoln Institute of Land Policy.

Bing, Y., K. Connelly, and M. E. Bell. 2009. "A Compendium of Countries with an Area Based Property Tax." Working paper WP09BY1. Cambridge, MA: Lincoln Institute of Land Policy.

Bryan, G., E. Glaeser, and N. Tsivanidis. 2021. "Cities." IGC evidence paper. International Growth Center, LSE, and University of Oxford (May).

Franzsen, R. C. D. 2020. "A Review of Property Transfer Taxes in Africa." In *Rethinking Land Reform in Africa: New Ideas, Opportunities, and Challenges*, 112–131. Abidjan, Ivory Coast: African Development Bank.

Glaeser, E., and J.-G. Abha. 2015. *The Urban Imperative: Towards Competitive Cities.* New Delhi: Oxford University Press.

Kelly, R. 2014. "Implementing Sustainable Property Tax Reform in Developing Countries." In *Taxation and Development: The Weakest Link? Essays in Honor of Roy Bahl*, ed. R. M. Bird and J. Martinez-Vazquez, 326–363. Cheltenham, UK: Edward Elgar.

Kelly, R., R. White, and A. Anand. 2020. *Property Tax Diagnostic Manual*. Washington, DC: World Bank.

McCluskey, W., R. Franzsen, and R. Bahl. 2017. "Challenges, Prospects and Recommendations." In *Property Tax in Africa: Status, Challenges and Prospects*, ed. R. C. D. Franzsen and W. J. McCluskey, 551–592. Cambridge, MA: Lincoln Institute of Land Policy.

McCluskey, W. J., R. Franzsen, M. Kabinga, and C. Kasese. 2018. "The Role of Information Communication Technology to Enhance Property Tax Revenue in Africa: A Tale of Four Cities in Three Countries." Working paper 88. International Center for Tax and Development.

McCluskey, W. J., and M. McCord. 2021. "Overview of the Urban Immovable Property Tax in Pakistan and Revenue Simulations." World Bank Report. Washington, DC.

Mohanty, P. K. 2014. *Cities and Public Policy: An Urban Agenda for India*. New Delhi: Sage Publications.

OECD (Organization for Economic Cooperation and Development). 2021. *Revenue Statistics in Asia and the Pacific 2021: Emerging Challenges for the Asia-Pacific Region in the COVID-19 Era*. Paris: OECD. https://doi.org/10.1787/ed374457-en.

Pethe, A. 2013. "Metropolitan Public Finances: The Case of Mumbai." In *Financing Metropolitan Governments in Developing Countries*, ed. R. Bahl, J. Linn, and D. Wetzel, 243–272. Cambridge, MA: Lincoln Institute of Land Policy.

UN-Habitat. 2020. *The Value of Sustainable Urbanization*. World Cities Report 2020. Nairobi: UN-Habitat. https://unhabitat.org/sites/default/files/2020/10/wcr_2020 _report.pdf.

United Nations. 2018. "Country Profiles." World Urbanization Prospects 2018. United Nations, Department of Economic and Social Affairs, Population Division. https:// population.un.org/wup/Country-Profiles/.

Wallace, S. 2018. "Property Transfer Taxes." Working paper WP-18-02. Pretoria, South Africa: African Tax Institute, University of Pretoria.

World Bank. 2006. *Where Is the Wealth of Nations? Measuring Capital for the 21st Century*. Washington, DC: World Bank.

PART 2

Case Studies

4

China: An Evolving Property Tax

ZHI LIU

China, unlike most other economies, does not have a broad-based annual property tax on the ownership of private residential properties. Several taxes are collected on the possession or transfer of real estate, but they are an ad hoc group of levies rather than a property tax system with clearly defined objectives (Bahl, Goh, and Qiao 2014, 55). As China rapidly urbanizes—96 percent of urban households own one or more residential properties—a local property tax could provide a sustainable source of municipal revenues.[1] It could also help correct distortions in the housing market, where the absence of a property tax encourages speculation and vacancy. The central government has been considering a local property tax since 2003, has supported pilot experiments in the cities of Shanghai and Chongqing, and is currently developing a property tax law as a necessary first step to introducing a local property tax nationwide. But this effort has sparked significant public resistance and heated policy debates. In the meantime, China's municipal governments have relied heavily on revenues from public land leasing for infrastructure and urban development.

This chapter is a revised, updated, and expanded version of Zhi Liu, "Land-Based Finance and Property Tax in China," *Area Development and Policy* 4, no. 4 (2019): 367–381. Copyright Regional Studies Association. The 2019 paper grew from a working paper I wrote and released in the African Tax Institute Working Paper Series (Z. Liu 2018). By permission of Taylor & Francis Ltd., http://www.tandfoline.com on behalf of Regional Studies Association.

This chapter describes the fiscal system and land-based finance in China and discusses the fiscal reform agenda, particularly the municipal finance challenges resulting from the decline of public land leasing revenues. It then discusses the current barriers to property tax implementation and proposes ways to overcome those barriers. The objective is to shed light on the importance of a property tax system in China's future municipal finance framework and housing markets and on the feasibility of property taxation.

The Fiscal System

China has five levels of government: central, provincial, prefecture, district/county, and village/township. Broadly, the term *local government (di fang zheng fu)* refers to any level of government under the central government. However, the central-local relationship in central-government documents often refers specifically to the relationship between the central and provincial-level governments, not the subprovincial governments (Z. Liu 2019).[2] This allows some room for provincial governments to define their fiscal relationships with lower-level governments.

Any government body at each level except the lowest (i.e., township) is a fiscal unit with revenue and expenditure assignments, as well as a budget. Township governments have their own budgets, but their revenues come from transfers from the higher-level government. All governments at each level are responsible for not only urban and rural public services but also economic development and social affairs within their administrative areas. These broad responsibilities are essentially the same for all levels of governments, except that national defense and foreign diplomatic affairs are reserved for the central government.

Table 4.1 shows the four broad sources of government revenues as of 2019: (1) general public budgetary revenues (comprising tax revenues and nontax revenues); (2) revenue from government-managed funds (such as land concession revenues, railway construction fund, and local education surcharges); (3) operating revenues from state-owned enterprises; and (4) revenues from social insurance funds. These four sources of revenues are managed and budgeted separately. Notably, tax revenues account for less than half of total government revenues.

The Tax-Sharing System

The current taxation system, known as the tax-sharing system, was adopted in 1994. All taxes are categorized into three groups: central taxes, local taxes, and shared taxes. Central taxes are collected and fully retained by

Table 4.1 Government Revenues, 2019 (RMB trillion)

			Central	Local	Total	% of Total
1	General public budgetary revenues		8.93	10.11	19.04	56.15
	Of which	Tax revenues	8.10	7.70	15.80	46.59
		Nontax revenues	0.83	2.41	3.24	9.55
2	Revenues from government-managed funds		0.42	8.05	8.47	24.98
	Of which	Land concession revenues	0.004	7.06	7.07	20.85
3	Operating revenues from state-owned enterprises		0.16	0.24	0.40	1.18
4	Revenues from mandatory social insurance funds		0.04	5.96	6.00	17.69
Total			**9.55**	**24.36**	**33.91**	**100.00**

Source: Ministry of Finance (2019).

the central government. Local taxes are collected and fully retained by local (or more precisely, provincial) governments.[3] Shared taxes are collected by the central government and shared in a predetermined proportion with the local government where the shared tax revenues are generated (Z. Liu 2019). The most important feature of this system is that the types and rates of all taxes are determined through a central-government process. Practically speaking, local governments do not have independent tax power or autonomy. The appendix lists all taxes under the three categories.

Table 4.2 shows tax revenues for selected years from 1995 to 2019. Note that the local share of total tax revenues is less than 50 percent for all years. Also, the share of total tax revenues over national GDP has declined steadily since 2015, largely as a result of the economic policy to reduce the tax burden on businesses.

In contrast, general public budgetary expenditures are highly decentralized. Local governments spend much more than the central government. Since the establishment of the tax-sharing system in 1994, local governments' share of general public budgetary expenditures has increased steadily from 70 percent in 1995 to about 85 percent from 2010

Table 4.2 Tax Revenues by Year, 1995–2019

Year	National GDP (RMB billion)	Total Tax Revenues (RMB billion)	Total Tax Revenues as % of GDP	Central Tax Revenues (RMB billion)	Local Tax Revenues (CNY billion)[1]	Local Share of Total Tax Revenues (%)
1995	6,079	597	9.8	312	286	47.8[2]
2000	9,922	1,258	12.8	657	601	47.8[2]
2005	18,494	2,878	16.7	1,605	1,273	44.2
2010	40,151	7,321	19.3	4,051	3,270	44.7
2015	68,905	12,492	18.1	6,226	6,266	49.8
2016	74,359	13,036	17.5	6,567	6,469	49.6
2017	82,712	14,437	17.5	7,570	6,867	47.6
2018	90,031	15,640	17.4	8,045	7,596	48.6
2019	98,652	15,800	16.0	8,102	7,698	48.7

Source: National Bureau of Statistics of China (http://www.stats.gov.cn/tjsj/ndsj/).

Note: This table does not show intergovernmental transfers from the central government to local governments.

[1] These are the tax revenues assigned to local governments, including revenues from all local taxes and the local share of shared taxes, but not intergovernmental transfers to local governments.

[2] The percentage is taken from the published share of local budgetary revenues over total budgetary revenues.

onward. In 2019, the total amount of general public budgetary expenditures was CNY 23.89 trillion, of which local governments spent CNY 20.37 trillion (85.3 percent), and the central government spent CNY 3.51 trillion (14.7 percent) and transferred CNY 7.44 trillion to the provincial governments.

Central-to-provincial transfers are meant to equalize the provision of basic public services across mainland China. The system is complex because the amount given to each targeted province is a result of central-government discretion and negotiation with each provincial government, not a formula. The transfers are in the form of grants that help close the gap between the relatively centralized revenues and the highly decentralized public expenditures. There are two types of central-to-provincial transfers: general-purpose transfers and earmarked transfers. In 2018, the central-to-provincial transfers amounted to CNY 6.16 trillion, of which general-purpose transfers accounted for 62.8 percent, and earmarked transfers accounted for 37.2 percent. In 2019, the central-to-provincial transfers amounted to CNY 6.68 trillion, but the share of earmarked transfers reduced to 10.2 percent, a result of a fiscal reform action that aimed to increase the share of general-purpose transfer and reduce the share of earmarked transfers.

Compared with the central-provincial fiscal framework, the intergovernmental fiscal framework at the subnational level is even more complex. Recall the four levels of subnational government: provincial, prefecture, district, and village. Significant variations exist among the provinces in terms of population, incomes, economic structure, level of urbanization, and fiscal capacity. There are several tax-sharing arrangements between the provincial and prefecture levels. For the local taxes with large and stable revenues, most provinces adopt a fixed share between the provincial and prefecture governments, and they assign revenues from small local taxes to the prefecture governments. Some provincial governments take all tax revenues generated from key industries with provincial significance (such as power generation and chemical industry in Ningxia Hui Autonomous Region, and finance and insurance in a few other provinces). In Zhejiang, Fujian, and Jiangsu Provinces, a quota is set for the total tax revenues generated from each prefecture; that quota amount is retained by the prefecture, and any excess above the quota is shared with the provincial government at an agreed proportion (Zhong 2017, 89–90).

The expenditure assignments are essentially similar among the provincial, prefecture, and county governments and are often criticized as being a one-size-fits-all pattern that ignores the comparative advantages of different levels of government in carrying out certain expenditure responsibilities. As a result, there is a tendency for higher-level governments to press lower-level governments to carry out mandates that the former cannot fully fund and implement. This results in lower-level governments, which have fewer financial resources and less implementation capacity, carrying a heavier burden of expenditure responsibilities. Similar misalignments also occur in the mandatory social insurance funds. For example, pension funds are collected and spent by the provincial- or prefecture-level governments within their jurisdictions, causing surpluses in some localities and shortfalls in others.

This situation is partly enabled by China's highly centralized political system. The top leader of a local government (the party secretary) is directly appointed by the next higher-level party committee. For example, the central party committee appoints the provincial party secretary, the provincial party committee appoints the prefecture party secretary, and so on (Z. Liu 2019). This centralized political system is to ensure that the central policy and directives get implemented by lower-level governments. To some extent, it is compatible with the tax-sharing system in which the central government maintains almost all taxing powers and the local governments are given little taxing power.

There are also intergovernmental transfers between the provincial- and prefecture-level governments. But this is perhaps the least known area of local public finance in China. There are essentially no centrally collected and published data on local-government transfers, although some provincial finance departments do track such data. It is unlikely that the provincial-prefecture transfers are strictly formula based.

Local Taxes on Real Estate

Five types of local taxes are collected on the possession or transfer of real estate properties: urban and township land use tax, farmland occupation tax, land appreciation tax, real estate tax, and deed tax.[4] As shown in table 4.3, total revenues from these five taxes have accounted for 22 to 25 percent of local tax revenues and 2 percent of national GDP in recent years.

According to China's tax code, an entity or an individual using land in cities, county seat towns, administrative towns, and industrial and mining districts shall pay an annual urban and township land use tax. The purpose is to encourage more efficient use of urban land. In practice, however, the tax is imposed only on land used for commercial purposes.[5] The tax base is the actual area of land occupied. The tax rates on each square meter of land are (1) 1.5–30 CNY for big cities (population over 1 million); (2) 1.2–24 yuan for medium-sized cities (population 500,000 to 1 million); (3) 0.9–18 yuan in small cities (population under 500,000); and (4) 0.6–12

Table 4.3 Revenues from Five Taxes on Real Estate Properties, 2013–2019 (CNY billion)

Tax	2013	2014	2015	2016	2017	2018	2019
Urban and township land use tax	158.2	185.2	205.1	225.6	236.1	238.8	219.5
Farmland occupation tax	171.8	199.3	214.2	202.9	165.2	131.9	139.0
Land appreciation tax	329.3	391.5	383.2	421.2	491.1	564.1	646.5
Real estate tax	182.8	205.9	209.7	222.1	260.4	288.9	298.8
Deed tax	384.4	400.1	389.9	430.0	491.0	573.0	621.3
Total	**1,225.6**	**1,381.9**	**1,402.1**	**1,501.8**	**1,643.8**	**1,796.7**	**1,925.1**
As % of local tax revenues[1]	**22.7**	**23.4**	**22.4**	**23.2**	**23.9**	**23.7**	**25.0**
As % of GDP	**2.1**	**2.1**	**2.0**	**2.0**	**2.0**	**2.0**	**2.0**

Source: Official website of the National Statistical Bureau (http://www.stats.gov.cn/tjsj/ndsj/).

[1] Local tax revenues do not include central-government transfers to local governments.

yuan in county towns, administrative towns, and industrial and mining districts (Z. Liu 2019; see Bahl [1999] for this tax's relevance to a local property tax). Local governments determine the exact rates on the basis of their local needs and affordability, with higher rates typically seen in more affluent provinces and lower rates in poorer provinces. Since 2013, the central government has allowed local governments to set rates higher than the ceiling subject to the approval of Ministry of Finance or lower than the floor (up to 30 percent lower) subject to the approval of the provincial government (State Council of the People's Republic of China 2013).

The farmland occupation tax is a one-time tax imposed on entities and individuals who use farmland to build houses or for other nonagricultural construction purposes. The aim is to preserve farmland, and the tax is based on the actual occupied area. Differentiated tax rates are adopted for different localities (mainly at the county level), ranging from 5 to 50 yuan/m². Higher tax rates are adopted in localities with less farmland per capita.

The land appreciation tax is a one-time tax levied on the incremental value received by those who transfer the right to use state-owned land and aboveground structures, and their attached facilities, and attain income from such transfer (Z. Liu 2019). The incremental value is the total income from the transfer minus the costs paid by the transferor for the land use rights, land development, structure construction, and the tax payments related to the transfer. The tax payments include individual income tax, deed tax, stamp tax, and value-added tax (which replaces the formerly imposed business tax).[6] Which of four levels of progressive tax rates (30, 40, 50, and 60 percent) is levied depends on the ratio of incremental value to the sum of costs and tax payments. A tax rate of 30 percent applies if the ratio is below 50 percent; 40 percent if between 50 and 100 percent; 50 percent if between 100 and 200 percent; and 60 percent if more than 200 percent. These rates are designed to help deter property speculation and raise revenues for local governments. In practice, this tax has not been levied on the transfer of private noncommercial residential properties.

The real estate tax is imposed on owners of houses and buildings within cities, county towns, administrative towns, and industrial and mining districts. So far, however, this tax has been implemented only on houses and buildings used for commercial purposes (e.g., rental units, service apartments, hotels, and office buildings), not on private noncommercial residential properties. According to the tax code, the real estate tax for owner-occupied houses is calculated at a tax rate of 1.2 percent on 70–90 percent of the original value of the property (Z. Liu 2019). The real estate tax for rented houses is calculated on the basis of the rental income, and the applicable tax rate is 12 percent. Rental of individually owned houses is taxed at 4 percent of rental income; rental of houses owned by enterprises and public institutions, social groups, and other entities is taxed at 4 percent.

The deed tax is a one-time tax imposed on the transferee (entities and individuals) for the right to use the land, for the right of ownership of the house, or for the price margin resulting from the exchange of land use rights and house ownership. The tax rates are 3–5 percent on the purchase price of the property (Z. Liu 2019). The range provides discretion to the provincial governments to determine a tax rate based on local economic conditions. To lower the financial burden on first-time homebuyers, purchase of a housing unit under 90 m^2 by individuals or households for whom this is the only housing unit is taxed at a preferential rate of 1 percent. Purchase of a housing unit over 90 m^2 that is the only housing unit of the buying household is taxed at half the applicable tax rate.

As noted earlier, the possession and transfer of private noncommercial residential properties are subject only to the deed tax. Applying these taxes to all residential properties would generate a huge, stable source of local revenues. A study estimated that there were 311 million residential housing units in urban China in 2019 (Ren, Xiong, and Bai 2019). Since 2003, the central government has been considering a property tax reform that would introduce an annual, broad-based, ad valorem local property tax system on the ownership of private residential properties, commercial properties, and industrial properties. A national property tax law is being drafted, but no details have been made public as of 2022. If the property tax system is created, restructure of the five taxes discussed in the preceding will be necessary. I return to a more detailed discussion of property tax reform later.

Land-Based Finance in Urban Development

China has experienced rapid urbanization since 1978, when Deng Xiaoping spearheaded economic reforms. Between 1978 and 2020, China's total population grew from 963 million to 1.41 billion, and its urban population grew from 18 percent to 64 percent of the total. Today, more than 902 million people live in cities, and that number is expected to top 1.13 billion (or 75 percent of the total population) by 2035.

The physical expansion and development of cities has been dramatic in the first two decades of this century. Most cities, large and small, have expanded in population and land area by several times. Large cities, megacities, and urban regions (or cluster cities) have emerged and serve as major economic centers of the nation. Development of the three largest cluster cities—the Beijing-Tianjin-Hebei Region, the Yangtze River Delta Region centered on Shanghai and Hangzhou, and the Greater Bay Area of Guangdong–Hong Kong–Macau—is expected to drive the national economy for the next few decades.

As of 2021, China has a total of 691 municipalities, with varied administrative ranks. Four municipalities are at the rank of provincial level: Beijing, Shanghai, Tianjin, and Chongqing, also known as the centrally administered municipalities (*zhi xia shi*). There are 293 municipalities at the prefecture level (*di ji shi*) and 394 at the county level (*xian*). In addition, 1,454 county towns (*xian cheng*) serve as the administrative seat of a county, and about 20,000 administratively are designated as townships (*jian zhi zhen*), mostly market towns serving rural areas. Some of the county towns and townships are large, with populations over 100,000.

Administratively, a municipality (*shi*) in mainland China is not exactly a city; it is an administrative area comprising both urban and rural areas. There is no government created specifically for an urban area. Usually, a municipality contains a central city built-up area and the surrounding rural districts or rural counties. A large municipality may contain several urban districts, one or two county-level cities, and several rural counties. This spatial arrangement allows sufficient geographic space for the municipalities to expand their urbanized areas. But it also complicates municipal financial management. A prefecture-level municipality has two levels of fiscal arrangements: the prefecture-level government itself and the county-level governments, each having its own revenue and expenditure assignments. In a few provinces, the provincial governments establish the direct fiscal relationship with the rural county governments within a prefecture, leaving the prefecture-level government to manage the finances of the central city areas.

The rapid urban development is driven primarily by rapid economic growth. But it is also made possible by the municipal governments' ability to mobilize and capitalize land resources. In the early years of economic reform, the central government initiated an open-door policy to take advantage of the investment opportunities from globalization and the abundant domestic supply of low-cost labor and cheap land (or more precisely, land without a market, which was a legacy of the planned economy). Special economic zones were set up in several coastal cities to attract business and manufacturing firms from outside mainland China. The local governments of these coastal cities allowed parcels of rural land to be leased for industrial plants. They also improved physical infrastructure and converted rural land into industrial parks. This government-led development approach succeeded greatly in attracting foreign direct investment and was later copied by many other cities in the 1990s and early years of the 2000s (Z. Liu 2019).

Local governments have long made economic growth a top priority, striving by whatever means possible within the legal and fiscal frameworks to achieve or surpass GDP growth targets set by the central government. Much public investment has flowed into infrastructure aimed at promoting local economic growth, during both economic upturns and economic downturns. However, municipal governments have limited fiscal means.

As mentioned, local governments possess essentially no tax power or autonomy and are not allowed by the Budget Law of the People's Republic of China to borrow directly from commercial banks or raise funds directly from the capital markets.[7] Facing these constraints, municipal governments have raised funds mainly through land-based financing mechanisms, including most significantly sales of land use rights (also known as land concessions or public land leasing) for real estate development, and indirect borrowing from commercial banks through local-government finance vehicles (LGFVs), often using land as a collateral.

Consequently, for the first two decades of this century, municipal governments have spent much more than the tax revenues they have (including intergovernmental transfers), with the fiscal gaps mainly covered by the revenues from public land leasing (or land concession revenues) and commercial borrowing by the LGFVs. As figure 4.1 shows, for most years between 2001 and 2019, land concession revenues were greater than 50 percent of the local general budgetary revenues (including both tax and nontax revenues). Land concession revenues were mainly used by local governments to fund capital investment projects (Z. Liu 2019). The large amount of land concession revenues (compared with local general budgetary revenues), together with LGFV borrowing, enabled China's rapid urban expansion and modernization over two decades. In practice, gross land concession revenues are used to compensate farmers for land taken and to fund the infrastructure needed to service the land. Subtracting these two outlays, net revenues are used to fund capital investment for other urban infrastructure (such as mass rail transit) and affordable housing (Z. Liu 2019).

The sales of land use rights for real estate development are a part of municipalities' land operations. In competition for investment and employment opportunities, most municipalities offer sizable industrial land for use by manufacturing firms at very low prices or even free of charge. Municipal governments believe that the newly attracted manufacturing firms bring in jobs and generate income and local tax revenues, that new jobs generate new demand for housing and other commercial services, and that the new supply of housing and services generates further local income and tax revenues. The costs of subsidizing industrial land are covered by the revenues from sales of land use rights for commercial and residential development.

Figure 4.1 Local General Budgetary Revenues and Land Concession Revenues, 2001–2019

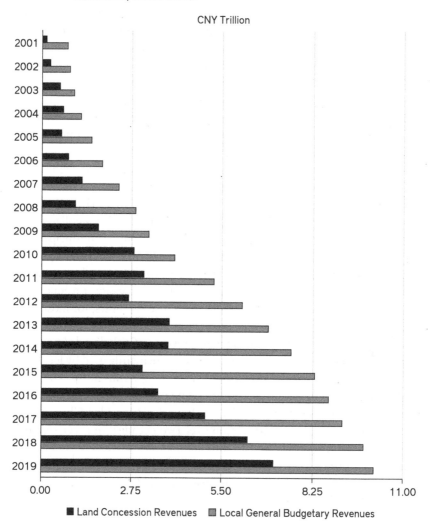

Sources: Official website of the National Statistical Bureau (http://www.stats.gov.cn/tjsj/ndsj/); Ministry of Land and Resources (2001–2017).

The prices of commercial and residential land—which are mainly determined by competitive bidding by developers—are many times (ranging from five to fifteen) higher than the officially set prices for industrial land. Figure 4.2 illustrates the mechanism of land-based finance. Heavily subsidized industrial land has led to considerable inefficiencies in industrial land use in many municipalities (Z. Liu 2019).

Figure 4.2 China's Land-Based Finance Mechanism

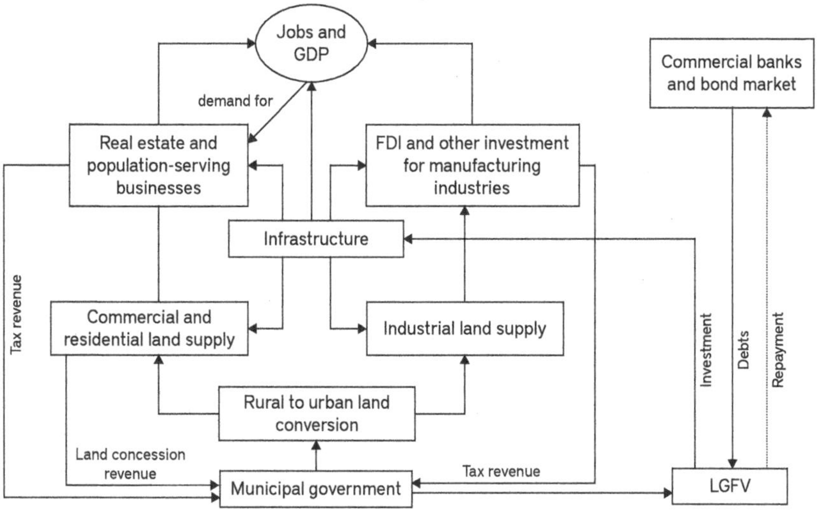

Note: FDI = foreign direct investment; LGFV = local-government finance vehicle.

Before the 2019 amendment to the Land Administration Law of the People's Republic of China became effective on January 1, 2020, this mechanism was made possible by the legal arrangement that gave local governments a monopoly power to supply land for urban development. Under the constitution of China, urban land is owned by the state and rural land by the village collectives. Before the 2019 amendment to the Land Administration Law, the state possessed the power to control and regulate land use, and only the state—which was represented by local governments—was given the legal power to convert rural land into urban land through land expropriation. Compensation to farmers for rural land taken by the government was set, not at the market price of the land, but at the agricultural production value (or the value of land in its original use). The Land Administration Law requires municipal governments to sell the use rights of the land to real estate developers for a certain period: 70 years for residential use, 50 years for commercial use, and 40 years for industrial use. This legal arrangement set the stage for land concessions across mainland China in this century (Z. Liu 2019).

The amended law permits village collectives to directly sell the use rights of their rural construction land for industrial and commercial development, without going through state expropriation. It also narrows the scope of state expropriation to a few strictly defined public purposes and requires compensation for taking land to be set at market-based, zonal-comprehensive land prices, plus social insurance.

Farmland is scarce in China, and municipal land operations are heavily constrained by the national farmland preservation policy. According to World Bank data for 2015, China's per capita arable land area is 0.09 hectare, compared with the world average 0.19 hectare. The national farmland preservation policy stipulates that a total of 1.8 billion *mu* (a unit of farmland equivalent to 667 m^2) of basic farmland (or high-grade farmland) must be preserved to maintain a sufficient food supply for a population of 1.41 billion. In implementation, each province must maintain a fixed quantity of basic farmland. Moreover, when a province takes farmland for urban development, the provincial government must generate farmland of the same amount and equivalent quality elsewhere within the province. This strict policy significantly limits the total amount of land supply for urban development, but it also drives up prices of public land leasing and thus the revenues per unit of land supply (Z. Liu 2019).

Urban land supply for residential use represents a small fraction of total urban land supply. Of the total amount of new land supply in a typical city, a significant portion (about 70 percent on average) is allocated to industry, infrastructure, public administration, and affordable housing—which generate little revenue for municipal governments. That leaves 20–30 percent of new land for commercial and residential development that generates land revenues. As a result of this limited supply, prices for residential land use rights have risen quickly (figure 4.3).

Land concession fees generate significant revenues for municipal governments but they also contribute to high housing prices. Analysis shows that the cost of land (i.e., the one-time payment of land concession fees made by the developer to the government) accounts for about 30 percent or more of the final sales price.[8] High housing prices and the expectation of price increases induce the sector to supply a large quantity of housing units every year, resulting in large inventories (i.e., unsold units) in many localities across the jurisdiction.

Despite high prices, housing demand remains strong in the major cities. The main reason is that many households purchase homes as the only viable means of investment. China has experienced rapid growth in household income since 2000, which has been accompanied by strong consumption growth and increases in the saving rate from 28 percent of household disposable income in 2000 to 38 percent in 2014 (OECD 2017).[9] But households have few investment options for their savings. The renminbi is not a freely convertible currency, and investing savings overseas is not

Figure 4.3 Chinese National Real Land Price Index, 35 Markets, Constant

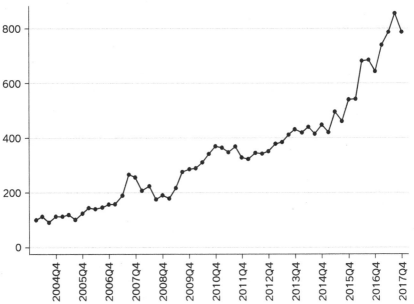

Quality Series (Quarterly: 2004q1–2017q4)
Source: Wu, Gyourko, and Deng (2017).

feasible for most households. Interest rates paid to domestic savings accounts are low owing to lack of competition in the commercial banking
sector and strong government interventions to control interest rates. The
domestic stock market is poorly regulated and not transparent, and many
investors have lost money or not made reasonable return since about 2005
despite the continuing growth of the economy. Many high-income and
middle-income households have purchased more than one housing property, many of which are left vacant because the carrying costs are low in
the absence of a property tax (Z. Liu 2019).

LGFV borrowing with land as collateral has also caused a local-
government debt problem. A 2013 national audit report revealed local
outstanding debts totaling CNY 17.8 trillion, which accounted for
28.6 percent of the national GDP (National Audit Office of the People's
Republic of China 2013). Efforts have been made since then to reduce local outstanding debts. The central government imposed a debt ceiling on
local-government borrowing and pledged that there would be no bailouts.
It permitted a small number of local governments to issue bonds to ease

their repayment pressures (Z. Liu 2019). These measures appear to have controlled the problem. According to the Ministry of Finance, the outstanding debt of local governments stood at CNY 25.7 trillion as of end of December 2020 (Ministry of Finance 2021) and accounted for 25.2 percent of the national GDP.

Since 2014, China's economy has entered a new growth stage, called by some the new normal. National GDP growth is no longer 10 percent annually as before. Instead, the rate has dropped to under 7 percent. Demand for land has cooled accordingly for most cities except the most economically viable cities at the top of the urban hierarchy. With a weakened land market, municipal governments are concerned about the sustainability of land-based finance in the near future. Prices for rural land, however, have also risen in recent years as farmers continue to press for higher compensation. This narrows the net revenues from land concessions (S. Liu 2018).[10] The 2019 amendment to the Land Administration Law may result in the biggest change. It permits village collectives to directly sell the use rights of their rural construction land for industrial and commercial development, without going through state expropriation. It also narrows the scope of state expropriation to a few strictly defined public purposes and requires that compensation for land taking be set at market- and zonal-based comprehensive land prices, plus social insurance. As a result, municipal governments face a new challenge: when land concession revenues become unsustainable, what will provide alternative sources of municipal revenues for urban development?

The land, housing, and local debt issues highlighted in the preceding are caused by distortions embedded in the urban growth model of many Chinese cities, which features a low cost for taking rural land from villages, the monopoly power of municipal governments in urban land supply, lack of investment alternatives for households, and the absence of a property tax on home ownership. All these have led to overexploitation of land for industrial development, housing vacancies, and an excessive housing supply that is a waste of land.

Fiscal Policy Reform and the Introduction of Property Tax

Property tax reform is an important part of China's ongoing fiscal policy reform. This section covers the dominance of indirect over direct taxation, the central-government-sponsored pilot programs underway since 2003, and milestones in fiscal policy and property tax reform since 2013.

Indirect Versus Direct Taxation

The current taxation system is dominated by indirect taxes. By definition, an indirect tax is one paid to the government by a firm or entity in the supply chain and can be passed on to the consumer in the price of a good or service. A direct tax is one paid directly to the government by a person or firm. In China, direct taxes include corporate income tax, individual income tax, vehicle purchase tax, vessel tax, deed tax, and real estate tax. According to tax revenue data published by the Ministry of Finance, direct tax revenues accounted for 38.8 percent of total tax revenues in 2019. In comparison, direct tax revenues usually account for over 50 percent of total tax revenues in Organization for Economic Cooperation and Development (OECD) jurisdictions (OECD 2019).

Because there is no annual property tax on the ownership of private residential properties yet, the share of tax revenues from individuals (instead of firms) is limited to individual income tax, which is small. As table 4.4 shows, individual income tax revenues accounted for 6.6 percent of total tax revenues in 2019. In comparison, 23.9 percent of the total tax revenues (including social security contributions) came from personal income tax and 5.8 percent from property taxes in OECD jurisdictions on average in 2017 (OECD 2019).

The dominance of indirect taxes is partly a legacy of China's planned economy, in which the government collected net revenues from state-owned enterprises as its main source of revenues. When its tax-sharing system was established in 1994, China was still a low-income economy. By design, the system taxed personal incomes only of foreigners and Chinese citizens with very high incomes and excluded most other people. In 2011, the central government raised the threshold for individual income tax from

Table 4.4 Individual Tax Revenues, 2013–2018 (CNY billion)

	2013	2014	2015	2016	2017	2018	2019
Individual income tax revenues	653	738	862	1,009	1,197	1,387	1,038
Total tax revenues (excluding social security contributions)	11,053	11,918	12,492	13,036	14,437	15,640	15,800
% of total	5.9	6.2	6.9	7.7	8.3	8.9	6.6

Source: Official website of the National Statistical Bureau (http://www.stats.gov.cn/tjsj/ndsj/).

CNY 2,000 per month to CNY 3,500 per month. The decision was very popular, but it substantially limited the number of individual income taxpayers to less than 50 million people, or less than 4 percent of the total population. In 2018, the central government further raised the threshold to CNY 5,000 per month. Given this system, most Chinese citizens are not used to paying direct taxes. This explains a strong social tendency to resist the introduction of broadly based direct taxes—notably, a highly visible property tax on the ownership of private residential properties.

Pilot Programs of Residential Property Appraisal and Taxation

The central government studied the need for and feasibility of property taxation on home ownership at the beginning of this century. This led Xie (2005, 2006) to recommend the introduction of the property tax. Scholars have also investigated needs and possible effects of the property tax in China (box 4.1). Given concerns about the absence of the building blocks of a modern, broad-based property tax system (such as property value appraisal), the central government has supported pilot programs to improve readiness for its introduction. In 2003, the government selected the centrally administered municipalities and provinces of Beijing, Chongqing, Liaoning Province (which in turn selected the city of Dandong), Jiangsu Province (city of Nanjing), Shenzhen, and Ningxia Hui Autonomous Region (city of Wuzhong) to develop mass appraisal capacity and to simulate property tax administration. This pilot program was later expanded to the city of Tianjin and to Anhui, Henan, and Fujian Provinces. In 2009, the central government further required every province to develop capacity for mass appraisal of property in at least one city, for the purpose of collecting the deed tax. As a result, some cities (including Hangzhou and Shenzhen) started to use mass appraisal for the assessment and collection of deed tax.

To support the pilot program, the State Administration of Taxation organized training courses for local tax officials on property tax law, assessment, and administration. Course development called on the expertise of the International Association of Assessing Officers (IAAO), Esri Canada (a provider of enterprise geographic information system [GIS] solutions), and the Rating and Valuation Department of Hong Kong.

To further test the feasibility and effectiveness of the property tax, in 2011 the central government initiated an experimental program in two cities, Shanghai and Chongqing. Table 4.5 describes the main design features of these pilots, which are limited in scope and do not involve broad-based

Box 4.1 Recent Perspectives on the Need for a Property Tax

The need for and impacts of a property tax in mainland China have increasingly been subjects of academic and policy inquiries in recent years. For example, Bahl, Goh, and Qiao (2014); Hou, Ren, and Zhang (2014); Lou (2013); and Man (2011) argue from the municipal finance perspective that a property tax on residential properties would be a stable source of municipal revenues and would help improve urban governance. Hong and Brubaker (2012) discuss how to integrate the property tax with the public land leasehold system. Zhang and Hou (2016) use household income data to estimate households' ability to pay local property tax under alternative exemption scenarios. Dale-Johnson and Zhu (2017) use a dynamic general equilibrium model to examine how different types and usage of property tax revenue and expenditure scenarios affect land price, house price, house rent, vacancy rate, and government revenue and land concession revenue. Zhang, Hou, and Li (2020) construct a static, partial equilibrium model to analyze the effects of a property tax on housing prices and housing rents. Hou, Ren, and Ma (2016) propose a design of the property tax system for mainland China.

In the tradition of Henry George (1879), who advocated taxing land value, most economists agree that a land value tax–a variant of the property tax that taxes only the land value and not improvements (or structures)–is a better type of property tax in terms of fairness and efficiency. Dye and England (2010) comprehensively assess the theory and practice of land value taxation. A major advantage of a land value tax is that, unlike a property tax on both land and improvements, it does not discourage investment in structures and improvements. In theory, a land value tax is most suitable for China, adopted perhaps by reforming the urban and township land use tax and land appreciation tax. However, in practice, this is not considered feasible, because the public land markets in Chinese cities are limited (especially in the built-up areas) and because land properties are not freely tradable. Without an active market across the urban area to generate necessary price information for land value assessment, it would be difficult to establish a tax base for taxation (Z. Liu 2019).

property taxes. Little is known about the outcomes to date, and revenue data are not publicly available, although Hou, Ren, and Zhang (2014, 46–47) reported that in 2011 (the first year) Shanghai collected CNY 90 million and Chongqing 150 million. Nonetheless, the pilot program is influential because other cities could learn lessons on property tax administration from Shanghai and Chongqing. Perhaps the biggest impact is that the pilot sends a strong signal to the public that the property tax will be implemented across the jurisdiction sooner or later.

Table 4.5 Property Tax Experiments in Shanghai and Chongqing

Design Features	Shanghai	Chongqing
Geographic coverage	The entire jurisdiction of Shanghai Municipality	All nine districts in the central city area
Properties to be taxed	For local resident households, all newly purchased housing units in addition to the first one owned by the same household For nonlocal resident households, all newly purchased housing units	1. All single detached commodity housing units 2. Newly purchased high-end housing units with purchase price over 200% of the average housing price in the central city area 3. Newly purchased housing units by households without Chongqing residential registration (hukou), without owning a firm, and without a job
Tax base	In the short term, 70% of the market transaction price In the long term, the appraisal value	In the short term, 100% of the market transaction price In the long term, the appraisal value
Tax rate	0.6%	For property types 1 and 2, progressive rates from 0.5% to 1.2%, depending on the purchase price For property type 3, 0.4%

Sources: Chongqing Municipal Government (2011); Shanghai Municipal Government (2011).

Milestones in Fiscal Policy and Property Tax Reform

Property tax reform was emphasized as an important part of the current round of fiscal policy reform that started after the Third Plenary Session of the 18th National Congress of the Communist Party of China, which was held in November 2013. The key objective is to optimize the tax system structure while maintaining the level of overall tax burden on the economy. Fiscal policy reform is also considered a key measure under the government's supply-side reform initiative that aims to cut the high tax and nontax burdens on the real economy. It requires an increase in direct tax revenues and a reduction in indirect tax revenues. Over the last few years, indirect tax revenues have been reduced by converting business tax to value-added tax, both of which are indirect taxes. Gao (2017) reported that the reduced amount of indirect tax revenues was about CNY 1 trillion a year.

This revenue reduction needs to be made up from other taxes if the level of public expenditures is to be maintained. The government recently introduced a resource tax and an environmental tax. But the revenues from these two new taxes are too small to close the gap. On the side of direct taxes, there is no room for higher corporate income tax because the policy's intent is to reduce the tax burden on enterprises. Therefore, attention has turned to personal income tax and private residential property tax. Otherwise, the government will have to rely on borrowing, which will increase the fiscal risks, especially at the local level, where the burden of local public debt is not small.

The Third Plenary Session of the 18th National Congress also established the principle of statutory taxation, that is, all new taxes must be established by law. Therefore, development of a property tax law becomes a critical milestone to cross before implementation nationwide. This principle is also written in the Legislation Law of the People's Republic of China.

The 19th National Congress of the Communist Party of China, held in October 2017, continued to emphasize fiscal policy reform, calling for deepening tax system reform and improving the local tax system. A key task is to continue increasing the share of direct taxes. Finance minister Xiao Jie outlined a three-part rollout of a property tax on home ownership (Xiao 2017). First, a property tax law has to be passed by the National People's Congress before local property taxes can be instituted. Second, the central government will give full authorization to local governments for implementation of a property tax, which indicates a certain degree of local flexibility on tax rates and exemptions. Third, the rollout will be taken step by step, implying that the cities that are ready may start their rollout. Furthermore, the residential property tax will be based on property value assessment, and other taxes on the construction and transaction of real estate properties will be lowered. Xiao (2017) remains the latest official statement about the broad direction of property tax reform. In March 2021, the central government announced the 14th Five-Year Plan for National Economic and Social Development and the Outline of the Long-Term Goals for 2035, which states that property tax legislation shall be advanced. In May 2021, the relevant central-government agencies convened a consultation meeting on pilot experiments of property tax reform. No details of the meeting were reported, but the news triggered speculation in the media that municipalities would be encouraged to launch experiments of property taxation.

By all indications, the government is determined to move ahead with a rollout, even though there is no specific timetable yet for the property tax law to be presented to the National People's Congress for approval. Even if the law is passed by the Congress in the near future, it will still take a few years for many municipalities to establish a working system of residential property assessment and administration. Therefore, it could be years before residential property tax becomes one of the main sources of municipal revenues (Z. Liu 2019).

No matter the timetable, a property tax will be significant in shaping urban governance in the future (Hou, Ren, and Zhang 2014; Lou 2013). Residential property tax is a local tax and its revenues are usually used by municipal governments to provide local public services that would constitute a portion of the residential property value. Thus, taxpayers would demand the right to influence and participate in municipal decision making and performance monitoring of municipal budget expenditures. This bottom-up pressure will fundamentally change the management style of municipal leaders, from responding mainly to higher-level directives to responding to the needs of urban residents.

Addressing the Barriers to Implementation

The political hurdles to an annual ad valorem property tax are high. Few homeowners in China—like those everywhere—will be happy to pay property tax. If new annual property tax revenues from urban areas account for 2 percent of the national GDP of CNY 101.6 trillion (the 2020 level), that would equate to CNY 2.032 trillion in total, or CNY 2,253 per urban resident (902 million urban residents in 2020) per year, or 5.14 percent of the disposable income for an average urban resident (CNY 43,834 in 2020). Given the likely exemptions that would benefit most low-income households, middle- and high-income households would bear much of the tax burden. Still, if many jurisdictions with lower per capita income can implement a property tax, why not China?

The resistance goes beyond affordability. Many Chinese homeowners argue that the purchase price of their home included a share of land concession fee for the use of public land underneath their home for 70 years and that the land concession fee was a proxy for property tax. This argument is incorrect because the land concession fee is a one-time payment for the lease of public land for 70 years; it does not include payment for public services typically covered by property tax revenues. Although the argument is incorrect, the land concession fee might be expected to be lowered in the presence of a property tax. Many homeowners also argue that it is not fair to impose a property tax after they made the decision to invest in property without prior knowledge about its introduction (Z. Liu 2019). Of course, this argument does not hold up to logic, because it precludes new taxes on assets, regardless of justification.

The readiness of cities to implement a property tax is another concern. Most cities, especially the smaller cities and towns, do not have the institutional capacity to undertake property tax assessment and administration, and building this capacity will take time and resources. However, the pilot programs for property tax assessment and simulated administration helped cities develop some aspects of the capacity, especially in property valuation. Thanks to the rapid and extensive land and housing property development since the new millennium, China's property appraisal profession has grown, reaching over 250,000 employees, 60,000 of whom are certified appraisers.

Many cities have developed or are developing a property market database that permits the use of computer-assisted mass appraisal (CAMA). With the assistance of international consultants such as Esri Canada, the city of Shenzhen developed a GIS CAMA system and 3D smart model (Nunlist 2017). Davis et al. (2019) assessed the housing property market data from a number of Chinese cities and concluded that Chinese cities could use CAMA that conforms to the IAAO valuation standards. Peking University–Lincoln Institute Center for Urban Development and Land Policy funded a study that used camera drones to help localities create a 3D property database (Wihbey 2017, 17–18).

In short, the barriers to implementing property tax reform are mainly political rather than technical. Despite the political hurdles, the pain of property tax can be reduced for the public, and the rest of this chapter offers measures that could help. These include reforming the price structure of public land leasing, starting with a wide base and a low tax rate, grandfathering based on time of home purchase, allowing time for ownership adjustments, and taking a stepwise approach to implementation. These provisional measures may lead to a smaller amount of property tax revenues in the early years, but the value of starting early outweighs the costs of further delays.

Reform the Price Structure of Public Land Leasing

The current price structure for public land leasing consists of a one-time payment of land concession fee only. It is deficient and unsustainable. With no annual rental charge on public land leasing and no property tax for recouping part of the costs of public services, real estate developers could bid a higher land concession fee up front. Although the mayor (who typically serves a four-year term) would at first gain substantial revenues for capital investment, subsequent mayors would have less and less land concession revenues when the city expansion slows down. This situation would be further compounded by the expected significant growth in operating and maintenance expenditures required for infrastructure.

Under the public land leasing system, the ideal price structure would consist of, first, a land concession fee up front to determine the most efficient use of newly supplied land; second, an annual leasing fee for the use of public land; and third, a property tax to finance public infrastructure and services. The second and third components could be bundled together because both can be levied annually on the basis of the same property assessment value (Z. Liu 2019). This is essentially the structure adopted in Hong Kong. China should reform the price structure of publicly owned land by introducing the property tax and public land rental charge. This structure would also give municipalities some flexibility to use the annual leasing fee of public land as a policy tool to stabilize land costs.

Start with a Low Tax Rate and Wide Base for Private Residential Properties

Given the urgency of strengthening the municipal finance system as the traditional land-based finance loses steam, introducing a property tax right away is best—perhaps by adopting a wide tax base and a very low rate to start with. The rate may be determined locally by municipal governments and depend on the affordability of their urban households. Some exemptions may be justified for very low-income households. Moreover, cities could learn a lot from international experiences, such as deferred tax payments for property owners with low cash incomes.

The acceptance by urban households of the property tax is extremely important to changing the culture of not paying direct taxes. Getting acceptance, however, will require tremendous political will and luck. Once a property tax with a low rate is accepted, municipal governments will have opportunities to gradually raise the property tax rate to a point that balances affordability and revenue needs for public services (Z. Liu 2019). This gradual approach would also allow time for taxpayers to understand the potential benefits of the property tax, such as revenues paying for urban services that increase private property values.

Adopt a Grandfathering Approach

If it is difficult to implement a broadly based property tax right away, an alternative would be to grandfather it, by which an old rule continues to apply to existing housing units while a new rule will apply to all new housing units. Specifically, a property tax would be imposed on the new owners of housing units that are built on the new land under the new land price structure proposed in the preceding. This is similar to the property tax experiments of Shanghai and Chongqing. It would also be imposed on the current owners of housing units built on land under the old price structure, when the current land leasing term expires and is extended to the next term. This alternative is transitional.

Home ownership in urban China is a rather recent phenomenon, starting after the 1998 housing marketization reform, and most homes still have 50 years or more in their land leasing term. Therefore, if this alternative is adopted, it will take many years before all residential properties become subject to the new property taxation. But doing it now may be better than delaying it. An alternative to grandfathering is an interim user charge for urban services, assessed on the basis of zones of public services and amenities.

Allow Time for Adjustment Before the Law Takes Effect

Most of today's urban homes were built and purchased after the housing marketization reform of 1998. Many households own multiple homes and keep them vacant, a phenomenon caused by various distortions, such as lack of household investment alternatives, a weak social safety net, and very low carrying costs in the absence of a property tax (Z. Liu 2019). Therefore, a property tax would provide an incentive for owners of multiple housing units to sell extra or vacant housing units or rent them out.

Considering that these owners purchased their properties when no property tax existed, the government should allow them time to reorder their housing investment portfolio after the national property tax law is passed by the National People's Congress. A simple way is to make the law effective two to three years after its approval. Hou, Ren, and Ma (2016) proposed an adjustment period of two to five years.

Allow Ready Municipalities to Implement Property Tax First

China has many municipalities, county seat towns, and administrative townships. As discussed, most of these cities and towns are not ready to implement a residential property tax, because they lack institutional capacity for property value assessment and property tax administration. However, some large municipalities have been making a significant effort to establish a city property database and develop property valuation methodologies, and some are ready to implement a property tax (Z. Liu 2019). It thus makes a great deal of sense for the central government to allow these ready municipalities to proceed with implementation after the national property tax law takes effect. At the same time, the central government and provincial governments may consider funding a capacity development program to assist other municipalities in developing a property assessment and administration system. The central government could use a financial incentive program based on the intergovernmental transfer system as a reward to municipalities that make real effort to roll out the property tax (Z. Liu 2019).

Conclusion

China missed a prime opportunity to implement property tax reform, before its housing boom, and today's homeowners are very reluctant to accept such a tax. If a property tax is not implemented, however, finding a sustainable source of local revenues will continue to challenge municipalities. In a broad sense, a property tax on the ownership of private residential properties is a significant missing piece of China's taxation reform strategy, which aims to achieve a better balance between indirect taxes and direct taxes. It is also a significant missing element of housing policy needed to discourage speculation and vacancy.

Appendix

Taxes by Category Under the Tax-Sharing System

	Central	Local	Shared (central-to-local ratio)
Turnover taxes		Excise tax	Value-added tax (50:50)
			Corporate income tax (60:40)
			Individual income tax (60:40)
Resource taxes		Resource tax	
		Urban and township land use tax	

Taxes by Category Under the Tax-Sharing System (*continued*)

	Central	Local	Shared (central-to-local ratio)
Specific-purpose taxes	Vehicle purchase tax	Urban maintenance and construction tax	
		Farmland occupancy tax	
		Fixed asset investment orientation regulation tax	
		Land appreciation tax	
Property taxes		Real estate tax (only on commercial properties)	
		Inheritance tax (not yet levied)	
Behavior taxes		Vehicle and vessel tax	
		Stamp tax	
		Deed tax	
		Vessel tonnage tax	
Customs duty	Custom duty		

Notes

1. According to a survey of 30,000 urban households across China carried out by the People's Bank of China, 96 percent owned one or more residential units as of October 2019. For one of the many reports on this survey, see https://finance.ifeng.com/c /7w4ii9mecW8. (The source is People's Bank of China 2020. "The Survey of Assets and Liabilities of Urban Households in China in 2019," posted on the Wechat public platform "China Finance" by the Department of Statistics and Analysis, the People's Bank of China on April 24, 2020. However, due to the political sensitivity of the data, the posting was soon removed from the public. And the report must have been made confidential, and has not been seen since then.)

2. Provincial-level administrations comprise twenty-three provinces, five autonomous regions, four centrally administered municipalities (Beijing, Tianjin, Shanghai, and Chongqing), and two special administrative regions (Hong Kong and Macau).

3. In 2018, tax administration reform took place at every level of subnational government. The central-government tax bureau merged with the local tax bureaus. This reform merged the collection management of central and local taxes but did not affect the tax-sharing arrangements.

4. Xu and Wang (2004) provide an early discussion of China's land and property taxes.

5. Some cities issue land use right certificates to buyers of new housing units, and the certificates are used as a basis for levying the urban and township land use tax.

6. For a private property transfer, an individual income tax of 20% is imposed on the net income received by the transferor. The net income is the total income from the property sale minus the cost of the original purchase and the tax payments made at the time of the sale. Moreover, a value-added tax of 5% is imposed if the transferor owned the property for less than two years. This tax replaces the business tax that existed for many years. Transferors who owned the property for more than two years are exempted from the value-added tax. The stamp tax is imposed on the final price at a rate of 0.05%.

7. An amendment to the Budget Law in 2014 permits local governments to sell bonds directly to raise funds for public investment projects. In implementation, however, only a handful of provincial-level governments are allowed to sell bonds under the quotas set by the State Council.

8. The share of land cost in housing sale price varies substantially across mainland China. The share is highest in first-tier cities (Beijing, Shanghai, Guangzhou, and Shenzhen) and a few second-tier cities where market demand remains very strong, but it is much lower in smaller cities where demand is less strong. This could be inferred from housing prices varying significantly across mainland China and the real cost of housing construction showing little change over time and across regions. Liu and Wang (2014) found that the real cost index of housing construction on mainland China fluctuated between 100 and 110 during 2005–2012.

9. The household saving rates for most Organization for Economic Cooperation and Development jurisdictions are below 10% (OECD 2017).

10. According to S. Liu (2018, table 22.6), the cost to convert rural land to urban land increased from 56.1% of total concession revenues in 2008 to 79.8% in 2015.

References

Bahl, R. W. 1999. *Fiscal Policy in China: Taxation and Intergovernmental Fiscal Relations.* Ann Arbor: University of Michigan Press.

Bahl, R. W., C. Goh, and B. Qiao. 2014. *Reforming the Public Finance System to Fit a More Urbanized China.* Beijing, China: Financial and Economic Publishing.

Dale-Johnson, D., and G. Zhu. 2017. "Transition to Property Tax in China: A Dynamic General Equilibrium Analysis." Working paper. Cambridge, MA: Lincoln Institute of Land Policy.

Chongqing Municipal Government. 2011. "Provisional Measures for Launching the Pilot Experiment of Property Taxation on Certain Personally Owned Housing Types." Public Notice announced on January 27, 2011.

Davis, P., M. McCord, P. Bidanset, and M. Cusack. 2019. "Nationwide Mass Appraisal Modeling in China: Feasibility Analysis for Scalability Given Ad Valorem Property Tax Reform." Working paper. Cambridge, MA: Lincoln Institute of Land Policy.

Dye, R. F., and R. W. England. 2010. *Assessing the Theory and Practice of Land Value Taxation.* Policy focus report. Cambridge, MA: Lincoln Institute of Land Policy.

Gao, P. 2017. "Taxation Reform Under the New Normal of Economic Development." [In Chinese.] *Economic Herald*, no. 225 (December).

George, H. (1879) 1997. *Progress and Poverty.* Reprint, Robert Schalkenbach Foundation, 1997.

Hong, Y.-H., and D. Brubaker. 2012. "Integrating the Proposed Property Tax with the Public Leasehold System." In *China's Local Public Finance in Transition*, ed. J. Y. Man and Y.-H. Hong. Cambridge, MA: Lincoln Institute of Land Policy.

Hou, Y., Q. Ren, and H. Ma. 2016. *Research in Scheme Design of China's Local Property Tax.* [In Chinese.] Beijing: Economic Science Press.

Hou, Y., Q. Ren, and P. Zhang. 2014. *The Property Tax in China: History, Pilots, and Prospects.* New York: Springer.

Liu, S. 2018. "The Structure of and Changes to China's Land System." In *China's 40 Years of Reform and Development, 1978–2018*, ed. R. Garnaut, L. Song, and C. Fang, 427–454. Acton: Australian National University Press.

Liu, Zhi. 2019. "Land-Based Finance and Property Tax in China." *Area Development and Policy* 4 (4): 367–381.

Liu, Z., and J. Wang. 2014. "An Analysis of Urban, Land and Housing Issues." In *Blue Book of New Urbanization (2014)*, ed. W. Li, M. Song, and T. Shen. [In Chinese.] Beijing: Social Sciences Academic Press.

Lou, J. 2013. *Rethinking of Intergovernmental Fiscal Relations in China.* [In Chinese.] Beijing China: Finance and Economics Press.

Man, J. Y. 2011. "Local Public Finance in China: An Overview." In *China's Local Public Finance in Transition*, ed. Joyce Y. Man and Y.-H. Hong Cambridge, MA: Lincoln Institute of Land Policy.

Ministry of Finance. 2019. *National Government Final Accounts.* [In Chinese]. http://yss.mof.gov.cn/2019qgczjs/index.htm.

———. 2021. "Report on the Local Government Debt Issuance and Outstanding Amount as of December, 2020." [In Chinese.] (January 26).

Ministry of Land and Resources. 2001–2017. *China Statistical Yearbook of Land and Resources* [In Chinese]. Beijing, China: The Geological Publishing House.

National Audit Office of the People's Republic of China. 2013. "The National Audit Results of Government Debts." Public notice, December 30, 2013.

Nunlist, T. 2017. "Virtual Valuation: GIS-Assisted Mass Appraisal in Shenzhen." *Land Lines*, October. https://www.lincolninst.edu/publications/articles/virtual-valuation.

OECD. 2017. "Household Savings (indicator)." https://doi.org/10.1787/cfc6f499-en, accessed December 30, 2017.

———. 2019. *Revenue Statistics 2019: Tax Revenue Trends in the OECD.* Paris: OECD. https://doi.org/10.1787/0bbc27da-en.

Ren, Z., C. Xiong, and X. Bai. 2019. *The 2019 Report on China's Housing Stock.* [In Chinese.] Guangzhou, China: Hengda Institute, Evergrande Group.

Shanghai Municipal Government. 2011. "Provisional Measures for Launching the Pilot Experiment of Property Taxation on Certain Personally Owned Housing Types." Public Notice, January 28, 2011.

State Council of the People's Republic of China. 2013. The Provisional Regulation of the People's Republic of China on the Urban and Township Land Use Tax. State Council Order No. 17.

Wihbey, J. 2017. "The Drone Revolution: UAV-Generated Geodata Drives Policy Innovation." *Land Lines*, October. https://www.lincolninst.edu/publications/articles/drone-revolution.

Wu, Jing, J. Gyourko, and Y. Deng. 2017. "Wharton/Tsinghua Chinese Residential Land Price Indexes." http://real-faculty.wharton.upenn.edu/gyourko/chinese-residential-land-price-indexes/.

Xiao, J. 2017. "Speeding Up the Establishment of a Modern Fiscal System." [In Chinese.] *People's Daily*, December 20, 2017.

Xie, F. 2005. *A Study of Real Estate Taxation in China*. [In Chinese.] Beijing: China Land Press.

———. 2006. *Designing China's Real Estate Tax System*. [In Chinese.] Beijing: China Development Press.

Xu, S., and D. Wang. 2004. "Land and Property Taxation in China." In *International Handbook of Land and Property Taxation*, ed. R. M. Bird and E. Slack, chap. 13. Cheltenham, UK: Edward Elgar.

Zhang, P., and Y. Hou. 2016. "Ability to Pay Local Property Tax, Tax Burden Distribution and Redistributive Effects." [In Chinese.] *Economic Research* 2016 (12): 118–132.

Zhang, P., Y. Hou, and B. Li. 2020. "Property Tax, Housing Prices, and Housing Rents: Theoretical Modeling and Implications for the Timing of Property Tax Implementation in China." [In Chinese.] *Finance and Trade Economics* 2020 (11).

Zhong, X. 2017. *Local Finance*. 4th ed. [In Chinese.] Beijing: Renmin University of China Press.

5

Hong Kong: A Well-Administered Property Tax System

MIMI BROWN

The Hong Kong Special Administrative Region (HKSAR) of the People's Republic of China is on China's southern coast near the Pearl River Delta and shares a border with Shenzhen, part of Guangdong Province. Hong Kong consists of three main territories: Hong Kong Island, Kowloon Peninsula, and the New Territories, including some 262 outlying islands. Though Hong Kong is tiny relative to most other Asian jurisdictions, covering a total area of roughly 1,107 km², less than 25 percent of that land is developed, and some 40 percent falls within country parks and nature reserves. The territory's population of roughly 7.5 million and density of 6,830 people/km² are almost on par with the numbers for Greater London (8.8 million and 5,590 people/km²).

Hong Kong is the world's seventh-largest trading economy, characterized by free trade, low taxation, and minimal government intervention. It is also a major service hub for the Asia-Pacific region, although far less so than in the late 20th century. With GDP per capita of HKD379,586 (USD 48,421) as of 2019, Hong Kong is second only to Singapore among the Asian jurisdictions.[1]

Sections of this chapter are based on *The History of Rates in Hong Kong*, 3d ed., (2013), *Property Rates in Hong Kong: Assessment, Collection, and Administration*, 3d ed., (2021), and Rating and Valuation Department website published by The Government of the Hong Kong Special Administrative Region (HKSAR). Permission has been granted by the Rating and Valuation Department, HKSAR.

Following British rule, from 1842 to 1997, China assumed sovereignty under the "one country, two systems" principle. The constitutional document, the Basic Law of the Hong Kong Special Administrative Region of the People's Republic of China, is intended to ensure that the political situation in place when China took over will remain in effect for 50 years and that Hong Kong will remain within the common law system. The Basic Law designates a system of governance led by a chief executive and an executive council, with a two-tiered system of semirepresentative government and an independent judiciary. The main administrative and executive functions of government are carried out by 13 policy bureaus, 56 departments, and other government agencies.

This chapter describes Hong Kong's land tenure and registration systems and then turns to a description and analysis of the territory's primary form of recurrent property taxes, known as rates. It explores collection and recovery of rates, other property-related taxes, and future challenges facing Hong Kong's property tax system.

Land Tenure and Registration Systems

Given Hong Kong's unique history, the land tenure system warrants a historical perspective. The registration system, which is based on deeds rather than titles, is another British colonial artifact and one that is slated to change.

Land Tenure Based on Leasehold

In Hong Kong, virtually all land is leasehold, except for a small plot of land granted to the Church of England for the construction of St. John's Cathedral in Central (the central business district of Hong Kong Island). Under the Government Leases Ordinance (Cap. 40), enacted in 1973, holders of all renewable land leases in Hong Kong are required to pay an annual rent equivalent to 3 percent of the ratable value (the estimated market rent at a designated date) of the land upon renewal of the lease.

In the early 1980s, there were widespread concerns over the future of Hong Kong, as the lease term of land in the New Territories approached expiry in 1997. This uncertainty was removed upon the signing of the Sino-British Joint Declaration in December 1984. The Joint Declaration states that sovereignty over the whole of Hong Kong would return to China and that land leases and related matters would fall under the provisions of Annex III in the declaration. In essence, from May 27, 1985 (the date of entry into the Joint Declaration), to June 30, 1997, normal land grants throughout Hong Kong had terms expiring not later than June 30, 2047. They were granted at a premium and nominal rental until June 30, 1997, after which an annual rent equivalent to 3 percent of the ratable value of the property would be charged. Leases expiring before June 30, 1997, with the exception of short-term tenancies and leases for special purposes, might also be extended to 2047 under the provisions of the Joint Declaration.

According to the HKSAR government, at least 30,000 land leases will expire by 2047. There have been public concerns over whether the government has the power to extend land leases expiring in 2047 and, if so, how to do so. Article 7 of the Basic Law states that, although all land within Hong Kong is state property, the HKSAR government has constitutional power and function to manage and grant land, with no time limit, within the territory in accordance with its land policies. The revenues derived therefrom shall be exclusively at the disposal of the HKSAR government. Articles 120–123 ensure continuation of existing land lease and renewal policy. They provide the legal basis for land policy after reunification. Specifically, Article 123 gives a blanket authorization and imposes no restriction on the HKSAR's power to grant leases beyond 2047. Thus, in the realm of land administration, the year 2047 is not a time limit. Indeed, new leases of land under the government land disposal program after reunification normally have a lease term of 50 years from the date of sale, beyond 2047. For example, Sha Tin Racecourse received a 50-year special-purpose lease in June 2016.

Deed Registration System

Hong Kong is one of the few common law jurisdictions that still operate a deed registration system for recording land and property transactions, rather than a title registration system. The Land Registration Ordinance (Cap. 128), under which the registration of deeds is conducted, was enacted in 1844 and is one of the oldest pieces of Hong Kong legislation still in use. Searches on land records have been supported by computerization of land registers and imaging of instruments for more than two decades. However, land registers remain simply an index to registered instruments. This significantly affects the efficiency of conveyancing and other dealings in property. Thus, buyers of property or land buyers, since 2005, have had to hire a lawyer to review each title document for transactions in order to ascertain the seller's title.

Since 1988, the government has been discussing conversion to a title registration system, a system long ago adopted by jurisdictions such as the United Kingdom and Australia. The Land Titles Ordinance, passed in 2004 but not yet enacted, aims to simplify the land and property registration system. The new law would give legal recognition to a registered person as the true owner and do away with any need to review title documents, thereby avoiding high legal fees and administrative delays. But the law will not come into effect until stakeholders and officials reach a consensus on a number of contentious issues.

Conversion of more than 3 million land registers under the deeds registration system dating back over a hundred years will be challenging. The main issues include whether existing land titles would be automatically converted under the new system, whether landlords would have a grace period for making a claim to the property to sort out unregistered interests, and whether a compensation cap would be needed if landlords suffer any loss of ownership due to fraud. As of 2022, the government is pursuing consensus with the major stakeholders with a view to enable early implementation of a title registration system in Hong Kong.

Taxation of Property: Rates

Hong Kong's principal method of recurrent property taxation is via property rates. Except for certain specific exemptions, all properties in Hong Kong are liable to rating assessment. Property rates are a percentage of the estimated ratable value of the property. The ratable value is determined according to open market rental evidence at the valuation date.

The Rating and Valuation Department assesses property rates under the Rating Ordinance (Cap. 116) and government rent (similar to ground rent in other jurisdictions) under the Government Rent (Assessment and Collection) Ordinance (Cap. 515). Staffed by valuation and other relevant professionals, the department's major responsibilities include

- accounting and billing of rates and government rent;

- provision of property valuation services to government bureaus and departments;

- provision of property information to government bureaus and departments, public bodies, and the private sector;

- administration of the Landlord and Tenant (Consolidation) Ordinance (Cap. 7); and

- provision of advisory and mediating services to the public on landlord and tenant matters with respect to residential properties.

Further details of the department's functions and services can be found at its website, www.rvd.gov.hk.

Apart from forming the bases for charging rates, ratable values are also used as a basis for charging government rent under the Government Rent (Assessment and Collection) Ordinance (Cap. 515), and the Government Leases Ordinance (Cap. 40).

In land- and property-related legal cases (normally initially heard by the Lands Tribunal), ratable values determine which level of court will have ultimate jurisdiction over application for recovery of land, determination of land title, and so on. Furthermore, ratable values determine the compensation ordered by the Lands Tribunal when hearing applications for repossession of leased properties and when applying provisions of the Landlord and Tenant (Consolidation) Ordinance (Cap. 7). Valuation professionals have an important role to play in giving advice on rates (box 5.1).

Box 5.1 Valuation Professionals' Education and Training

Before the formation of the Hong Kong Institute of Surveyors (HKIS) in 1984, the valuation profession in Hong Kong comprised mainly full members of the Royal Institution of Chartered Surveyors (RICS), a U.K. professional institute. Holders of diploma or higher certificate in Estate Surveying from local technical or polytechnic institutes were required to pass examinations set by RICS and also obtain supervised professional training before being accepted as full members of RICS.

With the RICS decision to reduce its operations in Hong Kong as 1997 (the hand-over date from the United Kingdom to China) loomed, HKIS was founded. The institute, with 85 founding members, was incorporated under the Hong Kong Institute of Surveyors Ordinance (Cap. 1148) in January 1990. In 1991, a registration board was set up under the Surveyors Registration Ordinance (Cap. 417) to administer the registration of surveyors.

As a professional institute, in addition to its primary roles in setting standards for professional services, establishing codes of ethics, and determining requirements for becoming a professional surveyor, it offers advice to the government on land supply, development strategies, town planning, building safety, construction quality, property management, and housing. In April 2019, HKIS members numbered 10,464, of which 6,891 were corporate members and the rest associate members, probationers, and student members.

Participating in international platforms on surveying matters, HKIS has reciprocal agreements with RICS and other national surveying bodies in Australia, Canada, China, Japan, Malaysia, New Zealand, and Singapore (Hong Kong Institute of Surveyors 2019).

Key Milestones

The rating system in Hong Kong was introduced more than 175 years ago, in 1845 (Brown 2013). Property rates were originally levied to maintain the police force. Subsequently, rates were used to fund other municipal services such as street lighting, water provision, and a fire brigade. Since 1931, revenue raised from property rates has been part of the government's consolidated revenue. A uniform charge of 17 percent of the ratable value was levied in all rated areas for services provided by government (Choi 2021, 5).

The earliest Rating Ordinance stipulated annual preparation of a valuation list, but resource constraints made the task difficult, and the practice of adopting an existing valuation list continued until 1973. Long periods between revaluations gave rise to huge increases in ratable values when revaluations did occur. To remedy this, revaluations since 1984 occur on a three-year cycle. Since April 1999, revaluation has occurred annually (Choi 2021, 7).

Not all the territory of Hong Kong was included within the rating system. For example, no property rates were levied in the New Territories. Over time, new rating areas were phased in, and from April 1988, the whole territory of Hong Kong has been subject to rates.

Liability for Rates

Rates are levied on the actual occupation of properties. The unit of assessment is a tenement, defined in section 2 of the Rating Ordinance (Cap. 116) as "any land (including land covered with water) or any building, structure, or part thereof which is held or occupied as a distinct or separate tenancy or holding or under any licence." A rating appeal case further defined the unit of assessment, a tenement, as consisting of land, buildings, and other structures. These three elements are ratable only if they are held or occupied as a distinct or separate tenancy, holding, or license (Choi 2021, 10).

Under the United Kingdom's rating law, the four commonly applied tests of ratability on which Hong Kong practice rests are that

- there must be actual occupation;
- the occupation must be exclusive;
- the occupation must be of some value or benefit to the possessor; and
- the possession must not be too transient (Choi 2021, 15).

In addition to these four tests, rate liability in Hong Kong exists only if the land is held or occupied under one of the three limited forms of tenure, and thus freehold land does not constitute a tenement.

On plant and machinery, the Rating Ordinance stipulates,

For the purpose of ascertaining the rateable value of a tenement . . .

(a) subject to paragraph (b), all machinery (including lifts) used as adjuncts to the tenement shall be regarded as part of the tenement, but the reasonable expenses incurred in working such machinery shall be allowed for in arriving at the rateable value of the tenement;

(b) no account shall be taken of the value of any machinery in or on the tenement for the purpose of manufacturing operations or trade processes. (Rating Ordinance, Cap. 116, sec. 8)

Ratable plant, under section 8A of the Rating Ordinance, includes cables, ducts, pipelines, railway lines, tramway lines, oil tanks, and settings and supports for plant or machinery.

Liability for Payment and Rates Payable

Rates in Hong Kong are a tax on occupation of a tenement. Under the Rating Ordinance, both the owner and occupier of a tenement are liable for payment of rates. However, primary liability rests with the occupier in the absence of any agreement to the contrary. This dual liability is a special feature of the Hong Kong rating system.

How Rates Are Calculated

Rates payable are the percentage (tax rate) of the ratable value for each tenement included in the valuation list. The tax rate is annually prescribed by the Legislative Council. Since 1999 the tax rate has been a fixed 5 percent; previously, they ranged from 4.5 percent to 18 percent.

If a tenement is supplied with unfiltered government water only or lacks any fresh water, the amount of rates payable will be reduced by 7.5 percent and 15 percent, respectively. However, nowadays there are very few tenements without a supply of fresh or unfiltered water.

Rate concessions protect ratepayers, at least in the short term, from increases in rate liability. In addition, the Rating Ordinance provides for refunds and exemptions to ratepayers in times of economic difficulty such as in 2003 and in 2020, when Hong Kong was affected by the SARS (severe acute respiratory syndrome) outbreak and COVID-19 pandemic, respectively.

Ratable value, the basis of assessment, is defined in section 7(2) of the Rating Ordinance (Cap. 116) as

> an amount equal to the rent at which the tenement might reasonably be expected to let, from year to year, if—
>
> (a) the tenant undertook to pay all usual tenant's rates and taxes; and
>
> (b) the landlord undertook to pay the Government rent, the costs of repairs and insurance and any other expenses necessary to maintain the tenement in a state to command that rent.

The ratable value is the estimated annual rental value in the open market. In standard industry practice, the ratable value is an agreed annual rent negotiated between a hypothetical landlord and a hypothetical tenant for a vacant property in its actual physical state (Choi 2021, 32).

Unauthorized or illegal properties or structures are also liable for rates. However, their assessments neither imply legal status nor confer legal sanction or authorization on them.

Introduced into the rating law in Hong Kong in 1973,

> the "tone of the list" provision was amended in 1981 to provide that the rateable value was to be ascertained by reference to the value as at a designated date known as the "relevant date." General changes in value after the relevant date are not material, so any increase or reduction in value since that date would not affect the rateable values. In recent years, the relevant date has been fixed at 1 October for the Valuation List to take effect on 1 April in the following year. (Choi 2021, 33)

Which method of valuation to apply depends on the availability of market rental evidence. Three valuation approaches are commonly used:

- Valuation by reference to rents (comparison method).
- Valuation by reference to receipts and expenditures.
- Valuation by reference to costs (contractor's method).

The majority of properties are valued by reference to open market rents. In the absence of rental evidence, incomes and expenditures indicate the rent that occupiers might reasonably be expected to pay. This method takes the gross receipts and deducts the cost of purchases to find the gross profit from which the working expenses are deducted to arrive at the divisible balance. The divisible balance is shared between the tenant and the landlord as the hypothetical rent payable for the property.

In the *China Light & Power* case, the tenant's share was determined by means of a return on capital, which was based upon the relevant Weighted Average Cost of Capital (WACC) at the valuation date. This took account of the company's amount of equity, the cost of the equity, the amount of debt and the cost of that debt. The cost of equity was determined by reference to the Capital Asset Pricing Model (CAPM) where the rate of return is based upon the return for a risk-free investment plus a premium to reflect the risk associated with the particular operation of the ratepayer. . . . The Tribunal commented that WACC was not definitive, but required adjustment by standing back and looking at the whole evidence. (Choi 2021, 37)

The contractor's method is used for rating assessments of specialized unique properties such as oil depots, golf courses, and recreation clubs. The practice is to use the financial market rate or the property market yield to decapitalize the effective capital value to arrive at the annual value.

Revaluation Timetable

To provide a sound and equitable tax base, the ratable values, on which rates are charged, must be updated regularly to reflect changes in market rental values. The frequency of general revaluation in Hong Kong is not specified in the Rating Ordinance. Instead, section 11 empowers the chief executive of the HKSAR to direct at any time the commissioner of Rating and Valuation to prepare a new valuation list and designate a date to ascertain ratable values of tenements. Since 1999, general revaluations have been conducted annually.

The preparation of a new valuation list involves four main stages:

COLLECTION OF RENTAL INFORMATION

Several hundred thousand request forms are sent out to ratepayers (occupiers) when the designated valuation reference date approaches. Ratepayers are required, under law, to complete and submit the forms physically or electronically within 21 days. Rental information can also be obtained from landlords. The Rating and Valuation Department has tracked and refreshed the details of about 382,000 rental records annually, comprising about 228,000 domestic and 154,000 nondomestic properties. These rental details provide very useful evidence for valuations carried out by the department. In the 2019/2020 valuation list, there are 2,121,273 domestic assessments and 410,000 nondomestic assessments (RVD).

Rental information is entered into the computerized Rental Information System. Following the exclusion of suspect rents, the information is analyzed and adjusted to accord with the basis of ascertaining ratable values.

REVIEW AND UPDATE OF RATABLE VALUES

The ratable value is assessed using the valuation reference date of October 1. Residential units, offices, and factories are mostly valued using the rental comparison method, making extensive use of computer-assisted mass appraisal techniques. The department updates buildings' valuation characteristics and the relativity between assessments to improve the techniques' accuracy (Choi 2021, 79). During the review, new quantity allowances and floor-level adjustments or patterns are established, and independent variables used in the multiple regression analysis are set by valuation staff. Adjustments are made to account for changes in market preference or physical and environmental changes.

DECLARATION AND PUBLIC INSPECTION OF THE VALUATION LIST

Since 2005, the valuation list has been prepared in digital format only, accessed by the public via the department website (www.rvdpi.gov.hk). The new list, usually completed in March of each year, contains the address, description, and ratable value of every tenement and is available for public inspection until the end of May. A summary of the 2020 list is shown in table 5.1.

Postrevaluation Statistical Audit

A statistical audit after the revaluation, following standards of the International Association of Assessing Officers (IAAO 2013), based in the United States, evaluates the accuracy of the appraisal using a set of ratio studies. Instead of capital values, the Rating and Valuation Department uses rental values in the ratio studies. All assessments are grouped by property type for analysis. For the 2019/2020 ratable values, the audit confirmed they were within the acceptable limits of 0.9–1.1 for mean, median, and weighted ratable value-to-rent ratios. The relativity equities between different property groups were within 5 percent of the overall ratios.

Compliance Check During Revaluation

The department implemented the Automated Property Valuation System in 2009 to enable just-in-time online comparison of valuations with avail-

Table 5.1 Valuation List: Distribution of Assessments and Ratable Values by Category as of April 1, 2020

Category	Number of Assessments	% of Total	Ratable Value (HKD million)
Domestic premises	1,904,852	74.1	375,159
Shops and other commercial premises	130,443	5.1	119,721
Offices	76,017	3.0	84,699
Industrial-cum-office premises	3,661	0.1	2,002
Factories	96,411	3.8	30,122
Storage premises	2,398	0.1	7,235
Car parking spaces	293,872	11.4	16,031
Other	61,344	2.4	96,841
Total	**2,568,998**	**100**	**731,811**

Source: HKSAR–Rating and Valuation Department.

able rental evidence for a property or by district, defined by users. The relativity equities between property groups and the bias within property groups is also available. Ratio studies can be conveniently conducted at any time during the revaluation.[2]

Updating the Valuation List

The commissioner of Rating and Valuation maintains and updates the list. Deletions occur if a tenement has been structurally altered; if a tenement should be separately assessed or, conversely, if two tenements should be valued together; or if a tenement ceases to be liable for assessment to rates. When a property, such as a new building, becomes liable to rates, an interim valuation will be made and included in the list. The commissioner may alter a valuation list to correct errors, such as in a description or calculation (Choi 2021, 54–55).

Proposals, Objections, and Appeals

Hong Kong ratepayers have free access to professional valuers and the Rating and Valuation Department and ample opportunity to discuss with them the valuation and assessment before considering any formal objection or appeal. The formal procedures are simple and the submission has historically been free of charge. These accessible and inexpensive practices underpin the Hong Kong rating system and are conducive to the successful application of property rates as an equitable and effective indirect tax.

Any aggrieved person may propose to the commissioner of Rating and Valuation altering an entry in a new valuation list or may object to a correction, deletion, or insertion to an existing valuation list. A person not satisfied with the commissioner's decision on the proposal or objection may lodge an appeal with the Lands Tribunal. The judgment of the tribunal on facts and valuation matters shall be final, but further appeal on any point of law can be made to a higher court.

An aggrieved person can propose to the commissioner an alteration of the valuation list after the declaration of a new list in March and before June 1 of that year. The person serving a proposal can be a third party—neither the owner nor the occupier—but the person must be aggrieved. Copies of the proposal must be served on both the owner and the occupier, and the aggrieved person must notify the commissioner of such service between April and May. The owner or occupier has 14 days to send comments on the proposal to the commissioner and the person serving the proposal. The commissioner must issue a decision before December 1 of the year in which a new list comes into force.

If the notice is for correction, deletion, or interim valuation, an aggrieved owner or occupier may, within 28 days, serve the commissioner a notice of objection stating the grounds of objection as provided in the ordinance. The commissioner is required to issue a decision within six months after the expiration of the 28-day objection period. The commissioner does not have the power to alter the assessment of a tenement not subject to a valid proposal or objection. Inconsistencies arising from the alteration of the assessment with another similar tenement can be rectified only in the following revaluation.

If dissatisfied with the commissioner's decision, a person may appeal to the Lands Tribunal (box 5.2) and must copy the notice of appeal to the commissioner within 28 days of service of the decision. An appellant who is a third party must also serve copies of the notice of appeal on the owner and occupier, both of whom may speak at the appeal hearing. Grounds of appeal are confined to those stated in the proposal or objection.

As shown in table 5.2, the relatively low number of proposals, objections, and appeals in the last half of the 2010s suggests that few ratepayers find cause for concern after annual revaluations and new assessments.

Notwithstanding any outstanding proposal, objection, or appeal, rates must be paid as demanded. In exceptional circumstances, the commissioner may defer payment of all or part of the rates due, pending a decision to the tribunal.

Box 5.2 THE LANDS TRIBUNAL

The Lands Tribunal in Hong Kong was established by statute in 1974 to settle disputes between claimants and the government concerning land matters. It was modeled on the similar organization of the Lands Tribunal for the United Kingdom. It consists of legal and valuation experts who hear and decide cases on valuation disputes. Through the tribunal, the public may contest a professional valuation without incurring the expense of a long legal process. The decision of the tribunal is final on issues of valuation and findings of fact. Further appeals can be made only on points of law to the Court of Appeal and eventually to the Court of Final Appeal. Upon request by a party to the dispute, the tribunal may send a question of law to the Court of Appeal. In addition, the tribunal may, within one month of issuing a decision, review the decision either on its own motion or upon application by any party (Choi 2021, 64–65).

Exemptions

Rate exemptions take two forms: exemption from assessment to rates and exemption from payment of rates granted by administrative means. Tenements listed as exempt from assessment to rates in the Rating Ordinance (Cap. 116, sec. 36(1)) are mainly

- agricultural land and buildings, including New Territories dwellings occupied in connection with agricultural operations;
- New Territories village houses within designated areas, complying with the prescribed size, height, and type criteria;
- tenements built for public religious worship and used wholly or mainly for such purpose;
- cemeteries and crematoria;
- properties owned and occupied for public purposes by government bodies;
- government properties occupied as dwellings by public officers in government employ;
- Housing Authority properties occupied for public purpose by the government;
- military land; and
- properties whose ratable value does not exceed the prescribed amount (HKD 3,000 in 2022).

Table 5.2 Proposals, Objections, and Appeals, 2015/2016–2019/2020

	2015/2016	2016/2017	2017/2018	2018/2019	2019/2020
Proposals					
Cases completed	50,304	48,688	40,190	40,566	39,092
RV confirmed	38,657	37,657	30,286	31,453	27,830
RV reduced	1,417	1,386	1,685	1,544	1,644
Miscellaneous	10,230	9,645	8,219	7,569	9,618
Objections					
Cases completed	3,572	4,431	3,914	2,755	7,481
RV confirmed	2,878	4,186	3,315	2,243	7,115
RV reduced	289	97	382	86	177
Miscellaneous	405	148	217	426	189
Appeals					
Cases completed	87	196	143	206	132
RV confirmed	1	1	-	-	5
RV reduced	-	-	-	-	-
Consent order	32	58	63	85	42
Withdrawn/lapsed	54	137	80	121	85

Source: RVD (2016–2020, table 12).

Notes: RV = ratable value; miscellaneous = cases that were found invalid, subsequently withdrawn by objectors, or found to have alterations not related to the ratable value, e.g., amendment to the tenement's description or deletion of the assessment.

The main classes of tenements exempted under different provisions in the ordinance from payment of rates are

- nonpurpose-built tenements used wholly or mainly for public religious worship;

- tenements that are occupied but not owned by the government;

- nongovernment-owned tenements occupied as dwellings by public officers by virtue of their employment;

- consular premises; and

- other tenements as authorized by the chief executive.

In essence, tenements likely to be permanently exempted are exempted from assessment, whereas those meriting temporary exemptions are exempted from payment, thus allowing closer monitoring of the exemption position. As of April 1, 2018, about 30,100 tenements, representing less than 2 percent of the total number of assessments in the valuation list, were exempted from payment of rates.

Proposals to exempt more classes of property have been resisted in the past. In lieu of exemption, the government added the amount of rate payments to its subventions for eligible charitable and similar organizations. Apart from avoiding hidden subsidies, this arrangement allowed a much stricter exemption policy and has avoided many potential challenges regarding eligibility for exemption. Also, the government has more flexibility to meet policy objectives in changing circumstances.

Computer-Assisted Mass Appraisal Techniques

Following a 1986 comprehensive exercise to input property data into computer systems, the Rating and Valuation Department completed the 1988–1989 general revaluation using computer-assisted mass appraisal (CAMA) for the first time for residential, office, and industrial premises. Since 2004, advanced CAMA techniques using a geographic information system (GIS) have facilitated the assessment of shops, retail premises, village houses, advertising signs, and other types of properties. The department now has over 35 computer programs running 24 hours a day. The major computer programs are fully integrated with one another, and the property and valuation data are stored in a central repository (Choi 2021). CAMA is extremely useful in analyzing rental patterns and formulating consistent value estimates. However, the responsibility of determining assessment levels, making accurate valuations, and ensuring that assessments comply with the requirements of the Rating Ordinance remains with the professional valuers.

The department employs four CAMA applications worthy of elaboration.

Reference Assessment Approach

Many properties have similar property attributes and valuation characteristics, such as residential flats, offices, flatted factories (high-rise buildings occupied by several manufacturers), and industrial-cum-office premises. Groups of detached, semidetached, or terraced houses also have similar attributes.

> Under the [reference assessment approach], a typical property unit within a building is selected as the "reference assessment." Mathematical relationships between the reference assessment and each of the other units selected in the building . . . are then established with regard to the attributes affecting the unit's rental value. Once the basic rate, i.e., dollar value per square metre per month ($/m²) for the reference assessment is determined based on the result of sophisticated rental and multiple regression analyses, the rateable values of . . . [other tenements in the building] can be generated automatically by the computer, with reference to the unit's floor area and other pre-determined adjustments relative to the reference assessment. (Choi 2021, 81)

This approach depends on the relationship between the reference assessment and the other related units, and a change to the reference assessment may trigger the need for a new set of relativities. To avoid this, the department has since 2014 used virtual reference assessments, which have the same set of valuation characteristics as the original reference assessment. Changes to the original, actual reference assessment no longer affect the other units, thus minimizing maintenance work.

Multiple Regression Analysis

The assessment of the reference tenements can be done manually or with the aid of a statistical software package called the Statistical Analysis System. The software performs a multiple regression analysis to predict the effects of property attributes and characteristics (independent variables) on property values. Ratable values (dependent variables) are the result.

Predictors (independent variables, such as location, building age, grade, and floor level) are used for residences, offices, and flatted factories.

The number of models is dynamically determined by valuation staff according to similar characteristics of properties in the model.

Two types of regression models are normally specified for each administrative district, or urban area, each having a different functional form or a different set of significant variables. The first type is the objective model, which includes only the property and transaction characteristics as independent variables, such as floor area, location, building age, grade, lift access, or date of rental agreement. The second type is the subjective model, itself broken into two types. Subjective model A includes the current ratable value as one of the independent variables and other physical characteristics, which are included because the ratable value has been refined over the years through proposal reviews by valuers' professional judgment to reflect attributes not captured in the original assessment. Subjective model B differs from model A by including building variables. Building variables are dummy variables created for buildings with significant value impact. Value contribution, positive or negative, is singled out in model B to even further improve the variations explained by the model.

Upon comparison of the actual with the estimated rents from the regression models, a decision is made as to which model should be adopted for the district or type of properties. Unless the current ratable values in a district show systematic or widespread problems, the subjective model is considered more reliable than the objective model (Choi 2021).

Indexation

When generating or adjusting ratable values in bulk and on a uniform basis, indexation is performed. It is often applied to reassess car parking spaces and commercial properties such as arcade shops.

Integrated Property Data Base

The department developed in-house an integrated property database, which is essentially a GIS incorporating textual data. It comprises parcel maps, zoning, and building plans integrated with textual property data stored in a document management system (Choi 2021, 92).

Apart from easily locating a particular property and retrieving its related data, valuation staff may also select properties on the map with specific characteristics or with rental records. The database generates maps showing the ranges of rent or ratable value factors in different colors, which facilitates value and rental analyses. The spatial tools also enable a user to define the location and shape of a particular property on the maps, upload the building plans, and calculate the floor areas using AutoCAD functions.

Since its initial application in the 2006/2007 general revaluation to reassess street and arcade shops, further enhancements to the database extended its functionality to types of properties such as village houses and advertising signs. Through integration of property data from the public and the private sectors, the integrated property database supports government plans to provide easier access for members of the public when obtaining property-related information.

Collection and Recovery of Rates

In 1995, the commissioner of Rating and Valuation took on the responsibilities, previously the Treasury's, of collecting rates to provide an improved one-stop service to ratepayers. The dual role of assessor and collector raised concerns about potential conflicts of interest. But these initial concerns proved unfounded because all rates revenue collected goes to the government as general revenue and is unrelated to the funding provided by the government to the collector.

The commissioner-collector issues demands for rates, maintains rates accounts, and recovers rates arrears. The Treasury continues to provide a centralized collection service for rates and other government fees and charges. These collection services were outsourced in 2001 to the Hong-kong Post (121 post offices) and later extended to some 1,400 convenience stores. Property rates can be paid in advance in four quarterly installments and are due in January, April, July, and October. Rates can be recovered retrospectively for a maximum of up to two years for tenements that are newly assessed to rates (Choi 2021, 97–98).

The collector is directly responsible for issuing rates demands and administering the electronic payment methods available to ratepayers. However, the printing and enveloping of rates demands are outsourced to a private contractor. In 2004, a consolidated billing and payment service was introduced so that ratepayers with multiple properties can opt to receive one bill covering all their properties. The share of payments made by electronic means grew from 36 percent in 2017–2018 to 63 percent in 2019–2020 (Choi 2021, 98). Payment methods include banking autopay, payment by phone, ATM, Internet, by post, and in person at post offices or in convenience stores (box 5.3).

Surcharges and Recovery of Arrears

Rates not paid by the due date may be subject to a surcharge of 5 percent and a further 10 percent if still unpaid after six months. They are recoverable as a debt to the government (Rating Ordinance, Cap. 116, sec. 22(3)). The definition of *owner* includes mortgagee, therefore both are liable.

Box 5.3 Customer-Centric Service Delivery

The Rating and Valuation Department has since 1993 provided customers with multiple customer-centric service delivery channels.

1993: Payment by phone is introduced, and soon after the 24-hour interactive voice processing system is launched. The system handles inquiries on rates and tenancy matters and also provides automated retrieval of forms, property statistics, press releases, confirmation of payment, and replacement bills.

1997: The department engages external service providers to issue combined demands for rates and government rent to ratepayers with multiple properties. Other outsourced tasks include printing and enveloping of bills and requisition forms, surveys for statistical compilations, updating of payers' records, and operating the telephone inquiry service.

1998: An automated hotline provides information via telephone about the age and floor area of residential properties. Public access to such information has greatly improved the transparency of the property market in Hong Kong.

2001: The telephone hotline includes information on permitted use of properties.

2002: The government call center with 24-hour operators now also answers telephone inquiries on the Rating and Valuation Department's services.

2009: The Property Information Online system debuts, replacing the outdated telephone-based interactive system. Supported by a powerful bilingual search engine with five different search paths, the public can obtain, at a small fee, ratable values of properties for the last three years of assessment and property account balances for rates and government rent. Frequent users can apply for a subscriber account. The system integrates over 2.5 million records held by the Rating and Valuation Department and the Land Registry.

2013: The Property Information Online system allows ratepayers to view information on the salable area[3] of their residential properties free of charge.

Ongoing: The department publishes property reviews annually, with monthly updates, providing a year-end summary of stock, actual and forecast completions of properties in Hong Kong, and statistics on prices and rentals (see https://www.rvd.gov.hk/en/publications/property_market _statistics.html). The department's website also releases property information such as average ratable values of private domestic units in selected developments. The department has been heavily involved in providing property information to concerned policy bureaus on housing development and market activities.

Table 5.3 Arrears Amount as a Percentage of Annual Demands

Financial Year	No. of Recovery Actions	Account with Outstanding Rates at Financial Year End	Arrears as % of Annual Demands	Arrears Amount (HKD million)
2008/2009	38,800	30,900	0.76	65
2009/2010	41,500	27,500	0.66	58
2010/2011	41,600	25,700	0.51	52
2011/2012	29,100	26,400	0.45	52
2012/2013	33,800	24,100	0.41	47
2013/2014	29,200	25,400	0.39	57
2014/2015	24,700	37,400	0.40	93
2015/2016	22,900	31,900	0.42	106
2016/2017	25,600	28,700	0.48	120
2017/2018	28,800	25,600	0.48	107
2018/2019	27,200	21,300	0.40	77
2019/2020	24,800	27,000	0.40	92

Source: HKSAR–Rating and Valuation Department.

Legal action is taken in the Small Claims Tribunal if arrears do not exceed HKD 50,000, in the District Court if above that amount. If the outstanding rates remain unsettled after the court's judgment, the commissioner may prohibit the property from being sold until the charge is released. However, the ordinance is silent on further stringent measures such as allowing distress and sale of goods as provided in similar statutes of the United Kingdom and Singapore. As evidenced by table 5.3, collection levels are exemplary.

Rates Refund Owing to Vacancy

Vacant properties up until 1973 were entitled to a full refund of rates paid. To discourage speculation in new properties, rate refunds for vacant residential units were abolished in 1973. In 1995, refunds were also abolished for vacant nondomestic units. However, vacant open land not previously used and not intended for parking motor vehicles continues to be eligible for a full refund of rates.

Other Property-Related Taxes

In addition to rates, Hong Kong levies two other types of property-related taxes. One type is stamp duties on property transactions. The other, known as property tax, applies to owners of land or buildings who earn income from those properties. Whereas rates are a form of tax levied on occupation of landed properties, property tax is imposed on owners of land or buildings in Hong Kong who give the rights of using their properties to others in return for payment or charges.

The government has considered imposing a steep special tax on vacant residential units to encourage developers to expedite the supply of new homes. Property developers and owners strongly oppose this tax, and it remains to be seen whether this proposed empty homes tax will ever be implemented. The later section "Pros and Cons of the Proposed Vacancy Tax" discusses the tax.

Property Tax on Rented Properties

Rates in Hong Kong are charged at 5 percent of the ratable value, which is the estimated rental value of a property. Rates are levied whether the property is owner occupied, tenant occupied, or vacant. Property tax is levied on properties in Hong Kong without regard to owners' residency or nationality. The Inland Revenue Department collects the property tax, which is payable annually by the owner at the current standard rate of 15 percent of the net assessable value of the property. Assessable value (AV) is the annual rental income of the property less the combination of rates paid by the owner and bad debts. From the AV, deduct 20 percent for repairs and expenses to arrive at the net assessable value (NAV).

Rental income includes rent, a license fee to use the premises and a lump sum premium, service charges, and management fees paid by the tenant to the owner. Property owners who receive rental income are assessed property tax at the standard rate. By electing to receive a personal assessment (relief for certain individual taxpayers who are subject to salary tax and property tax), taxpayers may claim deductions such as mortgage interest and personal allowance to reduce their tax liability.

Stamp Duties on Property Transactions

Stamp duty, or a tax on the transfer or sale of immovable property in Hong Kong, is charged at a rate that varies with the amount or value of the property. The commissioner of Inland Revenue, who is also the collector of stamp revenue and estate duty commissioner, enforces the ordinances related to stamp duty.[4]

As valuation advisor to other government bureaus and departments, the commissioner of Rating and Valuation in 2019/2020 received from the Stamp Office of the Inland Revenue Department 86,949 cases for examination and valuation. A total of 9,270 valuations revised the stated considerations or provided them for properties transferred without stated consideration (RVD). To address the heavy workload, CAMA techniques, using multiple regression analysis, are applied to scrutinize the stated consideration submitted by taxpayers in property sale transactions for stamp duty purposes.

Property values in Hong Kong have seen a considerable rise, and stamp duty rates have been increased in response. Despite this, rates continue to be dramatically different depending on whether the buyer is a Hong Kong permanent resident or a company and whether the property is residential or nonresidential.

There are three main categories of stamp duties related to transfer of properties: ad valorem stamp duty, special stamp duty, and buyer's stamp duty.

Ad Valorem Stamp Duty

Home prices have dramatically increased since 2010, which many blame on the demand from nonresidents and speculators or investors. The government introduced new stamp duties as a cooling measure for the housing market. Hong Kong permanent residents buying their first homes are substantially exempted from many of these stamp duties. First-time home buyers pay ad valorem stamp duty at the time of purchase (table 5.4). This stamp duty applies to Hong Kong permanent residents who are buying their first homes or switching homes (and have no property registered under their names at the time of transaction). The duty also applies to people who acquire homes under registered companies, instead of as individuals. People who sell a home before buying another must pay the full duty, but if they buy a home within six months of selling the first, they may apply to the Inland Revenue Department for a tax refund (Inland Revenue Department 2021).

As of November 2016, non-first-time home buyers pay a flat-rate stamp duty of 15 percent of the consideration or value of the property (whichever is higher). As of February 2013, buyers of nonresidential property pay a stamp duty that is usually twice as much as that for residential property, hence it is also known as double stamp duty.

Special Stamp Duty

The special stamp duty for residential properties took effect October 27, 2012, and is calculated on the basis of the stated consideration or of the market value of the property (whichever is higher). If the seller or transferor holds the property for six months or less before disposal, the rate is 20 percent. If the property is held more than six but less than twelve

Table 5.4 Ad Valorem Duty for First-Time Home Buyers

Purchase Price (HKD)	Stamp Duty Rates
0–2,000,000	HKD 100
2,000,000–2,351,760	HKD 100 + 10% of excess over 2 million
2,351,760–3,000,000	1.5%
3,000,000–3,290,320	HKD 45,000 + 10% of excess over 3 million
3,290,320–4,000,000	2.25%
4,000,000–4,428,570	HKD 90,000 + 10% of excess over 4 million
4,428,570–6,000,000	3%
6,720,000–20,000,000	3.75%
20,000,000–21,739,120	HKD 750,000 + 10% of excess over HKD 20 million
21,739,120–	4.25%

Source: https://www.gov.hk/en/residents/taxes/stamp/stamp_duty_rates.htm.

months, the rate is 15 percent. If held more than 12 but less than 36 months, the rate is 10 percent.

Buyer's Stamp Duty

Any residential property transaction executed on or after October 27, 2012, must pay a buyer's stamp duty of 15 percent, unless purchasers are Hong Kong permanent residents acquiring the property on their own behalf.

Estate Duty

The Revenue (Abolition of Estate Duty) Ordinance, which took effect in February 2006, abolished estate duty to facilitate development of Hong Kong as an asset management center, related to more local and foreign investors holding assets in Hong Kong. Asset management services create employment opportunities and make Hong Kong more competitive as an international financial center.

Challenges Facing Hong Kong's Property Tax System

Hong Kong's approach to property taxes has many positive attributes and is often cited at international conferences on property taxation as an example of a modern taxation system. Taxes levied on the occupation of landed properties form a simple, broad-based system that is well understood by the general public and has been a stable and reliable source of revenue for the government since 1845. As of April 1, 2020, the valuation list contained 2.569 million assessments with a total ratable value of HKD

731.8 billion, and the government rent roll contained 2.007 million assessments with a total ratable value of HKD 449 billion. For 2019/2020, the Rating and Valuation Department collected rates revenue of HKD 21 billion and government rent of HKD 13.3 billion. By March 31, 2020, rates arrears stood at less than 0.4 percent of annual rates demanded (RVD 2020, 5–28).

Nevertheless, Hong Kong's property tax regime faces many challenges similar to those faced in other jurisdictions with relatively mature systems and practices. This final section explores five key issues.

Safeguarding Revenue from Rates and Government Rent

The Audit Commission in 2015/2016 examined the Rating and Valuation Department's efforts to safeguard revenue from rates and government rent.[5] Among the commission's recommendations—such as improving timeliness in taking actions and improving cost-effectiveness in certain areas of work—one stands out for urgent rectification. The department should "take measures to improve the accuracy of rental information furnished in Form R1As [rental requisition forms] for GRs [general revaluations] and closely monitor the situation" (Audit Commission 2016, chap. 1).

The commission found that the department's annual rental verifications from 2010/2011 to 2015/2016, when 240 cases were selected to ascertain the accuracy of the reported rents, the average in-order rate was 71 percent. Discrepancies were found in 28 percent of the sampled cases. Another recommendation was for improvement of the return rate of rental requisition forms. Of some 307,000 Form R1As issued for annual general revaluation from 2010/2011 to 2015/2016, about 56,400 (18 percent) ratepayers failed to complete and return their forms. The department had prosecuted some cases (primarily repeat offenders) and issued warning letters to others, but the commission noticed an upward trend on the nonreturn rate in those five years.

Given the reality of limited resources and competing priorities, decision makers will need to make sound judgments as to how to go about rectifying these problems. An obvious solution, if additional funding can be found, is to devise further computer programs to assist valuation staff in screening out unreliable reported rents.

Reviewing and redesigning the rental requisition forms to make them easier to use would improve the return rate. Timeliness in effecting ratepayers' change of address and more marketing campaigns to emphasize the importance of reporting rental information promptly should also improve the situation. Announcements are made on television and radio to remind payers to pay their rates and government rent on time during the due month in each quarter.

Capturing Further Efficiency Gains amid Annual General Revaluation

For the 2020/2021 general revaluation, the ratable values took effect on April 1, 2020, and were based on market rents at the designated reference date of October 1, 2019. The exercise resulted in an average decrease in ratable values of 1.5 percent for rates and 1.4 percent for government rent; 50.2 percent of the properties experienced an average decrease of 6.4 percent, and 44.3 percent had no change in ratable values (RVD 2021). The remaining 5.5 percent of the properties had their ratable value increase by 5.5 percent on average (table 5.5).

In the seven general revaluations preceding the 2020/2021 general revaluation, the annual movements of ratable values range from –1.5 to +6 percent. This clearly demonstrates that Hong Kong's vibrant property market activities and transactions of significant values make annual general revaluations well justified from cost and equity perspectives. Although challenging, this annual workload has presented opportunities for the department to streamline workflows. Manual procedures were automated using computers. Modern technologies such as GIS have been extensively deployed to facilitate valuation work that maintains a sound and equitable tax base.

The public understands and accepts the department's work, and this explains in part the low rate of arrears, which has been reduced from 1 percent in 2004/2005 to around 0.4 percent of the annual rates demanded in later years, a remarkable achievement (RVD 2021). Nevertheless, the quest for efficiency gains and customer service improvements continues.

Gauging the Impact of Rates and Concessions on Government Revenue

On the one hand, there are good reasons to justify an annual review of the tax base. On the other hand, rates account for only a small percentage of government revenue in Hong Kong—4 to 6 percent—and rates concessions are eating into that number.

The government has granted rates concessions as a regular measure, perhaps as a political tool to seek public endorsement of its fiscal policies (table 5.6). Supposedly a financial relief measure that should be well received, this practice of rates concessions has sparked occasional yet strong debates. Some stakeholders, for example, argue that high-value properties,

Table 5.5 General Revaluation Results

Year	No. of Assessments in Valuation List April 1	Overall Average Increase/ Decrease (%)	Increase			No Change (%)	Decrease	
			%	Amount of Increase (%)			%	Amount of Decrease (%)
2014/2015	2,418,892	5.0	84.5	8.3		13.6	1.9	−9.1
2015/2016	2,434,626	6.0	88.9	7.9		10.4	0.7	−6.2
2016/2017	2,454,450	4.0	89.5	6.5		9.5	1	−10.3
2017/2018	2,477,584	1.4	37.6	7.3		53.3	9.1	−6.8
2018/2019	2,504,588	4.4	88.7	6.4		10.1	1.2	−5.7
2019/2020	2,531,346	4.8	90.5	6.9		8.8	0.7	−8.7
2020/2021	2,568,998	−1.5	5.5	7.1		44.3	50.2	−5.4

Source: RVD (2021).

Table 5.6 Rates Concessions Since 2014/2015

Year	Apr.–Jun.	Jul.–Sept.	Oct.–Dec.	Jan.–Mar.
2014/2015	Concessions to April and July qtrs., subject to ceiling of HKD 1,500 per qtr. for each ratable tenement			
2015/2016	Concessions to April and July qtrs., subject to ceiling of HKD 2,500 per qtr. for each ratable tenement			
2016/2017	Concessions subject to ceiling of HKD 1,000 per qtr. for each ratable tenement			
2017/2018	Concessions subject to ceiling of HKD 1,000 per qtr. for each ratable tenement			
2018/2019	Concessions subject to ceiling of HKD 2,500 per qtr. for each ratable tenement			
2019/2020	April 2019–December 2019: Concessions subject to ceiling of HKD 1,500 per qtr. for each ratable tenement			
	January 20–March 20: Concessions subject to ceiling of HKD 1,500 per qtr. for each ratable domestic tenement and ceiling of HKD 5,000 per qtr. for each ratable nondomestic tenement			
2020/2021	Concessions subject to ceiling of HKD 1,500 per qtr. for each ratable domestic tenement and ceiling of HKD 5,000 per qtr. for each ratable nondomestic tenement			
2021/2022	April 2021–September 21: Concessions subject to ceiling of HKD 1,500 per qtr. for each ratable domestic tenement and ceiling of HKD 5,000 per qtr. for each nondomestic tenement			
	October 2021–March 2022: Concessions subject to ceiling of HKD 1,000 per qtr. for each ratable domestic tenement and a ceiling of HKD 2,000 per qtr. for each ratable nondomestic tenement			

Source: Financial Services and Treasury Bureau, Government Secretariat.

properties held by companies, or commercial properties should not receive concessions. The government announced in its 2021/2022 budget that it has directed the Rating and Valuation Department to review the rating system with a view to introduce a progressive element and to regularly provide rates concessions to owner-occupied properties. The government will also consider shifting the primary liability for rates payment from the occupier to the owner of a property to reflect that the owner has ultimate responsibility for a property.

As shown in table 5.7, for example, revenue from rates in 2019/2020 was about HKD 20,980 million, reflecting a loss of about HKD 15,603 million due to rates concessions granted that year. To put this in perspective, however, in 2019/2020 financial year, the government made HKD 599 billion in total revenue, an aggregate of operating and capital revenues, of which 24 percent was from sale of government land (table 5.8). Meanwhile, the city sits on fiscal reserves of more than HKD 960 billion.

Pros and Cons of the Proposed Vacancy Tax

As mentioned previously, the government has proposed introducing special rates on vacant residential units to encourage developers to expedite the supply of new homes. The proposed tax rate will be set at 200 percent of the ratable value of the properties, which is roughly 5 percent of the property value, based on the average yield of 2.5 percent for residential property as of March 2018.

The ordinance will be amended to require owners, mainly developers, of new private residential units with an occupation permit of 12 months or more to inform the government annually on the occupancy status of the units. Units that have not been occupied or rented out for more than half the last 12 months will be considered vacant and subject to the special rates.

The proposals will need to be approved by the Legislative Council before they become law. As expected, the real estate sector has been overwhelmingly skeptical about the efficacy of the empty homes tax. Many believe the new tax will have little impact on rising home prices. In October 2020, the government withdrew the bill, citing an ailing economy and ambivalence of legislators and community members. Yet the government spokesperson emphasized that the initiative could be revived in future when more data about vacant flats have been collected.

The Rating and Valuation Department has been tasked with administering the proposed new tax, which will be operated as a separate and distinct tax regime. However, the resources required to set up and administer the new tax regime are not likely to be covered by the revenue collected—the bane of many unpopular taxes. It may also distract the department from its core responsibilities.

Balancing High Property Values and Low Recurrent Property Taxes

Hong Kong is known worldwide as a low-tax city. The government has reserves considerably exceeding 12 months' expenditure. The interest re-

Table 5.7 Number of Rating Assessments and Rates Contributions to Government Operating Revenue and GDP

Year	No. of Assessments in Valuation List as of April 1	Rates Revenue (HKD million) [revenue loss due to concessions]	Gov't Operating Revenue (HKD million)	Rates as % of Gov't Revenue	Calendar-Year GDP (HKD million)	Rates as % of Calendar-Year GDP
2013/2014	2,400,530	14,911 [11,570]	355,292	4.2	2013 2,150,437	0.69
2014/2015	2,418,892	22,272 [6,138]	393,934	5.7	2014 2,273,380	0.98
2015/2016	2,434,626	22,733 [7,767]	381,532	6.0	2015 2,413,195	0.94
2016/2017	2,454,450	21,250 [10,518]	411,727	5.2	2016 2,502,716	0.85
2017/2018	2,477,584	22,203 [10,722]	442,759	5.0	2017 2,662,920	0.83
2018/2019	2,504,588	17,167 [17,768]	454,416	3.8	2018 2,831,345	0.61
2019/2020	2,531,346	20,980 [15,603]	433,854	4.8	2019 2,844,560	0.74
2020/2021	2,568,998	18,710 [773]	440,351	4.2	2020 2,688,535	0.70

Sources: HKSARG–Rating and Valuation Department Annual Summary 2020/'21. https://www.rvd.gov.hk/doc/en/annualsummary/full.pdf (Accessed 9 April 2022).

Rates Revenue and Total Government Revenue. Central Statistics Department–HKSARG. https://www.censtatd.gov.hk/en/web_table.html?id=193 (Accessed 9 April 2022).

ceived on these reserves alleviates the tax burden, keeping it light. The ceiling for personal income tax is set at 17 percent, and that for corporate tax is 16.5 percent. Hong Kong deliberately has no capital gains tax, no estate duty, no dividend or interest tax, no sales tax, and no value-added tax. Duties on alcohol apply only to spirits.

Chapter 5, Article 106, of the Basic Law states that the HKSAR will have an independent taxation system separate from that of mainland China. Article 106 stipulates that Hong Kong have an independent public finance system and no obligation to transfer tax revenue to the central government in Beijing (Davis 2019).

Over the years there has been consistent criticism from some quarters that government revenue relies too much on the sale and lease of government sites to private developers. In the 2019/2020 financial year, 24 percent of Hong Kong's HKD 599 billion revenue came from land sales (see table 5.8). The administration has been criticized for seeing land for its potential to generate money for the capital works fund, rather than for the general welfare of the community. The policy of keeping recurrent tax low while relying on land sales revenue may have led to Hong Kong housing being the world's least affordable for almost a decade.[6] As pointed out by a former Hong Kong Monetary Authority chief executive, the city policy on land is a de facto tax imposed on its residents. He warned that sky-high land and property values would stunt economic development in what was already the world's least affordable market.

I concur with this critique. However, in addition to promoting an efficient and equitable land-based tax system in Hong Kong, a broader perspective finds other determinants that can enhance economic and social well-being. Housing affordability, which is a key determinant in individual well-being and overall economic growth, is such an issue. Solutions include expanding the housing supply and deploying public finance more strategically. To this end, the HKSAR government is consulting the public on the Land-Sharing Pilot Scheme, which seeks to unlock privately owned agricultural lots for both public and private housing development through public-private partnership (Legislative Council 2019). This pilot scheme bears monitoring in the coming years.

Proposed Modifications to the Rating System

In the 2022/2023 budget, the government proposes revising the rating system. The proposals require legislative approval, which is likely. If the revisions are enacted, owners will receive a rates concession for one residential property beginning in 2023/2024. In 2024/2025, a progressive system for residential property will be imposed (table 5.9).

Table 5.8 Property Tax Contributions to Government Operating Revenue Compared with Capital Revenues from Sales of Government Land (HKD million)

Year	Operating Revenue				Capital Revenue		Total[2] Government Revenue
	Direct Taxes	Indirect Taxes		Total Operating Revenue	Funds	Total Capital Revenue	
	Property Tax	Stamp Duties	General Rates		Land Premium[1]		
2012/2013	2,259	42,880	11,204	344,606	69,563	97,544	442,150
2013/2014	2,584	41,515	14,911	355,292	84,225	100,054	455,346
2014/2015	2,939	74,845	22,272	393,934	77,804	84,734	478,668
2015/2016	2,998	62,680	22,733	381,532	60,893	68,475	450,007
2016/2017	3,372	61,899	21,250	411,727	127,970	161,397	573,124
2017/2018	3,448	95,173	22,203	442,759	164,811	177,078	619,837
2018/2019	3,624	79,979	17,167	454,416	116,861	145,358	599,774
2019/2020	2,807	67,198	20,980	433,854	141,728	164,901	598,755

Source: HKSARG-Financial Services and the Treasury Bureau, Government Secretariat. https://www.fstb.gov.hk/en/treasury/pub_finance/docs/Financial%20statistics%20(22-23%20OE)_eng.pdf.pdf (Accessed 9 April 2022).

[1] Land owners making land transactions, such as lease modifications, land exchanges, or private treaty grants, must pay a land premium, which reflects the benefits to the government of the land value. The Rating and Valuation Department determines the benefit assessments; the Lands Department collects them.

[2] Total government revenue is the aggregate of government operating and capital revenues.

Table 5.9 Proposed Rates Concessions

Ratable Value (HKD)	Rate (%)
First 550,000	5
Next 250,000	8
Next 800,000	12

Notes

1. The Hong Kong dollar has been pegged at about HKD 7.8:USD 1 since 2005. By allowing trading within a range of HKD 7.85 and HKD 7.75 to USD 1.00, the Hong Kong Monetary Authority has narrowed the gap between Hong Kong and U.S. interest rates. This also avoids the Hong Kong dollar being used as a proxy for speculative bets on a renminbi revaluation. The stock and flow of the monetary base is fully backed by foreign exchange reserves.

2. According to the *Standard on Ratio Studies* issued by IAAO, appraised value divided by sale price ratios can be used to evaluate the level and uniformity of mass appraisal models. In Hong Kong, rental values instead of capital values are used in the ratio studies.

3. Salable area is defined in the Residential Properties (First-hand Sales) Ordinance enacted in 2012 as the floor area of a residential property, including balcony, utility platform, and verandah. It is measured from the exterior of the enclosing walls of the residential property and includes internal partitions and columns but excludes any common part (such as shared space in a condominium complex) outside the enclosing walls.

4. The relevant ordinances are Betting Duty Ordinance (Cap. 108), Estate Duty Ordinance (Cap. 111), Inland Revenue Ordinance (Cap. 112), Stamp Duty Ordinance (Cap. 117), Tax Reserve Certificates Ordinance (Cap. 289), Business Registration Ordinance (Cap. 310), and Hotel Accommodation Tax Ordinance (Cap. 348).

5. Under the Audit Ordinance (Cap. 122), the director of the Audit Commission is the external auditor of the accounts of the HKSAR government, has wide powers of access to the records of departments, and has an independent role. The director submits reports to the president of the Legislative Council, whose Public Accounts Committee reviews them.

6. According to the 15th Annual Demographia International Housing Affordability Survey (2019), Hong Kong housing has been the world's least affordable for nine consecutive years. Its 2018 median multiple, which is median house price divided by median pretax gross household income, of 20.9 rose from 19.4 in 2017. The survey, conducted by Urban Planning Policy Consultancy Demographia in 2018, covered 309 cities in China, the United States, Australia, United Kingdom, Canada, Singapore, New Zealand, and Ireland.

References

Audit Commission. 2016. "Efforts of the Rating and Valuation Department in Safeguarding Revenue on Rates and Government Rent." (April 5). https://www.aud.gov.hk/pdf_e/e66ch01.pdf.

Brown, M. 2013. *The History of Rates in Hong Kong.* 3rd ed. Hong Kong: Rating and Valuation Department, HKSAR. https://www.rvd.gov.hk/doc/en/hist_rate.pdf.

Choi, Ly. 2021. "Property Rates in Hong Kong: Assessment, Collection and Administration." 3rd ed. Rating and Valuation Department, Hong Kong Special Administrative Region. https://www.rvd.gov.hk/doc/en/property_rates.pdf.

Davis, H. 2019. "Hong Kong's Tax System Explained." *South China Morning Post*, March 2. https://www.scmp.com/news/hong-kong/hong-kong-economy/article/2188256/hong-kongs-tax-system-explained-why-levies-are-so.

15th Annual Demographia International Housing Affordability Survey: 2019. St. Louis Metropolitan Area (MO-IL), United States. http://demographia.com/dhi2019.pdf.

Hong Kong Institute of Surveyors. 2019. "35th Anniversary Commemorative Publication 2019." Hong Kong. https://www.hkis.org.hk/archive/materials/category/HKIS_35-booklet-_Low-res.pdf.

IAAO (International Association of Assessing Officers). 2013. *Standard on Ratio Studies*. Kansas City, MO: IAAO. https://www.iaao.org/media/standards/Standard_on_Ratio_Studies.pdf.

Inland Revenue Department. 2021. "Ad Valorem Stamp Duty (AVD)." FAQ. Last revised November 8, 2021. https://www.ird.gov.hk/eng/faq/index.htm#avd.

Legislative Council. 2019." Land Sharing Pilot Scheme." Briefing paper. HKSAR. https://www.legco.gov.hk/yr19-20/english/panels/dev/papers/dev20191126cb1-160-4-e.pdf.

Rating Ordinance, Cap. 116. https://www.elegislation.gov.hk/hk/cap116?xpid=ID1438402621171002.

RVD (Rating and Valuation Department). 2016. "Annual Summary." HKSAR. https://www.rvd.gov.hk/doc/tc/AS_fullbook/AS_2015-16_fullbook.pdf.

———. 2017. "Annual Summary." HKSAR. https://www.rvd.gov.hk/doc/tc/AS_fullbook/AS_2016-17_fullbook.pdf.

———. 2018. "Annual Summary." HKSAR. https://www.rvd.gov.hk/doc/tc/AS_fullbook/AS_2017-18_fullbook.pdf.

———. 2019. "Annual Summary." HKSAR. https://www.rvd.gov.hk/doc/tc/AS_fullbook/AS_2018-19_fullbook.pdf.

———. 2020. "Annual Summary." HKSAR. https://www.rvd.gov.hk/doc/tc/AS_fullbook/AS_2019-20_fullbook.pdf.

———. 2021. "Annual Summary." HKSAR. https://www.rvd.gov.hk/doc/en/annual summary/full.pdf.

6

India: A Macro View of the Property Tax System and Insights into Delhi's System

OM PRAKASH MATHUR

India's property taxation and municipal government finances have attracted significant attention since the 1990s for two reasons.[1] First is the recognition that urbanization is important to national economic growth and poverty reduction goals and strategies. This represents a major shift in India's development thinking, which until the late 1980s focused on rural development. As a result, the goal of sound municipal finance has emerged as an important national issue.

Second is the 74th amendment, enacted in 1993, to the Constitution of India. Aimed at decentralization and empowerment of municipalities, the amendment contains two provisions relating to municipal finances.

- Under Article 243 Y, state governments are mandated to constitute a state finance commission once every five years to recommend which state-level taxes and other revenue sources should be assigned to municipalities and which taxes should be shared between a state and its municipalities.

- Insertion of item (3)(c) into Article 280 of the Constitution requires the central Finance Commission to recommend, once every five years, measures to strengthen municipal finances.[2]

These two articles have brought about major changes in the structure of municipal finances and triggered reforms to bolster performance of the property tax system. Key reforms include the transition from annual rental value to capital value and unit-area value as the base for property taxes, establishment of state-level property tax boards, indexation of property values, introduction of property identification based on a geographic information system (GIS), assignment of unique identification numbers to properties, online tax payment, and reduction and rationalization of stamp duties. The success of these reforms has been uneven.

This chapter provides (1) a macro view of property taxation across India, including the impact of economy-wide changes stemming from the two constitutional articles; (2) an in-depth analysis of the property tax system and performance in the National Capital Territory of Delhi, including insights on how changing the valuation system has affected productivity; and (3) an analysis of the broad structure of property transfer taxes and stamp duties, which are important revenue sources for state governments and have significant revenue implications for local (municipal) governments. Box 6.1 describes data sources.

Notwithstanding the much-discussed empowerment of local governments by the changes to the Constitution, municipal finances remain the weak link in India's national fiscal system. The same weakness can be seen in Delhi. A 2019 World Bank comparative assessment of jurisdic-

---

Box 6.1 Data Sources

The data on municipal finance used in this study are drawn from multiple sources, especially the studies conducted by and for the central Finance Commissions, reports of the Delhi State Finance Commissions, budgets of the municipal corporations of Delhi and other local bodies, and the central government's annual publications *Indian Public Finance Statistics* and *Economic Survey*, and the Reserve Bank of India's *State Finances: A Study of Budgets*.

Beginning with the 11th Finance Commission, all have commissioned studies and carried out their own work on facets of the finances of municipalities. These studies have helped create a statistical database on the finances of municipalities. Updated quinquennially, this database has made it possible to, for example, assess the size of the municipal sector in terms of GDP, define the fiscal roles of the different constituents in municipalities' finances, and estimate the untapped potential of municipal revenues. Studies chartered by the 15th Finance Commission have added data on the status of property taxes in the 29 Indian states and in several larger cities. This database now forms the foundation for much of the research work on municipal finance in the jurisdiction, including this chapter.

tions characterizes India's municipal property tax system as one of the most underperforming systems (World Bank 2019a; and see Kelly 2018). India's own Ministry of Finance described the current situation as a low-equilibrium trap, a status quo preferred by all governmental tiers, with the central and state governments using their powers to control and influence lower tiers of government and the lower tiers unable and unwilling to tax their proximate citizens (GOI 2018a).

Overview of India's Fiscal Structure

Only 31 percent of India's 1-billion-plus population lives in settlements designated as "urban, but that is changing fast: the United Nations (2019) projects that India's urban population will reach 607 million by 2030, up from 377 million in 2011. Metropolitan cities (those with populations over 1 million) account for nearly 43 percent of the jurisdiction's urban population. GDP grows at a fast clip—7.2 percent in fiscal year (FY) 2017–2018 and an estimated 6.8 percent in FY 2018–2019 (GOI 2020a, chap. 1)—but India is classified as a low- to middle-income jurisdiction on the basis of its per capita income of INR 135,050 (USD 2,020). Lack of infrastructure is viewed as a primary constraint on economic growth (GOI 2020b).

India is a union of twenty-eight states and eight federally administered territories. The functions and finances of the central (union) and state governments are laid out in the seventh schedule of the Constitution in the union list, state list, and concurrent list.[3] The functions of the union government are generally those required to maintain macroeconomic stability; state governments are responsible for public order, police, public health, education, agriculture, and industries and minerals that are not in the union list.

Distribution of Tax Powers

The distribution of tax powers between the union and states is based on the principle of separation, with the exception of the goods and services tax (GST), introduced in 2017. Most of the broad-based and productive taxes fall within the tax powers of the union government and are taxes on income other than agricultural income, corporation tax, custom duties, union excises, and stamp duties on specified transactions. Tax powers assigned to the states include taxes on land revenues, agriculture income, land and property, motor vehicles, entertainment, trades, professions, and callings and excise duty on liquor and stamp duties. The GST, which amalgamates many union and state taxes, is a dual tax levied by the union and the states.

The 74th Amendment Act, 1992, constitutes a major step toward strengthening local governments and operationalizing the Directive

Principles of State Policy. The 74th Amendment parallels the decentralization initiatives of other parts of the world.[4] It is broad-based, and inter alia, reflects the importance of setting appropriate mechanisms for planning and development at local levels and of bringing greater balance, order, and stability to state-local functional and fiscal relations.

The 74th Amendment, however, does impose expenditure responsibilities on municipalities. The amendment consists of a schedule of functions (schedule 12) that makes a strong commitment to decentralization. The list of functions is illustrative and envisions municipalities performing such functions as economic and social development planning, urban planning, urban poverty alleviation, urban forestry, environmental protection, and slum improvement and upgrading. The significance of schedule 12 functions lies less in an enlarged scope of functions for municipalities and more in the functions having a redistributional and developmental orientation. State government power in determining the spending responsibilities of municipalities, however, continues to be absolute and inviolable.

The 74th Amendment does not specify municipalities' revenue base. State-local fiscal relations in India have historically been ad hoc and tentative, and thus there is a need for stability in their relations. The constitutionally mandated state finance commissions recommend taxes, duties, tolls, and fees that should be assigned to or appropriated by municipalities or that should be shared between a state and its municipalities. The state finance commissions advise on what grants-in-aid municipalities should receive and on any other measure that would improve the finances of municipalities. The amendment entails a major vertical and horizontal restructuring in state-municipal fiscal relations, giving states a unique opportunity to redesign their fiscal systems into ones that are coherent and flexible for rapidly changing local needs and responsibilities.

The 74th Amendment did not alter the rights of state legislatures over which taxes should be assigned to and shared with municipalities. This arrangement implies that municipalities in India do not possess general competency powers, or ability to take actions not explicitly prohibited or assigned elsewhere; they possess the legally delegated powers and functions under the doctrine of ultra vires, which limits local choice and diversity.

The tax powers of municipalities are embedded in the principle of benefit taxation and consist of taxes on land and buildings; and taxes on advertisements, professions, trades, callings and employment, nonmotorized vehicles, and local entertainment. These tax objects are less mobile and not easily exportable and thus fit the textbook model of tax instruments conforming to the rule that each jurisdiction pays for its own benefits.

The tax powers of municipalities are subject to the same restrictions as imposed by the state on their functional responsibilities. State governments shape the fiscal space for municipalities and define local tax policies, including tax rates and who pays taxes. India as of 2019 comprised more than 4,000 urban local governments, making the management of intergovernmental fiscal relations complex.

Adding (3)(c) to Article 280 of the Constitution was perhaps the most important initiative in reshaping intergovernmental fiscal relations. It recognizes that (1) municipalities are the responsibility of not just state governments but also the central government, which has a vital stake in financing municipal activities; and (2) municipalities have a claim on the divisible pool of central-government resources because many of their functions enumerated in schedule 12 were drawn from the concurrent list of the Constitution.

Unfortunately, these changes have not increased municipal budgets, as shown in tables 6.1 and 6.2. Studies by Finance Commissions indicate a dip in the share of municipal tax revenue in total tax revenue

Table 6.1 Tax Revenues Across Governmental Tiers as % of Total Revenues

Governmental Tier	FY 2012–2013	FY 2017–2018
Center	42.5	41.0
State	55.7	57.6
Local (municipal government)	1.8	1.4

Source: Ahluwalia et al. (2019b).

Table 6.2 Structure of Municipal Revenues

	% of GDP	
Constituents of Municipal Revenues	FY 2012–2013	FY 2017–2018
Tax revenues	0.32	0.25
Nontax revenues	0.20	0.18
State grants, including shared revenues	0.34	0.33
Central-government transfers	0.04	0.05
Finance Commission grants	0.04	0.07
Other	0.10	0.12
Total	**1.05**	**1.00**

Source: Ahluwalia et al. (2019b).

between FY 2012–2013 and FY 2017–2018 and a decline in municipalities' own revenues as a percentage of GDP in the same years. Moreover, municipal fiscal space has shrunk as a result of the abolition of octroi and absorption of several local taxes in the GST. One hypothesis for the shrinkage is that the poor performance of property taxes may be both a cause and an effect of the problems that characterize municipal finance in India.

Property Taxes in India: A Macro View

Despite the well-known advantages of property taxes as a revenue source for local governments,[5] India has not used them extensively. Land and property taxation has not been an important part of India's tax policy strategy, and the reforms made since 1990 to boost productivity and performance have not been institutionalized in formal property tax protocols. Mohanty (2016) notes that property taxes are unpopular with taxpayers for several reasons: They are levied on potential income from property assets and not on current income. The benefits received by taxpayers often do not correspond with the taxes paid. Property taxes are more conspicuous compared with income or sales tax. For these reasons, property taxes yield little revenue. In FY 2017–2018, property taxes in India generated an estimated INR 255 billion, accounting for only 0.14 percent of GDP (Ahluwalia et al. 2019a). These shares have changed little over the years, notwithstanding an extraordinarily large surge in land and property values and prices. In several states, the revenue significance of property taxes is much lower than portrayed in this aggregate figure.

General Framework

The seventh schedule of the Constitution of India provides for taxes on land and property, which are levied by municipal governments in accordance with the procedures laid down by state municipal legislations. These procedures describe the tax bases, valuation methods, tax structures, tax coverage, rebates and exemption policies, and measures for dealing with delays, defaults, and disputes. Municipal governments' autonomy in formulating property tax policy is severely limited, although they can decide on the tax rates within certain ranges and design collection strategies. Because property tax policies are made by state governments, there is significant interstate diversity in almost every sphere of property taxation. Thus, for instance, a tax on land and property is an obligatory tax in some states and an optional tax in others.

Three aspects of India's property taxation framework need some elaboration.

Valuation

Properties are valued for tax purposes in India by one of three methods:

- Annual rental value.

- Unit-area value.

- Capital value and variants of the method.

Annual rental value is the gross annual rent a property may reasonably be expected to earn from year to year. Many states have in recent years switched from using the annual rental value method to the unit-area value method, prompted by the area-based system's perceived simplicity in making valuations, ability to separate property valuation from rent control legislation, and better prospects for addressing the growing divergence between the taxable assessed value and the market value of properties. The unit-area value takes into account property characteristics—location, type of construction, nature of use, and so on—when making a valuation and is seen as simple, transparent, fair, and easy to implement (Kapoor and Ghosh 1992). Bengaluru implemented the unit-area value system and had noticeable gains (M. Rao 2013; V. Rao 2008).

Mumbai uses the third method, capital value. In this method, the market value of property is determined via the stamp duty ready reckoner, which is annually updated tables for calculating stamp duty. The Municipal Corporation of Greater Mumbai, which is responsible for the municipality's rules for fixing capital values, calculates it as follows:[6]

$$\text{Capital value} = BV \times UC \times NTB \times AF \times FF \times BA,$$

where

BV = base value of building according to the ready reckoner,

UC = use category factor,

NTB = nature and type of building,

AF = age of building,

FF = floor factor, and

BA = built-up area.

Weights are assigned to all.

Exemptions and Rebates

Exemptions from local property taxation constitute an important ingredient of a property tax system. The main objectives in providing exemptions are social justice and equity considerations, compensation to properties that have merit or public good, and avoiding high administrative and collection costs related to properties yielding little tax revenue. Residential properties below a prescribed minimum size, charitable organizations, places of worship, ancient monuments, properties used for sheltering the destitute, orphanages, organizations that run philanthropic activities, and burial and cremation grounds receive exemptions.

According to a 2009 study, exempted properties account for approximately 10–11 percent of the total number of properties (Mathur 2009). Article 285 of the Constitution exempts union government property on the grounds that the sovereign cannot tax itself. Similarly, Article 289 exempts state property from union taxation.

Most state statutes provide rebates for owner-occupied properties. Other rebates and reliefs are in state laws and justified on grounds of equity. Yet application has been inequitable because many rebates create unequal tax treatment among property users.

Tax Rates

At least four types of rate structures are in use: (1) statutory specification of maximum and minimum tax rates, with some flexibility for municipal government to determine the exact rate; (2) rate structures discriminating according to use of the property and other factors; (3) a consolidated rate combining all surcharges, such as a water tax or a sewerage tax; and (4) progressive rate structures that generally tax nonresidential properties at higher rates.

Property Tax Revenue Mobilization

Property tax revenues in India are estimated at about INR 255.1 billion (FY 2017–2018), or 0.15 percent of the jurisdiction's GDP. From FY 2012–2013 to FY 2017–2018, the annual growth rate of property tax revenues has been impressive: approximately 12–13 percent in nominal terms. Table 6.3 summarizes the property tax revenue contributions to the national, regional, and local economies.

As seen in table 6.3, property tax revenues in India are equivalent to about 0.15 percent of the jurisdiction's GDP and are inconsequential compared with the average of about 0.6 percent for developing jurisdictions, 0.68 percent for transitional economies, and 2.1 percent for Organisation for Economic Co-operation and Development jurisdictions (see Bahl and Martinez-Vazquez 2008). Property tax revenues account for 0.83 percent of the combined tax revenues of the central, state, and local governments. Moreover, time series data on the share of property tax revenues in total government revenues (and as a percentage of GDP) show it declining since

Table 6.3 Fiscal Role of Property Taxes, FY 2017–2018

National Economy	
Property tax revenues as % of	
GDP	0.15%
Tax revenues of the union, states, and municipalities	0.83%
Direct tax revenues of the union	2.60%
Regional Economy	
Property tax revenue as % of	
Tax revenue of state governments	1.46%
Direct tax revenues of state governments	6.30%
Local, Municipal Economy	
Property tax revenues as % of	
Tax revenues of municipalities	59.40%
Own revenues of municipalities	34.80%
Total revenues of municipalities	14.90%
Total expenditures of municipalities	19.30%
Per capita property tax revenues	INR 688

Sources: Ahluwalia et al. (2019b); GOI (2018a, 2018b); Reserve Bank of India (2017–2018).

FY 2002–2003. Revenues from property taxes account for 5.5 percent of the direct tax revenues collected in the jurisdiction. Note that the overall structure of tax revenues favors indirect taxes, whose yields are close to 12 percent of GDP. According to the government of India's *Economic Survey*, India compared in a group of advanced and emerging economies "has the lowest share of direct taxes in total taxes," and "under-collection of direct taxes relative to potential afflicts the Center [government] as much as [state and local governments]" (GOI 2018a).

Property tax revenues constitute 1.5 percent of the total tax revenues of state governments. That percentage represents, in part, the degree of tax devolution from the state to local and municipal governments. Direct tax revenues, which consist mostly of corporation tax and income tax, contribute 6.3 percent to local and municipal governments. State governments' access to direct taxes is limited to agricultural income. Property taxes have a significant role in local and municipal government finances, accounting for close to 60 percent of the tax revenues, 35 percent of own revenues of municipalities, and 15 percent of the total municipal revenues. This compares well with the average for other jurisdictions. Property tax revenues cover about 19.3 percent of municipal expenditure.

Significant interstate variation exists in property tax revenue productivity (table 6.4). Measured as a percentage of gross state domestic product (GSDP), the revenue productivity of property taxes in states such as Maharashtra (0.335 percent), Karnataka (0.206 percent), and Gujarat (0.404 percent) is high compared with that in Bihar and Jharkhand, where the percentages are 0.012 and 0.031, respectively (FY 2017–2018). As an instrument of local revenue, property tax is almost nonfunctional in such states. The productivity of property taxes has also declined perceptibly in states such as Andhra Pradesh, Tamil Nadu, and West Bengal, with improvements observed in Madhya Pradesh and Rajasthan.

Available data sets on property tax revenues do not permit ascertaining the extent to which interstate variations are caused by differences in coverage and collection rates, scale of exemptions, or periodic valuation. A 2009 jurisdiction-wide study on property taxation in 33 cities with over one million population (2001) noted across-the-board inefficiencies, attributable, on the one hand, to systemic issues such as the absence of a system that mandates municipalities to undertake a formal count of properties and the absence of the concept of market value in the determination of property values and, on the other hand, to operational factors like low coverage of properties for taxation purposes, low rates of tax collection, and the inability to effect revisions in property values even when required by law (Mathur, Thakur, and Rajadhyaksha 2009).

Impact of Key Parameters

To what extent are property tax revenues affected by parameters such as economic growth, urbanization, and decentralization? This question is important for two reasons. India's economy as measured by GDP grew from 2005 to 2017 at a compound average annual rate ranging between 3.7 percent and 10.2 percent, impressive by most standards. An important feature of this growth is the jurisdiction's economic structure changing from one in which a significant proportion of GDP accrued from the primary sector to one in which knowledge-based activities have gained primacy. As a result, the urban share of GDP has grown at a faster rate than the rural share. According to the Central Statistical Office (CSO 2017), 52.6 percent of GDP accrued in urban areas (FY 2011–2012), which is projected to rise to about 60 percent by FY 2021–2022.

In conjunction with economic growth, urbanization has emerged as an important development in recent decades. Consisting of statutory cities and towns, and over 3,570 census towns, and a population of over 377 million in 2011, India has the second-largest urban system in the world. The pattern of urbanization suggests a noticeable shift toward large cities

Table 6.4 Interstate Variation in Property Tax Revenues

	FY 2012–2013		FY 2017–2018	
State	**Property Tax Revenues as % of Municipal Revenues**	**Property Tax as % of GSDP**	**Property Tax Revenues as % of Municipal Revenues**	**Property Tax as % of GSDP**
Andhra Pradesh	32.2	0.158	24.7	0.118
Bihar	0.9	0.004	0.7	0.012
Chhattisgarh	13.2	0.061	25.5	0.162
Gujarat	9.4	0.124	9.1	0.404
Haryana	10.1	0.072	21.7	0.014
Jharkhand	1.9	0.006	1.8	0.031
Karnataka	16.3	0.237	16.8	0.206
Kerala	9.7	0.041	7.8	0.042
Madhya Pradesh	6.9	0.109	5.8	0.148
Maharashtra	15.8	0.383	18.3	0.335
Odisha	3.5	0.015	3.2	0.016
Punjab	8.1	0.066	8.1	0.052
Rajasthan	2.1	0.014	3.9	0.022
Tamil Nadu	13.7	0.133	11.7	0.128
Telangana	30.1	0.234	36.3	0.213
Uttar Pradesh	6.7	0.055	8.1	0.059
West Bengal	14.4	0.171	10.9	0.118
India	**13.1**	**0.138**	**13.8**	**0.149**

Source: Ahluwalia et al. (2019b).

Note: GSDP = gross state domestic product. States not listed are excluded because of their special characteristics.

(population of more than 1 million). In 2011, large cities accounted for 43 percent of India's urban population. Prima facie, high economic growth and increasing levels of urbanization boost property values and consequently potential for increased property tax revenues. Decentralization as embodied in the two articles of the 74th Amendment is also seen as an important factor in influencing local (urban) government revenues, including property tax revenues. Bahl and Martinez-Vazquez (2008, p. 45) tested the hypothesis that "fiscal decentralization drives the intensity of use of the property tax." They measured (national) fiscal decentralization as subnational government expenditures as a percentage of total government expenditure. The same method was attempted here for Indian states.[7]

Property Taxes in Delhi: A Micro View

Although the Constitution of India provides for land and property taxation, there is great variation in the actual practice among states and even among cities. It is important, therefore, to understand how tax policy changes have played out at the local level. The case study of the National Capital Territory (NCT) of Delhi provides a snapshot of the city's governance system and economy and then an in-depth analysis of the revenue performance of the property tax in Delhi.

Governance and Economy

Delhi, as the capital city and as a union (federal) territory with a directly elected legislature, enjoys a unique place in India's federal structure. The National Capital Territory of Delhi Act, 1991, defines the powers of the Delhi government that have shaped the functional and fiscal relationship between the central government, the government of the NCT of Delhi, and its local governments.

Delhi's population grew from 16.8 million in 2011 to 20.6 million in 2021, and its per capita income of INR 365,529 (FY 2018–2019) is roughly three times that of the national average (table 6.5). It has a vibrant small-scale manufacturing base and a buoyant services and trade sector that contributes over 80 percent of Delhi's GDP. The share of agriculture and other primary-sector activities in Delhi's GSDP accounts for only about 2 percent. The NCT maintains a surplus on its revenue account.

The union government shares responsibility for Delhi's management, administration, and finance with the government of the NCT and its five local governments. Under this arrangement, the NCT is endowed with all functions enumerated in the state list with the exception of public order, police, and land. These functions vest in the union government. Local governments in the NCT are responsible for providing essential services to Delhi. The functional portfolio of local governments was substantially trimmed; and electricity distribution, water supply, sewage disposal, and so on, were transferred out to the Delhi government. The functions of the New Delhi Municipal Council are similar to those of other local governments in Delhi.

The financial arrangements between the union government and NCT are complex. All taxation powers ordinarily available to a state under the seventh schedule of the Constitution devolve to the NCT, but other NCT financial arrangements are determined outside the mandated center-state fiscal relations.[8] In this arrangement, Delhi government revenues (excluding grants) constitute 6.5 percent of its GDP, which is significantly lower than the average for all states.

Table 6.5 Demographic, Economic, and Fiscal Profile of Delhi

Population, 2011	16.8 million
Urban population, 2011	16.3 million
Population density, 2021	13,890/km²
Urban population, 2021	20.6 million
Per capita GSDP, FY 2017–2018	INR 328,985
Per capita GSDP, FY 2017–2018	USD 5,100
Annual growth rate of GSDP (FY 2012–2013 to 2017–2018)	11.3%
Number of housing units, 2011	4.5 million
Population below the poverty line, 2011	9.9%
Slum population as % of total population, 2011	14.7%
NCT's own revenue as % of GSDP	6.7%

Source: NCT of Delhi (2019).

Despite its high income and expanding economic base, poverty and de-privation in Delhi continue to be a matter of serious concern. Close to 10 percent of Delhi's population is below the poverty line as measured by calorie intake. Nonfood poverty, as manifested in indicators such as the percentage of households in slum settlements, is high: 14.7 percent according to the 2011 census (GOI 2011).

Housing and Service Delivery

Delhi's housing market has grown substantially over the years. However, it is a fragmented mix of public housing for employees of the government of India, the state government, and their affiliated organizations; housing developed by the Delhi Development Authority, a central-government agency responsible for the preparation of a master plan for Delhi and the development and management of lands under the control of the central government; private housing on private lands; private housing in group housing societies and cooperatives on lands developed by the Delhi Development Authority; unauthorized housing developed either in violation of Delhi's master plan or on illegally subdivided agricultural lands; slum settlements recognized as such by the government, mostly on lands owned by the Delhi Development Authority or other governmental agencies; and slum settlements not recognized as such by the government. According to the census of India (GOI 2011), a little over 30 percent of households live in one-room tenements. Unauthorized housing accounts for 25 percent of Delhi's housing stock. According to the Delhi government's 2019 *Economic Survey*, about one-third of Delhi lives in substandard housing, which includes 695 slum clusters, 1,797 unauthorized colonies and old, dilapidated areas, and 762 villages (NCT of Delhi 2019, 10). A state finance commission report estimates that almost 46 percent of settlements in the NCT of Delhi are either "unauthorised" or "unauthorised-regularised" (NCT of Delhi 2017, table 6.16), meaning that such unauthorised properties will be given access to municipal services such as water.

No assessment of the effects of this structure of housing on property valuation and taxation has been published, but they are thought to be substantial, shown in large proportions of nontaxpaying properties and low-value properties. In the East Delhi Municipal Corporation, 82 percent of properties are low-value properties. Properties in Delhi paying property tax account for between 19 and 25 percent of the total (NCT of Delhi 2017, para. 6.81, table 6.23).

The Municipal Corporation of Delhi is responsible for local service delivery in the NCT (excluding the areas governed by the New Delhi Municipal Council and the Delhi Cantonment Board). To improve efficiency in service delivery, in 2011 the Municipal Corporation of Delhi was trifurcated into the East Delhi Municipal Corporation, North Delhi Municipal Corporation, and South Delhi Municipal Corporation. Local governments in Delhi are regulated and governed by the Delhi Municipal Corporation Act of 1957 (as amended by the Delhi Municipal Corporation Act 12 of 2011), the New Delhi Municipal Council Act of 1994, and the provisions of the Cantonment Board Act of 1924. The Delhi Municipal Corporation Act lays down the obligatory and discretionary functions of the three municipal corporations in Delhi. The functions consist of construction and maintenance of streets, building regulations, sanitation and burial grounds, public safety and suppression of nuisances, and maintenance and regulation of markets and slaughterhouses. With the exception of the maintenance of markets and slaughterhouses, all other services are nontradable services. The corporations levy obligatory and discretionary taxes to pay for these services (table 6.6).

Property Tax Reform in the NCT of Delhi

Delhi significantly reformed its property tax system in 2004, replacing its annual rental value approach to measuring the tax base with a unit-area value system. The transition to this new system and the structure of the unit-area value system are discussed in the following.

Annual Rental Value

In the annual rental value system, rental value is defined as the annual rent a property can reasonably be expected to earn. The system was plagued

Table 6.6 Obligatory and Discretionary Taxes: Local Governments in Delhi

Obligatory Taxes	Discretionary Taxes
Property tax on building and vacant lands	An education cess
A tax on vehicles and animals	A local rate on land revenues
A theater tax	A tax on profession, trade, callings, and employment
A tax on advertisements other than advertisements published in the newspapers	A tax on consumption of electricity
A duty on transfer of property	A betterment tax on the increase in urban land values caused by the execution of any development or improvement work
A tax on building applications payable along with the application for sanctioning of building plan	A tax on boats and on tolls

Source: Delhi Municipal Corporation Act 1957 as amended up to 2011.

by judicial pronouncements on the meaning of *reasonably* and *standard rent* under the rent control act. There were also many anomalies and disparities in applications of the tax. An expert committee recommended property tax reform in Delhi. It cited lack of transparency and objectivity, collusion, corruption, legal lacuna, and administrative difficulty with annual rental value, noting that "there have been ingenious designs for evading the tax by camouflaging of actual monthly rent through pugrees, [which are] lump sum payments in the form of security and advance rent, and entering into other types of agreements to give a color other than 'rent.' Further, the present method of assessment was a cumbersome process with discretion and arbitrariness. Moreover, there was no provision for self-assessment by the tax payer" (NCT Delhi 2003, 17) It recommended replacement of annual rental value with unit-area value.

Unit-Area Value

The unit-area value system came into effect in the Municipal Corporation of Delhi in 2004; the New Delhi Municipal Council adopted it in 2009. The Delhi Cantonment Board continues to rely on an annual rental value system. The tax base in a unit-area value system is the product of the estimated unit-area value and the actual area of the property. Implementation of the unit-area value system in Delhi requires estimations of

- the gross annual value of property, which is the sum of unit values multiplied by the entire area of the property (unit values depend on the market and characteristics of the area with respect to capital and rental values, quality of infrastructure services, location, economic status of occupants, and other characteristics of the area);

- the net annual value of the property, which takes the gross annual value and adjusts it for property-specific factors such as age, structure, use, and occupancy; and

- tax liability, which is the product of net annual value and tax rate.

Delhi's unit-area value system has statutory provisions related to the levy of a service charge in slum and resettlement colonies, the taxation of union properties, and the appointment of a Hardship and Anomaly Committee, but its chief features are the following:

- Classification of buildings and vacant lands. All districts, subdistricts, colonies (smaller areas that make up a subdistrict), and lands in Delhi have been classified into eight categories, from A to H,[9] on the basis of the capital value of land, annual rental values, age of the colony, the level of services, location of the colony, type of colony (planned, unplanned, or unauthorized), economic status of the occupants, and the road on which the colony is situated.

- Specifying unit-area values. How this is done to estimate gross annual values is described in the next section.

- Adjusting gross annual value. Estimations of the net annual value of properties consider the structure (permanent, semipermanent, or temporary), age (properties constructed before 1960, between 1960 and 1979, between 1980 and 1999, and in 2000 or after), occupancy (occupied by owner or tenant), and use (public purpose, recreation, education, public utility, hospitals and nursing homes, industries, business and offices, mercantile establishments and shops, star hotels, and banks). Weights for each factor are given in a table.

  i. An institutional system for classification. A municipal valuation committee, as mandated by the Delhi Municipal Corporation Act of 1957, Article 116, periodically recommends classification of vacant lands and buildings, base values, and increases or decreases in values. This allows a buoyant property tax system. Its recommendations are valid for three years. The Act also provides for indexation of unit area values if base unit values are not revised on the completion of a period of three years.

- Self-assessment system. The centralized system of tax assessment and billing is replaced by self-assessment.

Revenue Simulation Exercise

The property tax is a fiscal instrument for raising revenues for local governments, but it also should be consistent with the equity goals of the local government and be politically acceptable. Delhi's unit-area value system's design was based on a revenue simulation exercise in 2003 that aimed at generating unit values for the property tax zones, A to H, to yield a predetermined level of tax revenue.[10] The exercise surveyed 60,000 properties across property tax zones to collect data on the area and rental values related to the age of properties, their usage, the nature of structures, and type of occupancy. This data set fed a model to produce ranges of unit values consistent with the predetermined revenue target. Among the many assumptions made were that 70 percent of properties would pay taxes and that the tax rate would initially be 10 percent and then rise to 11–12 percent. The Municipal Corporation Act stipulates that the rate may range between 6 percent and 20 percent of the annual value of a building.

The revenue simulation exercise recommended unit values (INR/m^2) for the tax zones: A was valued at 630; B, 500; C, 400; D, 320; E, 270; F, 230; G, 200; and H (rural areas), 100.

The model results showed that properties in zones

- A and B (20 percent of the covered area) would contribute 33 percent of revenues;

- C, D, and E (40 percent of the covered area) would contribute 42 percent of revenues; and

- F and G (40 percent of the covered area) would contribute 25 percent of revenues.

These values have been used for estimating property tax liability since the unit-value area system was introduced in 2004. Neither the classification of colonies, the unit values, nor the tax rates have changed, despite recommendations from successive municipal valuation committees. Nor have the municipal corporations exercised their statutory powers to index the unit-area values to the consumer price index (as laid down in the act). This explains, in part, the slow growth of property tax revenues in the NCT of Delhi (box 6.2).

Box 6.2 POLITICS AND PUBLIC RESPONSE

Politics and public response play an important part in determining the classification of buildings and colonies and setting unit-area values. The main tasks of municipal valuation committees are to make recommendations on matters relating to the classification of vacant lands and buildings, setting unit-area values, and determining factors for increase or decrease in unit values. With the exception of the first committee, which recommended the adoption of the report of the expert committee on unit-area valuation and classification of colonies, subsequent committees' recommendations proposing reclassification of certain colonies (putting them into higher property tax zones and hiking up the unit-area values) have been summarily rejected by the standing committees, the political wing of the municipal corporations, on grounds that these recommendations will place a heavy burden on property owners, who constitute their electorate.

Under Article 116 B of the Delhi Municipal Corporation Act of 1957, municipal valuation committees are to publish public notices of their proposals and invite response from citizen groups in colonies affected by reclassification or change in unit-area values.

Invariably, the citizen groups have not only opposed reclassification and increase in unit values but favored downgrading their colonies to lower property tax zones. They argue that the quality of life in their colonies has deteriorated, and the occupants of the colonies (property owners) belong to the lower castes and other disadvantaged groups. Both claims attest to the observation, in the government of India's *Economic Survey 2017–18* (GOI 2018a), that "a status quo" is preferred by all levels of government. It applies to citizen groups as well.

Property Tax Revenue Performance

As shown in table 6.7, property taxes are the principal source of tax revenue for local governments in the NCT of Delhi and are equivalent to 0.30 percent of the state GDP. In FY 2015–2016, local governments (the three municipal corporations, the New Delhi Municipal Council, and the Delhi Cantonment Board) collected, under the unit-area valuation system, INR 16,510 million from property taxes, or 16.3 percent of their total municipal revenues and 21 percent of municipal own revenues.

A comparative time series analysis helps reveal the effects of the transition to the unit-value area system of property assessment and of the trifurcation of the Municipal Corporation of Delhi. I compared property tax revenues for FYs 2002–2003, 2006–2007, and 2014–2015, when the assessment procedure changed and the structure of the Municipal Corporation of Delhi changed. The results of this analysis show the impact of

Table 6.7 Delhi's Property Tax Revenues,
FY 2015–2016

Indicators	Delhi
Property tax revenues (INR million)	16,510
As % of state GDP	0.30
As % of state government's tax revenues	5.50
As % of total revenues of municipalities	16.30
As % of own revenues of municipalities	20.90
As % of own tax revenues of municipalities	38.50
As % of municipal expenditure	16.20

Source: NCT of Delhi (2017, table 6.6).

Note: The figures relate to the three corporations, New Delhi Municipal Council, and Delhi Cantonment Board. The most recent data available were for 2016. Data beyond 2015/2016 were in a form not possible to aggregate.

the two reforms on property tax revenues. Three points emerge from the analysis.

- As a percentage of GSDP, property tax revenues have twice dipped sharply. The first dip was between FY 2002–2003 and FY 2006–2007 when the property tax assessment system transitioned from annual rental value to unit-area value. The second was FY 2006–2007 to FY 2014–2015, when the Municipal Corporation of Delhi divided into three municipal corporations. The total decline was significant, from a high of 0.98 percent (FY 2002–2003), comparable with the average for several emerging economies, to a low of 0.29 percent (FY 2014–2015). Juxtaposing this decline with the municipal finance data suggests that this was not an isolated instance of a fiscal instrument losing its primacy but part of a larger context, in which the fiscal space of Delhi's local governments has shrunk vis-à-vis the state economy and property taxes have been crowded out by state transfers that now account for over 30 percent of local-government revenues.

- In nominal terms, property tax revenues have risen at impressive rates, 16.6 percent in the first years of the unit-area value system and 6.7 percent in the years following division of the Municipal Corporation of Delhi. As a percentage of GSDP, property tax revenues ranged between 0.40 and 0.49 percent in the first years and remained within 0.29 and 0.34 percent after the division. An increase in the number of taxpaying properties accounts for the increase in nominal property tax revenues to a noticeable extent. However, the three factors that bring buoyancy to the property tax system—unit-area values, classification of vacant lands and buildings, and tax rates— have remained unchanged since FY 2004–2005, notwithstanding the recommendations made by the successive municipal valuation committees to adjust them in line with developments in the housing market. The inability to adjust the unit-area values is one of the most disappointing features of the system, rendering the statutory provisions regarding the municipal valuation committee and indexing of unit-area values fruitless. The Act also provides for "indexation of unit area values" if base unit values are not revised on the completion of a period of three years.

- The number of taxpaying properties, about 1.049 million in FY 2015–2016, increased at an average 4.2 percent per year after implementation of the unit-area value system under a unified Municipal Corporation of Delhi and about 1 percent under a trifurcated Delhi.[11] These taxpaying properties account for 18–25 percent of properties in Delhi. The third state finance commission estimated 963,119 tax-paying properties for FY 2003/2004, or about 38 percent of the total (NCT of Delhi 2006, table 12-26, p. 531). That the coverage ratio has declined after unit-area value implementation raises serious questions about the effectiveness of the self-assessment system that replaced billing of tax liabilities but did not have the ability to locate nontaxpaying properties. The lack of a formal count of properties and a common definition of the term *property* are major handicaps in tapping the potential of this tax in Delhi (box 6.3).

Box 6.3 Database on Delhi Properties

The number of properties in the Municipal Corporation of Delhi is an approximation at best. No local or state statute requires a formal count of properties. The census of India occurs every 10 years. The self-assessment system of property tax and the trifurcation of the Municipal Corporation of Delhi have resulted in no formal count of properties in property tax zones, properties mandatorily exempted from taxes, properties liable for taxes, or properties that default on payment of taxes. The number of taxpaying properties in table 6.5 was furnished by the three corporations, the New Delhi Municipal Council, and the Delhi Cantonment Board. See the Report of the Delhi Fifth Finance Commission, 2016–2021.

Property Transfer Taxes

Property transfer taxes in India include capital gains taxes, stamp duties, and registration fees. They are a significant revenue source for local governments.

A capital gains tax is levied by the central government. Section 54 of the Income Tax Act exempts from income tax any long-term capital gains arising from transfer of a residential property if the capital gains are used to acquire or construct another residential home within a specified period, subject to compliance with other conditions. Revenues from capital gains tax are not separately identified.

Stamp duty is levied by both the central government and the state governments (table 6.8). Conceived as a duty to provide evidentiary value to a transaction, instrument, or document, the central government levies stamp duty on instruments specified in the union list; state governments, on instruments and documents in the state list. Entry 91 of the union list empowers the central government to fix the rates of stamp duty on documents related to banking, industry, and commerce such as bills of lading and letters of credit. These are, however, collected by the states, and revenues are assigned to them. Entry 63 of the state list provides for rates of stamp duty on documents other than those listed in the union list. The levy and collection of duties on such instruments is laid down in the Indian Stamp Act of 1899 and the State Stamp Acts, drawn up in line with the 1899 Act. Stamp duties have long been debated and discussed, particularly with regard to high rates of duty adversely affecting the efficient allocation of resources and economic growth (Alm, Annez, and Modi 2004). Some rationalization of and reduction in stamp duty have taken place.

Registration fees are fees over and above the stamp duties on recording the execution of a document such as a stamp duty paper. Only when a

Table 6.8 Stamp Duties of All States

Fiscal Year	Stamp Duty (INR million)	% Change	% of Total Revenue Receipts	Stamp Duty (USD million)
2013/2014	773,172		5.6	14,057
2014/2015	847,263	9.6	8.3	14,121
2015/2016	925,383	9.2	5.0	14,120
2016/2017	930,405	5.4	4.2	13,866
2017/2018	1,034,823	11.2	4.1	13,867

Source: Reserve Bank of India (2014–2015, 2018–2019).

document is registered and duty paid does a document become legally enforceable. Stamp duties and registration fees are an important source of revenue for state governments.[12] The Reserve Bank of India (2018) estimates that stamp duty revenues amounted to 4.1 percent of the total revenue receipts of all states. Annual growth rates of stamp duty receipts have fluctuated, reflecting conditions in the property market.

The government of NCT of Delhi levies stamp duty on instruments laid down for states under Entry 63 of the state list (table 6.9). As in states, stamp duty and registration fees are among the most important sources of revenues for the Delhi government. The declining percentage of the share of stamp duty receipts in the total revenues of the Delhi government reflects the slowdown in the property market of the 2010s.

Stamp duty receipts are shared between the state government and large local (urban) bodies in some states; in others, municipal corporations levy a surcharge on the stamp duty collected by the state (table 6.10). The Delhi Municipal Corporation Act and the New Delhi Municipal Council Act prescribe an upper limit of 5 percent as the rate surcharge; these rates now are 4 percent if the vender or donee is a woman and 6 percent if a man.

In FY 2015–2016, stamp duty and registration fee, accruing to local governments in Delhi, accounted for 16 percent of the total revenues and 68.8 percent of total property tax receipts. These shares show the revenue importance of the surcharge in the finances of local governments, somewhat similar to the stamp duty receipts in the finances of the government of NCT in Delhi. Local governments in Delhi, notably, have no role in determining the rate of the stamp duty, nor do they have a role in fixing the circle rates, or the minimum value for property transactions, which are often used for assessing the transaction value of property. Determination

Table 6.9 NCT of Delhi Revenues from Stamp Duty

Fiscal Year	Stamp Duty (INR million)	Stamp Duty (USD million)	% Change	% of Total Revenue Receipts
2013/2014	29,690	485		10.6
2014/2015	27,798	463	−6.40	9.4
2015/2016	34,336	524	+23.50	9.8
2016/2017	30,980	461	−9.77	8.4
2017/2018	40,330	625	+30.29	9.5

Source: Reserve Bank of India (2014–2015, 2018–2019).

Table 6.10 Local (Urban) Government Revenues from Stamp Duty

Fiscal Year	Receipts (INR million)	% Change	% of Property Tax Receipts	% of Revenue of All Local (municipal) Governments	Receipts (USD)
2012–2013	10,873		78.9	19.0	199
2013–2014	9,678	−11.0	71.0	16.9	176
2014–2015	11,290	3.7	79.6	16.9	188
2015–2016	11,371	0.7	68.8	16.0	173

Source: Reserve Bank of India (2014–2015, 2018–2019).

of circle rates is the responsibility of the Delhi government and is said to vaguely reflect the market value of properties. Over time, the difference between circle rates and market rates have significantly narrowed.

Conclusion

Past studies on India's property tax system have focused on its narrow tax base (the outcome of both the low proportion of properties forming a part of the municipal tax register and the large scale of statutorily exempted properties), the inability of the assessment system to capture the market value of properties, and a high rate of tax delinquency. A World Bank study (2019b) characterizes India's property tax system in terms of undervaluation, incomplete register, ineffective administration, and policy inadequacies. Interestingly, studies undertaken even before 1990 had the same refrain, especially those conducted for India's National Commission on Urbanization.

Consistent with these inadequacies, India's property tax reform agenda has centered on updating the municipal tax register, establishing a state-level valuation board, and indexing property values. The World Bank (2019b) proposes eliminating inefficient exemptions; building up a GIS-based, accurate property roll; adopting modern valuation approaches; and making property tax administration more efficient.

Neither the assessment of the system nor the proposed reform agenda should come as a surprise. A coverage ratio of 18–25 percent or even 40 percent can rarely be adequate to make property taxes a viable revenue instrument. Nor can a unit-area value or capital value format of assessment without periodic adjustment to property values be expected to generate revenues adequate for local governments to meet their expenditure responsibilities. These are fundamental to any good property tax system.

Box 6.4 The (Un)Willingness to Tax

The government of India's *Economic Survey* sees states' potential unwilling-ness to tax as possibly stemming from the very proximity of a state and its citizens on which decentralization is premised. There is another possibility, as the survey notes: "The status quo can be an equilibrium desired by all actors with higher tiers (both Centre and states) using their devolution powers to control and influence lower levels; and the latter, unable and unwilling to tax their proximate citizens, need outside resources even if they are not always [united]. But this is a low equilibrium, perhaps even a trap" (GOI 2018a).

Or is it a result of the low level of the jurisdiction's development, as seen in low per capita income, low level of urbanization, and low quality of housing stock?

Or is it because of uncoordinated and disjointed implementation of reforms?

This chapter sheds light on the weak connections among property taxa-tion and municipal finance and the Indian economy, on the one hand, and on how politicians and citizen groups can frustrate institutional reforms such as establishment of municipal valuation committees intended to im-prove the property tax system, on the other. This chapter points to the inconsequential impact of the range of initiatives such as the change in the system of valuation, establishment of new institutions like the prop-erty tax boards, statutory provisions for indexation of property values, self-assessment of property taxes, and GIS-based enumeration of properties on property tax revenues, giving rise to several possibilities (box 6.4).

The Indian property tax system is rudimentary and based on an imper-fect understanding of the role of the property tax. Many research studies have yet to grapple with questions such as what it costs to administer a property tax system, how well benefits are capitalized into property val-ues, whether transfers crowd out the need for property tax reform, and the effect on property values of using circle rates, or guidance values. The importance of such questions is barely recognized, and the database from which to make evaluations is inadequate. Much work remains to be done.

Notes

1. Before 1990, studies on municipal finances were few and did not recognize the po-tential link between local government finances and urban economic growth. The two developments discussed in the text coincide with the publication of the World Bank's policy paper *Urban Policy and Economic Development: An Agenda for the 1990s* (1991), and Roy Bahl and Johannes Linn's book *Urban Public Finance in Developing Countries* (1992).

2. The central Finance Commission recommends how to distribute the net proceeds of taxes that are divided between the union and the states. Adding item (3)(c) expands

Article 280's scope to include making recommendations on the measures that would strengthen the finances of municipalities (and rural local bodies).

3. The concurrent list contains functional responsibilities assigned to both the union and the state governments.

4. Article 5 of the Treaty on European Union 1992 on Decentralization set out the principle of subsidiarity that led a large number of countries in the developing world to amend constitutions or adopt legislation to decentralize powers to local governments.

5. A voluminous literature discusses property taxation benefits, generally, and newly imposed, particularly. Three such publications are central: Bahl, Martinez-Vazquez, and Youngman (2008); McCluskey (1999), and Oates (2001). See also Brunori and Bell (2010, 3).

6. For details, see https://cvs.megm.gov.in. For additional details on Mumbai property tax, see Pethe (2013). The capital value method has been questioned in court, and property owners have been given the option of using the erstwhile method of valuation.

7. To examine the relationship between property tax productivity and the economic characteristics of Indian states, I performed a regression analysis with per capita property tax revenue as the dependent variable and the percentage of urban population, per capita net domestic product, expenditure decentralization, and revenue decentralization as explanatory variables. The sample includes 17 of the 28 states; the remainder were excluded on account of data problems. The results of the simple correlation analysis show a positive association between per capita property tax revenues and both income and urbanization. Data is too limited for estimating the marginal impacts with a multiple regression analysis. Still, these results reinforce the conclusion that property taxation is primarily an urban tax, one that can benefit significantly from the ongoing increase in urban property values.

8. Delhi, as a union territory, is outside the purview of the central Finance Commission and not entitled to receive any share of central taxes such as income tax, corporation tax, and union excise duties. The union government instead provides a grant to the NCT, but the NCT alleges that the grant is less than what it would receive from the Finance Commission if NCT were a state.

9. The expert committee recommended 7 (A to G) categories of colonies; H was added subsequently to represent rural areas.

10. C. E. Info Systems (2003), a consulting firm, designed and developed the revenue simulation model.

11. During the census decade 2001–2011, the housing stock in the NCT (an urban area) increased at an annual average rate of 3.4%.

12. Stamp duty includes revenues from transactions other than real properties. Duties on property transactions are estimated to account for nearly 80% of total stamp duty revenues.

References

Ahluwalia, I. J, et al. 2019a. "Finances of Municipal Corporations in Metropolitan Cities of India, New Delhi." New Delhi: Indian Council for Research on International Economic Relations.

Ahluwalia, I. J., et al. 2019b. State of Municipal Finances in India. New Delhi: Indian Council for Research on International Economic Relations.

Alm, J., P. C. Annez, and A. Modi. 2004. *Stamp Duties in Indian States: A Case for Reform.* Working Paper 3413. Washington, DC: World Bank Policy Research, World Bank.

Bahl, R. W., and J. F. Linn 1992. *Urban Public Finance in Developing Countries.* New York: World Bank/Oxford University Press.

Bahl, R. W., and J. Martinez-Vazquez. 2008. "The Determinants of Revenue Performance." In *Making the Property Tax Work: Experiences in Developing and Transitional Countries.*, ed. R. Bahl, J. Martinez-Vazquez, and J. Youngman, pp. 35–56. Cambridge, MA: Lincoln Institute of Land Policy.

Bahl, R. W., J. Martinez-Vazquez, and J. Youngman. 2008. *Making the Property Tax Work: Experiences in Developing and Transitional Countries.* Cambridge, MA: Lincoln Institute of Land Policy.

Brunori, D., and M. Bell. 2010. "The Property Tax and Local Autonomy." In *The Property Tax and Local Autonomy,* ed. M. E. Bell, D. Brunori, and J. Youngman. Cambridge, MA: Lincoln Institute of Land Policy.

C. E. Info Systems. 2003. "Exercise on Revenue Simulation Model." New Delhi.

Central Statistical Office. 2017. "National Accounts Statistics. Statement 8.19."

GOI (Government of India). 2011. *Census of India 2011.* India: Ministry of Home Affairs, Office of the Registrar General and Census Commissioner.

———. 2018a. *Economic Survey 2017–18.* 2 vols. New Delhi: Ministry of Finance, Department of Economic Affairs, Economic Division. https://mofapp.nic.in /economicsurvey/economicsurvey/pdf/055-067_Chapter_04_ENGLISH_Vol_01 _2017-18.pdf.

———. 2018b. *Indian Public Finance Statistics, 2016–17.* New Delhi: Ministry of Finance.

———. Ministry of Finance. *Economic Survey.* New Delhi.

———. 2020a. *Economic Survey 2019–20.*

———. 2020b. "Report of the Task Force on National Infrastructure Pipeline." Mimeo. New Delhi: Ministry of Finance.

Kapoor, R. M., and P. K. Ghosh. 1992. "Composite Area Linked System for Property Tax Reform in India." *Urban and Regional Development Studies* 4 (2): 45–61.

Kelly, R. 2018. "International Experience in Property Taxation." PowerPoint presentation at the Consultative Workshop on Property Taxation in India, World Bank, New Delhi.

Mathur, O. P., D. Thakur, and N. Rajadhyaksha. 2009. Urban Property Tax Potential in India. National Institute of Public Finance & Policy. New Delhi.

McCluskey, W. J., ed. 1999. *Property Tax: An International Comparative Review.* Aldershot, UK: Ashgate.

Mohanty, P. K. 2016. *Financing Cities in India: Municipal Reforms, Fiscal Accountability and Urban Infrastructure.* New Delhi: Sage.

NCT (National Capital Territory) of Delhi. 2003. "Report of the Expert Committee on Property Tax Reforms." New Delhi.

———. 2006. *Third Delhi Finance Commission, 2006–2011: Report.*

———. 2017. *Fifth Delhi Finance Commission, 2016–2021: Report.* New Delhi. (October). http://it.delhigovt.nic.in/writereaddata/Odr201982138.pdf.

———. 2018. "Economic Survey of Delhi, 2017–18." New Delhi.

———. 2019. "Economic Survey of Delhi, 2018–19." New Delhi.

Oates, W. E., ed. 2001. *Property Taxation and Local Government Finance: Essays in Honour of C. Lowell Harris.* Cambridge, MA: Lincoln Institute of Land Policy.

Pethe, A. 2013. "Metropolitan Public Finances: The Case of Mumbai." In *Financing Metropolitan Governments in Developing Countries*, ed. R. Bahl, J. Linn, and D. Wetzel, 243–272. Cambridge, MA: Lincoln Institute of Land Policy.

Rao, M. G. 2013. "Property Tax System in India: Problems and Prospects of Reform." New Delhi: National Institute of Public Finance and Policy.

Rao, V. U. A. 2008. "Is Area-Based Assessment an Alternative, an Intermediate Step, or an Impediment to Value-Based Taxation?" In *Making the Property Tax Work: Experiences in Developing and Transitional Countries*, ed. R. Bahl, J. Martinez-Vazquez, and J. Youngman, 241–267. Cambridge, MA: Lincoln Institute of Land Policy

Reserve Bank of India. 2013–2014; 2014–2015; 2017–2018; 2018–2019. *State Finances: A Study of Budgets*. Mumbai. https://rbi.org.in/Scripts/AnnualPublications.aspx?head=State+Finances+%3a+A+Study+of+Budgets#.

United Nations. 2019. *World Urbanization Prospects: The 2018 Revision*. ST/ESA/SER.A/420. New York: Department of Economic and Social Affairs, Population Division.

World Bank. 1991. *Urban Policy and Economic Development: An Agenda for the 1990s*. Washington, DC.

World Bank. 2019a. "Property Taxation in India: India's Position, International Experiences, Issues and Ideas for Reform." Note for the 15th Finance Commission. Mimeo.

World Bank. 2019b. "Property Tax Reforms: Reform Performance and Challenges." Paper presented at the 15th Finance Commission, New Delhi. Mimeo.

7

Indonesia: Devolution of the Property Tax

RIATU MARIATUL QIBTHIYYAH

Indonesia's property tax, the land and building tax (*pajak bumi dan bangunan*), has been levied since the 1600s, when it was a fee on rural land (Booth 1974; Kelly 2004). Today, Indonesia has six types of land and building taxes: two urban (residential and commercial); rural (agricultural); plantation; forestry; and mining (including oil and gas). Urban and rural property taxes have been devolved to local governments, and the last three taxes on natural resources (*pajak bumi bangunan perhutanan, perkebunan, dan pertambangan*) remain central-government shared taxes. The property transfer tax, which is not an annual property tax, has also been devolved to local governments.

This chapter describes the legal framework and political context for property taxes in Indonesia. It then discusses the revenue performance, tax rate and base structure, tax administration, key shortcomings, and reform options. The focus is on the urban and rural property tax and the property transfer tax. Property taxes on natural resources are not examined in the same detail.

The Legal Framework and Political Context for Property Taxation

The evolution of property tax policies and regulations since 1959 is summarized in figure 7.1. The key laws and policy changes are outlined here.

Figure 7.1 Policies and Regulations on Property Tax in Indonesia

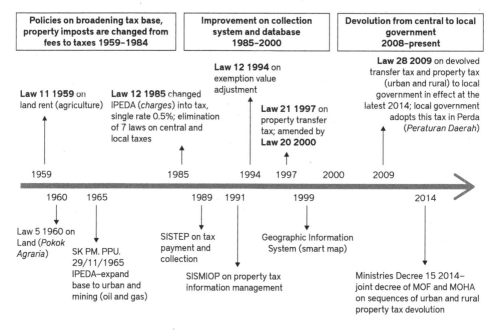

Sources: Booth (1974); Kelly (1992, 1993, 2004, 2012); Qibthiyyah (2016).

- Law 12 1985 on Property Tax changed a fragmented, fee-based type of tax into a more simplified recurrent property tax that was a land and building tax with a single rate and relatively broad-based coverage. Law 12 1985 did not differentiate the property tax base by sector or by specific type of land or property.

- Law 12 1994 on Property Tax made minor adjustments of exemption values and penalties but did not change policies covered by Law 12 1985.

- Law 21 1997 on Property Transfer Tax enacted the property transfer tax (*bea pengalihan hak atas tanah dan bangunan*). It was later amended by Law 20 of 2000 on Property Transfer Tax. Like all property taxes at that time, the property transfer tax was a central-government tax.

- Between 1988 and 1999, policies issued at the ministerial level were designed and implemented to help modernize the property tax administration system (Kelly 1992, 1993, 2004). For example, the government introduced a property identification number system and a computer-assisted property tax information management system; designated tax offices and banks that accept property tax payment; and began to use spatial mapping via a geographic information system (GIS) to improve the fiscal cadastre.

- Law 28 2009 on Provinces and Local Taxes and Charges devolved urban and rural property tax, as well as the property transfer tax, to local governments. The property tax devolved to the provincial level in DKI Jakarta Province.[1] The property tax devolution was part of an effort to broaden the revenue base of subnational governments.

In 2011, the city of Surabaya was the first local government to adopt the property tax. It was followed by 17 other local governments in 2012. Most others did not follow suit until 2013 or 2014, because local regulations needed to be prepared and issued, including changes in the administrative system (Von Haldenwang et al. 2015).

The devolution gave flexibility to local governments in setting and designing the urban and rural property tax rate structure and giving preferential tax treatments, and it decentralized full responsibility for administration (including valuation) to the local governments.

Expenditure responsibilities devolved to local governments as part of a major fiscal decentralization initiative in 2001 (Hofman and Kaiser 2004). But those responsibilities placed a heavy administrative burden on local governments, some of whose civil service capabilities were already strapped.[2] The urban and rural property tax devolution was also intertwined with priorities of the central government on planned administrative improvements during 2014–2019. Another reason for the devolution of urban and rural property taxes was that the central government had neither incentive nor interest in improving management of the property tax. Expectations were that devolution of urban and rural property tax would lead to increased property tax revenue mobilization in the long run. To date, the increases have been modest. The reasons for this are discussed in the remainder of this chapter.

Note that devolution does not mean a complete separation of the central government from property tax matters. The central government provides technical assistance and training, and it also has some influence in local-government tax policy, sometimes resulting in reduced revenues. For example, the tax directorate decree on property tax (Directorate General Tax Regulation No. 20 2015) allows the central government to limit urban and rural property tax bases.

Revenue Performance

Property tax revenue in Indonesia is relatively small, even compared with that in other low- and middle-income jurisdictions (see, e.g., Bahl and Martinez-Vazquez 2008; B. Lewis 2003; C. Lewis 2019; Von Haldenwang et al. 2015). Table 7.1 shows that the three major components of Indonesian property taxes (including transfer taxes) accounted for only 0.42 percent of GDP in 2019. Moreover, property tax revenues have been growing at a slower rate than the national economy.

The shares of the different types of property taxes are shown in figure 7.2. The fastest-growing components of overall property taxation are the property transfer tax and the urban and rural property tax. But it also shows that recurrent property taxes (urban and rural tax and natural resource tax) have become less important in the overall tax system over the last decade. If this trend continues, it will call into question the stability of the revenue flow from property taxes in future years, as discussed later in the chapter.

Natural Resource Property Tax Revenues

The majority of property tax revenues before 2015 came from the central-government taxes on natural resources (forestry, plantation, and mining).

Table 7.1 Property Tax Revenues by Type (selected measures)

	2010	2015	2019
Property tax revenue (% of GDP)			
Urban and rural	0.11	0.13	0.15
Natural resources	0.31	0.25	0.13
Property transfer taxes	0.12	0.10	0.14
Total property tax	0.53	0.49	0.42
Property tax revenue (% of total own-source revenues)			
Urban and rural	7.86	7.08	7.83
Natural resources	21.64	13.50	7.20
Property transfer taxes	8.29	5.50	7.49
Total property tax	37.78	26.07	22.52
Property tax revenue (% of total central-government tax revenues)			
Natural resources	2.90	2.34	1.37

Sources: Calculated from DGT Annual Report (2010, 2015, 2019); DGFB (2021a); and Indonesia Premium Database (2021).

Note: For 2010, before devolution, own-source revenues (the total revenues of local and provincial governments) refers to total revenues plus urban and rural property taxes and property transfer taxes.

Figure 7.2 Property Tax Revenues by Type (as % of total property taxes)

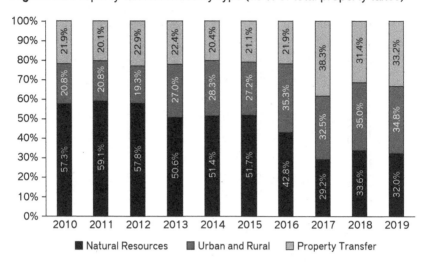

Sources: DGT Annual Report (2015–2018); Panjaitan and Fitri (2019); Qibthiyyah (2016); BPK (2019).
Note: Oil and gas are part of the mining property tax, which is a natural resource tax.

Those relatively high natural resource revenues taxes were probably due to valuation that considered the economic use (surface and below surface) of the land and to high commodity prices. As shown in figure 7.2, central-government natural resource revenues in 2015–2019 experienced a downward trend. By 2019, natural resource revenues were less than revenues raised, respectively, from urban and rural property taxes or from property transfer tax. This decline in natural resource revenues is partly due to exemptions given to the oil and gas sector.[3]

Property taxes on natural resources remain a central-government levy, which shares the revenues raised, less the collection fee of 9 percent, with provinces and local governments. Central, provincial, and local governments receive 10, 16.2, and 64.8 percent, respectively (Law 33 2004 on Intergovernmental Transfer). At less than 1.5 percent of central-government tax revenue in 2019, however, the share of natural resource revenues for the central government is very small.

Historically, natural resource tax revenues have been dominated by the mining sector, especially from oil and gas, which in 2015 accounted for approximately 87 percent of total central-government property tax revenues. But between 2015 and 2019, revenues relative to GDP declined precipitously, due to tax incentives given to the oil and gas sector and inefficiency in

Table 7.2 Property Taxes in DKI Jakarta Province (selected measures)

	2013	2014	2015	2016	2017	2018	2019
DKI Jakarta Urban and Rural Property Taxes							
Property tax revenue per capita (IDR thousand)	338.61	561.49	748.35	682.08	733.22	847.08	915.83
Property tax revenue as % of total city revenue	8.54	12.91	17.23	13.03	11.73	14.52	15.44
Property tax revenue as % of total city own-source revenue	12.57	18.09	22.61	19.00	17.32	20.53	21.05
Property tax revenue as % of total city tax revenue	14.45	20.91	25.37	22.18	20.83	23.69	23.87
DKI Jakarta Property Tax Revenues (% of national tax revenues)							
Urban and rural property tax	27.29	43.78	49.91	43.72	40.84	43.80	41.82
Property and land transfer tax	33.30	39.79	30.66	39.31	30.72	25.93	26.02
DKI Jakarta Property Transfer Tax							
Property tax revenue per capita (IDR thousand)	343.03	367.33	338.61	381.22	653.00	452.45	544.55
Property tax revenue as % of total city revenue	8.66	8.44	8.21	7.28	10.42	7.63	9.18
Property tax revenue as % of total city own-source revenue	12.74	11.83	10.77	10.61	15.39	10.89	12.52
Property tax revenue as % of total city tax revenue	14.64	13.68	12.48	12.38	18.51	12.57	14.19
DKI Jakarta Land Parcel Registry and Building Permits							
% of recorded land parcel registry	75.25	79.50	84.34	79.40	79.10	91.80	No data
Number of building permits issued	14,969	3,727	No data	No data	11,181	11,239	10,763

Sources: DKI Jakarta Province Central Bureau of Statistics (2013–2019); DGFB (2021b).

collections. There was, however, an increase in the number of payers of property tax for the mining sector, from 4,760 in 2016 to 5,090 in 2017 (DGT Annual Report 2017).

Urban and Rural Property Tax Revenues

Urban and rural property taxes are the basic annual levy on lands and buildings and have long been a low revenue producer. Rural property taxes experienced negative growth before devolution. The comparatives in table 7.1 show urban and rural property tax revenues in 2010 (before devolution) and in 2015 and 2019 (after devolution). The results suggest a small increase, from 0.11 percent of GDP, in 2010 to 0.15 percent of GDP, in 2019.[4] Clearly, when all central- and local-government property taxes are lumped together, and even if transfer taxes are included, Indonesia has low property tax effort. This was true in the predevolution period, and it is true in the postdevolution period.

An interesting question is whether urban and rural property taxes are essentially an urban tax—that is, whether more than a few local governments will greatly benefit from devolved taxes. As discussed and shown in Kelly (2012), the top dozen or so of the 519 local governments account for 70 percent of urban and rural property tax revenues. According to 2015 data, 16 local governments (including the province of DKI Jakarta)—out of a total of 435—contributed around 75 percent of total national urban and rural property tax revenues. By contrast, these same 16 local governments together account for 38 percent of total GDP. This top-heavy concentration holds even when expanded to 100 local governments sorted by size of realized urban and rural property tax revenues. More than 94 percent of national property tax revenues are concentrated in less than one-third of local governments, and these regions account for 71 percent of overall GDP.

An example of the concentration of property tax revenues is the province of DKI Jakarta, the capital region, where urban and rural property tax revenues in 2015 contributed nearly half of national property tax revenues (see box 7.1). On a per capita basis, property tax revenues from DKI Jakarta more than doubled from 2013 to 2016 (table 7.2). This is not unexpected. Even if there are no changes in the property tax rate or exemptions policy, property tax revenues are likely to increase because of faster urban development. For example, as shown in table 7.2, in 2017–2019, DKI Jakarta issued more than 10,000 building permits each year. In 2019, property tax revenues, referring to total urban and rural property taxes and property transfer taxes, in DKI Jakarta composed about two-thirds of the total (national) revenues of property taxes.

Box 7.1 Property Taxation in DKI Jakarta Province

DKI Jakarta, the capital city of Indonesia, is the wealthiest and most populous city. It has a special provincial status and oversight responsibility for cities and municipalities within its borders. DKI Jakarta consists of one administrative district (the Thousand Islands) and five administrative cities: North Jakarta, West Jakarta, Central Jakarta, South Jakarta, and East Jakarta. The total area of DKI Jakarta is 7,659 km^2 (662 km^2 for land and 6,998 km^2 for water areas) with a population of 11,063,324 in 2019. The population density is 16,704/km^2. Annual per capita income in 2019 was IDR 266.79 million or around USD 19,100, and around 70 percent of domestic money circulation occurs here. The economy of Jakarta is diversified.

The devolution of property tax (Law 28 2009) applied also to DKI Jakarta Province. The urban and rural property tax rate in DKI Jakarta is shown in the table. The bracket structure is progressive up to the maximum statutory rate allowed by law.

Taxable Property Value (IDR million)	Tax Rate (%)
<200	0.01
200–<2,000	0.10
2,000–<10,000	0.20
10,000+	0.30

The property tax rate is stipulated by provincial law (*peraturan daerah*, or PERDA). Per PERDA No. 16 2011 of DKI Jakarta, nontaxable property value is IDR 15 million. For example, if property value is IDR 500 million, then the urban and rural tax payment will be

$$(500 \text{ million} - 15 \text{ million}) \times 0.1\% = \text{IDR } 485,000.$$

Property values have been adjusted three times, the last stipulated by province of DKI Jakarta Governor Decree 24, in 2018. Taxable property value is based on classification of land value area (*zona nilai tanah*) issued by a central-government agency, the Agrarian Ministry, with detail at the block and street level. Policies to improve valuation aim to close or minimize the assessed value and the market value. However, the decree includes additional exemptions or administrative relief of property tax payment in DKI Jakarta. For example, land and property valued below IDR 1 billion is exempt from tax.

The devolution of urban and rural property tax in DKI Jakarta has been in effect since 2012. Property tax revenues have more than doubled since. Box Figure 7.1 compares DKI Jakarta realized and target revenues from urban and rural property taxes.

Box Figure 7.1 DKI Jakarta Realized and Target Revenues from Urban and Rural Property Taxes

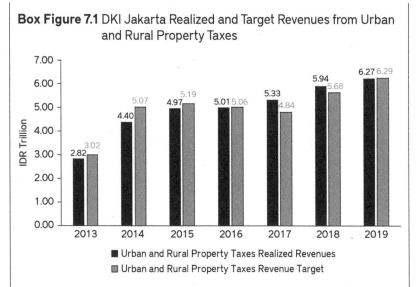

Source: DKI Jakarta summary of budget and realized province taxes data (DGFB 2021b).

Urban and rural property tax revenues have been growing, at a rate of 55 percent in the early period of devolution and more moderately since then. DKI Jakarta realized urban and rural property tax revenues that exceeded the moderate revenue targets in 2017 and 2018. These revenues could grow further if land values were regularly updated and collection was better. In DKI Jakarta, property tax payment at ATMs has been possible since 2014, a year that saw a high increase in urban and rural property tax revenues.

As shown in table 7.2, urban and rural property taxes have contributed more than 20 percent of total tax revenues for DKI Jakarta and have surpassed revenues from the property transfer tax every year since 2014.

Property Transfer Tax Revenue

The property transfer tax was devolved to local governments in 2011, before the urban and rural property tax was devolved. In 2010, revenues from the transfer tax exceeded those from urban and rural property tax revenues and had risen to around 0.12 percent of GDP. By 2019, revenues had increased to 0.14 percent of GDP (see table 7.1) and accounted for nearly 8 percent of own-source revenues of local governments. This increase in transfer tax revenues coincided with a significant number of land use changes, growing urbanization, and improved enforcement. But unlike the relatively stable recurrent urban and rural property tax, the revenue take from the transfer tax is volatile because revenues tend to follow fluctuations in property markets.

The experience with property transfer taxes in DKI Jakarta has been similar. Property transfers follow market sales, and revenues grow rapidly in periods of housing and land value appreciation. Revenues from property transfer taxes in DKI Jakarta reached 18 percent of total tax revenues collected in 2018 but slowed in subsequent years. Legal changes also had an impact. In 2016, DKI Jakarta Governor Decree 193 exempted from property transfer taxes any property transfers due to inheritance for any property with value less than IDR 2 billion. Another governor decree in 2017 expanded the exemption.

The Property Tax Structure and Property Valuation

The jurisdiction over property taxes in Indonesia is divided between the central government and the local governments. Of the recurrent levies, the urban and rural property taxes are assigned to the local governments and the forestry, plantation, and mining taxes are assigned to the central government (but are returned to local governments on a formula basis). If a property tax has not been assigned by law, it falls under the jurisdiction of the central government.

Property tax policy regarding exemptions is in Law 12 1994 and Law 28 2009. These laws exclude from property taxation lands and buildings used for or by government administration, international organizations, foreign (diplomatic) facilities, education, health facilities, religious activities, cemeteries, and forest conservation.

Urban and Rural Property Taxes

The urban property tax is sometimes referred to as a tax on land ownership, meaning residential housing and commercial buildings, and the rural property tax sometimes as the tax base of the agricultural sector, or land and property in rural areas. In reality, the tax structure is no different between urban and rural governments. Urban and rural property taxes are a local-government tax; and thus policies on tax rate, coverage and valuation of the tax base, exemptions and preferential treatments, and administration of the tax are mostly made by the local governments. Local governments have significant discretion to structure the property tax.

Tax Rate Schedule

Law 28 2009 sets a maximum tax rate on urban and rural property tax of 0.3 percent of taxable value. Local governments can adopt virtually any rate structure that they want, so long as the highest tax rate does not exceed 0.3 percent.[5] Some local governments use a flat maximum rate of 0.3 percent, but most apply a multiple or graduated tax rate and properties below a certain threshold are exempt from tax. DKI Jakarta's minimum tax rate is 0.01 percent, and Bengkulu Selatan Municipality's is 0.05 percent.

Several local governments levy lower urban and rural property tax rates on property in conservation areas or on properties that are heritage buildings, such as in South Aceh, Aceh Besar, Way Kanan, Bandung, Bojonegoro, Jayapura, Boven Digoel, and some municipalities in South and Central Kalimantan. Some local governments apply a higher rate for properties deemed to pose environmental risks.

Coverage of the Tax Base

The tax base is the market value of land and buildings. Local governments have some discretion to exempt properties from taxation or to provide special preferential tax treatments. They also have de facto powers to influence the size of the tax base through their assessment practices and their discovery of properties to be included on the tax roll. However, coverage is constrained by the relatively high proportion of properties that are not registered (Van der Eng 2016).

By law the minimum threshold exemption for the value of land and buildings is IDR 10 million (about USD 700). Some local governments set lower exemptions. For example, the municipality of Nagan Raya in Aceh Province and the municipality of North Konawe in Southeast Sulawesi have established a threshold value of IDR 7 million and 6 million, respectively (PERDA Konawe Utara No. 1 2013; QANUN Nagan Raya No. 14 2011). Other local governments have higher threshold levels, which the law allows, but this reduces the size of the tax base.

Valuation of Property

The valuation of properties for urban and rural property tax is the responsibility of the local government (Government Regulation 55 2016 enacted in terms of article 79b of Law 28 2009). Land valuation in Indonesia is based on market value (comparative sales approach), and residential buildings are typically valued by the cost approach. The approaches to valuation in the central-government era and the devolution era are much the same. Property information is mostly collected from the owner, then entered in the database. Local valuers (who may be contractors) then rely on third-party information (property sales data, construction costs, and special values) to identify land and building values in different zones of the local government. These zonal values and certain individual property assessments are used to develop the tax roll.

This valuation practice has not led to a buoyant property tax base. Observers have offered several reasons. First, the information base inherited from the central government was problematic because of errors in property identification and an already dated valuation roll. Second, the capacity of local-government staff, particularly valuers, was not adequate to maintain an accurate, updated roll. Third, the political costs of increasing values and therefore tax liabilities dampened enthusiasm for increasing taxable values. This led to assessed values that were on the order of 50 percent of market values (Von Haldenwang et al. 2015). Other evidence from a small sample of local governments places the assessment ratio near this same level (Prayogo 2020, 30–31).

The failure to revalue is a problem. Since devolution of urban and rural property taxes, many local governments have reassessed their tax base, in line with Law 28 2009, by which local governments' must conduct revaluations of urban and rural property tax at least every three years. A three-year cycle is similar to that in many jurisdictions at the same level of development. It is likely that the larger urban governments, where valuation capacities are better, have revalued more frequently. A 2009 survey by the Directorate General of Tax showed that 177 of 288 local governments (out of a total of more than 500) in Indonesia had updated land values in the previous three years, while many had not carried out any revaluation (Prayogo 2020, 31).

Local governments have some discretion on the frequency of the tax base valuation. Revaluation can be initiated by a governor decree, for DKI Jakarta, or by a mayor decree, for municipalities. But revaluation may not be politically feasible in regions where the head of the local government is considering reelection. It also may be that the local government does not have the capacity to conduct property tax revaluation (McCluskey 2016; Von Haldenwang et al. 2015). The relatively low urban and rural property tax revenues of local governments translate to low investment in updating coverage of the property tax base. McCluskey's (2016) view is that a less uniform revaluation schedule is needed, one depending on local characteristics. Large urban areas may need more frequent valuation than rural areas.

Natural Resource Property and Land Tax

The central-government natural resource property tax covers three sectors: plantation, forestry, and mining. Individuals and companies are obligated to pay this tax if they have received a permit from the central government for the activity. The permit determines the coverage.

Tax Rate and Base

The tax rate for natural resources is 0.5 percent. The tax base covers different uses of the land, determined by a schedule of valuation rules. Areas related to natural resource activity are usually classified as productive or nonproductive areas; productive areas generally carry a higher tax. The government defines each classification, for each sector, that will be identified in the filing of the tax object (tax base) declaration. The type of permit assigned to a productive area may also affect coverage. For example, if the resource is forestry, a permit may pertain to plantation areas or logging activities. Whether the tax base is considered forestry or plantation, property tax will depend on the areas and the activity noted in the permit.

Valuation Method

The tax base valuation refers to the unit values set by the central-government tax office in the respective regions using guidelines from the Directorate General of Tax.[6] The income approach to valuation is used. For example, the property tax for plantations requires the valuation of the tax base to relate to the size of productive areas, type and age of plants, and the production income. Tax offices in the regions provide a tax object declaration form for taxpayers to complete with information such as (1) size of productive and nonproductive areas; (2) type and age of plants and the size of areas planted with each; (3) unit costs of investment, which are determined by the government; (4) types and amenities of properties and sizes of areas, and unit costs for each type of property; (5) emplacement areas, referring to land in which properties are built; and (6) other land use—for example, undeveloped land and or land used for roads.

Property Transfer Tax

Property transfer tax is an important tax for local government, especially for the larger cities. As shown in table 7.1, the property transfer tax for local governments produces about the same revenue as does the urban and rural property tax. As mentioned previously, the revenue from urban property tax in DKI Jakarta has been greater than that for the transfer tax since 2004 (see box 7.1).

Tax Rate Schedule and Preferential Rates

Law 28 2009 mandates a property transfer tax rate of 5 percent, levied on the buyer and based on the value of the transaction. A separate capital gains tax charged through the income tax is levied on the seller.

A central-government regulation (*Peraturan Pemerintah* [PP] 34 2016) allows local governments to reduce the property transfer tax rate to 2.5 percent. However, given that the standard 5 percent tax rate is set by national law, it is not legal to levy a reduced tax rate through a regulation. Therefore, this policy seems not to be binding for local governments. Furthermore, the central government offers tax incentives for the property sector to develop real estate investment trusts, including lowering transfer tax rates from 5 percent to 1 percent.

Coverage of the Tax Base

Local governments were involved to some extent in setting policies for property transfer tax even before devolution in 2011. Suratman and Masrizal (2014) note that local government can set the exemption level of property transfer tax. The tax base exemption of the property transfer tax is IDR 60 million (USD 4,210) and IDR 300 million (USD 21,060) if the property is transferred as part of an inheritance. In 2011, most local governments set the exemption level of property transfer tax at less than IDR 60 million (about USD 4,200), but six local governments set a lower exemption level (Suratman and Masrizal 2014). Some local governments set the exemption level higher than IDR 60 million; for example, DKI Jakarta exempts from property transfer tax any property transaction with a value less than IDR 2 billion (Governor Decree of DKI Province No. 126 2017).

The property transfer tax is excluded from the tax base for property transactions in which the property will be used for government administration. Exclusions also apply to the property of diplomatic missions, property used by international organizations stated in Ministry of Finance Decree, and property transferred for religious use or donated land or buildings (i.e., *wakaf*, or charitable donation under Islamic law).

The tax is paid at the time of transaction when the ownership status of land and or property changes hands. The declared value of a transaction is the base value used to calculate tax liability.

Registering a land title requires paying the property tax and property transfer tax. However, in 2013, only 32 percent of land plots were registered (Van der Eng 2016), which may signal a high rate of undeclared transactions of property. This in turn implies lower property tax transfer revenues for local governments.

Property Tax Management and Collections

Another major issue related to recurrent property taxes is collections and the management of tax arrears discussed here.

Method of Collection

The government determines the amount of taxable land and property and the type of applicable property tax and issues a tax object identification number and registration (figure 7.3). Distribution of the urban and rural property tax bill is coordinated with the appropriate lower-level administration. The tax bill is sent in the first quarter of the year, and the due date is in the third quarter. The distribution schedule of the tax bill is community specific.

When there is a transaction between a buyer and seller, a notary public issues a deed of sale for the property. The property transfer tax is based on the transaction value as recorded in the deed of property transfer issued by public notary (or the locally assessed value, whichever is higher). Upon payment of the property transfer tax, the government issues a property title certificate (figure 7.4). Delinquent urban and rural property tax bills must be settled as a requirement for the issuance of a property deed. The property transfer tax must be paid before submitting a request for a new or a change in a property title certificate.

A major issue related to property transfer taxation is a probable widespread underdeclaration of transaction value (Suratman and Masrizal 2014).

Figure 7.3 Administration of Urban and Rural Property Taxes

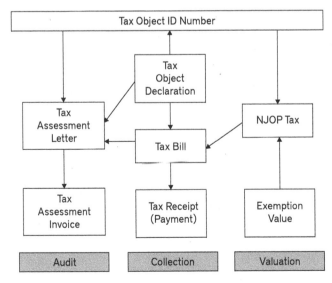

Sources: Adapted from Fiscal Policy Office (2015) and Government Regulation 55 2016.

Figure 7.4 Administration of Property Transfer Tax

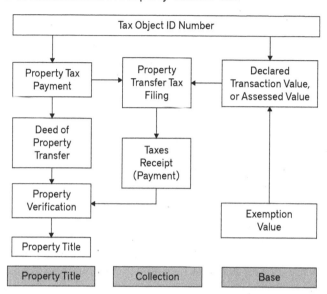

Sources: Adapted from Fiscal Policy Office (2015) and Government Regulation 55 2016.

The provision in Law 28 2009 for a minimum property transfer value to be set at the locally assessed value is hardly ever enforced. Even if it were enforced more often, the locally assessed value is well below true market value, setting up a vicious circle for underassessment. The property transfer tax may be based on a transaction value even lower than locally assessed value, but that lower value is recorded by public notary in the deed of property transfer (Dewi 2016; Kuswanto 2014; Suratman et al. 2015). As shown in figure 7.3, the property is verified and measured by a land registry office (a central-government agency) if there is a request for a property title certificate. Unlike the urban and rural property tax process, the property transfer tax process does not include an audit.

Penalties and Enforcement

Box figure 7.1 and figure 7.3, especially 7.3, are based on a study by the Fiscal Policy Office (2015). The description of the administration of urban and rural property tax in this section relies extensively on this 2015 study. As shown in box figure 7.1, an audit on urban and rural property tax examines information declared for the valuation and information as stated in the tax object declaration. This includes taxpayers' payment (or nonpayment) of the tax bill. If information on the tax object declaration is incorrect, the local-government tax office will send the taxpayer a tax assessment letter. Providing incorrect information that results in underreporting garners a penalty that is 25 percent of the difference between the correct tax amount and the underdeclared tax amount. This penalty is stated in Law 12 1994 and is also explained in the Directorate General (DG) Tax Regulation No. 20 2015 or the respective local-government regulations for urban and rural property tax. If taxpayers have not paid or have delayed payment of the property tax, the penalty applied is 2 percent per month of the unpaid tax amount, compounded up to two years. The annual tax bill sent to taxpayers consists of only property tax owed in one year, not accumulated unpaid taxes (arrears). Taxpayers receive a separate notification of arrears and associated penalties.

Compliance Costs

To make paying property taxes easier, some local governments have cooperated with the banking sector to allow urban and rural property tax payments to be made at ATMs. As discussed in box 7.1, DKI Jakarta introduced this payment method in 2014. Local governments also use technology to send tax bills—for example, sending text messages with notifications and reminders of tax payments or providing online tax bills. South Tangerang, a city adjacent to DKI Jakarta, introduced in 2016 an online program, called SIMPPEL *(Sistem Penyampaian SPPT PBB elektronik)*, that citizens can use to access property information, sign up to receive tax bills via email, and edit property information. The city of Denpasar adopted efiling of the property transfer tax in 2016 (Mayor Decree City of Denpasar No. 17 2016).

Property Tax Collections

The records inherited from the central government at devolution have both duplicate records and missing data, which causes problems for billing and collections. Some municipalities have staff and resources to enforce collections. Those municipalities without resources have a significant amount of uncollected taxes and growing arrears in property tax collections. Even before devolution, the collection rate was about 80 percent (C. Lewis 2019; Prayogo 2020). Even though collection has been decentralized to over 500 local governments, it is still not clear where the responsibility lies for monitoring and oversight.

Arrears

As shown in figure 7.5, arrears collections surged in 2011–2013. This may have been due, in part, to better tax collection of property tax that can be claimed as central-government revenues (Qibthiyyah 2016).

Before devolution, revenue from urban and rural property tax belonged to the central government. The effort to collect arrears starting in 2011 has not been sustained. Qibthiyyah (2016) found low collection of property tax arrears after 2014 by many local governments. For a majority of these governments, arrears collection reaches only about 10 percent of their property tax revenues. This low level may be due to weak enforcement, complicated by a database that does not enable full tracking of delinquent taxpayers.

The revenue potential of collections from arrears could be significant. Indonesia's Supreme Audit Agency (BPK [*Badan Pemeriksa Keuangan*]) audits the financial reports of agencies in the central government and at subnational-government levels. According to the audited financial report of local governments for 2014 (BPK 2019), property tax arrears were around IDR 18.4 trillion, 0.18 percent of GDP. Urban and rural property tax arrears are quite large relative to total local collections (figure 7.6), even in regions with a relatively high level of revenues, such as in the DKI Jakarta

Figure 7.5 Percentage of Arrears Collection by Central Government, 2010–2014

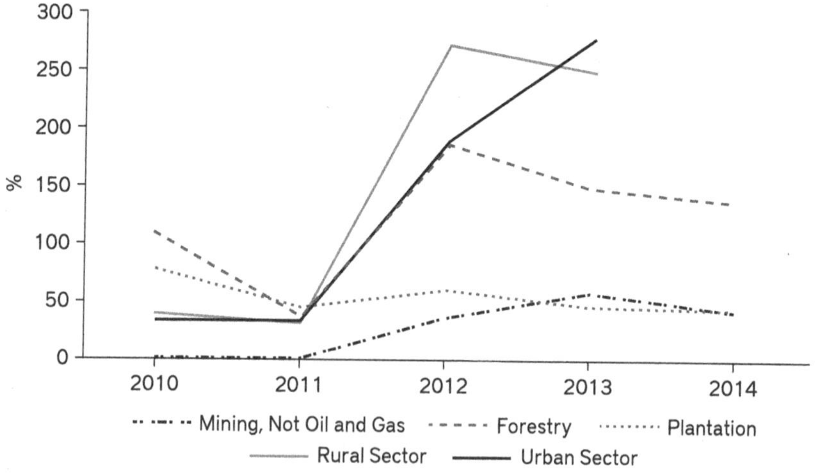

Source: Qibthiyyah (2016, fig. 4).

Figure 7.6 Ratio of Urban and Rural Property Tax Arrears to Revenues, 2015–2018

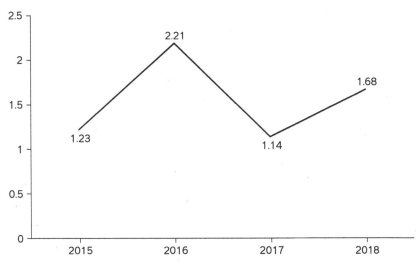

Source: Aggregated from provinces' and local governments' audited financial reports (BPK 2019).

and Badung (Bali). In 2018, urban and rural property tax arrears in Badung were more than 50 percent of property tax revenue collected (Nusa-Bali.com 2019). There is not enough data to calculate the arrears inherited from the central government at devolution compared with low arrears today due to a low collection rate. Nor are data available to examine the extent to which arrears recovery was in the form of cash collections or write-offs.

Problems and Issues

Property taxation devolution raised hopes for increased revenue mobilization. This has not materialized. Moreover, revenue mobilization is unlikely to grow significantly without reforms in the system. The constraints to revenue growth have several forms.

Narrow tax base

Limited coverage of properties in the tax base and the underassessment of taxable properties and property transactions, which seems to remove 50 percent of market values from the system, are the main reasons for the narrow tax base. Some of the reduction is due to exclusions and statutory rate caps, and some of it is due to flawed administration. These structural problems and policy issues are magnified by the very low statutory rate and weak collection effort.

VALUATION

A major constraint to revenue mobilization is the undervaluation of urban and rural properties and the undervaluation of property transactions. Recurrent valuations are often out of date, and they are partly based on comparative sales values of properties, which are very low. The property transfer tax is often based on declared values or assessments under the recurrent property tax, both of which are also low. A key to increasing property tax revenues in Indonesia is to do regular revaluations and to move assessments closer to market value levels.

CAPACITY CONSTRAINTS

In the years after devolution, the largest 100 local governments accounted for more than 90 percent of property tax collections. The smaller local governments, the other 400, are challenged by a lack of oversight and management, a limited supply of qualified appraisers, and an inadequate number of enforcement officials. The problems are compounded by the need to collect property tax under a relatively uniform tax administration system and policies. Not all local governments will be enthusiastic about reforms that will not yield significant revenue. Even the central government, which currently handles a smaller number of taxpayers, takes the position that the number of appraisers is inadequate. The 259 qualified appraisers for the central government are distributed to its regional-level tax offices and are responsible for natural resource property tax (DGT Annual Report 2017).

LIMITED COMPLIANCE

Property owners should know about property tax payments Some of the low level of property tax compliance may have to do with taxpayers' lack of awareness of their responsibility for paying the tax. Affordability is usually not an issue for local taxes, including property tax, because tax bills are small enough that many residents consider them an invisible tax. After devolution of urban and rural property tax, some local governments adjusted the tax base value to be closer to market value. These policy changes led to higher tax bills and made the tax more visible (and more objectionable) to residents. Property owners should be sensitized to the need for the property tax, such as paying for public services that they support. Finally, local governments do not rigidly enforce the hard penalties available to them for tax delinquencies.

LOW TAX COLLECTION RATE AND HIGH ARREARS BALANCES

The final step in mobilizing property tax revenue is collection. Some estimates place the collection rate in Indonesia around 80 percent, which is quite low by comparison with the higher-income jurisdictions in Asia. The combination of this low collection rate, an assessment ratio of around 50 percent, and low statutory tax rates goes a long way toward explaining Indonesia's weak revenue performance. Low collection rates of course, go hand-in-hand with increasing arrears. Tax arrears have not been managed well during the devolution of urban and rural property tax from central government to local governments.

LACK OF POLITICAL WILL

Any remedies require local voters to pay higher taxes. National and community leaders have seen the political costs of reforming the property tax and the administrative costs as being too high relative to possible gains for the nation or community.

Reform Options

The devolution of the property tax to local governments was in step with a major reform in the decentralization of government finance. Local-government ownership of the tax would, in theory, give them funds for local services, and this would in turn make elected local politicians more accountable to voters. But of the 514 local governments, some had more capacity to take on these tax administration tasks than others, and the devolution has not only not solved all the old problems but has brought on other problems.

The central government does not exhibit overwhelming support for improving the property tax system. Part of this may be due to the influence of certain interest groups with land and property taxes. In 2015, the Minister for Agrarian Affairs and Spatial Planning at the central level proposed eliminating urban and rural property tax (Aji 2015). There may also be a broader concern about the increased visibility of the property tax. When revenue from the central-government property tax was shared with local governments, the central government had little reason to improve tax collections. With the property tax now the purview of local governments, they have an incentive to promote policy and administrative improvements in property taxation to increase revenues and improve local public services.

Reform of property tax might focus on revenue mobilization, either by broadening the base, increasing rates, or improving administration (Kelly 2004; Kelly, White, and Anand 2020; B. Lewis 2003; McCluskey 2016; Suratman et al. 2015). The following are some reform paths that might be taken.

Upgrade Valuations

The one reform that might double land and property tax revenues is to bring valuation closer to market levels. This would have three benefits: (1) increase property transfer tax revenues by perhaps 50 percent; (2) potentially, double land and property tax revenues; and (3) provide market value information for valuation and revaluation. If local politicians could get past their fear of the consequences of such actions, they could take four steps: The first is to levy (and enforce) heavy penalties on underdeclaration of property values with respect to property transfer taxes. The second is to adopt a capital gains tax on land transactions that would introduce a self-reinforcing component into the process. The third is to use this market sales information in assessing the value of properties in the annual property tax base. The fourth is to improve valuation skills through the delivery of training to local-government officials (Ministry of Finance 2018). Local universities could scale up the effort to reach all 514 local governments.

Revenue mobilization will increase with revaluation of the property tax base. Although this is expensive if done correctly, local governments will greatly benefit. Revaluations are needed at intervals frequent enough to avoid large increases in taxpayers' bills. Law 28 of 2009 calls for a regular revaluation cycle for local governments, and larger urban governments should follow the same cycle. The law stipulates a three-year cycle, but a less uniform period of valuation may be sufficient for the economic development and property markets of the very diverse local governments in Indonesia.

Finding a more practical way to value land and buildings is also needed, because a full survey of the tax roll is not feasible for many local governments (Van der Eng 2016). Moreover, many local governments have a limited number of qualified valuers available to undertake this task. Given these constraints, local governments might begin to focus more on the use of computerized mass appraisal; however, this puts further demands on resources, such as better data.

Increase the Collection Rate

Low collection rates are not an unusual feature of taxation in the poorer jurisdictions of Asia, and the approaches to improve collection are similar across these jurisdictions, including Indonesia. The most popular routes are tougher enforcement, lower effective tax rates and lower compliance costs, providing better information to taxpayers, and offering incentives to pay taxes. To some extent, Indonesia has used all these. Tougher enforcement would probably get the best results. Indonesia, like most Asian jurisdictions, has penalties in place to punish those who evade, but harsh treatment for not paying such a small tax could backfire.

A related problem is the accumulation and collection of arrears. Lower collection rates for the annual property tax lead to greater arrears, and taxpayers with significant arrears are hesitant to pay their current property tax bill for fear of becoming too visible to the tax authorities. Some local governments have approached this problem with an amnesty. Amnesties can be popular with delinquent taxpayers, but they also can be seen as penalties on those who have been paying their taxes all along. Some local governments in Indonesia issued district-head (*bupati*) or mayor decrees to forgive property tax arrears. Different areas use different schemes. For example, in Kutai Barat, property tax arrears forgiveness is granted by the *bupati* only for arrears of IDR 5 billion or less. Arrears higher than IDR 5 billion would need approval of the local house of representatives (the Regional People's Representative Council, or Dewan Perwakilan Rakyat Daerah).

Eliminate Barriers to the Flow of Information

The database on property markets is limited. For example, in 2004, a residential and commercial property price survey by Bank Indonesia, the central bank, included only the metropolitan area of DKI Jakarta. The survey has since been expanded to 18 of the 98 cities. In recent years, the Central Bureau of Statistics issued statistics on costs related to property construction. However, these property market data cover only metropolitan areas and large cities. Property price data and land registration are also still an issue (Van der Eng 2016). Only 32 percent of land plots are registered, which implies low tax base coverage.

Making registration data for all related taxes more accessible would improve information flow. Local governments usually have a different administration unit for each type of local tax. The data management system is not coordinated, and the result is that the database is not fully used, even within the local government itself. Merging the administration of annual urban and rural property tax, property transfer tax, and in the future, value capture instruments could remove barriers to the flow of information where clear efficiencies are to be had from joint administration (ADB 2021).

Reduce Exemptions and Tax Preferences

Local governments have discretion to grant exemptions to property tax in addition to those exemptions stipulated in Law 28 2009. Some of these local exemptions for property tax create horizontal inequities in the tax and are costly in terms of revenue sacrifice. For example, in DKI Jakarta, a preferential treatment that started in 2019 exempts teachers from paying property tax. Amending the 2009 law is not feasible, but local governments could require that proposed preferential treatments be supported by a fiscal note on revenue costs and that they be vetted periodically to assure their continued usefulness. This would also make the property tax more transparent to taxpayers.

Simplify the Tax

Many local governments have adopted complicated rate structures for their urban and rural property taxes that feature multiple rates. However, some of these local governments are less urbanized than others and do not have the capacity to implement a complicated property tax. Higher rates and multiple levels of property tax may be feasible for large metropolitan areas, but such a structure is less practical for most local governments. Moreover, there is little evidence that these structures have distributed tax burdens more fairly or increased revenue mobilization. A simple flat-rate structure, supported by assessments at market value levies, might be a better approach.

Notes

1. The official name of the city is Daerah Khusus Ibukota Jakarta Raya (DKI Jakarta), meaning "Special Capital City Region." The government unit administration of DKI Jakarta differs from that of other provinces under Law 29 2007 on Province of DKI Jakarta as capital city of Indonesia.

2. ADB (2012) reports that in 2008 about half the jurisdiction's 4 million civil servants had insufficient qualifications.

3. Property tax exemption involves a 100% tax exemption on oil and gas preexploration and an exemption up to a maximum 100% on oil and gas revenues (*tubuh bumi*) during exploration. This policy came into effect in 2017 in Government Regulation No. 27 2017.

4. Only aggregated data on local-government property tax are available and only from publicly available local-government financial reports. Most of these reports provide only a total amount of urban and rural property taxes, with no separate data for urban and rural property taxes.

5. The draft of Law on Financial Relation of Central and Lower Level Government submitted to legislature in 2021 (KONTAN 2021) proposes to increase the maximum rate of urban and rural property taxes to 0.5%.

6. Tax Directorate Regulation PER-31 2014 on Plantation Property Tax, Tax Directorate Regulation PER-42 2015 on Forestry Property Tax, and Tax Directorate Regulation PER-47 2015 on Property Tax in Mining, and PER-45 2013 on Oil and Gas Sector Property Tax.

References

ADB (Asian Development Bank). 2012. "Republic of Indonesia: Local Government Finance and Governance Reform." Technical Assistance Report (Project Number 42221), Capacity Development Technical Assistance, Asian Development Bank. https://www.adb.org/sites/default/files/project-document/73044/42221-022-ino-tar.pdf.

———. 2021. *Innovative Infrastructure Financing Through Value Capture in Indonesia.* Asian Development Bank. http://hdl.handle.net/11540/13684.

Aji, W. 2015. "Serius Soal Penghapusan PBB, Menteri Ferry Surati Presiden," February 10, 2015. https://www.tribunnews.com/nasional/2015/02/10/serius-soal-pengha pusan-pbb-menteri-ferry-surati-presiden.

Bahl, R., and J. Martinez-Vazquez. 2008. "The Property Tax in Developing Countries: Current Practice and Prospects." In *Making the Property Tax Work: Experiences in Developing and Transitional Countries*, ed. R. Bahl, J. Martinez-Vazquez, and J. Youngman, 35–57. Cambridge, MA: Lincoln Institute of Land Policy.

Booth, A. 1974. "IPEDA—Indonesia's Land Tax. *Bulletin of Indonesian Economic Studies* 10 (1): 55–81.

BPK. 2010–2019. "Provinces and Local Governments Audited Financial Report."

Dewi, A. R. 2016. "Assessment Sales Ratio (ASR) as Performance Indicator of Property Transaction Value (NPOP)." [In Bahasa.] *BHUMI: Jurnal Agraria dan Pertanahan* 26 (1): 96–108.

Directorate General of Fiscal Balance (DGFB). 2021a. "Taxes Revenues Budget and Realization." [In Bahasa.] Ministry of Finance, Government of Indonesia.

DGFB. 2021b. "DKI Jakarta Summary of Budget and Realized Province Taxes Data." DKI Jakarta Province audited Financial Reports 2013–2019. [In Bahasa.] Ministry of Finance, Government of Indonesia. https://djpk.kemenkeu.go.id/?p=5412.

DGT (Directorate General of Tax) Annual Report 2010–2019. Ministry of Finance, Government of Indonesia. https://pajak.go.id/id/tahunan-page.

DKI Jakarta Province Central Bureau of Statistics. 2013–2019. "DKI Jakarta Province in Numbers 2014–2020." [In Bahasa.] https://jakarta.bps.go.id/publication.

Fiscal Policy Office. 2015. "Evaluation on Devolution of Urban and Rural PBB to Local Governments: Some Lesson Learned. In Study of Plan to Devolve Natural Resource PBB (PBB P3)." [In Bahasa.] Ministry of Finance, Government of Indonesia.

Hofman, B., and K. Kaiser. 2004. "The Making of the "Big Bang' and Its Aftermath: A Political Economy Perspective." In *Reforming Intergovernmental Fiscal Relations and the Rebuilding of Indonesia*, ed. J. Alm, J. Martinez-Vazquez, and S. M. Indrawati, 15–46. Cheltenham, UK: Edward Elgar.

Indonesia Premium Database. 2021. Government Revenue: Domestic: Land and Building Tax CEIC Data,

Kelly, R. 1992. "Implementing Property Tax Reform in Developing Countries: Lessons from the Property Tax in Indonesia." *Review of Urban and Regional Development Studies* 4 (2): 193–208.

———. 1993. "Property Tax Reform in Indonesia: Applying a Collection-Led Implementation Strategy." *Bulletin of Indonesian Economic Studies* 29 (1): 85–104.

———. 2004. "Property Tax Reform in Indonesia: Emerging Challenges from Decentralization." *Asia Pacific Journal of Public Administration* 26 (1): 71–90.

———. 2012. "Strengthening the Revenue Side, in Indonesia." In *Fiscal Decentralization in Indonesia a Decade After Big Bang*, 173–206. Jakarta: University of Indonesia Press.

Kelly, R., R. White, and A. Anand. 2020. *Property Tax Diagnostic Manual*. Washington, DC: World Bank.

KONTAN. 2021. "Supporting Local Economy, Government Submitted RUU HKPD." [In Bahasa.] June 28, 2021. https://nasional.kontan.co.id/news/dorong -ekonomi-daerah-pemerintah-ajukan-ruu-hkpd.

Kuswanto, D. 2014. "The Accuracy of Property Transaction Value (NPOP) of BPHTB to Market Value." Thesis. Gajah Mada University [in Bahasa].

Lewis, B. 2003. "Property Tax in Indonesia: Measuring and Explaining Administrative (Under-) Performance." *Public Administration and Development* 23 (3): 227–239.

Lewis, C. 2019. "Raising More Public Revenue in Indonesia in a Growth- and Equity-Friendly Way." OECD Working Paper. https://doi.org/10.1787/a487771f-en.

McCluskey, W. 2016. "Simplifying Cost Valuation Method. TA 8877—TRAMPIL." Asian Development Bank and Ministry of Finance.

Ministry of Finance. 2018. "E-Learning on Local Finance Technical Assistance." [In Bahasa.] https://djpk.kemenkeu.go.id/elearning-djpk/mod/page/view.php?id=103

NusaBali.com. 2019. "IDR 200 Billion PBB-P2 Not Paid by Taxpayer," August 1, 2019. [In Bahasa.] https://www.nusabali.com/berita/56656/rp-200-miliar-pbb-p2-belum-dibayar-wajib-pajak.

Panjaitan, J. Y., and H. Fitri. 2019. *Perkembangan Realisasi Penerimaan Perpajakan Periode 2013–2018 dan Target dalam RAPBN 2019.* Budget Office Review, Expert Council, Indonesia House of Representatives.

PERDA DKI Jakarta No. 16 2011. "Province Law on Urban and Rural Property Tax (PBB P2)."

PERDA Konawe Utara No. 1 2013. "Local Government Law on Urban and Rural Property Taxes." [In Bahasa.] https://peraturan.bpk.go.id/Home/Details/14331/perda-kab-konawe-utara-no-1-tahun-2013.

Prayogo, S. G. 2020. "A Strategy to Increase Property Tax Revenue in Indonesia." Master's thesis, Duke University, Durham, NC.

QANUN Nagan Raya No. 14 2011. "Local Government Law on Local Taxes." [In Bahasa.] https://jdih.naganrayakab.go.id/dih/detail/c7574599-0e47-4911-9358-c9c3267920ed.

Qibthiyyah, R. 2016. "Evaluation of PBB P3 Revenue Sharing, TA-8877-TRAMPIL." Asian Development Bank and Ministry of Finance.

Suratman, E., C. F. Ananda, H. Paddu, and A. Adji. 2015. "Evaluation on Implementation of Law 28 2009 on Local Taxes and Charges." [In Bahasa.] Tim Asistensi Desentralisasi Fiskal (TADF), Ministry of Finance.

Suratman, E., and M. Masrizal. 2014. "Policy Brief NPOP-TKP (Rp 60 Juta) dalam rangka Penentuan Cluster NPOP-TKP sebagai Bahan Revisi UU 28 Tahun 2009. Property Transfer Tax Exemption Policy of IDR 60 million." Tim Asistensi Menteri Keuangan untuk Desentralisi Fiskal [Technical Assistance to Minister of Finance on Fiscal Decentralization]. Directorate General of Fiscal Balance, Indonesia Ministry of Finance.

Van der Eng, P. 2016. "After 200 Years, Why Is Indonesia's Cadastral System Still Incomplete?" Discussion Paper No. 2016-03. Canberra: Center for Economic History, Australian National University.

Von Haldenwang, C., A. Elfert, T. Engelmann, S. Germain, G. Sahler, and A. S. Ferreira. 2015. "The Devolution of the Land and Building Tax in Indonesia." Bonn: German Development Institute. https://www.die-gdi.de/en/studies/article/the-devolution-of-the-land-and-building-tax-in-indonesia/.

8

Japan: Challenges to a Mature Property Tax System

ANDREW DEWIT

Japan's population is highly urbanized, with close to 92 percent of the jurisdiction's total population living in cities. But among Organization for Economic Cooperation and Development (OECD) member jurisdictions, Japan is also markedly bifurcated between very dense city-regions and remote villages. The key element is topography: Japan is an archipelago composed of four main islands, and roughly 75 percent of the land is mountainous. In consequence, about half the population is clustered in the three city-regions of Tokyo, Osaka, and Nagoya. These city-regions compose only 5.2 percent of the national territory and are in relatively close proximity (500 km) along the Pacific coast. By contrast, 7 percent of the population lives in remote communities. Both the remote and the rural areas are rapidly aging and depopulating, in large part because of out-migration to the city-regions (OECD 2016). The rural municipalities' challenges of maintaining attractive levels of public services are further compounded by declining property values, higher levels of vacant residential houses and condominiums than the 2018 national average of 13.6 percent, and higher indeterminate land ownership than the national average of 20.1 percent in 2016 (Kashiwagi 2018).

This chapter describes Japan's fiscal system and the intergovernmental context for property taxation. Although focused on the principal recurrent tax on immobile property and land—the fixed asset tax (FAT; *koteishisanzei*)— it also describes two comparatively minor, municipal recurrent taxes on property, the city planning tax (CPT; *toshikeikakuzei*) and the business office tax, and it briefly addresses other national and prefectural taxes relevant to Japan's overall property and land taxation regime. The chapter then reviews the property tax base and the exceedingly complex assessment, administrative, and other pertinent details of the FAT and CPT. It situates the FAT in the context of Japanese policy makers' efforts to bolster municipal tax bases and economies to cope with unprecedentedly severe demographic and other challenges. It includes a case study of Tokyo Metropolitan Government's property taxation and a summary and assessment of ongoing reforms and much-needed changes.

The Fiscal System

Property and land taxation plays an important role in Japan's public financing structure, particularly at the municipal level, in a fiscal regime often described as centralized in terms of taxation but very decentralized on the expenditure side. Indeed, Japanese public finance scholars have long emphasized that the most conspicuous feature of Japan's intergovernmental finance is a large role for subnational expenditures that is not matched by adequate subnational revenue autonomy (Jinno 2017; Mochida 2008). In fiscal year FY 2017, subnational governments (prefectures and municipalities) accounted for 58 percent of total general government spending but collected just 39 percent of total tax revenues of JPY 102.2 trillion (figure 8.1).

The national-level inheritance and gift taxes are significant, at JPY 2.23 trillion. So too is the prefectural real estate acquisition tax, which totaled

Figure 8.1 Ratio of National and Subnational Taxes, FY 2017

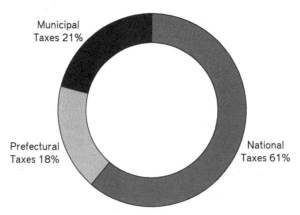

Municipal
Taxes 21%

Prefectural
Taxes 18%

National
Taxes 61%

Source: MIC (2019a).

Figure 8.2 Principal Municipal Tax Revenues, FY 2017

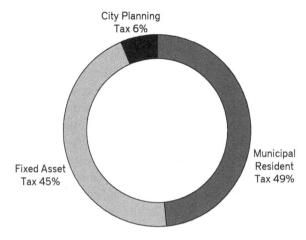

Source: MIC (2019a).

JPY 407 billion in 2017. But Japan's property and land taxation regime is concentrated at the municipal level (Miyazaki and Sato 2018). Figure 8.2 shows the principal municipal taxes and their amounts for FY 2017. The FAT and CPT together comprise JPY 10.53 trillion, or about half of municipal taxes, a share that has remained generally consistent over the 2010s. Well under half of Japan's municipalities choose not to levy the CPT, with some analyses suggesting that the CPT is substituted for by higher FAT rates (Tanashita and Imanishi 2006).

Figure 8.2 also shows that second to the aggregate revenue share from property and land taxation is the municipal resident tax, or inhabitant tax, which comprises taxes on individuals' incomes and on businesses' incomes. In addition, there is a flat per capita levy. The remaining municipal taxes are largely imposed on tobacco and other consumption.

Japanese subnational governments are responsible for such services as public welfare (excluding pensions), primary and secondary education, public works, public safety, and general administration. Many of these are delegated functions, such as welfare services, wherein the relevant central agencies set standards for local service delivery. Total prefectural expenditures in FY 2017 were JPY 50.7 trillion, and municipal expenditures were even larger at JPY 56.5 trillion. These expenditures were far in excess of their respective revenues from taxes, fees, and debt finance. The resultant gap between subnational spending and own revenues (particularly taxes) is a persistent feature of Japanese public finance and requires a large role for earmarked and general intergovernmental transfers. In FY 2017, earmarked transfers represented 12.1 percent of prefectural revenues from all sources and 15.3 percent of municipal revenues from all sources. In addition, general transfers composed 17 percent of prefectural revenues and 14.5 percent of municipal revenues.

Reducing these intergovernmental transfers, bolstering local fiscal and administrative autonomy, and maintaining intergovernmental equity have long been principal subjects in debates over the reform of Japanese public finance. The underlying arguments are deeply normative and echo the experience of the centralized wartime state and postwar high growth that was based on centrally directed industrial policy (Akizuki 2001). Put simply, institutionalist public finance scholars view earmarked and general subsidies as key mechanisms through which Japanese central-government agencies have structured subnational fiscal and economic options since the 1950s (Ide 2013; Takahashi 2012). Public finance analyses with a more econometric bent highlight transfers as a source of moral hazards and other distortions (Bessho 2016, 2017; Miyazaki 2018).

Reflecting this general agreement on the need for reform, intergovernmental transfers have been the focus of large-scale initiatives for fiscal and administrative decentralization. These initiatives have gained generalized, bipartisan support in the attentive public debate and party politics. More than two decades of reforms have significantly reduced the central agencies' capacity to direct subnational-government spending and taxation. Agency delegation by the central agencies (*kikan inin jimu*) was abolished through the 1999 Devolution of Power Law, implemented in 2000 (Y. Ichikawa 2019). The subsequent 2004–2006 Trinity Reform to local taxes, national disbursements, and grants saw a total of roughly JPY 3 trillion in tax revenues transferred to subnational governments (H. Ichikawa 2007). These reforms have increased the subnational share of revenue and subnational governments' ability to make autonomous decisions. Even so, the intergovernmental fiscal gap and numerous fiscal rules continue to define the constraints and opportunities for local governments in the Japanese fiscal system (DeWit and Steinmo 2002). Policy makers seek to maintain a balance between constitutionally mandated intergovernmental equity and the need for expanded local capacity to address increasingly diverse challenges. In particular, Japan confronts the developed world's most rapid aging and population decline. These challenges are framed by a 2018 gross public debt of 226 percent of GDP, the highest level ever recorded among OECD member jurisdictions (OECD 2019).

Japan's overall tax reform has focused on raising the national consumption tax, so as to broaden the tax base, increase tax revenue and revenue stability, and move toward fiscal sustainability. Subnational governments have benefited, with their portion of the 10 percent consumption tax (increased from 8 percent as of October 2019) increasing from 1.7 percent to 2.2 percent. The subnational share of the 10 percent tax rises to 3.72 percent after adding the 19.5 percent of national consumption tax revenues earmarked for general grants. Though it seems likely there will be future increases in the consumption tax, the next increment is almost certainly a few years away.

In this context, property and land taxation revenues are recognized as critical to fiscally sustainable local government. High levels of national debt impede the central government's capacity to maintain current levels of intergovernmental transfers, particularly because the Ministry of Finance seeks to achieve a primary budget surplus in FY 2025 (the official government target). Reforms to shared income and consumption tax bases have sought to increase local-government revenues and independent tax options while still limiting regional fiscal disparities. Increased property and land taxation, especially in areas outside Tokyo, is often suggested as one underexploited means to bolster local-government revenue autonomy. And indeed, recent reforms have eliminated or relaxed national limits on property and land taxation rates and otherwise broadened the scope for local action.

Increasing property and land taxation burdens in the regions is politically contentious among local governments and with local taxpayers. Japan's property and land taxation regime is strongly rooted in benefit tax principles, a concern that has inhibited revenue increases in the past (Kitazato 2003). Raising local burdens also risks exacerbating already powerful incentives for students and the working-age population to abandon the regions and concentrate in Tokyo and other major cities. The central agencies continue to use property and land taxation, especially its exemptions, to foster industrial policy, disaster resilience, regional revitalization, and other policy goals. Figure 8.3 illustrates Japan's levels of government; box 8.1 describes the governance structure.

As shown in table 8.1, population density is relatively high, at 347.8 persons/km^2 (third highest among OECD jurisdictions), and municipal fragmentation is relatively low. These features are important for controlling the per capita cost of delivering public services and for maintaining aging infrastructure, yet another critical challenge. Japan's average number of inhabitants per municipality and average number of municipalities per 100,000 inhabitants are considerably higher than the respective figures for OECD member jurisdictions as a whole, yet its average municipal area, 215 km^2, is roughly equivalent to the OECD average of 211 km^2.

Figure 8.3 Japan's Three Tiers of Government

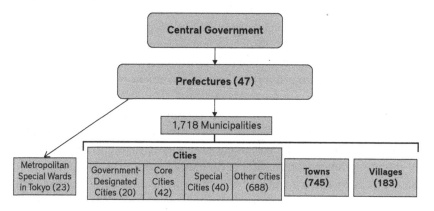

Box 8.1 Japan's Intergovernmental System

Japan is a unitary state, with three tiers of government, as shown in figure 8.3: the central (national) government; 47 prefectures, or regional-level governments; and 1,718 municipalities (792 cities, 745 towns, and 183 villages, in 2014). Tokyo Metropolitan Government is a prefecture containing 23 special wards. Cities are subdivided further into 20 designated cities (cities of over 500,000 residents, designated by cabinet ordinance), 42 core cities (cities of over 200,000 residents, designated by cabinet order), 40 special cities (also over 200,000), and 688 others (DeWit 2021). The 20 designated cities and the 23 special wards of Tokyo possess administrative and fiscal autonomy largely comparable to prefectures within their own municipal jurisdictions. The special cities can provide some degree of prefectural-level services (such as welfare, planning, and environmental services).

The 47 prefectures possess considerably stronger administrative and fiscal powers than their municipal counterparts, and they also have significantly different tax systems and spending responsibilities. The prefectures do not rely on property and land taxation to a significant extent. But to maximize administrative efficiency, Tokyo collects the FAT and CPT on behalf of its 23 special wards.[1]

Property and land taxation rate setting is almost wholly undertaken by the municipalities, within the overall framework of the Local Tax Law (*chihouzei-hou*). Special measures and exemptions are a product of the Local Tax Law and local ordinances. In general, the Local Tax Law defines the ambit of these items, and local ordinances define their precise implementation.

Japan's constitution explicitly stipulates local autonomy within the framework of the Local Tax Law. Authority to revise the Local Tax Law is vested in the National Diet and involves annual negotiations between the Ministry of

Internal Affairs and Communications and the Ministry of Finance. Furthermore, the constitution mandates that local governments have the autonomy to levy taxes on the basis of local bylaws. Hence, the Local Tax Law defines the types and mechanisms of local taxes, including the tax base and range of rates (e.g., standard and maximum rates), and the constitution nominally guarantees local autonomy within that overall framework. This legal-administrative structure is a compromise between the prewar era's marked differentiation between local taxes and rates and the wartime period's extreme fiscal centralization.

Japanese intergovernmental expenditure allocation is based on spatial competency. Thus, municipal governments provide local welfare, primary education, local roadbuilding and maintenance, and other functions that have limited cross jurisdictional spillovers. For their part, the prefectural governments undertake secondary education, construction and maintenance of regional roads and riparian works (e.g., flood control and irrigation), and other functions deemed appropriate to the regional level. The central government's role includes not just the conventional realms of national defense and the national currency but also national roadways, large river systems, and nationwide public welfare such as postsecondary education, health care, and pensions.

Within the central government, the main agencies that oversee subnational finance are the Ministries of Internal Affairs and Communications and of Finance. A National Tax Agency collects national taxes and–for efficiency–some subnational taxes (e.g., the local consumption tax), but the allocation of national revenues for intergovernmental disbursement is negotiated by the two ministries. The Ministry of Internal Affairs and Communications is the key agent in intergovernmental finance, representing subnational fiscal and administrative stability at the national level. It negotiates with the Ministry of Finance to expand local fiscal autonomy and either limit cuts to fiscal transfers or secure expanded local taxation in exchange for reduced transfers. One factor complicating this bargaining is that Japanese subnational taxation is roughly balanced among assets, income, and consumption, leading to considerable tax base overlap with the central government's taxes.

This governance structure is evolving, with greater voice for subnational governments, which are directly represented by six national associations. These associations are composed, respectively, of prefectural governors, city mayors, city legislative representatives, town and village mayors, and representatives of town and village legislatures. The associations are quite active and generate a considerable volume of studies and recommendations for fiscal reform. Since June 2011, the six national associations have met with the Ministry of Internal Affairs and Communications and other central-government agencies in a legally mandated forum for cooperation at least twice per year. At these proceedings, the subnational associations present proposals to the ministry and other central agencies for changes to subnational taxes, intergovernmental transfers, and other relevant items. Traditionally, the Tokyo Metropolitan Government took a leadership role in the association of prefectural governors and argued for interregional equity. This role has abated somewhat, under pressure from rising costs in a rapidly aging society. After all, the Tokyo Metropolitan Government bears a significant share of costs for general and specific grants that foster interregional equity. But Japan's overall political culture retains a strong commitment to equity, reflected in mainstream discourses on fiscal reform. Interregional equity is also institutionalized in intergovernmental transfers that guarantee a nationwide basic minimum in public services.

Table 8.1 Municipal Fragmentation in Japan and OECD Member States, 2018

	Avg. No. of Inhabitants	Avg. No. of Municipalities/ 100,000 People	Avg. Municipal Area (km²)
Japan	72,831	1.4	215
OECD jurisdictions	9,693	10.3	211

Source: OECD (2018).

Revenue Performance

As noted earlier, Japanese subnational governments levy taxes on assets, income, and consumption. The composition of the subnational tax base has expanded greatly since the mid-1980s, when the main revenue sources were property and land taxation (primarily the FAT), plus business and personal income taxes piggybacked onto the national levies. Since the 1990s, there has been a general trend toward increasing the earmarked subnational share of the nationally collected consumption tax. Revenues from the FAT have been generally stable, within the range of JPY 8 trillion to 9 trillion. Tables 8.2 and 8.3 show Japan's GDP, total national and subnational tax revenues, and the role of property taxes. Property tax revenue has been quite stable over the period, but it has not kept pace with increasing local expenditures.

Table 8.2 details Japan's real GDP and property and land taxation revenues (represented by the FAT) over 2008–2018. The table indicates that FAT revenues have generally been stable, within the range of JPY 8.5 trillion to 9 trillion. However, over the same period, real GDP increased by 7.1 percent. In consequence, the FAT burden of 1.76 percent of GDP in 2008 declined to 1.67 percent of GDP in 2018.

Table 8.2 Real GDP and Property Tax Revenues, 2008–2018

Year	2008	2009	2010	2011	2012	2013	2014	2015	2016	2017	2018
Real GDP (JPY trillion)	499.2	472.0	492.0	491.5	498.8	508.8	510.7	516.9	520.0	530.0	534.5
FAT (JPY trillion)	8.78	8.78	8.86	8.87	8.49	8.56	8.68	8.63	8.77	8.88	8.94
FAT as % of GDP	1.76	1.86	1.80	1.80	1.70	1.68	1.70	1.69	1.71	1.68	1.67

Source: MIC (2019b).

Table 8.3 FAT Revenues and Expenditures, 2008–2017

Year	2008	2009	2010	2011	2012	2013	2014	2015	2016	2017
FAT (JPY trillion)	8.78	8.78	8.86	8.87	8.49	8.56	8.68	8.63	8.77	8.88
Total tax (JPY trillion)	85.4	75.4	78.0	79.3	81.5	86.6	94.6	99.1	98.3	102.2
Total revenues (JPY trillion)	158.5	143.5	145.2	147.3	152.2	158.9	170.9	181.8	183.6	186.7
Subnational revenue (JPY trillion)	92.2	98.4	97.5	95.0	93.8	96.2	97.5	97.5	97.6	98.5
Local expenditure (JPY trillion)	48.4	52.0	52.1	52.9	54.2	54.9	56.0	56.5	56.5	No data
FAT as % of total tax revenues	10.3	11.6	11.4	11.2	10.4	9.8	9.18	8.71	8.92	8.67
FAT as % of total revenues	5.54	6.12	6.10	6.02	5.58	5.39	5.08	4.75	4.78	4.76
FAT as % of total subnational government revenues	9.5	8.9	9.1	9.3	9.1	8.9	8.9	8.9	9.0	9.0
FAT as % of local expenditures	18.14	16.88	17.04	16.77	15.66	15.59	15.50	15.27	15.52	No data

Source: MIC (2019b).

On the basis of its revenue performance over the decade, FAT would not appear to be the answer to filling a revenue mobilization gap. Shown in table 8.3, the statistical profile of revenue mobilization over the 2008–2017 period suggests that FAT revenues

- have generally been stable in nominal terms, staying within the range of JPY 8.5 trillion to 9 trillion, but they have declined as a percentage of total revenues raised;

- declined to 8.67 percent in FY 2017, down from 10.3 percent in 2008, of total subnational government revenues, after having reached a peak of 11.6 percent in 2009; and

- covered about 18 percent of subnational government expenditures in 2008, but by 2016, the share had fallen to a little more than 15 percent.

Table 8.4 outlines the revenues from the three major components of the FAT, for 2008 to 2018. The table shows that, over the decade, revenues from buildings (residences, offices, factories, etc.) have consistently exceeded revenues from land. In Japan's property and land taxation regime, the FAT levies on buildings and land are assessed separately (albeit not with split rates). Before 2002, revenues from land exceeded those from buildings.

Table 8.5 lists revenues forgone by exemptions, as calculated by the Ministry of Internal Affairs and Communications for 2015 (the most recent year for which data are available). The table shows that the total assessed cost of exemptions for 2015 was just under JPY 237 billion, of which 56.2 percent was due to exemptions pertaining to dwellings, 3.4 percent for land, and 40.4 percent for depreciable assets.

Overview of Property Taxes

This section describes Japan's three main types of property taxes, including tax rates and revenues from each. As noted earlier, the FAT is the jurisdiction's principal recurrent tax on immobile property and land. There are also two comparatively minor, municipal recurrent taxes on property: the CPT and the business office tax.

FAT

Municipalities (and Tokyo Metropolitan Government for its 23 special wards) levy the FAT on agricultural and residential land, structures (residential buildings, factories, and other buildings), and depreciable assets (e.g., construction equipment, machinery, and factory equipment). The

Table 8.4 Japan FAT Categories and Revenue, 2008–2018 (JPY trillion)

Year	2008	2009	2010	2011	2012	2013	2014	2015	2016	2017	2018
Total	8.78	8.78	8.86	8.87	8.49	8.56	8.68	8.63	8.77	8.88	8.94
Buildings	3.73	3.66	3.78	3.87	3.55	3.65	3.75	3.68	3.77	3.86	3.81
Land	3.41	3.47	3.48	3.44	3.40	3.37	3.38	3.39	3.38	3.37	3.44
Depreciable assets	1.64	1.65	1.61	1.56	1.54	1.54	1.55	1.57	1.61	1.65	1.69

Source: MIC (2019b).

Table 8.5 Total Value of FAT Exemptions, by Category, 2015

	Buildings	Land	Depreciable Assets
Value (JPY billion)	133.0	8.1	95.6
% of total	56.2	3.4	40.4

Source: MIC (2019b).

Local Tax Law grants the municipalities the authority to levy the FAT via their own ordinances and in accordance with the Local Tax Law.

The standard FAT rate is 1.4 percent of assessed value (explained in detail later). For land, this is about 70 percent of the public valuation and is applied at the same rate across property classes in the same jurisdiction. Taxing at a level lower than 1.4 percent is allowed, but in most cases would result in reduced intergovernmental grants and reduced local tax revenue.[2] As one example of recent decentralization reforms, the maximum FAT rate of 2.1 percent was abolished in 2004, giving municipalities greater taxation autonomy. Table 8.6 summarizes key aspects of the FAT.

Table 8.7 shows that 1,566 (91.1 percent) of the 1,719 municipalities (including Tokyo) levy the tax at the standard rate of 1.4 percent, and only 153 (8.9 percent) opt to tax above the standard rate, referred to in Japanese as *chouka kazei* (excess taxation). The term is not pejorative but rather taken as an indicator of tax effort.

Tax effort varies by population. Japan's 28 large cities with populations exceeding 500,000 all levy the FAT at the standard rate of 1.4 percent. Of cities at the next category of population size, below 500,000 but over 50,000, 454 (92.8 percent) levy the FAT at the standard rate, and 35 (7.2 percent) tax at the higher rates of between 1.4 and 1.8 percent. Of the 275 cities with populations under 50,000, 224 (81.5 percent) levy the FAT at 1.4 percent and 51 (18.5 percent) opt for rates over 1.4 and below 1.8 percent. When it comes to Japan's 744 towns and 183 villages (some of which have populations in the tens of thousands), 860 (92.8 percent) of the combined total of 927 levy the FAT at the standard rate, and 153 (8.9 percent) tax over the standard rate but under 1.8 percent. None of Japan's cities, towns, and villages impose a levy above 1.8 percent, let alone over the 2.1 percent limit that was abolished in 2004.

CPT

The tax base of the CPT, similar to the FAT's, is land and buildings; however, the CPT is not levied on depreciable assets. The CPT revenues totaled

Table 8.6 FAT Characteristics, FY 2018

Object of taxation	Land, buildings, and depreciable assets
Taxing authority	1,718 municipalities (cities, towns, and villages) plus Tokyo Metropolitan Government (on behalf of its 23 special wards) assess, levy, and collect the tax
Taxpayers	Registered owners of land, buildings, and depreciable assets in cadastre as of January 1. As of FY 2018, the cadastre lists 40.91 million persons owning land; 41.48 million persons owning buildings; and 4.50 million persons owning depreciable assets.
Taxation standard	Valuation, with land and buildings being assessed every three years (the most recent assessment being 2018 and the next scheduled for 2021)
Tax rate	Standard tax rate: 1.4%
Tax value thresholds	Land: JPY 300,000 Buildings: JPY 200,000 Depreciable assets: JPY 1.5 million
Imposition date	January 1 of the taxation year
Tax revenues[1]	JPY 8.94 trillion, of which land = JPY 3.87 trillion (43.32%); buildings = JPY 3.88 trillion (43.44%); and depreciable assets = JPY 1.67 trillion (18.66%).

Source: MIC (2019b).
[1] Data for tax revenues are from FY 2017, but other data are FY 2018.

JPY 1.227 trillion in FY 2017. The CPT was adopted in 1956 to cope with the stresses of high postwar economic growth on urban infrastructure (Fukui et al. 2017). Thus, its revenues are, in principle, earmarked to finance city planning and land readjustment projects. But in practice, the CPT revenues flow into general revenues. The Local Tax Law allows municipalities to set the CPT tax rate as high as 0.3 percent. Many municipalities either do not levy the tax or set the rate below the 0.3 percent limit. In FY 2018, 647 of the 1,719 municipalities levied the CPT (table 8.8).

In 2021, the most recent comprehensive data on CPT tax rates was for FY 2015, when 651 of 1,719 municipalities imposed the levy. Many imposed it at less than the standard tax rate of 0.3 percent, as shown in table 8.9. This standard rate is the maximum rate allowed under the Local Tax Law.

Table 8.7 FAT Rates by Municipal Population, 2018

| Tax Rate Municipal Pop. | Below Standard Rate <1.4% | Standard Rate 1.4% (A) | Excess Taxation | | | | | | |
			>1.4%–<1.6%	>1.6%–<1.8%	>1.8%	Subtotal (B)	Total (C)	A÷C (%)	B÷C (%)
>500,000	0	28	0	0	0	0	28	100	0
50,000–500,000	0	454	34	1	0	35	489	92.8	7.2
<50,000	0	224	48	3	0	51	275	81.5	18.5
Towns and villages	0	860	52	15	0	67	927	92.8	7.2
Total	**0**	**1,566**	**134**	**19**	**0**	**153**	**1,719**	**91.1**	**8.9**

Source: MIC (2019a).

Table 8.8 CPT Characteristics, FY 2018

Object of taxation	Land and residences within municipal boundaries: 42.23 million plots and 30.10 million buildings
Taxing authority	Municipalities that have city planning areas: 647 tax-levying municipalities
Taxpayers	Owners of land or buildings: 21.83 million landholders, 27.10 milllon building owners
Taxation base	Value (appropriate current price), with FAT standard as appropriate price valuation
Tax rate	Up to 0.3%
Tax value thresholds	Land, JPY 300,000; buildings, JPY 200,000
Imposition date	January 1 of the taxation year
Tax revenues[1]	JPY 1.277 trillion (of which land, JPY 680 billion; buildings, JPY 596.7 billion)

Source: MIC (2019b).

[1] Data for tax revenues are from FY 2017, but other data are FY 2018.

Table 8.9 CPT Rates, FY 2015

Tax Rate	No. of Municipalities Imposing Tax Rate	% Imposing Tax Rate
0.3%	328	50.4
>0.2%–<0.3%	269	41.3
<0.2%	54	8.3

Source: MIC (2015).

Business Office Tax

A somewhat hybridized form of property and land taxation is the business office tax (BOT; *jigyoushozei*), first instituted in 1975 to cope with the stresses of rapid urbanization in large cities. As of January 1, 2019, the 77 cities that levy the BOT are those with populations over 300,000 and the special wards of Tokyo Metropolitan Government. In precise legal terms, this is a tax on use (*shiyou*) rather than possession (*shoyuu*) per se. The object of the tax is firms whose office facilities exceed a floor area of 1,000 m², employ more than 100 workers who are deemed regular staff according to the BOT, or both. The tax rates are JPY 600/m² of floor space and 0.25 percent of the total amount of employee salaries. Generally, businesses with under 800 m² of office space within the given municipality are exempt from reporting requirements, and those with less than

1,000 m² of office space are exempt from taxpaying obligations. In addition, firms are exempt from tax-reporting requirements if they have fewer than 80 staff within the municipality, and they are exempt from taxpaying obligations if their total number of staff (total number in the relevant municipality minus staff not subject to tax regulation, such as part-time workers) is under 100 people.

Revenues from the BOT in FY 2017 totaled JPY 371.2 billion, of which JPY 253.1 billion (71.4 percent) were derived from real estate assets and JPY 95.3 billion (28.6 percent) were derived from the levy on the aggregate amount of employee salaries. The tax revenues are, in principle, earmarked for the upkeep and improvement of transport-related assets such as roadways; parks, green space, and other public areas; water mains, sewers, waste-treatment facilities, and other infrastructure for delivery or disposal; canals and other waterways; schools, libraries, and other facilities for education and culture; hospital, day care, and other health and welfare-related facilities; work related to pollution control; work related to disaster prevention; and other work, such as for urban development or otherwise maintaining or enhancing the urban environment.

The Property Tax Base, Administration, and Assessment

Japan's recurrent property tax system is revenue productive but complicated, as described in the following, which also identifies its strengths and weaknesses.

Types of Land

There are 23 different types of land in Japan for the purposes of the property registration law. These types of land generally differentiate by function, such as residential land, water supply lands, railway lands, school lands, and similar roles ("Types of Land," n.d.). The FAT definition of land is based on the land-registration law and its elements, but it aggregates the 23 different types of land into a total of 10 categories (Management of Information and Appraisal Council, n.d.).

Table 8.10 provides an accounting of the types of land pertinent to the FAT, listing their area in units of 10,000 hectares and in terms of the percentage of total national lands. The total area and percentage of urban areas are at the bottom of the table for comparison.

The FAT Base

The tax base for the FAT is not market value but rather the assessed value of the taxable fixed property listed in the FAT registration cadastre compiled

Table 8.10 Distribution of Lands, 2012

Type of Land	Area (10,000 hectares)	% Total
Agricultural land	454	12.0
Mountains and forests	2,506	66.4
Wilderness	34	0.9
Waterways	134	3.6
Roads	137	3.6
Residential lands	190	5.0
Housing	116	3.1
Industrial	15	0.4
Other residential	59	1.6
Other lands	324	8.6
Total	**3,780**	**100**
Urban areas[1]	**127**	**3.4**

Source: MLIT (2017).

[1] Urban areas are high-population-density districts, based on the 2010 census.

by each municipality. The FAT assessment is one of Japan's four publicly undertaken assessments of land values and can be summarized as roughly 70 percent of the public valuation undertaken annually by the Ministry of Land, Infrastructure, Transport, and Tourism (see box 8.2). The FAT assessment is also undertaken for buildings, using a replacement cost approach. Regarding depreciable assets, the valuation is derived from the

---

Box 8.2 PROPERTY TAX ASSESSMENT

Some of the important features of the property tax assessment system in Japan are summarized in the following table.

Assessment	Assessment Authority	Frequency of Assessment	Results Are Published
FAT valuation	Municipality	Triennial	April–June
Basic valuation	Prefecture	Annual	September
Public valuation	Ministry of Land, Infrastructure, Transport, and Tourism	Annual	January 1
Road tax rating	National Tax Agency	Annual	January 1

Source: Kyoto Association of Real Estate Appraisers (n.d.).

Municipalities triennially revise the FAT assessment valuation. As of 2021, the most recent year of assessment revision was 2018, and the next assessment revision is scheduled for 2021. The basis of assessment revision is roughly 70 percent of the public valuation, and the revision is compiled for municipal residents' property holdings as of January 1. In principle, the result of the triennial assessment is reported to taxpayers between April and June, depending on the individual municipality's relevant bylaw.

Prefectures assess the basic valuation, employing real estate appraisers for the purpose. The mechanism for assessment is an annual survey, on July 1, of over 20,000 land parcels nationwide. Each land parcel assessment is done by more than one real estate appraiser. The sample results are then generalized, and land values are announced on or about September 20 of the same year.

The Ministry of Land, Infrastructure, Transport, and Tourism annually compiles the public valuation, on the basis of holdings of January 1. The sample includes 23,000 parcels nationwide (many overlapping with the basic valuation survey sample). Each land parcel assessment is done by more than two real estate appraisers and sets reference values that are then generalized for all land values. The results are published annually in mid-March and inform assessments for taxation purposes.

The National Tax Agency annually performs the road tax rating, on the basis of January 1 data. The public valuation, traded market values, and real estate appraisals form the basis of this assessment. And as the assessment's name implies, it applies to parcels adjacent to roads. Hence, most of the reference base for this assessment is within urban and developed rural areas. The assessment results are generally about 80 percent of the public valuation noted earlier and are published in early July. The National Tax Agency uses the assessments for levying transfer and gift taxes on real estate, and it uses the FAT assessment valuation in areas where the road tax rating cannot be determined, such as some rural areas and many agricultural and forested or mountainous regions.

amount of depreciation or depreciable expense incurred in generating income reported for the national corporate or individual income tax.

The FAT assessments for land, buildings, and depreciable assets are undertaken by the municipalities in accordance with a nationally unified formula. The overall formula for assessing the value of taxable fixed property is determined by the minister of Internal Affairs and Communications, the Japanese central-government agency responsible for subnational governments' finances. The ministry's uniform formula for valuing assets and computing assessments is key to ensuring that each municipality's assessment is essentially unified and thus that the property tax system is fair and equitable (Kitazato 2004).[3]

In practice, however, Japan's valuation and assessment of land, dwellings, and other assets for the FAT is quite complicated. Indeed, the ministry's guide to assessments is reputedly as thick as a telephone book. This complexity results in limited understanding among taxpayers, onerous assessment procedures in staff-strapped local governments, and numerous mistaken assessments that undermine taxpayer trust. The problem is further exacerbated by interaction with the three other public property assessments (see box 8.2).

Registering Land

Registering land as residential, which secures eligibility for special tax measures (discussed later), is not automatic. Rather, the owner must file a "Notification of Residential Land, etc. for Fixed Assets Tax Purposes" (for the first five items listed here) or a "Notification of Disaster-Damaged Residential Land for Fixed Assets Tax Purposes" (for the sixth and last item listed here) with the municipal tax office that has jurisdiction over the area in which the land is located. The filing deadline is January 31 of the year in which the land is to become taxable.

Conditions making land eligible for special tax measures are the following:

- Acquisition or construction of a new residential building.

- Demolition of all or part of a residential building.

- Reconstruction of a residential building.

- Conversion of all or part of an existing building (e.g., from a shop to a house).

- Change in land use (e.g., conversion to a parking lot).

- Destruction of, or damage to, a residential building through natural disasters and similar events.

The Legal Affairs Bureau of the Ministry of Justice maintains a registry of fixed property (land and buildings). The ministry's branch offices throughout the jurisdiction register property in their respective areas and report purchases or transfers of property to the municipalities. In turn, the municipalities use the national registry to check that their registries are current. As explained later, the increasingly dire problem of tracing land and building ownership suggests these mechanisms are inadequate and in need of reform.

Valuing Land

In principle, land is reassessed every third year on the basis of the Ministry of Land, Infrastructure, Transport, and Tourism's public valuation, actual market prices of several similar tracts of land, and other survey evidence. Under normal circumstances, that assessed value is maintained for the subsequent two years. In practice, however, assessments are undertaken whenever required—for example, when land plots are subdivided or consolidated or when dwellings are newly built, expanded, or renovated.

The triennial FAT assessments are undertaken by real estate appraisers, contracted by the municipal offices. Land and buildings are valued separately. Land assessments are performed according to the 10 different types of land relevant to property taxation (e.g., residential land, agricultural land, and mountains and forests). In each municipality, multiple plots of land are selected to be a standard for assessing other areas types of land. This selection of standard plots begins with defining districts with roughly similar characteristics, such that the selected standard plot will be representative of nearby plots. Then a major roadway bordering the standard plot is chosen. An assessment is then made of the standard residential plot, or standard residential land (*byoujun takuchi*), and about 70 percent of the assessed value is posted as the road tax rating (*rosenka*). This roadside land valuation is then used as the basis for assessing other values along other (nonmajor) roadways. These valuations for roadways and plots are based on distances from the nearest railway station, the dimensions of the roadway, and other relevant factors. The values of residential plots are then expressed per square meter. Outside cities, the assessment omits the use of roadways as a guide to valuation. Instead, the plots near a standard residential land plot are assessed in proportion to that standard plot.

Agricultural Land

The taxable value of agricultural land is assessed in a manner similar to residential land. The assessment starts with selecting standard plots of agricultural land in each area. One key difference from residential land assessment is that agricultural land is divided into general agricultural land (*ippan nouchi*) and urban agricultural land (*shigaichikuiki nouchi*). General agricultural land is situated outside municipal city-planning areas and assessed against the value of standard plots relevant to that category.

In contrast, urban agricultural land is farmland within city-planning areas. This agricultural land is separated into three distinct categories: (1) land deemed to be in a productive green land district; (2) land deemed to be general urban area agricultural land; and (3) agricultural land deemed to be in one of the 190 designated cities in the three major metropolitan areas (centered on Tokyo, Nagoya, and Osaka). Agricultural land in de-fined urban areas of the municipality and in a productive green land dis-trict is assessed as agricultural land and is also taxed as agricultural land. Agricultural land designated as general urban area agricultural land is as-sessed as residential land but taxed as agricultural land. Agricultural land in the third category, within one of the designated cities, is both assessed and taxed as residential land.

In practice, the FAT burden per 10 ares (equivalent to 1,000 m²) varies considerably according to the category. For general agricultural land, the burden per 1,000 m² is JPY 1,000. The burden rises severalfold if the land is classified as urban agricultural land in a productive green land district. The burden rises an order of magnitude, to several tens of thousands of JPY per 1,000 m², if the land is general urban area agricultural land, and it then rises a further order of magnitude, to several hundred thousand JPY per 1,000 m², if the agricultural land is in one of the 190 designated cities in the three major metropolitan areas.

Hence, the average assessed value of farmland in Japan is JPY 70/m², which is roughly equivalent to 0.2 percent of the value of residential land. One reason is that the assessment of fields is discounted 45 percent to the public valuation and other varied assessments of market prices. The low burden of assessment and taxation is thought to be a major reason that about 400,000 hectares of Japan's farmland lies idle. These issues are dif-ficult to address because they are national policy and concern multiple stakeholders. The OECD argues that Japan's problem of idle farmland is "due to the production quota system and the complex web of laws govern-ing land ownership, transfer, use and taxation" (OECD 2015, 2).

Residential Land

Just as Japanese agricultural policy influences the assessment and taxation of agricultural land, Japanese housing policy influences the assessment and taxation of residential land. There are significant incentives to use vacant land (*sarachi*) for housing and to thus deem it residential land (*takuchi*) for tax purposes. The scale of these incentives derives in part from rapid post-war growth that saw large population flows from the rural, agricultural sector to the industrializing and urban areas. The incentives also reflect the role of structures, especially homes, as commodities expected to de-preciate rapidly in value and to be replaced within a few decades.

Incentives for residential land are displayed in table 8.11, The table shows that, in accordance with national law, plots of residential land 200 m² or less are taxed on the basis of one-sixth of the assessed value of the plot, as small-scale housing-use land (*shokibo juutaku youchi*). Portions of lots that exceed 200 m² are taxed at one-third of the assessed value, as general

Table 8.11 Special Measures for Tokyo Residential Land, FY 2019

Residential Land Area		FAT	CPT
Small-scale	Up to 200 m²	⅙ assessed value	⅓ assessed value
General	More than 200 m²	⅓ assessed value	⅔ assessed value

Source: TMG (2019).

housing-use land (*ippan juutaku youchi*). In other words, the tax base for residential land is one-sixth of the assessed value for up to 200 m² and one-third of the assessed value for the portion that exceeds 200 m². The table shows that these incentives also apply to the CPT, at least as levied by Tokyo Metropolitan Government on behalf of its 23 special wards.

Valuing Dwellings

In practice, the taxable value of a house or building is determined by direct assessment by the relevant municipal authorities (in the city office's Fixed Asset Assessment Division). The Local Tax Law accords the appropriate municipal tax-assessment officers the legal authority to visit the premises and undertake an assessment. Refusal to cooperate with the assessment team (usually two people from the division, who are obliged to show identification when requested) or other obstruction can be subject to penalty. The taxpayer or a representative must be at the premises to allow entry so that the inside walls, ceilings, fixtures, and other particulars can be assessed. The assessment differs if the building is new as opposed to existing. In both cases, however, the assessed value is the result of numerous grading factor points (such as the reconstruction cost) multiplied by the value assigned per grade. Recent changes have also introduced a floor-level adjustment, because of the increasing number of tall buildings. The great complexity of Japanese building assessment, in terms of materials and other aspects, appears to reflect Japan's lack of standardization in methods of construction.

In assessments, the reconstruction cost is defined as the cost of building the same structure as the one under assessment, calculated by aggregating the estimated prices of the materials and other items used to build it. The reconstruction costs cover only the replacement value of the materials, exclusive of the structure's design and construction. The depreciation adjustment accounts for aging of the structure. Depreciation rates differ significantly by type of building, but all are set so that even after

65 years (for offices built of reinforced concrete), 20 percent of the initial reconstruction cost remains.[4] A correction regarding interregional differences in the price levels (relative to the level in Tokyo) is among the allowable adjustments, which also include measures to incorporate costs of design and construction.

Tax Reductions and Exemptions for Structures

A host of tax reductions and exemptions apply to Japan's FAT levied on buildings, especially residential housing and condominiums. The most commonly cited is the tax reduction for new detached homes. This reduction is especially important in light of the relatively short lifetime of houses, noted previously.

Tax rules provide a FAT reduction of 50 percent for the first three taxable years. This reduction applied to new houses built by March 31, 2020, with a dwelling floor space of 50–280 m^2. For new condominiums (over three floors), the 50 percent FAT reduction was for the first five taxable years, with the stipulation that per-unit floor space be a maximum of 120 m^2.

Even larger tax reductions are provided for long-term, high-quality houses (*chouki sairyou juutaku*) that are built to be used over many decades, are crafted with special attention to the living environment, and otherwise meet guidelines set by authorities in the Ministry of Land, Infrastructure, Transport, and Tourism. These homes are part of the 200-Year Lifespan House initiative of the ministry. The initiative aims to raise the market share of long-term, high-quality houses from 8.8 percent in 2010 to 20 percent by 2020 were met. Up to March 31, 2020, these long-term buildings were eligible for 50 percent FAT reductions for five years if the building was a general residence. If the building was a condominium of three stories or greater, with a per-unit floor space not exceeding 120 m^2, the FAT reduction is for seven years.

Similarly, remodeling a home to enhance the safety and comfort of an elderly resident was eligible for a two-thirds reduction in the FAT for five years, for work undertaken between October 20, 2011, and March 31, 2015.

Other reductions that apply to the FAT aim at bolstering the durability of homes, their energy efficiency, their deployment of renewable energy (e.g., solar and solar heating), and their accessibility for disabled residents. A typical example is earthquake proofing: From January 1, 2013, through March 31, 2020, home renovations aimed at earthquake proofing were targeted at homes built before January 1, 1982. The reduction was 50 percent of the FAT for one year and was applied to 120 m^2 of dwelling space.

Tokyo Metropolitan Government also has even more robust tax-reduction and exemption measures, largely centered on bolstering structures against earthquake and fire threats. Up to March 31, 2020, Tokyo exempted the entirety (not just 50 percent) of the FAT and the CPT for three years for the replacement of residential buildings constructed before January 1, 1982. The measure was to encourage greater earthquake proofing of buildings throughout Tokyo's 23 special wards. And if a building constructed before January 1, 1982, was not replaced but rather renovated for earthquake proofing, it was eligible for a full year of complete exemption from the FAT and the CPT. A special FAT and CPT exemption of two years was possible if the renovated structure was originally noncompliant with earthquake resistance standards and was at risk of blocking roadways in the event of an earthquake.

Tokyo has specific fireproofing districts (*funenka tokku*) where reconstruction of structures, subject to certain restrictions on area and original building materials, can result in exemption from the FAT and CPT for five years from completion of the rebuild.

Defining Depreciable Assets

As noted earlier, the FAT applies to land and buildings, as the CPT does, but also to depreciable assets. In FY 2018, the revenues from taxing these assets via the FAT was just over JPY 1.69 trillion.

The taxable value of these tangible business assets accounts for the cost and amount of depreciation. The valuation of depreciable capital excludes items subject to the automobile or light-vehicle tax (e.g., light forklifts). It also excludes intangibles (software, patents), deferred assets, capital that has a depreciation period of less than a year or a value of less than JPY 100,000, and leases involving assets with an acquisition cost of less than JPY 200,000. Depreciable assets with a value of less than JPY 1,500,000 (the tax threshold) are not subject to taxation via the FAT.

Other FAT Exemptions

Also exempt from the FAT are many of the 23 types of land discussed previously and detailed in the property registration law, often with the stipulation that the property be for public use.[5] Religious properties are also exempt, as are schools and care facilities for the elderly and disabled persons owned by social-welfare corporations. Fixed assets owned by the national government, prefectures, municipalities, and embassies and consulates of foreign jurisdictions are also exempt.

In consequence of these tax rules, all the assets owned by local public corporations, including social housing, hospitals and health facilities, day care centers, libraries, museums, research facilities, and the like, are exempt from the FAT (as well as the CPT). The scale of this exemption is quite significant. For example, Japan's social housing, or public rental housing (*kouteki chintai juutaku*), totaled almost 1.1 million units as of the end of 2018. The assessment takes into account the cost of replacement, depreciation over years in use, and other factors.

Adjusting Asset Burdens

Japan's FAT assessment was altered to cope with rapid urbanization, the emergence of the 1980s bubble economy, and the subsequent collapse followed by low growth and accelerating aging coupled with depopulation. Before the 1980s, assessed property values were very low compared with market prices. This led to concern that low property taxation fueled land speculation. A large-scale reform was undertaken in 1994. Since that year, Japan has deployed special measures to adjust tax burdens on land caused by the effects of the 1980s asset bubble. Yet just before the 1994 tax reform, the FAT assessment's triennial result came out (in FY 1993) and showed a 350 percent nationwide increase in assessed property values. The best course of action was thought to be gradual increases of a maximum 15 percent over a three-year period, via a burden adjustment mechanism (*futan chousei sochi*). The adjustment also set the FAT assessment of land at 70 percent of the Ministry of Land, Infrastructure, Transport, and Tourism's public price valuation (Jinno and DeWit 1998).

As the 1990s unfolded, land prices dropped precipitously, and assessments were further adjusted in light of the new reality. One measure was adjustment rates (a ratio of taxable value to real assessed value) that moderated tax shifts (Kitazato 2004). In recent years, the key issue has been moderating the potential for rapid shifts in tax burdens, increases and decreases in the value of the underlying asset, via burden adjustment mechanisms that cope with rising residential and commercial land values in big cities (especially in the Tokyo Metropolitan Government region) while the regions experience a general decline. The mechanism takes the current year's valuation as 100 and then adds 5 percent to the previous year's valuation. If the previous year's valuation plus the 5 percent adjustment is less than the current year's valuation (i.e., 100), then that result becomes the valuation. For example, if the land valuation rises 7 percent over the previous year, the actual increase in taxable value will be only 2 percent (Ichinomiya City 2019). Tokyo Metropolitan Government calculates a tax burden level by dividing the FY 2018 taxable value of the asset by the 2019 assessed value and then multiplying the result by 100. The result is the "level of discrepancy between the price and the standard taxable value" (TMG 2019, 40). A tax burden level of 100 percent or more on residential land leads to no change in the regular standard taxable value (meaning the assessed value multiplied by one-sixth or one-third, depending on the size of the residential plot). But for tax burden levels below 100 percent, the tax payable gradually increases.

As for commercial land in Tokyo, a tax burden level of 70 percent or more leads to a reduction of the legal upper limit (70 percent of the price) of the applied standard taxable value. For burdens between 60 and 70 percent, the standard taxable value for the previous year is applied. Burdens of lower than 60 percent lead to a gradual tax increase.

Tax Collection

Since the early years of this century, Japan's fiscal crisis and demographic challenges have led Japanese municipal authorities to tighten their collection of FAT and other taxes. Virtually all the municipalities strongly encourage taxpayers to pay the tax levied on their property by providing ample notice of assessment and explaining the purposes of property taxation. In most of Tokyo's wards and municipalities, taxpayers receive notice of their FAT and CPT (where applicable) levy in June, which is also the first month for payment of the quarterly burden. The subsequent payment deadlines are in September, December, and February. The tax levy can also be paid in one lump sum in the initial payment period (e.g., June, if that is the month of initial notice), though no discount is gained through a lump-sum payment. In most Japanese municipalities, the payment deadlines for the FAT and CPT are the last day of April, July, December, and February. An example of a variation is the city of Yokohama's FAT and CPT payment deadlines being April 30, July 31, January 4, and February 29.

Ministry of Internal Affairs and Communications surveys for 2017 indicate that collection of the FAT and CPT were, respectively, 99.3 percent and 99.4 percent of assessments. The options for payment include ordinary banks and postal banks, most convenience stores, the Pay-easy network (Japan Multi-Payment Network Management Organization, which allows payment via the Internet or ATMs, and the postal service (i.e., a registered bank transfer). Bank transfers can also be set up to automatically forward the tax payment from the taxpayer's account to the municipality's account at a specified time. Beginning in 2015, Tokyo has also included FAT payments among the taxes that can be paid via credit card. The Tokyo Metropolitan Government has quite detailed web pages on the property and land taxation assessment and payment system in English, Chinese, and Korean.

Tax Delinquency

The laws and regulations use carrots and sticks to cope with delinquency, as the high collection rates attest. First, taxpayers are strongly advised to contact the assessment office in the relevant municipality if they find it difficult to make the required tax payment. All evidence indicates that the municipal authorities are quite willing to negotiate, preferring to receive some cash rather than having to seize and dispose of assets. Resolution mechanisms include postponement of payment, reduction of the burden, and other measures deemed suitable for any given case.

If a taxpayer misses a payment or does not pay the full amount without prior consultation, the municipality issues a reminder and also makes contact via telephone or dispatches staff to visit the noncompliant taxpayer. From the point of delinquency, the municipality also begins charging a late penalty on the taxes in arrears. This penalty (*honsoku no wariai*) is in principle a 2.6 percent rate of interest for the first month of arrears, a rate that increases to 8.9 percent the next month. In practice, these rates of penalty are adjusted to align with changes in the prime rate. A special rate (*tokurei no wariai*) is also calculated annually by the minister of Finance and based on the annual average for new short-term borrowing at domestic banks from October to September of two years prior. The special rate is 1 percent above this prevailing rate of bank interest.

If the above measures fail to induce the delinquent taxpayer to pay the sum in arrears within 10 days, the municipal authorities are legally empowered to investigate the taxpayer's financial and property assets (such as an automobile). Assets are valued by, for example, visiting the taxpayer's place of work, questioning financial institutions where the taxpayer conducts transactions (such as maintaining a savings account), and directly inspecting assets at the delinquent's residence. After assessing assets, the authorities are empowered to seize them to cover the amount in arrears directly or via proceeds raised through public auction. These steps are all codified in the Local Tax Law.

Property and Land Taxes in Tokyo

As of March 31, 2019, the total population under the authority of the Tokyo Metropolitan Government (TMG) was 13.86 million, an increase of over 103,000 residents from the previous year. During this same time, Japan's total population declined by 330,587, to 126.85 million. The TMG encompasses 2,191 km², and its economic output in 2014 of JPY 94.9 trillion was 19.4 percent of Japan's GDP.

The TMG itself is a regional government that comprises 23 special wards (e.g., Shinjuku-ku, Toshima-ku), 26 cities, 5 towns, and 8 villages.

This structure dates back to 1943, at the height of World War II in the Pacific Theater, when the former Tokyo Prefecture and Tokyo City were merged for greater efficiency. As an administrative entity, TMG's relationship with its wards is comparatively unique, even within Japan. The TMG undertakes several of the functions that the wards would ordinarily perform (being administratively equivalent to cities): it collects property and land taxation revenues on behalf of the wards, but it also provides regional water supply, firefighting, and sewerage services. The metropolitan-wide provision of these services is unusual, because Japanese cities ordinarily perform them as part of the urban package of spatially defined public services. It is generally more efficient and effective to leave these functions to the municipal authority, which has the best understanding of local conditions coupled with the closest relationship to citizen-voters. But Tokyo's density of over 15,000 inhabitants/km^2 within the 600 km^2 area of the 23 special wards changes the fiscal and administrative math. This density allows service-delivery efficiencies and intercity equity to be maximized through a regional system that is simultaneously closely consultative. This collaboration is institutionalized in a Metropolitan-Ward Council (TMG 2018).

Residential and commercial land values in TMG are much greater than elsewhere in the jurisdiction, reflecting its density and other attributes as a global city. The assessment of land values nationwide released July 1, 2019, by the National Tax Agency indicated that these differences have grown. Nationwide, average values of all land increased 0.4 percent for 2019. But in TMG these property values rose by 2.2 percent. The other large city-regions also saw their overall land values increase, whereas the majority of municipalities saw declining values. The TMG generally finances over 70 percent of its spending via taxes. This level of revenue autonomy is far higher than the 30–40 percent average among Japanese subnational governments. And as a result of its high property values, the TMG is able to finance much more of its overall revenues from all sources via the FAT.

Table 8.12 shows that between 2008 and 2018, FAT revenues consistently composed more than 16 percent of revenues from all sources. This table also displays FAT revenues as a share of TMG's total tax revenues for the same period. The data show that TMG's FAT revenues exceeded 22 percent of total tax revenues during the decade.

Table 8.13 displays Tokyo's CPT revenues as a share of total taxation for 2008–2018. The ratio has fluctuated from 3.6 percent in 2008 to a high of 5.2 percent for 2011 and 2012, and it was 4.6 percent for 2018.

In 2016, TMG's per capita revenues from the FAT of JPY 107,900 were considerably higher than the national average of JPY 70,100 (MIC, 2019b). Also in FY 2016, TMG's FAT revenues were JPY 642/m^2 for residential

Table 8.12 Tokyo's Property Tax Revenues, 2008–2018

Year	2008	2009	2010	2011	2012	2013	2014	2015	2016	2017	2018
FAT (JPY trillion)	1.43	1.06	1.11	1.13	1.11	1.11	1.14	1.16	1.18	1.19	1.24
Total own-source revenue (JPY trillion)	6.86	6.60	6.26	6.24	6.15	6.26	6.67	6.95	7.11	6.95	7.46
Total city tax revenue (JPY trillion)	5.51	4.76	4.15	4.22	4.12	4.28	4.67	5.22	5.21	5.91	5.23
FAT as % of own-source revenue	20.9	17.0	17.7	18.1	18.1	17.7	17.1	16.7	16.6	17.1	16.6
FAT as % of city tax revenue	26.0	22.4	26.8	26.9	26.8	26.0	24.5	23.1	22.6	23.4	23.7

Source: Hato (2019).

Table 8.13 Tokyo's CPT Revenues, 2008–2018

Year	2008	2009	2010	2011	2012	2013	2014	2015	2016	2017	2018
CPT (JPY 100 billion)	1.96	2.02	2.14	2.19	2.14	2.16	2.21	2.21	2.28	2.30	2.40
Total revenue (JPY 100 billion)	55.1	47.6	41.5	42.2	41.2	42.8	46.7	52.2	52.1	59.1	52.3
% revenues	3.6	4.2	5.1	5.2	5.2	5.1	4.7	4.4	4.4	4.5	4.6

Source: Hato (2019).

land, 5.7 times the national average of JPY 113. The gap in revenues from commercial property was even more pronounced: TMG's JPY 5,248/m² was 16 times the national average of JPY 322.

Recent and Ongoing Reforms

Japan's property and land taxation collection, appeals, and enforcement mechanisms are generally sound. But with accelerating population aging and depopulation, the institutions for keeping track of asset ownership are encountering severe difficulties as local economies flounder. Major reforms to the property and land taxation tax regime have focused on clarifying ownership of abandoned residences, incentivizing urban agriculture, and addressing the larger (and more contentious) issues of local revitalization and industrial policy.

Clarifying Ownership of Abandoned Residences

A reform to the FAT is a special measure to incentivize disposal of Japan's increasing number of empty residences (*akiya*). The Statistics Bureau of the Ministry of Internal Affairs and Communications compiles five-year comprehensive data on empty residences, which indicate that, as of October 2018, Japan's total housing stock stood at 62.42 million houses, a 3.0 percent increase from 2013. During the same five years, the number of empty, and presumably abandoned, homes increased by 0.1 percent, or 260,000 units, to a total of 8.2 million units. This latter figure represented 13.6 percent of the total housing stock. Significant regional variations saw a high of 21.3 percent in Yamanashi Prefecture, a low of 10.2 percent in Saitama Prefecture (adjacent Tokyo), and 10.6 percent in Tokyo itself (MIC 2018b).

Public health threats posed by increasing numbers of uninhabited dwellings led to the Special Measures for Empty Residence Law of 2015. The law's provisions allow municipal officials to enter "specified empty residences" (*tokutei akiya*) suspected of being permanently uninhabited and posing risks. The law confers on officials powers of administrative guidance and the authority to levy penalties. The law also specifically permits use of FAT-related data to determine ownership. Moreover, as of May 2015, the law allows the land on which an uninhabited dwelling stands to be declared vacant land (*sarachi*) rather than residential land (*takuchi*). As noted earlier, these two designations of land result in a sixfold difference in the FAT levy, because residential land under 200 m² is given a special tax exemption of one-sixth vacant land.

The object of the tax change was to incentivize homeowners to either repair, sell, or dispose of the house. But the ownership of lands and buildings is increasingly uncertain because of registration costs and other reasons. Hence, the threat of an increase in the FAT burden is often not sufficient to settle the matter, leaving the municipality shouldering the cost. Indeed, the first use of the new law to dispose of an abandoned house occurred October 26, 2015, in Kanagawa Prefecture's Yokosuka City. The city officials had received complaints that the structure was in danger of collapsing into the street, and upon passage of the law a check of the premises' FAT registration confirmed that ownership was unclear. In other words, there was no party to pay the fee for disposal of the premises. Because of the danger of the building's collapse, the city had to assume the JPY 1.5 million cost (*Yomiuri Shimbun* 2015).

Compounding the building ownership problem is the increasing uncertainty over land ownership, due to outdated institutional mechanisms for recording ownership. We have seen that Japan undertakes extensive cadastral surveys, but it still relies on local real estate ledgers to verify ownership and has no legal requirement for landowners to update title information. Moreover, transferring the deed to land and a structure—for example, in the event of an owner's death—can cost hundreds of thousands of yen. Especially in areas outside Tokyo and other built-up urban areas where properties have considerable value, a tract of agricultural or forest land may have minimal value. Although the tax burden may be low, the pecuniary and other costs of claiming ownership are apparently deemed too great in an increasing number of cases. Thus, many properties are simply left unclaimed (Shoko 2018).

This ownership problem is quite serious. An authoritative 2017 study by Japan's National Spatial Planning Association (affiliated with the Ministry of Land, Infrastructure, Transport, and Tourism) warned that ownership of 4.1 million hectares of land—an area larger than Kyushu, the Japanese archipelago's third-largest island, at 3.68 million hectares—was unclear (NSPA, 2017). Moreover, the 4.1 million hectares of land represented 20.1 percent of all surveyed plots, the breakdown being 14.5 percent densely inhabited district, 17.4 percent residential district, 16.9 percent farmland, and 25.6 percent forested area. The association's research suggests that, at present trends, the total could increase to 7.2 million hectares by 2040, not far below the 8.35 million hectares of Japan's northern island of Hokkaido. The association also warned that, left unresolved, the issue could lead to a JPY 6 trillion cumulative loss in tax revenues and economic activity, a conservative assessment because the association could not assess the management, disaster risk, and other costs unclaimed land represented.

A March 2016 Tokyo Foundation survey of all Japanese subnational governments found significant concern over these issues. Of the 888 local governments that responded to the survey, 63 percent (557 subnational governments) indicated that unclear ownership of property was a problem. Of these, fully 87 percent declared that it made FAT management more difficult. At the same time, 61 percent of these governments were not able to provide data on the annual average FAT revenue of such properties over the previous three years. This inability of subnational governments suggests countermeasures have significant costs and will require a coordinated and nationally led response.

One step to resolving these issues was taken by the Ministry of Justice in May 2019. The ministry amended the law on property registry, making two significant changes. The first, effective November 22, 2019, bolsters legal authority for searches of ownership. The second, effective November 1, 2020, allows court-appointed management to take charge of properties whose ownership cannot be established. These measures are regarded as a first step in disposing of assets, such as through sales by government or private parties. The Ministry of Land, Infrastructure, Transport, and Tourism also announced on November 18, 2019, that it intended to formulate a strategy to cope with the problem. The Research Center for Property Assessment System (RECPAS) has also proposed integrating all records, overcoming institutional sectionalism, and sharing data (RECPAS 2019). Box 8.3 explains the role of RECPAS.

This gradual move toward a strategy on unclear property ownership is expected to benefit property and land taxation revenues. We have seen

---

Box 8.3 Collaboration on Assessment and Data Accuracy

Japan has four main public-sector property valuations. The results of these assessments are aggregated at the Research Center for Property Assessment System (RECPAS). These survey results are readily available in a very user-friendly manner (in Japanese) to any interested party via the RECPAS Internet portal, making the otherwise confusing and inordinately complicated multiple assessments more accessible.

Japanese policy makers promote collaboration among subnational governments and other interests concerning property taxation through the RECPAS. This agency was founded May 1, 1978, as an incorporated foundation. It bears some similarity to other national organizations of local governments, tax professionals, academics, and other parties to exchange information on best practices and research how to improve them—for example, the Canadian Property Tax Association (https://cpta.org). However, in contrast to other property tax associations, RECPAS's main membership consists of the subnational governments (all 1,765 of them). Other organizations (15 public-service corporations and 24 private firms) are supporting members (as of April 2015). Among those supporting organizations is the Japan Association of Real Estate Appraisers, governed by the Ministry of Land, Infrastructure, Transport, and Tourism.

The RECPAS budget for FY 2015 was just under JPY 420 million, of which JPY 140 million was from subnational governments. Its organizational goals center on analysis of the conditions of all relevant property (land, buildings, and depreciable assets) and research on the theory and practice of improving assessments. It is also devoted to helping balance the valuations among different kinds of property. The RECPAS also has an important educational role. Its approximately 30 annual training seminars train local officials in charge of the valuation of fixed assets, aiding them in improving their appraisal techniques. The RECPAS produces a wide range of video and written material to this end. Moreover, every two months it publishes a magazine (in Japanese) *Property Assessment Information* (*Shisan Hyouka Jouhou*) that focuses on enhancing assessment mechanisms and is distributed to subnational governments and related institutions.

The RECPAS thus performs a crucial role in linking the subnational governments; the Ministries of Internal Affairs and Communications and of Land, Infrastructure, Transport, and Tourism; real estate appraisers, and other stakeholders in assessing and collecting the FAT.

Moreover, it aids municipal governments in locating and assessing assets so they can maintain accurate and fair property taxation. One means is dissemination of the standard specification for research on fixed assets (revised in March 1999). This specification was developed to use aerial photography in assessing changes in structures and other related elements. The RECPAS itself conducts research on fixed assets when requested by municipalities by using the standard specification.

The RECPAS committee on "Standardization of Research on Present Situation of Fixed Assets" regularly reviews the standard specification to respond to rapid development of computer technologies. Indeed, automation and other information and communications technologies are used quite extensively to improve assessments and spot changes in the municipal asset profile. These technologies use 3D analysis of aerial photography, artificial intelligence processing, and related technologies to maximize the accuracy of surveys and minimize the time to do them, a benefit for Japanese local governments, which have severe personnel shortages.

---

that Japan has very high rates of FAT collection on assessed property whose ownership is clear. But we have also seen that there is a lot of property whose title is unclear. The National Spatial Planning Association survey of 2017 projected forgone tax revenues (of all types) between 2017 and 2040 at approximately JPY 60 billion. The association did not offer a breakdown by tax category, but some significant portion of this total would be FAT and other property and land taxation revenues. At the very least, it seems reasonable to suggest that rather more FAT and other property and land taxation revenues could be expected through bringing these assets into the assessment regime. But perhaps even more revenues could be generated by turning these lands to productive purposes.

Incentivizing Urban Agriculture

As discussed earlier, Japan has very low taxation of most farmland. In tandem with the extremely complex rules governing land ownership and transfer, the low burden has incentivized the idling of about 97,000 hectares of farmland. Another factor is the aging population. The average age of agricultural households rose from 61.1 years in 2000 to 66.7 years in 2017. At the same time, urban farming is argued to be impeded by high taxation of urban farmland.

In April 2015, these problems were addressed through the Basic Law to Promote Urban Farming. The law requires the central and subnational governments to work toward expanding productive green zones and alleviating the FAT and inheritance tax burden on urban farmland. Advocates of the reform point out that the area of urban agricultural land has declined markedly. In the years between 2003 and 2018, total urban agricultural land area fell from 143,000 hectares to 69,000 hectares. Within this decline, farmland deemed productive green land dropped from 15,000 hectares to 13,000 hectares, with 3,224 hectares (24 percent of the total) being in the TMG. Along with the Basic Law, the government has implemented tax incentives, which took effect April 1, 2016, to consolidate farmland and impose greater burdens on unused farmland via the FAT. The changes to the FAT will remove the limited assessment (45 percent in FY 2015) and halve the FAT burden if the land is leased to a "farmland bank" (*nouchi banku*).

Addressing Industrial Policy and Revitalization Issues

Distortions for industrial policy purposes are another shortcoming of Japan's property and land taxation regime. In December 2015, the Japanese cabinet approved investment incentives that reduce the FAT's burden on depreciable assets. Depreciable assets represented 18.1 percent (JPY 1.54 trillion) of all FAT revenues in FY 2012, so the proposal elicited great concern in the Ministry of Internal Affairs and Communications and among the subnational governments. The Ministry of Economy, Trade, and Industry and other interests are keen to enhance investment incentives. They also insist that property tax levies on depreciable assets (specifically machinery and equipment, which provide roughly one-third of the FAT's revenue base from depreciable assets) are a rarity among the major economies. They argued for, and secured, a reduction to apply to small- and medium-sized enterprises' purchases of equipment and machinery, exempting them from half the normal FAT applied. Calculations indicated that the measure could lead to as much as JPY 18.3 billion in forgone revenues. The initial ministry-led efforts to exempt far more of the depreciated assets tax base was, however, contained to this more restricted measure.

A potentially larger issue involving the FAT (and the intergovernmental fiscal system) concerns the local revitalization (or regional revitalization) incentives for expanding regional business offices or moving business offices from major urban centers (especially the TMG area) to smaller cities and towns. In FY 2015, special tax measures were introduced to encourage firms to relocate their offices, open research facilities, or transfer portions of their office functions to areas outside the Pacific Coast city-regions, with particularly attractive incentives for moving out of the TMG's 23 special wards.

The measures applied to the purchase price of an office facility include a 15 percent front-loading of the depreciation and a 4 percent tax exemption. In addition, there is a JPY 600,000 per person tax exemption for increased employment (up to a maximum of JPY 6 million for 10 employees). Moreover, the block-grant intergovernmental subsidy, known as the local allocation tax, covers an expanded list of revenue losses incurred by the local government in its efforts to attract business firms through the use of local tax reductions. An additional measure uses the local allocation tax to cover revenue losses from the FAT and the real property acquisition tax (*fudousan shutokuzei*) due to the local governments' use of special tax measures to attract firms.

When the relocation is from one of TMG's 23 wards, the special measures that apply to the purchase price of the office facility is a front loading of 25 percent in the depreciation as well as a 7 percent tax exemption. Moreover, the per-person employment subsidy is a JPY 900,000 tax exemption in the first year with the possibility of additional measures in subsequent years, to a possible maximum of JPY 1.4 million over three years. In addition, the block-grant intergovernmental subsidy, the local allocation tax, is used to cover an expanded list of revenue losses incurred by the local government in its efforts to attract business firms through the use of tax reductions in its local taxes. Not only does the local allocation tax cover revenue losses from special measures in the FAT and the real estate acquisition tax (*fudousan shutokuzei*), but the local business tax (*houjin jigyouzei*) is also included.

Firms that relocate to the Tokyo, Chubu, and Kinki areas are not eligible for these incentives. Moreover, relocations to these larger urban

subnational governments are not eligible for coverage by the local allocation tax for revenues forfeited via the use of special tax reductions. TMG's
tax commission reports have been quite critical of this measure. But the
cabinet's special advisory commission on local revitalization deems it
quite successful. Their figures indicate that the measure has, as of 2018,
led to 1,600 local revitalization programs and additional regional employment of 21,421 persons (Cabinet Local Revitalization Office 2021).

Directions for Reform

As discussed, Japan's property and land taxation regime provides a reasonably large and stable flow of revenues to its subnational governments, especially the municipalities. At the same time, the regime is beset with numerous problems. Comprehensive reforms are essential, both to simplify
important aspects of the overall system and to maintain—indeed, bolster—
local fiscal autonomy.

Simplify the FAT

Perhaps the most striking issue with Japan's property and land taxation
regime is the complexity of valuations and assessments for the FAT,
resulting from policy makers having to develop a system addressing the
diversity of land types, construction styles, and other matters. Political
culture seems to play a role: similar complexity is seen in Japan's intergovernmental general grant, the so-called local allocation tax, whose
complexity reflects a desire to ensure adequate attention to such regional
differences as climate conditions (Yoneyama 2008). The FAT's complicated valuation and assessments have long been a concern because of the
great scope for errors and delegitimization of the tax. A Ministry of Internal Affairs and Communications survey in 2012 determined that
97 percent of local governments between 2009 and 2011 had recorded
mistakes in their FAT assessments (Kanazawa 2019). More recently, municipal governments are compelled to meet the needs of increasingly diverse local societies with limited staff, indicating that simplification of the
FAT seems imperative (Horikawa 2018).

The mechanisms used to adjust the FAT burdens are also quite problematic. The fiscal authorities are, of course, constrained by the legacy effects of choices made in previous years. But the current mechanisms to
adjust burdens over time and across land types (including agricultural land)
are evidently very difficult for taxpayers to understand. Particularly controversial is that property tax burdens can rise even as the asset value falls.
The authorities, national and subnational, do a very poor job of explaining

this to taxpayers. Because of the importance of the property and land taxation regime in Japan, it is advisable that the various levels of government, RECPAS, and other actors collaborate on simplifying the FAT and increasing transparency on burden adjustments.

Undertake Coordinated Reform

Another prominent challenge is that the neediest local governments—those with the most rapidly declining and aging populations—have constrained fiscal options. Administratively, they are able to increase their property taxes, owing to the removal of top rates and other decentralization reforms. Yet increasing reliance on the property and land taxation regime has significant political risks for the economically and fiscally weaker local governments.

For one thing, most regional property values are already declining owing to factors that include the world's highest rate of aging. In many of the regional municipalities, shrinking populations further accelerate the rapid aging of the demographic profile. Adding higher FAT and other property taxes to this difficult context would seem to further encourage the flow of young, able-bodied students and workers to Tokyo and other city-regions. Indeed, the political feasibility of property and land tax increases seems limited—no local governments tax at levels close to the FAT's former top rate of 2.1 percent. Significant tax measures would be politically contentious, at least for individual governments. But a national debate on increasing revenues from the FAT and perhaps integrating the CPT should be possible, in tandem with reforms to simplify the FAT.

The evidence suggests that—at least outside TMG and the other large city-regions—Japanese subnational governments' challenges are almost certain to worsen. There are virtually no prospects for large-scale migration to shift demographic trends. The regions also face rising per-capita maintenance costs for water, transport, and other critical infrastructure networks built for larger populations and more vibrant economies. In addition, unclear property ownership exacerbates disaster risks and local burdens, such as for disposing of decrepit and abandoned residences. These issues are chronic and do not manifest themselves in an abrupt fiscal crisis that expands the scope for activist reform.

Yet we have also seen that the Japanese policy-making community is moving toward comprehensive measures to cope with the problem of land and other property ownership. Those policy measures are unfolding in a political and policy-making context that already views compact cities as essential to bolster disaster resilience and cope with rising infrastructure upkeep and the other unsustainable costs of sprawl. There seems to be no reason to stop at reforms for clarifying property ownership. Comprehensive reform could also include measures to reduce the complexity of the FAT, so as to reduce the risk of errors and taxpayer distrust. It seems advisable to combine these large-scale reforms with a much more strategic use of local revitalization tools. Japan's issues are without precedent, which suggests that the required countermeasures will be as well.

Notes

1. For this reason, Japanese fiscal and other data used in this chapter summarize the number of municipalities as 1,719, comprising the 1,718 municipalities and Tokyo Municipal Government's special wards (represented as one municipality because Tokyo collects the FAT and CPT on their behalf).

2. Japan's intergovernmental grant (the local allocation tax) is calculated on the basis of standard tax rates. Because most local governments receive some grant amount (determined by fiscal need), taxing under the 1.4% FAT standard rate would automatically affect their calculated fiscal need. See MIC (2018a, 13).

3. The formula (in Japanese) for each element of the FAT (land, buildings, and depreciable assets) is at the website of the Ministry of Internal Affairs and Communications, https://www.soumu.go.jp/main_sosiki/jichi_zeisei/czaisei/czaisei_seido/ichiran08.html.

4. See the details (in Japanese) on buildings and the FAT at the website of the Ministry of Internal Affairs and Communications, https://www.soumu.go.jp/main_sosiki/jichi_zeisei/czaisei/czaisei_seido/ichiran13/pdf/kaoku.pdf.

5. The exempt properties include irrigation and drainage waterways (*youakusuiro*), public-use roadways (*koushuuyou douro*), precinct lands (*keidaichi*), mineral-spring lands (*kousenchi*), water supply lands (*suidouyouchi*), canal lands (*ungayouchi*), reservoirs (*tamechi*), dikes (*tsutsumi*), and farmland and village waterways (*kousei*). Also exempt are cemeteries (*bochi*). In addition, the FAT exemption extends to types of properties held by independent administrative corporations (*dokuritsu gyousei houjin*), land-improvement districts (*tochi kairyou ku*), associations (*tochi kairyou rengou*), and land-development public corporations (*tochi kaihatsu kousha*) and used for their operations.

References

Akizuki, K. 2001. "Controlled Decentralization: Local Governments and the Ministry of Home Affairs in Japan." World Bank Institute. (May). http://siteresources.worldbank.org/WBI/Resources/wbi37170.pdf.

Bessho, S. 2016. "Case Study of Central and Local Government Finance in Japan." Working paper No. 599. Asian Development Bank. https://www.econstor.eu/handle/10419/161475.

Bessho, S. 2017. "A Case Study of Central and Local Government Finance in Japan." In *Central and Local Government Relations in Asia: Achieving Fiscal Sustainability*, ed. N. Yoshino and P. J. Morgan. Cheltenham, UK: Edward Elgar.

Cabinet Local Revitalization Office. 2021. "Concerning the Local Base Bolstering Tax System." [In Japanese.]. Cabinet Office, Government of Japan. https://www.chisou.go.jp/tiiki/tiikisaisei/pdf/03pamphlet.pdf.

DeWit, A. 2021. "Tokyo Sustainable Megacity: Robust Governance to Maximize Synergies." In *Sustainable Megacity Communities*, ed. W. W. Clark, 211–238. Oxford: Elsevier.

DeWit, A., and S. Steinmo. 2002. "The Political Economy of Taxes and Redistribution in Japan." *Social Science Japan Journal* 5 (2): 159–178.

Fukui, E., K. Samakura, N. Nakai, and M. Numata. 2017. "Concerning the City Planning Tax and Taxation Methods Relevant to City Planning in an Era of Depopulation." [In Japanese.] *Journal of the City Planning Institute of Japan* 52 (3), October 37–49.

Hato, N. 2019. "An Outline of Property Taxation in the Tokyo Metropolitan Area." [In Japanese.] Summary Report for Author by Tokyo Metropolitan Government Tax Office, Fixed Assets Tax Section Manager (April 19).

Horikawa, H. 2018. "Issues with the Fixed Assets Tax." [In Japanese.] Japanese Real Estate Appraisers Academic Association Special Edition, Vol. 31, No. 4, March: 66–67.

Ichikawa, H. 2007. "Recent Local Financial System Reform (Trinity Reform)." Japan Council of Local Authorities for International Relations (CLAIR report), July.

Ichikawa, Y. 2019. "The Political Process of the 2000 Decentralization Reforms, Part 1." [In Japanese.] *Jichisoken*, no. 492 (October). http://jichisoken.jp/publication /monthly/JILGO/2019/10/yichikawa1910.pdf.

Ichinomiya City. 2019. "About the Burden Adjustment Mechanism." [In Japanese.] September 9, 2019. https://www.city.ichinomiya.aichi.jp/zaimu/shisanzei/1043976 /1000141/1040426.html.

Ide, E. 2013. "A Political Dispute over the Local Public Finance Equalization Grant: The Legacy of Shoup's Policy Choices." In *The Political Economy of Transnational Tax Reform*, ed. W. E. Brownlee, E. Ide, and Y. Fukagai, 336–364. Cambridge: Cambridge University Press.

Jinno, N. 2017. "The Decentralization of Local Public Finance." [In Japanese.] Report to Japanese National Governors' Association (May 12). www.nga.gr.jp /ikkrwebBrowse/material/files/group/2/02%20shiryou1.pdf.

Jinno, N., and A. DeWit. 1998. "Japan's Taxing Bureaucrats: Fiscal Sociology and the Property Tax Revolt." *Social Science Japan Journal* 1 (2): 233–246.

Kanazawa, K. 2019. "Is Your Fixed Asset Tax Valuation Base Correct? Mistaken Assessments Continue Nationwide." [in Japanese.] *Nishi Nihon Newspaper*, December 25.

Kashiwagi, M. 2018. "The Current State of Indeterminate Land Ownership and Its Implications for the Fixed Assets Tax." [In Japanese.] March: https://www.canon -igs.org/research_papers/180424_kashiwagi.pdf.

Kitazato, T. 2003. "Japanese Fixed Property Tax." Paper presented at the Innovations in Local Revenue Mobilization World Bank Seminar, Washington, DC (June 23–24). www1.worldbank.org/publicsector/decentralization/June2003Seminar /Japan.pdf.

———. 2004. "Property Tax in Japan." In *International Handbook of Land and Property Taxation*, ed. R. M. Bird and E. Slack, 107–116. Cheltenham, UK: Edward Elgar.

Kyoto Association of Real Estate Appraisers. n.d. "The Relationship Between Real-Estate Appraisals and Real Prices." [In Japanese.] https://www.kantei-kyoto.or.jp /?page_id=15.

Management of Information and Appraisal Council, n.d. "Formulating the Standards for Certification of Land." [In Japanese.] www.miaj.gr.jp/publication/kotei23th_pdf /23-4-1.PDF.

MIC (Ministry of Internal Affairs and Communications). 2015. "Data Concerning 2015 Local Finance." [In Japanese.] Tokyo: Statistics Bureau, MIC.

———. 2018a. "FY 2016 Settlement: White Paper on Local Public Finance, 2018." [In Japanese.] Tokyo: MIC.

———. 2018b. "The 2018 Survey on Housing and Lands." [In Japanese.] Tokyo: Statistics Bureau, MIC. https://www.stat.go.jp/data/jyutaku/2018/pdf/g_gaiyou.pdf.

———. 2019a. "Local Public Finance White Paper 2018." [In Japanese.] Tokyo: MIC .

———. 2019b. "Concerning the Fixed Assets Tax." [In Japanese.] Tokyo: MIC.

———. n.d. "Summary Reports on Fixed Assets Valuations and Related Matters." [In Japanese.] Annual data. Tokyo: MIC. https://www.soumu.go.jp/main_sosiki/jichi_zeisei/czaisei/czaisei_seido/ichiran08.html.

Miyazaki, T. 2018. "Regional Inequality in Fiscal Capacity and Allocation of Tax Sources: Do Local Allocation Taxes Correct the Inequality?" *Policy Research Institute* 14 (2): 347–368.

Miyazaki, T., and M. Sato. 2018. "Property Tax and Land Use: Evidence from the 1990s Reforms in Japan." REITI discussion paper series 18-E-072. (October). https://www.rieti.go.jp/jp/publications/dp/18e072.pdf.

MLIT (Ministry of Land, Infrastructure, Transport, and Tourism). 2017. "Concerning Areal Goals in Draft Final Report of 5th National Land Plan." [In Japanese.] Tokyo: Land Policy Bureau, MLIT. (May 28).

Mochida, N. 2008. "Local Government Organization and Finance: Japan." In *Fiscal Decentralization and Local Public Finance in Japan*, ed. A. Shah, 149–188. New York: Routledge.

NSPA (National Spatial Planning Association). 2017."Final Report of Research Commission on the Unclear Land-Ownership Problem." [In Japanese.] National Spatial Planning Association. (December). https://www.kok.or.jp/project/pdf/fumei_04_02.pdf.

OECD (Organization for Economic Cooperation and Development). 2015. "Agriculture: Assuring the Long-Term Health of Japan's Food and Agricultural System." Japan policy brief. (April). www.oecd.org/policy-briefs/japan--assuring-long-term-health-of-food-and-agriculture-system.pdf.

———. 2016. "OECD Territorial Reviews: Japan 2016." Paris: OECD.

———. 2018. "Subnational Governments in OECD Countries: Key Data." Paris: OECD.

———. 2019. "OECD Economic Surveys: Japan." Paris: OECD. (April).

RECPAS (Research Center for Property Assessment System). 2019. "A Mid-Term Report on Issues Posed for the Fixed Assets Tax due to Unclear Ownership of Lands and Structures." [In Japanese.] Japan Research Institute for Property Assessment System. (November).

Shoko, Y. 2018. "Tackling the 'Missing Landowner' Crisis: Stopgaps and Structural Reforms." Tokyo Foundation for Policy Research. (October 16). https://www.tkfd.or.jp/en/research/detail.php?id=582.

Takahashi, M. 2012. "Political Economy of Intergovernmental Fiscal Relationship and Local Government Deficit in Japan." *Keio Economic Studies* 48: 111–116.

Tanishita, M., and A. Imanishi. 2006. "Determinants of City Planning Taxation and Tax Rates in Japanese Municipalities." [In Japanese.] *Journal of the City Planning Institute of Japan*, 41 (3): 631–634.

TMG (Tokyo Metropolitan Government). 2018. "The Structure of the Tokyo Metropolitan Government (TMG)." https://www.metro.tokyo.lg.jp/ENGLISH/ABOUT/STRUCTURE/index.htm.

———. 2019. "Guide to Metropolitan Taxes, 2019." Tokyo Metropolitan Government. https://www.tax.metro.tokyo.lg.jp/book/guidebookgaigo./

Tokyo Foundation. 2016. "Unclear Land Ownership: A Survey of Subnational Governments." [In Japanese.] (March).

"Types of Land." n.d. [In Japanese.] Your District Registration and Survey Consultant Center. www.to-ki.jp/data/chimoku.html.

Yomiuri Shimbun. 2015. "In the First Application of the Special Law for an Abandoned Residence, the City Does the Removal." [In Japanese.] October 26, 2015.

Yoneyama, H. 2008. "Allocation of Tax Revenue to Promote Local Government Independence." [In Japanese.] Fujitsu Research Institute Research Report No. 326. (October).

9

Republic of Korea: A Unique Two-Tier System of Land and Property Taxation

YOUNGHOON RO

This chapter provides an overview of the land and property tax regime in the Republic of Korea. It then turns to a deeper analysis of the two most important recurrent property and land taxes in the system: the local property tax on land and buildings and the central-government gross real estate tax. The latter is levied only on owners whose nationwide aggregate holding value of land and housing exceed certain threshold values and is a form of personal wealth tax. This chapter focuses on the rationale for this two-tier property tax system, its problems, and its successes with revenue generation, equity, and land use. The transfer tax on real property, which accounts for significant revenue, is given separate attention. The final section considers issues that require attention if future reforms are to be successful.

Overview of the System of Land and Property Taxes

Taxes on real property in Korea have long been an important revenue source for local governments. All land and property taxation components are summarized in figure 9.1, a two-dimensional rendering of property-related taxes, one dimension showing the Organisation for Economic

---

The description of the property tax in this chapter is largely based on Ro (2001b).

Cooperation and Development (OECD) classification criteria and the other stages of acquisition, holding, and transfer of property. Using this cross classification, we can compare the revenue dependency on property-related taxes with both the base of the tax and the timing of the levy. The Korean property tax system has three legs: first, an annual property tax on land and buildings; second, a national tax on real property wealth that kicks in when landholders exceed a threshold; and third, a set of property transfer taxes that are levied when real estate assets change ownership (Ro 2001c).

Korea's rate of revenue mobilization ranks high compared with other Asian jurisdictions and even compared with OECD jurisdictions, as shown in figures 9.2 and 9.3. This high rate is mostly due to Korea's growing property values and its heavier taxation on transfer and registration taxes on real property sales. However, the effective tax rates on owning or holding real estate (the recurrent property taxes) are low: around 0.2 percent to 0.3 percent of the market price for both land and buildings, a reflection of land and buildings being assessed for tax purposes at only around one-third to one-half the true market price.

The strong performance of transfer taxes is primarily because local governments collect acquisition and registration taxes at the time of a change in property ownership. Note that the tax on capital gains realized upon transfer of a property is normally not counted as a property tax in Korea, in contrast to the OECD (see figure 9.1). If it were included, the proportion of taxes imposed on property in total tax revenues becomes quite pronounced in Korea.

Box 9.1 KOREAN GOVERNANCE

The Republic of Korea is a unitary jurisdiction with three tiers of government administration: a central government, regional governments (17), and local governments (228). Non-central governments have two levels: an upper level of eight metropolitan or special cities and nine provinces, and a lower level of thirty-two counties (called *gun*), seventy-seven cities (*si*), and sixty-nine municipalities (*gu*). After Seoul Special Metropolitan City, the six most populous cities are Busan, Incheon, Daegu, Daejon, Gwangju, and Ulsan. These are treated as provinces (*do*), as are Jeju Island (formally Jeju Special Self-Governing Province) and Sejong (a special self-governing city). Local property taxes are levied and collected by district-level municipalities (autonomous *gu*) in seven major metropolitan cities and by counties in the nine provinces. About 80 percent of the Korean population lives in urban areas.

Figure 9.1 Classification of Property-Related Taxes in Korea

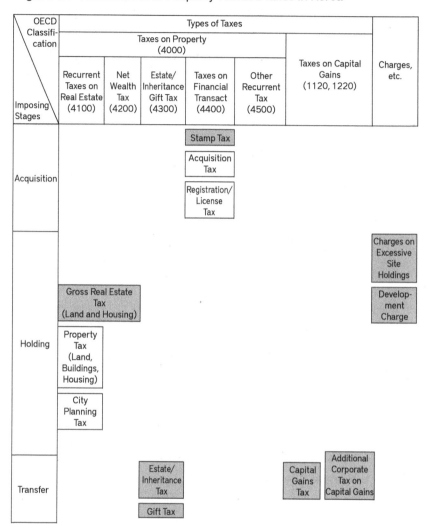

OECD Classification / Imposing Stages	Types of Taxes						
	Taxes on Property (4000)					Taxes on Capital Gains (1120, 1220)	Charges, etc.
	Recurrent Taxes on Real Estate (4100)	Net Wealth Tax (4200)	Estate/ Inheritance Gift Tax (4300)	Taxes on Financial Transact (4400)	Other Recurrent Tax (4500)		
Acquisition				Stamp Tax			
				Acquisition Tax			
				Registration/ License Tax			
Holding	Gross Real Estate Tax (Land and Housing)						Charges on Excessive Site Holdings
	Property Tax (Land, Buildings, Housing)						Development Charge
	City Planning Tax						
Transfer			Estate/ Inheritance Tax			Capital Gains Tax	Additional Corporate Tax on Capital Gains
			Gift Tax				

Source: Ro (2001c).
Note: Taxes in shaded boxes are national taxes.

Figure 9.2 Property and Land (Real Estate) Tax as Percentage of Total Tax Revenue for Selected OECD Jurisdictions

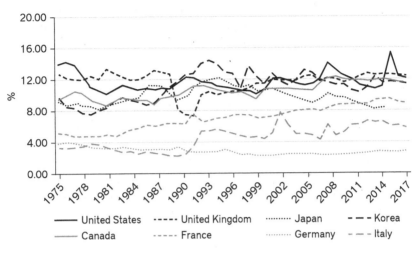

Source: OECD (2018).

Figure 9.3 Recurrent Taxes on Real Estate

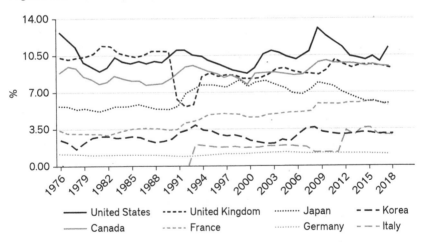

Source: OECD (2018).

Korea imposes an annual tax on property and land based on the capital market value of privately owned property. If an individual's aggregate holdings (second stage in figure 9.1) of housing or land, or both, across the jurisdiction exceeds a threshold, the excess is subject to an additional national tax, called the gross real estate tax.

Local Property Tax on Land, Buildings, and Housing

The recurrent property tax in Korea is complicated, involving the tax base, a progressive rate structure, valuation, and overlapping administration. Together with gross real estate tax (discussed later), they are a unique system with two levels of recurrent property tax (local and central) that have several intended and unintended effects on the economy. The backbone of the property tax system in Korea is the local property tax on land and buildings. Its features are similar to those levied in many other Asian jurisdictions.

Unit of Taxation and Taxpayer

The owner of a taxable property as of the base date of assessment (June 1 of each year) is obligated to pay the local property tax on land, buildings, and housing units. If the title holder's identity is uncertain, the tax authorities may collect from (1) the registered owner on the property tax roll; (2) the primary successor when inheritance is in progress and registration has not occurred; (3) the purchaser who signed a sales contract to obtain the right to use the taxable property free of charge by yearly installments; or (4) the user of the property.

Tax Base and Rates

The tax is based on the capital market value of privately owned property, which may include land, structures, and other real property such as boats and aircraft. This discussion focuses on land and structures and not aircraft and boats. Cities, municipalities, townships, and counties (rural equivalents) impose their own in rem local property tax on land, buildings, and housing units within their jurisdictions (Ro 2004). The use of land determines its tax category and the tax rate schedule to be applied. Each taxpayer's landholdings are broken down into one of three categories and subject to each category's tax rate schedules:

GENERAL AGGREGATE TAXATION CATEGORY RATE

The first schedule is progressive, in which rates rise from 0.2 to 0.5 percent. This schedule is called the "General Aggregate Taxation Category Rate" and is applied to speculative land, or land withheld from

Table 9.1 General Aggregate Land Taxation Rate of Local Property Tax (KRW thousand)

Tax Base	Tax Amount
<50,000	0.2% of tax base
50,001–100,000	100 + 0.3% of amount exceeding 50,000
>100,001	250 + 0.5% of amount exceeding 100,000

Source: Local Tax Act, Article 111.

the use that would bring the highest current returns in hopes of reaping a higher sales price or higher annual returns later. In Korea, policy makers and taxing authorities also define excessive landholding (in terms of land use intensity) as speculation (table 9.1).

SPECIAL AGGREGATE TAXATION CATEGORY RATE

The second schedule is also progressive, with rates ranging from 0.2 to 0.4 percent. It is called the "Special Aggregate Taxation Category Rate," to be applied to commercial building sites (table 9.2).

FIXED RATE

All other lands, buildings, and housing units not covered by the first two categories are taxed at a fixed rate. Farmland and forestland receive a preferential tax rate of 0.07 percent, and luxury properties like golf courses and villas receive a higher rate, 4 percent (table 9.3).

For residential property, a house's value is progressively taxed, from 0.1 to 0.4 percent (table 9.4). For example, if the standard market value of a house is KRW 500 million (KRW 1,165 = USD 1), its taxable assessed value is computed by multiplying the above market value by the assessment ratio of 60 percent (500 million × 60 percent = 300m). The resulting 300 million puts it in the highest bracket of statutory tax rate, 0.4 percent. The property tax due is KRW 570,000 according to the rate schedule of table 9.4.

Table 9.2 Special Aggregate Land Taxation Rate of Local Property Tax (KRW thousand)

Tax Base	Tax Amount
<200,000	0.2% of tax base
200,001–1,000,000	400 + 0.3% of amount exceeding 200,000
>1,000,001	2,800 + 0.4% of amount exceeding 1,000,000

Source: Local Tax Act, Article 111.

Table 9.3 Fixed-Rate Taxation on Land under Local Property Tax

Taxable Objectives	Tax Rate (%)
Farmlands tilled by the owner (dry fields, rice paddies, orchards), pastures, and forests	0.07
Golf courses, villas, and high-priced resorts	4.00
Other	0.20

Source: Local Tax Act, Article 111.

Table 9.4 Local Property Tax Rate on Houses

Assessed Tax Base (standard market value; KRW thousand)	Tax Amount (KRW thousand) at Statutory Tax Rate	Effective Tax Rate (%)
<60,000 (100,000)	0.10% of tax base	0–0.060
60,000–150,000 (100,000)	60 + 0.15% of amount exceeding 60,000	0.060–0.078
150,001–300,000 (250,000)	195 + 0.25% of amount exceeding 150,000	0.078–0.114
>300,001 (500,000)	570 + 0.40% of amount exceeding 300,000	0.114

Source: Local Tax Act, Article 111.

The product of the nominal tax rate and the assessment ratio is called the *effective property tax rate* because it represents the actual percentage of the market value of property that is taken as property tax each year. In this example, the effective property tax rate for the house is 0.114 percent (570,000 ÷ 500 million). The last column of table 9.4 shows the effective tax rates for each tax base bracket.

Surtaxes

Surtaxes (imposed by central-government law) are added to the local property tax bill.

- In urban areas designated by the National Land Planning and Utilization Act and stipulated by the relevant local council resolution, a pro rata amount of tax, calculated by applying 0.14 percent to the tax base on land, buildings, and housing, is imposed in city areas.

Table 9.5 Local Resource and Public Facility Tax
(KRW thousand)

Tax Base	Tax Amount
<6,000	0.4% of tax base
6,001–13,000	2.4% + 0.5% of amount exceeding 6,000
13,001–26,000	5.9% + 0.6% of amount exceeding 13,000
26,001–39,000	13.7% + 0.8% of amount exceeding 26,000
39,001–64,000	24.1% + 1.0% of amount exceeding 39,000
>64,001	49.1% + 1.2% of amount exceeding 64,000

Source: Local Tax Act, Article 146.

- Local resource and facility tax may be imposed at the progressive rate schedule of 0.4–1.2 percent on the value of buildings that house firefighting facilities, garbage disposal facilities, irrigation facilities, or any other public facilities that finance these activities (table 9.5).

- A local education tax is imposed at 20 percent of the amount of property tax.

Exemptions, Preferences, and Collections

Properties for nonprofit use, roads, lands for public interest, real estate owned by governments, and lands for public utilities are tax exempt. Properties owned and used by education institutions, nursing homes, job training institutes, and lands and facilities inside local industrial zones are eligible for tax reduction.

Notices for half the local property tax due are sent in July and for the other half in September. In December, homeowners whose house values exceed KRW 600 million or KRW 900 million, depending on the number of houses owned, are subject to an additional tax, the gross real estate tax on housing, but the local property tax is deducted from the additional tax as a credit. The collection rate is consistently above 95 percent. The 2019 collection rate of the local property tax was 98 percent.

Assessment of Local Property Tax

Property tax liability is calculated by multiplying the nominal property tax rate by the assessment ratio (the percentage of the value of the property that is taxed) and the value of the property. The standard market prices for all parcels of land, single detached houses, and condominiums are publicly declared each year by the end of the first quarter. The determination of property values is the responsibility of a designated, central-government assessment agency, the Korea Real Estate Board.[1] The board is governed by the Ministry of Land, Infrastructure, and Transportation. By law, the central government and the local government with the property in its jurisdiction collaborate in valuation and assessment.

The first step in the process is to classify all properties (land, buildings, and housing) by type. Residential land and improvements on it are valued as a whole each year, and those values are announced annually. Land and the land portion of nonresidential properties is valued separately from improvements and that value is also announced. These official values of housing and land are determined after a notice and appeals process between local authorities and property owners, under the guidance of the Ministry of Land, Infrastructure, and Transportation and the real estate board, and announced around May.

The tax base for local property tax is stipulated in the national Local Tax Act to be the product of multiplying their standard market price by the fair market price ratio. This ratio is the assessment ratio of taxable value to public appraisal value. On the basis of these standard values of land and buildings, local governments were supposed to be allowed to set the assessment ratio within the range of 50 to 90 percent for land and buildings and 40 to 80 percent for housing units, considering the local real estate market trends and fiscal conditions. But a presidential decree froze the nationally uniform assessment ratios at 60 percent for housing and 70 percent for land and commercial buildings (table 9.6). See a fuller discussion in the later section "Double Taxation."

In general, the laws on the annual tax on property and land are very clear, but some accountability issues remain. The authority to impose the local property tax belongs to each local jurisdiction where the property and land are located, but local jurisdictions have very limited power in setting their taxable values. Normally, they adopt the central government's announced annual public values for land and properties with little adjustment. When the local government's tax department faces taxpayer complaints and disputes about the increase of taxable value over last year's, departments tend to refer them to the Ministry of Land, Infrastructure, and Transportation and the agency it sponsors, the Korea Real Estate Board. The board often dodges disputes on the nonuniform assessment ratios among various classes of real estate by arguing that their published prices are used not only for the tax purpose but have many other uses. In 2020, the ministry, which sets government policy on real estate, announced that 2019 apartment valuations would go up by an average 14.2 percent, another double-digit increase after a 10.2 percent rise in 2018.

Table 9.6 Assessment Ratios for Local Property Tax and Gross Real Estate Tax (GRET)

Type		Appraisal Stage	Local Property Tax Range (%)	Central-Government GRET Range (%)
Housing		Publicly declared value	40–80 (60)	60–100 (85 → 90 → 95)
Nonresidential property	Building	Replacement cost formula	← the same	–
	Land	Publicly declared value	50–90 (70)	60–100 (85 → 90 → 95)
Land		Publicly declared value	50–90 (70)	60–100 (85 → 90 → 95)

Sources: Act on Public Announcement of Real Estate Values; Local Tax Act; Gross Real Estate Tax Act.

Note: Percentages in parentheses are those effective from 2019 onward; the ranges show the statutory ratios stipulated in the tax laws for the local property tax and GRET.

Computer-Assisted Mass Appraisal

Until 1995, the lower-level municipal governments were responsible for assessing the value of land and buildings in their jurisdictions each year. These same lands were valued independently by the national government in the assessment of its own land-related taxes. Local governments had the authority to determine taxable land value on the basis of a unit land price. It was called the current standard value for taxation and recorded on the cadastre (*Ji-Juk*) and the land tax roll maintained by the local government.

Another real estate valuation was introduced in 1990, after passage of the Act on Public Announcement on Real Estate Values, on land (publicly declared land value) and in 2005 on housing (publicly declared housing value) as an important tax reform measure. Originally, it was intended for valuations in the national tax administration of the gross real estate tax, but it was expanded into local tax assessment. First, the publicly declared value was announced to give guidelines in the local assessment of taxable value, or current standard value for taxation. Valuation records were available for public inspection. In 1996, the Local Tax Act was amended to prohibit local governments from maintaining their own land valuation system and to require them to apply a certain percentage of the publicly declared value—the standard market price—as their taxable land and housing value.

Therefore, this assessment ratio represents only the relative degree of local assessment compared with the central government's publicly declared value and should not be confused with the ratio of assessment to sales price, which is the ratio of taxable value to fair market value.

In the absence of reliable sales price information in both the land registry and the local property tax roll, Korea developed a two-tier valuation system for annual appraisal of almost 30 million parcels of land. Land valuation in Korea is a unified system based on a computer-assisted mass appraisal (CAMA) method. First, out of the population of land parcels, 450,000 are selected as standard parcels, and these are appraised by professional fee appraisers in the private sector. Second, with these official values of standard parcels as benchmark references, values for all the individual land parcels nearby are calculated using comparison matrix tables, which contain the estimated coefficients of factors affecting the unit price of land. A parcel's size, location, shape, usage, proximity to amenities, and other characteristics are surveyed and the observed difference of these attributes from those of the standard parcels are measured and multiplied by the estimated coefficients of the multiple regression equations obtained using the sample parcels.

Gross Real Estate Tax

A unique feature of Korea's property tax regime is the separate property tax, gross real estate tax (GRET), imposed by the central government on total holdings of real property. This section discusses the GRET's important effects as a wealth tax and as a tax to control housing markets. It can also impose significant administrative costs.

History

The GRET was introduced in 2005 as an extension of the previous aggregate land value tax, which had been in effect for 10 years. The land levy portion of the GRET is similar to the old aggregate land value tax in that it is a unique version of land value tax in line with Henry George's 1879 (1992, 433–472) idea: public services ought to be financed by the value land creates—the economic rent of land—even if that rent does not come close to being a single land tax. But the GRET is quite different from the single tax in that improvements on the land (building structures) are also taxed. Land and improvements on nonresidential properties are separately assessed, but both are taxed under the land and building categories of the GRET.

The aggregate land value tax was introduced into the tax system as a part of the land policy reform package of 1990 to emphasize the landowners' responsibility for putting their private land into socially desirable uses, called *Toji-Gong-Kae-Nyum*, or "the public concept of (private) land." Before the aggregate tax, the annual land tax was a land-component levy of the property tax, which simply taxed each unit of land at a single flat rate. The newly enacted tax, however, expanded the scope of the tax base by aggregating all the lands owned by each taxpayer on a national basis, and it became the genesis of land wealth tax in Korea. Since 1990, all information on land asset ownership has been recorded in the database of the unified national land valuation system.[2]

Objectives

When the aggregate land value tax was conceived in the late 1980s, policy makers explicitly or implicitly laid out the following objectives: promoting more intensive land use, encouraging more productive use of scarce resources, lessening the inequities of land ownership and income redistribution, and decreasing land speculation. But the initial statutory tax rates were set much too low to elicit these desirable behavior changes from landowners. And political sensitivities, particularly in regard to the liquidity constraints of many middle-class property owners, appeared to preclude ever raising these rates to a level that might significantly alter major investment and consumption decisions. At the time, the aggregate land value tax was viewed as complementing the capital gains tax on land. Because of the absence of a mechanism to ensure the proper reporting of market transaction price data to the tax authorities, taxation on capital gains from land relied on a presumptive approach, and the effective tax rate was quite low.[3]

Korea's land price inflation in the 1980s and the housing price boom in the first decade of the 2000s triggered the inception of the aggregate land value tax and GRET. The first land price inflation period of 1964–1970 saw a more than 50 percent rate of change per annum. Although inflation rates for the second (1975–1980) and third (1987–1990) periods were not as high as those of the first, the second and third periods witnessed a 27.4 percent and 22.3 percent annual appreciation rate, respectively. And housing prices escalated again in 2003–2007 during the global financial crisis. This land and housing price inflation led to significant speculation. Figure 9.4 provides an overview of housing market trends in Seoul and the jurisdiction more generally from January 1992 to July 2019.

Economists and policy makers in Korea have long been interested in employing tax policy tools to address land price inflation. Indeed, many former administrations have relied on real estate taxes as a tool for fiscal stimulus or a deterrent to real estate speculation. The aggregate land value tax was an attempt to stabilize speculation-driven land price inflation and

Figure 9.4 Housing Market Trends in Seoul and Korea: Housing Composite Price Index (November 2017 =100)

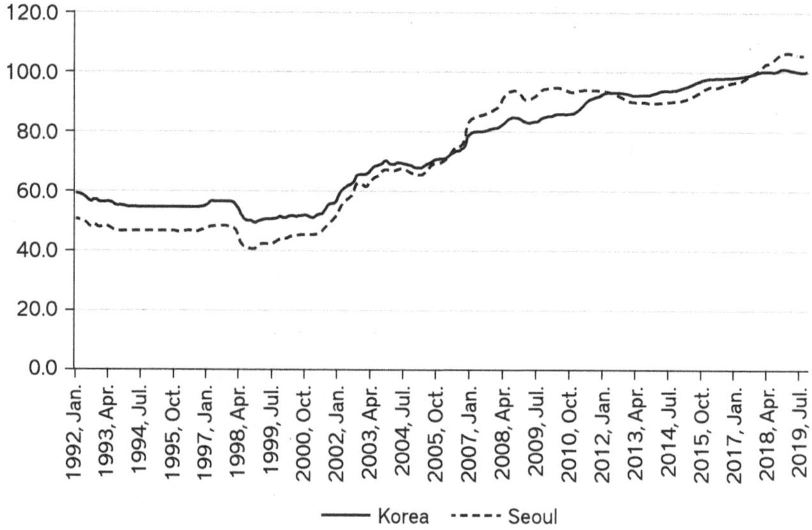

Sources: MOLIT (2020).

to lessen the degree of land ownership concentration. It used a progressive rate for the total value of nationwide landholdings by a given taxpayer. The aggregate land value tax was administered by the national government, and the same tax rates were used in all local jurisdictions. The introduction of the GRET in 2005 to replace the aggregate land value tax was a result of the government's determination to respond to housing price inflation through fiscal tools. It included housing wealth directly in the tax base and has been levied annually, but only on the top 1–2 percent of real estate landholders.

GRET Base

Two noteworthy features of the GRET base are its parallels with a wealth tax and how it treats land and improvements. A third feature, the relatively high threshold at which GRET rates kick in, is also reviewed here.

Korea's GRET can best be described as a form of personal wealth tax, with wealth defined in terms of real estate holdings and not allowing debt deductions. It is levied annually on total housing and landholding values across the whole jurisdiction. It is an ad valorem tax rather than a unit tax and a personal tax rather than an in rem tax (against an object). The tax is levied on each owner's national land and property holding total value, and the taxation unit is either an individual or an equivalent legal entity such as a corporation. The GRET is reassessed annually, on the basis of the capital market value of land or on proxies for capital value such as presumed or actual rental income.

Before 1990, before the aggregate land value tax and GRET, the property tax system in Korea was graded, in the sense of differential treatment, for residential and nonresidential property taxation. Land and building components were separately assessed using different methods, though there were no intentional objectives of encouraging more intensive land use by taxing land heavier than improvements. Also, the aggregated land value of that for residential use was taxed under a progressive rate of 0.2–5.0 percent and that for nonresidential land use was taxed under a less progressive rate of 0.3–3.0 percent, but the buildings were valued by replacement cost and subjected to the seemingly more progressive tax rate schedule of 0.3–7.0 percent. Since 2005, with the GRET for housing and the local property tax on the housing capital value as a whole, graded property taxation remained only for nonresidential property. A policy shift toward heavier land taxation by aggregating personal holdings and using progressive tax rates still exists in land categories of the local property tax and GRET. Because three types of land classes and three tax rate schedules are applied, depending on land usage, the GRET is designed to be a non-neutral differential land tax. Tables 9.1 to 9.5 and tables 9.7 to 9.10 provide more detail.

Tax Base and Rate Schedule

Recall the three categories for the local property tax on land, buildings, and housing: general, special, and fixed (see tables 9.1–9.3). Tax rate schedules for two kinds of land and housing are as follows. Table 9.7 shows the progressive rate schedule of the general category. Table 9.8 reports the progressive rate schedule of the special category.

Tables 9.9 and 9.10 apply to personal total residential holdings, or housing wealth. An even more progressive rate schedule applies for ownership

Table 9.7 General Aggregate Land Taxation Rate of GRET (KRW thousand)

Tax Base	Tax Amount
<1,500,000	1.0% of tax base
1,500,001–4,500,000	15,000 + 2.0% of amount exceeding 1,500,000
>4,500,001	75,000 + 3.0% of amount exceeding 4,500,000

Source: Gross Real Estate Tax Act, Article 14.

Table 9.8 Special Aggregate Land Taxation Rate of GRET (KRW thousand)

Tax Base	Tax Amount
<20,000,000	0.5% of tax base
20,000,001–40,000,000	100,000 + 0.6% of amount exceeding 20,000,000
>40,000,001	220,000 + 0.7% of amount exceeding 40,000,000

Source: Gross Real Estate Tax Act, Article 14.

of three or more houses compared with up to two houses. Mortgage debt is not an allowed deduction, but age and longer ownership are allowed deductions. For example, if a single homeowner is more than 70 years old and has owned the house for at least 15 years, that owner may deduct 30 percent of the value plus 50 percent of the value for the holding period. The consequent taxable rate is $(1 - 0.30) \times (1 - 0.50) = 0.35$. These rate schedules are described in tables 9.9 and 9.10.

Table 9.9 GRET Housing Taxation Rate, Fewer Than Three Houses (KRW thousand)

Tax Base	Tax Amount
<300,000	0.6% of tax base
300,001–600,000	1,800 + 0.8% of amount exceeding 300,000
600,001–1,200,000	4,200 + 1.2% of amount exceeding 600,000
1,200,001–5,000,000	11,400 + 1.6% of amount exceeding 1,200,000
5,000,001–9,400,000	72,200 + 2.2% of amount exceeding 5,000,000
>9,400,001	169,000 + 3.0% of amount exceeding 9,400,000

Source: Gross Real Estate Tax Act, Article 9.

Table 9.10 GRET Housing Taxation Rate, Ownership of Three or More Houses (KRW thousand)

Tax Base	Tax Amount
<300,000	1.2% of tax base
300,001–600,000	3,600 + 1.6% of amount exceeding 300,000
600,001–1,200,000	8,400 + 2.2% of amount exceeding 600,000
1,200,001–5,000,000	21,600 + 3.6% of amount exceeding 1,200,000
5,000,001–9,400,000	158,400 + 5.0% of amount exceeding 5,000,000
>9,400,001	378,400 + 6.0% of amount exceeding 9,400,000

Source: Gross Real Estate Tax Act, Article 9.

Administration and Valuation

The GRET aggregates the value of an individual's holdings in land and housing across the jurisdiction. For the tax to be fair, homogeneous administrative rules and uniform assessments need to be applied in every aspect of valuation and tax computation. Valuation methods and administration standards are established at the central-government level by the Ministry of Land, Infrastructure, and Transportation. The fractional assessment ratio is between 60 and 100 percent.

The local authorities input land and housing characteristics into the unified CAMA-based system to come up with the official prices. To maintain property cadastres and tax rolls, they regularly collect other sources of information, like the Ministry of Justice's title registry data. For smooth functioning of the GRET, several ministries of the central government and local governments must coordinate very closely.

Intergovernmental Arrangements and Political Economy Implications

Both the local property tax and the GRET are legislated by the National Assembly in the state-level Tax Act, with some minor taxable value and rate adjustment power left to local governments. Proceeds of the local property tax belong to each local government, and GRET revenues collected by the National Tax Service are distributed to local governments according to a formula (determined by the central government's budget office) that takes into account the local governments' financial conditions (50 percent), social welfare (35 percent), regional education (10 percent), and scale of real estate holdings tax collected locally (5 percent). Under this scheme, local governments in Korea must accept the central government's tax law and apply it uniformly.

The political economy aspect of the annual tax on property and land in Korea is important. Revenues from the local property tax do not represent a sizable portion of a metropolitan government's budget, and officials are not aggressive in raising their assessments in the face of owners' resistance. Hence, fiscal accountability issues ensue. Table 9.11 shows that the GRET share is fairly insignificant, at around 0.7 percent.

Property Transfer Tax

An important part of the Korean property tax system is the property transfer tax, or acquisition tax. *Acquisition* in the law refers to sale, exchange, inheritance, donation, contribution in kind to a corporation, construction, repair, land reclamation, and so on, with or without compensation. Taxable objects like automobiles, aircraft, ships, forests, mining and fishing rights,

Table 9.11 Decomposition of Total Property Taxes in Local and Central Levies

Category		Item	2015 Amount (KRW million)	% Total tax revenues	2016 Amount (KRW million)	%	2017 Amount (KRW million)	%
National Tax Service total collected			217,223,873		243,111,437		266,174,209	
	Central-levied	GRET	1,399,035		1,293,892		1,651,974	
	Personal property and land taxes	Special surtax for GRET	266,596		240,399		302,104	
		Subtotal	**1,665,631**	0.77	**1,534,291**	0.63	**1,954,078**	0.73
Local tax collection			70,977,794		75,531,651		80,409,137	
	Local-level	Property tax	9,293,705		9,929,915		10,662,094	
	Property and land taxes	Additions in city districts	3,337,883		3,583,000		3,850,218	
		Local resource facilities tax	1,227,449		1,161,802		1,253,866	
		Local education tax	1,206,100		1,290,563		1,379,200	
		Subtotal	**15,065,138**	21.23	**15,965,281**	21.14	**17,145,378**	21.32
Total tax collections			288,201,667		318,643,088		346,583,346	

Sources: Author's calculations using National Tax Service (2016, 2017, 2018), and Ministry of Interior and Safety (2016–2018, 2018b).

time-sharing resort membership, and golf and sports club memberships are also subject to the tax. But more than 90 percent of the tax proceeds come from real estate sales, and the tax is imposed on the purchaser. The base for the acquisition tax is the value reported by the acquirer (purchaser) at the time of acquisition. See Ro (2013) for a detailed analysis of the acquisition tax.

The taxable value is the actual price of acquisition, which is multiplied by the applicable tax rate to determine tax liability. Rates include 2.3 percent for inheriting farmland, 2.8 percent for original acquisition, 3 percent for farmland sales, 4 percent for real estate sales other than houses, and rates for residential property sales that depend on the purchase price range (1 percent if less than KRW 600 million, 2 percent if 600 million to 900 million, and 3 percent if more than 900 million). Because of the sizable differentiation in rates of 1, 2, or 3 percent, there is a price-notch effect in market transaction volume data, with cutoff points of KRW 600 million and KRW 900 million. If a sale is not reported or the value is not indicated, or if the reported value is less than the standard market price, the standard market price is considered to be the value at the time of acquisition.

Nationwide, the acquisition tax is almost 29 percent of the total local-government tax revenue (24 percent of Seoul government's local tax revenue), and it is more than twice the share of nationwide land and property tax revenues and almost double the share in Seoul. Therefore, about 63 percent of total taxes on property collection (OECD's "Taxes on Property" heading in figure 9.1) is accounted for in the financial and capital transactions subcategory ("Taxes on Financial Transact" heading in figure 9.1), which is 2.4 times the amount of recurrent property and land-holdings tax ("Recurrent Taxes on Real Estate" heading in figure 9.1) revenue in OECD Revenue Statistics for 2016 (OECD, n.d.).[4] Even if the revenue proceeds initially go to the provinces and metropolitan cities, some fraction of the yields are transferred to their constituent lower-level governments in the form of specific grant-in-aid or block-grant programs.[5] Table 9.12 reports the acquisition tax's rate change history for a 10-year period.

Education tax and a special rural development tax are surtaxes of the main acquisition tax in some locations. Starting in 2020, when multihouse ownership in areas with soaring property prices became a national concern, new purchases by people already owning multiple houses in these areas became subject to the special rate of up to 12 percent.

Policy debates regarding the acquisition tax concern its effectiveness in boosting or curbing housing market activity. Reductions in acquisition

Table 9.12 Property Transfer Tax Rates for Housing and Land (%)

	Jan. 1, 2011–Mar. 21, 2011	Mar. 22, 2011–Dec. 31, 2011	Jan. 1, 2012–Sept. 23, 2012	Sept. 24, 2012–June 30, 2013	July 1, 2013–Aug. 27, 2013	Aug. 28, 2013–Dec. 31, 2019	Jan. 1, 2020–
Property transfer tax	4.0	2.0	4.0	2.0	4.0	1.0 (<600 million) 2.0 (600 million–900 million) 3.0 (>900 million)	1.0 (<600 million) 2.0 (600 million–900 million) 3.0 (>900 million) ≤12.0 (2+ houses)
Special rural development tax (10% of tax amount)	0.2	0.5	0.2	0.5	0.2	0.2	0.2
Education tax (20% of tax amount)	0.4	0.2	0.4	0.2	0.4	0.1 0.2 0.3	0.4
Total	4.6	2.7	4.6	2.7	4.4	1.1 2.2 3.3	4.6

Source: Local Tax Act, Ministry of Interior and Safety.

tax rates can be especially contentious. For example, during the depressed housing market of 2011–2013, the central government tried lowering the transaction costs associated with the sale of a property to decrease moving costs by halving the housing transfer tax (see table 9.11). But the acquisition tax levied by provincial governments accounts for almost 26 percent of the total local tax revenue. Because of the tax's revenue importance, the on-and-off rate cuts caused controversy. First, provincial governments, especially the major metropolitan cities losing the tax revenue, were not receptive to the rate reductions if cities were not fully compensated through intergovernmental grants. The central issue became whether the transfer tax reduction would stimulate enough transactions to offset the revenue loss. The sales transaction elasticity with respect to price became the core of the policy debate. Second, the government's preferential transfer tax treatments toward lower-priced houses and sales promotion period transactions created simultaneous price-notch and time-notch problems.[6]

Revenue Performance of Property Tax

The property tax in Korea, including both recurrent and acquisition taxes, is equivalent to about 2.2 percent of GDP. Recurrent property taxes account for less than half this amount.

In 2017, recurrent local and national taxes on real property as a percentage of total government revenues was around 5.51 percent when all surtaxes are included (see table 9.11). Property taxes on land and buildings accounted for less than 2 percent of total government revenues throughout the 1980s. With the *Toji-Gong-Kae-Nyum* measures of (land) tax reform in 1990, the ratio continued to rise, until it reached 4.32 percent in 1995 and then plateaued at 4 percent.

But the importance of the local property tax as a local revenue source can be seen in its proportion of the local tax amount excluding national taxes (see table 9.11). The share of recurrent taxes on real property, including the local property tax, in total local tax revenue was around 21 percent from 2015 to 2017. That the same ratio declined to around 18 percent for cities indicates that county governments in rural areas are more dependent than metropolitan city governments on the local property tax as a revenue source.

Although local-government dependence on property-related taxes has eased somewhat in recent decades, property taxes, especially the land value tax, will continue to be the primary source of recurrent local-government revenue. Property taxes are a good choice for local governments (Rosengard

1998). They often do not play a policy role at the national level, even in jurisdictions with a long history of local autonomy. Korea, however, is still decentralizing, and traditions of fiscal centralization continue to influence the local property tax system. First, all local-government taxes are uniform and their structures are nationally determined. This may have the advantage of minimizing economic distortions and simplifying administration, but it comes at the cost of reducing local autonomy. The rates and base of local taxes, including the property tax, are enumerated in the Local Tax Act passed in National Assembly. Each local government, whether it is a provincial or lower-level government, can make only minor adjustments. Therefore, the realignment of the two-tier property tax system—the local property tax and then the GRET—was designed with the central government's specific policy objectives: giving a revenue mobilization role to the local property tax and pursuing real estate market stabilization and distribution policy goals through the GRET. But the question is still open as to whether this tax policy setup has been effective in lessening the real estate ownership concentration and curbing the speculation-motivated demand. And the absence of local fiscal autonomy has put a serious crimp in the revenue mobilization objective.

Korea's tax-to-GDP ratio of 27.4 percent in 2019 is well below the (unweighted) OECD average 33.8 percent. But taxes on property account for 11.7 percent of total tax revenue and 3.3 percent of GDP.[7] Among the 35 OECD member jurisdictions, Korea had the fourth-highest property tax share in 2016, after Iceland (34.2 percent), the United Kingdom (12.6 percent), and Canada (12.0 percent).[8]

Table 9.13 shows the revenue performance of property taxes of Korea at the national and city levels from 2015 to 2017 (refer to box 9.1 for definitions of cities). Revenue is composed of taxes, nontax receipts, and subsidies and grants from upper-level governments. "Property tax revenue" in the upper three rows includes all the recurrent taxes on real estate: local property tax, GRET, and the surtaxes of local resource and facility tax, special levy in city areas, pro rata portion of the education tax, and special tax for rural areas, and so on. To differentiate the revenue potential of property tax levied by local government from the overall property tax, the local property tax revenue as a percentage of local-government tax revenue is also reported.

The local property tax revenue constitutes more than 21 percent of total local-government tax revenues in the whole jurisdiction, but the share of local property tax in city-level government revenues is less than 6 percent (see table 9.13). Other revenue sources like the acquisition tax, local income tax, and local consumption tax are more important in terms of fiscal ca-

Table 9.13 Revenue Performance of Property and Land Taxes

Measures	2015	2016	2017
National			
Property tax revenue as % of GDP	1.07	1.07	1.10
Property tax revenue as % of total government revenue	3.13	3.08	3.13
Property tax revenue as % of total government tax revenue	5.81	5.49	5.51
Local property tax revenue as % of local-government tax revenue	21.23	21.14	21.32
Local property tax revenue as % of total local-government revenue	8.59	8.60	8.63
Acquisition tax revenue as % of GDP			1.04
City			
City property tax revenue as % of total city own-source revenue[1]	12.43	12.39	12.70
City property tax revenue as % of total city revenue	5.89	5.86	5.95
City property tax revenue as % of total city tax revenue	17.91	17.94	18.05
Property tax revenue per capita (KRW thousand)	183	195	210

Sources: Author's calculations using IMF (2018); MOIS (2018a, 2018b); National Tax Service (2016, 2017, 2018); OECD 2018.

[1] Own-source revenue = local tax revenue + nontax receipts.

pacity. Property and land tax for Seoul, the largest metropolitan city government, composed approximately 14 percent of revenue in 2018 and 2019 (table 9.14).

Of recurrent tax revenues, the local property tax constitutes 21.3–22.9 percent of county-level governments' tax revenue, 25.6–26.5 percent of city-level governments', and only 8.9–9.1 percent of metropolitan city and provincial-level governments' (table 9.15). The overall tax base of the local property tax is comprehensive, and the real estate database and tax rolls are maintained by both the central and the local levels. Registration of land and property deeds is required to update the current ownership status by the jurisdictional body of the jurisdiction. And the Ministries of the Interior and Safety and of Land, Infrastructure, and Transportation share the database necessary for real estate taxation. Still, there are problems: assessments have not been uniform because of disagreements between local and central governments during property booms, and the central government has continued to grant exemptions from the local property tax without sufficient compensation to local governments for revenue loss.

Table 9.14 Seoul Metropolitan Government Local Tax Revenue Budget, 2018 and 2019

	2018		2019	
Classification	KRW 100 Million	%	KRW 100 Million	%
Ordinary taxes				
Acquisition tax	4,395	25.7	4,274	24.0
Leisure tax	132	0.8	131	0.7
Property and land tax	2,369	13.9	2,615	14.7
Tobacco consumption tax	624	3.6	565	3.2
Automobile tax	1,102	6.4	1,132	6.4
Inhabitant tax	505	3.0	545	3.1
Local consumption tax	1,213	7.1	1,359	7.6
Local income tax	4,848	28.4	5,239	29.5
Subtotal	15,188	88.8	15,860	89.2
Earmarked taxes				
Regional resource and facilities tax	276	1.6	285	1.6
Local education tax	1,396	8.2	1,419	8.0
Subtotal	1,672	9.8	1,704	9.6
Revenue from the previous year	237	1.4	222	1.2
Total	**17,096**	**100.0**	**17,786**	**100.0**

Source: Seoul Metropolitan Government (2019).

Issues with Property and Land Taxation

The performance of the property tax in Korea is admirable in terms of how it is administered and in terms of the total revenue generated by its taxes on property ownership and transfers of ownership. But like all jurisdictions, Korea has issues to be addressed, including tax burdens and double taxation. These are discussed here.

Distribution of the Tax Burden

Both the tax laws and the tax administration contribute to an unfair tax burden distribution between residential and nonresidential properties. While the land and building components of residential property are valued and taxed as one unit in the tax law provisions, nonresidential property is presumed to be composed of land and building components that are taxed under different rate schedules. Because of infrequent updates to transaction

Table 9.15 Tax Collection by Local Governments and Sources, 2017 (KRW 100 million)

Tax	Total	Provincial and Metropolitan City Tax	City Tax	County Tax	%
Ordinary taxes					
Acquisition tax	234,867	234,867			**29.0**
Registration and license tax	16,077	16,077			
Leisure tax	10,510	10,510			
Property and land tax	**106,621**	**54,622**	45,935	6,064	**13.0**
Tobacco consumption tax	36,026	14,607	17,819	3,600	
Automobile tax	77,723	30,251	39,822	7,650	
Inhabitant tax	18,633	8,709	8,626	1,298	
Local consumption tax	72,738	72,738			
Local income tax	144,395	73,311	62,270	8,814	**18.0**
Subtotal	**717,590**	**515,692**	**174,472**	**27,426**	**89.2**
Earmarked taxes					
Regional resource and facilities tax	15,126	14,873			2.2
City planning tax	–3	–3	253		4.4
Local education tax	64,230	64,230			2.0
Subtotal	**79,353**	**79,100**	**253**	**0**	**9.9**
Revenue from the previous year	7,150	3,140	3,481	529	0.9
Total	**804,091**	**597,932**	**178,206**	**27,955**	**100.0**

Source: Ministry of Interior & Safety (2017).

records and nonstandardized attributes in the commercial and industrial properties market, nonresidential real estate tends to be appraised at levels lower than residential property. Also, the lack of rental income information by the taxing authority makes it difficult to adopt the net rental value approach in determining the fair market value for taxing these properties. The sum of separately determined tax assessment values of land and structures in nonresidential property is below the fair market value obtained through a comparative market transaction method. Because only owners of land and property are subject to land and property taxes, renters are not directly liable, and owner-occupiers have a different tax burden. However, there is also the question of whether the incidence of the property tax falls on capital in the Korean real estate market. Does the property tax structure and administration lead to perverse incentives for land use? With the lessened tax burden for nonresidential use, there are incentives for property to be categorized as mixed-use property.

Property and Land Taxes Are Controversial

Any taxpayer who is liable for property taxes on housing as of the date of taxation and whose aggregate of publicly notified housing value exceeds KRW 900 million for owner-occupiers or KRW 600 million for multi-house owners must pay the GRET. Likewise, a person whose aggregate landholding value exceeds KRW 500 million or KRW 8 billion in the general-aggregation category or special-aggregation category, respectively, is subject to the GRET.

An estimated more than 70,000 residential properties exceed this threshold, the value of which has not been updated for more than 15 years, while housing prices have skyrocketed. In this sense, property taxes are controversial and unpopular among the housing rich during housing price inflation and a slowdown of income growth. Trapped by the liquidity constraint on tax payments, housing-rich and income-poor cohorts like the retired and elderly feel the tax burden is too severe, because the unrealized increase in housing wealth is subject to (progressive rate) taxation without taking into account the ability to pay. The reference date of ownership that determines who is obligated to pay the tax is June 1 every year. Retirees whose lifetime savings is their home are enraged by the double-digit increase in local property and GRET taxes and health insurance premiums.

Tax Burdens and Land Use Impacts

One of the main objectives of introducing the aggregate land value tax in 1990 was to discourage the concentrated distribution of land ownership.

Ro (2001a) examined the individual taxpayer's land ownership concentration between 1993 and 1996. The Gini coefficient increased from 0.6544 in 1993 to 0.6708 in 1996, which can be interpreted as no improvement in lessening the land ownership concentration.

Also, the introduction of the GRET was motivated by the need to address the housing-wealth concentration problem. Ro (2012) estimated the housing tax burden and equity impacts of the local property tax and GRET using sample household data. The total burden from the local property tax and GRET compared with current income was 1.98 percent on average in 2011. But the tax burdens by income quintile regress as the ratio declines and the income quintile goes up: 5.51 percent (the lowest-income group) > 2.15 percent > 1.41 percent > 1.12 percent > 0.89 percent (the highest-income group). The effective rate on the total local property tax and GRET was 0.19 percent. A separation of the distributional effects into local property and national GRET parts showed that the regressivity of the local property part dominates the progressivity of the national GRET part, with the Suits index[9] of −0.10 for the former and 0.21 for the latter types of taxes.

Double Taxation

In 2015, the Korean Supreme Court ruled that the formula for calculating the credit for the local property tax payment to avoid double taxation with the GRET was not appropriate (Ruling Annulling GRET Levy 2015.6.23). Its decision was clear that the change in rules by presidential decree in 2009 did not support the legitimacy of less than full deduction of the local property tax in determination of the GRET. The double taxation issue arose because both the local property tax and the GRET were levied on the same real estate asset holdings, first by local government as in rem tax and then by central government as a personal tax. The central government exempts owners of one house from paying GRET for up to KRW 900 million and owners of multiple houses for up to KRW 600 million. Therefore, housing wealth above these thresholds was subject to double taxation, first by local jurisdictions as local property tax and then by central government as the GRET. In the equation for GRET determination,[10] the specific fractional assessment ratios for both the local property tax and the GRET are stipulated differently in the presidential decrees; in 2019 housing was 60 percent for the local property tax and 85 percent for the GRET. The discrepancy in assessment ratios between 60 percent for one tax and 85 percent for the other led to double taxation. But in the GRET, the way the assessment ratio is multiplied after the threshold amount is deducted and then put into the tax rate schedule is quite different from the way the ratio is multiplied and then put into the rate schedule for the local property tax. This inconsistency in integrating in rem local property tax into personal GRET results in more serious double-taxation issues in which multihouse owners have a different rate schedule applied, especially in the form of ownership shares.[11]

The Backdrop for Reform

The taxation of land and property in Korea has changed dramatically as the jurisdiction modernizes. The recurrent annual taxes now feature a rule-based land and building tax focused on taxing the residential and nonresidential sectors. It is broad based and supported by technological advances in collection and valuation methods. The GRET, another annual property tax but focused more on achieving macroeconomic objectives and equity, is now levied by the national government (with the proceeds directed back to the local governments). The primary revenue producer in the real estate tax system is the property transfer tax (acquisition tax).

The difficult problems with the recurrent property tax system that have emerged are that it has not achieved its revenue potential, even in this time of rapid increases in land and property values. This is due partly to underassessment, partly to low statutory tax rates, and partly to the limited coverage of the GRET. A result of this weak revenue mobilization from annual property taxes is that local governments in Korea are left with little discretion to generate more resources.

Korea has three issues to deal with in formulating a reform program. First, designing and implementing an equitable personal progressive land and property tax is very difficult. Raising land value assessments for the aggregate land value tax during the stable and depressed land market of 1990–1995 increased the tax yield only 3-fold compared with the increase of land value assessments of 2.5-fold. The average annual 24 percent yield increase in revenues came mainly from the increases in land value reassessments and not from the progressive tax rate structure in effect during this period. Because of strong resistance to revaluation from landowners, local tax officials could not raise the taxable base high enough for any significant bracket creep. Local tax officials knew that continually increasing the aggregate land value tax burden would face strong resistance from taxpayers because of their cash-flow difficulties. Also, the difficulty of maintaining uniform assessment ratios among classes of lands belonging to the same progressive rate band forced the previous aggregate land value tax and the current GRET to become part of the equity issue.[12] A property tax system with a progressive rate structure, like the GRET, is especially difficult to implement because the distribution of tax burdens is sensitive to assessment uniformity.

Second, the feasibility of two-tier local and central property taxation depends on close intergovernmental relationship and tax administration cooperation. Throughout the nation, approximately 30 million taxable objects (land and housing units) are listed in the local property tax and GRET tax rolls, and at least one-fourth of them require updates to their ownership and physical characteristics changes. The annual administration cost incurred by every level of local government and the central government in maintaining the land valuation system reached almost USD 100 million, but the quality of the resulting official value of individual parcels has not been checked against actual market transaction data. As fiscal decentralization progressed after the first local elections of mayors, governors, and councilors in 1995, local-government fiscal autonomy took on more importance because property and land taxes came to be recognized as an own revenue source for local governments. But the current local property tax and GRET system does not provide much room for local-government autonomy. Even though local governments are allowed to use revenues raised from the local property tax at their discretion, they do not have much discretion over tax rates and adjusting the assessed values. Thus, increasing the share of recurrent property taxes and reducing the transfer tax burden while maintaining revenue neutrality would entail a total overhaul of the local tax system. The amount of revenue resulting from the change makes it unlikely that 270 upper- and lower-level local governments would agree to it.

Third, stabilizing the property market is not the primary objective of local government, and the property tax is not the appropriate fiscal tool to achieve it. The two main goals of introducing the aggregate land value tax in the 1990s and the GRET in 2005 were to stabilize the land and housing markets and to change the ownership concentration among individuals. The traditional in-rem land tax effect has theoretical underpinnings, but little is known about the actual capitalization process of this personal land and housing wealth tax. Also, it is questionable whether the increased landholding tax and housing wealth tax burden caused the rate of increase in land prices to be less than they otherwise would have been.

A comparison of land ownership concentration between 1993 and 1996 finds no significant change in land ownership distribution leading to a more equitable state, even when the increase of the aggregate land value tax burden was imposed in 1995. Moreover, tax avoidance avenues are always open. It has always been possible for taxpayers to reduce the aggregate tax and GRET burden by transferring a title to other members of a household with fewer real estate holdings. This and similar loopholes might have contributed to this tax's low effectiveness in reducing the concentration of real estate ownership.

Notes

1. The Korea Appraisal Board was a professional appraisal and assessment institution established in 1969. After a refocusing of its activities, the board was rebranded as the Korea Real Estate Board.

2. The United States and other high-income jurisdictions have made few major reforms in property taxation field, but Korea has experimented with fairly drastic reforms from 1990 to 2020. California's approval of Proposition 13 in 1978 and Pittsburgh's restructuring of its property tax system in 1979 could be regarded as major reforms at the subnational level (Oates and Schwab 1997). Korea's 2005 property tax reforms that introduced GRET, the inauguration of other central-government land taxes and charges, and the national land valuation system (Official Land and Property Value System) in the 1990s are examples. For a detailed description of these taxes and changes, see Ro (1996).

3. Korea has a more than 40-year-long history of taxing capital gains realized from real estate. The capital gains tax is separate from other individual ordinary income. It has its own tax rate schedule and tax base calculation, different from the comprehensive income tax. Even though the capital gains tax–translated from the Korean name of "the tax on the income from alienation of asset," has been imposed on the seller's total annual net gains from chargeable capital assets, it has not been developed as a special form of personal income tax in terms of source, characteristics, and timing of income. Very narrow form of capital assets like real estate and the right to use it have only been taxed, and hence the capital gains tax has been used as a fiscal tool used by the central government to stabilize boom-bust cycles in land and housing markets.

4. The OECD Recurrent Taxes on Real Estate subcategory tax includes financial transfer taxes, such as stock transaction tax, stamp duties, and vehicle registration tax, so that determining the real estate–related transfer tax revenue is difficult.

5. Various forms of property transfer taxes are prevalent at the city, state, and provincial levels of many jurisdictions. For example, real estate transfer tax and real property transfer tax are imposed by New York State and New York City. Also, deed recording tax and deed transfer tax are imposed in Washington, DC. In Canada and Australia, land transfer taxes have long been imposed by provincial governments. The United Kingdom has the national stamp duty land tax (formerly stamp duty) with 0%, 2%, 5%, 10%, and 12% marginal progressive tax rates. The effects of these property transfer taxes on both public finance and property markets have been a subject of attention in the academic literature. See Dachis, Duranton, and Turner (2011) and Harris (2013).

6. Ro (2013) addresses some of the economic inefficiency caused by these notches.

7. Most of the chapter follows OECD classification criteria of taxes. But the amount of each tax collected and the subtotals of some subcategories are all based on the original figures of actual collections published in the official Korean government statistics. The international comparisons are based on the data reported in the jurisdiction sections of the IMF, Government Finance Statistics (2018) and OECD, Revenue Statistics (2018).

8. The OECD uses a different definition of property tax revenues than the government of Korea. The government's share of property tax revenues to GDP is 2.14%; according to the OECD, it is 3.3%.

9. Suit's index is a measure of progressiveness of a certain tax or a set of taxes named for economist Daniel B. Suits. It is calculated by comparing the area under the Lo-

renz curve to the area under a 45-degree proportional line. The most progressive tax when the richest taxpayer unit pays all the tax has a Suits index of 0, and a regressive tax when the less wealthy pay a greater fraction of their wealth has a negative value.

10. The GRET for housing after deducting the local property tax payment tax credit for an individual i is calculated by the following equation when the local property tax on house j owned by an individual i with share α_{ij} is aggregated across local jurisdictions and the person's gross housing wealth exceeds KRW 600 million.

$$GTax_i = G\left\{\left(\sum_{i=1}^{J} DV_j \times 0.6 \times a_{ij}\right) - 600mil.\right\} \times 0.85 - \sum_{i=1}^{J} PTax_j$$
$$\times P\left\{\left(\sum_{i=1}^{J} DV_j \times 0.6 \times a_{ij}\right) - 600mil.\right\} / P\left\{\sum_{i=1}^{J} DV_j \times 0.6 \times a_{ij}\right\}$$

where

$G(\cdot)$ and $P(\cdot)$ are GRET and local property tax rate schedule functions, respectively, and DV and AV are declared value and assessed value, respectively.

11. For a detailed analysis, see Ro (2012, 184–185).

12. The taxation structure for the land portion of the GRET is the same as that for the previous aggregate land value tax.

References

Dachis, B., G. Duranton, and M. A. Turner. 2011. "The Effects of Land Transfer Taxes on Real Estate Markets: Evidence from a Natural Experiment in Toronto." *Journal of Economic Geography* 12 (2): 327–354.

George, H. 1992. *Progress and Poverty*. New York: Robert Schalkenbach Foundation. First published 1879.

Harris, B. H. 2013. "Tax Reform, Transactions Costs, and Metropolitan Housing in the United States." Paper presented at the 106th Annual National Tax Association Conference, Tampa, FL (November 21–23).

IMF. 2018. *Government Finance Statistics*. Washington, DC: International Monetary Fund.

Ministry of Interior and Safety. 2016–2018. *Statistical Yearbook of Local Tax*, 2016–2018. Seoul, South Korea.

———. 2017. *Financial Yearbook of Local Government*. Seoul, South Korea.

———. 2018a. *Statistical Yearbook of Local Tax 2016–2018*. Seoul, South Korea.

———. 2018b. *Consolidated Local Governments Finance*. Seoul, South Korea.

MOLIT. 2020. *Housing Market Trends in Seoul and Korea*. Ministry of Land, Infrastructure, and Transportation, Seoul, South Korea.

National Tax Service. 2016, 2017, 2018. *National Tax Statistical Yearbook*. Seoul, South Korea

Oates, W., and R. Schwab. 1997. "The Impact of Urban Land Taxation: The Pittsburgh Experience." *National Tax Journal* 50 (1): 1–21.

OECD. 2018. *Revenue Statistics*. Paris: Organization for Economic Co-operation and Development. https://stats.oecd.org/index.aspx?DataSetCode=REV (accessed 01 March 2022).

Ro, Y., ed. 1996. *Land Taxation in Korea: A Critical Review of Current Policies and Suggestions for Future Policy Direction.* Seoul: Korea Institute of Public Finance.

———. 2001a. "Does Progressive Land Value Tax Induce More Equitable Distribution of Land in Korea?" Paper presented at the 57th Congress of 2001 International Institute of Public Finance (IIPF). Linz, Austria (August 27–30).

———. 2001b. Land Value Taxation in South Korea." Working paper WP01YR1. Cambridge, MA: Lincoln Institute of Land Policy.

———. 2001c. "Policy Proposals on Land Taxation in Korea." [in Korean]. Final draft of research project submitted to Ministry of Land and Transportation, Seoul, Korea.

———. 2004. "Real Estate Taxation in Korea." *Tax Notes International* 35 (10): 893–899.

———. 2012. *Net Wealth Tax and Aggregated Real Estate Tax in Korea.* [In Korean.] Seoul: Korea Institute of Public Finance.

———. 2013. *Acquisition Tax Reduction for the Vitalization of Housing Transactions and Its Effect on Local Tax Revenues.* [In Korean.] Sejong: Korea Institute of Public Finance.

Rosengard, J. K. 1998. *Property Tax Reform in Developing Countries.* Boston: International Tax Program Harvard University / Kluwer Academic.

Seoul Metropolitan Government. 2019. *Financial Yearbook of Seoul Government.* Seoul, South Korea.

10

Malaysia: Property and Land Taxes in a Federal System

DZURLLKANIAN ZULKARNAIN DAUD AND SALFARINA SAMSUDIN

Malaysia's population as of 2021 is estimated at 32.6 million. Urbanization has slightly increased since 1970, rising from about 75 percent of the population to 76.2 percent by 2019 (Department of Statistics Malaysia 2020; Embong 2011; Rofiei et al. 2016). The World Bank classifies Malaysia as a developing jurisdiction, with an upper-middle-income ranking and steady economic growth (Royal Institution of Chartered Surveyors 2019). Malaysia is divided into thirteen states and three federal territories. Eleven states and two federal territories (Kuala Lumpur and Putrajaya) are in Peninsular Malaysia, and two states (Sabah and Sarawak) and one federal territory (Labuan) are in East Malaysia.

Malaysia is a parliamentary democracy with a constitutional monarch as the head of state (Gökçe 2013). The three levels of government—federal, state, and local—divide powers and functions among them. The federal government has jurisdiction over foreign affairs, finance, transportation, and other sectors mentioned in the constitution. The state governments oversee land, local governments, Islamic religious affairs, agriculture, and forestry. Although local governments serve as local planning and licensing

We thank Madam Siti Maizun Arshad from the Valuation Department of Kuala Lumpur City Council and Dr. Soeb Pawi from the Valuation Department of Kulai Municipal Council for their fruitful discussion and data assistance. We also thank our editors and anonymous reviewers for helpful comments on earlier versions of this chapter.

authorities, they have the competence to impose certain types of taxes according to the provisions of the Local Government Act (Act 171) 1976. The 154 local governments in Malaysia are divided into four categories, as shown in table 10.1.

In Malaysia, local governments are under the jurisdiction of state government and are intermediaries between the state and the people within their jurisdictions. Their primary role is to provide services, such as environmental, social, public, and security services, and to ensure that policies are conducted fairly at all levels of the society (Md Khalid, Mat Nurudin, and Mohd Zain 2017). The three federal territories governed directly by the federal government of Malaysia are Kuala Lumpur, Putrajaya, and Labuan. Kuala Lumpur is the capital city of Malaysia, and Kuala Lumpur City Council performs the local-government duties.[1]

Table 10.1 Local Governments in Malaysia

State or Federal Territory	City Hall	Municipal Council	District Council	Special / Modified Council	Total by State
Peninsular Malaysia					
Johor	2	6	7	1	16
Kedah	1	4	6	1	12
Kelantan	0	1	11	0	12
Melaka	1	3	0	0	4
Negeri Sembilan	0	4	4	0	8
Pahang	0	3	8	1	12
Perak	1	4	10	0	15
Perlis	0	1	0	0	1
Pulau Pinang	2	0	0	0	2
Selangor	2	6	4	0	12
Terengganu	1	2	4	0	7
Kuala Lumpur	1	0	0	0	1
Putrajaya	0	0	0	1	1
East Malaysia					
Sarawak	3	4	19	0	26
Sabah	1	2	21	0	24
Labuan	0	0	0	1	1
Total for Malaysia	**15**	**40**	**94**	**5**	**154**

Source: Local Government Department, Ministry of Housing and Local Government, Malaysia (2019).

This chapter provides an introduction to land ownership and property rights and an overview of land and property taxes in Malaysia. It then describes the details of property tax law and practice, and it explores the administrative process and capacity issues currently faced by Kuala Lumpur City Council. The closing section highlights issues and challenges with regard to property tax practice and policy, including a spotlight on attempts at reform to date, and offers some thoughts on the way forward.

Land Tenure and Property Rights

Land is primarily in private ownership, and Malaysia operates a cadastre-based land administration system (Asian Development Bank 2020). There are 7.3 million land parcels, of which 98 percent are legally registered and surveyed (Nordin 2010). By law, state governments have the right and responsibility to administer the land in their jurisdictions. Land laws in Malaysia are governed by the National Land Code (Act 828), which applies to the states in Peninsular Malaysia, except for Penang and Malacca, both of which are governed by the National Land Code (Penang and Malacca Titles) Act 1963.

Land registration in Malaysia is based on the Torrens system, in which property rights are certified by registered titles and land ownership entails an indefeasible interest in land and guarantee that the person named on the title displayed in a land register is the rightful owner. A uniform system has emerged with respect to land tenure, title registration, transfer of land, leases and charges, easements, and other rights and interests in land. A title document clearly defines the location of the land, category of land use, ownership of transfer, constraints, and all subsequent transactions or dealings in the land. These details are registered when the title document is obtained at the state registry or district land office.

Tenure of land in Malaysia falls into two broad categories: levied freehold and leasehold. Freehold of land lasts indefinitely and can be transferred from one person to another (La Croix 2017). However, this tenure may have restrictions, which are stated in the title deed. Some state regulations give government the right to acquire land for socially beneficial services. Leasehold of land normally refers to leases from the state authority, usually granted for up to 99 years. Other periods of leasing may be shorter—for example, 60 years. The property returns to the state upon lease expiration, and the landholder will not be entitled to any compensation (Zainuddin 2010). If the lease is reaching the expiry date, the landholder can renew or extend the lease by paying a lease extension premium. The fee depends on property type, extension length, or other aspect.

Overview of Real Estate Taxes

As in most jurisdictions, Malaysia's taxes on real estate fall into two categories: taxes on acquisition and transfer of real estate and recurrent taxes on the holding of real estate. In Malaysia, the first category includes stamp duty and capital gains taxes. The federal government imposes these for revenue raising, but they also are used to control inflation in the property market and to verify ownership. The second category includes quit rent and the recurrent property tax. Quit rent is under the control of the state government, and property tax is levied by local governments. Table 10.2 shows the types of taxes within each category, the relevant level of government, and the law governing each tax.

Stamp Duty

The stamp duty is a federal tax levied under the Stamp Duty Act 1949. Duties are imposed on instruments and not transactions; *instrument* is defined as any written document specified in the First Schedule of the act. In general, stamp duty is levied on legal, commercial, and financial instruments and is collected by the Inland Revenue Board of Malaysia. Stamp duties are levied on both an ad valorem and a fixed-amount basis. The ad valorem duty rate varies depending on the type and value of the instrument.[2] For immovable properties, stamp duty is the tax placed on documents during the sale or transfer of any property, which includes sale and purchase agreements or memorandums of transfer. According to Aliasak and Sa'ad (2015), this provision is purposely to ensure that the transaction of property is validated and that the purchaser right is secured after the transaction.

Table 10.2 Basic Features of Land and Property Taxes

Tax Category	Tax Type	Government Level	Relevant Law
Taxes on acquisition and transfer of real estate	Stamp duty	Federal	Stamp Duty Act 1949
	Real property capital gains tax	Federal	Real Property Gains Tax Act 1976
Taxes on possession and operation of real estate	Quit rent / land tax	State	National Land Code (Act 828); State Land Rules
	Property tax / assessment tax	Local	Local Government Act 1976

Table 10.3 Stamp Duty for Real Estate
Transactions, 2020

Property Price (MYR)	Stamp Duty (%)
<100,000	1
101,000–500,000	2
500,001–1 million	3
>1 million	4

Source: Inland Revenue of Board Malaysia
(2020).

The valuation that determines the amount of stamp duty owed is carried out by officers from the Valuation and Property Services Department,
Ministry of Finance (Ab Latif et al. 2018). These officers inspect the property, analyze comparisons, decide value, and produce a valuation report
(Rosman et al. 2019). The valuation report is sent to the Inland Revenue
Board of Malaysia for the notification of the stamp duty payable. The duty
is based on the monetary value of the consideration or the market value of
the property, whichever is higher.

In the 2019 budget, the government announced a stamp duty increase,
from 3 percent to 4 percent, for properties costing more than MYR 1 million (about USD 240,000). Enactment of the increase for 2020 is shown in
table 10.3.

Real Property Gains Tax

The real property gains tax is the sole tax on capital gains in Malaysia. It
is imposed on the revenues from the disposal of real property and on the
shares of a real estate company. The Real Property Gains Tax Act 1976
ensures that profits made from the sale of land are taxed. This tax was designed to raise revenue and to prevent property speculation (Zainuddin
2015). The tax rate depends on the duration of holding. The basis of the
tax is the original purchase price less miscellaneous expenditures and less
a standard exemption level. Effective January 1, 2019, the tax was increased
for property sold after six years. Table 10.4 summarizes the tax rates applicable to the various entities.

As seen in table 10.4, real property gains tax rates are slightly different
for companies and citizens. The rates decrease three years after acquisition for companies and citizens, to a low of 5 percent for citizens holding
property for more than six years. As is the case in many other Asian jurisdictions, noncitizens are charged a higher rate.

Table 10.4 Real Property Gains Tax Rates, 2020

Years Held After Acquisition	Company Rate (%)	Individual Rate for Citizens and Permanent Residents (%)	Individual Rate for Noncitizens (%)
<3 years	30	30	30
4 years	20	20	30
5 years	15	15	30
6+ years	10	5	10

Source: Inland Revenue Board of Malaysia (2020).

Quit Rent

In Malaysia, every registered land parcel is subject to an administrative tax, known as quit rent, under National Land Code 1965 provisions (Adnan, Suratman, and Samsudin 2021). It is an annual land tax payable to the state government and is levied on the landowner, whether freehold or leasehold and whether unimproved or improved. Each state government has autonomy to determine its own tax rate schedule. The quit rent payable within states also varies according to the size and locality of land parcels and the category of land use. Each state authority has different rates for agricultural and building or industrial land. Table 10.5 shows the quit rent rates for Kuala Lumpur.

Quit rents are the largest source of own revenue for state governments in Malaysia. The National Land Code 1965 mandates landowners to pay quit rents by a certain date. The last date for payment of quit rent varies from state to state, but most states set May 31 as the deadline. Payments after the deadline are subject to penalty. Landowners can lose their properties if the state forfeits the property.

Table 10.5 Quit Rent Rates for Residential, Commercial, and Industrial Land in Kuala Lumpur

Land Use	Rate of Rent per Annum (MYR/m^2)		
	Town Land	Village Land	Jurisdiction Land
Residential	0.65	0.50	0.30
Commercial	4.00	4.00	3.00
Industrial	3.30	3.30	1.60

Source: Federal Territories Director of Lands and Mines (2019).

Recurrent Property Tax

Property taxes are collected by the local councils. The recurrent property tax in Malaysia refers to the tax levied on the ownership or occupation of immovable properties—for example, houses, shops, factories, and offices (Umar, Kasim, and Martin 2012). The tax rate varies among local governments according to the targeted collection amount of each (Daud, Alias, and Muthuveerappan 2008). The revenues pay for developing and maintaining infrastructure and services in the local authority administrative areas (Pawi 2013). The property tax system is the main source of local-government revenue.

The Recurrent Property Tax System in Peninsular Malaysia

In Peninsular Malaysia, the property tax system is guided by the Local Government Act (Act 171) 1976. Section 39(a) of Act 171 states that revenue of a local authority is all the taxes, rates, rents, license fees, dues, and other sums or charges payable to the local authority—making the property tax the largest source of revenue for municipalities. Local governments have autonomy as prescribed by the act to levy the tax. Taxpayers will receive benefits from the tax in the form of tangible and intangible services, community facilities, infrastructures and development projects (Alias 2000; Pawi et al. 2011). The property tax is an important instrument for steering local planning and development.

Base of the Property Tax

According to Section 130, rates depend on the annual value of the holding or on the (capital) improved value of the building as determined by the local authorities (Halim et al. 2017). Annual tax rates are imposed on the property's estimated, reasonable gross annual rent if the landlord pays for repair, insurance, maintenance or upkeep, and all public rates and taxes.[3] According to the section 2 of the Local Government Act 1976, improved value of holding means the price that an owner willing, and not obliged to sell, might reasonably expect to obtain from a willing purchaser with whom he was bargaining, for sale and purchase of the holding.

Annual value is the most widely used means of assessment, except in the states of Johor and Malacca, where the capital improved value is used as the basis of property rates (table 10.6).

In general, a residential unit's property tax liability is 0.1 percent to 0.5 percent of the improved value, or 1 percent to 10 percent of the annual value. However, as shown in table 10.7, the tax rates vary according to use of the property. Agricultural and vacant lands are taxed at lower rates and

Table 10.6 Property Tax Bases Adopted by Local
Governments

Local Governments	No. of Local Governments Using	
	Annual Value	Improved Value
Peninsular Malaysia	84	20
East Malaysia	50	–
Total	**134**	**20**

commercial and industrial lands at the highest rates. Minimum and maximum rates are imposed by the state governments.

The range of rates shown in table 10.7 suggests considerable variation across the 150-some local governments in Malaysia. In particular, statutory tax rates in Kuala Lumpur are low relative to the rest of the jurisdiction; however, property values in the capital city have doubled or tripled since 2010. For the other local authorities that assess annual values, the rate of growth of residential properties has risen between 5 and 13 percent.

In Malaysia, different rates are often applied to different classes of land and property, such as whether they are used for residential, commercial, or industrial purposes. Tax rates also are sometimes differentiated by area if there are certain public services that benefit only particular areas in a city. The actual tax rate levied varies from one local authority to another. The more improved or built up a property is, the higher its value. This contributes to the higher property tax. Tax rates are set by discussion among members of the council chaired by the mayor and on the basis of the total annual value of all assets, the maximum target budget (potential tax revenue) to cover annual expenses, and the proposed budget for the year. The tax increase usually does not exceed 20–25 percent from the previous year.

Exemptions and Reliefs

Section 134 of the law exempts properties used exclusively for public purposes or religious worship; licensed burial grounds or crematoria; public schools; and places for charitable, science, and literature and fine arts purposes. These exemptions must be approved by the local governments.

Section 135 of the law states that if any holding or part thereof is used exclusively for recreational, social, or welfare purposes and not for pecuniary profit, the state authority may at its discretion exempt such holding

Table 10.7 Property Tax Rates Imposed by Local Governments

Property Tax Base	Residential (%)	Commercial (%)	Industrial (%)	Agriculture / Vacant Land (%)
Annual value				
Kuala Lumpur City Council	2.00–7.00	8.00–10.00	8.00–10.00	1.00–7.00
Other local governments (except Kuala Lumpur City Council and local government in states of Johor and Melaka)	5.00–13.00	6.00–13.00	6.00–13.00	2.00–7.00
Improved value				
Local governments in the states of Johor and Melaka	0.15–0.35	0.20–0.50	0.25–0.75	0.05–0.25

Source: Daud, Alias, and Muthuveerappan (2008).

Figure 10.1 Application Process for Exemption from or Reduction of
Property Tax

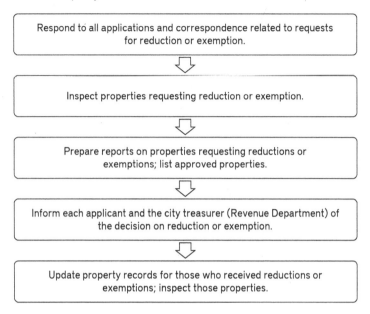

or such part thereof from the payment of all or any rates, or reduce the
rate. The property tax paid by the government on government-owned
buildings—either federal or state buildings—is a contribution in lieu of
tax. Other uses such as common areas are exempted from tax. The steps
state authorities take to make exemptions or reductions of assessment tax
are in figure 10.1.

Valuation and Assessment

The Department of Valuation and Property Services is responsible for
all matters related to rating valuation and assessment (Daud et al. 2013).
The department's property valuers identify the properties to be taxed,
manage and update the property data and information, revalue all properties every five years, determine the necessary tax rates, update the valuation roll, identify changes of ownership, entertain appeals, collect unpaid
taxes, and handle applications for rebates.

Valuation and assessment departments of local governments are administered by the state secretary of the government office, which approves
or disapproves rates proposed by local authorities. When considering

approval, the Department of Valuation and Property Services determines the annual value or improved value for every holding by applying only valuation procedures (Aliasak and Sa'ad 2015).

Methods for Valuation

Any of the accepted valuation methods—comparative rentals or sales, profit and investment, or cost—may be used, depending on the property's nature, available comparable data, type of use, and location. The comparative method is used to value properties that are commercial, residential, vacant land, or industrial. Comparisons of sales records for similar properties are adjusted and analyzed to obtain differences that determine assessments (Daud et al. 2013), and special properties are valued using profit and investment methods and cost methods. The staff measure land and buildings (survey property) and create records in the local authority's valuation department. In this way, proper records on all the properties in the local authority areas can be kept systematically.

Section 140 of the Local Government Act empowers a representative of the local authority to enter, inspect, and survey any holding within the local authority area. It also empowers the local authority to require the owners or occupiers of any holding to furnish information on the area, situation, quality, use, and rent necessary for the preparation of the valuation list. One who fails to furnish the correct information within two weeks or hinders the local authority from entering, inspecting, or surveying property may be fined up to MYR 2,000, imprisoned up to six months, or both.

BOX 10.1 EXAMPLE OF CALCULATION OF TAX

The property tax is imposed on either an annual value (AV) or improved value (MV) basis. There is a significant difference in the tax rate between annual value and improved value.

For property tax based on annual value, if the AV is MYR 12,000 and the tax rate is 3 percent, then the property tax owed per year is calculated as follows:

Property tax = AV × tax rate

$$= 12{,}000 \times 3\%$$
$$= (12{,}000 \times 3) \div 100$$

Tax payable = MYR 360

For property tax based on improved value, if the MV is MYR 300,000 and the tax rate is 0.15 percent, then the property tax payable owed per year is calculated as follows:

Property tax $= MV \times$ tax rate

$\qquad = 300{,}000 \times 0.15\%$

$\qquad = (300{,}000 \times 0.15) \div 100$

Tax payable $=$ MYR 450

Most valuation lists are computerized, and a few local authorities use digital maps. After all returns have been received, a critical analysis of values is made, using the adequate and correct information both from the surveys and from the returns. This analysis is very important because valuation accuracy is critical to enforce the property tax. Box 10.1 shows examples of how property tax is calculated.

Revaluation

The local government performs revaluations to determine the amount and rate of tax to be charged (Kamarudin and Daud 2014). The property tax is the biggest source of local-government revenue. The revaluation of the property tax roll updates all annual values or improved values for land and buildings to the current value. This keeps it consistent, accurate, and equitable. It ensures that property owners pay fair, effective rates. Updating property records also finds properties not yet listed and verifies the fairness of property taxes (e.g., revaluating renovated houses or improved properties). Revaluation work is mostly outsourced to private valuation firms.

Objection Process

The Local Government Act 1976 granted to taxpayers the right to object for certain grievances (Section 142 of the LGA 1976). These include over- or undervaluing a property, charging tax on a property that is nontaxable by the act, and omitting a property from the valuation list (Muhammad and Ishak 2013). The objection must be in writing to the local authority and no later than 14 days before the valuation list is revised. All persons making objections will be allowed the opportunity to be heard either in person or represented by an authorized agent.

Property Taxation in Kuala Lumpur

Kuala Lumpur's population is about 1.7 million, or less than 1 percent of the national population (Department of Statistics Malaysia 2020). It is the largest city and growing rapidly, covering 243 km². Since 1961, Kuala Lumpur has been governed by a single corporate entity. Its mayor is appointed by the Ministry of Federal Territories. Kuala Lumpur City Council is responsible for public health and sanitation, waste removal and management, town planning, environmental protection and building control, social and economic development, and general maintenance functions of urban infrastructure.

Tax Administration

Kuala Lumpur City Council derives its revenue mainly (about 49 percent) from property taxes. It established a valuation unit in 1958 that became the Property Management and Valuation Department in 1975. The department makes valuations and assessments on about 645,658 private properties in the Federal Territory of Kuala Lumpur. As of 2020, the division has 302 personnel, including 32 valuation officers and 97 assistant valuation officers.

Taxable property in Kuala Lumpur is divided into four categories: residential, commercial, institutional, and industrial (table 10.8), which are further categorized according to whether they are within the 93.2396 km² of the city center or beyond it. The area within 36 square miles is considered a prime area. It has high density and is the most expensive.

Residential units account for about 85 percent of all properties in metropolitan Kuala Lumpur, and about two-thirds of these are in the outer suburbs. Commercial and industrial properties tend to be more heavily concentrated within the inner 93.2396 km², near amenities and the main

Table 10.8 Taxable Properties in Kuala Lumpur

Property Type	No. of Units Within City Center (93.2396 km²)	No. of Units Outside City Center
Residential	167,939	354,554
Commercial	51,307	46,943
Institutional	58	37
Industrial	993	4,089
Subtotal	**220,297**	**405,623**
Total	**625,920**	

Source: Kuala Lumpur City Hall (2018).

attractions of the city. Overall, there are about 2.88 persons per property in metropolitan Kuala Lumpur.

Section 137 of the Local Government Act 1976 allows the local authorities to make revaluations every five years or at a frequency determined by the state-level authorities. Kuala Lumpur City Council in 2013 independently carried out in-house revaluation work and used a computerized valuation and administration system. This revaluation was for a tax roll last updated 22 years before, in 1992. Table 10.9 describes the 2021 property tax rates imposed by Kuala Lumpur City Council in 2020. The rates depend on use or location of the property. Commercial and industrial properties received the highest rates both before and after revaluation. However, the rates were lowered for all types of properties to soften the impact of the new tax roll. This reduction is in step with the strategy of reducing the amount of arrears for each state.

The annual value and revenue for the general revaluation of January 1, 2014, is in table 10.10.

The revaluation in 2014 increased taxable annual value by 47.7 percent. The property tax increase was capped at 0, 10, or 25 percent, according to property ownership. The maximum of 25 percent avoids open-ended increases in property tax and lessens the burden on taxpayers in Kuala Lumpur. Tax revenue under the new roll would have increased by 19.63 percent but was capped with rate adjustments to 8.86 percent (see table 10.10).

In accordance with section 142 (2) of the Local Government Act 1976, each objection received a hearing. Hearings were held over three months, from January 6, 2014, to March 24, 2014. Out of 235,374 objections received, only 36,041, or 15 percent, of property owners attended their hearings.

Table 10.9 Property Tax Rate Imposed by Kuala Lumpur City Council

Type of Property	% Within City Center (93.2396 km²)	% Outside City Center (93.2396 km²)
Commercial / industrial	10	8
Service apartment	7	5
Residential / institution	4	4
Low-cost flat	2	2
Vacant commercial land	7	5
Vacant residential land	5	5
Special areas and villages	1	1
Other than villages: buildings	2	2
Other than villages: vacant land	1	1

Source: Kuala Lumpur City Council (2020).

Table 10.10 Annual Value, Revenue, and Capping for the Revaluation of January 1, 2014

Property Rate (%)	No. of Properties	Annual Value (MYR million)	Revenue Without Capping (MYR million)	Capping of Increase of Assessment
10	37,825	5,897	590	25%
8	39,308	1,535	123	25%
7	16,563	901	63	25%
5	40,165	989	50	10%–25%
4	289,155	4,615	185	0%–10%
2	70,919	339	7	0%–10%
1	5,921	137	1	10%
Total	**499,856**	**14,413**	**1,018**	**MYR 926 million**
Increase		**4,654** **(47.70%)**	**167** **(19.63%)**	**MYR 75 million** **(8.86%)**

Source: Kuala Lumpur City Council (2019).

Revenue Performance in the Postrevaluation Period

Property tax revenue growth was strong in Kuala Lumpur after revaluation. Table 10.11 summarizes the growth: the total revenue from property tax rose by about 25 percent between 2016 and 2020. Most of this increase was due to an increase in the coverage of the base and to the progressivity of the rate structure. The population also increased during this period.

The percentage of tax arrears remained significant, as is evident from table 10.12. Arrears amounted to approximately 21 percent of revenues due in 2018.

Table 10.11 Property Tax Revenue in Kuala Lumpur

Year	No. of Taxable Properties	Total Annual Value (MYR million)	Property Tax Revenue (MYR million)
2016	539,389	15,960	1,081
2017	557,114	16,737	1,093
2018	584,638	17,514	1,217
2019	645,659	18,559	1,308
2020	670,730	19,234	1,353

Source: Kuala Lumpur City Council (2021).

Table 10.12 Total Property Tax Revenue and Arrears, 2016–2018

Year	Total Current Revenue (MYR million)	Total Arrears (MYR million)	Total Current Revenue + Arrears (MYR million)	Arrears as % of Total Revenue + Arrears
2016	1,081	339	1,420	23.89
2017	1,093	321	1,414	22.70
2018	1,217	330	1,547	21.32

Source: Kuala Lumpur City Council (2020).

Collection, Enforcement, and Exemption

The types and number of properties exempted from tax for 2018 are shown in table 10.13. Categories A and B are properties often exempt from property taxes; and C is recreational, social, and welfare properties. However, the values of these public-use properties have never been published (or otherwise been made available to the public), and it is therefore not possible to determine the revenue forgone as a result of the relief given.

Issues and Challenges

Malaysia's property tax system is beset with problems; and reforms to address these involve policy choices, modernization, and management and administrative improvements.

Table 10.13 Tax Exemption by Category, 2018

Property Type	Category	Classification Under Section 134 of the Local Government Act 1976	No. of Exempt Properties
Public places for religious worship; licensed public burial grounds or crematoria; public schools; public places for charitable purposes or for the purposes of science, literature or the fine arts	A	Full exemption of the whole property	90
	B	Full exemption of part of the property	17
	C	Full or partial exemptions of recreational, social, or welfare property	103
Total			**210**

Sources: Local Government Act (Act 171) 1976; Kuala Lumpur City Council (2018).

Revenue Mobilization

Revenue mobilization is a choice that jurisdictions make according to their desired size of government, taxable capacity, and preferences for tax types. In other words, no one can prescribe a normative level of taxation for Malaysia or recommend the role that property taxes should play. These questions are answered in the political process. We can, however, estimate property tax revenues in Malaysia and discuss the capacity for increasing them.

In 2020, during the COVID-19 pandemic, federal government revenues decreased by 14 percent, to MYR 227.3 billion, and to a revenue amount equivalent to 15.8 percent of GDP. Stamp duty and real property gains tax were lower, at MYR 8 billion (table 10.14) following the exemptions announced in the economic stimulus package.

Collectively, stamp duty and real property gains tax are equivalent to 1.9 percent of GDP.[4] As shown in table 10.15, in 2019, stamp duty revenue

Table 10.14 Property Transfer Tax as Percentage of Total Government Tax and GDP, 2019

Type	Total Revenue (MYR million)	As % of Total Federal Government Tax Revenue	As % of GDP
Stamp Duty	6,213	3.3	1.5
Real Property Gains Tax	1,800	1.0	0.4
Total Taxes on Transfers	**8,013**	**4.3**	**1.9**

Source: Ministry of Finance (2017).

Table 10.15 Property Transfer Taxes as Percentage of GDP in Kuala Lumpur, 2019

Tax	Total Revenue (MYR million)	As % of Kuala Lumpur GDP
Stamp duty	713	0.5
Quit rents	616	0.5
Recurrent property tax	1,353	1.0
Total property tax	2,682	2.0

Source: Kuala Lumpur City Council (2020).

from properties was 0.5 percent of Kuala Lumpur GDP. Quit rent generated MYR 615,811,452.80, also accounting for 0.5 percent of GDP. The level of recurrent property taxes in Kuala Lumpur is low and well below the average for all low- and middle-income jurisdictions in the world. The amount was only 1 percent of Kuala Lumpur GDP in 2019.

Infrequent Property Revaluation

Whether the goal of property taxation in Malaysia is to increase or decrease revenue, it is important for property valuations to keep up with property market values. Otherwise, revenues will flag, and the tax will become increasingly unfair in distribution of burden (Wong et al. 2017). In the best management, valuations will be kept current and revenue needs will be met by changing the tax rate.

The property market in Malaysia is active, and property values change regularly. The consensus seems to be that there is a pressing need to consider updating the valuation lists of local governments. Valuation lists are outdated in most localities (Usilappan 2006). For most of the local authorities in Malaysia, revaluations have not been done for more than 10 years, and the value of the properties has likely increased by more than 50 percent or even 100 percent.

The chief barriers to regular revaluations every five years are the large number of taxable properties to be valued, skilled staff shortages in some local-government areas; and valuations done manually. Revaluation frequency is also constrained by taxpayer resistance.

Inadequate Tax Collection and Enforcement

Collection and enforcement are a problem for many local governments. Tax arrears grow and constrain local governments not only in development and services but also in disruption of daily administration. Across Malaysia's 13 states, property tax revenue as a percentage of local-government income ranged from a low of about 30 percent in Sabah to more than 55 percent in five states (Johor, Melaka, Selangor, Perlis, and Pulau Pinang). Property tax arrears as a percentage of income ranged from about 16 percent of collections in Sarawak to close to 64 percent in Perlis; most other states faced arrears of 20–35 percent.

The law provides extensive remedies if taxes are unpaid, but implementation of the law has been piecemeal. Local authorities are either unable or unwilling to demand tax arrears (Mohd Ayub and Mohd Anuar 2018). The law clearly allows local governments to demand payment from the defaulted owners, and tax arrears must be settled within 15 days from the date of the notice being issued. If no payment is forthcoming, local authorities may confiscate movable items from the property. To alleviate the owner's burden, local authorities may allow the owner to pay in installments (Umar, Kasim and Martin 2012).

Given the large amount of national arrears, how property taxes are collected should be reviewed. Pawi (2013) finds that weak financial management is a factor in local authorities achieving low tax revenue collection. Ghani (2014) contends that arrears are caused by local governments' internal problems such as cumbersome and slow assessment methods and lack of staff for collections. Tenants also cause arrears when they receive the property tax bill and do not notify the owner of the property, who then suffers late payment charges.

Another challenge faced by the local authority is the presence of empty buildings and abandoned properties. Mohd, Ayub, and Mohd Anuar (2018) state that tax arrears on these buildings are difficult to collect because of, for example, absentee property owners or properties in bankruptcy. According to Section 160 of the LGA 1976, property owners and purchasers must notify local authorities of the transfer. Mohd, Ayub, and Mohd Anuar have discovered other issues, such as the previous owner of the property refusing to settle the assessment rate arrears and the current owner assuming that the assessment rate arrears must be borne by the previous owner.

Slow Adoption of Information Technology

The property tax system in Malaysia has difficulty integrating property information collected by separate but related agencies. For example, the information systems for property data in the local authority and for ownership registration in the land office are not integrated or linked. Property registration is under the state authority, and any change of ownership on the title is not directly conveyed to the local government. Hence, the property transfer information is not properly executed in the local system, which affects the availability of reliable data (Ismail 2013; Mohd, Ayub, and Mohd Anuar 2018). A lack of reliable data poses challenges when the local government tries to identify the owner for tax assessment and collection.

A related concern is the hesitancy to adopt technological advancements in the revaluation process, even though it has the potential to reduce administration costs considerably. Appraisals in Malaysia mostly still involve the manual valuation or revaluations of the properties and only limited computer applications. This manual approach is one of the main reasons for the slow process of determining values. Only a limited number of local governments have adopted mass appraisal techniques in their revaluation work (Kamarudin and Daud 2013). Malaysia could adopt technologies that would streamline the property tax valuation, administration, and

Box 10.2 Property Tax Reforms

Computer-Assisted Mass Appraisal

Universiti Teknologi Malaysia has developed a computer-assisted mass appraisal (CAMA) system that several local governments, including Putrajaya Corporation and Hang Tuah Jaya Municipal Council, use to make valuations and revaluations. This system has been relatively successful because it supports local authorities in performing a revaluation every five years. The CAMA system application provides a cost-effective data management system and database of property records. The CAMA system is easy to use, and it can make complex and voluminous calculations more quickly and accurately than a manual system. The system frees up human resources so that appraisers can devote more time to collecting information to value property.

Electronic-Local Authority

Another system, the Electronic Local Authority (e-PBT), is a revenue management, accounting, complaint, and report system. Created in 2004, the system assists the local authorities in conducting daily operations involving revenue collection, financial processing, and accounting transactions. The client-server and Web application consists of five main systems and twenty-one subsystems that integrate to generate statements and reports. Moreover, e-PBT allows the public to go online and review license accounts, rental accounts, and complaints and make payments. However, the public-facing part of e-PBT is not being fully utilized, presumably because customers prefer direct over-the-counter service. Only 14 local authorities provided e-PBT online in 2019 compared with 64 in 2012.

collection (box 10.2). If implemented, the approaches outlined in this chapter would likely reduce costs, increase accuracy, improve data consistency, and shorten the time needed for processes.

Notes

1. A city hall is a local authority at a higher level than municipal council status if certain criteria are met, including that the municipality's total population exceeds 500,000 and its annual revenue exceeds MYR 100 million. The Federal Territory of Putrajaya is the administrative capital and the Federal Territory of Labuan is an offshore international financial center. These territories are under special or modified council, Putrajaya Corporation and Labuan Corporation, respectively.

2. The ad valorem stamp duty for some benevolent transfers between family members can be fully or partially exempted.

3. As defined in Section 2 of the Local Government Act 1976 (as amended).

4. This is below other Asian jurisdictions and below the percentage of GDP reached by three of the so-called Asian Tigers: 3.27% in Hong Kong, 3.14% in South Korea, and 2% in Singapore.

References

Ab Latif, S. N. F., S. H. Rosman, A. H. Nawawi, and M. I. Abdullah,. 2018, July 25–27. *Types of Knowledge Involved in a Stamp Duty Valuation Process* [Paper presentation]. Knowledge Management International Conference (KMICe) 2018, Miri Sarawak, Malaysia.

Alias, B. 2000. "Analysis of Factor That Contributes to the Accumulation of Uncollected Rates in Local Governments in Malaysia." PhD diss., Universiti Teknologi Malaysia.

Adnan, M. Z., R. Suratman, and S. Samsudin. 2021. "Key Geographical Features on Malaysia's Land Tax System: A Comparison Study in Negeri Sembilan, Malaysia." *IOP Conference Series: Earth and Environmental Science* 683 (1): 8.

Aliasak, M. H. H. and M. F. Sa'ad. 2015. "Role of Real Estate Valuation Surveyors in the Malaysian National Taxation." *Proceedings of Postgraduate Conference on Global Green Issues (Go Green)*, UiTM (Perak), Malaysia.

Asian Development Bank. 2020. *Mapping Property Tax Reform in Southeast Asia*. Manila: Asian Development Bank.

Daud, D.Z., Kamarudin, N., Franzsen, R., and McCluskey, W. 2013. "Property Tax in Malaysia and South Africa: A Question of Assessment Capacity and Quality Assurance." *Journal of Property Tax Assessment & Administration* 10 (4): 5–18.

Daud, D., B. Alias, and C. Muthuveerappan. 2008 August 27–29. *Property Tax Administration and Capacity Building for Local Governments in Malaysia* [Paper Presentation]. The CASLE Conference on Urban Development, Regeneration and Finance, Belfast, Northern Ireland.

Department of Statistics Malaysia. 2020. *Federal Territory of Kuala Lumpur*. https://www.dosm.gov.my.

Embong, A. R. 2011. "Urbanisation and Urban Life in Peninsular Malaysia." *Akademika* 81 (2): 23–39.

Federal Territories Director of Lands and Mines. 2019. *Quit Rent*. https://www.ptgwp.gov.my/portal/web/guest/hasil-main

Ghani, S. N. A. 2014. *Internal Problems in Collecting Property Tax Arrears at Local Authority (Case Study: Iskandar Malaysia)*. [In Malay.] Master's thesis. Universiti Teknologi Malaysia.

Gökçe, A. F. 2013. "Federal Parliamentary Democracy with a Constitutional Monarchy: Malaysia." *Journal of Academic Social Science Studies*, 6.

Halim, N. Z. A., S. A. Sulaiman, K. Talib, O. M. Yusof, M. A. M. Wazir, and M. K. Adimin. 2017. "Identifying the Role of National Digital Cadastral Database (NDCDB) in Malaysia and for Land-Based Analysis." *International Archives of the Photogrammetry, Remote Sensing and Spatial Information Sciences* 42 (4/W5): 81–89.

Inland Revenue Board of Malaysia. 2020. *Stamp Duty*. https://www.hasil.gov.my/en/stamp-duty/.

Ismail, M. F. 2013. *The Factors of Assessments Tax Arrears and Method of Implementation and Payment (Case Study: Johor Bahru City Council)*. [In Malay.] Master's thesis. Universiti Teknologi Malaysia.

Kamarudin, N., and D. Daud. 2014 June 16–21. *Computer-Assisted Mass Appraisal (CAMA) Application for Property Tax Administration Improvement in Malaysia* [Paper Presentation]. FIG Congress 2014: Engaging the Challenges, Enhancing the Relevance, Kuala Lumpur, Malaysia.

Kuala Lumpur City Council. 2018–2021. Annual questionnaire and interview with City Council officials. University of Technology, Malaysia.

La Croix, S. 2017. *Land Tenure: An Introduction*. Honolulu: East West Center.

Local Government Department, Ministry of Housing and Local Government, Malaysia. 2019. *Local Authority Statistics*. http://jkt.kpkt.gov.my/index.php /pages/view/187.

Md Khalid, S. N., S. Mat Nurudin, and Z. Mohd Zain. 2017. "Local Government Administrative Concepts in Malaysia: A Study on Understanding of Public Administrative Students." *Journal of Global Business and Social Entrepreneurship* 3 (7): 98–108.

Ministry of Finance. 2017. *Malaysia Economic Report: Economic Performance and Prospects*. Kuala Lumpur.

Mohd, E., Z. A. Ayub, and H. Mohd Anuar. 2018. "The Challenges of Local Authority in Malaysia in Assessment Rates Arrears Collection." *International Journal of Law, Government and Communication* 3 (13): 34–43.

Muhammad, S. H., and M. B. Ishak. 2013. "Objection Hearing on Property Assessment Rate Charges in Malaysia." *Civil and Environmental Research* 3 (5): 49–59.

Nordin, A. F. 2010. *Country Report 2010: Malaysia*. Kuala Lumpur.

Pawi, S. 2013. *A Model of Property Tax Management of Malaysia Local Authorities* [In Malay]. Doctoral Dissertation. Universiti Tun Hussein Onn Malaysia.

Pawi, S., D. Martin, W. Z. W. Yusoff, F. Shafie, I. Suziella, N. F. P. Ibrahim, and N. Ismail. 2011. "Assessment Tax Performance of Local Government in Malaysia." *Social Science Letters* 1 (1): 47.

Rofiei, R., N. M. Tawil, K. A. Kosman, and A. I. Che-Ani. 2016. "Understanding the People's Needs of Living in City: Scenario in Malaysia." *Journal of Engineering Science and Technology* 11 (5): 704–713.

Rosman, S. H., A. H. Nawawi, S. N. F. Ab Latif, and M. I. Abdullah. 2019. "The Effectiveness of Training Programmes Towards the Level of Knowledge of the Personnel Involved in Stamp Duty Valuation." *IOP Conference Series: Earth Environmental Science*, 385 (1): 012026. http://dx.doi.org/10.1088/1755-1315/385/1/012026.

Royal Institution of Chartered Surveyors. 2019. *International Models for Delivery of Affordable Housing in Asia*. Insight Paper (May). https://www.rics.org/globalassets /rics-website/media/knowledge/research/insights/international-models-for -delivery-of-affordable-housing-in-asia-rics.pdf.

Umar, M. A., R. Kasim, and D. J. Martin. 2012 December 18–19. *An Overview of Property Tax Collection as a Tool for a Sustainable Local Government Reform in Malaysia* [Paper presentation]. Proceedings International Conference of Technology Management, Business and Entrepreneurship, Melaka, Malaysia.

Usilappan, M. 2006. "Real Estate in Malaysia, Challenges, Insights and Issues." University of Malaya Press, Kuala Lumpur.

Wong, W. C., K. N. Taufil Mohd, and N. A. Hiau Abdullah. 2017. "Announcement Effects of Dividend Tax Cuts and Corporate Policies: Evidence from Malaysia REITs." *Pacific Rim Property Research Journal* 23 (2): 213–226.

Zainuddin, Z. B. 2010. *An Empirical Analysis of Malaysian Housing Market: Switching and Non-Switching Models*. Doctoral dissertation. Lincoln University, New Zealand.

Zainuddin, N. 2015. "Overview of Real Property Gains Tax in Malaysia." *Emerging Tax Issues in Asia*, 7–9.

11

Pakistan: Rebuilding the Tax Base

RAJUL AWASTHI

This chapter briefly reviews the fiscal environment in Pakistan, the chal-lenges to property taxation by the land and property market, and the potential impacts of urbanization on revenue mobilization from the prop-erty tax. To provide more context for Pakistan's complicated federally based property tax system, the chapter examines the property tax in the nation's four provinces, with an emphasis on Punjab and Sindh. A final sec-tion explores some of the major options and challenges for reform.

The urban immovable property tax has a long history in Pakistan, hav-ing been originally introduced by the British colonial administration. It is regulated in the four provinces by legislation originally passed in 1958 (with subsequent amendments). As is discussed at some length in this chap-ter and in studies of property taxation in Pakistan, each province deter-mines its base depending on how it values properties.

Overview of the Fiscal and Institutional Environment

Pakistan is a federation, with powers and revenue-raising responsibilities shared between the federal government and four provincial governments (table 11.1). The 18th amendment, of 2010, to the Constitution of Pakistan

---

The author thanks Irum Touqeer and Clelia Rontoyanni, who provided excellent comments and input. They both work in the Governance Global Practice of the World Bank and are based in Islamabad, Pakistan.

Table 11.1 Provincial Economy and Disparity, 2017

Province	Population	% Urban Population	Per Capita GDP (USD)
Punjab	110,012,442	26.7	1,557
Sindh	30,439,893	52.0	1,748
Balochistan	12,344,408	27.6	771
Khyber Pakhtunkhwa	30,523,371	8.8	740

Sources: Adapted from CLGF (n.d.) and Wikipedia (2022). USD 1,557 = PKR 274.4

Note: This table excludes the Islamabad Capital Territory.

expanded powers of the provinces and devolved delivery of key services to them (Pasha 2011). The federal government retains core or shared responsibility for functions including tertiary education, tax and trade policy regulation, and transmission and distribution of electricity.

The third tier of government, local governments, is defined by the Constitution. However, each province also has its own legislation and assignment of ministries. Districts are administrative divisions, and below them are the *tehsils* (city municipalities). Rural local governments are called union councils or village councils. District councils within *tehsils* are local-government units (neighborhood councils).[1]

International agencies (World Bank 2016b; 2019b) and independent studies (Cevik 2016; Piracha 2016) have documented for many years that the government of Pakistan must increase tax revenues to ensure its fiscal sustainability. Pakistan's overall tax revenue performance has improved significantly since 2015, to about 13 percent of GDP in 2018, but it falls short of the 15 percent that is considered the minimum that developing jurisdictions need to fund basic government functions (World Bank 2017; 2019b). It also falls below the level needed to address budget deficits and create fiscal space for public spending on infrastructure, education, and health. Pakistan's recurrent expenditures account for 80 percent of government expenditure, but rigidity in the amounts defined for these expenditures means public spending cannot easily be cut (Aamir et al. 2011; Ellis, Kopanyi, and Lee 2007; World Bank 2019b). As Martinez-Vazquez and Cyan (2015, 1) put it, "There is a near universal agreement that more funds should be raised in taxes."

About 80 percent of the revenues of provincial governments come from intergovernmental transfers from the federal government (table 11.2). The share of total tax revenue collected by the provinces remains small at about 9 percent of total receipts, but has been growing, from 0.4 percent of GDP in fiscal year 2010/2011 to 1.2 percent in fiscal year 2017/2018. The Constitution assigns the following taxes to the provinces: general sales

Table 11.2 Provincial Own-Tax Revenue as % of Total Revenue, 2019–2020

Provinces	Own Taxes (PKR billion)	Total Revenues (PKR billion)	Share (%)
Punjab	189.8	1,459.3	13.0
Sindh	182.6	842.5	21.7
Khyber Pakhtunkhwa	25.1	595.0	4.2
Balochistan	16.2	344.2	4.7

Source: Pakistan's Fiscal Operations 2019–20, Ministry of Finance, Government of Pakistan (as reported in Finance Division (n.d.).

tax on services, tax on professions, agricultural income tax, motor vehicle tax, urban immovable property tax, and other taxes related to real estate (e.g., stamp duty and capital value tax). The tax assessment and collection duties are split between the federal and provincial governments as is usually done in a federal jurisdiction (box 11.1).

Property taxation in Pakistan continues to be challenged by the developing system of real estate markets (Nabi and March 2011). Rural land ownership concentration and poverty significantly limit coverage of the property tax. The land administrative system also offers challenges for the property tax, with parallel customary systems and unregistered ownership compromising the development of the full cadastre and the use of property transfer taxes. This is particularly evident in Sindh. Finally, the extremely low rate of

---

Box 11.1 Tax Administration in Pakistan

The World Bank (2019b, 10–11) describes Pakistan's Federal Board of Revenue (FBR) as

> the only federal tax authority, and it comprises the Inland Revenue and Customs. The FBR collects most of the country's tax receipts (86% in FY17/18), primarily from GST [goods and service tax], income tax, and customs duties. The FBR is a statutory body established by the Federal Board of Revenue Act of 2007 (amended in 2012) to replace the Central Board of Revenue. According to the FBR Act, the Chairman and the members of the FBR Board are appointed by the Federal Government. The Chairman also holds the position of Secretary of the Revenue Division in the Ministry of Finance (MoF) and therefore reports to the Minister of Finance, Revenue, and Economic Affairs). The dual role of the FBR Chairman gives the FBR a strong role in tax policy, especially as the Revenue Division has few staff and limited capacity.

The World Bank continues,

> At the provincial level, the structure of the tax administration is more complex. Each province has three revenue authorities: (a) the Excise and Taxation Departments, which collect the [urban immovable property tax], the tax on professions, the motor vehicle tax, and provincial excises; (b) the Boards of Revenue, which collect the agricultural income tax, land taxes, stamp duty, and other taxes on property transactions; and (c) the revenue authorities that collect the [general sales tax on services] (Sindh Revenue Board, Punjab Revenue Authority, [Khyber Pakhtunkhwa] Revenue Authority, and Balochistan Revenue Authority). However, tax policy is clearly the domain of the provincial Finance Departments. (World Bank 2019b, 11; see also Bahl, Wallace, and Cyan 2015)

formal financing of housing affects property taxation because it limits the availability of accurate data on housing values and prices. As a result, fair market value estimations of property values are difficult to make. This is a critical constraint in property valuation. A limitation of this analysis is the uneven amount of data and information available in the four provinces.

Urbanization and Property Taxation

Pakistan's population is growing and becoming increasingly urban. It now has the highest rate of urbanization in South Asia. According to the 2017 population census (Pakistan Bureau of Statistics 2021), 36.4 percent of the population lives in urban areas, compared with 32.5 percent in 1998. Other estimates, based on a modified definition of urban settlements, suggest that the ratio of urban to rural population could be 40.5 percent and even higher. Administrative city boundaries have not been adjusted for decades and leave out many peri-urban areas. For example, according to the 2017 census, more than 49 percent of Islamabad Capital Territory's population is classified as rural.

Increasing urbanization may increase demands for a stronger property tax. Housing, infrastructure, and local public services are already stressed, and the municipal finance base is not adequate to cover the fiscal needs (Abbas and Cheema 2021). Meanwhile, urban infrastructure investments that are taking place and are generating increasing land values are not being captured by the land and property tax system. A well-administered property tax, levied at an adequate effective rate, could begin to address some of these expenditure needs and value-capture possibilities. In particular, Punjab is in a position to capture the gains from urbanization. Its five largest cities, all with a population of more than a million people in

2019, increased population by 60 percent between 1998 and 2017. Land and property prices grew correspondingly (Wani, Shaikh, and Harmon 2020).

Recurrent Property Taxes

Provincial governments in Pakistan levy three annual property taxes: the urban immovable property tax, the farmhouse tax, and the luxury house tax. All are imposed under provincial-government law and are assessed and collected under provincial-government auspices. The three are summarized in table 11.3, along with the transfer tax regime, which is discussed later in this chapter.

Urban Immovable Property Tax

In three Pakistan provinces, the urban immovable property tax (UIPT) is the tax levied on the annual rental value of property. Punjab, Sindh, and Balochistan operate under the Urban Immovable Property Tax Act 1958, and the tax is based on the annual rental values of residential, commercial, and industrial properties (Piracha and Moore 2016). In Khyber Pakhtunkhwa, it is the North West Urban Immovable Property Tax Act, 1958, and property taxation there has been based on property location since 1997 (McCluskey and McCord 2021). The UIPT is the principal component of the recurrent property tax regime in Pakistan. The four provincial governments have full discretion to determine the rate and base of taxation (Bahl and Cyan 2009; Piracha and Moore 2015).

The UIPT as a percentage of national GDP is approximately 0.13 percent, which is below that of other low- and middle-income jurisdictions. There is considerable variation among the provinces: UIPT revenue is estimated at 0.18 percent of provincial GDP for Punjab, 0.10 percent for Khyber Pakhtunkhwa, 0.07 percent for Sindh, and 0.01 percent for Balochistan (McCluskey and McCord 2021). This revenue performance of the property tax is among the lowest in Asia.

The statutory property tax rates differ among provinces but are usually levied as a flat percentage against the annual rental value (Auditor General n.d.). The rental value is a presumptive estimate by the provincial government of how much rent the property could have earned (McCluskey and McCord 2021). The calculations of rental value follow a similar approach in the four provinces, though each produces its own property valuation table using its own parameters. In addition, the Federal Board of Revenue in 2019 began publishing its valuations of immovable properties in bigger cities[2] to use in assessing the capital value tax. The board values are generally higher than district council rates but are still lower than actual market values.[3]

Table 11.3 Overview of Federal and Provincial Property-Related Taxes

Tax	Based on	Level of Taxation	Who Pays?		
			Buyer	Seller	Owner
Urban immovable property tax	Ownership	Provincial			X
Farmhouse tax	Ownership	Punjab only			X
Luxury house tax	Ownership/ wealth	Punjab only			X
Capital value tax	Transfer	Provincial/ Federal Board of Revenue for Islamabad	X		
Stamp tax	Transfer	Provincial	X		
Town fee/ registration fee	Transfer	Provincial	X		
Withholding tax	Transfer	Federal	X	X[1]	
Tender/auction fee	Transfer	Federal		X	
Capital gains tax	Transfer	Federal		X	
Income tax from property	Ownership/ income	Federal			X

Sources: Pakistan laws; World Bank (2016a, 2019b).

Note: [1] Seller and buyer both pay if the property value is more than PKR 4 million.

Because the annual rental value of a property in Pakistan depends on factors stipulated by the provincial governments, the annual rental value for similar properties can differ among provinces. The factors that influence the annual rental value of properties are generally location and service amenities, how much of the property is land and how much is improvements (covered area), what size bracket the building or land falls into, and whether the property is rented or owner occupied.

Cyan (2017b, 8) explains the assessment method when describing Punjab's approach. The gross annual rental value (GARV) is calculated in the following:

$$GARV = \{[(LA \times R_i) + (CA \times R_j)]\ 12\}\ T_k,$$

where

LA is land area in square yards,

CA is covered area in square feet,

R is the valuation rate assigned from the valuation table. The subscripts $(i, j, . . .)$ refer to property features such as size of the plot, size of covered area, size thresholds for both land and covered area, occupation status, location on a main road, primary occupant, and main use of property, and

T_k is 1 for most residential and industrial properties. Properties with special features, k, are multiplied by T to inflate or deflate the assessment.

When assigning valuation rates, the valuers use their discretion, based on their surveys of other properties in the province and other information. Further, they determine the additional multiples that will be used for special features. So the effective tax rate has several components: the statutory tax rate, the valuation rates for land and buildings, and the rate for special properties. "The valuation rate $R_{i,j}$ works as a compound of valuation and rate. When it is read with the property factors T_k, it further adds to the rate component of the tax calculation" (Cyan 2017a, 9).

The approach is relatively simple, despite having to account for several factors. It is not a transparent approach, however, because determination of the valuation rates is so subjective—that is, the extent to which they reflect market values and the extent to which they reflect views about how tax rates should match up to market values. Whether the determination really captures market value influences is also suspect because provincial valuations seem to fall well below market levels.

All provinces use a similar method of valuation and a similar formula, though their valuation rates, special property factors, and classifications of property may differ. After selecting the property category, according to the province's property valuation table, the annual rental value is calculated to determine the property tax obligation. The calculation for residential properties in Punjab and Sindh is shown here (Khyber Pakhtunkhwa and Balochistan modify the calculations):

i) (Total **Land Area** of a Property)×(Sq. Yard **Rent** Prescribed in Valuation Table)=**A**

ii) (Total **Covered Area** of a Property)×(Sq. Foot **Rent** Prescribed in Valuation Table)=**B**

iii) (A+B)×12 = Gross Annual Rental Value (**GARV**)

iv) GARV—10% of GARV=Annual Rental Value (**ARV**)

v) ARV×Tax Rate = Property Tax Obligation

The property valuation tables are developed by the respective provincial taxation departments. The table entries reflect market rental values of both residential and commercial property. They tend to be infrequently updated. The Punjab table was last revised in 2014 after a 13-year hiatus, and the Sindh table was last revalued in 2001.

Property Tax Revenues

Table 11.4 shows UIPT tax revenues overall and by province. Whereas Punjab's property tax revenues show a clear, although small, upward trend, Sindh's and Balochistan's property tax revenues have fluctuated greatly over the last four years. Khyber Pakhtunkhwa was able to steadily raise the revenue received from property tax, but its baseline was very low. In contrast to the other three provinces, Khyber Pakhtunkhwa's property tax grew its share of the overall provincial tax revenues (from 0.9 percent in 2014/2015 to 2.5 percent in 2018/2019). UIPT collection rates vary among the provinces. However, on average the annual collection rate is between 50 and 60 percent.

These data can be used to show the concentration of property tax revenues in Punjab. About 75 percent of property taxes in Pakistan were collected in Punjab Province, which contains 58 percent of the national population and accounts for 59 percent of GDP. If we consider the property tax revenue raised per PKR of GDP to be a crude indicator of property tax effort, we can grade Punjab as having made significantly higher effort than the other three provinces (table 11.5).

Punjab

The UIPT is a potentially important source of revenue for Punjab Province. Its collections in 2018 were 40 percent of total direct taxes of the province, although its share in total own-source revenues (including direct and indirect taxes) is only about 5 percent. The UIPT is levied under the Punjab Urban Immovable Property Tax Act of 1958, by Punjab's taxation department (Excise, Taxation, and Narcotics Control Department). Past research on Punjab property taxation concludes that it has not come close to reaching its revenue potential (Abbas and Cheema 2021; Cyan 2017b; Piracha 2016; World Bank 2006). Most observers would agree. Cyan (2017b) estimates that removing most exemptions and increasing the assessment ratio to 75 percent of market values could increase property tax revenues fivefold.

TAX BASE AND VALUATION FOR UIPT

Punjab's UIPT is levied on the annual rental value of buildings and land. The rental value of the property depends on its location and rating

Table 11.4 Provincial Tax Revenue Totals

Province		2014	2015	2016	2017	2018
Punjab	Total provincial tax (PKR billion)	233.109	238.015	324.063	375.084	475.512
	Property tax (PKR billion)	**5.42**	**7.34**	**8.16**	**9.23**	**10.01**
	Property tax/provincial tax (%)	2.3	3.1	2.5	2.5	2.1
Sindh	Total provincial tax (PKR billion)	188.170	219.407	286.913	336.320	403.683
	Property tax (PKR billion)	**2.14**	**1.91**	**1.97**	**2.00**	**2.02**
	Property tax/provincial tax (%)	1.1	0.9	0.7	0.6	0.5
Khyber Pakhtunkhwa	Total provincial tax (PKR billion)	28.679	27.349	31.212	36.159	43.696
	Property tax (PKR billion)	**0.267**	**0.266**	**0.376**	**0.262**	**1.135**
	Property tax/provincial tax (%)	0.9	0.9	1.2	0.7	2.5
Balochistan	Total provincial tax (PKR billion)	5.940	5.921	9.402	14.985	21.771
	Property tax (PKR billion)	**0.122**	**0.080**	**0.092**	**0.113**	**0.122**
	Property tax/provincial tax (%)	5.0	3.0	2.0	2.0	1.0
All provinces	**Total property tax revenue (PKR billion)**	**7.95**	**9.60**	**10.60**	**11.60**	**13.29**

Source: World Bank 2019b.

Table 11.5 Provincial Property Tax Revenues

Province	As % of Total Property Tax	As % of Total Population	As % of Total GDP	Property Tax Revenue as % of Provincial GDP[1]
Punjab	75.3	58.4	59.1	0.18
Sindh	15.2	25.4	28.5	0.07
Khyber Pakhtunkhwa	8.5	16.2	9.3	0.10
Balochistan	0.9	6.5	3.1	0.01

Sources: Table 11.2; Wikipedia (2022).
[1] McCluskey and McCord (2021).

area, listed in Punjab's property valuation tables. Notably, Punjab's valuations differentiate between residential and commercial property, and between owner-occupied property and rented property (tables 11.6 and 11.7). The tax is levied at the statutory rate of 5 percent of annual rental value (Punjab ET&NCD 2021c).

The Punjab valuation tables list eight zones (A to G, moving from high to low values). Neighborhoods are assigned to categories on the basis of property surveys carried out by the taxation department. Valuation rates are based mostly on expert judgment. The valuation tables show the following pattern of residential assessed values (see table 11.6): a steep gradient for all categories between rental and owner-occupied residences, lower rates of assessment for buildings exceeding 3,000 square feet of covered area than for smaller buildings, and valuation preference for owner-occupied over rental properties. Roughly the same pattern exists for commercial properties, except that the assessed values for rented commercial properties are much higher than for owner-occupied buildings (see table 11.7). Whether tables 11.6 and 11.7 reflect the actual pattern of rents or discretionary policies is not clear.

ASSESSMENT RATIO

In Pakistan, ratio studies are not carried out, including for the assessment ratio, which is the ratio of assessed value to total market value. However, a moment's reflection about the structure of the assessment formula suggests that there will be wide disparities in the assessment ratio across property types and across zones and that significant horizontal inequities are built into the system.

Table 11.6 Punjab's Residential Property Valuation Assessment Table for Urban Immoveable Property Tax (UIPT), July 1, 2021

Residential Category	Rented				Owner Occupied			
	Rate (PKR) on Land (Sq. Yd.)		Rate (PKR) on Covered Area (Sq. Ft.)		Rate (PKR) on Land (Sq. Yd.)		Rate (PKR) on Covered Area (Sq. Ft.)	
	Up to 500	Exceeding 500	Up to 3,000	Exceeding 3,000	Up to 500	Exceeding 500	Up to 3,000	Exceeding 3,000
A	23.00	18.40	23.00	18.40	4.60	3.68	4.60	3.68
B	17.00	13.60	17.00	13.60	3.40	2.72	3.40	2.72
C	14.00	11.20	14.00	11.20	2.80	2.24	2.80	2.24
D	11.00	8.80	11.00	8.80	2.20	1.76	2.20	1.76
E	8.20	6.56	8.20	6.56	1.64	1.31	1.64	1.31
F	6.50	5.20	6.50	5.20	1.30	1.04	1.30	1.04
G	4.00	3.20	4.00	3.20	0.80	0.64	0.80	0.64

Source: Punjab ET&NCD (n.d.).

Table 11.7 Punjab's Commercial Property Valuation Assessment Table for Urban Immoveable Property Tax (UIPT), July 1, 2021

Commercial Category		Rented				Owner Occupied			
		Rate (PKR) on Land (Sq. Yd.)		Rate (PKR) on Covered Area (Sq. Ft.)		Rate (PKR) on Land (Sq. Yd.)		Rate (PKR) on Covered Area (Sq. Ft.)	
		Up to 500	Exceeding 500	Up to 3,000	Exceeding 3,000	Up to 500	Exceeding 500	Up to 3,000	Exceeding 3,000
A	Main road	120.00	96.00	120.00	96.00	40.00	32.00	40.00	32.00
	Secondary	96.00	76.80	96.00	76.80	32.00	25.60	32.00	25.60
B	Main road	80.00	64.00	80.00	64.00	26.70	21.40	26.70	21.40
	Secondary	64.00	51.20	64.00	51.20	21.40	17.10	21.40	17.10
C	Main road	56.00	44.80	56.00	44.80	18.70	15.00	18.70	15.00
	Secondary	44.80	35.80	44.80	35.80	15.00	12.00	15.00	12.00
D	Main road	40.00	32.00	40.00	32.00	13.40	10.70	13.40	10.70
	Secondary	32.00	25.60	32.00	25.60	10.70	8.60	10.70	8.60
E	Main road	30.00	24.00	30.00	24.00	10.00	8.00	10.00	8.00
	Secondary	24.00	19.20	24.00	19.20	8.00	6.40	8.00	6.40
F	Main road	20.00	16.00	20.00	16.00	6.70	5.40	6.70	5.40
	Secondary	16.00	12.80	16.00	12.80	5.40	4.30	5.40	4.30
G	Main road	15.00	12.00	15.00	12.00	5.00	4.00	5.00	4.00
	Secondary	12.00	9.60	12.00	9.60	4.00	3.20	4.00	3.20

Source: Punjab ET&NCD (n.d.).

Exemptions

The property tax base in Punjab is eroded significantly by exemptions. These have grown over the years and do not seem meant to relieve excessive property tax burdens. Box 11.2 provides a comprehensive list of exemptions. Properties within cantonments are not exempt, but the property tax revenue belongs to the cantonment board. Cantonments are permanent military stations, which are administered by cantonment boards controlled by the Military Lands and Cantonments Department in the Ministry of Defense. Cantonments were established under and are governed by the Cantonments Act of 1924. Among the most important other exemptions in terms of revenue sacrifice are the following:

- Properties of less than five-*marla* area (151.25 sq yards) are exempt from taxation, without any means test. A study of six districts in Punjab found that this exemption moved more than 60 percent of properties off the tax roll (Cyan 2017b).

- Retired government employees living in houses above a certain size are exempt, again with no means test.

- Owner-occupied properties are valued at about 20 percent of comparable rented properties. This contributes to the regressivity of the tax system.

Special tax preferences are also offered, as is noted in box 11.2.

Box 11.2 Property Tax Exemptions in Punjab

The following lists all exemptions:

- Residential houses constructed on a land area less than five *marla* other than those in the A category of the residential property valuation assessment table.
- Property not capable of commanding an annual rent exceeding PKR 4,320.
- An owner-occupied single house not capable of commanding an annual rent exceeding PKR 6,480.
- Tax liability of up to PKR 1,2150 per annum is exempted for buildings owned by widows, minor orphans, or disabled persons.
- One residential house of up to one *kanal* (about 506 m²) owned and occupied by a federal or provincial retired government employee.
- Buildings owned by the government or a local authority such as a corporation, municipality, or town committee.

- Mosques and other religious buildings.
- Buildings and lands used as public parks and playgrounds, schools, boardinghouses, hostels, libraries, and hospitals.
- Properties whose rents are devoted exclusively to religious or prescribed public charitable institutions.

FARMHOUSE TAX

An additional farmhouse tax was levied by the government of Punjab (under the Finance Act 2011) on farmhouses outside existing rating areas of property taxation, with a minimum covered area of 5,000 square feet and that were constructed after 1980 at differentiated tax rates (Punjab ET&NCD 2021a).

LUXURY HOUSE TAX

A luxury house tax was imposed by Punjab in 2014 as a one-time tax on residential houses above a specified value and in the rating areas of the UIPT or in cantonment areas (Punjab ET&NCD 2021b). The liability to pay this tax rested jointly with the owner and occupier.

TAX ADMINISTRATION AND COMPLIANCE

The Punjab offers an online tax calculator for its citizens. The PT-1 is the basic register for all documents relating to property taxation, including property descriptions, ownership, possessions, use, and annual rental value. Any person filing an appeal or revision is required to attach a copy of the PT-1 form along with the appeal or revision (Punjab ET&NCD 2021c).

The property tax payment must be deposited on or before September 30 (Punjab ET&NCD 2021c). Time allowed for payment is 30 days from the date of serving the demand notice. The tax payment can be made to the Treasury or at any commercial bank of Pakistan. Payment can also be made by check or even by mobile phone via e-Pay Punjab.[4]

Compliance incentives include a rebate equal to 5 percent of the amount of the annual tax if the amount of the annual tax is paid in a lump sum on or before September 30. A late payment surcharge at the rate of 1 percent of the gross payable tax is imposed on the first day of every month if the payment is delayed (Punjab ET&NCD 2021c).

PROPERTY TAX REVENUE PERFORMANCE

Recurrent property tax revenues in Punjab make up a small fraction (3 percent) of the total provincial tax collection despite an increase in investment in urban property, both residential and commercial, over the last several years. As Punjab's then minister of Finance, Aiesha Ghaus Pasha, stated, the valuation tables still do not reflect the actual market value of urban property, and urban property remains one of the most undertaxed areas in Punjab (Jamal 2018). A major digitization effort began in 2014, and all 36 districts have now digitized property records (World Bank 2019c). Over 1 million new properties were identified during digitization and are now included in the tax base. Geographic information system (GIS) mapping is in process.

Sindh

Property tax is levied and collected under the Sindh Urban Immovable Property Tax Act, 1958. The tax is levied at a rate of 25 percent on the annual rental value of the property (Sindh ET&NCD 2021). As with Punjab, the property tax base is the gross annual rent, which is calculated in much the same way in all three provinces except for KPK, which still uses area as the basis. However, each province takes a slightly different approach, and different valuation parameters are used. Accordingly, the valuation tables are different. One important contrast to Punjab is that the taxation department of Sindh does not assign different rental values to properties on the basis of occupancy (rented versus owner occupied).

Annual rental value is determined as follows:

$$\text{Annual tax value} = (a + b) - [10\% \ (a + b)],$$

where

$$a = \text{size of plot} \times \text{rate} \times 12,$$

$$b = \text{covered area} \times \text{rate} \times 12.$$

Although Sindh's tax rate (25 percent) is five times Punjab's tax rate (5 percent), the annual rental values in the property valuation table issued by Sindh's taxation department are correspondingly lower. If the rental value of similar properties in each province is compared (e.g., residential, improvements only, most expensive category), Sindh's property valuation table gives a rental value between PKR 0.5 and 0.6 per square feet, whereas Punjab's rental values are between PKR 3.68 and 18.40 per square feet. Therefore, nongovernment sources suggest that the final tax amount for similar properties in the two provinces is roughly similar (Zameen Blog n.d.b).

The province of Sindh divides all rating areas into five valuation zones (Karachi, Hyderabad, Mirpur Khas, Sukkur, Nawabshah). Over 90 percent of total UIPT is collected from Karachi. Hyderabad brings in 5 percent, and the other three zones total less than 5 percent. All properties in those five valuation zones are sorted into three groups: residential properties, commercial properties, and industrial properties. Recall that Punjab had only two categories: commercial and residential.

The value of properties in those three groups further varies depending on the characteristics of the property that can be found in each valuation table. Some factors are similar to Punjab's—for example, the differentiation between land and improvements (covered area) for residential properties. However, Sindh's taxation department asks owners if their property is an apartment or a house. Moreover, not only commercial but also residential property is grouped by category, A through D (Sindh ET&NCD 2021). Residential properties in Sindh are sorted by property division area or locality. The respective valuation tables of the five valuation zones can differ from one another.

EXEMPTIONS

Exemptions apply if a property does not exceed a certain size (e.g., 120 square yards), for ownership (e.g., property owned by widows), and according to the property's purpose (e.g., charity, worship, government work, or public health). Box 11.3 lists exemptions. The last survey of properties was undertaken in 1998.

Box 11.3 UIPT PROPERTY TAX EXEMPTIONS IN SINDH

The Urban Immovable Property Tax Act 1958 contains the following exemptions:

- Building and lands owned by the federal, provincial, or local government and used for a public purpose.

- A building or land whose annual rental value does not exceed PKR 864.

- A building used for residential purposes built on a plot not more than 120 square yards.

- One apartment with covered area not exceeding 600 square feet on any floor of a residential building.

- Buildings and lands or portions thereof used exclusively for libraries, public parks, and playgrounds, and buildings and lands used exclusively for public worship or public charity including mosques, churches, *dharma salas*, *gurdawaras*, orphanages, poorhouse burial or burning grounds, or other repositories for the dead.

- Buildings and lands whose annual rental value do not exceed PKR 48,000 and are owned by widows, minor orphans, or permanently disabled persons.

- Buildings and lands or portions thereof other than commercial properties declared as protected heritage under the Sindh Culture Heritage (Preservation) Act 1994.

COLLECTIONS

Low collection rates are due to a factors including lack of good information and communication technology, insufficient resources, and little enforcement. Politics also plays a major role. Many leading politicians are large landlords and have no appetite for increasing property taxation, the obvious outcome of updating valuations. The valuation roll appears to be incomplete. The number of residential properties in Karachi of approximately 700,000 is incompatible with a population of 22 million.

REVENUE PERFORMANCE

Property tax revenues in Sindh are very low, only about 0.5 percent of total provincial taxes in 2018. Improvement requires a reform program that touches several fronts. In particular, the coverage of the tax is limited, exemptions from the base are too extensive, and valuation is well below the legal base.

Only about 50–60 percent of properties are accounted for in the property tax register.[5] The precise number of potential taxable properties is impossible to estimate from the current property tax records, but for the city of Karachi, with a population of some 20 million and an average household of seven to eight persons, 1.5 to 2 million properties could be assessed to property tax (World Bank 2019a). Extrapolation of the FY 2017/2018 revenue collection of PKR 2 billion indicates that this number of taxable properties would increase revenues to about PKR 7.2 billion—an increase of more than 5 billion. A World Bank survey of Karachi is expected to be completed by the end of 2023. Another World Bank project is already surveying properties in Sukkur, the second-largest city. As a result of these projects, property registers will be updated in the two largest cities in Sindh, accounting for about 95 percent of property tax revenue (World Bank 2019a, 2019c).

The property tax has the potential to generate far higher levels of revcnuc, but this will require a significant review of legislation for, administration of, and approach to valuations. Similarly, property valuation tables have not been updated for almost 20 years. A proposal for revision of property valuations has been awaiting government approval for about two years.

Khyber Pakhtunkhwa

The demand for local public services in Khyber Pakhtunkhwa has significantly increased, raising interest in strengthening property taxes (both UIPT and property transfer taxes). Abbas and Cheema (2021) lay out a strong case for placing more reliance on land and property taxation and argue for a comprehensive reform package. I draw on their study and other past work to offer a brief outline of the practice in Khyber Pakhtunkhwa and the problems faced.

Revenue raised from the UIPT in Khyber Pakhtunkhwa is very low. In 2018, the amounts were about 2.5 percent of provincial tax revenues. Starting from such a low base, and not having a solid structure in place, suggests that achieving increased revenue mobilization will be slow. The following outlines obstacles to increased revenue mobilization and discusses the features of a reformed structure.

TAX MORALE

Widespread unwillingness to pay higher property taxes is a taxpayer morale problem (Abbas and Cheema 2021). This constraint is present in all jurisdictions to some extent, but it can be made more or less binding in Pakistan depending on the actions of the provincial government. A major difficulty is that once tax preferences are given, they are hard to withdraw. That said, the granting of new tax preferences can be partially controlled by proper vetting such as fiscal notes as a requirement for giving exemption extensions.

The willingness of the population to accept a property tax change depends on perception of whether the tax is fair (in terms of horizontal and vertical equity) and whether the government uses the revenues to deliver an adequate level of local public services. In fact, the property tax system in Khyber Pakhtunkhwa has horizontal and vertical inequities introduced by exemption and valuation regimes and provides a low quality of public services.

EXEMPTIONS AND PREFERENTIAL TREATMENTS

Tax exemptions and tax preferences significantly narrow the property tax base in Pakistan. Though we do not have a firm estimate of the tax expenditure in Khyber Pakhtunkhwa, evidence from Punjab suggests that it might be considerable (Cyan 2017b). Exemptions and tax preferences are meant to reduce the tax burden on low-income families and on those providing important social goods. But in practice exemptions are given as political favors. Other types of property tax relief are for political gain or due to lobbying of social engineers to, for example, encourage more investment in housing or better use of land.

Several forms of property tax relief have been adopted in Khyber Pakhtunkhwa, and some have significant consequences in terms of revenue loss. Three important examples: First, the five-*marla* exemption in Punjab as previously discussed places a high floor on tax liability for owner-occupied residential property. Because it is not means tested, some higher-income occupants benefit from the relief. Moreover, it is restructured to favor owner occupants. There is a paucity of empirical work on the incidence of property taxes in Khyber Pakhtunkhwa, but it is not a stretch to argue that the five-*marla* exemption is regressive.

Second, the exemption of government property is problematic, especially in decentralized jurisdictions where there may be two or three levels of government involved. In major cities and provincial capitals, government properties use services provided by local governments and take up space that might otherwise be occupied by taxpaying uses of land. As in all of Pakistan, in Khyber Pakhtunkhwa the case is strong for tracking the revenue cost and for compensating the local government. The solution in Khyber Pakhtunkhwa is to tax government buildings at only 20 percent of assessed value.

Finally, some tax relief is not given as exemptions but is built directly into the valuation system, such as lower assessments on land than on improvements, lower assessments on residential than on commercial and industrial land, and generally lower assessments on owner-occupied than on rented properties.

VALUATION

The Khyber Pakhtunkhwa valuation system builds certain tax relief (penalty) measures directly into its assessment regime, whereas it ought to estimate the amount for which a property could be let in a competitive market. The valuation approach taken in Khyber Pakhtunkhwa is area based. Properties are surveyed and categorized, and values are assigned to each category, according to location and use. For residential property, the province of Khyber Pakhtunkhwa has divided all rating areas into five valuation zones, each with different rental values for properties (e.g., township versus nontownship) and for size brackets. Values are subjective estimates by experts. The provincial government rebates 30 percent of the total tax calculated for former divisional headquarters of provincial government buildings and 50 percent for all other rating areas (KPK ET&NCD 2021).

Some properties receive preferential treatment. For example, improvements are assessed more heavily than land, a bias against development. And, as in Punjab, there are biases in favor of owner-occupiers and against nonresidential uses of land.

A reworking of the valuation system has been recommended by Abbas and Cheema (2021). It would resemble a banded system with zonal values adjusted to reflect factors such as access to roads, public transportation, and the like.

Tax rates are fundamental to the amount of revenue raised. In theory, all properties would be assessed at market levels. The statutory tax rate is the political variable that determines the amount of revenue to be raised. In Khyber Pakhtunkhwa, however, the political economy has led to assessment practices and exemptions that are part of the effective tax rate.

The property tax in Khyber Pakhtunkhwa is levied at a statutory rate of 25 percent of the annual rental value (KPK ET&NVD 2021). Khyber Pakhtunkhwa, like Sindh, treats industrial areas separately with a rate of PKR 2.5 per square feet. The tax rates are determined by zone for commercial properties. Property tax liability is levied by estimating the gross annual rent, which is calculated according to the province valuation table.

Balochistan

In Balochistan, UIPT is levied on the basis of the annual rental value of properties. In contrast to other provinces, the provincial government of Balochistan imposes two different tax rates: 10 percent for properties with an annual rental value below PKR 12,000, 15 percent for properties above PKR 12,000 (Balochistan ET&NVD, n.d.).

Balochistan's Excise and Taxation Department does not differentiate between covered and noncovered areas. However, like the other provinces, it allows a deduction of 10 percent from the gross annual rental value to calculate the annual rental value. The annual rental values are based on surveys conducted every five years (Balochistan ET&NVD 2021). During these property surveys, Excise and Taxation officials visit every house and building in their respective jurisdictions and distribute PT-4 forms to be returned by the owner or tenant as a self-assessment. The owner or tenant then receives a notice of demand. No property valuation tables are available on public government websites, which limits transparency to taxpayers.

Property Transfer Taxes

The other form of property tax imposed in Pakistan is that levied against transfers of properties. These taxes have significant revenue potential, depending on how they are levied, and in some jurisdictions outweigh the revenue contributions of the annual property taxes (Bahl and Bird 2018, chap. 6). In Pakistan, however, the laws and the administration of transfer taxes are significantly flawed, mainly because of underdeclaration of transaction prices, and reform has been slow to come. Some reforms could move transfer taxes toward capturing more of their considerable revenue potential. This section examines the main sources of transfer tax on real property in Pakistan and speculates about options for reform.

The different types of property transfer taxes levied in Pakistan are summarized in table 11.8.

Capital Value Tax

The capital value tax is a former federal tax that was transferred to the provinces through the 18th constitutional amendment, effective as of April 19, 2010. The federal government still levies the tax for the Islamabad Capital Territory. The capital value tax is paid by the buyer at the time of the acquisition of an asset (e.g., immovable property). It is based on the capital value of an acquired asset that is calculated according to local district council rates if the property value is not mentioned in the transaction (FBR, n.d.). The tax rate is 2 percent of the value of the transaction. Previously, the capital value tax was levied only in urban areas. Some have reported that there are plans for an extension to rural areas (Zameen Blog, n.d.b).

All property transfers that are gifts, exchanges, surrenders, or powers of attorney are subjected to capital value tax. However, transactions between spouses, parents, grandparents, and siblings through gift and inheritance are excluded.

In the Finance Bill 2018, the federal government recommended abolition of district council rates. This includes property rates set by the Federal Board of Revenue on the transfer of property and district council rates (provincial rates for the collection of stamp duty). The Finance Bill 2018

Table 11.8 Property Transfer Taxes

Tax	Base	Rate (%)
Capital value tax	Registered value	2
Stamp duty	Registered value	3
Registration fee	Registered value	Up to 1
Withholding tax	Federal Board of Revenue value	1–4
Public auction or tender fee	Auction sales price	Depends on filing status
Capital gains tax	Federal Board of Revenue valuation table	Depends on holding period

Sources: Bahl, Wallace, and Cyan (2015, 2011); Cyan 2017a; Zameen Blog (n.d.b).

stipulated that provinces abolish district council rates and reduce the stamp duty and capital value tax to 1 percent (Zameen Blog, n.d.b).

Stamp Tax

Stamp duty is a provincial tax applicable under the Stamp Act of 1899. It is levied at 3 percent of the district council value of a property and is paid by the buyer at the time of the acquisition of the property. It is required for most legal documents. The stamp tax was merged with the capital value tax for easy registration and for the convenience of buyers in the province of Punjab (Zameen Blog, n.d.a).

Registration Fee and Town Tax or Fee

Registration and town fees can each reach 1 percent of the property value depending on the province. They may or may not be payable separately. In Punjab, for instance, the registration fee is part of the stamp duty bill and only town fee, capital value tax, and stamp duty are still visible on the bill.

Withholding Tax

According to the Federal Board of Revenue, withholding tax is a federal tax payable by both buyer and seller if the value of property is greater than PKR 4 million (FBR 2021). Withholding tax is paid by the seller only if selling the property within five years of buying it (Zameen Blog, n.d.a). It must be paid when registering or attesting to the transfer of any immovable property. It acts as an advance on other taxes and, hence, is refundable when the buyer files income tax returns (Zameen Blog, n.d.a).

The government created two different sets of rates for filers and nonfilers to incentivize people to file their income taxes (Zameen Blog, n.d.a). The withholding tax for buyers who are nonfilers is 4 percent of the Federal Board of Revenue rates. It is 2 percent for buyers who are filers. For sellers who are filers, withholding tax is 1 percent of the board rates and zero if the property is sold within five years of purchase. It is 2 percent for sellers who are filers (FBR 2021; KPMG 2017).

Auction or Tender Fee

Any person making a sale by public auction or tender of property or goods must pay this federal tax. For filers the tax is 10 percent of the gross sales price of the property. For nonfilers it is 15 percent of the gross sales price.

Capital Gains Tax

The capital gains tax is a federal tax and is payable by the seller. The tax base is the profit made on the sale of a capital asset (property). According to the Finance Act 2017, the rate of taxation is 10 percent for the first year of holding, 7.5 percent if sold during second year, and 5 percent if sold during the third year. After three years it is zero (KPMG 2017). These gains are calculated according to the fair market value, based on the Federal Board of Revenue's valuation tables. For capital gains tax rate application, different holding periods are considered for open plot and a constructed property, per the Finance Act 2019.

Problems and Reform Options

A long-standing problem with property transfer taxes in Pakistan is the undervaluation of the tax base. The transfer tax rates are high enough to give buyers and sellers an incentive to understate the true value. The government's response to this is a backup option of using its valuation tables as the tax base if the declared values are deemed too low. In fact, however, the government's valuation tables are also well below the market value of properties in Pakistan. An analysis of capital value tax and stamp duty records shows that the tax base used for the transfer tax amount was the district valuations in more than 90 percent of the cases studied (Cyan 2017a).

Resolving this problem relies on rethinking the valuation methods used and better reflecting market values. At present, the provincial government does not do a rate study to examine the extent to which assessments capture full market value or to examine the disparities in assessments made. One independent analysis finds that the ratio of assessed value to market value is between 0.3 and 0.8 and that the Federal Board of Revenue tables for Lahore value residential properties by 60 percent more than the district valuation tables (Cyan 2017a).

Administration of the property transfer tax has long been plagued by the absence of coordination among levels of government and departments (Bahl, Wallace, and Cyan 2015). Land records are maintained separately in different agencies, and there is little coordination and information sharing among them (Cyan 2017a, 5).

The property tax structures and administrations in the provinces of Pakistan might be described as systems that are not well designed, poorly administered, and heavily driven by political interests. Their very weak revenue performance is the expected result of these flawed systems.

Nothing short of comprehensive reform and administrative makeover is necessary to make the property tax in Pakistan a viable revenue option for financing local public services. But this has been known for some time, and the attempts at modernization of UIPT have a long history in Pakistan. What to do is not the issue. Reports have been commissioned in the last decade or before by the government, the World Bank, the Asian Development Bank, and others with a view to developing proposals for updating and modernizing the UIPT (Abbas and Cheema 2021; Bahl, Wallace, and Cyan 2015; World Bank 2019a, 2019b). The obstacle has been and still is unwillingness to move toward a viable property tax.

Punjab

The Punjab Excise and Taxation Department has made some progress in broadening the tax base and improving the collection and administration of the property tax. Among the notable improvements in recent years are

- digitization of property records;

- inclusion of over 1 million new properties in the tax base;

- revision of valuation tables;

- reduction of the tax rate from 25 percent to 5 percent; and

- strengthened enforcement measures (Kelly, White, and Anand 2020; McCluskey 2020).

As a result of these measures, property tax collections have increased from PKR 3.2 billion in FY 2010/2011 to PKR 10.01 billion in FY 2017/2018, an increase of 313 percent (McCluskey and McCord 2021). During the same period, GDP in Punjab has increased by a much larger percentage, and the effective rate of property taxation has fallen.

Despite these improvements, the Punjab government is not exploiting the full potential of the property tax. The Department of Excise and Taxation collected only about PKR 10 billion in FY 2017/2018, which is far below potential. The policy, the legislation, and the administration need to be comprehensively reformed to become a modern property tax system making full use of information and communication technology.

The national and provincial governments have acknowledged the potential to raise higher levels of revenue from the property tax. This could largely be achieved by broadening the tax base, rationalizing exemptions, and further improving and expanding the automation agenda. The necessary reforms to accomplish this have been known for a long time and have been discussed by government on numerous occasions. The long-standing problem is with the political economy and with opposition to reform. The following are reform areas that might be targeted.

- Critically review exemptions and eliminate those that cannot be justified by nonpolitical criteria, such as inability to pay or the provision of social goods. Such a policy review could bring the list of exemptions into line with international best practice. Attention should be paid to less visible tax preferences that are built into the valuation system, particularly the five-*marla* exemption.

- Move toward a value-based assessment property tax system, rather than one based on physical measurements, expert judgment about valuation, and preferential treatment for preferred types of property. The current valuation methodology, which relies on government-produced valuation tables, is simple and easy to use. But it does not reflect market values and contains many discretionary elements that distort the assessed values and lead to unfair treatment of some taxpayers. One suggestion is a zone approach to value, based on a detailed analysis of the market rental values and amenities that might affect values in these zones. These reviews could be conducted annually, predicated on beacon properties that indicate market rental value movements. Legislation (such as the Urban Immovable Property Tax Act 1958) needs a comprehensive review with particular attention given to definitions, for example of "rating area," the valuation methodology for high-value specialized properties.

- The rollout of information and communication technologies to all districts managed by the Excise and Taxation Department is complete. But the system needs further development to make it a fully automated system so that it relies less on manual systems and so that discretion, particularly in relation to enforcement from the tax inspector and constables, is removed. The first step—aiding taxpayers to make payments by introducing an epayment system and opening up payments via commercial banks—has already been implemented.

Sindh

Tax revenue collection in the province of Sindh is highly concentrated. Of the fifteen taxes, almost 99 percent of own-source revenue comes from nine taxes with six taxes related to property: a tax on services (49 percent), infrastructure tax (27 percent), property transfer taxes (12 percent, which includes stamp duty, registration fee, and capital value tax), the UIPT (at less than 2 percent), and three more with the remaining six taxes contributing less than 1 percent to total revenue. The UIPT is seen as a tax that has significant untapped revenue potential. The same may be said for the taxes on property transfers. As with Punjab, in Sindh the issue is less identifying reforms than it is carrying out the reforms. Five areas might be targeted for early reform.

- The Sindh government is not exploiting the full potential of the property tax. The Department of Excise and Taxation collected only about PKR 2 billion in 2020, which is far below potential. Initial conclusions on the administration of property tax are that the Sindh government is not taking advantage of a significant taxable capacity in the province. Of the five urban areas—Karachi, Hyderabad, Mirpur Khas, Nawabshah, and Sukkur—only three levy and collect the property tax. Notifications for the remaining rating areas must be issued.

- The potential revenue, even without any major changes to the tax regime, is estimated at PKR 7.2 billion. This estimation is based mainly on an increase in the tax base in Karachi, a city with an estimated population of over 20 million but where only 800,000 or so properties are on the property tax rolls. The number of taxable properties should be at least 1.5 million to 2 million (World Bank 2016a).

- There is a need for a comprehensive reform of the property tax regime. The policy, the legislation, and the administration must all be comprehensively reformed to put in place a modern property tax system making full use of information and communication technology. The current tax base appears to be significantly underreported, on the basis of international metrics, and needs to be properly assessed. An extensive, province-wide survey using modern geospatial mapping to uncover hidden properties is necessary. Informal estimates made by the Excise and Taxation Department are that 50–60 percent of properties in Karachi are not in the property register.

- Although annual rental value, as the basis of property valuation, is simple and easy to use, its results do not match values very well. No significant increases in tax revenues have taken place over the years because, as the tax structure was based on fixed rates that have not kept pace with inflation. Various studies recommend a different approach to valuation—more reflective of market values. Moreover, revaluation should be more frequent. The valuation table was revised in 2016—the previous revision was in 2001—but has not been implemented. As an interim measure, the new, unapproved valuation table could be updated to be closer to market values. A detailed analysis of market rental values should be done annually and use beacon properties to obtain a view on the average zone rates and to more closely monitor market rental value movements. The Valuation Tables should be recalibrated to more closely approximate market values. The size of Karachi calls for more zones, currently numbering four. .

- Property values have grown over the years, but property tax revenues have not. Part of the problem is that the province has given away much of its tax base with preferential treatments—reliefs and exemptions. A review of the area-based exemption needs to be undertaken, and consideration should be given to using a value-based exemption for residential property. Properties below the prescribed value would be exempt.

- Collection levels are low, whether targeted collections or full-liability collections. The systems are largely manual, and customer service is not a priority. The administration suffers from weak billing, collection, and enforcement. Enforcement procedures are almost nonexistent, and when taken they are not timely, leading to high levels of arrears. There is no clear policy for writing off irrecoverable debts.

Notes

1. There are 129 district councils across the 4 provinces, 619 urban councils made up of 1 city district, 4 metropolitan corporations, 13 municipal corporations, 96 municipal committees, 148 town councils, 360 urban union committees, and 1,925 rural councils. Additionally, there are 3,339 neighborhood, *tehsil*, and village councils in the northernmost province of Khyber Pakhtunkhwa.

2. See https://www.fbr.gov.pk/valuation-immovable-properties/51147/131220. Accessed 05 April 2022.

3. Using survey data, Cyan (2017a) estimated assessment ratios that varied widely, depending on property type and market value. In his sample, the ratios varied from 25% to 80%.

4. See the e-Pay Punjab website, https://epay.punjab.gov.pk.

5. This range is based on informal estimates made by the director general of Sindh's Excise and Taxation Department in conversations with me.

References

Aamir, M., A. Qayyum, A. Nasir, S. Hussain, K. I. Khan, and S. Butt. 2011. "Determinants of Tax Revenue: A Comparative Study of Direct Taxes and Indirect Taxes of Pakistan and India." Special issue, *International Journal of Business and Social Science* 2 (19): 173–178.

Abbas, A., and A. Cheema. 2021. *Reforming Property Tax in Khyber Pakhtunkhwa: Introducing an Efficient, Effective and Equitable Tax Policy*. Sustainable Energy and

Economic Development (SEED), UKAID. https://cdpr.org.pk/wp-content/uploads /2018/02/Reforming-Property-Tax-in-KP.pdf.

Auditor General. n.d. Audit Report on the Accounts of Revenue Receipts of Government of The Punjab—Audit Year 2016–17, Auditor General of Pakistan.

Bahl, R., and R. Bird. 2018. *Fiscal Decentralization and Local Finance in Developing Countries*. Cheltenham, UK: Edward Elgar.

Bahl, R., and M. Cyan. 2009. "Local Government Taxation in Pakistan." International Studies Program Working paper 09. Atlanta: Andrew Young School of Policy Studies, Georgia State University.

Bahl, R., M. Cyan, and S. Wallace. 2011. "Challenges to Intergovernmental Fiscal Relations in Pakistan: The Revenue Assignment Dimension." In *Decentralization in Developing Countries: Global Perspectives on the Obstacles to Fiscal Devolution*, ed. J. Martinez-Vazquez and F. Vaillancourt, 131–154. Cheltenham, UK: Edward Elgar.

Bahl, R., S. Wallace, and M. Cyan. 2015. "The Potential of Provincial Taxation." In In *Decentralization in Developing Countries: Global Perspectives on the Obstacles to Fiscal Devolution*, ed. J. Martinez-Vazquez and F. Vaillancourt, 488–548. Cheltenham, UK: Edward Elgar.

Balochistan ET&NVD. n.d. "Property Tax", Excise, Taxation, and Narcotics Control Department, Government of Balochistan. Accessed February 23, 2022. https:// balochistan.gov.pk/wp-content/uploads/2020/08/Property-Tax1-Copy.pdf.

Cevik, S. 2016. "Unlocking Pakistan's Revenue Potential." FAD working paper 16/182. Washington, DC: International Monetary Fund.

CLGF. n.d. "The Local Government System in Pakistan: Country Profile 2017–18." Commonwealth Local Government Forum. Accessed October 18, 2021. https:// www.clgf.org.uk/default/assets/File/Country_profiles/Pakistan.pdf.

Cyan, M. R. 2017a. "Analysis of Stamp Duty and Capital Value Taxes in Punjab: Gap Analysis and Recommendations. Unpublished paper.

———. 2017b. "The Revenue Potential of the Urban Immovable Property Tax in Punjab." Unpublished paper.

Cyan, M. R., and J. Martinez-Vazquez. 2015. "Pakistan's Enduring Agenda for Tax Reforms." In Martinez-Vazquez and Cyan 2015, 1–77.

Ellis, P., M. Kopanyi, and G. A. Lee. 2007. "Property Taxes in the Large Cities of Punjab Province, Pakistan." *Journal of Property Tax Assessment and Administration* 4 (2): 31–51.

FBR. 2021. "Withholding Income Tax Rates Card." Federal Board of Revenue, Pakistan. (June 30). https://download1.fbr.gov.pk/Docs/20218151182834653202189138454560UPDATEDWHTRateCardupto30thJune2021.pdf.

———. n.d. "Valuation of Immovable Properties." Federal Board of Revenue, Pakistan. Accessed April 05, 2022. https://www.fbr.gov.pk/valuation-immovable -properties/51147/131220.

Finance Division. n.d. "Pakistan: Summary of Consolidated Federal and Provincial Budgetry Operations, 2019–20." https://www.finance.gov.pk/fiscal/July_June_2019 _20.pdf.

Jamal, N. 2018. "Punjab Property Tax Collection Remains Far Behind." *Dawn, The Business and Finance Weekly*, March 26. https://www.dawn.com/news/1397466 /punjab-property-tax-collection-remains-far-behind.

Kelly, R., R. White, and A. Anand, eds. 2020. *Property Tax Diagnostic Manual*. Washington, DC: World Bank Group.

KPK ET&NCD. 2021. "Property Tax." Excise, Taxation, and Narcotics Control Department, Government of Khyber Pakhtunkhwa. https://www.kpexcise.gov.pk/app/.

KPMG. 2017. "Amendments Through Finance Act 2017." (June). https://home.kpmg/content/dam/kpmg/pk/pdf/2017/06/Finance%20Act%202017.pdf.

McCluskey, W. J. 2020. "Case Study: Punjab Province, Pakistan." In *Property Tax Diagnostic Manual*, ed. R. Kelly, R. White, and A. Anand, 137–145. Washington, DC: World Bank Group.

McCluskey, W. J., and M. McCord. 2021. "Overview of the Urban Immovable Property Tax in Pakistan and Revenue Simulations." World Bank Report.

Nabi, I., and H. S. March. 2011. "Reforming the Urban Property Tax in Pakistan's Punjab. Development Policy Research Centre," Working Paper, Lahore University, Pakistan.

Pakistan Bureau of Statistics. 2021. "Final Results (Census-2017)." https://www.pbs.gov.pk/content/final-results-census-2017.

Pasha, A. G. 2011. "Fiscal Implications of the 18th Amendment: The Outlook for Provincial Finances." World Bank Policy Paper Series on Pakistan, PK 02/12. Washington, DC: World Bank. https://openknowledge.worldbank.org/handle/10986/18707.

Piracha, M. M. 2016. "Sub-National Government Taxation: Case of Property Taxes in Punjab, Pakistan." Ph.D. diss., University of Sussex.

Piracha, M., and M. Moore. 2015. "Understanding Low-Level State Capacity: Property Tax Collection in Pakistan." ICTD Working Paper 33. Institute of Development Studies. (March). https://opendocs.ids.ac.uk/opendocs/bitstream/handle/20.500.12413/11182/ICTD_WP33.pdf.

———. 2016. "Revenue-Maximising or Revenue-Sacrificing Government? Property Tax in Pakistan." *Journal of Development Studies* 52 (12): 1776–1790.

Punjab ET&NCD. 2021a. "Farm House Tax." Excise, Taxation, and Narcotics Control Department, Government of Punjab. Available at https://excise.punjab.gov.pk/farm_house. accessed October 18, 2021.

———. 2021b. "Luxury House Tax." Excise, Taxation, and Narcotics Control Department, Government of Punjab. Available at https://excise.punjab.gov.pk/luxury_houses. accessed October 18, 2021.

———. 2021c. "Property Tax." Excise, Taxation, and Narcotics Control Department, Government of Punjab. Available at https://excise.punjab.gov.pk/property_tax#h3. accessed October 18, 2021.

———. n.d. https://excise.punjab.gov.pk/system/files/Valuation_Table_New.jpg.

Sindh ET&NCD. 2021. "Property Tax." Excise, Taxation, and Narcotics Control Department, Government of Sindh. http://excise.gos.pk/taxes/property-tax/. accessed on October 18, 2021.

Wani, S., H. Shaikh, and O. Harman. 2020 "Urban Property Taxes in Pakistan's Punjab." Policy brief. International Growth Center. (October). https://www.theigc.org/wp-content/uploads/2020/11/Wani-et-al-2020-Policy-Brief.pdf.

Wikipedia. 2022. "List of Pakistani Administrative Units by Gross State Product." Last modified February 10, 2022. https://en.wikipedia.org/wiki/List_of_Pakistani _administrative_units_by_gross_state_product.

World Bank. 2006. "Property Taxes in the Punjab, Pakistan." Washington, DC: World Bank Infrastructure and Energy Department, South Asia Region. https:// openknowledge.worldbank.org/handle/10986/8277.

———. 2016a. "A Report on Reforming the Urban Immoveable Property Tax in Sindh." Washington, DC: World Bank.

———. 2016b. "A Review of the Urban Immovable Property Tax in Punjab." Washington, DC: World Bank.

———. 2017. Project Information Document/Integrated Safeguards Data Sheet (PID/ ISDS), Pakistan Housing Finance Project. P162095.

———. 2019a. "Competitive and Livable City of Karachi Project." PAD 128942. (June). https://projects.worldbank.org/en/projects-operations/project-detail/P161402.

———. 2019b. "Pakistan Raises Revenue Project." Project Appraisal Document. P165982.(May).https://documents1.worldbank.org/curated/en/458051560736948947 /pdf/Pakistan-Raises-Revenue-Project.pdf.

———. 2019c. "Pakistan: Punjab Public Management Reform Program." Implementation Completion and Results Report: IDA-53140-PK, Report No. ICR00004836. https://projects.worldbank.org/en/projects-operations/project-detail/P132234.

Zameen Blog. n.d.a. "Property Fees Applicable to Real Estate Investments." Accessed October 18, 2021. https://www.zameen.com/blog/6-types-of-property-fees-you -may-not-know-about.html.

———. n.d.b. "Understanding Property Tax Rates in Pakistan." Accessed October 18, 2021. https://www.zameen.com/blog/understanding-property-tax-rates-in -pakistan.html.

12

Philippines: Policy, Administration, and Revenue Mobilization

NIÑO RAYMOND B. ALVINA

This chapter examines how real property taxation has evolved and performed as a fiscal decentralization instrument. It starts with an overview of taxing powers and the fiscal performance of local-government
units and then discusses property-related taxes at the local and national
levels. Subsequent sections address property tax exemptions, administration, valuation, and revenue performance. The chapter concludes with an
analysis of the last decade of important reform programs and ongoing initiatives and summarizes the prospects for change. Property tax reform in
the Philippines is nothing new, and past structures continue to affect the
choices of feasible options for change. The appendix summarizes the history of property taxation in the Philippines.

Overview of Local-Government Taxing Powers and Fiscal Performance

The tax assignments of local governments in the Philippines are reported
in table 12.1. Provinces are mainly responsible for real property tax, and cities[1] have broader responsibilities. Cities can tax what both provinces and municipalities are authorized to tax, and they are allowed to exceed their
maximum rates by up to 50 percent for most taxes. Local government
units (LGUs) can also impose regulatory fees and user charges or operate

Table 12.1 Key Taxing Powers by Level of Government

Tax Base	Province	City	Municipality	Barangay
Real property[1]	Yes	Yes	Share	Share
Local business[2]	No	Yes	Yes	Yes[3]
Franchise	Yes	Yes	No	No
Real property transfers	Yes	Yes	No	No
Printing and publication	Yes	Yes	No	No
Sand, gravel, and other quarry resources	Yes	Yes	Share	Share
Delivery vans and trucks	Yes	Yes	No	No
Amusement places	Yes	Yes	Share	No
Professionals	Yes	Yes	No	No
Community tax	No	Yes	Yes	Share

Source: Local Government Code of 1991.

Notes: Share indicates the percent of RPT collection that is retained by the municipality or barangay where the property is located. As a provincial imposition, 35% goes to the province, 40% to the municipality where the property is located, and 25% to the barangay where the property is located. As a city imposition, the city gets 70% of the RPT, while 30% is shared by the barangay where the property is located (50%) and the remaining 50% is distributed to all other barangays.

[1] Includes idle land tax, socialized housing tax, and special levy.
[2] As defined in Local Government Code of 1991 sec. 143 (a)–(h).
[3] For stores or retailers with fixed business establishments as provided in the law.

economic enterprises in the exercise of their corporate powers. Barangays (barrios or villages) are the smallest unit of government.

Depending on the type of tax, the rates that local governments can impose are determined by a tax ceiling or are fixed, but these can be adjusted once every five years by up to 10 percent through local legislation. All local impositions of provinces, cities, municipalities, and barangays must be enacted in a local tax ordinance passed by the *sanggunian* (the local legislative council), approved by the local chief executive, and reviewed by higher local-government levels. This means that tax ordinances of barangays are reviewed by the municipality or city that has jurisdiction over them and ordinances of component cities and municipalities by the province.

The bulk of operating income of most local governments comes from intergovernmental transfers, mainly the internal revenue allotment. This allotment is a guaranteed annual formula-based block grant equaling

40 percent of the gross internal revenues collected three years previously by the Bureau of Internal Revenue. The bureau collects the revenue from personal and corporate income tax, estate and donor's taxes, value-added tax and other national set percentage taxes, excise taxes, documentary stamp tax, and other internal revenue taxes.

In terms of vertical distribution of the internal allotment, provinces get 23 percent, cities 23 percent, municipalities 34 percent, and barangays 20 percent. Horizontally, each LGU type receives amounts distributed according to population (50 percent), land area (25 percent), and equal sharing (25 percent). The barangay share is determined according to population (60 percent) and equal sharing (40 percent).

From FY 2018 to FY 2020, internal revenue allotment transfers grew by an average 10.07 percent, because of improved national tax effort, as shown in table 12.2. Sixty-seven percent of the total revenues of local governments came from the allotment, and provinces and municipalities notably relied on it for more than 80 percent of their regular incomes (table 12.3), and a majority of villages depend on it for at least 90 percent. Conversely, only 29 percent of the annual regular income of LGUs come from locally sourced revenues (table 12.4), and only the cities have a high degree of revenue autonomy. This low dependence of cities on the internal revenue allotment, however, is mostly evident in highly urbanized metropolitan cities, because rural cities have relatively high dependence on the allotment, and their local revenues remain low compared with other cities of the same size or income classification.

Table 12.2 Growth of Internal Revenue Allotment of LGUs, 2018–2020

LGU Type	Internal Revenue Allotment Share (PHP billion)			Growth (%)			
	2018	2019	2020	2018	2019	2020	Avg.
Province	122	132	149	7.28	8.87	12.75	9.63
City	120	132	149	7.40	10.52	12.75	10.22
Municipality	178	196	221	7.35	9.85	12.75	9.98
Barangay	103	115	130	7.43	11.51	12.75	10.57
Total	**523**	**576**	**649**	**7.36**	**10.10**	**12.75**	**10.07**
Net increase (year over year)	36	53	73	–	–	–	–

Source: DOF-BLGF (2021).

Table 12.3 Share of LGUs' Annual Regular Income (ARI) and Internal Revenue Allotment (IRA)

LGU Type	ARI (PHP billion)			IRA (PHP billion)			IRA as % of ARI			
	2018	2019	2020	2018	2019	2020	2018	2019	2020	Avg.
Province	152	159	174	121	132	149	80	83	86	83
City	262	290	307	119	132	149	46	46	49	47
Municipality	229	249	268	178	196	221	78	81	82	80
Total	**644**	**691**	**749**	**418**	**460**	**519**	**65**	**67**	**69**	**67**

Source: DOF-BLGF (2021).

Table 12.4 Share of LGUs' Locally Sourced Revenues (LSR) to Annual Regular Income (ARI)

LGU Type	ARI (PHP billion)			LSR (PHP billion)			LSR as % of ARI			
	2018	2019	2020	2018	2019	2020	2018	2019	2020	Avg.
Province	152	159	174	22	23	21	15	15	12	14
City	262	290	307	134	149	150	51	51	49	50
Municipality	229	242	268	35	39	38	15	16	14	15
Total	**644**	**691**	**749**	**192**	**211**	**209**	**30**	**31**	**28**	**29**

Source: DOF-BLGF (2021).

Even with these increases in the internal revenue allotment allocations under the Local Government Code (LGC) of 1991, the devolved expenditure responsibilities of the local governments were not sufficiently addressed. A long and drawn-out legal battle on the proper interpretation of the tax base of the internal revenue allotment was resolved with finality in 2019 when the Supreme Court ruled that limiting the internal revenue allotment base to internal revenue collections and excluding the tax collections from customs operations was unconstitutional, and the allotment should be drawn now from all national taxes. Had the ruling been retroactive, a staggering PHP 1.512 trillion might have been allocated. The application of the ruling, however, is prospective, and all national taxes collected by the national government in FY 2019 will be the base for the FY 2022 allotment. The internal revenue allotment will be called the national tax allotment. This is estimated to increase allocations by 27 to 30 percent in aggregate levels. In two years' time, the fiscal position of most local governments that depend on internal revenue allotments will change. The national tax allotment could have negative effects on local property tax effort, because local taxpayers and political leaders find the national transfers to be a more acceptable source of revenues.

In addition to the internal revenue allotment, local governments receive grants, extraordinary aid, and other shares from the national taxes, where such a source of tax was collected. The 5 percent (as a share to the total income) refers to the grants, aids, and other shares from national taxes received by the LGUs. Tobacco-producing provinces and municipalities, however, can receive as much as 60 to 65 percent of their shares from the tobacco excise tax.

LGUs have improved their domestic resource mobilization and increased revenue collections from real property tax, local business tax, regulatory fees, service or user charges, and derived income from their operations of hospitals, public markets, and transport terminals, among others. However, a large part of this improvement comes from the bigger and richer LGUs. This easily offsets the more than 47 percent of the LGUs (800 lower-income and rural provinces, cities, and municipalities) that usually depend on national transfers for at least 90 percent of their income. Provinces' and municipalities' own revenues, for example, make up around 15 percent of their income, and for cities it is approximately 50 percent. From FY 2018 to FY 2020, at least 29 provinces, 20 cities, and 769 municipalities relied on national transfers for at least 90 percent of their income.

Given the concentration of commercial and economic activities in urban areas and capital towns, local business tax is their main income and contributed 59 percent (cities) and 38 percent (municipalities) of their total local revenues in 2018–2020. The local business tax is assessed and collected by city and municipal treasurers as a fixed tax or percentage tax, or combination of both, on the preceding year's gross receipts of businesses.[2]

Provincial governments depend mainly on real property tax and property-related taxes, regulatory fees and user charges, and revenues from economic enterprises, as shown in table 12.5, but they can also impose and collect percentage tax on businesses printing and publishing books, cards, posters, leaflets, handbills, certificates, and receipts and businesses that have a franchise from the national government, taxing their prior year's gross receipts or a percentage of capital investment if the business is newly started.

The total collections from locally sourced revenues remained only a little over 1 percent of GDP from 2018 to 2020, indicating that local revenue generation capacity has not tracked national tax effort and economic

Table 12.5 Individual Local Taxes as % of Total Local Income

LGU Type	Real Property Tax				Business Tax				Other Taxes			
	2018	2019	2020	Avg.	2018	2019	2020	Avg.	2018	2019	2020	Avg.
Province	18	19	20	19	7	8	8	8	4	5	5	5
City	18	17	18	17	56	58	62	59	6	6	5	6
Municipality	13	12	13	13	36	37	41	38	3	3	3	3

LGU Type	Regulatory Fees				Service/User Charges				Receipts from Economic Enterprises			
	2018	2019	2020	Avg.	2018	2019	2020	Avg.	2018	2019	2020	Avg.
Province	2	2	2	2	40	41	37	39	28	26	28	27
City	7	7	6	7	5	6	5	5	7	6	5	6
Municipality	13	13	13	13	12	12	11	11	23	24	20	22

Source: DOF-BLGF (2021).

growth. Internal revenue allotments have grown along with an increased base of national taxes collected.

All local governments in the Philippines can borrow from any domestic banks or lending institutions, but they are very conservative—loan proceeds constitute about 4 percent of both the annual regular incomes and expenditures. Annual debt servicing is also generally below the 20 percent statutory expenditure limit, and over the last six years the average ratio of LGU debt stock to GDP is only 0.59 percent, far from the average 5 percent debt-to-GDP ratio in developing jurisdictions.

Design and Structure of Local and National Property-Related Taxes

The power to tax real properties and property-related transactions in the Philippines is exercised by both national and local governments. At the local-government level, it is primarily a mandate of provinces and cities. They are in charge of the overall property tax administration, including property identification, appraisal and assessment, records management, and collection and enforcement. Provincial and city governments have the authority to decide on the property values, tax rates, imposition of interest and penalties, application of discounts, relief for property owners and taxpayers, and enforcement within their jurisdictions.

Local Property-Related Taxes

At the local level, the main tax on land and property is the real property tax. Another six property-related taxes are also levied. All seven real property and property-related taxes imposed by LGUs accrue on specific dates, have predetermined purposes, and are shared with lower-level LGUs (table 12.6).

Basic Real Property Tax

Under LGC of 1991, the basic real property tax is an annual ad valorem tax on land, buildings, improvements, and machinery. The tax rate depends on jurisdiction—provinces can impose a tax rate of up to 1 percent, and cities are allowed up to 2 percent. This tax is the only local tax whose proceeds are shared by all LGUs,[3] regardless of type, class, or level of urbanization, making it perhaps the most sustainable source of local revenues. A 2018 survey by the Bureau of Local Government Finance found that 95 percent of provinces have set their property tax rates at the maximum of 1 percent. Because of their broader revenue-raising powers, only 18 percent of all cities imposed the maximum 2 percent rate.

Table 12.6 Accrual, Payment, and Sharing Arrangements of Local Property-Related Taxes

Tax	Date of Accrual	Payment Scheme	Sharing of Proceeds				
			Provincial Tax			City Tax[1]	
			Prov.	Muni.	Brgy.	City	Brgy.
Basic real property tax	Jan. 1	One-time or quarterly installment (Mar. 31, Jun. 30, Sep. 30, Dec. 31)	35%	40%	25%	70%	30%
Special education fund tax			Divided equally		Not applicable	100%	Not applicable
Idle land tax			100%	Not applicable	Not applicable	100%	Not applicable
Socialized housing[2] tax			As per ordinance[3]	Not applicable	Not applicable	100%	Not applicable
Special levy on land	First day of next quarter after effectivity	Annual installments: 5 to 10 years	100% to the funding LGU	Not applicable	Not applicable	100%	Not applicable
Local transfer tax	Within 60 days of transfer	One time	100%	Not applicable	Not applicable	100%	Not applicable
Tax on quarry resources	Upon extraction	One time	30%	30%	40%	60%	40%

[1] For the municipality of Pateros, the lone municipality within metropolitan Manila, the sharing of basic real property tax is 35% to the municipality, 35% to metro Manila, and 30% to barangays. Similarly, all real property taxes other than the basic may likewise be imposed and collected by Pateros. Throughout this chapter, the municipality of Pateros is treated as a city.

[2] Socialized housing is known as affordable housing in some other regions.

[3] The sharing arrangement between provinces and their component municipalities is not provided by law, and local ordinances may assign shares.

Administration of the basic real property tax depends on two components: the assessed value according to property classification and actual use and the applicable statutory tax rate. These components serve as policy levers for LGUs in deciding on how much tax will be collected. The assessed value is set as a percentage of the market value of the property. This is computed by first determining the applicable unit market value of the property, as indicated in the current and approved schedule of fair market value (also called the schedule of market value), according to its property classification (whether residential, agricultural, commercial, industrial, mineral, or timberland). The corresponding assessment level for each property class (land and machinery is detailed in table 12.7) is then applied, on the basis of the property's actual use, to arrive at the final assessed value on which the final tax rate will be applied.

Under LGC of 1991, real properties shall be listed, valued, and assessed in the name of the natural or juridical person owning or administering the property or having legal interest thereon. The person is required to prepare and file with the local assessor a sworn detailed description and declaration of the true value of property, whether previously declared or undeclared, taxable or exempt. This must be done once every three years, coinciding with the mandated period of revaluation of property values at the local level. The requirement also applies when any person acquires property or when improvements are made, and the local assessor must be notified within 60 days after property acquisition or upon completion or occupancy of the improvement, whichever comes earlier. This is useful when transaction data are unavailable to support market value determination.

Table 12.7 Real Property Tax Assessment Levels on Land and Machinery

Land		Machinery	
Property Class	*Maximum Assessment Level (%)*	*Property Class*	*Maximum Assessment Level (%)*
Residential	20	Residential	50
Agricultural	40	Agricultural	40
Commercial	50	Commercial	80
Industrial	50	Industrial	80
Mineral	50		
Timberland	20		

Source: LGC of 1991.

When self-declaration of the property is not made within the prescribed time, the local assessor is authorized to make the declaration in the name of the defaulting owner or against an unknown owner, without a sworn statement. The local assessor compares owner-declared values with the schedule of fair market value and with similar property transaction records or market information on sale, lease, rental, or construction.

Special classes of lands, buildings, machinery, and improvements are assessed differently according to use, taking 10 percent of the assessed value for local water districts and for government-owned or government-controlled essential public services (supply and distribution of water or generation and transmission of electric power) and 15 percent for properties used for hospitals or for cultural or scientific purposes, as prescribed under LGC of 1991. Roads, lots, and streets in subdivisions are also assessed on the basis of the cost of cementing, asphalting, or paving per square meter. These properties become exempt if they are donated or turned over to the local government.

For other buildings and improvements not considered a special class, the assessment levels are up to a maximum of 80 percent, as summarized in table 12.8. For residential buildings or structures that have a total market value of up to PHP 175,000 (about USD 3,446), the level is zero, but they are still on the tax rolls and assessed for real property tax. This threshold, however, was set in 1991 and is not indexed to inflation, leaving many properties with severely outdated property values.

Table 12.8 Schedule of Assessment Levels for Buildings and Other Structures

	Assessment Level			
Value (PHP thousand)	Residential (%)	Agricultural (%)	Commercial and Industrial (%)	Timberland (%)
0–175	0	–	–	–
176–300	10	–	–	45
301–500	20	25	30	50
501–750	25	30	35	55
751–1,000	30	40	50	60
1,001–2,000	35	45	60	65
2,001–5,000	40	50	70	70
5,001–10,000	50	–	75	–
10,001+	60	–	80	–

Source: LGC of 1991.

As mentioned (see table 12.6), six other taxes are imposed on real property by local governments; four are recurrent and two are a one-time tax. The four recurrent ones are the additional levy for the special education fund, the additional ad valorem tax on idle lands, the special levy by local-government units, and the socialized housing (affordable housing) tax. A nonrecurrent or one-time tax on transfer of real property ownership may also be imposed by provinces and cities. Another one-time tax can be imposed on the extraction of quarry resources by provinces and highly urbanized cities.

Levy for the Special Education Fund

The special education fund tax has a maximum rate of 1 percent on the assessed value of real property.[4] Proceeds of this additional levy, collected by the local treasurer, exclusively accrue to the special education fund of the local school boards and are automatically released to them. The fund is generally intended for operations and maintenance of public schools; construction and repairs of school buildings, facilities, and equipment; research; purchase of books and periodicals; and sports development. As a rider tax, the levy started in the 1960s to support financing for public education, and in 1987,[5] at a time when all public secondary school teachers were nationalized. In its early design, 80 percent of the proceeds of the levy were remitted to the national treasury to help stabilize education spending by the central government, and the remaining 20 percent accrued to local school boards in every province, city, and municipality. With the passage of LGC of 1991, the sharing arrangement was abolished, and the full tax revenue collected for the special education fund is now under the control of local school boards, which are chaired by the local chief executive.

Idle Land Tax

Provinces and cities may impose an additional ad valorem tax on idle lands at a rate not exceeding 5 percent of their assessed value. This tax is designed more to promote better land use and to curb land banking and speculation than to be a revenue tool.

Idle lands are agricultural lands of more than one hectare and suitable for cultivation, dairying, inland fishery, and other agricultural uses of which half remains uncultivated or unimproved. Nonagricultural lands are deemed idle if the lot is more than 1,000 m^2 and half remains unused or unimproved.

Many provinces and cities have legislated the idle land tax, but very few have successfully implemented it.[6] Among the problems are what really makes a land idle, the cycle for reassessment, the time horizon for newly acquired lots to be developed, and the proper listing and recording of these idle lands. Only 12 of 81 provinces and 43 of 146 cities reportedly impose the tax, of which only a couple of provinces and 19 cities collect it (BLGF 2015).

Special Levy on Land

Akin to land value capture and having the characteristics of a betterment tax, this special levy originated in the 1970s on land that benefits from public work projects or improvements funded by the province or the city. This levy aims to recover public expenditures but not more than 60 percent of the actual cost of such projects and improvements, including property acquisition costs. To date, however, this tax has been imposed by few provinces or cities. Many local authorities take the view that their local capital investment projects, which are relatively small, are outright public goods that should not be burdened with a cost-recovery objective. There is also little fiscal need to impose it because for decades many LGUs received substantial support from the national government for public works.

Imposing special levies on real property has been considered. The levies would be development charges or special assessments on buildings in highly urbanized areas declared by the national government as special economic zones. However, the legality of these initiatives is still under study.

Socialized Housing Tax

Another recurrent tax imposable by provinces and cities is the socialized (affordable) housing tax, which is the only local-government taxing power not provided in LGC of 1991. The tax was legislated in 1992 under the Urban Development and Housing Act as an additional tax premised on the constitutional principle that the ownership and enjoyment of property carries a social responsibility to raise funds for local urban development and housing programs for the underprivileged. The rate is 0.5 percent, and it is levied only on lands in urban areas that are valued above a total assessment of PHP 50,000.[7]

The tax is not used often and it is not popular when implemented. For instance, in 2011, Quezon City, a special city in metro Manila, used it for five years to fund housing projects for the poor.[8] Every real property in the city with an assessed value over PHP 100,000, which is higher than the threshold provided by law, was levied with this additional tax. Estimates were that it would generate at least PHP 185 million per year, and the city earmarked the funds to purchase and develop land, improve socialized housing facilities, and construct core houses, sanitary cores, and medium-rise buildings and similar structures for marginalized people

(*BusinessWorld* 2011). The tax was expected to finance public-private partnership agreements of the city government and the National Housing Authority with the private sector.

Quezon City gave a tax credit to taxpayers who paid the tax during the five-year period, at a rate of 20 percent for every year from the sixth to tenth year after implementation. The tax was challenged in the courts for its purpose and design. In 2015, the city government won the case when the Supreme Court ruled that the tax ordinance was constitutional (*Jose J. Ferrer, Jr. v. City Mayor Herbert Bautista*, G.R. No. 210551 [June 30, 2015]).[9] The affordable housing tax is no longer implemented in Quezon City because the revenue and social objectives have been deemed achieved by the city government.

Tax on Transfer of Real Property Ownership

Provinces and cities can also impose a one-time tax on the transfer of real property ownership by sale, donation, barter, or any other mode of transferring ownership or title of real property. The tax rate is a maximum of 50 percent of 1 percent for provinces or 75 percent of 1 percent for cities of the total amount for acquiring the property or as listed in the schedule of fair market value, whichever is higher.

The tax must be paid to the local treasurer by the seller, donor, transferor, executor, or administrator within 60 days of the date of the execution of the deed or of the date of the decedent's death. For properties transferred upon the owner's death, this tax may be difficult to settle within the prescribed period. Taxpaying heirs may have to deal with huge tax obligations and penalties imposed by the province or city that have accrued over time. Some local governments use zonal values as the basis for this tax, even if it is not allowed by LGC of 1991.

Tax on Quarry Resources

For quarry resources, such as sand, gravel, rock, and other earth resources, provinces and highly urbanized cities can impose an ad valorem tax of up to 10 percent of the fair market value of resources extracted from public lands or from the beds of seas, lakes, rivers, streams, creeks, and other public waters within their territorial jurisdictions. The assessment is made upon or before extraction and is based on the schedule of fair market value. The tax must be paid immediately. Many provinces have benefited significantly from this tax imposition, more than from real property tax, notwithstanding the revenue lost when the extracted volume is more than what was declared for tax purposes. Clamor has been growing to shift this taxing power to municipalities and cities for better monitoring and revenue sharing.

National Property-Related Taxes

At the national level, five nonrecurrent property-related taxes are imposed and collected by the Bureau of Internal Revenue. These include the capital gains tax, estate tax, donor's tax, value-added tax, creditable withholding tax, and documentary stamp tax. The taxes are based on the zonal values prescribed by the Bureau of Internal Revenue or the actual price in consideration, whichever is higher.

Capital Gains Tax

The capital gains tax is levied on the presumed capital gained from the sale, exchange, or disposition of land and buildings. The tax rate is fixed at 6 percent of the gross selling price or current fair market value, whichever is higher.[10] The base of this tax depends on either the fair market value as determined by the commissioner of Internal Revenue through zonal valuation or the fair market value as shown in the schedules of fair market value of the provincial and city assessors. Capital gains from the sale of a principal residence is exempt if all proceeds are used for the acquisition or construction of a new principal residence within 18 months. A taxpayer can use this exemption, however, only once every 10 years. Otherwise, a portion of the gain presumed to have been realized from the sale or disposition becomes subject to the capital gains tax.[11]

Estate Tax

Estate tax and inheritance tax is levied on the net value of the decedent's estate, whether resident or nonresident. The value of the gross estate less allowable deductions is taxed. The estate is appraised at its fair market value prevailing at the time of death of the property owner. In 2018, the rate of estate tax was reduced to 6 percent.

Donor's Tax

A donor's tax is imposed on gifts of real property between two or more persons who are living at the time of the transfer. A one-off tax, its rate is 6 percent on real properties with total fair market value above PHP 250,000, according to the fair market value as determined by the Bureau of Internal Revenue or the schedule of values fixed by the provincial and city assessors, whichever is higher.

Value-Added Tax

A 12 percent value-added tax is levied on the sale, barter, exchange, or lease of goods or properties, including real properties held primarily for sale or lease in the ordinary course of trade or business. This tax does not apply to sale of real properties for low-cost and specialized housing,[12] sale of a residential lot valued at PHP 1.5 million and below or house and lot and other residential dwellings valued at PHP 2.5 million and below, and lease of residential units whose monthly rental rate per unit is less than PHP 10,000, regardless of the amount of aggregate rentals received by the lessor for the year.

Creditable Withholding Tax

A creditable withholding tax is imposed by the Bureau of Internal Revenue on the sale of ordinary assets of the seller. The rate of this tax ranges from 1.5 to 6 percent and is based on the selling price of the property.

Documentary Stamp Tax

The documentary stamp tax is imposed for the stamp duty levied on documents or instruments for the assignment, transfer, or conveyance of real property at a rate of 1.5 percent of the consideration or value received. In practice, this tax is PHP 15 for the first PHP 1,000 of the consideration or fair market value, whichever is higher, and an additional PHP 15 for every subsequent PHP 1,000 or part thereof in excess of PHP 1,000.

Exemptions from Local Property Taxes

Local governments do not have discretionary powers to grant exemptions from local property-related taxes. Exemptions are clearly laid out in the 1987 constitution or provided specifically by LGC of 1991 for ownership, character, or usage of real property. The real properties owned by the national government, local governments, and cooperatives registered with the Cooperative Development Authority are tax exempt. LGC of 1991, however, withdrew the tax-exempt status of government-owned or government-controlled corporations, making them liable for real property tax and property-related taxes. But when the beneficial use of a government-owned real property is granted to a taxable person, the property will be listed, valued, and assessed in the name of the possessor, grantee, or public entity if the property is sold or leased.

Charitable institutions and religious buildings—churches, temples, parsonages, convents, mosques, and nonprofit or religious cemeteries are not taxed. The exemption extends to all lands, buildings, and improvements actually, directly, and exclusively used and devoted for religious, charitable, or educational purposes. Also tax exempt are machinery and equipment used by local water districts or by government corporations that supply and distribute water or electric power, and that used for pollution control and environmental protection. International treaties and obligations make certain organizations exempt from property taxes, like embassies and premises of diplomats and the Red Cross, among others. Legislation exempts franchises of specific telecommunication corporations.

Under special laws, companies or individuals operating in special economic zones are exempt from real property tax as part of the tax holiday or incentive structure for investors. For example, eligible enterprises and industrial parks may be entitled to a three-year exemption from payment of the real property tax for every piece of equipment it acquires for its operation.

The assessor must value exempt properties and record them on the assessment rolls, but these records are incomplete. Declarations of exempt properties may be unreliable, assessors may not be able to gain access to the properties, or LGUs have no comparable transactions in the property market.

Local Property Tax Administration

Today's policies on assessment for the real property taxes and property-related taxes discussed above were largely influenced by the real property tax administration and local resource mobilization projects introduced in the 1970s.

Rosengard (1998) notes that the real property tax administration projects in the 1970s and 1980s in almost half of LGUs were implemented in political and economic environments that ranged from martial law to the people power revolution, from economic growth to oil price shocks, but they also included long-lasting peace in many parts of the jurisdiction and agrarian reforms. These early projects increased local tax revenues, the number of tax-mapped land parcels, and property values because of revaluation, but the project left much to be done in collection efficiency.

Overview of the Process and Key Players

Real property tax administration involves two main local actors—the assessor in the first three phases (property identification, appraisal and assessment, and records management) and the local treasurer for tax collection and enforcement. The assessors, who must be licensed and registered real estate appraisers, are appointed by the local chief executive and follow the technical guidelines and regulations on real property appraisal and assessment provided by the Department of Finance and the Bureau of Local Government Finance. Local treasurers are appointed and supervised by the secretary of Finance.

In the first phase, property identification, the provincial and city assessment offices take the lead in mapping and field inspection to accurately identify the property owners and the attributes of the real properties, such as location, boundaries, and actual use. Local assessors produce the tax map; the tax map control roll; and related data sets of properties to establish a credible and reliable system for property identification numbering, tax records maintenance; and the total land area of provinces, cities, or municipalities. The local assessment office establishes a complete inventory of all real properties, provides a permanent link between real properties and office records, identifies the ownership of every piece of real property, and accounts for the total land area of provinces, cities, or municipalities (DOF-BLGF 2006).

In the second phase, real properties are appraised and assessed. The process starts with a field appraisal and assessment sheet, a manual or electronic form to collect the data from the field inspection. Then the tax declaration is produced, an official property assessment record issued and maintained by assessors indicating the market and assessed values of the property. It contains pertinent information on property boundaries, history of issuance or cancellation, and related annotations or memoranda to indicate changes in property records.

In the records management phase, the data from the field appraisal and assessment sheet are converted into official LGU property records that will eventually link to the office of the city or municipal treasurer for tax collection purposes. In this stage, the records are stored at the municipal or city level, but copies are sent to and maintained by the province, together with the tax declaration, property record and ownership forms, assessment roll, and records of assessments and canceled assessments. The municipal or city treasurer will then maintain the real property tax account register to record all taxes due and payments.

The last phase of real property tax administration is collection and enforcement; and this involves billing, collecting, and recording of payments and enforcing administrative and judicial remedies. A notice of assessment is issued by the assessor, and the tax bill is issued by the treasurer.

Receipt of a notice of assessment legally binds the new or revised valuation, assessment, and classification of the property. For instance, when a property is assessed for the first time or if the valuation is adjusted, the notice of assessment must be issued within 30 days. Courts have ruled on the primacy of this document; its absence would render any tax collection action or demand by the local government illegal. Public announcement and posting of notices on real property tax payment deadlines in public places is the general practice of most LGUs.

The collection and enforcement of all local real property and property-related taxes are primary responsibilities of the city or municipal treasurers, and the revenue shares set by law accrue exclusively to their respective general and special funds.[13] The city or municipal treasurer retains only the share of the city or the municipality concerned, and the respective shares to the province and barangay are remitted accordingly. The collection function may also be deputized to the barangay treasurer, who must be bonded, but capacity and risk issues associated with tax collections mean this is hardly ever done. In large jurisdictions, satellite collection offices are commonly set up by the city or municipal treasury officers during collection periods. Barangay officials are directed by the mayor and local treasurer to distribute the notices or tax bills to the property owners, or they must at least assist in tax advocacy campaigns.

In treating real property tax and special education fund payments, local treasurers are required to apply payments first to prior years' delinquencies, interests, and penalties, if any, and credit the remainder for the current period.

The collection method of property taxes varies by LGU—some allow electronic payment, using credit and debit cards, others have mobile or off-site payment facilities, and some allow payments at bank facilities, usually government financial institutions, where local governments maintain their regular deposits. More than half of the surveyed LGUs in 2018 indicated that they already have real property tax billing and collection information systems, mostly provided by private firms (DOF-BLGF 2018).

If property taxes become delinquent, interest is applied at 2 percent per month on the unpaid amount or a fraction thereof, until the delinquent tax is fully paid, but only up to a maximum of 36 months, or 72 percent interest. The local treasurer can further institute remedies by administrative action or judicial action. Unpaid property taxes constitute a local-government lien on the subject property that is superior to all other liens, charges, or encumbrances. It is extinguished only upon payment of the tax and the related interest and expenses.

When the period to pay the property taxes has expired, the local treasurer will issue a warrant of levy and prepare a duly authenticated certificate showing the name of the delinquent owner of the property or person having legal interest therein, the description of the property, the amount of the tax due and the corresponding interest. Within 30 days after service of the warrant of levy, the treasurer advertises for two weeks the sale at public auction of the property to recover the tax delinquency and expenses of sale. The property owner can prevent the auction anytime by paying the tax. Within 30 days after the sale, the local treasurer must report the sale to the local council and deliver to the purchaser a certificate of sale of the subject property. Within one year after the auction, the delinquent real property can still be redeemed by paying the delinquent tax, expenses of sale, and interest; otherwise, the deed of conveyance to the purchaser becomes final. If there is no purchaser, the property is acquired by the province or city, and it may be sold and disposed of publicly, and the proceeds of the sale will accrue to the general fund.

Assessment Appeals

Redress is available for protests on assessments. No protests are entertained by the local treasurer unless the taxpayer first pays the tax, and the official receipts are marked "paid under protest." This makes the notice of assessment, together with other assessment records, indispensable in determining the propriety of the protest. The protest must be formally filed in writing within 30 days from payment of the tax, and the local treasurer renders a decision within 60 days.

Pending resolution of the appeal, the payment is held in trust by the local treasurer. If the taxpayer eventually gets a favorable decision, the amount paid in excess will be refunded or applied as a tax credit against current or future property tax liabilities. But if the decision is against the property owner or after the 60-day period, the taxpayer has to avail of the administrative remedies and redress mechanisms under the jurisdiction of the local board of assessment appeals.

Every province or city is required to establish a local board of assessment appeals, chaired by the registrar of deeds, whose members are the provincial or city prosecutor and the provincial or city engineer. Any question on the property assessment or dissatisfaction with the action of the local assessor on property assessments may, within 60 days from the date of receipt of the written notice of assessment, be filed with the appeals board. The board must resolve the issue within 120 days from the date of receipt of the appeal. Any further appeals of the board's decision are resolved by the Central Board of Assessment Appeals. The highest quasi-judicial administrative body, the central board has appellate jurisdiction on all assessment cases of the local board and must receive notification within 30 days after receipt of the local board's decision. Under LGC of 1991, the central board was transformed into an independent body with detailed jurisdiction and powers to better safeguard the objectives of the government and the property taxpayers, and it has exclusive jurisdiction to hear and decide all appeals on decisions, orders, and resolutions of the local board of assessment appeals.

Tax Relief

Local governments can grant relief or deferral on property-related taxes, especially in times of economic hardship, such as general crop failures, substantial price decrease of agricultural products, or natural calamities. This can be done by the LGU through an ordinance. However, in practice, many LGUs have used a broader-based general amnesty of real property taxes that does not meet the economic hardship conditions.

A 2018 Bureau of Local Government Finance survey found that 56 LGUs have granted amnesty to taxpayers in the last two decades, mostly in urbanized regions with high-value residential, commercial, and industrial properties (DOF-BLGF 2018). As relief, some LGUs wrote off the unpaid real property tax, others provided relief on the interest and penalties, and some combined both approaches. Only 60 percent of the surveyed provinces and cities responded that the purpose of their amnesty was due to economic hardship or calamity. Other LGUs' amnesty programs were to encourage delinquent taxpayers to pay up. But this strategy could backfire if delinquent taxpayers believe another amnesty could come in the near future.

Local governments reported that around 666,570 taxpayers (48 percent from provinces, 52 percent from cities) from 1999 to 2019 benefited from the real property tax amnesty program, and approximately PHP 7.59 billion in revenues have been written off (PHP 6.6 billion, or 87 percent, of which were forgone by provinces and PHP 1 billion, or 13 percent, by cities). Nonetheless, the amnesty programs yielded an estimated PHP 28.6 billion (PHP 8.6 billion, or 30 percent, of which went to provinces and PHP 20 billion, or 70 percent, to cities). This may be understated because the participating LGUs in the survey account only for about half the total number of provinces and cities. The president of the Philippines may also forgive or reduce property taxes for any taxable year when public interest requires. Since 2011, five executive orders have been issued.[14]

Property Valuation

Real property market values in the Philippines are conservatively estimated to be about 268 percent larger than the assessed values for property tax purposes of LGUs, as of FY 2020 (DOF-BLGF 2021).[15] Conversely, roughly 27 percent of the recorded and declared market values of LGUs account for the base of the property taxes. Property valuation in the Philippines is inefficient and inequitable because of multiple, overlapping valuation systems that result in wide disparities in property values for the same property at a given time. More than 20 central-government agencies perform or require valuation-related functions, such as national taxation, expropriation, agrarian reform, socialized housing, mortgage, lease, sale, or imposition of fees.[16] At the subnational level, there is weak legal compliance with LGC of 1991 for updating property valuations for real property taxation purposes.

The LGU property valuation system is primarily for revenue generation, using the mass appraisal technique as a general rule. But it is not uncommon for LGUs to rely on the sworn statements of property owners for their valuations, which are usually underdeclared, and market investigation is limited by resource constraints of LGUs.

Technically, all real properties, whether taxable or exempt, are required to be appraised at the current and fair market value in the property's locality. The schedule of fair market value is developed by the local assessor and required to be updated every three years, to be legislated by the local council. The schedule is a table of base unit values for all kinds of real properties (excluding machinery) and the basis for computing the basic real property tax and other recurrent local taxes on real properties imposed by provinces and cities.

In preparing the schedule, the assessor is guided by three valuation methods prescribed by the Department of Finance (DOF-BLGF 2010; DOF-BLGF 2018; MRPAAO 2006, No. 1-04;): the market data, income capitalization, and cost approach.

In the market data approach, market value is estimated on the basis of recorded prices paid in actual property transactions and listings in the market. Also called the comparable sales approach, it is commonly used in estimating the value of the land by analyzing the sales data of properties that are similarly situated and near the same date of transaction to arrive at the most probable sale price of the land being appraised. Local assessors obtain sales and transaction data from the records of the registrar of deeds, notaries public, sworn statements of property owners, insurance companies, banks, building permits, and certificate of registration of machinery, among others. Property values published in foreclosure notices, financial statements of companies, business intelligence products, and web-based property listings, whenever necessary, are also considered in the analysis. Market data use is practical when the market is active and has sufficient reliable and credible data to make objective comparisons. Abstraction is also used to estimate first the value of buildings and improvements and subsequently arrive at the residual value of the land. Simply put, and as provided under existing rules of the Department of Finance,[17] the value of buildings is deducted from the transaction or sales price to estimate the value of the land. The method excludes transfers with special consideration, quitclaims, and so on, and must be proximate to the base valuation date or planned general revision of assessments, usually using the records of the last two to three years, depending on property market conditions.

Income capitalization is based on the value of an income-earning property not being more than the returns derived from it and attendant risks. The income produced by the property for its use is analyzed against the associated expenses to arrive at the net income capitalized at the rate that an investor would expect as reasonable return or the interest prevailing in the locality, and the capitalized value of the income represents the present value of the property.[18]

Valuation of buildings and other land improvements uses the cost approach, particularly reproduction or replacement cost, taking the established standards and costs of materials and labor for such structures. Essentially, the cost of reproducing an exact replica is estimated. After the unit base construction cost is established, it is multiplied by the size of the property, and then a depreciation amount is deducted to arrive at the depreciated cost. The Department of Finance prescribes certain computations to use in cost-estimation methods (MRPAAO 2006): The quantity survey calculation adds up costs for materials, labor, fees, licenses, and so on. The unit-in-place calculation estimates the unit costs for various property components. The index calculation applies an adjustment factor from an index to the original cost. The comparative calculation uses the known construction cost of similar property.

The assessor's judgment finds the one of the three approaches to values that will be most sound, logical, and defensible, and the other approaches may be used to complement it. Because local governments do not have the resources to undertake detailed and individualized valuations, assessors use a mass appraisal for lands, base unit construction cost for buildings and improvements, individualized valuation for machinery, and specialized appraisal for special-purpose properties.

Metro Manila has the peculiar practice of the prior coordination of its member cities and municipalities every time the schedule of fair market value is updated or revised,[19] established in 1976 under Presidential Decree No. 921. The old law required that the schedules of fair market value in metro Manila must be jointly prepared by the city assessors of each district. Because this requirement was not repealed by LGC of 1991 and is considered a good law, it is still practiced today. Assessors concur on the schedule of fair market value in harmony with the current regulations on property valuation and assessment.

Local Compliance with Mandatory Property Revaluation

Property values and revision of property assessments and classifications followed a five-year cycle under Presidential Decree No. 464 of 1974. In 1979, the revaluation period was shortened to three years. Under LGC of 1991, all provinces, cities, and the lone municipality within metro Manila are mandated to update real property assessments and classifications every three years. LGU compliance has been generally dismal. With the decentralization of approval of property values and appointment of assessors, the property tax base of most LGUs had become obsolete, even if the central government retained technical supervision and coordination of assessment operations—there was neither carrot nor stick to make the LGUs comply.

In 2000, Hernando de Soto, in his book *Mystery of Capital*, estimated that 60 percent of the jurisdiction's properties are dead capital (or assets informally held and with legal constraints to freely selling or using as collateral) amounting to about PHP 6.92 trillion (USD 133 billion) in 2021 prices. De Soto believes that 57 percent of city dwellers and 67 percent of rural residents in the Philippines live in housing that is dead capital that cannot be realized owing to inefficiencies in land administration and management systems and policies. Up until about 2005, LGU valuations were 10 to 15 years outdated, thus making the schedule of fair market value a misnomer. Although compliance was high immediately after passage of LGC of 1991, noncompliance rose to 83 percent in 1993, and by 2008 it was only 25 percent. Most LGUs, including the newly created cities, used the old valuations.

From 2010 to 2013, compliance percentages of all provinces and cities were as low as between 4 and 15 percent. In 2010 the Department of Finance and the Department of the Interior and Local Government began a massive information campaign in the national dailies. Three years into the campaign, the Bureau of Local Government Finance published LGU progress in the national dailies, and compliance significantly increased the next year, 2014, to 20 percent. Compliance further picked up in FY 2018 and reached 46 percent in FY 2020, when 43 of 81 provinces and 60 of 146 cities revised their property valuations, as summarized in table 12.9. Closer scrutiny, however, reveals that many revaluations were based on a previously deferred schedule of fair market value or on transactions beyond the prescribed three-year cycle.

Local governments shy away from revaluation primarily because they do not want to burden local taxpayers. There are no penalties under the law for noncompliance and no administrative sanctions or incentives. Local

Table 12.9 LGU Compliance in Property Revaluation, 2010–2020

Updated Schedule of Fair Market Value	2010	2011	2012	2013	2014	2015	2016	2017	2018	2019	2020
No. of provinces[1]	9	7	11	5	18	29	33	31	35	33	43
No. of cities[1]	4	11	22	4	27	32	41	40	48	49	60
Total	13	18	33	9	45	61	71	71	83	82	103
% of compliant LGUs	**6**	**8**	**15**	**4**	**20**	**27**	**33**	**32**	**37**	**37**	**46**

Source: DOF-BLGF (2021).
[1] Author's estimation, based on 81 provinces and 146 cities.

officials generally commingle the technical aspects of property revaluation with its political dimensions—that the components of property taxation can be dealt with separately and that the tax itself is not strictly value driven, because the tax rate and assessment levels are flexible policy levers to mitigate any sudden hikes in tax. In LGUs with low tax-collection efficiency, officials usually do not favor revaluation as a strategy. They contend that adjustments on property values will result only in bigger arrearages and ballooning collectibles.

Many assessors dispute the attribution that they do not regularly prepare new valuation schedules and point to the politicized environment that makes compliance with the revaluation requirement challenging. The common notion on the ground is that updating the property values will bring an undesirable political backlash to incumbent officials because the revaluation cycle coincides with local elections. Newcomer local chief executives usually do not wish to introduce reforms during their first term of office that would increase local impositions. Often, updating the tax base or rationalizing local tax measures occur only during the second or last term of office or when political capital is sufficient to absorb negative backlash associated with increased local taxes.

Assessors also lament that their proposals for revaluation are given low priority once presented to the local council and that it is hard to champion this reform if there is no imprimatur from the local chief executive. Consideration on a proposed schedule of fair market value is deferred in local councils by at least two to three years. By the time the schedule of fair market value is approved, a budget for enforcing the new values is not always assured, and when the implementation falls on an election year, it is deferred anew, thereby resulting in more years of delay in implementation of an already outdated schedule.

Many LGUs, regardless of the size of their property tax base, could remedy their outdated valuations by gradually increasing the assessment levels and tax rates. They could argue that they have not yet reached the tax ceilings and that revaluation is much easier to do and less costly to administer than thought. For the tax collectors, real property tax is easier to collect from commercial and industrial properties than from residential and agricultural areas because businesses cannot operate unless their taxes, regulatory fees, and service fees are paid during renewal and registration in the first quarter of the year. This explains why tax delinquencies are mostly accruing from residential and agricultural properties or from a very few big companies with pending tax assessment appeals.

In high-income cities, updating property values is not an urgent concern, because their tax base grows as properties are assessed after property sales, subdivisions and buildings are constructed, and improvements and other taxable structures are added on existing properties. This is true in 70 percent of high-income and highly urbanized cities where their total locally sourced revenues continue to grow, because they can churn out more revenues from other sources, such as local business taxes or from operations of economic enterprises. This situation is not in itself unintentional—mayors argue that it is better to go after other local revenue sources because their tax bases are sectors that can easily generate revenues.

For instance, the better-performing cities in metro Manila, such as the city of Manila, Quezon City, and Makati City, are assured of very high, yet disproportionate, property tax revenues compared with secondary and urban cities across the jurisdiction. Assessments in these cities are shown in table 12.10. Manila's taxable property units assessed using the 2014 schedule of fair market value could still generate in 2018 more than PHP 7 billion in basic real property tax revenues,[20] excluding special education fund and other property-related taxes. Quezon City and Makati City would have bigger base and real property tax intake if the property values were valued at market levels, because these cities still use 1996 and 1997, respectively, valuation schedules. Even if the property tax bases of these cities are decades old, they still collect basic real property tax of PHP 4.38 billion and PHP 4.56 billion, respectively.

The costs of outdated values are easily illustrated in the rural areas when compared with the going rates in the property market in the same locality, based on the existing tax ordinances and the unit-based analysis of lands according to property classes of provinces and cities with the oldest schedules of fair market value. For instance, in FY 2018 some LGUs reported residential lands with the low value of PHP $5/m^2$ and agricultural properties whose values were unbelievably less than PHP $1/m^2$. Some provinces reported revenue-generating commercial and industrial lands with inordinately low valuations officially set in the assessor's records at less than PHP $25/m^2$.

For national property-related taxes, the bases used by the Bureau of Internal Revenue in the past were the self-declared valuations of transacting parties or the appraisals of local assessors. However, the values set by the assessors were too low, property transactions were likely underdeclared, and the system was prone to abuse and tax leakages. This prompted the national government to devise a new valuation system for the Bureau of Internal Revenue to use. Under the National Internal Revenue Code (NIRC) of 1997, the bureau's commissioner subdivided the jurisdiction into zones and assigned property values according to an internal process to arrive at market-based or transaction-driven valuations.

But over time, zonal valuations also lagged market levels because of infrequent updating. There was no statutory requirement for a zonal revaluation

Table 12.10 Property Tax Revenue from Real Property Units (RPUs) of Metro Manila Cities, FY 2018

	City of Manila	Quezon City	Makati City
No. of RPUs	393,569	301,606	205,824
No. of taxable RPUs	385,165	283,714	203,658
No. of exempt RPUs	8,404	17,892	2,166
Assessed value (PHP billion)	391	244	264
Estimated tax revenues: basic property + special education fund (SEF) taxes (PHP billion)	Basic: 7 SEF: 4 **Total: 11**	Basic: 4 SEF: 2 **Total: 7**	Basic: 5 SEF: 3 **Total: 7**
Valuation setup in assessment office	Department of Assessment; with 51 local assessment operations officers	Property Valuation Standard Division, with 172 filled positions	Appraisal Division, with 16 appraisers and centralized computer system
Date of last revision	2014	2017's was suspended; reverted to 1996 level	1997

Note: RPUs are land, buildings, and machinery.

or review period, but in 2017, Republic Act No. 10963, the Tax Reform for Acceleration and Inclusion (TRAIN) Law, mandated that the Bureau of Internal Revenue update zonal valuations every three years and follow the Philippine valuation standards. Spatial planning is discordant, and the comprehensive land use plans of local governments either are not in place or are already outdated,[21] and thus zonal values in most LGUs are usually higher than the schedule of fair market value because they are based on the average of the two highest recommended values or best data available.

By the time new assessments take effect, for both the schedule of fair market value and the zonal values, the base value is already outdated. Over time, the gap in values increases inordinately. The huge variance in values was validated in 2004 by a comparative survey commissioned by the Department of Finance in 19 cities and municipalities (DOF-BLGF 2004). It found that schedules of fair market value were lower than zonal values by 13 to 94 percent, zonal values were lower than private appraisers' values by up to 930 percent, and schedules of fair market value were lower than private appraisers' values by up to 7,474 percent.

In urban areas, the variance is significantly higher. In a rapid survey of values (per square meter) of prime properties in metro Manila conducted in 2017, the market valuation on Ayala Avenue in Makati City was 18 times more than the recorded values of the government—PHP 40,000 according to the schedule of fair market value, PHP 439,000 according to zonal valuation, but the going rate is PHP 700,000 to PHP 1,000,000. In Legazpi Village, a high-end residential area in Makati City, the recorded appraisal of the city assessor for the same year is only PHP 29,000, and the zonal valuation's rate is PHP 320,000, but the prevailing rate is approximately PHP 500,000. This scenario is the same in many highly urbanized and developed cities where property markets are active but the valuation schedules used by government are outdated by at least a decade.

Outdated valuations undermine more than taxation. The system also contributes to huge delays in government infrastructure projects when valuation disputes require lengthy court litigation for right-of-way acquisition, thus impeding economic growth and resulting in cost escalation, unrealized revenues, and fewer socioeconomic benefits.[22]

Revenue Performance

Real property tax and property-related taxes lag the booming property market in the Philippines. In the 2010s, property developments, township projects, and residential subdivisions also grew, particularly in secondary cities across the jurisdiction.[23]

From FY 2010 to FY 2019, real estate's gross value added grew. This is a measure of the increase in the value of the economy owing to production of goods and services by real estate enterprises. Ownership of dwellings has been growing at an average annual rate of 10.66 percent. Real property tax revenues, in contrast, registered a lower average annual growth of 8.41 percent, and from FY 2010 to FY 2016 the ratio of real property tax to gross value added declined, and the ratio of real property tax to GDP during the same period shows a corresponding trend, as summarized in table 12.11.

Because of the failure to assess at current market values, the government, particularly LGUs, missed capturing the potential revenue growth in the size of the real property market (BLGF 2018). The failure is magnified by the importance of real property tax in the overall tax structure. Although the nominal amounts of revenue grew substantially after fiscal decentralization, the share of real property tax compared with aggregate local income shows a stark contrast.

Before fiscal decentralization, 10-year average data (1982 to 1991) indicate that real property tax constituted 35 percent of the local revenues. In the first 10 years after LGC of 1991 was passed (1992 to 2001), real property tax's

Table 12.11 LGU Collection of Recurrent Property Taxes

Year	Total[1] (PHP billion)	Growth (%)	Real Estate GVA[2] (PHP billion)	Growth (%)	GVA[2] as % of GDP	Real Property Tax as % of GVA[2]	Real Property Tax as % of GDP
2010	33	4.90	540	10.70	5.75	6.12	0.35
2011	36	8.90	597	12.90	5.88	6.03	0.35
2012	39	9.20	672	10.50	6.07	5.85	0.36
2013	41	5.00	760	12.60	6.31	5.43	0.34
2014	45	10.20	831	12.10	6.29	5.47	0.34
2015	48	6.50	930	10.10	6.67	5.21	0.35
2016	51	4.90	996	11.80	6.58	5.11	0.34
2017	62	21.70	1,076	9.80	6.50	5.75	0.37
2018	66	6.69	1,190	10.53	6.51	5.55	0.36
2019	70	6.12	1,256	5.55	6.43	5.58	0.36
Avg.	**49**	**8.41**	**885**	**10.66**	**6.30**	**5.61**	**0.35**

Source: DOF-BLGF (2021); Philippines Statistics Authority (n.d.).
[1] Total is real property tax + special education fund tax.
[2] GVA = gross value added by real estate, including renting and business.

share of local revenues declined and contributed only 12 percent of the total local income. Similarly, real property tax as a share of tax revenues of LGUs declined from a 62 percent average from 1982 to 1991 to 50 percent during the first decade after the LGC of 1991. Analysis of real property tax's contribution to total annual regular income makes apparent its poor performance—from a high of 21 percent of annual regular income before passage of LGC of 1991 down to 12 percent from 1992 to 2001 and only 10 percent during the last five years (2014 to 2018), as summarized in table 12.12.

Collection of real property tax has been consistently low, averaging only 57 percent from 2001 to 2010, excluding delinquencies or arrears. Revenue inefficiency is also aggravated by lack of computerization—in 2005, only 16 percent of LGUs had computerized real property tax administration systems—and poor collection levels, thus making property tax collection administratively costly. From 2016 to 2018, collection efficiency irregularly improved but had a three-year average of only 65 percent (table 12.13). The collection rate inconsistency is due to two divergent trends: the number of taxable real properties declining and the assessed values and collectible real property tax growing by PHP 10 billion. The tax rate (the ratio of tax liability to assessed value), including the basic real property tax and the additional levy for the special education fund, averaged 2.34 percent.

Figure 12.1 depicts the distribution of real property tax and the special education fund tax to local governments. Local property taxes are a minor source of revenues for provincial and municipal governments, but 30 percent of city government tax revenues are from property taxes. Reliance on property taxation is especially pronounced in highly urbanized, commercial, or industrialized cities. By regional distribution, 41 percent of all real property tax concentrated in the National Capital Region (metro Manila) from FY 2018 to FY 2020. High-value properties and volume of transactions have always been concentrated within metro Manila. If Central and southern Luzon peripheral regions are considered, the total real property tax share of these three urbanized regions would account for 73 percent of the total nationwide.

Before fiscal decentralization in 1991, shown as the dotted vertical line at 1991 in figure 12.2, property taxation was the single most important and stable source of own revenues of LGUs. When the local taxing and revenue-raising powers were expanded and the national transfers were increased in LGC of 1991, the significance of real property tax declined, whereas the local business tax consistently grew and now overshadows real property tax.

In fact, the property tax share to GDP has not fared significantly well since fiscal decentralization (shown as the vertical dotted line at 1991 in figure 12.3). Initially, the ratio of real property tax to GDP consistently

Table 12.12 LGUs' Fiscal Performance Pre- and Post-LGC of 1991

	Pre-LGC		Post-LGC			
	10-Year Avg. 1982–1991		10-Year Avg. 1992–2001		5-Year Avg. 2014–2018	
	PHP Billion	%	PHP Billion	%	PHP Billion	%
Locally sourced revenues	**7**	**60**	**26**	**31**	**181**	**32**
Tax revenues	*4*	*34*	*20*	*24*	*133*	*24*
Real property tax	2	21	10	12	54	10
Local business and other taxes	1	13	10	12	79	14
Nontax revenues	*3*	*27*	*6*	*7*	*48*	*9*
Fees and charges	–	–	3	3	27	5
Income from local enterprises	–	–	3	4	21	4
Internal revenue allotment	**5[1]**	**40**	**53**	**64**	**345**	**61**
Other transfers	**–**	**–[2]**	**1**	**1**	**23**	**4**
Loans	**–**	**–**	**3**	**3**	**13**	**2**
Total annual regular income	**12[1]**	**100**	**83**	**100**	**562**	**100**
Real property tax as % of locally sourced revenues	*–*	*35*	*–*	*38*	*–*	*30*
Real property tax as % of tax revenues	*–*	*62*	*–*	*50*	*–*	*40*
Real property tax as % of annual regular income	*–*	*21*	*–*	*12*	*–*	*10*

Source: DOF-BLGF (2021).

[1] Author's extrapolation from Budget Operations Statement of LGUs. Pre-LGC, national transfers were reported as external sources, which may also include all other external sources of revenues.

[2] Bold and italic highlight emphasizes the ratios or percentage of shares as processed data from the above rows.

Table 12.13 Real Property Tax and Special Education Fund Profile, FY 2016–2018

	2016	2017	2018	Avg.
No. of taxable real property units	32,530,804	33,089,630	30,960,873	32,193,769
Assessed values (PHP billion)	3,571	3,818	4,161	3,850
Collectible basic real property tax (PHP billion)	48	49	60	52
Collectible special education fund tax (PHP billion)	36	40	38	38
Total collectible real property tax (PHP billion)	84	89	98	90
Reported real property tax collections (PHP billion)	51	62	64	59
Collection efficiency (%)	61	70	66	65

Source: DOF-BLGF (2021).

increased during the first decade of LGC implementation but suddenly declined in 2004. After a slight recovery in 2005, following years saw a mostly downtrend, from 2006 to 2016. Election years also exhibit consistent drops in the ratio of real property tax to GDP, such as in 1980, 1988, 1992, 1998, 2001, 2004, 2007, 2010, 2013, and 2016, when local revenues are relatively lower but expenditures are higher.

Taking all local property-related taxes of LGUs together, including the property transfer tax, the revenues raised in the Philippines in 2020 were about 0.42 percent of GDP (table 12.14). This is a low revenue yield compared with other Asian jurisdictions.

National property-related taxes have overtaken the overall performance of local property taxes. The Bureau of Internal Revenue started revising zonal values in 2010, and collection strategies and data analytics were also

Figure 12.1 Composition of Annual Regular Income of LGUs, FY 2020

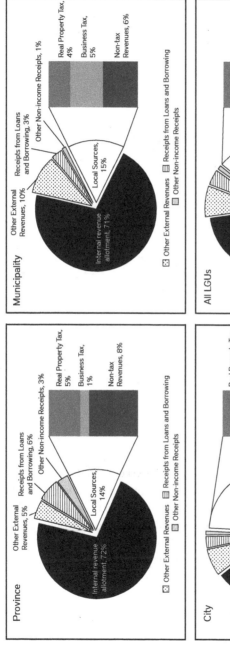

Province

Other External Revenues, 5%
Receipts from Loans and Borrowing, 6%
Other Non-income Receipts, 3%
Real Property Tax, 5%
Business Tax, 1%
Non-tax Revenues, 8%
Local Sources, 14%
Internal revenue allotment, 72%

⊡ Other External Revenues   ⊞ Receipts from Loans and Borrowing
      ▨ Other Non-income Receipts

City

Real Property Tax, 14%
Business Tax, 28%
Non-tax Revenues, 8%
Local Sources, 49%
Internal revenue allotment, 40%

⊡ Other External Revenues   ⊞ Receipts from Loans and Borrowing
      ▨ Other Non-income Receipts

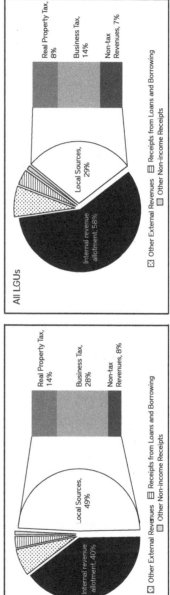

Municipality

Real Property Tax, 4%
Business Tax, 5%
Non-tax Revenues, 6%
Receipts from Loans and Borrowing, 3%
Other Non-income Receipts, 1%
Other External Revenues, 10%
Local Sources, 15%
Internal revenue allotment, 71%

⊡ Other External Revenues   ⊞ Receipts from Loans and Borrowing
      ▨ Other Non-income Receipts

All LGUs

Real Property Tax, 8%
Business Tax, 14%
Non-tax Revenues, 7%
Local Sources, 29%
Internal revenue allotment, 58%

⊡ Other External Revenues   ⊞ Receipts from Loans and Borrowing
      ▨ Other Non-income Receipts

Source: DOF-BLGF (2021).

Figure 12.2 Share of Local Tax Revenue Sources, 1972–2020

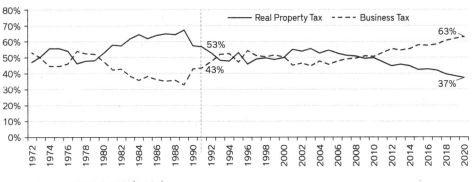

Source: DOF-BLGF (2021).

Figure 12.3 Real Property Tax to GDP Ratio, 1972–2020

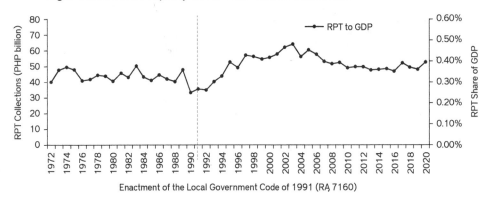

Enactment of the Local Government Code of 1991 (RA 7160)

Source: DOF-BLGF (2021).

intensified given the very active property market in real estate subsectors. By 2017, the aggregate collections from capital gains tax, estate tax, donor's tax, documentary stamp tax, and value-added tax reached PHP 67.12 billion and exceeded the total LGU collections from property tax. The difference between local and national collections nearly doubled in 2018, when national collections from property-related transactions reached 0.43 percent of GDP (table 12.15).

Twenty-First Century Reform Programs

Recognizing the revenue dimension in land administration, reforms in property valuation were initiated by the Department of Finance from 2000 to 2012, as part of the local resource mobilization and fiscal decentralization

Table 12.14 Overall Performance of Local Property-Related Taxes

Year	Basic Real Property Tax	Special Education Fund Tax	Local Transfer Tax	Special Levy	Idle Land Tax	Total[1]	As % of Locally Sources	As % of Regular Income	As % of GDP
				(PHP billion)					
2016	24.69	25.65	4.75	0.01	0.32	55.42	36.95	10.82	0.37
2017	29.68	30.87	5.07	0.01	0.38	66.01	38.79	11.87	0.40
2018	30.08	31.79	6.24	0.05	0.41	68.57	35.76	10.65	0.38
2019	33.98	35.49	7.27	0.03	0.41	77.18	36.58	11.16	0.40
2020	34.98	35.08	5.24	0.02	0.34	75.66	36.13	10.11	0.42
Avg.	**30.68**	**31.78**	**5.71**	**0.02**	**0.37**	**68.57**	**36.84**	**10.92**	**0.39**

Source: DOF-BLGF (2021).

[1] Excludes revenues from the socialized housing tax and tax on quarry resources.

Table 12.15 Overall Performance of National Property-Related Taxes

Year	Capital Gains Tax[1]	Estate Tax	Donor's Tax	Documentary Stamp Tax	Value-Added Tax	Total Property Taxes	Total Collections	As % of Total Collections	As % of GDP
				(PHP billion)					
2014	31.85	3.49	1.96	0.03	2.35	39.68	1,334.76	2.97	0.31
2015	35.96	3.34	2.29	1.01	1.82	44.42	1,441.57	3.08	0.33
2016	39.10	4.72	1.92	2.54	0.94	49.22	1,575.78	3.12	0.34
2017	49.38	5.00	2.47	5.96	4.31	67.12	1,780.80	3.77	0.42
2018	54.72	3.65	3.50	9.52	3.04	74.44	1,962.64	3.79	0.43
Avg.	**42.20**	**4.04**	**2.43**	**3.81**	**2.49**	**54.98**	**1,619.11**	**3.40**	**0.37**

Source: Bureau of Internal Revenue (2019).

[1] *The amount also includes the final capital gains tax for onerous transfer of real property classified as capital assets.*

programs that were supported by development partners. Building on lessons from the decades of real property tax administration projects, the department implemented a property valuation program to strengthen institutional responsibilities on property valuation and taxation, pursue legislative reforms in appraisal and assessment (including the professionalization law as discussed next), set national standards and methods for property valuation, and provide formal valuation education programs for government appraisers and assessors to build capacity. The department set up pilot programs of the reform in selected cities, developed a computerized property valuation system, and strengthened national and local property tax enforcement through tax policy studies and pilot simulations by the Bureau of Local Government Finance and the National Tax Research Center.

Professionalization and Capacity Development

The valuation profession in the Philippines had been characterized as fragmented, having developed without uniform formal training of appraisers. Adherence to valuation guidelines, such as standards and code of conduct, was spotty, and practitioners had few licensing requirements. Government oversight was lax (Bates 2004). In 2009 a law on professionalization of property appraisers, particularly the local government assessors and assessment staff, was implemented. It transformed real estate appraisal into a professional undertaking, now regulated, licensed, and supervised by the Professional Regulation Commission. The law established a regulatory and human resource framework for property valuation in the government sector (Segovia 2009), wherein civil service positions that perform appraisal and assessment are to be duly licensed and registered real estate appraisers.

Politicization in the appointment of LGU assessors was regarded as a contributing factor in the inefficiencies and poor quality in local-government valuations. But under the new law, no one can be appointed as real property appraiser in any national-government entity or as assessor in any LGU unless that person has passed the licensure examination for real estate service. Ten years after the law's passage, the number of licensed real estate appraisers was 10,701.[24] Despite this substantial growth, many local assessor positions reportedly remain unfilled.

The professionalization program for government appraisers was complemented by formal higher education programs and continuing professional development courses on land valuation and management, in partnership with the Central Queensland University in Australia and the University of the Philippines Open University. These are offered as diploma and master of land valuation and as management programs through an online, distance-learning platform.

Valuation manuals have been developed to raise the quality of valuations at the LGU level. The first *Philippine Valuation Standards* was published in 2009, which was later amended in 2018, while the *Mass Appraisal Guidebook* for assessors was issued in 2010. The Basic Course on Mass Appraisal was rolled out in 2011 comprising structured training programs on valuation of land, buildings, plant and machinery, equipment, and special purpose properties; valuation testing; and tax policy studies.

Revaluation Pilot Programs

The Department of Finance's property valuation program chose Naga City, Iloilo City, and Mandaue City for pilot programs in revising their schedule of fair market value using the valuation standards and tools developed by the project. In 2008, the first pilot implementation was successfully completed in Naga City, a city in southern Luzon. Revising its 12-year-old schedule of property values increased the base unit market values of residential lands by 100 to 500 percent, commercial lands by 55 to 200 percent, and agricultural lands by 42 to 209 percent. With these increases, the aggregate market value of properties soared by 147 percent. Consequently, assessed values also increased, by 110 percent, and increase of 40,025 real property units increased the tax roll. In total, 87 percent of the city's real property units were affected by the increases in property values and 12 percent saw a decrease in assessed value.

Not surprisingly, the proposed schedule of fair market value of Naga City was controversial. But in active social marketing and consultations with people's organizations, business groups, and property owners, the city mayor personally committed to putting a reliable system of property valuation in place. He argued that the schedule is a fundamental requisite to ensure equity in the distribution of tax burdens. In response to the huge increases in real property tax owed, the mayor assured the public that increases in property tax liabilities would be gradually phased in and that the revenues generated would finance the city's capital investments, especially infrastructure projects that enhance real property values.

Eventually, the city council adopted the updated schedule of fair market value and the tax policy options. To further cushion the impact of increased real property tax, the local council applied lower assessment levels and placed a cap on the increases in property values in the computation of the real property tax. Collections increased that year by 3 percent, partly because more taxpayers paid early and applied for advance payment discounts (a 69 percent increase over 2008). This resulted in an initial decline in total real property tax collections by 4 percent, and delinquency and penalty payments declined from prior years.

The revenues generated could have been bigger in 2009 if Naga City had fully and directly applied the values under the 2008 schedule of fair market value and if no tax policy considerations had been made. But these measures were a calibrated response by the city to ensure that the reform would not unduly burden taxpayers. When the new values were fully phased in, collections in 2011 were 27 percent above 2010 revenues. For the mayor, an important factor in gaining acceptability of the schedule reform was to engage the people not only when taxes were being raised but also when government funds were being spent, which leads to ownership by the people in the governance process (Robredo 2010).

The Bureau of Internal Revenue also adopted Naga City's proposed schedule as basis for its zonal values in that city, and for the first time, there was a uniform basis for national and local taxation purposes. The Revenue District Office noted that adoption of a single valuation base made the computation and collection of property-related taxes much easier for Bureau of Internal Revenue examiners and collectors. In 2009, collections of the capital gains tax and documentary stamp tax by Naga City's Bureau of Internal Revenue grew by 68 percent and 63 percent, respectively, and its year-on-year total collections in May 2012 rose by as much as 16 percent because of its updated zonal values following the Naga City schedule of fair market value.

This successful demonstration of a single valuation base for national and local tax purposes provides a working model to better understand the local challenges and peculiarities in property valuation and taxation in the jurisdiction. It is a guide for how to address these implementation bottlenecks in other cities and provinces. The Department of Finance, through the Bureau of Local Government Finance, scaled up this project in two phases of a capacity-building project. Funded by the Asian Development Bank, the project supported seven secondary and rural cities, four of which were able to update and enforce their schedules of fair market value, and six municipalities on projects related to land administration.

In this pilot work, a paradigm shift was critical for local stakeholders of the reform, especially elected officials and public officers if they were to be introduced to new ways of doing things. Local-government decision makers and key actors had to understand that the reform must be institutionalized and sustained beyond the project life and that broadening a tax base over time is better than imposing a one-time increase in the tax rate on a small tax base that is not growing.

Outside the project, other LGUs updated their schedules of fair market value to comply with the directives made by the central government and with local champions who recognized the urgent need to act on the long-pending revaluation proposals. But adoption of updated schedules by LGUs will result only in sudden revenue increments. Although that is the primary goal of the reform, the equity aspect of the property tax itself will be meaningless if tax compliance, valuation coverage, and collection efficiency remain low and penalties to enforce the tax remain weak, because then only diligent taxpayers are burdened by increased property taxes.

Other Reform Strategies

The Bureau of Local Government Finance applied a novel approach from 2014 to 2015 to persuade LGUs to update their schedules of fair market value and improve their collection performance. The bureau's Tax Watch campaign published weekly ads in national newspapers to increase transparency on tax payments and to encourage people to be conscientious in paying taxes. The ads listed local governments showing those with updated valuations and those with outdated valuations.[25] Full-page ads ranked provinces and cities by the age of their schedules and by the unfunded public goods and services forgone because of outdated property values.

The ads gained traction with the public and drew immediate action and commitment of local chief executives to comply with the revaluation requirement. As a communication strategy, the ads received mixed reactions. Some perceived them as a call to action for local governments and a good transparency mechanism for the public to better understand how property tax revenues should benefit them. For others, it was a shame campaign with political repercussions for LGUs being branded as noncompliant with LGC of 1991. It was effective, nevertheless. A number of LGUs began revising their schedules of fair market value and passed pending proposals. Total real property tax revenues rebounded in 2015 and 2016.

A related but more direct approach was adopted in 2016 to 2017 when the Secretary of Finance formally informed the individual provincial governors and city mayors of the estimated forgone revenues due to outdated property valuations and their noncompliance with the law, with specific recommendations on how to improve their property tax administration and reduce their dependence on intergovernmental transfers. Building on earlier strategies, this resulted in improved real property tax collections and higher revaluation compliance in FY 2017 and FY 2018, as discussed in previous sections.

Ongoing Initiatives and Looking Forward

Since 2017, the Philippines has identified the proposed Real Property Valuation and Assessment Reform Act (RPVARA) as the centerpiece reform to establish a better regulatory regime on property valuation under the Comprehensive Tax Reform Program of the Rodrigo Duterte administration.

The RPVARA has a broad agenda. It seeks to (1) adopt international standards and rationalize the valuation process; (2) establish a single valuation base for all national and local property-related taxes and use it as a benchmark for other governmental purposes, such as socialized housing, leases, just compensation, and right-of-way reference; (3) insulate valuation from undue politicization by recentralizing to the secretary of Finance approval of property valuations of LGUs, while local governments continue to regulate the tax rates and assessment levels; (4) enhance the statutory procedures and timelines in the conduct of property revaluation and integrate tax impact studies in every revaluation; (5) develop a national property information system and database linked to local governments and key agencies to support appraisal work and tax compliance; (6) improve the selection and appointment of assessors in the LGUs; (7) establish central and regional consultative forums to discuss crosscutting issues on property valuation and taxation; (8) strengthen the appeals process on property valuation and assessment; (9) reorganize the Bureau of Local Government Finance to supervise and review the valuations of LGUs; and (10) enforce specific penal sanctions on LGUs and involved government officials for noncompliance with the law.

The RPVARA is expected to have a direct long-term positive impact not just in boosting government revenues but also in ensuring that the new legal framework will establish an equitable and efficient valuation system. The estimated incremental revenues from updating the property valuations and optimizing their collection efficiencies could reach up to PHP 30.46 billion (PHP 23.08 billion for provinces and PHP 7.38 billion for cities), which would also result in incremental benefits for the real property tax shares of the municipalities and barangays. The increase in real property tax collections from this reform could potentially improve the ratio of real property tax to GDP from 0.37 percent to 0.54 percent. The education sector stands to gain from this reform proposal because it would increase the proceeds that local school boards receive from the special education fund tax.

But legislative reforms are not easily implemented, and this is especially true when reforms affect important interest groups. Since 2004, efforts to legislate property tax administration reforms at the LGU level have been regarded as going against the spirit and intent of local autonomy. But evidence shows that even when administrative measures of oversight agencies have scaled up good property valuation and tax practices of some model LGUs, or at least tighten compliance enforcement, the gains were usually short term and not wide ranging, because the actual implementation on the ground was still rife with political concessions that distorted efficiencies in property taxation. The lackluster performance of property tax as a policy instrument is a compelling reason to take back a decentralized power that does not work in the best interest of public finance.

Even elected officials of LGUs favorably view the proposed recentralization of valuation review and approval of schedules of fair market value of LGUs, although recentralization passes the buck to the central government. Local elected officials are generally happy with the proposed shift in policy, because any increase in values can be tempered by exercising their autonomy to decide the rates and assessment thresholds that suit their local constituencies' capacity to pay and other political or socioeconomic considerations.

Unless the pending structural reforms are instituted, the property tax system in the Philippines will not be a good contributor to strengthening the revenue autonomy and mobilization of local governments. But as the cycle of reforms in the last five decades shows, success will not come from only a valuation-pushed strategy or only a collection-led approach; a right mix is needed in a scalable reform program to make the two components of property tax administration work efficiently to broaden the tax base, achieve high tax compliance and collection efficiency, and promote good local fiscal governance.

Appendix: A Brief History of Property Taxation in the Philippines

Property taxation in the Philippines is believed to have started during the latter part of the Spanish colonial era, evolving from the impositions of the *urbana* tax,[26] a city tax that was levied on income, and the territorial tax, which was levied on the value of property and later became the tax on rural property, imposable by municipalities in the islands of Luzon and the Visayas.[27] Taxes on land were indirectly levied on male tenants as personal taxes or tributes, normally in an in-kind payment for the privilege to work on the land of the *encomienda*.

Under the U.S. occupation (first half of the 20th century), real property taxation in the jurisdiction was formalized with the enactment of Act Nos. 82 and 83 in 1901, which respectively organized the municipal- and provincial-government structures and gave them the mandate to levy and collect the annual ad valorem tax on real property. During this period, both the province and the municipality could levy the same tax on the same property but at different tax rates and earmark revenues for specific public purposes.[28]

Over time, the laws on property taxation and assessment were consolidated in the Administrative Code of 1916 under the Jones Act, and eventually they were legislated separately in the Commonwealth Acts of 1932 and 1939. This continued as the governing laws with the postwar strengthening of local governments under the Local Autonomy Act of 1959.[29]

In 1972, under the Ferdinand Marcos administration, major reforms in property taxation took place. Presidential Decree Nos. 25 and 76 set the rules on appraisal, assessment, distribution, and use of property tax. In 1974, Presidential Decree No. 464, the Real Property Tax Code, was enacted and became the comprehensive law that directed the course of real property tax administration in the jurisdiction, which was continuously implemented with the enactment of Local Government Code (LGC) of 1983.[30] This led local governments to assume greater responsibility to exercise their revenue-generating authorities and to pilot best practices and innovations in real property tax administration, local resource mobilization, and municipal finance. The real property tax administration projects were led by the Ministry of Local Government and Community Development, and supported by the World Bank and the U.S. Agency for International Development.

A decade later, President Marcos transferred supervision of these projects, their technical and administrative support and personnel, appropriations, equipment, and records, to the Ministry of Finance. That made the Ministry of Finance, now the Department of Finance, the lead agency overseeing all subsequent long-term programs and projects related to real property tax administration. It was a strategic move because the key actors in real property tax administration—the local treasurers, who collect local taxes, and the assessors, who perform property appraisal and assessment—are jointly under the administrative and technical supervision of the Finance Department. As part of the Ministry of Finance, the Office of Local Government Finance (now the Bureau of Local Government Finance) led the project implementation and coordinated the development of the local fiscal cadastre through tax mapping operations, updating of property values through mass appraisal, and revision of assessments and property classifications.

With the people power revolution and the new democratic government led by President Corazon Aquino, the 1987 constitution was ratified. It guaranteed greater local autonomy to all territorial and political subdivisions of the state. Congress enacted a law to provide a more responsive and accountable local-government structure instituted through a system of decentralization. On October 10, 1991, Republic Act No. 7160 was passed; An Act Providing for a LGC of 1991 set the new legal framework on real property tax administration of local-government units.[31] LGC of

1991 effectively decentralized most of the powers the central government had had under decree 464, the Real Property Tax Code, particularly in the setting of property values, review of tax rates, and appointments of provincial, city, and municipal assessors. Among the other notable differences under LGC of 1991 is its removal of minimum property tax rates, stipulation that fixed assessment levels be updated, and definition of the technical role of the Department of Finance in setting rules and regulations for the classification, appraisal, and assessment of real property and supervising the property assessment operations of local-government units.

During this period, reforms initiated under decree 464 and the implementation of LGC of 1991, although speckled with transition difficulties, delivered better results and higher revenue performance from real property tax. But this promising trend, as in the early phase of decree 464, waned, and the promise of property tax as a sustainable and progressive revenue tool to achieve genuine and meaningful autonomy was, to a large extent, faced again with design and implementation constraints, political challenges, administrative bottlenecks, and capacity limitations.

Notes

1. Each city's charter categorizes it as an independent component city, a component city, or a highly urbanized city. Residents of independent component cities cannot vote for provincial elective positions. A component city is considered part of its province, and its city council ordinances must be reviewed by the provincial council. A highly urbanized city shall have a minimum of 200,000 inhabitants who must have a minimum annual income of PHP 50 million based on 1991 constant prices.

2. This is provided under section 143 of the Local Government Code (LGC) of 1991 as the basis of municipalities and cities in imposing the local business tax. The businesses are manufacturers, assemblers, repackers, processors, brewers, distillers, rectifiers, and compounders of liquors, distilled spirits, and wines or manufacturers of any article of commerce; wholesalers, distributors, or dealers in any article of commerce; exporters and manufacturers, millers, producers, wholesalers, distributors, dealers, and retailers of essential commodities; contractors; retailers; banks and other financial institutions; peddlers engaged in the sale of any merchandise or article of commerce; and any other business not covered by the foregoing but deemed taxable by the local council.

3. The local tax on quarry resources, which is based on the fair market value upon extraction, is also shared by all LGUs, but this tax is based on derivation and is shared only by local governments that have these natural resources.

4. The special education fund tax was created by Republic Act No. 5447, 1968 (https://lawphil.net/statutes/repacts/ra1968/ra_5447_1968.html). The Philippine Supreme Court ruled in *Demaala v. COA*, G.R. No. 199752 (February 17, 2015), that the special education fund tax may be imposed at a lower rate than the fixed rate of 1% provided by LGC of 1991 (https://elibrary.judiciary.gov.ph/thebookshelf/showdocs /1/59833).

5. Executive Order No. 189, issued on 10 June 1987 (https://www.officialgazette .gov.ph/1987/06/10/executive-order-no-189-s-1987/).

6. For some cities, like Marikina City in metro Manila, the idle land tax improves the local environment by requiring owners to pay higher taxes on vacant lots unless they clean their properties and put them to productive use by planting or fencing.

7. The Urban Development and Housing Act of 1992 was created by Republic Act No. 7279 (https://www.officialgazette.gov.ph/1992/03/24/republic-act-no-7279/).

8. City Ordinance No. SP-2095, S-2011, the Socialized Housing Tax of Quezon City, enacted on October 17, 2011. http://quezoncitycouncil.ph/ordinance/SP/sp-2095,%20s%202011-1.pdf.

9. Find this Supreme Court en banc decision at https://www.chanrobles.com/cralaw/2015junedecisions.php?id=503.

10. Being a national tax, capital gains tax revenues are shared via internal revenue allotment and represent 40% of all national taxes shared with LGUs.

11. As provided under sec. 24 (D) of the National Internal Revenue Code of 1997, as amended by Republic Act No. 10963, or the Tax Reform for Acceleration and Inclusion Law 2017 (https://www.officialgazette.gov.ph/downloads/2017/12dec/20171219-RA-10963-RRD.pdf).

12. These are defined under Republic Act No. 7279 and related laws, such as Republic Act Nos. 7835 and 8763, wherein price ceiling per unit is PHP 450,000 or as determined by the Housing and Urban Development Council and the National Economic and Development Authority.

13. The city or municipal treasurer must post tax due dates by January 31 at the city or municipal hall. The notice must also be published in a newspaper of general circulation in the locality once a week for two consecutive weeks. The payment may be a single one or four equal installments. The quarterly deadlines are March 31, June 30, September 30, and December 31.

14. Generally, these executive orders supported the energy sector. The executive orders are the instruments signed and issued that caused the condonation or reduction of RPT by the President of the Philippines and benefited the energy sector to stabilize energy prices and manage the fiscal position of government corporations engaged in the power industry. This may interest readers to illustrate an overriding authority of the President on the taxing powers of local governments when the public interest so requires. See the latest news on the most recent EO issued (https://www.bworldonline.com/duterte-orders-lower-property-taxes-for-ipps-penalty-condonation/).

15. The aggregate reported market value of all taxable and exempt real properties recorded by LGUs reached PHP 17.695 trillion in FY 2020, but LGUs use outdated valuations.

16. The following government agencies are among them: Bureau of Internal Revenue, Bureau of Local Government Finance, Land Management Bureau, Land Management Service, Forest Management Bureau, Department of Agrarian Reform, Bureau of Land Acquisition and Distribution, Department of Agriculture, Department of Public Works and Highways, Board of Investments, Bureau of Trade Regulation and Consumer Protection, Land Registration Authority, Registry of Deeds, Commission on Audit, National Power Corporation, Bangko Sentral ng Pilipinas, Land Bank of the Philippines, Development Bank of the Philippines, National Housing Authority, National Home Mortgage Finance Corporation, Home Guaranty Corporation, Home Development Mutual Fund, Social Security System, Government Service Insurance System, and Philippine Reclamation Authority.

17. The rules are in sec. 21 (A) (2), Local Assessment Regulations No. 1-92 of the Department of Finance (https://blgf.gov.ph/local-assessment-regulations-no-1-92/).

18. Sec. 21 (B) of Local Assessment Regulations No. 1-92 of the Department of Finance,https://blgf.gov.ph/local-assessment-regulations-no-1-92/.

19. In 1976, Presidential Decree No. 921 (https://www.officialgazette.gov.ph/1976/04/12/presidential-decree-no-921-s-1976/7) created four districts in metro Manila:

(1) Manila; (2) Quezon City, Pasig City, Marikina City, Mandaluyong City, and San Juan City; (3) Caloocan City, Malabon City, Navotas City, and Valenzuela City; and (4) Pasay City, Makati City, Paranaque City, Muntinlupa City, Las Piñas City, Taguig City, and Municipality of Pateros.

20. Pegged on 85% collection efficiency and maximum rate of 2%, and including barangay shares of real property tax.

21. The author concludes that 12.5% of LGUs have no comprehensive land use plans. For LGUs with comprehensive land use plans, 51.6% are fairly current, but 48.4% are severely outdated.

22. For example, the Batangas Port Development Project in 1999 was designed to decongest commercial port operations in metro Manila and make it an international trade port capable of handling container cargo for foreign trade. The Philippine Ports Authority began its expropriation proceedings against 185 lots owned by 231 entities, with a total area of 1,298,340 m^2, with a first offer of PHP 337/m^2 based on the valuation of the land acquisition team of the port authority. Property owners were unsatisfied with the offer and elevated the expropriation issue to the courts, which ruled in 1999 that the unit-based valuation should be PHP 5,500 m^2. The case then went to the Supreme Court, which reduced the value to PHP 5,000 m^2. Eventually, in 2009, the Supreme Court's final ruling was that the fair property valuation should be only PHP 425/m^2.

23. Arcadis (2019) estimates that a total of 337,000 residential condominium units were built in metro Manila in 2018 and an additional 61,000 units by 2021. The housing deficit for socialized housing, however, is estimated to reach 7.67 million units by 2022 and 10.1 million units by 2030, according to the Housing Industry Roadmap of the Philippines (Arcadis 2019). On a bright note, the retail, lifestyle, and industrial sectors of real estate are experiencing movement. In 2018, the existing stock for retail spaces reached 6.5 million m^2, which is anticipated to grow by a further 697,000 m^2 by 2021.

24. In 2021, the PRC reported licensing 10,546 appraisers, 31,444 brokers, and 318 consultants. This is based on internal monitoring of BLGF/inquiry with the Professional Regulation Commission.

25. See examples of Tax Watch campaign advertisements at https://www.dof.gov.ph/advocacies/tax-watch/. The four ads in this campaign were Tax Watch No. 42, "Provincial Profile: Schedule of Market Values," *Philippine Daily Inquirer*, June 4, 2014, p. 5; Tax Watch No. 43, "City Profile: Schedule of Market Values," *Philippine Star*, June 11, 2014, p. A13; Tax Watch No. 78, "Provinces Forego up to PHP 9.4 Billion in Real Property Taxes," *Philippine Star*, March 4, 2015, p. 11; and Tax Watch No. 79, "Cities Miss up to PHP 20.3 Billion in Real Property Taxes," ("Tax Watch Notice, 2015, https://www.dof.gov.ph/tax_watch/cities-rpt/ March 11, 2015).

26. Provided under the Royal Decree of June 14, 1878, the *urbana* tax is a 5% direct tax on urban property based on the net profits of each proprietor, as discussed in *La Compañia General De Tabacos v. The City of Manila*, G.R. No. L-4393 (January 8, 1909) (https://lawphil.net/judjuris/juri1909/jan1909/gr_l-4393_1909.html).

27. Provided under the Royal Decree of May 22, 1893, and based on a percentage of the real value of the property, whether cultivated or not. The municipal court determines the percentage, attended by the representative of the principality and of the reverend or parish priest.

28. For provinces, the annual tax could not exceed ⅜ of 1% of the property's value as assessed in accordance with the municipal code. The proceeds were assigned as follows: ⅛ of 1% only for the construction and repair of provincial roads and bridges and ¼ of 1% could be levied at the discretion of the provincial board and applied to any purpose. For municipalities, the tax was set at a minimum of ¼ of 1% and maximum of ½ of 1% of the assessed value of lands, buildings, and improvements. The proceeds of at least ¼ of 1% were used for free public primary schools and construction of

school buildings. The proceeds in excess of the minimum rate could be used for any municipal purpose at the discretion of the municipal council. Act No. 82, A General Act for the Organization of Municipal Governments in the Philippine Islands, 1901 (https://www.chanrobles.com/acts/actsno82.html); Act No. 83, A General Act for the Organization of Provincial Governments in the Philippine Islands, 1901 (https://thecorpusjuris.com/legislative/acts/act-no-83.php).

29. Commonwealth Act No. 3995 of 1932, An Act Revising and Compiling the Assessment Laws, consolidated all laws relating to the assessment and collection of real property taxes (https://lawyerly.ph/laws/view/l40e1). Commonwealth Act No. 470 of 1939 (https://www.chanrobles.com/commonwealthacts/commonwealthactno470.html) repealed Act No. 3995 and continued, as the Assessment Law of 1940, until the 1970s. The Local Autonomy Act was enacted on June 19, 1959, as Republic Act No. 2264, An Act Amending the Laws Governing Local Governments by Increasing Their Autonomy and Reorganizing Provincial Governments (https://lawphil.net/statutes/repacts/ra1959/ra_2264_1959.html). Further postwar legislation strengthened local governments under the Local Autonomy Act of 1959.

30. Presidential Decree No. 25 of October 20, 1972, required all natural and juridical persons owning or administering real property to file sworn statement of the true value of such property (https://www.officialgazette.gov.ph/1972/10/20/presidential-decree-no-25-s-1976/). Presidential Decree No. 76 of December 6, 1972, amended decree no. 25 and provided new guidelines on the appraisal and assessment of real property tax, as well as the distribution and use of proceeds (https://www.officialgazette.gov.ph/1972/12/06/presidential-decree-no-76-s-1972/). Presidential Decree No. 464's title is Enacting a Real Property Tax Code, 1974 (https://www.officialgazette.gov.ph/1974/05/20/presidential-decree-no-464-s-1974/). Local Government Code of 1983 was enacted in section 8 of Batas Pambansa Blg. 337, February 10, 1983 (https://lawphil.net/statutes/bataspam/bp1983/bp_337_1983.html).

31. See Local Government Code of 1991 at https://www.officialgazette.gov.ph/1991/10/10/republic-act-no-7160/.

References

Arcadis. 2019. *Construction Cost Handbook: Philippines 2019*. Makati City, Philippines: Ardadis. https://www.arcadis.com/en/knowledge-hub/perspectives/asia/research-and-publications/construction-cost-handbook.

Bates, M. 2004. *Developing a Framework for the Appraisal of Real Estate in the Philippines: Inception Report and Blueprint for Future Actions*. Technical report. (September–November.) Makati City, Philippines: USAID.

BLGF 2015 survey initiated by the author.

Bureau of Internal Revenue. 2019. Raw data.

Bureau of Local Government Finance. (BLFG). 2018. "Survey on LGU Schedule of Market Values."

BusinessWorld Online. 2011. "Quezon City Council OK's Socialized Housing Tax." October 18, 2011. www.bworldonline.com/content.php?section=Nation&title=Quezon-City-council-OK's-socialized-housing-tax&id=40107.

de Soto, H. 2000. *The Mystery of Capital*. London: Bantam Press.

DOF-BLGF (Department of Finance–Bureau of Local Government Finance). 2004. F19 Study under the Land Administration and Management Project, Phase 1.

———. 2006. *Manual on Real Property Appraisal and Assessment Operations*. Philippines. (January). https://blgf.gov.ph/wp-content/uploads/2015/08/ManualRPAandAO.pdf.

———. 2010. *Mass Appraisal Guidebook.* Philippines. https://blgf.gov.ph/wp-content/uploads/2015/11/Mass-Appraisal-Guidebook.pdf.

———. 2018. *Philippine Valuation Standards,* 2nd ed. https://blgf.gov.ph/wp-content/uploads/2015/11/Philippine-Valuation-Standards-Manual.pdf.

———. 2021. SRE Reporting System. https://blgf.gov.ph/lgu-fiscal-data/?s=SRE+Report.

MRPAAO. 2006. *Manual of Real Property Appraisal and Assessment Operations.* Manila, Philippines: Bureau of Local Government Finance.

Philippines Statistics Authority (PSA). n.d. Report Reference No. 2019-040 https://www.psa.gov.ph.

Robredo, J. 2010. "Single Valuation System: The Naga City Experience." Speech presented at the First National Congress on Property Valuation, Manila, Philippines.

Rosengard, J. K. 1998. "Philippines Case Study." In *Property Tax Reform in Developing Countries,* pp. 53–84. Boston: International Tax Program Harvard University / Kluwer Academic.

Segovia, P. 2009. "Human Resource Regulatory Regime to Support Real Property Valuation Reform in the Philippines." Paper presented at the 22nd Eastern Regional Organization of Public Administration Conference, Seoul, Korea.

13

Singapore: A Policy Strategy for Land and Property Taxation

LAY CHENG JASMINE LIM AND NIGEL WOODS

Singapore is a democratic parliamentary republic with a single central tier of government. It is one of Asia's most affluent jurisdictions, with per capita GDP of SGD 89,547 (USD 65,641) as of 2019. The economy is driven mainly by the services sector (notably financial services and tourism) and also by electronics manufacturing, oil refining, and shipping. By virtue of its strategic location, Singapore boasts the world's second-largest shipping port, after Shanghai. The city-state is recognized worldwide as a key financial center and ranked fourth in the Global Financial Centers Index for 2018, thanks to the stability of its financial system and the robustness of its regulatory infrastructure. Many consider Singapore's economy one of the world's most stable; it has no foreign debt, high government revenues, and a consistent surplus. Unemployment remains one of the lowest in the developed world at just 2.2 percent, and inflation has been consistently low, 0.4 percent in 2018.

In the World Economic Forum's annual Global Competitiveness Index for 2019, Singapore ranks first out of 141 jurisdictions, ahead of the United States, Hong Kong, the Netherlands, Switzerland, and Japan (WEF 2019). In addition to being a clear indicator of the economic attractiveness of Singapore for international investors, this ranking also acknowledges Singapore's openness, future readiness, health care, and transport infrastructure—all of which further enhance its global reputation as an ideal business location. Singapore also ranks first in the Heritage Foundation's

Index of Economic Freedom report 2020 (Miller, Kim, and Roberts 2020) and second in the World Bank's "Doing Business, 2020." Its success across these indexes is attributable to its highly developed free market economy and its open and corruption-free business environment.

A dramatic increase in Singapore's population in the latter half of the 20th century led to concerns about the availability of land resources to sustain growth. The population increased by 87 percent between 1990 and 2019. Population density increased from 4,814 residents/km^2 in 1990 to 7,866 in 2019.[1] To deal with the challenges of population growth and high density, and to avoid the overcrowding and poor living standards of the 1960s, the government has taken a comprehensive and interventionist approach to management of the property market and development activities. The approach relies on state ownership and control of housing (Phang and Helble 2016).

In the 1990s, Singapore embarked on an ambitious land reclamation program that increased its size to 726 km^2 over three decades, an increase of 14.7 percent. The Urban Redevelopment Authority has plans for a further 100 km^2 by 2030. Commercial, leisure, or tourism enterprises use the majority of the reclaimed land, allowing other areas to be developed for housing. Climate change has become a critical issue because much of the island state lies less than 15 meters above sea level.

Singapore has one of the lowest birth and population growth rates in Southeast Asia (Department of Statistics 2019a). Postwar population control policies and social changes induced this low population growth rate (currently 1.2 percent). Two of the population control policies were the stop-at-two policy and the financial, health, and educational incentives offered for smaller families. More recently, limited population growth results from young adults remaining single for longer, deciding to have their families later in life, and being concerned about the cost of living. A reduction in immigrant jobs further limits population growth as the jurisdiction attempts to balance immigration and population growth to ensure it retains a stable working-age population.

The age structure of the resident population has consistently risen since 1990, and the median age is now 41.1 years (Department of Statistics 2019b). The proportion 65 years old or more was 14.4 percent in 2019, compared with 6 percent in 1990 (Department of Statistics 2019c), and is expected to increase to 25 percent by 2030. An aging population will put pressure on public and individual finances to support elders' physical and health care needs. Tax revenues of the government (e.g., individual income tax, property tax) will decline as the working-age population declines. Singapore has a reputation for having a well-educated workforce. The percentage of residents with a university degree increased from 26.7 percent in 2009 to

37.5 percent in 2019 (Department of Statistics 2019d). An educated population attracts foreign investment and multinational companies, helping maintain Singapore's national competitiveness.

Singapore is one of the most culturally diverse jurisdictions in the world and has four official languages: Malay, Chinese, Tamil, and English. Singaporean society is based on Confucian traditions, including respect for authority, government, and bureaucracy. These traditions enable the nation to prosper and remain harmonious (Tan 2007). The highly disciplined, hardworking, law-abiding society positively contributes to the functions and efficiency of government. Hence, citizens pay their taxes, evincing few instances of nonpayment or tax evasion and few property tax appeals.

The remainder of this chapter describes Singapore's government structure and land administration, the tax base and revenue performance, and the property market. It then details the property and land tax system, its three main property-related taxes, and property tax administration. It concludes with an assessment of the system's overall effectiveness and offers a few ideas for improving what is already a highly effective and efficient property tax system.

Government Structure and Land Administration

The government structure follows the British Westminster model of three separate branches: the legislature (parliament), the executive (cabinet), and the judiciary (courts). In this system the legislature makes the laws, the executive administers the law, and the judiciary interprets the law. As a republic, Singapore has a president as the head of state and a prime minister as the head of government. Since 1966 it has been governed mostly by the People's Action Party, which has provided strong direction and leadership since the jurisdiction's independence in 1965. Singapore is known for being a benevolent, efficient society with a strong, highly structured, and organized government to help it function given its population density and diverse ethnicity (Tan 2007).

The government has 16 ministries of which the Ministry of Finance and the Ministry of National Development have direct impact on land and property. Directly under the ministries are statutory boards or agencies that are responsible for the day-to-day management and operation of government functions. The Inland Revenue Authority of Singapore is one such statutory board under the Ministry of Finance. The revenue authority is directly responsible for assessing, levying, and collecting taxes, including property tax and stamp duty, and for enforcing tax regulations. It shares all the sales and lease transaction data it gathers for property tax and stamp duty with government departments, including the Department of Statistics, to compile a statistical yearbook, and the Urban Redevelopment Authority, to construct residential and commercial price and rental indexes.

The Ministry of National Development oversees land, development, and urban planning. Of particular interest are the roles of the Housing Development Board (public housing) and the Urban Redevelopment Authority (planning and development control). The Housing and Development Board is a statutory board, set up in 1960, responsible for housing policy with a specific focus on provision of affordable apartments for owner occupation.

The Urban Redevelopment Authority is a statutory board, established in 1974, and the national land use planning authority. It prepares long-term strategic plans and local-area plans for both development and conservation. The board implements government land sales for commercial, hotel, private residential, and industrial developments (Hui and Ho 2004). It assesses the development charge, a tax on planning permissions, and one of the three main property taxes, which is detailed later in this chapter. Table 13.1 outlines some of the key laws and organizational structures governing the real estate market.

Tax Base and Revenue Performance

The government collects tax revenue from a number of sources. The total collected in 2019 was SGD 74.274 billion, representing a slight increase of 0.7 percent over 2018's SGD 73.738 billion. Singapore has a history of being a low-tax jurisdiction. Its ratio of tax revenues to GDP was 13.3 percent in 2019, well below the Asian average of about 21 percent (OECD 2021). The main contributors to tax revenue receipts were corporate income tax totaling SGD 16.732 billion, personal income tax SGD 12.368 billion, and goods and service tax SGD 11.164 billion. The full breakdown of taxes and their revenue performance in fiscal year (FY) 2017 to FY 2019 is shown in table 13.2.

The major property-related taxes are the stamp duty (SGD 4.199 billion) and property (asset) tax (SGD 4.762 billion). The third major property-related tax, the development charge, is grouped with several other taxes and therefore impossible to further disaggregate. Property tax collection for 2019 was SGD 4.762 billion, up 2.4 percent from 2018. The property tax element equates to just under 1 percent of GDP, as shown in table 13.2. Stamp duty revenue dropped from SGD 4.905 billion in 2017 to SGD 4.199 billion in 2019, due to the lower transaction volume in the property market.

Table 13.1 Principal Laws and Statutory Boards Governing Real Estate

Real Estate Concern	Law or Board
Development control and planning	*Planning Act 1998* All development or subdivision of land requires approval under the act. The Urban Redevelopment Authority develops the strategic land use plans (through zoning and permissible uses of land). These are reviewed every five to ten years. All changes of use and development density must be approved by the Urban Redevelopment Authority.
Industrial sites	Jurong Town Corporation is a state-owned real estate company and statutory board under the Ministry of Trade and Industry. It is the lead agency that deals with all industrial sites.
Land ownership / administration	*State Lands Act 1886 (chapter 314)* This act regulates the use and control of state land. The Singapore Land Authority manages state properties and assets. It also maintains the national land information database and is responsible for managing state land through land sales, leases, acquisitions, and allocations. The Singapore Land Authority issues land titles. The act details the six types of ownership, which include strata titles, occupational leases, and licenses.
Land registration	*Land Titles (Amendment) Act 2001* Since the 1960s, all land must be registered. The amendment mandates that records be held and maintained by the Singapore Land Titles Registry.
Property tax / stamp duty / development charge	*Property Tax Act (chapter 254), revised 2005* The Property Tax Act governs the Property Tax/Stamp Duty/Development Tax in Singapore, and these are administered by IRAS.
Public housing provisions	The Housing Development Board oversees public housing.

Note: "Singapore Statutes Online" provides access to Singapore's legislation, https://sso.agc.gov.sg/.

Table 13.2 Fiscal Position for FY 2017–2019

	FY 2017		FY 2018		FY 2019	
	SGD (billion)	% of GDP	SGD (billion)	% of GDP	SGD (billion)	% of GDP
Total tax revenue	75.817	15.8	73.738	14.4	74.274	14.6
Corporate income tax	14.944	3.1	16.032	3.1	16.732	3.3
Personal income tax	10.724	2.2	11.706	2.3	12.368	2.4
Withholding tax	1.532	0.3	1.590	0.3	1.637	0.3
Statutory boards' contributions	4.866	1.0	1.490	0.3	1.798	0.4
Assets taxes	4.440	0.9	4.649	0.9	4.762	0.9
Customs and excise taxes	3.133	0.7	3.075	0.6	3.264	0.6
Goods and services tax	10.960	2.3	11.137	2.2	11.164	2.2
Motor vehicle taxes	2.153	0.4	2.623	0.5	2.419	0.5
Vehicle quota premiums	5.796	1.2	3.616	0.7	2.865	0.6
Betting taxes	2.688	0.6	2.664	0.5	2.620	0.5
Stamp duty	4.905	1.0	4.607	0.9	4.199	0.8
Other taxes[1]	6.019	1.3	6.629	1.3	6.683	1.3
Fees and charges (excluding vehicle quota premiums)	3.279	0.7	3.490	0.7	3.409	0.7
Other	0.378	0.1	0.430	0.1	0.354	0.1

Source: IRAS (2017–2019a).

[1] Other taxes include the foreign worker levy, water conservation tax, development charge, and annual tonnage *tax.*

The Property Market

Singapore has been traditionally viewed as a safe destination for property investors because it offers a stable currency, solid economic growth, and a transparent property market. Thus, in 2020 it ranked fourteenth in the JLL Global Real Estate Transparency Index (JLL 2020). When the real estate market size is compared with the GDP per capita, Singapore ranks second, after Hong Kong, demonstrating the strength and global status of its real estate market (MSCI 2020).

Singapore has two distinct residential property markets: public housing subsidized by the Housing and Development Board and private-sector housing. The housing board's original remit was to clear slum housing and resettle residents into low-cost, state-built housing. This helped overcome the housing shortage and encouraged a property-owning democracy by providing housing stock in the shift toward higher rates of owner occupation.

The majority of public housing is publicly managed and developed by the housing board under 99-year lease agreements. To qualify for a housing board apartment, a buyer must be a Singapore citizen or a permanent resident, be over 21 years of age, and have a family. Single people younger than 35 or noncitizens cannot purchase new housing board apartments but can purchase resale ones. Other requirements concern household status (single, family, or multigenerational), minimum occupation period (five to seven years), and income (monthly income ceiling of SGD 7,000–SGD 21,000 depending on apartment size or location). A buyer may own only one housing board apartment, may not purchase a second private residential home until after the minimum occupation period, and must have received no more than one Central Provident Fund housing grant.[2] Foreigners can own private apartments or condominiums but must seek government approval to own landed residential property such as detached houses and bungalows. There are no equivalent restrictions on foreigners wishing to acquire commercial property.

Figure 13.1 shows the breakdown of public and private housing stock between 2000 and 2020. Subsidized public housing units dominate the housing stock, above 80 percent in 2000–2015 but slightly dropping in 2020 to 78.7 percent. The popularity of the public housing apartments relate to the additional incentives that allow social security savings with the Central Provident Fund to be used for down payments on public housing and mortgage interest payments, making home ownership more affordable. The role played by the Housing and Development Board in delivering affordable housing is lauded around the world, and many jurisdictions explore its lessons. However, the approach is not without problems. Concerns exist about the funding model, in which the money diverted from pension savings could lead to pension shortfalls. Similarly, the aging population and its downsizing implications could adversely affect housing supply. Nonlanded housing ownership (e.g., condominiums[3] and private apartments,[4] the two most popular types of private housing in Singapore's nonlanded residential sector) has experienced a double-digit growth (16 percent in 2020 compared with just 6.5 percent in 2000). Whereas landed housing (e.g., detached, semidetached, and terrace) units have shown a stagnant growth of approximately 5 percent over the same period, reflecting the excessive price of private landed property, which is unaffordable to a high proportion of the local residents.

Singapore has a high owner-occupation rate: 88 percent (table 13.3). This is the sixth-highest rate in the world and substantially higher than other developed jurisdictions such as the United States (65.4 percent), United Kingdom (65.2 percent), Germany (50.4 percent), and Hong Kong (49.8 percent) (Trading Economics 2022). Ching and Tyabji (1991) categorize

Figure 13.1 Housing Stock, 2000–2020

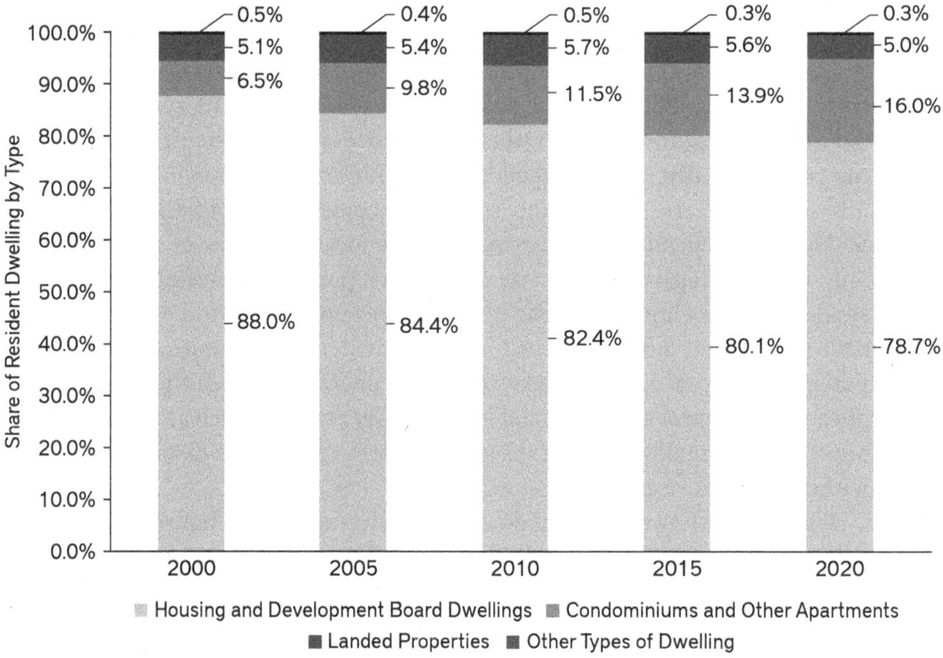

Source: Department of Statistics (2020a).

Table 13.3 Household Tenancy

	Total[1] (thousand)	Owner (thousand)	Tenant (thousand)	Home Ownership Rate (%)	Renter Rate (%)	Other[1] (%)
1990	661.7	578.9	78.6	87.5	11.9	9.5
2000	915.1	841.6	63.4	92.0	6.9	1.1
2010	1,145.9	998.9	132.5	87.2	11.6	1.2
2020	1,372.6	1,206.0	152.1	87.9	11.1	1.0

Source: Department of Statistics (2020b).
[1] Includes dwellings provided free by employers or others.

the Singapore housing policies into three areas: the supply side policy of affordable housing board apartments; the demand-side policy, which increases the buying power of owner-occupier purchasers; and tenure choice constrained through income ceilings, age requirements, and tenure-related policies.

Singapore is home to some of the world's most expensive luxury apartments, and the government is quick to intervene in the market if prices veer from market fundamentals. The government introduced two measures in July 2018 meant to cool the residential property market after house prices rose to a five-year high: raising the additional buyer's stamp duty[5] rates and tightening loan-to-value limits on residential property purchases. The additional buyer's stamp duty was raised by 5 percent for citizens and permanent residents buying second or subsequent homes and by 10 percent for commercial entities.

Before the change in loan-to-value limits, individual borrowers could borrow up to 80 percent of the value, or 60 percent if the loan term was more than 30 years or extended past the age of 65; the respective figures are now 75 percent and 55 percent. The two cooling measures increased demand for residential purchases immediately before the policies took effect in 2018 by buyers taking advantage of the higher limits and lower stamp duty rates.

The commercial market remained stable in 2019, despite some contraction in GDP growth and continued rises in interest rates, making Grade A office space affordable for corporations with notable increases in both co-working and technology sectors (CBRE 2019). Wong and Song (2019) predicts a healthy office rental market and a possible 10 percent average annual growth from 2018 to 2023 if Grade A office vacancy remains below the 10-year average of 6.3 percent. This potential rental growth could increase the commercial property tax roll, based as it is on annual rental values. Furthermore office rentals is also evidenced in the 2019 JLL (2019) Global Premium Office Rent Tracker, which ranks Singapore 14th in office rental expense, at an annual occupancy cost of USD 1259 per sq meter compared with the top three markets of Hong Kong (USD 3365), New York (USD 2282), Beijing (USD 1981), and London (USD 1955). Singapore's rental price is a little more than a third of that charged in Hong Kong. At the other end, JLL (2019), reports that Singapore's office rental is four times more expensive than its near neighbor Kuala Lumpur (USD 323 per square meter), demonstrating Singapore's attractiveness for investors seeking Southeast Asian opportunities. In contrast, the retail and industrial sectors demonstrate a relatively stable rental income, especially since about 2019, with these trends expected to continue in the short term.

Property and Land Tax System

Of Singapore's land and property taxes—property tax, stamp duty, and development charge—property tax and stamp duty are common to most developed jurisdictions but in Singapore have been adapted and shaped to foster development of a property-owning democracy. Development charge is not as common as a tax, but it also is closely linked to the obvious need to control the use of land given how scarce it is in this island state. This section briefly outlines the stamp duty and development charge before describing the property tax.

Stamp Duty

By the Stamp Duties Act, passed in 1929 and revised in 2006, stamp duty is payable for lease and tenancy agreements and transfer documents for all properties and is based on the declared amount. Given the openness of the market, cross-checks with the property tax system, and severe penalties for an incorrect declaration, there is virtually no evasion. The stamp duty is also payable for mortgage agreements and share transfers. There are three types of duty payable for property transfers at market value:

- Buyer's stamp duty rates are 1–3 percent for nonresidential and up to 4 percent for residential properties.

- Additional buyer's stamp duty is payable on purchases of second homes or residential investment properties; rates start at 12 percent and go to 30 percent.

- Seller's stamp duty is payable for transfers of property held for less than three years; rates start at 12 percent if property is held for less than one year and decrease in years two and three to 8 percent and 4 percent, respectively.

The second and third categories reflect the government's comprehensive and interventionist approach to management of the property market, particularly the residential sector. Over the years a constant aim of the government has been to create a property-owning democracy, hence the punitive stamp duty rates when residential accommodation is purchased to rent. As discussed later, the property tax rates for owners of rented residential accommodation are also much higher than those for owner-occupiers.

Another interesting and possibly unique feature of the stamp duty system is application of the additional buyer's stamp duty to site purchases by developers. Developers must pay the 30 percent additional buyer's stamp duty when they purchase land but can get it back if they sell the completed development within five years. This measure discourages land banking, a more serious issue in this small island state than in other jurisdictions.

Stamp duty is administered by the Property Tax Division in the Inland Revenue Authority of Singapore. The coordination has obvious benefits

Table 13.4 Stamp Duty Income, 2017–2019

		No. of Transactions	%	Amount (SGD)	%
2017	Sale and purchase agreement	81,056	19.2	4,525,483	85.6
	Lease agreement	227,956	54.0	599,136	11.3
	Mortgage agreement	79,721	18.9	39,170	0.7
	Share transfer	31,753	7.5	120,267	2.3
	Other	1,377	0.3	14	2.6×10^{-4}
	Total	**421,863**		**5,284,070**	
2018	Sale and purchase agreement	80,638	17.5	3,823,946	80.2
	Lease agreement	257,741	55.8	706,636	14.8
	Mortgage agreement	90,110	19.5	43,061	0.9
	Share transfer	32,045	6.9	193,078	4.1
	Other	1,136	0.2	11	0.0002
	Total	**461,670**		**4,766,732**	
2019	Sale and purchase agreement	76,139	16.2	3,628,835	77.7
	Lease agreement	283,306	60.3	833,640	17.9
	Mortgage agreement	76,123	16.2	36,958	0.8
	Share transfer	33,055	7.0	170,240	3.6
	Other	1,363	0.3	14	0.0003
	Total	**469,986**		**4,669,687**	

Source: IRAS Property Tax Statistics (2017–2019b).

in terms of connectivity and data sharing. Stamp duty is a significant source of revenue with annual yields similar to those of the property tax (table 13.4).

Table 13.5 shows the volatility of transfer tax revenue. The high income in 2018 reflected an active buyers' market and increased demand, thereby driving up private property price indexes. Property sales and leases contributed the lion's share of income, with sales on their own representing about 90 percent of the total collected. The additional buyer's stamp duty, representing only 25 percent of total residential sales, produced nearly as much income as the buyer's stamp duty, and the seller's stamp duty produced a fraction of either. Residential properties in 2019 brought in revenue from the buyer's stamp duty of SGD 1,147 million, additional buyer's stamp duty of SGD 1,171 million, and seller's stamp duty of SGD 23 million.

Table 13.5 Stamp Duty Income from Private Residential Properties, 2017–2019

		No. of Transactions	%	Amount (SGD)	%
2017	Buyer's stamp duty	33,774	72.6	1,518,469	48.1
	Additional buyer's stamp duty	12,138	26.0	1,574,245	49.9
	Seller's stamp duty	637	1.4	63,080	2.0
	Total	**46,550**		**3,155,795**	
2018	Buyer's stamp duty	29,833	74.5	1,744,217	53.2
	Additional buyer's stamp duty	9,440	23.6	1,450,278	44.2
	Seller's stamp duty	748	1.9	86,163	2.6
	Total	**40,021**		**3,280,658**	
2019	Buyer's stamp duty	20,947	77.0	1,147,472	49.0
	Additional buyer's stamp duty	5,690	20.9	1,171,815	50.0
	Seller's stamp duty	562	2.1	22,315	1.0
	Total	**27,199**		**2,341,602**	

Source: IRAS Statistics (2017–2019c).

Table 13.5 also demonstrates a significant reduction in the transaction amounts collected in 2017–2019. When the 2017 figures are compared with the 2019 figures, the number of transactions drop by 41.5 percent (influenced by the higher loan-to-value limits and increase in additional buyer's stamp duty), and tax revenue drops by 25.8 percent as a result of fewer property transactions.

Development Charge

The development charge is a tax on planning permission that increases land value. It is administered by the centralized planning authority, the Urban Redevelopment Authority. Normally the charge arises when land is rezoned to a higher-value use or when the plot ratio density has been increased. The owner pays the development charge when obtaining enhanced planning permission. The charge is calculated by the following formula:

Development charge = development ceiling – development baseline – development change exemption.

The development ceiling is provided by schedules of value for uses. The schedules are updated twice yearly on the basis of information supplied by the chief assessor of the Inland Revenue Authority of Singapore.

Development baseline is the value of the existing or previous planning permission. Development change exemption most commonly is the difference between the historical baseline of the site and the development baseline.

The example calculation on the Urban Redevelopment Authority website (https://www.ura.gov.sg/Corporate/Guidelines/Development-Control/Planning-Permission/Folder/DC-Charge-Rates/Example-Scenario-Calculating-DC) details a planning permission that increased the value of the land by SGD 1.85 million, from SGD 6.72 to SGD 8.57 million. The calculations result in a development charge of SGD 170,000, representing 9 percent of the development gain.

The yield from the development charge is included in "Other taxes" in table 13.2, which altogether totaled SGD 6.683 billion in 2019. No separate figures are available, but it is probably reasonable to assume that the revenue from the development charge is a significant amount given the scale of development activity and high property prices. Press comment on this tax indicates that the twice-yearly review of rates usually increases it, reflecting rising prices in the market, which is seen as an effective check on the market (*The Straits Times* 2021).

There is no capital gains tax in Singapore, reflecting the buoyancy of other tax revenues and making a direct incentive to investment.

Property Tax

The property tax was introduced in the early 19th century when Singapore was a British colony. It was based on the British rating system and was levied by local authorities. Since independence in 1965, the property tax has undergone significant change: it is now a purely fiscal levy, reflecting the single-tier governmental setup. Since 2010 it has been positioned as an asset tax. At the same time, the rates for residential properties were made highly progressive.

The Property Tax Act, revised in 2005, governs the property tax.

Basis of Assessment, Scope, and Liability

The basis of assessment is annual value, defined in part 1, section 2 (1), of the act, which

(a) in relation to a house or building or land or tenement, not being a wharf, pier, jetty or landing-stage, means the gross amount at which the same can reasonably be expected to be let from year to year, the landlord paying the expenses of repair, insurance, maintenance or upkeep and all taxes (other than goods and services tax); and

(b) in relation to a wharf, pier, jetty or landing-stage, means the gross amount at which the same can reasonably be expected to be let from year to year, the tenant paying the expenses of repair, insurance, maintenance or upkeep. (Property Tax Act 2005)

Further provisions in part 2, section 2 (3) and (9), allow the chief assessor to arrive at an annual value by estimating the value of the property and applying a decapitalization factor of 5 percent and by referring to gross receipts. The 5 percent of capital value method is used most often to value land and non-market-traded properties. The gross receipts method is used for profit-making trading properties that are rarely leased to tenants, such as hotels.

Section 2 (5) allows separately valuing excess land held with a house or building; apart from this the annual value is calculated on the basis of existing use.

The scope of the tax is set out in part 3, section 6 (1), of the act: "All houses, buildings, lands and tenements whatsoever included in the Valuation List." Agricultural land and buildings are included in the definition of "buildings" and "lands."

Section 6 (2) defines the owner as liable for the tax.

Tax Rates

There are no differential rates, and all commercial and industrial properties are taxed at a flat rate of 10 percent. This rate has remained unchanged since 2001, when it and a program of annual revaluations were introduced.

The tax rate for residential properties is highly progressive and differentiates between owner-occupied and non-owner-occupied properties. The progressive tax rates were introduced in 2010 at the same time as estate duty (death duties) was abolished. At that time the Minister of Finance stated,

> When we eliminated Estate Duties, I highlighted that we would retain property tax as a means of taxing wealth. Unlike Estate Duties, the burden of which was felt most significantly by the middle and upper-middle income groups rather than the rich, property taxes can be structured more equitably, with the rich paying the most. Property tax cannot be avoided through tax planning.

> A moderately progressive property tax system, together with an income tax system that collects more taxes from better-off individuals and a flat [goods and services tax] rate that everyone pays, will together form a fair system of taxes in Singapore. Everyone pays something, but the rich pay more. (Shanmugaratnam 2010)

The tax rate for owner-occupiers exempts the first SGD 8,000 of annual value and taxes the remainder in bands starting at 4 percent and peaking at 16 percent for over SGD 130,000. The rates for owners of rented residential properties start at 10 percent and peak at 20 percent for annual value over SGD 90,000 (table 13.6). In practice, this means that, at the bottom end of the market, an owner-occupier of the average Housing and Development Board property pays very little. We further comment on this later.

Tax Yield

The tax was redefined as an asset or wealth tax in 2010, and progressive rates for higher-value residential properties, both owner occupied and nonowner occupied, were introduced in 2019.

Table 13.6 Tax Rates for Non-Owner- and Owner-Occupied Residential Properties

Progressive Tax Rates for Non-Owner-Occupied Properties

Annual Value (SGD)	Rate (%) Effective Jan. 1, 2015
First 30,000	10
Next 15,000	12
Next 15,000	14
Next 15,000	16
Next 15,000	18
Annual value exceeding 90,000	20

Progressive Tax Rates for Owner-Occupied Properties

Annual Value (SGD)	Rate (%) Effective Jan. 1, 2015
First 8,000	0
Next 47,000	4
Next 15,000	6
Next 15,000	8
Next 15,000	10
Next 15,000	12
Next 15,000	14
Annual value exceeding 130,000	16

Source: IRAS (https://www.iras.gov.sg/taxes/property-tax/property-owners/property-tax-rates).

In 2019 there were 1,404,994 residential properties and 137,528 commercial properties, for a total tax base of 1,542,522 properties, a 42 percent increase over 2010.

Figure 13.2 charts the total increase in numbers over the nine-year period, from 1,210,008 to 1,542,522, an increase of 22 percent. At the same time, revenue grew from SGD 2,572 million to SGD 4,413 million, an increase of 42 percent, reflecting an increase in numbers and property price inflation. The dips in income in 2012 and 2016 owing to falling property prices show the vulnerability of the income stream from an asset tax with fixed tax rates. This could be a serious issue if the tax was funding local government, but in Singapore it is a fiscal levy, and government revenues have a constant surplus.

Table 13.7 shows the low yield from the public housing sector and the exceptional growth in private residence numbers. The Housing and Development Board sector is 65 percent of the total but yielded only 2.7 percent of the tax in 2019, an average bill of SGD 121 per property. Further, although no official figures are available, at least 20 percent of

Figure 13.2 Number of Properties and Property Tax Revenue Collected, 2010–2019

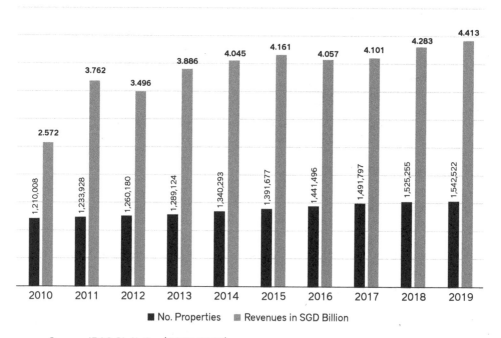

Source: IRAS Statistics (2010–2019).

Table 13.7 Breakdown of Property Tax, 2010 and 2019

Year	Property Type	No. of Dwellings	Income (SGD thousand)	Median Annual Value (SGD)	Revenue % of Total
2010	Housing and Development Board	836,041	112,520	8,100	4.44
	Private residential	259,342	536,166	24,000	21.16
	Commercial	76,825	896,014	42,000	35.37
	Industrial	35,591	838,790	36,900	33.11
	Other	2,209	150,000	150,000	5.92
	Total	**1,210,008**	**2,533,490**		
2019	Housing and Development Board	1,002,671	121,330	9,600	2.70
	Private residential	402,323	818,724	24,000	18.60
	Commercial	81,555	1,715,165	62,800	38.90
	Industrial	54,590	1,338,633	36,000	30.30
	Other	1,383	419,589	229,000	9.50
	Total	**1,542,522**	**4,413,441**		

Source: IRAS Tax Statistics (2010, 2019).

housing board properties are estimated to be below the SGD 8,000 annual value threshold and therefore pay no tax. At the top end, in contrast, the owner-occupier of a property with an annual value of SGD 150,000 paid SGD 12,580, an effective tax rate of 8.4 percent. If the same property was a rental or a second home, the bill would be SGD 20,000, an effective tax rate of 13.4 percent. Assuming this property is worth SGD 3 million, in capital value terms, these rates are the equivalent of 0.4 and 0.66, respectively, of 1 percent. This ties in with an average rate of 0.43 of 1 percent for all private-sector residential properties, calculated from published statistics of total income and average value for 2019. This outcome is clearly in line with the intention to create a "fair system of taxes," as the minister of Finance stated in 2010, for the rich to pay more (a higher effective rate) and by implication those on low and moderate incomes to pay significantly less. It also supports the government's key aim of a property-owning democracy by minimizing the costs of ownership for households with low incomes.

Exempt Properties

Exemptions from property tax are listed in part 3, section 6 (6), of the act:

- Places used for public religious worship.

- Public schools that receive grants-in-aid from the government.

- Buildings used for charitable purposes.

- Buildings used for purposes conductive to Singapore's social development.

This list is in common with most property taxes based on the British rating system. Also, the zero tax for the first SGD 8,000 of annual value for owner-occupied residential properties effectively exempts a significant proportion of poorer owners, which is wholly consistent with an asset or wealth tax.

Property Tax Administration

The Ministry of Finance sets property tax rates. The Property Tax Division of the Inland Revenue Authority of Singapore administers this tax and the stamp duty. The Property Tax Division is overseen by two statutory officers: the comptroller, who is in charge of both taxes, and the chief assessor, who is responsible for the assessment of annual values for the property tax. The chief assessor is statutorily independent, in that the comptroller may not alter or amend any values fixed by the chief assessor. The Property Tax Division has four functional valuation sections: residential, commercial, industrial, and valuation and stamp duty.

Figure 13.3 shows the organizational structure of the revenue authority; the Property Tax Division falls under the control of the International, Investigation, and Indirect Tax Group. A licensed valuer practicing in Singapore must have a relevant degree, at least two years' practical experience, and be a member of the Singapore Institute of Surveyors and Valuers. Licenses are issued by the revenue authority in accordance with the amended Appraisers Act 1906.

The remainder of this section describes Singapore's administrative processes related to property tax: assessment and valuation, objections and appeals, and collection and billing. These processes are highly efficient compared with most other Asian jurisdictions.

Assessment and Valuation

The chief assessor has the discretion to revalue all properties each year or to adopt the existing valuation list. In practice, revaluations take place every year.

Figure 13.3 Inland Revenue Authority of Singapore Organizational Structure

Source: IRAS (2019).

The Property Tax Division has a clearly stated strategy of using technology and data to reduce revaluation time and to improve the robustness of the valuation process. This includes digitizing end-to-end work processes and connecting digitally with other public bodies that supply data and with taxpayers.

Part 3, section 19, of the act obligates property owners to notify the chief assessor of all sales and leases within one month. Further provisions apply to notification of increase of rents on review and payment of premiums. The Property Tax Division also makes direct use of information from its involvement in stamp duties. The division has set up a computer application for taxpayers such as shopping mall owners that allows them to submit rental information and retrieve updated annual value and taxes due information, saving everyone time and effort and speeding up the valuation process.

The Property Tax Division has a digital connection to the Urban Redevelopment Authority and Building Construction Authority, which minimizes interference with property occupiers and improves the timeliness of the valuation process: 99.9 percent of new properties are valued within 12 months.

Most valuations use the comparative method. Given the nature of the urban landscape with its vast swaths of high-rise apartment blocks, the division uses automated valuation methods. In line with the division's stated strategy, technology creates dynamic valuation models for the main property types: residential, office, retail, and industrial. These models' statistical tools and business rules identify outliers and suggest property values. Interactive dashboards present pattern analysis results and trend recognition, and geospatial capabilities enhance the process.

Box 13.1 describes expenses of the Property Tax Division.

Objections and Appeals

Owners can make an objection to the chief assessor within 30 days of being notified of a new value, under part 3, section 20A, of the act. Any objection must be in writing and state precisely the grounds for the amendment sought.

There are no published statistics on objections and appeals, but informed opinion is that the number of objections for all properties is around 10,000 per annum, or 0.07 percent of the total. This is low compared with other jurisdictions; however, as noted several times already, the zero-to-small financial impact of the tax on most of the housing board sector has to be taken into account. We understand that most of objections are made against commercial assessments. If there are, say, 6,000 objections each year against the commercial assessments, this equals 4.4 percent of the total—this is within the expected range for annually reviewed as-

---

Box 13.1 THE COST OF PROPERTY TAX ADMINISTRATION

The annual report for 2018 (IRAS 2018) of the Inland Revenue Authority of Singapore identifies the functional cost of the Property Tax Division as 7 percent of total costs. If the costs of the various corporate support groups are apportioned to the functional tax divisions, the total cost of the division is SGD 47.64 million (11.3 percent of the total of SGD 421.9 million). With total revenue from the property tax and stamp duty of SGD 9.2 billion, this gives a cost of 0.52 of 1 cent per SGD collected. There is no breakdown of costs between the two taxes, but it is safe to assume that property tax accounts for a much larger share than stamp duty. If property tax accounts for, say, 80 percent of total costs, the cost is SGD 25 (about USD 18.50) per property. This looks about right when compared with other jurisdictions. For example, British Columbia Assessment Annual Plan Service Report (2018) maintains an annually revalued tax roll of 2.2 million largely heterogeneous properties in a vast geographic area; in 2018, this cost British Columbia USD 31.38 per property.

No breakdown of staffing figures is published for the Property Tax Division, but we believe there are approximately 80 valuation staff.

sessments. Although the revenue authority's annual report contains some statistics on timeliness of assessment for review and new properties, there are no data on how many objections are processed within an appropriate timescale, such as six months given the annual revaluation cycle. In most jurisdictions, this is normally a key performance indicator. Completion of, for example, 90 percent of objections within the first six or seven months of the year is bound to be an objective for the Property Tax Division, to allow valuer resources to concentrate on producing the annual revision of all assessments of annual value for the start of the next year.

Owners who are dissatisfied after the chief assessor issues a decision on an objection can appeal within 30 days to the Valuation Review Board under part 3, section 20A (7), of the act. The board sits as an independent expert panel with a chairperson and at least two others. Cases are decided by a majority vote, and if the vote is tied, the chair's vote decides the matter. Again, although there are no statistics published on the number of appeals to the board each year, an informed opinion was that 300 or so go to this stage. How many proceed to actual hearing is not published.

Following a decision by the Valuation Review Board, the appellant can make further appeal to the High Court of Singapore, which will rehear the case under part 4, section 35 (1) and (2), of the act. An interesting provision is that the chief assessor or the comptroller may appeal to the High Court on a point of law, per section 35 (3) of the act; in many jurisdictions this applies to both sides, the specialist tribunal being the final arbiter on matters of fact and value. The appeal process can be lengthy: a case (*HSBC Institutional Trust Services (Singapore) LTD v. Chief Assessor* [2019]SGHC 95) decided by the High Court in April 2019 for a cinema complex started with an objection lodged in 2008.

Collection and Billing

The property tax is billed yearly in advance and must be paid within one month, thereafter interest charges are applied. The tax is a first charge on the property, and as a last resort the property can be seized and sold to recover the tax debt.

The billing and collection processes employed by the Property Tax Division are in line with overall revenue authority policies to be customer-centric and make good use of digital services. Videos explain the basis of the taxpayer's bill; the videos use data integration and analytics to provide personalized property tax information tailored to each residential property owner. The revenue authority has begun combining the tax bill with the valuation notification. Digital property tax bills were piloted in 2017 with text messages (SMS notification) and, after a positive response from taxpayers, the program was ramped up to nearly 1 million and 1.02 million bills in 2018 and 2019. Electronic payment methods are also heavily promoted and employed.

In 2018, the rate of taxes paid on time was 94.9 percent; in 2019, it was 95.1 percent. Furthermore, the revenue authority reports a 98 percent satisfaction rate with its service, and nine out of ten individuals completed their tax returns on time, which is unheard of in the tax collection sphere. Part of this is surely due to good administrative practices, strict enforcement, and overall public awareness, but part of it may be due to the tax-paying culture mentioned earlier.

These outcomes clearly demonstrate the effectiveness of the Inland Revenue Authority of Singapore technology and customer strategies outlined earlier. Another factor, as noted earlier, is that for most residential taxpayers the bills are very small.

Conclusion

Singapore's economic success has led to a very healthy fiscal position and a regular government surplus of income and substantial reserves. The provision of affordable owner-occupied residential accommodation for nearly everyone with low to moderate incomes has led to the highest incidence of home ownership of any developed jurisdiction (91 percent as of 2018).

These factors and the absence of local government have led to the property tax's current form: an asset or wealth tax that hardly affects most properties occupied by people of low or middle income. The scale of other revenue streams also means that the tax rates for those owners who do pay can be set at modest levels in international terms. Bahl, Martinez-Vazquez, and Youngman (2010, 3) state, "Property Tax . . . revenues average 3 percent of GDP in [Organization for Economic Cooperation and Development] countries." The tax yield in Singapore at 1 percent of GDP is clearly well below this average.

Youngman (2016, 10) notes that "asset taxes face special disadvantages, especially the need for a cash payment without any necessary realization of income at the time the tax is due." By removing most owners with low or middle incomes from the tax net, Singapore has nullified that disadvantage.[6]

The efficiency of the tax's administration and collection by the Inland Revenue Authority of Singapore also contributes to its acceptability. The assessment processes appear to be highly efficient and under constant improvement. The nature of the built environment, no doubt, is a big help, given the large percentage of relatively homogeneous high-rise apartment blocks. In a different urban and economic environment, maintaining property values for all the housing board's stock and reviewing it annually might be difficult to justify for such a small return.

The accuracy of assessments may also be high, but because none of the normal performance indicators for an assessment system are published, it is not possible to verify. Most advanced assessment jurisdictions publish detailed figures on objections and appeals by sector; the results of the appeal process; and how many values were reduced, increased, and so on.

Potential Reforms

Could the tax be improved? One possible policy change would be to shift the tax base from annual value to capital value. On the face of it, for an asset tax, capital value seems more appropriate to use. On the residential side, the very best houses and apartments would end up with a larger share of the tax burden; and with 90 percent or more owner-occupation, more people are aware of sale than of rental prices. On the commercial side, it would also be fairer, because poorer properties have a much lower multiplier of rent to capital value than prime shops and offices. Owner-occupiers of secondary commercial property would benefit with a decreased share of the tax burden, and large-scale investors in prime commercial property would have an increased share—which could all be politically attractive. That said, there is no evidence on the ground of any lobbying for such a change. Both the relatively modest level of the tax, 10 percent of rental value, and the little or no tax for most residential taxpayers mean there is little public concern—all much different from those developed jurisdictions where the tax is three to four times higher relative to GDP.

On the operational front, the Property Tax Division of the revenue authority apparently administers the tax efficiently and effectively, but opportunities to improve the transparency of the assessment process and to exploit for public benefit the value inherent in the database may exist.

For example, the revenue authority's annual report contains no detail on tax operations, including the property tax assessment process. Headlines on press releases from the revenue authority claim, for example, "99.9% of New Properties Valued within 12 Months." In nearly all developed jurisdictions, particularly where all properties are revalued annually, published performance data cover key areas such as the timeliness of the objection process and the accuracy of the revaluation process. The 2018 annual report for British Columbia Assessment Annual Plan mentioned earlier and the Hong Kong Rating and Valuation Department are examples of good practice here.

The databases the Property Tax Division maintains on market transactions and the physical details of every property are a valuable resource. The division passes information to the Department of Statistics for compilation of the statistical yearbook and to the Urban Redevelopment Authority for the construction of the residential and commercial price and rental indexes. However, in many assessment jurisdictions today, advances in information technology have led to much more innovation in the use of and access to databases—from full and free access by the public to all the property records to the sale of products such as indicative valuations for properties backed by details of comparable transactions. Food for thought?

Notes

1. Singapore ranks third by population density, behind Monaco and Macau; however, it has the highest overall density for jurisdictions with a population of over 1 million.

2. Singapore's Central Provident Fund is a compulsory comprehensive savings and pension plan.

3. A condominium is defined in Singapore as a strata-titled (unit in a multistory building) development on a minimum land area of 0.4 hectare that provides residents with shared facilities. They are predominately owned by more affluent residents.

4. Apartments are multihousing units built on a smaller land parcel with no or very limited shared amenities.

5. Additional buyer's stamp duty is payable on the acquisition of residential properties and is based on the higher of either the consideration or market value. The rate applicable depends on the profile of the buyer at the date of purchase, whether the buyer is an individual or an entity, the buyer's residency status, and the number of residential properties owned. See https://data.gov.sg/dataset/duty-rates-for-stamp-duty.

6. It is not surprising, then, that searching for comments or stories in the press on the property tax found nothing of significance. Any articles typically were on the fairness of the property tax as a wealth tax, the lowering of rates for Housing and Development Board properties, and the move to efficient electronic billing.

References

Bahl., R., J. Martinez-Vazquez, and J. Youngman. 2010. "Whither the Property Tax: New Perspectives on a Fiscal Mainstay." In *Challenging the Conventional Wisdom on the Property Tax*, ed. R. Bahl, J. Martinez-Vazquez, and J. Youngman. Cambridge, MA: Lincoln Institute of Land Policy.

British Columbia Assessment Annual Service Plan Report. 2018. info.bcassessment.ca/about/Publications/2018 Annual Report.pdf.

CBRE. 2019. *Singapore Real Estate Market Outlook, 2019.* http://cbre.vo.llnwd.net/grgservices/secure/Singapore%20Real%20Estate%20Market%20Outlook%20 2019_AWoz.pdf?e=1648846662&h=283720eaea0868ea6238768c48a489ae.

Ching, L. K., and A. Tyabji. 1991. "Homeownership Policy in Singapore: An Assessment." *Housing Studies* 6 (1): 15–28.

Department of Statistics. 2019a. *Year Book of Statistics, Government of Singapore.* Singapore. https://www.singstat.gov.sg/-/media/files/publications/population/population2020.pdf.

————. 2019b. "Indicators on Population." Annual. Singstat Table Builder. https://tablebuilder.singstat.gov.sg/table/TS/M810001.

————. 2019c. "Key Indicators on the Elderly." Annual. Singstat Table Builder. https://tablebuilder.singstat.gov.sg/table/TS/M810611.

————. 2019d. "Resident Labour Force Aged 15 Years and Over by Highest Qualification Attained and Sex" (June). Annual. Singstat Table Builder. https://tablebuilder.singstat.gov.sg/table/TS/M182271.

————. 2020a. "Resident Households by Type of Dwellings." Annual. Singstat Table Builder. https://tablebuilder.singstat.gov.sg/table/TS/M810351.

————. 2020b. "Resident Households By Tenancy." Annual. Singstat Table Builder. https://tablebuilder.singstat.gov.sg/table/TS/M810401.

HSBC Institutional Trust Services (Singapore) Ltd v. Chief Assessor (2019) SGHC95. 2019. https://www.elitigation.sg/gdviewer/SUPCT/gd/2019_SGHC_95.

Hui, E. C.-M., and V. S.-M. Ho. 2004. "Land Value Capture Mechanisms in Hong Kong and Singapore: A Comparative Analysis." *Journal of Property Investment and Finance* 22 (1): 76–100.

IRAS Property Tax Statistics. 2010–2019. "Tax Statistics." *Annual Value and Property Tax by Property Type, Annual.* https://data.gov.sg/dataset/annual-value-and-property-tax-by-property-type-annual?view_id=2e9c7499-f9a5-4d9f-8b2d-de952f4cdb99&resource_id=ea3ae22f-a84f-4951-b86b-2ef6ccc3f541.

————. 2017–2019a. "Tax Statistics." *Total Government Operating Revenue and IRAS Collection, Annual.* https://data.gov.sg/dataset/total-government-operating-revenue-and-iras-collection-annual?view_id=b74a4432-b236-4568-8735-4c3eb6bf968e&resource_id=c6a3b31f-0067-4e7d-b7fa-6a5078a808fd.

————. 2017–2019b. "Tax Statistics." *Annual Value and Property Tax by Property Type, Annual.* https://data.gov.sg/dataset/annual-value-and-property-tax-by-property-type-annual?view_id=2e9c7499-f9a5-4d9f-8b2d-de952f4cdb99&resource_id=ea3ae22f-a84f-4951-b86b-2ef6ccc3f541.

————. 2017–2019c. "Tax Statistics." *Stamp Duty Assessed for Private Residential Properties, Annual.* https://data.gov.sg/dataset/stamp-duty-assessed-for-private-residential-properties-annual?view_id=e5715676-6ac6-4570-bc73-f34d1980f1c4&resource_id=d9f4f45c-80ea-49e3-b5d5-ce21cf464ded.

————. 2018. *Annual Report 2018-19.* https://www.iras.gov.sg/media/docs/default-source/uploadedfiles/pdf/iras-annual-report-fy201819-(1).pdf?sfvrsn=5215ecf4_5.

————. 2019. Annual Report 2019–2020. https://www.iras.gov.sg/media/docs/default-source/uploadedfiles/pdf/iras-annual-report-fy201920_oct.pdf?sfvrsn=c69e59f5_8.

JLL (Jones Lang LaSalle). 2019. "Global Premium Office Rent Tracker." https://www.jll.co.uk/content/dam/jll-com/documents/pdf/research/jll-global-premium-office-rent-tracker-q4-2019.pdf.

————. 2020. "Transparency, Digitization, Decarbonization." https://www.jll.co.uk/content/dam/jll-com/documents/pdf/research/jll-and-lasalle-global-real-estate-transparency-index-2020.pdf.

Miller, T., A. B. Kim, and J. M. Roberts. 2020. *2020 Index of Economic Freedom.* Washington, DC: Heritage Foundation. https://www.heritage.org/index/pdf/2020/book/Index_2020.pdf.

MSCI. 2020. *Real Estate Market Size, 2019/20.* https://www.msci.com/documents /1296102/19878845/MSCI_Real_Estate_Market_Size_2020.pdf/06a13e2c-0230 -f253-26fa-3318cecb1c59.

OECD (Organization for Economic Cooperation and Development). 2021. *Revenue Statistics in Asia and the Pacific: Emerging Challenges for the Asia Pacific Region in the Covid-19 Era.* Paris: OECD. https://www.oecd-ilibrary.org/sites/ed374457-en/index .html?itemId=/content/publication/ed374457-en.

Phang, S.-Y., and M. Helble. 2016. "Housing Policies in Singapore." ADBI Working Paper 559. Tokyo: Asian Development Bank Institute. (March). www.adb.org /publications/housing-policies-singapore/.

Shanmugaratnam, Tharman. 2010. "Towards an Advanced Economy: Superior Skills, Quality Jobs, Higher Incomes." Budget speech delivered in Parliament on February 22. https://www.mof.gov.sg/docs/default-source/default-document-library/singapore -budget/budget-archives/2010/fy2010_budget_statement.pdf?sfvrsn=252ea182_2.

Tan, C. H. 2007. "Confucianism and Nation Building in Singapore." *International Journal of Social Economics* 16 (8): 5–16.

The Straits Times. 2021. "Development Charge Rate Up to 10.9% for Non-Landed Residential Use, 0.7% Cut for Commercial Use." https://www.straitstimes.com /business/property/development-charge-rates-up-109-for-non-landed-residential -use-07-cut-for.

Trading Economics. 2022. "Home Ownership Rate." Accessed January 17, 2022. https://tradingeconomics.com/country-list/home-ownership-rate.

WEF (World Economic Forum). 2019. *The Global Competitiveness Report, 2019.* Insight report. Geneva: World Economic Forum. https://www3.weforum.org/docs/WEF _TheGlobalCompetitivenessReport2019.pdf.

Wong, S., and T. Song. 2019. "Steady Rental Growth: Office Q1 2019." Colliers International. (April 21). https://www.colliers.com/en-sg/research/2019-q1-singapore -office-quarterly-report-colliers.

Youngman, J. 2016. *A Good Tax: Legal and Policy Issues for the Property Tax in the United States.* Cambridge, MA: Lincoln Institute of Land Policy.

14

Taiwan: Implementation of a Split-Rate Property Tax

TZU-CHIN LIN AND WEN-CHIEH WU

Taiwan's split-rate property tax system can be traced back to the period when the Republic of China (ROC) was based in Nanjing. The land value tax was introduced by the ROC government in 1936. However, the ROC government did not tax buildings until 1943 when a building surcharge was collected. The building surcharge was later implemented in Taiwan after Japanese colonization ended. In 1949 the ROC government relocated from China to Taiwan. The building surcharge policy was replaced in Taiwan in 1968 by the building tax. The land value tax was not introduced in Taiwan until 1956. Imposition of the land value tax started in specified urban areas and was fully implemented in all of Taiwan beginning only in 1977, when Taiwan implemented a split-rate property tax system that included the land value tax and building tax.

A split-rate tax on real properties is levied at a higher rate on land than on buildings in Taiwan. This is intended to reduce the penalty on investments in improvements and to encourage more intensive land use. Besides, land is always assessed at each point in time in its highest and best possible use; therefore, taxes on land have no direct effect on either the form or timing of development of unused land parcels (Oates and Schwab 1997). Taiwan is often highlighted in the literature as one of a small number of jurisdictions that levy separate taxes on land and improvements.[1]

Taxation of land in Taiwan originated long ago in Articles 142 and 143 of the Constitution of the Republic of China. The constitution stated that the state shall pursue the equalization of land ownership and restriction of private capital to achieve a well-balanced national wealth. Private land is liable to taxation according to its value. To address the increment of land value that is not contributed by invested labor or capital, an increment tax shall be levied, and its revenue shall be shared by all.

The main goals of land use policy in Taiwan are to use land in its full capacity and to share the returns from land use. This requires assessing land, taxing land, purchasing land when needed, and returning the increment of land value to the public. These four measures were written into the Act of Equalization of Land Rights in Urban Areas, implemented in 1956. This short history led Lam and Tsui (1998) to conclude that the original purpose of introducing land-related taxation in Taiwan was not to finance local public services but to serve as a mechanism for speculative land value capture.

This chapter starts with an overview of Taiwan's property tax system and its components, which is followed by discussions of revenue performance, valuation, and administration. It then analyzes the shortcomings of Taiwan's system and concludes with a consideration of the prospects for reform.

Property Tax System

Unlike most jurisdictions, where *property tax* refers to a tax levied on the value of both land and buildings, Taiwan levies separate taxes on land and buildings. Both the land value tax and the building tax are imposed as local government taxes. A land value increment tax, a tax on capital gains from the sale of land, is also levied by local governments. In addition, the integrated real estate transaction tax, levied by the central government, is the latest addition under the umbrella of property tax. The taxes imposed on the annual value of property are called the property holding taxes. In other words, both land value tax and building tax are taxes paid for holding properties. Finally, deed taxes and stamp duties are also included in the real property tax regime.

The two tiers of government in Taiwan are central and local. Local governments consist of a total of 22 special municipalities, cities, and counties. These local governments are parallel administrative units as far as taxing power is concerned. Land value tax, building tax, land value increment tax, deed tax, and stamp duty are levied by local governments, and the integrated real estate transaction tax is levied by the central government. The five types of property taxes levied by local governments are subject to the same national government rate structure. Local governments fully retain the collection of these taxes. Although the valuation rules are also set by central government, properties are valued by local governments.

Land Value Tax

The annual land value tax is based on the assessed capital value of the property. The tax rate is determined using threshold value, which is the value for a hypothetical 700 m² parcel of land. The value of this hypothetical land per square meter is reached by summing the value of all land parcels within the local government boundaries and then dividing by the total area of those parcels, excluding land for industrial use, mining use, agricultural use, and tax-free land. In other words, it is an average value per square meter of land in the local government area, and it can vary from one local government to the next.

The values of all land parcels owned by the same owner in a local government are summed to arrive at the taxable value. The progressive tax system applied to this tax base has six brackets, as shown in table 14.1. If the summed value is lower than the starting threshold, the rate from the first bracket, 1 percent, applies. If the value is between the starting threshold and five times the starting threshold, the second bracket, 1.5 percent, applies. The third bracket is applicable to the portion of the summed value lying between five times and ten times the starting threshold. Its marginal tax rate is 2.5 percent. The threshold of each additional bracket increases by five times the starting threshold, and the marginal tax rate of each additional bracket increases by 1 percent. The threshold of the last bracket is 20 times the starting threshold, and its marginal tax rate is 5.5 percent. The goal of this tax rate structure is clearly to impose a higher effective tax rate on those who own more valuable property.

For owner-occupied residential land, the preferential flat tax rate is 0.2 percent of its assessed land value, but the amount of land cannot exceed 300 m² in urban areas and 700 m² outside urban areas. Owner-

Table 14.1 Land Value Tax Rates 2019

Tax Bracket	Tax Rate (%)	Threshold
1	1	Value < ST
2	1.5	ST < value < (5 × ST)
3	2.5	5 × ST < value < (10 × ST)
4	3.5	10 × ST < value < (15 × ST)
5	4.5	15 × ST < value < (20 × ST)
6	5.5	Value > (20 × ST)

Source: eTax portal (n.d.).

Note: ST = starting threshold value, the average value of 700 m² of land.

occupied residential land refers to land on which the owner or owner's spouse, parents, grandparents, children, or grandchildren reside. The preferential rate applies to the land parcel of only the main residence. The 0.2 percent preferential tax rate is also applicable to public housing or housing provided by private or state-run enterprises for their employees (Articles 9 and 17 of Land Tax Act).

Another preferential flat rate of 1 percent is applicable to land used or zoned for industry, mining, private parks, zoos, sports stadiums, temples, churches, places of scenic or historical interest, gas stations, and public parking. In addition, public land that is used for nonpublic purposes is levied at the preferential flat rate of 1 percent. Tax is exempted for public land used for public purposes (Articles 18 and 20 of Land Tax Act).

Building Tax

The building tax is levied annually by local governments, but the rate is set by the central government. As shown in table 14.2, the building tax for owner-occupied structures is 1.2 percent. Up to three buildings under the same owner can be claimed as owner-occupied structures and enjoy the

Table 14.2 Building Tax Rates, Since 2014

Type	Central Rate (%)	Taipei Rate (%)
Owner-occupied residential buildings	1.2	1.2
Residential buildings rented to public welfare use	1.2	1.2
Publicly owned buildings for residential use	1.5 (1–2 buildings) 3.6 (3 or more buildings)	1.5
Residential buildings rented as social buildings	1.5–3.6	1.5
Residential buildings for labor and student dorms	1.5–3.6	1.5
Non-owner-occupied residential buildings	1.5–3.6	2.4 (1–2 structures); 3.6 (3 or more structures)
Nonresidential buildings for business and hospital	3.0–5.0	3.0
Nonresidential buildings for nonbusiness uses	1.5–2.5	2.0

Source: Taipei City Revenue Service (2021).

lowest rate of 1.2 percent. Four or more buildings with the same owner are classified as non-owner-occupied structures on which a higher tax rate is applicable. The building tax rate for non-owner-occupied structures is between 1.5 percent and 3.6 percent. In Taipei City, a tax rate of 2.4 percent is applied to the first two non-owner-occupied structures and 3.6 percent to three or more.

According to Article 3 of the Building Tax Act, the value of a building attached to land, and additional use value from structure added to (or extended from) the building, must be taxed. In major cities, illegal additions to legal buildings are common. Once these are reported to the building management authority and determined to be illegal, they are added to the building tax file by the local tax authority. The tax rate of the illegally extended structure is the same as that for the legal building and varies by use, whether residential, business, or mixed use. Illegally extended structures and legal buildings are assessed by the same valuation.

Land Value Increment Tax and Integrated Real Estate Transaction Tax

The land value increment tax is levied when land is sold. It is a tax on the capital gain from the sale of land and was initially instituted to take away the unearned income.

To recoup the unearned income, a progressive tax rate structure was designed. The increment in land value between two transactions is broken into three brackets. The lowest bracket is for the value increment that is less than the last sales price. The second bracket is for the value increment that is more than the last sales price but less than two times that figure. The highest tax bracket is for the value increment that is two times or more of the last sales price. The sales price of land for calculating the value increment is determined by assessors, who are civil servants. The marginal tax rates progress from 20 percent to 40 percent as the value increment moves from the low to the high brackets (see table 14.3). Both the

Table 14.3 Land Value Increment Tax Rates

Tax Bracket	Holding <20 Years (%)	Holding 20–30 Years (%)	Holding 30–40 Years (%)	Holding >40 Years (%)
Low	20	20	20	20
Middle	30	28	27	26
High	40	36	34	32

Source: eTax portal (n.d.).

tax rate and base are uniform across Taiwan, but the tax is assessed and collected by local governments.

To discourage short-term, speculative holding of land and also to lessen the tax burden of a long-term holding (the value increment is likely to be substantial), a tax deduction applies if the land sold has had the same owner-ship for more than 20 years. The longer the duration of ownership before sale, the higher the tax deduction.

Before 2016, when a property (land with building) was sold, the land value increment tax was paid for the land portion of the sale, and a sepa-rate tax (income tax for building transaction) was paid for the building portion—that is, two different taxes were paid on the transaction. Under that tax structure, income from selling a building was considered a source of income in the year that the property was sold. A specific percentage set by individual local governments (for example, 48 percent for high-value buildings and 42 percent for others in Taipei) was multiplied by the as-sessed value of the building to estimate the taxable income from selling a building. This amount would be added to other sources of income in that year to arrive at the annual total income of an individual who was subject to national income tax. Therefore, two individuals who earned the same amount of income from selling buildings could pay different tax amounts.

The integrated real estate income tax was introduced in 2016. The new tax was proposed primarily in response to the criticism that the capital gain from selling a property was largely avoided under the existing tax struc-ture. The new integrated tax took the form of a capital gains tax. The cap-ital gains from sales of land and buildings would no longer be separated and would be subject to the same tax rate. The tax rates are progressive and decline the longer the seller holds the property (table 14.4). The thrust of this tax is to penalize the short-term holding of properties. Sellers who are not regular residents in Taiwan are subject to a tax rate of 45 percent

Table 14.4 Integrated Real Estate Income Tax Rates

Tax Bracket	Tax Rate (%)	Length of Ownership (applied between Jan. 1, 2016, and June 30, 2021)	Length of Ownership (applied from July 1, 2021)
1	45	<1 year	<2 years
2	35	1–2 years	2–5 years
3	20	2–10 years	5–10 years
4	15	>10 years	>10 years

Source: eTax portal (n.d.).

if they held the property for less than two years, and the rate is 35 percent if held more than two years. In addition, TWD 4 million (approximately USD 134,000) is exempted from the tax base if the seller was an owner-occupier for at least six years, and the tax rate is 10 percent. Despite "integrated" being part of the name of this tax, the income from selling a property is taxed separately from other sources of income.

Before 2016, some argued for repeal of both land value increment tax and income tax for building transaction, replacing them with the integrated real estate income tax. In the end, the pre-2016 income tax for building transaction was abolished, but the land value increment tax remains. The single most important reason for land value increment tax to be kept is that it was specified in the constitution, and revising the constitution is extremely difficult. As a result, when a property is sold, to avoid overtaxation on land, the taxable value of land value increment tax is deducted from the taxable value of integrated real estate income tax. That is to say, the seller of a property needs to pay both land value increment tax and integrated real estate income tax. The former tax is paid to the local government and the latter to the central government. To further curb short-term transactions, in 2021 some amendments were made to the integrated real estate income tax, primarily to its rate structure (see table 14.4).

In addition to the 10 percent owner-occupier preferential rate, the majority of taxpayers in Taiwan pay the 20 percent tax rate for land value increment tax, a failure of this tax to tax the well-off.

Deed Tax and Stamp Duty

The seller pays both land value increment tax and integrated real estate income tax after a property sale. The buyer pays both deed tax and stamp duty. Deed tax applies only to the building and not to the land it sits on. The deed tax for building sales is 6 percent, and the tax base is usually the same as that for the building tax. The rate of stamp duty is 0.1 percent, and the tax base is the sum of the tax bases of land value increment tax and building tax.

Revenue Performance

To understand the contribution of tax revenue of individual property taxes, we describe here the growth in Taiwan's property tax revenues and the composition of these revenues.

Taxes on Land Value, Buildings, and Land Value Increment

Table 14.5 shows that the broadly defined property tax revenue (the combination of land value tax, building tax, and land value increment tax) in

Table 14.5 Components of Property Tax Revenues

Year	Property Taxes as % of GDP	Holding Taxes as % of GDP	Property Taxes as % of Total Tax Revenue	Holding Taxes as % of Total Tax Revenue
2002	1.35	0.90	11.79	7.88
2003	1.45	0.90	12.75	7.88
2004	1.57	0.87	13.20	7.34
2005	1.54	0.86	11.88	6.67
2006	1.45	0.84	11.47	6.69
2007	1.39	0.84	10.81	6.51
2008	1.30	0.87	9.73	6.50
2009	1.30	0.89	11.02	7.54
2010	1.37	0.85	11.99	7.47
2011	1.40	0.86	11.41	6.96
2012	1.40	0.84	11.44	6.92
2013	1.55	0.87	12.92	7.29
2014	1.47	0.84	12.03	6.89
2015	1.51	0.83	11.89	6.58
2016	1.45	0.97	11.25	7.50
2017	1.47	0.95	11.79	7.61
2018	1.42	0.93	10.94	7.14
2019	1.44	0.91	11.09	6.99
2020	1.43	0.87	11.84	7.13

Sources: Ministry of Finance, ROC (2002–2007); Ministry of Finance, ROC (2008–2020); National Statistics (2002–2020).

Taiwan from 2002 to 2020 was approximately 1.3–1.6 percent of GDP, and the more narrowly defined annual property tax, or holding tax, revenue (land value tax and building tax) was around 0.9 percent of GDP.

The ratio of property tax revenue to GDP was below 1.4 percent for most of the first decade of the 2000s, and the ratio averaged 1.45 percent during 2010–2020. This means that the percentage increase in property tax revenues has been greater than the percentage increase in GDP over time. All told, property and land tax revenues in Taiwan have accounted for more than 10 percent of total tax revenues in recent years. On the basis of these data (which include both automatic and discretionary changes in revenues), the property tax has been buoyant.

The data in table 14.5 also show that property tax revenues in Taiwan heavily rely on collections in the largest urban areas. Table 14.6 shows that

Table 14.6 Property Holding Tax Revenues for Major Metropolitan Cities, 2020

	Land Value Tax		Building Tax	
	TWD Thousand	%	TWD Thousand	%
New Taipei	15,179,366	16.54	13,032,422	16.43
Taipei	27,842,756	30.35	15,089,684	19.02
Taoyuan	8,562,132	9.33	8,707,223	10.98
Taichung	6,479,285	7.06	9,376,715	11.82
Tainan	5,871,784	6.39	5,755,782	7.25
Kaohsiung	12,542,080	13.67	10,304,366	12.99
Metropolitan total	**76,477,403**	**83.35**	**62,266,192**	**78.50**
Jurisdiction total	**91,752,605**	–	**79,315,449**	–

Source: Ministry of Finance, ROC (2020).

the six largest metropolitan areas account for 83.35 percent of collections from the landholding tax and 78.50 percent from the building holding tax. Taipei and New Taipei City alone contribute close to half of the total national collections from the landholding tax.

Revenues from land value tax and building tax are a major source of financing for Taipei City (table 14.7). If land value increment tax is included, the fiscal importance of property taxation rises to over 80 percent. Other local taxes include deed tax, stamp duty, license tax, and amusement tax. Deed tax revenue is only 2.49 percent of local tax revenue. Stamp duty is 6.96 percent, but that includes non-property-transaction activities.

Table 14.7 Property Taxes Relative to Total Local Government Tax Revenue in Taipei City, 2020

Taxes	Amount (TWD thousand)	% of Local Government Tax Revenue
Land value tax	27,842,756	36.75
Building tax	15,089,684	19.91
Land value increment tax	18,070,687	23.85
Deed tax	1,893,517	2.49
License tax	7,433,330	9.81
Stamp duty	5,272,401	6.96
Amusement tax	149,095	0.19
Total local tax revenue	**75,751,470**	**100**

Source: Ministry of Finance, ROC (2020).

As shown in table 14.8, revenues of both land value tax and building tax grew from 2007 to 2020, whereas revenues from land value increment tax have gradually played a less important role. Two institutional changes may have led to this changing composition of tax contribution. First, the tax rates of land value increment tax were reduced in 2005 to 20, 30, and 40 percent from 40, 50, and 60 percent. Second, the tax base of land value tax has been on the rise nationwide since about 2005. The base of the building tax in several major cities has also significantly grown since the mid-2010s. The significant rise in both taxes was largely a response to soaring housing prices. The low taxes on owning property contributed to this housing price inflation.

Property Tax Administration

The property tax system in Taiwan is focused on the capture of the land value base and recoupment of a part of its increments. This section considers how the administration of the property tax accommodates these goals.

All parcels of land are required by law to be registered in the land registry office of the parcel's local government. This secures transaction safety and protects property rights. Buildings are not required by law to be registered; in practice, however, except for a fairly small number of very old buildings, almost all buildings are registered. The following covers the valuation of these parcels for property taxation and the collection of property tax.

Valuation

The traditions of property tax valuation in Taiwan are rich because of the split-rate system and the focus on land. The following discussions concentrate on the evolution of the valuation approach in Taiwan and on the separate valuation of land and buildings.

Table 14.8 Major Property Taxes in Taipei City
(as % of property tax revenue)

	2007	2012	2020
Land value tax	40.06	42.24	45.64
Building tax	20.76	24.23	24.73
Land value increment tax	39.17	33.51	29.62

Sources: Ministry of Finance, ROC (2007); Ministry of Finance, ROC (2012, 2020).

Evolution of the Current System

Before 1964, landowners self-assessed the value of their land and reported that figure to the government. After 1964, the government assumed responsibility for land assessment and made its assessments available to the public. The landowners then reported the value of their land to the government by referring to the government's values. Reassessment of land values was on a three-year cycle between 1977 and 2017. The reassessment cycle was shortened to two years after 2018. The reassessment could, however, be postponed if the government deemed it appropriate.

After the government-assessed value was introduced, if the owners' reported value was deemed too low, the government had the authority to order the landowners to revalue. The government could also purchase the land at the price the owners reported. The right to purchase land at this price was intended to incentivize owners to report land value honestly.

After 1986, the owners' reported value is required by law to be within 20 percent of the government-assessed land value. If the owners' reported value is 20 percent over it, 120 percent of the assessed value will be the tax base. If the reported value is 20 percent less than the assessed value, the government may purchase the land at the reported value or use 80 percent of the assessed value as the tax base. For owners who do not report their land value, 80 percent of the government-assessed value is automatically used as the tax value.

For the land value increment tax, a 1964 amendment requires local governments to value all parcels of land twice a year and make the valuation results available to the public. The interval of reassessing land was extended to once a year in 1968. The parties involved in a land sale were required by law to submit the sales price of the land in the transaction. If the submitted price is higher than the value appraised by the government, the submitted price will be adopted as the price to calculate the price difference between this and the previous sale as the tax base. If the submitted price is lower than the appraised value, the government may use the appraised value as the price to calculate the price difference or purchase the land at the price the parties submitted.

Because there are two different taxes on land, the government released to the public two sets of land values. Since 1964, the two sets of values were required by law to coincide every three years when the land was reassessed for land value tax. Between 1977 and 1986, the government exercised its discretion not to undertake reassessment for land value tax. When the government reassessed land in 1987, the assessed land value had to be raised dramatically to make up for the increase in land values over 10 years. This upward trend of land value, however, had been reflected year by year in the government-appraised land value for land value increment tax. It was the first time in history that the government revoked tax bills, and it offered 40 percent and 20 percent tax rebates for 1987 and 1988, respectively.

After this rather embarrassing experience and before the next reassessment, the law was amended in the early 1990s. Since then, the two government-assessed land values no longer need to periodically coincide with each other. It was a watershed in the history of land tax valuation in Taiwan. To make the rules even clearer, the central government issued guidance notes in 1999 and 2006 stating that the assessed land value (for land value tax) shall take into consideration the appraised land value (for land value increment tax) of that year, the previous assessed land value, local financial needs, socioeconomic conditions and tax burden of the taxpayers, and other factors.

Valuing Land

The land administration department in each local government is responsible for valuing land. Properties in the same area with similar attributes, land use, amenities, buildings, and proximities to transportation and other facilities are grouped together and assigned to the same land value section. In 2018, for example, Taipei had a total of 4,447 land value sections.

Assessors from the local land administration department are required to frequently collect price and related information from real estate agents, financial institutions, and other property professionals. Government assessors are civil servants who have passed an examination in which real estate valuation is one of the subjects. Local governments contract with private appraisers for auction of public land and other tasks. However, valuation of land for taxation purposes is done by government assessors. Assessed land value for individual properties is derived by subtracting the current value of the building from the sales price of an improved property. The building value is determined by taking into consideration the reproduction costs, the value effects of building depreciation, interior decoration, equipment expenditures during building construction, and expected profits of capital investment. The building value for land value tax differs from the building value serving as the tax value of building tax. Valuation of land, as described earlier, is an application of the extraction method (Appraisal Institute 2008, 366) or the widely documented land residual approach.

The median of estimated land values per square meter for sampled property sales in a land value section is designated as the representative sectional land value. The sectional land value indicates the general price level for improved sites within a section. For properties facing major roads, benefits of easy access are also taken into account. For example, a price premium is given to the part of a land parcel that is within 18 meters of a roadside in Taipei. The portion of land with better road access is therefore valued higher than land farther away from the road. This valuation practice is adopted nationwide.

Valuation results and supporting evidence are required by law to be presented to an expert committee. The committee is composed of seventeen members: seven officials from departments within the local government and ten appraisal-related professionals appointed by the local government. The appointment is for three years. This committee changes valuation results when its members deem it necessary. The valuation results cannot be announced to the public until committee members approve them. There is no explicit written criteria for the committee members when they are examining the valuation results. However, it is widely understood that a targeted ratio of assessed value to market value for land in a city as a whole is normally set when periodic assessment is undertaken.

In addition, regression-based housing price seasonal indexes have been published since 2015 (Real Estate Information Platform n.d.). There is one index for Taiwan and individual indexes for six major Taiwan cities (New Taipei, Taipei, Taoyuan, Taichung, Tainan, and Kaohsiung). Formerly, in the publication of this price index, a hedonic multiple regression methodology was applied. The price of a hypothetical standard housing unit was estimated over time to construct the price index. The methodology was changed to one that follows repeat sales occurring since the fourth quarter of 2018 (Real Estate Information Platform n.d.). Despite the demonstrated capability of applying the advanced automated valuation models, those models have not been used in valuation for taxation on land or buildings. Geographic information system (GIS) technology is widely employed in valuation—for example, in the display of valuation results presented to the members of valuation committees.

Valuing Buildings

The modern version of legislation on building tax appeared in 1967 with the Building Tax Act. The taxable value for the building tax is the capital (market) value of a building, and there is no longer a distinction between owner-occupied and rental buildings. Building value is derived from the cost approach, which is extensively documented in the valuation literature. The determination of building value takes account of (1) construction materials, building height, and building purpose (for example, a concrete 15-story residential building); (2) building depreciation; and (3) locational adjustment rate related to business activity, traffic, and the market for buildings near the taxed building (Article 11 of the Building Tax Act). Those value-contributing factors detailed in the act are reviewed every three years and updated if deemed necessary by the local-government expert committee.

Similar to the valuation of land, the valuations for buildings are submitted to an expert committee for approval. This committee is composed of governmental representatives and professionals in related domains from outside the local government. At least two-fifths of the committee members must be external professionals.

Despite the recommended three-year periodic review that is allowed, local governments tend not to raise the assessed building values. For example, the assessed building values in Taipei remained unchanged between 1981 and 2014 for buildings of 35 stories or fewer, and remained unchanged between 2005 and 2014 for buildings of 36 stories and higher. An enhanced assessed value took effect in 2014 (applying only to buildings completed after July 2014), and the building tax for concrete buildings in Taipei was estimated to rise by 1.2 to 2.9 times, varying with building height and other factors (Taipei City Revenue Service 2021). The tendency to not bring assessed building values in line with rising construction costs is commonplace nationwide.

Tax Collection and Payment

Tax bills are sent through the post office. Taxpayers can pay taxes at banks or convenience stores. They can have a bank or credit card company automatically pay land value and building taxes at a specified time. They can pay at an ATM or use Taiwan Pay (a tax payment method of the Ministry of Finance similar to Apple Pay). To save administration costs and be eco-friendly, documents related to tax bills such as payment requests and certificates can be also sent by email.

If taxpayers do not pay taxes due by the deadline, they owe a penalty of 1 percent of tax amount for every two days overdue. After 30 days, bank accounts are subject to seizure. The collection rate for property-related taxes in Taiwan is high. Taking New Taipei City (the second-largest city) as an example, the ratio of taxes collected to taxes owed was 96.11 percent for the land value tax, building tax, and land value increment tax in 2011 (Statistics Book of Revenue Service Office 2012).

Analysis of Problems

Taxes on land and buildings have given local governments in Taiwan significant and reliable tax revenues. To follow the spirit of the split-rate tax design, specific valuation approaches were developed and have been evolving. The Taiwan government has been consistent in trying to establish a sound tax system on land and buildings that embraces the teachings of Henry

George (1879). Despite the effort, the Taiwan property tax regime has drawbacks and some room for reform, as highlighted in the following.

Property Tax Revenue Is Too Low

Taiwan's total property tax revenues are about 1.5 percent of GDP. Recurrent property tax revenue is slightly less than 1 percent of GDP. By comparison with developing jurisdictions, this is well above the international average of 0.6 percent of GDP (e.g., Bahl and Martinez-Vazquez 2008). But compared with other Asian Tigers and many Organization for Economic Cooperation and Development jurisdictions, it is not high (OECD, n.d.). Property tax revenue accounts for 3–4 percent of GDP in both Canada and the United States, and 2–3 percent in Korea and Hong Kong. These comparisons suggest that a higher level of property taxes would not be out of line with other jurisdictions of similar incomes. *The Proposal for Tax Reform in Taiwan* (Academia Sinica 2014), among many others, highlights the low tax burdens of both holding and selling properties. Moreover, some local governments that rely heavily on this source of revenue face considerable expenditures.

Low Effective Tax Rate

Tsai (2001) compares the auction prices of a sample of selected foreclosure sites with their land value tax to roughly estimate the difference between the taxed value and the market value for certain types of property. The taxed-to-market-value ratio ranges between 8.9 percent and 37.6 percent, and averages 17.4 percent. This calculation suggests the effective rate of land value tax for these sample sites may be as low as 0.18 percent. This figure may be even lower given that an auction price is generally less than the market price. Peng, Wu, and Wu (2007) estimate the effective property tax rate in two areas of Taipei. The effective tax rate is estimated by dividing the sum of the land value tax payment and building tax payment by the sales price of a property. Effective rates range from 0.09 percent to 0.13 percent.

Failure of Self-Reported Assessments

Self-reporting of land value was expected to deter owners from under- or overassessing their land. Niou and Tan (1994), however, point out that, even with perfect information, landowners report land value to be less than the market price. If the government is not aware of the market value, the probability that landowners report truthfully remains close to zero.

In the earlier stages of property tax administration, the percentage of owners who self-reported assessed value was fairly high, around 98 percent in the late 1960s and early 1970s. This fell in the 1980s to less than 1.5 percent and has remained at that level. Owners who self-reported assessed value in 2018 were less than 0.03 percent. Self-reporting has not succeeded.

Unclear Effects of the Progressive Tax Rate on Land

A progressive tax rate structure was created for the land value tax to discourage concentration of landholding by a small group of owners. However, only about 8 percent of land parcels in Taiwan in 2011–2013 were subject to the higher rates, and less than 1 percent of land parcels paid the highest rate of 5.5 percent (Ministry of Finance 2014). Owners paying the 5.5 percent rate are likely private developers who are holding parcels for future development. Two investigations (Chen and Wang 2013; Wang and Zeng 2013) found that the burden of the land value tax declines with land values in two major Taiwan cities, Taipei and Kaohsiung. Because of the complicated tax structure, Huang (1999) called for a uniform tax rate for the land value tax. Academia Sinica (2014) even argued for the merger of land value tax and building tax into a unified property tax.

Poor Coordination Between Governmental Agencies

The land administration department assesses the land portion of a property value, whereas the revenue service department assesses building costs and depreciation and pays little attention to land values. Additionally, two different expert committees oversee valuation of land and buildings. Only a small number of experts sit on both committees, and no official communication between the committees is required. However, their decisions collectively decide the two tax bases, and consequently, the payment of property tax (the sum of land value tax and building tax).

A valuation dispute is required by law to be heard by the expert committee before it is sent to the administrative courts. Chen (2008) finds that the courts tend to defer to the decisions made by the committees. The courts largely examine the disputes from a legal perspective and pay very little attention to the valuation accuracy issues.

Because the expert committees meet only a few times a year, the experts are often left to make decisions without sufficient time and information. To make the situation even worse, governments can use expert committees as a cost-effective mechanism to stop disputes from entering the administrative courts.

The Prospects for Reform

The split-rate tax system in Taiwan was originally intended to be not only the major source of local government finance but also a measure to affect land use. Has this unique split-rate property tax lived up to its promise? A definitive conclusion is not possible, but given the evidence, it can be argued that it has much room for improvement.

One of the ongoing debates in Taiwan is about whether the government should continue with the split-rate tax or change to a conventional uniform rate for both land and buildings. To the best of our knowledge, no credible empirical studies that compare the performance of a split-rate with a uniform-rate system in Taiwan are available. One of the difficulties in undertaking this kind of comparative study is that all jurisdictions in Taiwan are required to adopt the same split-rate system. Laws are made by the central government and followed by all cities and counties.

Moreover, the valuation methods and formulas to apply are specified, leaving very little discretion to assessors. A major project, commissioned by the Ministry of the Interior, aims to build reliable statistical models that are capable of valuing property as a whole and the separate values of land and buildings that a split-rate system features. A joint working group was set up between the Ministries of the Interior and of Finance to discuss the possible merger of land value tax and building tax.

Two phenomena might define future developments. One is the increasing number of court cases that challenge the valuation results. Since the early 2010s, largely in response to increasing housing prices, governments have been under great pressure to raise assessed values on both land and buildings. It was widely agreed that a higher tax burden would deter property speculation, thus suppressing the price rise. However, the rise in tax burden has confronted local governments with legal disputes in valuation. The majority of court cases were brought by owners of high-end hotels, office towers, and luxury apartments. Challenges against valuation results were rarely seen in the past. In consequence, taxation's valuation methodology has been under scrutiny, including splitting values between land and buildings. A reasonable expectation is that an overhaul of valuation methods in property taxation will soon be required. Results of these legal challenges will to a significant extent determine whether the tax and valuation system will continue in its current form or be replaced by a new one, such as a uniform rate and assessment system.

Another recent change that will have far-reaching effects on future taxes is the requirement to report the sales price or rent when a property is sold or rented. This obligatory registration of price and rent took effect in August 2012. The attorney, real estate agent, or buyer is obliged to report title transfer within 30 days. For a leasehold, the real estate agent is required to report within 30 days after signing the contract. Failure to report a genuine price within the specified time will be fined TWD 30,000–150,000 (around USD 1,000–5,000). Partly because of the improved market transparency, Taiwan was already ranked 23rd out of 109 jurisdictions on the JLL global real estate transparency index, outperformed in Asia only by Singapore, Hong Kong, and Japan (Jones Lang LaSalle 2016). A transparent property market will certainly facilitate a better valuation. If the difficulties of splitting land and building values can be largely resolved, the present split-rate system is expected to remain. Otherwise, a new tax system might be called for.

Taiwan's tax system on land and buildings follows the teachings of Henry George. Over the last half century, Taiwan has distinguished itself from other jurisdictions in taxation through a number of novel designs. In practice, many of those innovations do not seem to meet their original promise. Strict legal scrutiny and improved market information will to a large extent define the direction in which this unique property tax system will move.

Note

1. See, for example, Brown (1997), Dye and England (2010), and Prest (1981), among others. Doebele (1997, 57) even wrote that "except in the Republic of China (Taiwan), the ideas of [Henty] George have not been supported by any major political party or by national policy in any of the so-called 'developing countries.'"

References

Academia Sinica. 2014. *The Proposal for Tax Reform in Taiwan*. [In Chinese.] Taipei, Taiwan: Academia Sinica.

Appraisal Institute. 2008. *The Appraisal of Real Estate*. Chicago: Appraisal Institute.

Bahl, R., and J. Martinez-Vazquez. 2008. "The Property Tax in Developing Countries: Current Practice and Prospects." In *Making the Property Tax Work*, ed. R. Bahl, J. Martinez-Vazquez, and J. Youngman, 35–57. Cambridge, MA: Lincoln Institute of Land Policy.

Brown, H. J., ed. 1997. *Land Use and Taxation*. Cambridge, MA: Lincoln Institute of Land Policy.

Chen, M.-C. 2008. "Compensation for Private Land Expropriated for Public Facilities." [In Chinese.] *Yue-Dan Financial-Economic Law Journal* 14:115–150.

Chen, T.-H., and H.-W. Wang. 2013. "A Study on the Equity of Property Tax in Taipei." [In Chinese.] *Journal of Taiwan Land Research* 16 (2): 89–139.

Doebele, W. A. 1997. "Land Use and Taxation Issues in Developing Countries." In *Land Use and Taxation*, ed. H. J. Brown, 57–69. Cambridge, MA: Lincoln Institute of Land Policy.

Dye, R., and R. England. 2010. *Assessing the Theory and Practice of Land Value Taxation.* Policy focus report. Cambridge, MA: Lincoln Institute of Land Policy.

eTax portal. n.d. Taxation Administration, Ministry of Finance, ROC. *Law Source Retrieving System of Taxation Laws and Regulations.* https://law.dot.gov.tw/law-en /index.jsp.

George, H. 1879. *Progress and Poverty.* Reprint, New York: Robert Schalkenbach Foundation, 1992.

Huang, Y.-H. 1999. "Reform of Taxes on Land and Buildings." [In Chinese.] Taipei, Taiwan: Chung-Hua Institute for Economic Research.

Jones Lang LaSalle. 2016. "Taking Real Estate Transparency to the Next Level." Global Real Estate Transparency Index. https://www.jll.co.uk/en/trends-and -insights/research/global-real-estate-transparency-index-2016.

Lam, A., and S. Tsui. 1998. "Policies and Mechanisms on Land Value Capture: Taiwan Case Study." Working paper. Cambridge, MA: Lincoln Institute of Land Policy.

Ministry of Finance. 2014. "Report of Analysis of the Structure of Land Value Tax as of Year 2012." Republic of China, Taiwan. [In Chinese.]

Ministry of Finance, ROC. 2002–2007. *Yearbook of Tax Statistics.* [In Chinese.] https:// www.mof.gov.tw/singlehtml/285?cntId=57475.

Ministry of Finance, ROC. 2008–2020. *Yearbook of Financial Statistics.* Ministry of Finance, ROC. https://www.mof.gov.tw/Eng/singlehtml/260?cntId=290009d7327a 40b9a6/572a21d6ffc52.

National Statistics. 2002–2020. Directorate General of Budget, Accounting and Statistics of Executive Yuan, Taipei City, ROC. https://eng.stat.gov.tw/mp.asp?mp=5.

Niou, E., and G. Tan. 1994. "An Analysis of Dr. Sun Yat-sen's Self-Assessment for Land Taxation." *Public Choice* 78 (1): 103–114.

Oates, W. E., and R. M. Schwab. 1997. "The Impact of Urban Land Taxation: The Pittsburgh Experience." *National Tax Journal* 50 (1): 1–21.

OECD (Organization for Economic Cooperation and Development). n.d. "Tax on Property (indicator)." Accessed August 6, 2021. https://doi.org/10.1787/213673fa-en.

Peng, C.-W., S.-T. Wu, and S.-H. Wu. 2007. "The Influences of Effective Property Tax Rates on Housing Values: Evidence from Ta-tung and Nei-hu Districts in Taipei City." [In Chinese.] *Journal of Taiwan Land Research* 10 (2): 49–66.

Prest, A. R. 1981. *The Taxation of Urban Land.* Manchester, UK: Manchester University Press.

Real Estate Information Platform. n.d. [In Chinese.] https://pip.moi.gov.tw/Upload /CustomFile/Doc/(%E5%B9%B3%E5%8F%B0)110Q3%E4%BD%8F%E5%AE %85%E5%83%B9%E6%A0%BC%E6%8C%87%E6%95%B8%E7%99%BC %E5%B8%83%E5%85%A7%E5%AE%B9.pdf

Statistics Book of Revenue Service Office. 2012. https://www-ws.gov.taipei/001/Upload /public/attachment/31161542681.pdf [In Chinese.]

Taipei City Revenue Service. 2021. https://tpctax.gov.taipei/News_Content.aspx?n =428605627B9B4FCE&sms=34DDC2994B075569&s=C2214FBE71F15C1A [In Chinese.]

Tsai, C.-Y. 2001. "Land Taxes in Taiwan: Problems, Impact and Reforms." [In Chinese.] *Journal of Taiwan Land Research* 3:37–83.

Wang, H.-W., and Y.-M. Zeng. 2013. "A Comparison of Effective Property Tax Rates and Their Implications for Fiscal Effort in the Cities of Taipei and Kaohsiung." [In Chinese.] *Taiwan Journal of Political Science* 56:119–156.

15

Thailand: A Reform of the Property Tax

DUANGMANEE LAOVAKUL

In the center of the Indochinese Peninsula in Southeast Asia, Thailand borders Myanmar and Laos to the north, Laos and Cambodia to the east, the southern leg of Myanmar and the Andaman Sea to the west, and Malaysia and the Gulf of Thailand to the south. The total area of Thailand is 513,140 km² with a population of about 66 million. The population density is 128.95 people/km². Bangkok is the capital and largest city in Thailand. The urban population is 34.47 percent of the total population.

GDP per capita in 2018 was USD 7,328 (THB 236,815). Economic growth slowed from 4.2 percent in 2018 to 2.3 percent in 2019. The economic impact of the COVID-19 pandemic has been severe, resulting in a spike in the unemployment rate, affecting middle-class households and the poor alike. In 2020, GDP growth contracted by 6.1 percent. The key drivers of contraction were declines in external demand on trade and tourism, supply chain disruptions, and weak domestic consumption.

This chapter traces the development of property and land taxation in Thailand up to the early days of the implementation of a new property tax law in 2020. The first sections describe the local-governance structure and the revenue regime for local governments. A description and analysis of long-standing property taxation practices in Thailand follows. The final sections outline the new property tax system that is still in its infancy, analyzes its potential strengths and weaknesses, and discusses the successes and failures of the transition. A brief section on other property-related taxes precedes final concluding comments.

Government Administrative Structure and Fiscal Relations

Thailand is a unitary state with very limited local-government autonomy. The 1997 constitution was the first to refer to decentralization, recommending that Thailand develop a plan and process to decentralize power to local governments. The 2007 constitution reaffirmed these goals and commitments, and the 2017 constitution, enacted after the 2014 coup, confirms the independent authority of local governments and their role in providing local public goods and services, education services, and regulating local finances. This suggests that political and fiscal decentralization are viewed as an important part of advancing Thai society. History, however, shows that decentralization in Thailand has not been smooth.

The National Decentralization Committee[1] formulates decentralization policy, sets the guidelines for the devolution of functions and personnel to local governments, designs revenue assignment and intergovernmental transfer formulas, and monitors and evaluates the devolution process and its impacts on local people. The chairperson of the committee is the prime minister or, if assigned by the prime minister, the vice prime minister, because a major responsibility of the committee is to reassign functions and revenues from the central government to local governments, which requires executive decisions and actions.

Thailand's local administrative structure is organized as a dual system, with local administration and local, autonomous self-government. Local administration consists of 76 provinces, further divided into districts and subdistricts. The minister of the Interior appoints the governor and other head officials for each province, and governors in turn answer to the Ministry of the Interior. Other line agencies appoint their own officials, who report back to their respective ministries, though they do work with the governors and other local administrators.

The structure of local, autonomous self-government is a two-tier system, with each tier independent from the other. The local administrators and their councils are directly elected. However, they are under the control and supervision of the provincial governors, district officers, and ultimately, the minister of the Interior, who retains the authority to approve their annual budget plans and local regulations, dissolve local councils, and dismiss local councilors. There are 7,850 local governments (table 15.1). At the upper layer of local administration are provincial administrative organizations, which coordinate and assist other local governments within their provinces in delivering public services. The lower level of local

Table 15.1 Local Governments

Type	No.
Provincial administrative organizations	76
Municipalities	2,472
Urbanized (*nakorn*) municipalities (30)	
City municipalities (187)	
Tambon municipalities (2,237)	
TAOs	5,300
Special local governments (Bangkok Metropolitan Administration and Pattaya City)	2
Total	**7,850**

Source: DLA (2020).

administrative bodies are municipalities and subdistrict administrative organizations, or *tambon* administrative organizations (TAOs). There are 5,300 TAOs in more rural and remote areas of the provinces. In addition, there are two special local units: the Bangkok Metropolitan Administration and Pattaya City. Because Bangkok's population is several orders of magnitude larger than the other local governments in Thailand, its government operates differently from other local governments. Merging some municipalities and TAOs to reduce administrative costs and to improve efficiency of local goods and services provision has been discussed.

Under the Budget Procedures Act of 1959, local governments (except Bangkok Metropolitan Administration and Pattaya City) receive their budgets not from the national budget but through the Department of Local Administration, part of the Ministry of the Interior. After passage of the New Budget Procedures Act in November 2018, local administrators submit their proposed budget to the minister of the Interior, who then passes the proposed budget with comments and recommendations to the director of the Budget Bureau, under the office of the prime minister. All local governments receive their approved budgets from the bureau without the budgets passing through the Department of Local Administration.

The structure of local-government revenues during 2011–2020 is shown in table 15.2. The share of locally levied tax revenue is quite low (about 9–10 percent). The combined share of centrally levied revenue, which is directly reallocated to local governments, and shared taxes is around 50 percent. Intergovernmental grants make up about 40 percent of local-government revenue. The proportion of local-government revenue to

Table 15.2 Local-Government (LG) Revenue Structure (%), 2011–2020

Type of Revenue	Budget Year									
	2011	**2012**	**2013**	**2014**	**2015**	**2016**	**2017**	**2018**	**2019**	**2020**
Locally levied revenue	9.87	9.09	9.03	9.80	9.59	9.95	10.29	9.99	9.93	5.58
Central government revenue allocated to LGs	33.14	30.39	30.78	30.40	29.79	30.25	32.51	33.83	31.97	31.13
Shared tax	16.69	15.82	18.89	17.94	16.69	17.53	17.62	17.64	17.02	16.71
Grants	40.30	44.70	41.30	41.86	43.93	42.26	39.59	38.53	41.08	46.58
LG revenue to total government revenue	**24.92**	**24.31**	**25.49**	**23.55**	**25.43**	**25.06**	**25.74**	**25.98**	**26.33**	**23.03**

Source: DLA (2021); author calculations.

total government revenue has slowly grown from around 25 percent in 2011 to 26 percent in 2019, suggesting that some degree of expenditure decentralization is in place. In 2020, the government announced a land and building tax deduction of 90 percent because of the COVID-19 pandemic. The proportion of local-government own-source revenue to total government revenue dropped to around 5 percent, prompting a central-government subsidy. As of 2021, the central government has provided a subsidy of THB 10,068 million to subdistrict municipalities and TAOs. The remaining local governments are still waiting for another THB 22,000 million in subsidy.

The Decentralization Plan and Process Act of 1999 and the laws preceding the 1999 act assign certain revenues to each type of local government. Local governments in Thailand have only limited power to raise their own tax revenues. Local-government revenues are divided into four categories (table 15.3). First, locally levied revenues (taxes and nontaxes) are building and land tax; local development tax; signboard tax; animal slaughter tax; bird nest collection tax; a retail tax on the sale of cigarettes, tobacco, and gasoline; hotel rental tax; fees, fines, and permission charges; revenue from property; revenue from public utility provision; and other small sources of revenue. Second, centrally levied revenue that is reallocated to local governments consists of value-added tax, specific business tax, alcohol and beer tax, excise taxes, motor vehicle tax and fees, property registration fees, gambling fees, mineral fees, petroleum fees, and miscellaneous revenue. Third is an additional shared tax from the value-added tax, of which no more than 30 percent goes to local governments, as specified under the Decentralization Plan and Process Act. Fourth are general and specific grants from the central government.

Property and Land Taxation Before the 2020 Reform

Before 2020, Thailand's recurrent property tax system was composed of two taxes: the building and land tax and the local development tax. The building and land tax dates back to 1932, the local development tax was adopted in 1965, and neither was substantially revised until 2020. The building and land tax applied mainly to commercial use, and the local development tax applied mainly to land used for residential and agricultural purposes. Local governments are responsible for collecting building and land tax and local development tax in their respective jurisdictions. The revenue from these taxes in 2019 was just 0.22 percent of GDP and 5.44 percent of total local-government revenue. Under the pre-2020 system, structural and administrative issues constrained the two property

Table 15.3 Sources of Local-Government Revenue

Type of Revenue	Provincial Administrative Organization	Municipality	TAO	BMA	Pattaya City
Locally Levied Revenue					
Tax revenue					
Building and land tax		✓	✓	✓	✓
Local development tax		✓	✓	✓	✓
Signboard tax		✓	✓	✓	✓
Animal slaughter tax		✓	✓		
Bird nest collection tax		✓	✓		
Retail sale of cigarettes, tobacco, and gasoline	✓				
Hotel rental tax	✓			✓	
Nontax revenue					
Fee, fine, and permission charge	✓	✓	✓	✓	✓
Revenue from property	✓	✓	✓	✓	✓
Revenue from public utility	✓	✓	✓	✓	✓
Miscellaneous revenue	✓	✓	✓	✓	✓
Centrally Levied Revenue Allocated to LGs					
Value-added tax[1]		✓	✓	✓	✓
Specific business tax		✓	✓	✓	✓

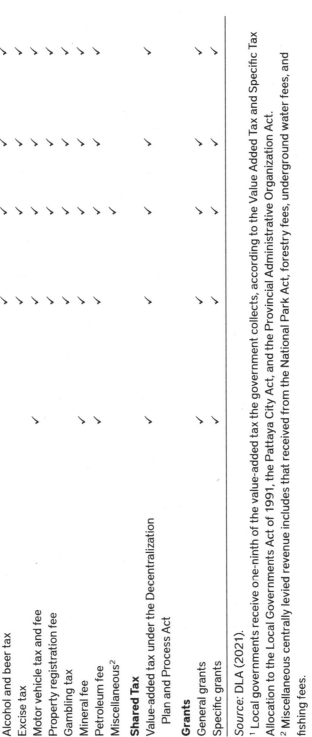

Alcohol and beer tax		✓	✓	✓
Excise tax		✓	✓	✓
Motor vehicle tax and fee	✓	✓	✓	✓
Property registration fee		✓	✓	✓
Gambling tax		✓	✓	✓
Mineral fee	✓	✓	✓	✓
Petroleum fee	✓		✓	✓
Miscellaneous[2]		✓		
Shared Tax				
Value-added tax under the Decentralization Plan and Process Act	✓	✓	✓	✓
Grants				
General grants	✓	✓	✓	✓
Specific grants	✓	✓	✓	✓

Source: DLA (2021).

[1] Local governments receive one-ninth of the value-added tax the government collects, according to the Value Added Tax and Specific Tax Allocation to the Local Governments Act of 1991, the Pattaya City Act, and the Provincial Administrative Organization Act.

[2] Miscellaneous centrally levied revenue includes that received from the National Park Act, forestry fees, underground water fees, and fishing fees.

taxes from efficient functioning. Furthermore, long-standing political forces resisted reforming these taxes.

Building and Land Tax Before 2020

The owners of property who rented or leased it or who used it for commercial or industrial purposes were liable for the building and land tax. If the owners had contested the assessment of the annual value, they could appeal to the local authorities. If they were not satisfied with the local authorities' decision, they could submit their petitions to a civil court to reconsider the assessment value. The civil court ruling was final.[2]

The coverage of the tax base included buildings and land used for all purposes, except for owner-occupied or vacant residences. Taxable property included land adjacent to the buildings and structures attached to the property and used for industrial purposes (machines, rice mills, sawmills, etc.). Royal palaces, properties used by the government and state enterprises for public activities, school and hospital properties that were not used for private profit, religious properties, and buildings unoccupied for the whole year were exempted. The method of determining the tax base was prescribed in the law. Local authorities assessed the annual value on the basis of the actual or imputed rental income of the property. For properties that were not rented, including those used for commercial or industrial purposes, the minister of the Interior announced the annual value as a percentage of the capital value of the property as a guideline for local authorities. The tax rate was a uniform 12.5 percent of the annual value for all localities, set by the central government. The tax base was reduced to one-third of the annual value for buildings with some attached structures or machines for industrial purposes.

The building and land taxes were collected and retained by local governments (municipalities and TAOs). Owners of taxable property declared their rental values to the local authorities annually. Local authorities adjusted disputed self-declared amounts according to the area's annual value. Past-due tax (by less than four months) was increased by 2.5–10 percent, depending on the number of past-due months. Local authorities could seize and sell properties with tax overdue by more than four months. Owners who did not pay were fined and sometimes jailed.

The building and land tax had several important drawbacks:

- The tax applied to the same tax base as the personal income tax, which included the rental income of the property. Thus, many property owners paid twice. However, the building and land tax applied to property generating income, whereas the personal income tax applied to income as such. Furthermore, rental income was measured quite differently under the two taxes, and Thailand's practice of measuring rental income differently under different taxes was similar to that in many other countries. Some justified the building and land tax as being a local tax financing local services.

- There was no standard annual rental value for a tax base. The tax base depended on self-declaration by property owners. However, there was no direct evidence of market rental value to estimate the tax base when owners used their buildings for commercial purposes. Finally, the tax base depended on the discretionary decisions of local officers, creating many incentives and opportunities for tax evasion and even corruption.

- A wide range of tax exemptions and deductions eroded the tax base, such as the exemption on owner-occupied residential property and vacant buildings. The tax office had difficulty separating the residential property from commercial property (such as rented property). The large number of dual-use properties, such as a shop on the bottom floor and family living quarters above it, were difficult to deal with. Proving whether properties were really vacant as reported was costly. The rate of the building and land tax—12.5 percent of the annual rental value—was high enough to give property owners an incentive to avoid or evade the tax. For example, some property owners did not report rental property or underreported the rental value. This all placed a heavy burden on tax administration.

- Some local authorities did not have capacity to monitor and enforce the tax. In addition, the fees and penalty for tax evasion were low and not strictly enforced.

Local Development Tax Before 2020

The individual or corporate entity whose name was on the title on January 1 was liable for local development tax for that year. People who were in possession of land were also liable. The tax base was the taxable value of the land, and the medium land price was the main factor determining the assessed land value.[3] The provincial governor appointed local appraisal committees for each jurisdiction, whose members varied in number and qualifications according to type of local government.

The local appraisal committee computed the medium land price, taking the average price of at least three recent land sales in the same district and without accounting for the value of improvements, structures, or crops included in their sale price. If there were no recent transactions, the medium land price was calculated using the average land price in nearby areas with similar land conditions and usage. The committee could also use other criteria to determine the average market value of the land. The medium land price was revised every four years and a new medium land price announced. Landowners dissatisfied with the new medium land price could appeal to the provincial governor for a revision.

Landowners submitted a list of their locally owned land to the municipalities and TAOs that collected local development taxes. Landowners who failed to submit land lists paid an additional 5–10 percent tax to local government. If past due, landowners paid an extra 24 percent of the tax. The local authorities could seize and sell land, and even imprison owners who did not pay tax.

The coverage of the tax base for local development taxes was narrow, composed of land, including mountains and water basins but exempting the following:[4]

- Royal palace land.

- Public land and state land used for state and public purposes without making any profit.

- Local-government land used for local and public purposes without making any profit.

- Land used for health care, education, or public charity purposes.

- Land used for religious purposes without making any profit.

- Land used for grave and crematorium purposes without making any profit.

- Land used for state railways, water utilities, electric utilities, state ports, and state airports.

- Land adjacent to buildings already subject to building and land taxes.

- Private land whose owners allowed the government to use the land for public purposes.

- International organization land.

- Foreign embassy land.

- Land specified in ministerial regulations.

Moreover, in some provinces, land used for residential and cultivation purposes was exempt, depending on property location. Land in Bangkok received some exemptions that depended on population density. Joint owners jointly received a specified amount of tax exemption. However, land with buildings used for business or rental purposes did not receive an exemption. Landowners could receive tax exemptions in only one province.

Problems with the local development tax included the following:

- The tax base, which is the assessed value of land from 1978–1981, has never been updated since then. The tax base was undervalued, leading to less tax revenue for the local government.

- The local development tax schedule was regressive in the top brackets.

- The buildings used for residential purposes were tax exempt for owner-occupiers, which benefited the wealthy.

- The tax base was significantly narrowed by tax exemptions and deductions.

- The nominal tax rate schedule for the local development tax was progressive if the medium land price was less than THB 30,000 per *rai* (2.53 *rai* = 1 acre) and regressive above that.

Revenue Performance Before 2020

Property and land taxes pre-2020 did not generate a significant amount of revenue for local governments. The building and land tax accounted for only about 0.2 percent of GDP, though its growth kept pace with GDP in 2012–2019 (table 15.4). The average growth rate in revenues for 2012–2019 was about 7.73 percent, roughly the same as the growth in land prices. On average during 2012–2019, building and land tax revenue remained at less than 5 percent of local-government revenue.

Revenue from the local development tax as a percentage of GDP was even lower than that raised by the building and land tax. It remained at about 0.007 percent of GDP in 2012–2019 (table 15.5). The combination of these two property taxes accounted for less than 0.2 percent of GDP (table 15.6). Thailand ranked near the bottom of developing jurisdictions in terms of property tax effort. Property taxes from Bangkok and Pattaya City totaled THB 15,228 million and THB 462 million, respectively, in 2019 and were equivalent to about 40 percent of total national property tax collections.

New Property and Land Tax System in 2020

In 2020, Thailand replaced the building and land tax and the local development tax with the land and building tax. This section describes the new system and the justifications for its components. The previous property and land tax system was not contributing significantly to either the budget

Table 15.4 Building and Land Tax Revenue as a Percentage of GDP, All Tax Revenue, and Local-Government Revenue, 2012–2019

| Year | Building and Land Tax Revenue (THB million) | GDP (THB million) | All Tax Revenue (ATR) (THB million) | Local-Government Revenue (LGR) (THB million) | Building and Land Tax | | |
					As % of GDP	As % of ATR	As % of LGR
2012	21,067	12,357,342	2,112,820	481,304	0.17	1.00	4.38
2013	23,103	12,915,158	2,306,629	535,369	0.18	1.00	4.32
2014	25,077	13,230,304	2,225,924	535,746	0.19	1.13	4.68
2015	26,940	13,743,480	2,279,082	591,309	0.20	1.18	4.56
2016	29,060	14,590,337	2,382,994	583,866	0.20	1.22	4.98
2017	32,008	15,488,664	2,455,843	603,112	0.21	1.30	5.31
2018	33,385	16,368,705	2,598,731	636,573	0.20	1.28	5.24
2019	35,449	16,898,086	2,700,183	671,427	0.21	1.31	5.28
Avg.	28,261	14,449,010	2,382,776	579,838	0.19	1.18	4.84

Sources: DLA (2021); Fiscal Policy Office (2021); author calculations.

Table 15.5 Local Development Tax Revenue as a Percentage of GDP, All Tax Revenue, and Local-Government Revenue, 2012–2019

Year	Local Development Tax Revenue (THB million)	GDP (THB million)	All Tax Revenue (ATR) (THB million)	Local-Government Revenue (LGR) (THB million)	Local Development Tax		
					As % of GDP	As % of ATR	As % of LGR
2012	904	12,357,342	2,112,820	481,304	0.007	0.043	0.19
2013	934	12,915,158	2,306,629	535,369	0.007	0.040	0.17
2014	896	13,230,304	2,225,925	535,746	0.007	0.040	0.17
2015	932	13,743,480	2,279,082	591,309	0.007	0.041	0.16
2016	954	14,590,337	2,382,994	583,866	0.007	0.040	0.16
2017	957	15,488,664	2,455,843	603,112	0.006	0.039	0.16
2018	939	16,368,705	2,598,731	636,573	0.006	0.036	0.15
2019	968	16,898,086	2,700,183	671,427	0.006	0.036	0.14
Avg.	936	14,449,010	2,382,776	579,838	0.007	0.039	0.16

Sources: DLA (2021); Fiscal Policy Office (2021); author calculations.

Table 15.6 Property and Land Tax Revenue as a Percentage of GDP, Local-Government Revenue, and All Tax Revenue, 2012–2020

Year	Property and Land Tax Revenue (THB million)	GDP (THB million)	All Tax Revenue (ATR) (THB million)	Local-Government Revenue (LGR) (THB million)	Property and Land Tax		
					As % of GDP	As % of ATR	As % of LGR
2012	21,971	12,357,342	2,112,820	481,304	0.18	1.04	4.56
2013	24,037	12,915,158	2,306,629	535,369	0.19	1.04	4.49
2014	25,973	13,230,304	2,225,924	535,746	0.20	1.17	4.85
2015	27,872	13,743,480	2,279,082	591,309	0.20	1.22	4.71
2016	30,013	14,590,337	2,382,994	583,866	0.21	1.26	5.14
2017	32,965	15,488,664	2,455,843	603,112	0.21	1.34	5.47
2018	34,324	16,368,705	2,598,731	636,573	0.21	1.32	5.39
2019	36,527	16,898,086	2,700,183	671,427	0.22	1.35	5.44
2020	3,317	15,698,286	2,473,038	629,027	0.02	0.13	0.53
Avg.	26,330	14,587,818	2,392,805	585,304	0.18	1.10	4.51

Sources: DLA (2021); Fiscal Policy Office (2021); author calculations.

needs of local governments or to an improved land policy, nor was it equitable. The explanations for this poor performance have long been known. Revenue growth was constrained because land values had not been reassessed since 1978, and low effective tax rates had led to a very low cost of holding unproductive land. The result was too much underused or vacant land, often held for speculation. Further, a preponderance of tax exemptions had narrowed the tax base. This led to low property and land tax revenues for local governments—one of the lowest in Asia—which in turn limited the fiscal independence of local governments.

This weak performance generated considerable interest in revising the laws, and proposals had been made since before 2000 for reforming the new property and land tax system (Varanyuwatana 2004). In fact, there were many draft land and building tax bills, proposed by many administrations, but until 2020, none made it through parliament. Property tax reform was long overdue.

A draft of the Land and Building Tax Bill was approved by the cabinet on March 21, 2017. The national legislative assembly appointed a committee to consider and revise the draft bill. A total of 85 meetings were held to make changes before the revised draft bill was submitted to the national legislative assembly for approval.[5] The national legislative assembly approved the new land and building tax bill on November 16, 2018. The Land and Building Tax Act was announced in the *Royal Thai Government Gazette* on March 12, 2019, and implemented on January 1, 2020, by local governments.

The objectives of the Land and Building Tax Act are

- to reform and modernize the property tax structure to eliminate the problems of the old system and unify the previous land and building tax and the local development tax;

- to stimulate land use, especially with respect to properties that have long been vacant;

- to stimulate fiscal decentralization by increasing revenue mobilization at the local-government level;

- to strengthen the capacity of local fiscal administrations and increase the transparency of their operations; and

- to generate enough revenue for local governments to significantly improve the delivery of local public services (Fiscal Policy Office, 2018).

The remainder of this section details the new law and describes some of the potential revenue and equity impacts.

Land and Building Tax Law

When the Land and Building Tax Act took effect in 2020, the Building and Land Tax Act of 1932 and the Local Development Tax Act of 1965 were repealed. The new law applies to owners of land and buildings and to people who have possessory rights (either through a government grant or lease to use the land).

Tax Base

The tax base is the capital value of land and buildings. It includes all land (including mountains and water basins), all habitable buildings or structures, and buildings and structures that can be used or can store merchandise for commercial purposes, including apartments and boats used as residential housing.

The bases to be taxed are:

- the assessed land values;
- the assessed building values; and
- the assessed condominium values.

If there is no assessed value of the property, the value will be estimated based on ministerial regulations first issued in 2019, which was finally announced in the government gazette on January 7, 2022 (Ratchakitcha 2020). This regulation will apply only to miscellaneous types of land and buildings. The assessed value of land, buildings, and condominiums is the same as the assessed value of property that is used for collecting the fee for registration of rights and legal transactions. These assessed values are determined by the provincial assessment subcommittees and supervised by the assessment value committee at the central-government level.

In general, local governments must survey all properties in their jurisdictions and calculate the land and building tax liability of each property owner. The new law is not a self-declaration system. The local authority instead informs the property owners of their tax liabilities. Taxpayers can appeal either the assessments of their property value or the taxes assessed on them to the local authorities and to the civil court, which will be the final ruling.

Exemptions and Deductions

In the earlier versions of the draft land and building tax bills, no properties used for residential and agricultural purposes were tax exempt. After the draft bill was made public, there was enough dissatisfaction that the government revised the bill to significantly increase the tax exemptions for main residences and agricultural properties.

In the final version of the bill, the following properties receive a tax exemption:

- State or government property that is used for state or government purposes without making any profit.

- International organization properties.

- Foreign embassy properties.

- International Red Cross properties.

- Nonprofit religious properties.

- Cemeteries and crematoriums.

- Nonprofit foundations and properties owned by charitable entities, according to criteria to be determined by the minister of Finance.

- Private property that governments use for public purposes, according to criteria to be determined by the minister of Finance.

- Property for common usage of joint owners, as determined by the condominium laws.

- Properties for providing utility, such as roads or common areas, according to the Land Allocation Act of 2000 and 2015 and the other laws under this act.

- Properties for providing utility, according to the Industrial Estate Authority Act of 1979 and the revised version and the other laws under this act.

- Other types of properties specified in ministerial regulations.

Individual owners (not corporations) who use their land and buildings for agricultural purposes receive a tax exemption for the value of the property not to exceed THB 50 million. Moreover, for the first three years after implementation of the new law, only natural persons (that is, individuals, not corporations) who use their property for agricultural purposes will receive a tax exemption. Property used for residential purposes will receive a tax exemption up to THB 50 million. If they own just the house, not the land, and they are registered in the house, they receive a tax exemption up to THB 10 million. These thresholds are quite high and will exclude most owner-occupiers from the tax base (ADB 2020, 42).

For some types of property (such as property used for public services), the owners can get a tax deduction of up to 90 percent of the amount of the tax. Property eligible for these deductions are specified in the Land and Building Tax Deduction Decree, announced on January 20, 2020 (Ratchakitcha 2021).

During a three-year transition period, taxpayers whose tax burden has increased under the new law pay the old tax amount plus only 25 percent of the increased amount of tax (the difference between the old and new taxes) in the first year, 50 percent in the second year, and 75 percent in the third year. In the fourth year, taxpayers pay the full amount of their tax liability.

Tax Rate Schedule

Properties are classified into two categories: used and vacant. For property that is used, three ceiling tax rates apply according to land and building usage:

- For agricultural usage of land and buildings, the maximum tax rate is 0.15 percent of the assessed value.

- For residential usage of land and buildings, the maximum tax rate is 0.3 percent of the assessed value.

- For usage other than agricultural or residential (such as commercial or industrial purposes), the maximum tax rate is 1.2 percent of the assessed value of land and buildings.

For vacant property, the imposed tax rates and the maximum tax rate are the same as the usage of property for other than agricultural or residential purposes. However, the tax rate increases by 0.3 percent every three years that the property remains unused. Its maximum tax rate is capped at 3 percent of the assessed value of lands and buildings.

The actual tax rate schedules are progressive with respect to the assessed value of the property classified by usage types (table 15.7). Under the law, the central government creates ceiling tax rates and adjusts them depending on the prevailing economic situation. The local governments have the authority to increase the tax rates above the rates set by the central government but may not exceed the ceiling rates set by the Land and Building Tax Act. The actual tax rates have been put in the transitional chapter of the law and applied for the first two years so that the taxpayers will know their tax liability. The actual tax rate, which will apply to the 2022 tax year, was announced in the Land and Building Tax Rate Determination Decree on December 13, 2021.

Table 15.7 Land and Building Tax Rates per Usage

Agriculture Use (max tax rate 0.15%)		Residential Use (max tax rate 0.30%)		Other Use (max tax rate 1.20%)	
Imposed Tax Rate					
Value (THB million)	Tax Rate (%)	Value (THB million)	Tax Rate (%)	Value (THB million)	Tax Rate (%)
0–75	0.01	0–50	0.02	0–50	0.30
75–100	0.03	50–75	0.03	50–200	0.40
100–500	0.05	75–100	0.05	200–1,000	0.50
500–1,000	0.07	100+	0.10	1,000–5,000	0.60
1,000+	0.10			5,000+	0.70

Source: Fiscal Policy Office (2018).

Collection and Enforcement

Collection and enforcement reside with the local governments (i.e., municipalities and TAOs). All the tax revenue they collect belongs to them. Delinquent taxpayers pay a fine of 10–40 percent of the total amount of the unpaid tax and an extra 1 percent of the total amount of the unpaid tax per month. If taxpayers refuse to pay their taxes without cause, they are fined and may be jailed. The local authorities can seize and sell properties to pay past-due taxes and associated fines.

Potential Long-Run Benefits

The new land and building tax is imposed on the value of land and buildings—making it a wealth-based tax. The tax is determined by the legal tax rates and the assessed values of land and buildings announced by the Treasury Department. These values are standardized without any discretionary decisions by local officers, to decrease opportunities for corruption in the tax assessment process.

The land and building tax is intended to follow the ability-to-pay and the benefit principles, in the belief that those who own the most property will benefit the most from the enhanced local-government services that will come from the tax. Thus, property owners who own higher-valued property will pay more tax than the owners who own less. Property owners get benefits from local development in their area, so it is proper that they bear some of the burden of financing those development projects.

Vacant properties are subject to a higher tax rate under the new regime. Property owners now bear some costs of property holding. The higher tax rate is expected to stimulate property owners to use their land in more productive ways or to sell it to somebody else who will. That said, the actual tax rates imposed on vacant land still are low compared with the average increases in land prices each year. Landowners thus may still not have adequate incentives to use their land more efficiently. Other landowners may look for avenues of tax avoidance, such as planting trees on their land to repurpose it as agricultural and thereby limit their tax liability.

Thailand has a very high concentration of land ownership, and the top 20 percent of landowners own around 80 percent of the total land (Laovakul 2016a). In theory, the new tax will cause large holders of vacant land to bear a higher cost of holding it, incentivizing them to get rid of land being held for speculation, and lead to less concentrated landholding. But this outcome depends crucially on the percentage increase in the value of land annually. The ceiling tax rate for vacant property is 3 percent. Land prices have been increasing on average about 7 percent a year. The effect on reducing landholding for speculation may not be as much as hoped for, at least in the short run.

The land and building tax is a local-government tax collected by local authorities. It is meant to lead to more fiscal decentralization by making local fiscal units more independent from the central government, at least on the expenditure side of their budget. The result could be local authorities that are more accountable, and thus responsive to, their constituents. In addition, local governments will have room to increase their tax rates if they need a larger budget to provide more public services in their area. This also will support the accountability features of fiscal decentralization (Laovakul 2016b).

The land and building tax was originally designed to generate significant sources of local revenue. Modifications added many tax exemptions and deductions, including tax relief in the transitional periods. The statutory rates are low. Thus, the new land and building tax will probably not produce much tax revenue for local governments, and some local governments may find that their tax revenues have decreased, especially in small and more remote jurisdictions.

Implementation Challenges

The new tax is still being implemented, and it is not likely to be fully completed for some time. This section makes a few preliminary observations about the tax's implementation, challenges to be overcome, and issues to be resolved.

Property Survey

To turn the law into a reality, local governments will have to survey every piece of property in their jurisdictions, recording the size, usage, and value of all the land and buildings. This is the only way to cover the legal tax base. Some jurisdictions have many parcels and buildings, so it will take time to fully document every piece of property and accurately value them. The survey process is costly, which will be a problem for small local governments with a limited budget. Although local governments have an incentive to find all these properties, it will take time for them to do so. And then it will take more time to calculate the tax liability of each parcel and to collect the amounts due. It could take years to put together the fiscal and physical cadastres.

Likely Gap Between Assessed Price, Market Value, and Revenue Targets

Even after the new system is fully in place, the assessed land value will likely still be lower than the market value of the land, and in some areas, it is likely to be much lower. The same will be true of the assessments on buildings. These shortcomings will compromise revenue productivity of the new tax. So will tax exemptions and deductions, low tax rates, and tax avoidance.

The implementation of the property tax reform has been slowed by the COVID-19 pandemic. The Treasury Department continues to use the assessed value of land and buildings that were in place in 2016–2019. The Treasury Department has not yet announced the new assessed value of land and buildings for 2020–2023.

Unknown Regulatory Details

Because the process and the details of implementing the new land and building tax are not the same as the old tax system, local authorities will have to understand the new law well enough to implement it correctly. They will also need to be able to explain it to the taxpayers in their jurisdictions. This will involve significant public relations and communications.

Although the tax is to be implemented by local governments, it was created by the central government. The Ministry of the Interior and the Ministry of Finance have yet to issue many ministerial regulations and rules concerning the new property tax. Some local-government officers are still confused about the new process—for example, how to measure the size of the buildings, how to define the types of some buildings. Some taxpayers who own vacant land that is subject to a higher tax rate are trying to avoid the tax by growing low-maintenance plants such as bananas or limes and claiming it as agricultural usage, which is subject to the lowest tax rate among all types of land usage.

Equity

The burden of the new property tax is not likely to be distributed fairly during the implementation period. If local governments cannot accurately survey all properties in their jurisdiction, some properties could be taxed at the wrong rate, generally lower than they should be. This will create unfairness. Likewise, assessments may not match market values, and in the absence of a new survey, some taxpayers may escape the tax net when the tax system is changed. Additionally, people who do not know about the new tax law or do not have enough information about the tax collection process may not cooperate with local officers and may be unwilling to pay the taxes. Some taxpayers will have moved to new addresses and not informed their local government and so may not have received the tax documents.

Revenues

Given the large number of tax exemptions and deductions and their collective erosion, the low actual tax rates, and the infrastructure for the new system not yet being in place, many local governments will receive less tax revenue than before. If the local governments do not have enough tax revenue, they will not have the budgets necessary to provide quality social services. This will push the burden of funding services back onto the central government, which will have to provide grants to subsidize the local governments. As part of the COVID-19 pandemic program, in 2020 and again in 2021, the central government announced a decree to reduce land and building tax liability by 90 percent.

Other Property-Related Taxes and Fees

Property taxes are also levied in respect of transactions. Three of these are local government taxes, as described in table 15.8. In 2019, they yielded revenues equivalent to about 0.26 percent of GDP. The local government taxes on property transfers are property registration fees and the specific business tax. In addition, there is a central government capital gains income tax and stamp duties. Details on these transfer taxes are described in table 15.8.

Table 15.8 Revenue from Property-Related Taxes and Fees, Selected Budget Years

Type of Property Transfer Tax (PTT)	Budget Year					
	2012	2015	2018	2019	2020	
1. Fees	**27,700**	**37,258**	**40,803**	**41,111**	**31,483**	
a. Property registration fees (LG revenue) (THB million)	27,320	36,816	40,264	40,554	30,942	
b. Other fees (CG revenue) (THB million)	380	441	539	556	541	
2. Specific business tax (THB million)	**21,886**	**30,492**	**34,876**	**35,194**	**31,989**	
a. LG revenue (97.0% of 0.3%) (THB million)	1,976	2,772	3,071	3,073	2,817	
b. CG revenue (3.0%) (THB million)	19,910	27,72-	31,705	31,995	29,081	
c. Tax collection expense (3.0% of 0.3%) (THB million)	No data	No data	99	127	91	
3. Withholding income tax on property transfers (THB million)	**20,689**	**23,802**	**27,547**	**27,001**	**23,253**	
4. Stamp duty (THB million)	**3,508**	**5,512**	**5,175**	**5,352**	**4,732**	
Total PTT revenue (THB million)	**73,783**	**97,064**	**108,400**	**108,658**	**91,457**	
LG PTT revenue (1.a + 2.a) (THB million)	**29,295**	**39,589**	**43,335**	**43,627**	**33,759**	
LG PTT revenue as % of total revenue	**40**	**41**	**40**	**40**	**37**	
LG PTT revenue as % of GDP	**0.24**	**0.29**	**0.26**	**0.26**	**0.22**	

Source: Department of Lands (2021).

Note: LG = local government; CG = central government.

Fees

Fees fall into two categories: surveyor fees and property registration fees. Surveyor fees belong to the central government. Property registration fees are allocated to local governments.

Property registration fees are collected on transfers of property rights, including sales, mortgages, preferential rights, and rents. The basic fee is 2 percent of the assessed value of the property or the price reported by the parties, whichever is higher. The assessed value of the property is determined by the Treasury Department, and the market price is generally about double the assessed value. Note that the market price is almost always higher than the sales price reported to the government. Often, the tax is based on the sale price reported by the two parties, which is much lower than the actual market price. The amount of THB 40,554 million and THB 30,942 million went to the local governments in 2019 and 2020, respectively.

For other kinds of property transfer and registration, the fee is less than 2 percent, depending on the types of transfers. For example, property transfers between parents and descendants or between spouses are charged a fee of 0.5 percent of the assessed value of the property. Preferential rates are given for agricultural credits from financial institutions and for registration for rent. The revenue from the property registration fees belongs to the local governments.

Specific Business Tax

Specific business taxes are payable on transfers by both companies and private individuals who have owned the property for less than five years. The tax rate is 3.3 percent of the assessed value on the tax roll or the reported price as given by the parties, whichever is higher. If the seller has owned the property for less than five years but the household registration certificate has been in the seller's name for at least one year, the seller can get the specific business tax exemption. Local governments get 0.3 percent (effectively 2.91 percent as a 3 percent collection fee is deducted; table 15.8) from the total amount of specific business tax on property. The revenue was THB 3,073 million and THB 2,817 million in 2019 and 2020, respectively.

Withholding Income Tax on Property Transfers

Both individuals and corporate entities making property transfers pay a withholding income tax levied under the Revenue Code, 1938, amended in 2021. The withholding tax for corporate entities is 1 percent of the assessed value or the price as given by the parties, whichever is higher. For individuals, this tax is calculated on the basis of the property's assessed value. The owners can deduct expenses from their tax basis according to the ownership period. The tax rate is listed in the personal income tax schedule. Individuals who buy and sell properties for profit file this as part of their personal income tax at the end of the tax year. People who inherit property or receive it as a gift and then sell it do not have to. The amount of withholding income tax was THB 27,002 million and THB 23,253 million in 2019 and 2020, respectively. These revenues belong to the central government.

Stamp Duty

Stamp duty is due only when the specific business tax is not applicable. For donations and contracts of sale, the stamp duty is THB 1 for every THB 200 or fraction of THB 200 of the assessed value or the price as given by the parties, whichever is higher. The stamp duty revenue goes to the central government. This revenue was THB 5,352 million and THB 4,732 million in 2019 and 2020, respectively.

Conclusion

Thailand's ambitious property tax reform aims to develop a modern property tax system. The new tax is expected to yield a 17 percent increase in annual revenues over the old system (ADB 2020, xiv).

Transition to the new system is underway in 2022, but several further necessary reforms are known. First are the exemptions in the new law that have severely narrowed the tax base. This is not an unusual outcome for a new system in which the focus is on getting the reform through a legislature. The residential housing exemption was set very high and shields all but the very wealthy from the tax. Many would argue that the tax exemption for farmers was set too high and gives preferences to more farmers than just the poor ones. Such features of the tax system lower revenue mobilization and harm equity goals.

A second problem is with the tax rates, which may have been set too low. For example, the ceiling rate for vacant land is 3 percent, but land prices have been increasing at 7 percent annually. The result is that landowners have less incentive to use their land efficiently and have less incentive to reduce land speculation.

A third issue is tax avoidance. With the higher tax rate for vacant land and a big tax exemption for agricultural usage, people who hold high-value land will try to change their vacant land to agricultural land to get a tax exemption.

A fourth issue has to do with educating taxpayers and local-government officers about the new law. The central and local governments need to clearly communicate to citizens the benefits they will receive in exchange for paying taxes under the new Land and Building Tax Law. Otherwise, confidence in local government and compliance will likely suffer.

Whether Thailand can resolve these problems remains to be seen.

Notes

1. The National Decentralization Committee is composed of central-government staffs from related ministries such as the Ministry of the Interior, Ministry of Finance, and Ministry of Education; representatives of local governments; and experts on decentralization who are mostly from academic institutions.

2. The pre-2020 system was governed by the Building and Land Tax Act B.E. 2475 (1932).

3. The "medium land price" used for calculating the tax base is the average land price in the period 1978–1981. Because of political conflicts and divisions, this archaic approach to assessment was used until quite recently.

4. Local Development Tax Act B.E. 2508 (1965).

5. Despite the widespread recognition that Thailand's property taxes needed reform, the political process was protracted. The people who have power to pass or influence bills normally are the people who own much of the property or are supported by wealthy property owners. The power of this group is one of the reasons it was so difficult to pass the Land and Building Tax Bill in parliament. Interest groups were fearful of paying higher taxes on their commercial or residential properties, and their resistance is evident in many exemptions in the final law.

References

ADB (Asian Development Bank). 2020. *Mapping Property Tax Reform in Southeast Asia.* Manila: Asian Development Bank.

Department of Lands. 2021. *Data on the Amount of Work and Revenue Collection of Land Offices* [in Thai]. Retrieved April 26, 2021. https://data.go.th/dataset/income-dol.

DLA (Department of Local Administration). 2019. *Land and Building Tax.* http://www.dla.go.th/work/tax9/2.pdf.

———. 2020, *September 9. Number of Local Government Organizations.* [in Thai.] Retrieved April 26, 2021. http://www.dla.go.th/work/abt/index.jsp.

———. 2021. *The Local Administration Organizations' Revenue Data.* [in Thai.] Bangkok: Department of Local Administration. http://www.dla.go.th/work/money/index.jsp.

Fiscal Policy Office. 2018. *The Importance Issues of the Land and Building Tax Act* [in Thai]. Retrieved April 26, 2021. www.fpo.go.th/main/getattachment/General-information-public-service/ประชาชนควรรู้/ภาษีที่ดินและสิ่งปลูกสร้าง/Land-Building-taxnew-(1).pdf.aspx?lang=th-TH.

———. 2021. *FIT_D101Government Revenue Dataset.* [in Thai.] Retrieved September 17, 2021. www.fpo.go.th/main/Statistic-Database.aspx.

Laovakul, D. 2016a. "Concentration of Land and Other Wealth in Thailand." In *Unequal Thailand: Aspects of Wealth and Power,* ed. P. Phongpaichit and C. Baker, chap. 2. Singapore: National University of Singapore Press.

Laovakul, D. 2016b. "Property Tax in Thailand: An Assessment and Policy Implications." *Thammasat Review of Economic and Social Policy* 2(1): 24–53.

Ratchakitcha. 2020. *Ministerial Regulation on Determining Criteria, Methods, and Conditions for Calculating the Value of Land or Buildings without Appraisal Value, B.E. 2562 (2019)* [in Thai.] http://www.ratchakitcha.soc.go.th/DATA/PDF/2563/A/001/T _0006.PDF.

———. 2021. *Royal Decree on Determining Land and Building Tax Rates, B.E. 2564 (2021).* [in Thai]. http://www.ratchakitcha.soc.go.th/DATA/PDF/2564/A/084/T_0001 .PDF.

Varanyuwatana, S. 2004. "Property Tax in Thailand." In *International Handbook of Land and Property Taxation*, ed. R. Bird and E. Slack, 159–164. Cheltenham, UK: Edward Elgar.

16

Vietnam: A Property Tax System in Transition

TRUONG BA TUAN

Vietnam has a unitary system of government, but the central government delegates significant decision-making powers to the local governments. Local governments in Vietnam are in a three-level hierarchy:
province, district, and commune. As of December 31, 2020, there were 63
provinces (including five large cities: Hanoi, Haiphong, Da Nang, Can
Tho, and Ho Chi Minh City), 707 districts, and 10,616 communes (GSO
2021). Each local level of government reports to the next higher level.

In 1986, Vietnam introduced Doi Moi, a program to transform from a
centrally planned economy to a market-based economy. Compared with
other formerly communist jurisdictions in Eastern Europe and the former Soviet Union, Vietnam has emphasized gradualism over radical
changes in its reform process. Its economy has grown rapidly, and in the
twenty-first century, Vietnam has had one of the fastest-growing economies in Asia. Rapid economic growth created favorable conditions for
Vietnam to improve the living standards of its people, and it has transformed from one of the poorest jurisdictions in the world to lower-middle-
income status. The poverty rate fell dramatically, from 14.2 percent in
2010 to less than 2.75 percent in 2020 (GSO 2021).

In parallel with the structural changes of the economy, the tax system in
Vietnam has undergone significant changes, including the gradual introduction of standard tax instruments, such as corporate income tax,

value-added tax, personal income tax, and environmental protection tax. In addition, tax policies, which had discriminated between domestic enterprises and foreign-invested enterprises, became one integrated system. There have also been considerable changes in tax policies related to land and property. Property taxation has evolved along with the development of land policy since the start of the economic reform, as reflected in four versions of the Law on Land (1988, 1993, 2003, and 2013). The proposed revision to the Law on Land 45/2013/QH13 in 2019 by the National Assembly has been postponed until 2022 because of its complexity.

Property- and land-related revenue has been important in the government budget since 2000, especially at the local levels. Currently, Vietnam imposes seven types of taxes and charges on land and property, detailed later in this chapter, but only two can be considered annual property taxes. The others apply to the acquisition, assignment, or transfer of land use rights or buildings. In 2020, all land- and property-related revenues combined accounted for 16.9 percent of total government revenue. That is a large share even by international standards. However, the annual property taxes play a very limited role in revenue mobilization for the government, largely due to a narrow tax base, a very low tax rate structure, and an inadequate assessment mechanism (Le 2018).

This chapter traces the development of property taxation in Vietnam and examines the need for reform. The chapter begins with a review of fiscal reform to date, including the development of the property tax regime. It then describes the seven types of land and real estate taxes and charges currently in force and analyzes their roles in revenue mobilization. The final section discusses the rationale and policy choices for future property tax reform and lays out options for strengthening the annual property tax.

Fiscal Reform to Date

Vietnam has undertaken extensive public finance reform, focusing on both financial management and government resource mobilization. Until 1989, all taxes were levied in terms of administrative decrees, rather than enacted laws. From 1990 to 1995, numerous tax laws replaced these administrative decrees and gradually built up the foundation of a new tax system to support the functioning of a market-oriented economy (Truong 2018). These tax laws included the Law on Turnover Tax (1990), Law on Excise Tax (1990), Law on Profit Tax (1990), Law on Export and Import Tax (1991), Law on Agricultural Land Use Tax (1993), Ordinance on Land and Housing Tax (1992), and Ordinance on Income Tax on High-Income Earners (1994). In the late 1990s, Vietnam embarked on a second phase of tax reform, marked by the introduction of modern tax laws, including the Law on Value Added Tax (1997) and the Law on Corporate Income Tax (1997).

A third phase of tax reform took place from 2001 to 2010, especially the tax overhaul to meet the requirements of the World Trade Organization in 2007. All discriminatory tax treatments between domestic enterprises and foreign-invested enterprises were eliminated. New tax laws were introduced, including the Law on Personal Income Tax 04/2007/QH12, Law on Natural Resource Tax 45/2009/QH12, Law on Nonagricultural Land Tax 48/2010/QH12, and Law on Environmental Protection Tax 57/2010/QH12.

Another wave of reform is underway, guided by the Tax Reform Strategy 2011–2020. In this phase, changes have been made to most major tax laws, focusing on broadening the tax base, rationalizing the tax rates, and improving tax administration and compliance. The standard corporate income tax rate was reduced to 20 percent and excise tax rates on demerit goods were increased. In 2015, the National Assembly approved the Law on Fee and Charge 97/2015/QH13, delegating significant autonomy to provincial governments in setting fees and charges for public services.

Tax policy reform has been accompanied by a corresponding reform in tax administration. In June 2019, the National Assembly approved the Law on Tax Administration 38/2019/QH14, strengthening the risk-based approach in tax administration and enforcement, promoting etaxation and einvoicing, and strengthening international cooperation on tax management. This law also provides the legal framework for the collection and administration of property-related taxes. The government issued Decree 126/2020/ND-CP, October 19, 2020, to guide its implementation.

Impact of Reform on Revenue Mobilization and Mix

These reforms have led to an impressive increase in revenue mobilization as shown in table 16.1. The ratio of government revenue to GDP increased from 23.3 percent in 1995 to 27.3 percent in 2010. Some backtracking occurred from 2011 to 2014, due to decreases in tax rates, expansion of tax incentives to stimulate investment, lower crude oil prices, and a decrease in trade revenue due to tariff cuts under various free trade agreements. Government revenue mobilization recovered in 2015, to a level of about 25 percent of GDP, a favorable ratio compared with other jurisdictions in the region (Truong 2021). In 2020, because of the COVID-19 pandemic, government revenue collection as percentage of GDP lowered to around 24 percent.

Table 16.2 shows positive structural changes in the composition of the tax mix of government revenue, in particular a move away from the sale

Table 16.1 Government Revenue from Selected Taxes (as % of GDP)

	1995	2000	2005	2010	2015	2020
Value-added tax	3.73	3.87	5.02	7.18	6.00	5.43
Excise on domestic goods and services	1.41	1.19	1.72	1.73	1.59	1.61
Corporate income tax	2.63	2.83	3.19	4.71	3.59	3.83
Personal income tax	0.23	0.37	0.46	1.22	1.35	1.83
Environmental protection tax	–	–	–	–	0.64	0.96
Trade taxes	5.80	3.04	2.59	3.43	2.37	1.22
Agricultural land use tax	0.68	0.40	0.01	0.00	0.00	0.00
Nonagricultural land use tax	0.14	0.08	0.06	0.06	0.04	0.03
Fee and charge revenue	1.69	1.32	1.20	1.54	1.14	1.11
Crude oil	2.65	5.33	7.28	3.21	1.61	0.55
Land use levy	0.09	0.23	1.55	2.29	1.65	2.74
Land rental fee	–	0.13	0.09	0.13	0.32	0.63
Sale of state-owned housing	0.39	0.19	0.14	0.10	0.05	0.02
Total	**23.32**	**20.55**	**24.98**	**27.27**	**24.27**	**23.96**

Sources: GSO (2021); MOF (2021); calculations by the author.

Table 16.2 Government Tax Revenue Mix in Vietnam (% of total)

	1995	2000	2005	2010	2015	2020
Value-added tax	16.0	18.8	20.1	26.3	24.7	22.7
Excise on domestic goods and services	6.1	5.8	6.9	6.3	6.5	6.7
Corporate income tax	11.3	13.8	12.8	17.3	14.8	16.0
Personal income tax	1.0	1.8	1.9	4.5	5.6	7.6
Environmental protection tax	–	–	–	–	2.7	4.0
Trade taxes	24.9	14.8	10.4	12.6	9.8	5.1
Agricultural land use tax	2.9	2.0	0.1	0.0	0.0	0.0
Nonagricultural land use tax	0.6	0.4	0.2	0.2	0.1	0.1
Fee and charge revenue	7.3	6.4	4.8	5.6	4.7	4.6
Crude oil	11.4	25.9	29.2	11.8	6.6	2.3
Land use levy	0.4	1.1	6.2	8.4	6.8	11.5
Land rental fee	–	0.6	0.3	0.5	1.3	2.6
Sale of state-owned housing	1.7	0.9	0.6	0.4	0.2	0.1
Other	16.7	7.6	6.7	6.1	16.2	16.6
Total	**100.00**	**100.00**	**100.00**	**100.00**	**100.00**	**100.00**

Sources: MOF (2021); calculations by the author.

of national resources, such as crude oil and minerals, and trade taxes. The decrease in trade tax revenue and crude oil revenue was compensated for by an expansion in consumption tax revenue (valued-added tax and excise tax) and income tax revenue (corporate and personal). The share of revenue from these taxes in total government revenue increased from around 40 percent in 2000 to around 53 percent in 2020.

Land- and property-related revenue significantly increased in this century, especially that from one-time-event revenue, such as land use levy and land rental fee.[1] The share of land- and property-related revenue in total government revenue increased from 8.6 percent in 2012 to 16.9 percent in 2020. However, most land- and property-related revenue comes from one-time-event sources. In 2020, these sources accounted for 83.6 percent of total land- and property-related revenue. Recurrent property taxes continue to play an insignificant role in revenue generation for the government, accounting for less than 0.14 percent of total government revenue, or 0.03 percent of GDP in 2020.

Further Reform Is Required

Because of strong demand for government expenditure, the government budget has been in persistent deficit, which has led to a rapid buildup of public debt in the 2010s. Since 2015, ensuring medium- and long-term public finance sustainability has been a critical challenge and has heightened interest in tax reforms that would strengthen revenue mobilization.

Prospects seem bright for a well-designed property tax in Vietnam's fiscal consolidation program. The property tax has several unique advantages over other potential taxes in terms of revenue mobilization and economic efficiency. Vietnam's Five-Year National Fiscal Plan 2016–2020, approved by the National Assembly in late 2016, addressed reforming the property tax in the face of rapid urbanization. But efforts have met resistance, as detailed later.

Land and Real Estate Taxes and Charges

Under the constitution of 2013, lands are owned by the people as a whole and are public properties. Therefore, in principle, there is no transfer of a land ownership right. The state grants land use rights to land users. The state allocates or leases land to individuals and organizations through issuance of land use right certificates, which may be exchanged, transferred, mortgaged, leased, and inherited. The transfer of land use right, not land ownership right, constitutes a very special legal institution in Vietnam. In addition, the Law on Land 45/2013/QH13 permits the state to recover the allocated land by compulsory land acquisition. Such recovery must be based on a national defense or security purpose or in the national or public interest. As of the end of 2019, 84.5 percent of Vietnam's total land area of 33,131,713 hectares was classified by the government as agricultural land. Nonagricultural land accounted for 11.8 percent, and the remaining 3.7 percent is unused land (MONRE 2021).

Vietnam is unlike many jurisdictions in that the institutional arrangements for taxing land and property are stipulated in both land laws and tax laws. Before 1992, only one type of tax was collected on land—namely, an agricultural land use tax. Following the reform in land policy initiated in 1993, other land-related taxes and charges were gradually introduced. Today, there are seven types of taxes and charges on land and real estate: (1) agriculture land use tax; (2) nonagricultural land use tax; (3) income tax on the transfer of real estate; (4) registration charge; (5) land use levy; (6) land rental fee; and (7) payment upon purchase of state-owned housing. Among these, only the agricultural land use tax and the nonagricultural land use tax are recurrent property taxes. All the others relate to the acquisition or transfer of land use rights.

Agricultural Land Use Tax

The current agricultural land use tax has its roots in the agricultural tax, which was adopted in 1951 under Government Directive 031/SL. Following the introduction of the Law on Land in 1993, the National Assembly approved the Law on Agricultural Land Use Tax 23-L/CTN, which revoked all previous regulations on agricultural tax. Agricultural land use tax liability is determined by the land size, and tax rates apply to each land category, such as that used for annual harvest or long-term production. The tax rate is defined in terms of kilograms of rice per hectare and is adjusted according to the grade of land (defined on the basis of soil quality, location, weather conditions, or irrigation system). The Law on Agricultural Land Use Tax stipulates six tax rates for annual harvest land and five tax rates for long-term production land. The tax payment is made by money, which is determined by multiplying the calculated tax liability by the price of rice. The price of rice is published annually by provincial people's committees. There is also a supplementary tax of 20 percent imposed on land area exceeding the standard threshold prescribed by the provincial people's committees in accordance with land policy regulations.

Initially, the agricultural land use tax was relatively important in revenue generation for the government. In 1993, revenue from agricultural land use tax accounted for 4.2 percent of total government revenue, much higher than revenue from personal income tax and natural resource tax then. However, from 1995 to the first years of the 2000s, the nonagricultural land use tax generated less revenue for the government. This was due to a rapid expansion in revenue from other taxes compared with agricultural land use tax revenue. In addition, a policy of agricultural land use tax exemption and reduction was adopted in 2003 by the National Assembly to support farmers and rural development. In particular, agricultural land assigned to households that is under the threshold land area, to poor communes, and to agricultural cooperatives receives a 100 percent tax exemption. All other taxpayers, including owners of commercial agricultural land, receive a 50 percent tax reduction. This policy was to remain in effect until 2010 but was extended to 2020, and in July 2020, the National Assembly extended this policy to 2025. In 2020, more than 12 million taxpayers were eligible for the agricultural tax reductions and exemptions (MOF 2020). By 2020, the agricultural land use tax generated almost no revenue (see table 16.2).

Nonagricultural Land Use Tax

Before December 31, 2011, the taxation of nonagricultural land and housing was governed by the 1992 Ordinance of Land and Housing Tax 69-LCT/HDNN8. However, despite the ordinance's name, Article 1 stipulated, "In [the] current situation, temporarily do not collect tax on housing" (Le 2018, 90). As a result, the tax base was confined to only nonagricultural land, including residential, commercial, and industrial land.

Certain types of land were exempted from paying the tax, such as land used for public interest, social welfare, or charity. The taxpayers were organizations and individuals who had the right to use taxable land. Tax liabilities were calculated on the basis of land area, land grade, and the applicable tax rate. There were 10 tax rates, depending on land types. Each tax rate is defined as a multiple (from three to thirty-two times) of agricultural land use tax rate applied to agricultural land of the highest grade in the local area. Therefore, the tax base was effectively linked with the price of rice, as discussed in the preceding, and not the value of the land. Revenue generated from this tax was extremely low (MOF 2021).

Since 2010, with the adoption of the Law on Nonagricultural Land Use Tax 48/2010/QH12, which replaced the previous Ordinance on Land and Housing Tax 69-LCT/HDNN8, there have been significant changes in the taxation of nonagricultural land, especially on the tax base, assessment mechanisms, and tax rate structure. These regulations took effect on January 1, 2012. The major features of the 2010 law are highlighted in the following.

Tax Base

The tax base is nonagricultural land, which includes residential, commercial, and industrial land. Nonagricultural land leased from the state and used for private purposes is also taxable. As in many other jurisdictions, certain categories of land are exempt, such as land used for public purposes, religious facilities, construction of government office buildings, or national defense and security. Any exempt land would become taxable if later used for commercial purposes or any purpose not defined as exempted. As of 2016, more than 18 million land parcels were under the coverage of nonagricultural land use tax (Pham 2017). A high percentage of these land parcels are small in size and value, especially in rural areas. This large and fragmented tax base has created an administrative burden for the local tax authorities in assessing and collecting the tax.

Taxpayers

Tax liability falls on the owners of the right to use land specified in their land use right certificate, including organizations, households, and individuals. If the certificate has not yet been issued, the current land user is considered the taxpayer. When leasing land from the state, the leaseholder is the taxpayer. If more than one person has the right to use the same parcel of land, the lawful representative is the taxpayer. As for land under dispute, the current land user is defined as the taxpayer, and tax payment is not grounds for the settlement of dispute over land use right. Business entities paying nonagricultural land use tax are eligible to deduct the amount of tax due as an expense. According to Pham (2017), there were around 17 million nonagricultural land use taxpayers in 2016, making the Law on Nonagricultural Land Use Tax 48/2010/QH12 the largest generator of tax in Vietnam in terms of number of taxpayers.

Value Assessment

Taxable value is defined as taxable land area multiplied by the price of one square meter of land. Taxable land area is the entire parcel of land allocated to the taxpayer. When the taxpayer has the right to use more than one parcel of land, the taxable area is the total of all taxable land parcels. For multistory buildings, a coefficient is used to determine the value of the land allocated to each apartment. The price of a square meter of land is based on a land price table published by the provincial people's committee (box 16.1). Valuation frequency is every five years.

With the introduction of the Law on Nonagricultural Land Use Tax 48/2010/QH12, Vietnam made the important shift from using the price of rice as the valuation basis to a more market value–based approach, which

---

Box 16.1. DEVELOPMENT OF LAND PRICE FRAME AND LAND PRICE TABLE

The government defines a land price frame, which provides the highest and lowest land prices by land use category for each province. Provincial departments of Natural Resources and Environment use the land price frame to formulate a land price table applicable in their jurisdictions. The land price table is submitted to the provincial people's committee, which is a state administrative agency. This exercise is completed before January 1 of the first year in a five-year cycle.

Before submission to the provincial people's committee, the land price table is reviewed by the committee's Land Price Appraisal Council, chaired by the president or a vice president of the committee. The land price table is also submitted to the provincial people's council for consideration before promulgation. The Law on Land 45/2013/QH13 allows consultancy on the development or adjustment of the land price frames or land price tables, and organizations licensed to provide land valuation services may be contracted by a provincial Department of Natural Resources and Environment to develop the land price table. The prices in the table are used in the calculation of nonagricultural land use tax liabilities and other taxes involved in the transfer of property.

---

is better for both efficiency and equity reasons. The remaining challenge for Vietnam is how to better correlate the land value used for tax purposes to the actual market value of land—that is, improve the assessment ratio. This would require significant changes in land legislation, especially in the land pricing mechanism as discussed later in this chapter.

Tax Rates

The nonagricultural land use tax in Vietnam is a central-government tax. The National Assembly sets the tax rates. Local governments have no discretion in changing the tax rate applied in their jurisdictions. A uniform standard tax rate of 0.03 percent is applied to both residential land under the standard land area threshold and nonresidential land.

As shown in table 16.3, residential landholdings exceeding the standard land area threshold prescribed by the provincial people's committee are taxed at a higher rate in accordance with a partially progressive rate structure, ranging up to 0.15 percent for a landholding greater than three times the threshold. The tax rates are the same for commercial and residential land use. Higher tax rates are applied to lands used improperly or vacant land. Illegally occupied lands are subject to the highest tax rate of 0.2 percent.

Table 16.3 Nonagricultural Land Use Tax Rates

Taxable Land Area	Tax Rate (%)
Area less than standard threshold	0.03
Area between the threshold and three times the threshold	0.07
Area greater than three times the threshold	0.15
Land use for underground works and high-rise apartments	0.03
Commercial and industrial land	0.03
Land use for inappropriate purposes	0.15
Illegally occupied or invaded land	0.20

Source: Law on Nonagricultural Land Use Tax 48/2010/QH12.

Note: Different thresholds for land area apply to rural and urban areas.

The rationale for choosing a standard tax rate of 0.03 percent was that it would maintain a tax liability equivalent to that under the Ordinance on Housing and Land Tax 69-LCT/HDNN8. In contrast, the objective of the progressive rate structure on residential land was to reduce land speculation and to increase land use efficiency (GOV 2009). However, as discussed later, the nonagricultural land use tax has created little revenue for the government, which means the law has had minimal effect on the government's objectives.

A progressive rate structure on residential land has created a number of issues. Under the Law on Nonagricultural Land Use Tax 48/2010/QH12, the progressive rate structure is designed with respect to total landholding rather than a single parcel holding. Taxpayers may own more than one land parcel in different districts or even in different provinces. Because the standard land area thresholds vary greatly among provinces, calculating tax liabilities for these taxpayers is difficult for the local tax authorities. Information and administrative capacity are needed to effectively link landholdings with individual taxpayers, especially when the lands are in different provinces.

The nominal tax rates on nonagricultural land are very low by international standards (Le 2018). Low tax rates together with low assessment value have led to a very low level of revenue mobilization, as discussed later. The nonagricultural land use tax is based on the land price table issued by the provincial people's committee, and the prices are normally below the market value of land. According to Ho Chi Minh City Real Estate Association (2018), the land price table for Ho Chi Minh City, the largest city in Vietnam, captures from 30 to 50 percent of market value. In 2018, on average, each nonagricultural land use taxpayer paid about VND 100,000 per year (less than USD 4.50), which was extremely low. For taxpayer households in rural and mountainous areas, and some other groups of tax-payers, the cost of collecting and administrating nonagricultural land use tax is considerably higher than the amount of tax collected. High administrative costs and little revenue collected have led to the nonagricultural land use tax becoming one of Vietnam's most inefficient taxes.

The minimal revenue from nonagricultural land use tax for local governments can be seen in Hanoi (table 16.4). Hanoi, population 7,523,000, is the second-largest city in Vietnam and has experienced rapid urbanization in this century, but its government collects very little from recurrent property tax. Revenues from property tax covered less than 1 percent of budget spending. Nonagricultural land use tax collected per capita in 2016 was just VND 51,000, an extremely small amount compared with the average public spending per household of VND 13.67 million. Yet in 2016, about 27 percent of national nonagricultural land use tax revenue was collected in Hanoi. This was the largest among the provinces and cities and double that of Ho Chi Minh City.

Exemptions and Reductions

The Law on Nonagricultural Land Use Tax 48/2010/QH12 contains an extensive list of land use tax exemptions and reductions as investment promotion measures and to meet social objectives. In particular, Article 9 lists nine types of exemptions and preferential treatments, with both public and private business entities eligible for them. For example, business entities providing public services such as education, vocational training, or health care, including private schools and hospitals, are exempt from paying the land use tax. Residential land below the standard land area threshold in regions with difficult socioeconomic conditions or used by poor households are also exempt. In addition, a 50 percent reduction is applied to investment projects in sectors eligible for investment promotion or projects in socioeconomic difficult regions.

Table 16.4 Hanoi's Revenue and Nonagricultural Land Use Tax, 2016

Total revenue (VND billion)	119,816
Land use levy (VND billion)	26,220
Total expenditure (VND billion)	103,043
Nonagricultural land use tax revenue (VND billion)	386
Nonagricultural land use tax revenue per capita (VND thousand)	51
Nonagricultural land use tax as % of total revenue	0.32
Nonagricultural land use tax as % of expenditure	0.37

Sources: Hanoi Statistics Office (2019); MOF (2019).

According to Pham (2017), total revenue forgone because of nonagricultural land use tax exemptions and reductions in 2016 was VND 157 billion, or 11 percent of total revenue from this tax. Residential land owned by individual taxpayers accounted for around 75 percent of total tax revenue forgone, and industrial and commercial land for most of the remainder. However, the actual revenue forgone is likely higher than this estimated amount. Few data relating to the revenue costs of tax incentives are available. There is always a lack of adequate data to identify and quantify the revenue loss and other implications of tax incentives, including nonagricultural land use tax exemptions and reductions. The concept of tax expenditures is also rather new in Vietnam (Truong 2018).

In addition, since July 1, 2016, with the enactment of the Law 106/2016/QH13, households and individuals who incurred an annual nonagricultural land use tax liability of less than VND 50,000 are exempted from paying the tax. This change was made to reduce the administrative costs of collecting nonagricultural land use tax of small amounts and to support low-income taxpayers. These taxpayers account for around 75 percent of the total number of nonagricultural land use taxpayers but generate less than 10 percent of the collected revenue. Total revenue collected from this group of taxpayers was just VND 159 billion, or USD 7 million (GOV 2015). Although all nonagricultural land use taxpayers on the tax roll are assessed, only the taxpayers owing more than VND 50,000 receive tax payment notifications. In 2019, this exemption policy was incorporated in the Law on Tax Administration 38/2019/QH14.

Administration and Collection

More than 17 million taxpayers are subject to the nonagricultural land use tax (MOF 2018b). The total land area of the tax's coverage by households and legal entities is 46,200 km^2 and 1,200 km^2, respectively (Pham 2017). Article 8 of the Law on Nonagricultural Land Use Tax 48/2010/QH12 explicitly requires taxpayers to register, declare, calculate and pay tax under the Law on Tax Administration (Le 2018). Calculating the tax liability is complex, and Circular 153/2011/TT-BTC of the Ministry of Finance elaborated on the declaration, calculation, and payment of the nonagricultural land use tax: taxpayers are responsible for declaring the property and giving description information on the property, such as location, land area, and land use in the nonagricultural land use tax declaration form. On the basis of the information provided by the taxpayers, the tax liability is calculated by the local tax authorities by applying appropriate tax rate and assessment values. A tax payment notification then will be issued and sent to the taxpayers.

The General Taxation Department collects the nonagricultural land use tax, and all types of taxes, but can authorize other agencies to collect on its behalf for certain types of tax and for tax delinquency. This authorization is carried out through a contract between local tax authorities and the collecting agencies. The communes' people's committees, which are an arm of the local government, are normally the collecting agencies. The authorized collecting agency is entitled to a collection fee, which is a percentage of the collected revenue, ranging from 5 percent to 8 percent, depending on the region. The highest rate of 8 percent applies to the mountainous provinces in the northern region and the provinces in the Central Highlands. For Hanoi and Ho Chi Minh City, the rate is 5 percent. The rate for the remaining provinces and cities is 6 percent. Collection fee proceeds go to the commune's budget. However, not many local governments are willing to make collections because the nonagricultural land use tax yields very low revenue, and the collection fee is very small.

Tax on Transfer of Land Use Right

Following the 1993 changes in land policy, the National Assembly in 1994 approved the Law on Land Use Right Transfer Tax 35-L/CTN, under which individuals, organizations, and business entities pay a tax on the transfer of a land use right. As the name indicates, the tax was applied only to the transfer of land use right, not the improvement on land, such as buildings. This tax had the characteristics of a transfer tax on land as found in other jurisdictions. The taxable value was based on the value of land use right, which was calculated on the basis of land area and land price as determined by the provincial people's committee. Originally, there were five tax rates, ranging from 5 percent to 30 percent. In 1999, the tax rate structure was simplified and reduced significantly to 2 percent for the transfer of agricultural land use right and 4 percent for the transfer of other types of land use right. This change was made with a view to reduce the undocumented transactions that avoided the tax, because the previous rates were considered relatively high. In 2003, enactment of the Law on Corporate Income Tax 09/2003/QH11 changed the approach of taxing income from transfers of land use right. In particular, as of January 1, 2004, business entities were no longer subject to the land use right transfer tax, but they were required to pay income tax on the capital gains from transfers of real estate, including lands and buildings. The tax is levied on the difference between the selling price and the original price and allowable expenses. The tax rate is 20 percent, which is the same as the tax rate applied to other types of business income.

Starting January 1, 2009, in accordance with the Law on Personal Income Tax 04/2007/QH12, individuals having income from the transfer of real estate, including land use rights, were subject to personal income tax instead of paying the tax on the transfer of land use rights. Originally, there were two options for paying the tax. The first was to pay the tax on the basis of the net gain, which was the sale proceeds minus the original purchase costs of the real estate and related expenses. The second option applied if taxable capital gain income could not be determined, such as when information on the original purchase price of the real estate was not available. In these cases, a tax rate of 2 percent was imposed on value of sale proceeds.

In 2015, the first option, to declare and pay personal income tax on the basis of the net gain, was abolished to simplify the method of taxing income from real estate transfer of individuals. The sale proceeds are now determined on the basis of the transaction value in transfer contracts. If the value stipulated in the contract is lower than the value determined by the provincial people's committee, the tax liability is based on the land price table and house price provided by the provincial people's committee. This revision was made to deal with underdeclaration of sale proceeds by people to reduce their tax obligation. Indeed, the revenue collected from transfers of real estate by individuals jumped by 41.6 percent in 2015.

Registration Charge

A registration charge was introduced in Vietnam in 1987. In addition to incurring income tax, the transfer of land and houses is subject to a registration charge, imposed on the buyer upon registration of the title. The registration charge is regulated by the Law on Fee and Charge 97/2015/QH13 and Decree 140/2016/ND-CP of the government (amended in 2019). Unlike jurisdictions where the registration charge is based on a fixed amount, Vietnam's registration charge is 0.5 percent of the transfer value. The transfer value is determined based on land price table and housing price as stipulated by the provincial people committee. This serves as the minimum value on which the registration charge is imposed. In the case where the value stipulated in the transfer contract is higher than the value determined by using land price table and house price provided by the provincial committee, the registration charge is calculated based on the value stipulated in the contract.

To some extent, the property registration charge is a transaction tax in that the payable amount is also based on the transfer value. However, the registration charge is imposed on the buyer, not the seller, as in the land use right transfer tax discussed earlier. In addition, the maximum registration charge for a property is limited to VND 500 million. Various transfers are exempted from paying the registration charge, including transferring land and houses among family members or transferring land for public use. In 2020, the registration charge on the transfer of land and houses accounted for 0.42 percent of total government revenue and 2.51 percent of total land- and property-related revenue (MOF 2021).

Land Use Levy

In 1987, the first Law on Land was approved by the National Assembly, and land use rights were assigned to individuals and households for a period of up to fifteen years. However, such a land use right was not tradable until 1993, when the Law on Land 24-L/CTN was enacted. Now, land use rights may be inherited, transferred, exchanged, leased, or mortgaged. This law recognizes that land has value and that the state has the right to collect a land use levy when assigning land to individuals, households, organizations, or business entities.

The collection of a land use levy was based on a pilot program in Ba Ria–Vung Tau Province in 1991 to mobilize financial resources for infrastructure development (Le 2018). The way the land use levy is imposed has changed, especially how the base of the levy is calculated. According to the Law on Land 45/2013/QH13, a land use levy is collected when the state allocates land for use by individuals, business entities, or organizations or when a land use purpose changes, such as when converting from agricultural land to nonagricultural land or converting from a levy-free allocated land use to a levy-paid one. For the latter, the collection of the land use levy may not involve the change of ownership, as it does for collecting tax on transfer of land use rights.

In addition, as stipulated in the Law on Land 45/2013/QH13 and Decree 45/2014/ND-CP, the land use levy is reduced or exempted to promote investment or for social objectives, such as the development of private schools, hospitals, or social housing. In 2016, total revenue forgone because of these exemptions and reductions was VND 3,802 billion, accounting for 3.85 percent of land use levy revenue (Truong 2018).

The levy on land use rights is determined by a number of factors, including land use purpose, land area, land price, and the terms of the land use. Previously, the land use levy was based on the land price table, whose prices are normally below the market value. With the changes in land legislation, other mechanisms to determine the land use levy have been gradually added. One mechanism uses the land price table, or the specific land price determined by the provincial people's committee. Another

mechanism uses a competitive auction process. The Law on Land 45/2013/
QH13 clearly specifies which cases will use the land price table, specific
land prices, or competitive auctions. The majority of the land use levy is
collected according to specific land prices or through auctions.

In terms of revenue generation, since its introduction in 1994, the land
use levy has gradually become the most important revenue source for local governments. In 2019, the share of the land use levy revenue in total
local-government revenue was 21.7 percent. This ratio tends to be higher
in large cities, such as Hanoi and Ho Chi Minh City.

Land Rental Fee

In 1993, with the adoption of the Law on Land 24-L/CTN, lease of land
use right was first allowed in Vietnam. Since then, land rental policy has
been extensively amended. Land rental is collected when the government
leases lands to organizations, business entities, or households and individuals for commercial uses. However, individuals or business entities
that lease land from the state do not have the right to transfer this land
use right.

Land rental amount is based on factors including land area, lease term,
rental tariff, and the type of land lease. The rental tariff is determined as
a percentage of the specific land price stipulated by the provincial government or through an auction. The rent can be paid annually or prepaid
in full for the whole duration of the lease term. There is always a limit on
the lease term, depending on the land use purposes. The maximum lease
term for commercial and industrial land is 70 years. Individuals and business entities who lease land from the government are also liable to pay the
nonagricultural land use tax discussed earlier.

As with other sources of revenue from land, land rental revenue remains
local. There is some discretion granted to the provincial government in
reducing the land rental tariff as a fiscal instrument for investment pro-
motions. According to the Ministry of Finance, total revenue forgone
because of land rental exemptions and reductions in 2016 was about VND
7,875 billion, or 33.34 percent of total land rental revenue. Land rental exemption and reduction policy is one of the most expensive investment
promotion instruments in terms of revenue forgone, ranking just after corporate income tax incentives (Truong 2018).

Payment on Purchase of State-Owned Housing Stock

Vietnam is transitioning from a centrally planned to a market-oriented
economy. In the past, certain public employees were eligible to rent houses
from the state. In 1994, the government adopted Decree 61/ND-CP to

sell the state housing stock. Under this program, those leasing state-owned housing units, mostly housing stock in large cities, could buy their houses from the state and also acquire the land use right. Since this program began, more than 90 percent of the state-owned housing stock has been sold.

All revenue collected from these sales is kept by the local governments. Initially, sales of state-owned housing stock generated significant revenue for local governments. As time went on, the number of houses being sold dropped significantly and revenues also. New-house purchases are also taxable under the provisions of the Law on Nonagricultural Land Use Tax 48/2010/QH12 similar to other residential properties.

Analysis of Land and Property Revenue

From 2012 to 2020, when detailed data are available, land- and property-related revenue averaged about 2.94 percent of GDP per year, equivalent to 11.9 percent of total government revenue. As indicated in table 16.5 (and see table 16.1), land- and property-related tax revenue has increased significantly in the 2010s. However, there is a very strong reliance on one-time-event revenue sources. In 2020, the land use levy accounted for nearly 67.7 percent of total land- and property-related revenue (MOF 2021). This poses great concerns about the sustainability of revenue from land, because the supply of land is limited.

For more than two decades, Vietnam has made substantial efforts to decentralize its public finance system.[2] This was mandated in large part by the Law on State Budget 47-L/CTN approved by the National Assembly in 1996 and its revisions in 1998 and 2002. In 2015, the Law on State Budget 83/2015/QH13 was passed by the National Assembly and has brought important changes to budgetary management, such as setting a medium-term fiscal framework, moving toward performance-based budgeting, and strengthening fiscal autonomy of local governments. The Law on State Budget 83/2015/QH13 has established key principles and a framework for spending assignment, revenue sharing, and intergovernmental fiscal transfers.

Table 16.5 Land- and Property-Related Revenue

	2012	2015	2018	2019	2020
As % of total government revenue	8.6	10.0	15.0	14.9	16.9
As % of GDP	2.0	2.4	3.9	3.8	4.1

Sources: GSO (2021); MOF (2021); calculations by the author.

In terms of revenue assignment, under the Law on State Budget 83/2015/ QH13, 20 revenue items are assigned as own revenue sources for local budgets, including license tax, natural resource tax (except from crude oil), lottery, nonagricultural land use tax, agricultural land use tax, land rental, land use levy, and user fees and charges. However, local authorities currently have very little autonomy over their revenue sources. All the tax bases and tax rates are centrally determined. They have discretion only to set certain types of user fees and charges under the provisions of the Law on Fee and Charge 97/2015/QH13. However, provincial legislative bodies (the provincial people's councils) possess delegated authority to decide on how to share the revenue from land- and property-related taxes or charges among the three levels of local government. Consequently, the sharing mechanisms vary greatly among provinces.

In some provinces, certain land and property revenue items are assigned exclusively to the district budget or commune budget, but in other provinces, they are retained at the provincial-level budget. For example, in Hanoi, nonagricultural land use tax revenue collected from households is allocated exclusively to the commune budget, but in Ho Chi Minh City, it is shared between district and commune budgets. In both cities, nonagricultural land use tax revenue collected from business entities is allocated to the district budgets. In most provinces, revenue from land use levies and land rental are assigned to the provincial budget. These two sources of revenue account for the largest shares in total revenue from land and property taxes. District and commune budgets are financed with smaller revenue-yielding items, such as agricultural land use tax, nonagricultural land use tax, or property registration charges.

Land- and property-related revenue is divided into three categories: one-time-event revenue, recurrent revenue, and transfer revenue. Tables 16.5, 16.6, and 16.7 show key trends from 2012 through 2020.

One-Time-Event Revenue

One-time-event revenue accounts for more than 80 percent of total revenue from land and property transactions. In 2020, this source of revenue was about 3.4 percent of GDP (table 16.6), which is high compared with other Asian jurisdictions. One-time-event revenue is composed of the land use levy (2.74 percent of GDP); land rental revenue (0.63 percent of GDP), which has increased sharply in recent years because of adjustments in land rental policies and the expansion of land available for rent; and proceeds from sales of state-owned housing (0.02 percent of GDP).

Revenue from land and property transactions as part of total revenue is shown in table 16.7.

Table 16.6 Land- and Property-Related Revenue by Item (% GDP)

	2012	2015	2018	2019	2020
One-time-event revenue	**1.63**	**2.01**	**3.23**	**3.13**	**3.39**
Land use levy	1.39	1.65	2.67	2.55	2.74
Sale of state-owned housing	0.05	0.05	0.05	0.03	0.02
Land rental	0.19	0.32	0.51	0.56	0.63
Transfer tax revenue	**0.30**	**0.37**	**0.61**	**0.67**	**0.63**
Registration charge	0.04	0.07	0.10	0.01	0.10
Income tax on real estate transfer	0.25	0.30	0.51	0.57	0.53
Recurrent revenue	**0.04**	**0.04**	**0.03**	**0.03**	**0.03**
Agricultural land use tax	0.00	0.00	0.00	0.00	0.00
Nonagricultural land use tax	0.04	0.04	0.03	0.03	0.03
Total land- and property-related revenue	**2.0**	**2.4**	**3.9**	**3.8**	**4.1**

Sources: MOF (2018, 2021); calculations by the author.

Table 16.7 Structure of Land- and Property-Related Revenue (% of total)

	2012	2015	2018	2019	2020
One-time-event revenue	**83.0**	**83.2**	**83.4**	**81.7**	**83.6**
Land use levy	70.7	68.0	68.9	66.5	67.7
Sale of state-owned housing	2.7	2.0	1.2	0.7	0.6
Land rental	9.6	13.3	13.3	14.6	15.4
Transfer tax revenue	**15.0**	**15.3**	**15.7**	**17.4**	**15.5**
Registration charge	2.3	2.8	2.55	2.52	2.51
Income tax on real estate transfer	12.7	12.5	13.2	14.8	13.0
Business entities	6.9	5.8	7.1	8.6	6.7
Individuals	5.8	6.7	6.0	6.2	6.3
Recurrent revenue	**2.0**	**1.5**	**0.9**	**0.9**	**0.8**
Agricultural land use tax	0.1	0.1	0.0	0.0	0.0
Nonagricultural land use tax	1.9	1.5	0.9	0.9	0.8
Total land- and property-related revenue	**100.0**	**100.0**	**100.0**	**100.0**	**100.0**

Sources: MOF (2018, 2021); calculations by the author.

Both the land use levy and the land rental revenue are anticipated to decline, because of the finite supply. Another issue is the stability of the revenue yield, which is particularly important to local governments. Since its introduction in 1993, land use levy revenue has fluctuated from year to year and is unpredictable. This source of revenue tends to be high in times when the real estate market is booming, such as late in the first decade of the 2000s. In addition, as noted earlier, land rent can be paid annually or in a lump sum; most lessees pay the lump sum. With limited land available, the policy of allowing payment for the whole duration of the lease might affect intergenerational equity. Although this practice tends to benefit the current government, it may create fiscal burdens for future governments. Future local governments will be expected to provide basic infrastructure and services for land that was leased by a past government, and land whose lease payments are long gone. The potential benefits of an effective recurrent property tax regime for Vietnam are becoming clearer.

Property Transfer Tax Revenue

Individuals or business entities that transfer or register their land use right and houses pay a property transfer tax. This revenue includes income tax on real estate transfer and registration charge. The real estate transfer tax, similar to the capital gains tax imposed in other jurisdictions, accounts for about 13 percent of total land- and property-related revenue in 2020 and is equivalent to about 0.45 percent of GDP. In 2020, income tax on real estate transfers accounted for 83.9 percent of total transfer revenue, and the rest (16.1 percent) came from registration charges. Because of changes in the scope and method of taxing discussed earlier, revenue from this tax fluctuated year to year in the 2010s.

Recurrent Property Tax Revenue

Recurrent property taxes include the agricultural land use tax and nonagricultural land use tax. As the laws have changed and as Vietnam has urbanized, recurrent property revenue importance has shifted to the nonagricultural land use tax. In the early 1990s, revenue from land and property was derived almost exclusively from the agricultural land use tax.[3]

The Law on Nonagriculture Land Use Tax 48/2010/QH12 had the objective of improving revenue mobilization; however, it has not led to any noticeable improvement in recurrent property tax revenue. The role of recurrent property tax revenue has steadily declined since 2012 (see table 16.6). Revenues fell from the equivalent of 1.2 percent of GDP in 1992 to 0.03 percent in 2020 (MOF 2021).

Most nonagricultural land use tax revenue is collected in urban and economically well-developed areas. In 2019, the top 10 provinces and cities with the largest revenue from this nonagricultural land use tax accounted for 71.7 percent of the total. More specifically, the amount of nonagricultural land use tax revenue collected in Hanoi and Ho Chi Minh City accounted for 26.7 percent and 20.4 percent, respectively. The remaining 53 cities and provinces accounted for less than 45 percent of the total nonagricultural land use tax revenue (MOF 2021).

Reforming the Property Tax: A Way Forward

The long-term history of land and property taxation in Vietnam has been one of an emerging system shaped by socioeconomic, political, and governance changes. As the preceding sections have made clear, now may be an opportune time for another sea change in the property tax regime—the establishment of a more revenue-productive recurrent property tax system. This section addresses the potential of such a reform.

The Case for Reform

Real property and land taxation in Vietnam began modernizing at the end of the last century in terms of how the base is defined and measured. It has taken an important place in the national tax system of revenue mobilization, and it can strongly influence land use outcomes. However, further reform of the property tax system is needed, for both fiscal and economic reasons.

Further Legislation on the Recurrent Property Tax

From a legal perspective, it is not only necessary but also timely to review the legislation on the recurrent property tax, including the Law on Agricultural Land Use Tax 23-L/CTN, and the Law on Nonagricultural Land Use Tax 48/2010/QH12. Property taxes are implemented in almost all jurisdictions (Bird and Slack 2004) and offer advantages over other taxes in terms of revenue generation for the local governments, equity, and economic efficiency (Bahl and Martinez-Vazquez 2007). The 2010 Law on Nonagricultural Land Use Tax 48/2010/QH12 was intended to improve revenue mobilization for the local governments, to promote efficient land use, and to strengthen state management on land (GOV 2009), but it failed to produce these results, especially that of revenue mobilization.

Because of a narrow tax base, many tax exemptions and preferential treatments, low nominal tax rates, and inadequate valuation mechanisms, the nonagricultural land use tax remains a minor tax. In particular, the standard legal tax rate of 0.03 percent is very low by international standards. A rigid land value tax assessment mechanism has also led to a very low assessment ratio. Using the prescribed land price table for assessing land value for taxing purposes has limited local-government ability to capture increased real estate values resulting from economic growth and infrastructure development. Consequently, local governments have relied more on revenue from one-time property transactions or from intergovernmental transfers from upper-level governments to finance local infrastructure and public services.

The Law on Agricultural Land Use Tax 23-L/CTN has had less effect since 2003, when the tax exemption and reduction program was introduced. Although exempting subsistence farms and small-scale agricultural land use can often be justified, excluding large-scale commercial agricultural land use has no good rationale. Vietnam should revise the tax laws on agricultural and nonagricultural land use. Review of land- and property-related taxes has begun by the government and the National Assembly—for example, the Tax System Reform Strategy 2011–2020 and the Five-Year National Fiscal Plan 2016–2020.

Tax Revenue Mobilization

With a persistent budget deficit and rising public debt, Vietnam needs to increase its tax revenue mobilization effort. Government revenue as a percentage of GDP is a respectable 25 percent, and property taxes are at a respectable percentage of GDP. However, reliance on unsustainable capital revenue and nontax revenue, such as state-owned enterprise divestment proceeds and one-time property transaction revenue, increases. Pressure for more public spending for both capital and recurrent purposes is unrelenting (Truong and Dao 2018). Vietnam is undergoing a demographic transition with a rapidly aging population, which will create demand for public services. Rapid urbanization will also lead to greater demand for infrastructure development to improve the jurisdiction's competitiveness, whereas tax revenues will be reduced by continuing trade liberalization. Furthermore, outstanding public debt has increased significantly in the 2010s (Truong and Dao 2018).

In this context, reforming the tax system to strengthen government revenue mobilization is a critical issue. Property tax is a good candidate for increasing tax revenue given that the share of urban population in Vietnam has increased from 25 percent to more than 35 percent in the last 15 years (GSO 2021). Land value is also rapidly increasing.

Although land- and property-related revenue has played an important role in the government budget, it has been overshadowed by revenue from the land use levy and land rental fees. These taxes have some characteristics of capital revenue, but both the land use levy and land rental fees will phase out naturally when all vacant land is fully used or when all land use right certificates are issued.

Land use levy revenue from the conversion of agricultural land to commercial and residential land will fall in the future, because the stock of land available for the conversion is limited. According to the General Department of Land Administration (2019), as of 2018, most land in Vietnam has already been issued land use right certificates (92.9 percent of agricultural land, 98.3 percent of urban residential land, 96.1 percent of rural residential land, and 98.2 percent of forest land).

To ensure fiscal sustainability, Vietnam should consider a stronger and more stable, efficient, and equitable annual property tax. Rapid urbanization in this century has generated substantial new private wealth because a large part of agricultural land has been converted to residential and commercial land use. However, both the tax rate and the valuation ratio are low, and the existing recurrent property tax system has not captured the increase in the land value, especially in large cities.

Fiscal Decentralization

Continuing progress toward fiscal decentralization is necessary. Since the start of the economic reform in the 1980s, a variety of measures to promote fiscal decentralization have been introduced. The principles for spending assignments, revenue arrangements, and intergovernmental fiscal transfers all are stipulated in the Law on State Budget 83/2015/QH13. Compared with many other jurisdictions in the region, Vietnam is a highly decentralized jurisdiction (World Bank and Government of Vietnam 2017), and provincial governments have considerable autonomy in shaping local policies and managing their fiscal resources. However, Vietnam's type of decentralization is more *deconcentration* than *devolution*. In 2017, local governments were responsible for more than three-fourths of total capital spending and over half of total recurrent spending.

The fiscal autonomy of local governments (provincial, district, and commune) in revenue raising is very limited. They cannot impose taxes or fees that fall outside the regulations of central government. All revenue from the agricultural land use tax and from the nonagricultural land use tax is allocated to local governments, but those taxes yield little revenue. The recurrent property tax as a measure to promote fiscal decentralization has not been effectively explored, especially in terms of how it might be used to improve the fiscal autonomy of local governments.

Local governments must find the resources to finance public infrastructure and services essential to support their rapidly urbanizing populations. Local governments need a stable revenue source to provide an appropriate level of public services to their citizens. A stronger recurrent property tax could be part of the answer to this revenue gap. The government has made substantial infrastructure investment, leading to rapid increases in land and property values, but the mechanism to recapture part of this value increase is inadequate.

Property Tax Reform Initiatives

The government of Vietnam has been exploring a house and land tax since 2008. In September 2009, a draft Law on Housing and Land Tax was submitted to the National Assembly for consideration. The draft proposed including both land and buildings in the tax base but not industrial and commercial buildings and more heavily taxing land than residential buildings (GOV 2009). However, the National Assembly opposed parts of the draft, especially the proposal to tax residential buildings. Consequently, the Standing Committee of the National Assembly omitted buildings in the tax base, effectively opting to tax only land. The committee also changed the name of the law to reflect its definition of tax base (SCNA 2010). Consequently, the Law on Nonagricultural Land Use Tax 48/2010/QH12 was approved by the National Assembly in late 2010.

In 2018, a second attempt to reform the property tax in Vietnam was initiated by the Ministry of Finance. The proposal reiterated the necessity for establishing a new property tax system and called for including both land and buildings in the tax base. Land and buildings were proposed to be taxed separately by different assessment methods: land value would remain subject to assessment under the nonagricultural land use tax, and buildings would be assessed on the basis of standard construction cost norms issued by the Ministry of Construction for each class of buildings—for example, villa or high-rise apartment. There were also allowances for depreciation of old buildings.

The Ministry of Finance proposed limiting the taxation of buildings to those whose value exceeded a certain threshold. The ministry gave two options for consideration in the draft: a construction value of more than VND 700 million, and a construction value of VND 1 billion. No exemption threshold was proposed for land. This tax rate structure would have taxed land and buildings at the same rate. There were also two options for the standard tax rate: 0.3 percent or 0.4 percent. Unused land and illegally occupied lands would be taxed at higher rates than the existing nonagricultural land use tax regime. Residential land would be taxed at more than 10 times the current rate of 0.03 percent. According to the Ministry of Finance (MOF 2018a), the proposed tax would have strengthened revenue mobilization from land and buildings by more than 12 times the existing nonagricultural land use tax regime. In particular, the tax on buildings worth more than VND 700 million would have brought in between VND 23.3 trillion and VND 31 trillion per year, depending on which options for the tax rate and deduction threshold were selected. The Ministry of Finance favored the more revenue-productive option of taxing residential buildings worth more than VND 700 million at the tax rate of 0.3 percent, arguing that selecting the other option would eliminate 80–90 percent of residential buildings from the tax base (MOF 2018a).

Again, controversy erupted over the proposed tax. The media, real estate industry, and academia reacted strongly to the proposal, especially on what buildings to include in the tax base. Some thought the tax was too weak because the proposed exemption threshold on buildings was too low, whereas others thought that taxing buildings would negatively impact low-income homeowners. Some thought all owner-occupied houses should be exempted. Faced with strong reactions from the public, the ministry withdrew the proposal. Opposition to changing property taxation is commonplace. People object to higher property taxes. This underlines the need for an effective public awareness campaign to ensure that relevant stakeholders are fully informed about the impacts of proposed policy changes.

Options for Reform

Reforming the property tax system involves defining the tax base, taxpayers (owner, occupier, or beneficiary), and structure of the tax rate; deciding on the assessment basis (area or ad valorem); finding a valuation approach to use; and finally, improving tax administration. International experience suggests great diversity in the property tax regimes that depend on legal and institutional systems, administration structures, and historical legacies of taxing land and buildings. Improving revenue from property taxation has enormous potential if the tax is properly designed. Building on this chapter's analysis of existing land- and property-related taxes and learning from internationally best practices and from the failures of recent property tax reform initiatives, the following section discusses policy choices available for reforming Vietnam's property tax system.

Property Tax Base

Some jurisdictions tax only land, others tax only buildings, and others tax both land and buildings (Bird and Slack 2004). Each tax base definition has advantages and disadvantages. The choice of the tax base depends on practical reasons, such as the availability of data on land and buildings. If buildings are included in the tax base, building information must be identified, collected, and managed and buildings must be valued. Taxing both land and buildings is more administratively costly. Although using construction cost norms for the calculation of the tax base of buildings, as in the recent two reform initiatives in Vietnam, is easier and cheaper to do, it may not result in a correct estimate of the current market value of the buildings. In addition, under the existing institutional arrangements in Vietnam, the determination of land value for tax purposes is the responsibility of the provincial people's committees. In assessing land value, local tax authorities are not required to develop separate land valuation mechanisms. However, if buildings are included in the tax base, the local tax authorities will likely be required to assess the value of buildings on the basis of the market information on buildings or of standard construction cost norms developed by the Ministry of Construction.

Little market information on the value of the building stock exists, and thus Vietnam should not tax buildings until administrative capacities of the local tax authorities improve enough to accurately assess buildings' market value. Any property tax reform initiative should focus on the consolidation, rationalization, and modernization of the existing two current taxes on land. The Ministry of Finance plans to propose a new law on property tax in 2023 or 2024. Restricting the reform to these two land taxes would make it more acceptable because people are familiar with paying the land tax.

To eliminate the negative impacts of property tax on low-income households and farmers and to reduce the administrative costs for the tax authorities, the reform could introduce a threshold to eliminate low-value residential land from the tax base. The threshold should be established with respect to property value rather than the amount of tax payable, which is the stipulation in the current Law on Tax Administration 38/2019/QH14. A tax-exempt threshold will eliminate low-value land from the tax base, especially in rural areas. In addition, small-scale agricultural land use should be also exempted from paying the tax.

Unlike other tax liabilities, property tax liability is visible, and it is billed periodically (Bahl and Martinez-Vazquez 2007). This makes property tax reform very difficult because property owners are more likely to know exactly what they have to pay. There is also no direct relationship between tax liability and the capacity to pay it. Some—the poor and certain of the elderly—are unable to pay the tax. Thresholds that eliminate low-value residential land from property tax coverage would help this issue. Owners of low-value property tend to benefit more from thresholds, which will make the new tax more acceptable and improve its chances.

Over time, as the real estate market matures and more information on market value for buildings becomes available, the tax base can be expanded to include buildings. The expansion should be restricted to residential buildings, at least initially. It is much more difficult to assess nonresidential building value than residential building, and taxing commercial and industrial buildings may hurt ongoing efforts of the government to improve the business environment and reduce the cost of doing business.

Because taxing buildings is a multifaceted challenge, a pilot program could help. Vietnam could choose its five largest cities, Hanoi, Haiphong, Da Nang, Can Tho, and Ho Chi Minh City, to take part in such a pilot program. Their rapid urbanization has great potential to increase revenue from land and buildings. The pilot program would identify problems and issues before rolling out nationally.

Property Tax Exemptions

When designing property tax structures, the experts try to minimize revenue loss, administration complications, and possibly opening doors to political favorites. However, in every jurisdiction, some types of property are excluded from the tax base according to a variety of factors (Bird and Slack 2004). These factors include ownership (e.g., government-owned property, public parks and schools, or properties owned by international organizations), property use (e.g., for farming, health, education, or charitable purposes), or sociodemographic characteristics of property owners (e.g., the aged or the disabled). Vietnam is not an exception to this practice. The Law on Nonagricultural Land Use Tax 48/2010/QH12 lists many tax exemptions and reductions. These exemptions have substantially reduced the property tax revenue. According to Pham (2017), revenue forgone from 2012 to 2016 accounted for 10–11 percent of total revenue collected from the nonagricultural land use tax. Exemptions and reductions introduced in 2003 have also dramatically reduced the revenue from the agriculture land use tax. In 2016, the revenue forgone because of these exemptions and reductions was VND 6,869 billion, or 0.61 percent of total government revenue (MOF 2020).

The larger the tax base, the lower the tax rate for an equivalent amount of revenue. Therefore, when consolidating the two recurrent property taxes, the size of the tax base should be as broad as possible. Tax exemptions should be reviewed carefully and regularly to avoid revenue loss. Even well-intentioned exemptions must be reviewed to ensure that the intended objectives are being achieved. In the 2018 property tax reform discussed earlier, agricultural land would have received a permanent exemption. The exemption of small-scale agricultural land may be justified as support for low-income farmers or to reduce administrative costs of taxing low-value land. However, excluding large agricultural lands used for commercial purposes is not justified. Exemptions should be simple, transparent, and easy to enforce. Once established, changing or removing these exemptions can be difficult. Therefore, eligibility conditions for exemptions need to be targeted and selective and be based on both theoretical and practical reasoning. To assess the costs and benefits of property tax exemptions, Vietnam should establish a reporting mechanism for local tax authorities to collect data relating to property tax exemptions, such as the number of eligible properties. This would allow the government to estimate the revenue forgone because of exemptions.

Property Valuation and Assessment

Property value assessment is the basis of any property tax system, and the methodology for establishing tax liability should be clear to taxpayers. The two major methods of assessment are area-based assessment and value-based assessment (Ali, Fjeldstad, and Katera 2017; Bird and Slack 2004). Market value is generally regarded as a better method because it captures the effects of location and public amenities available in the property's neighborhood.

The Law on Nonagricultural Land Use Tax 48/2010/QH12 moved from area-based assessment to value-based assessment. Under the current Law on Land 45/2013/QH13, land value could be determined from the land price table or through specific land price mechanisms, depending on the purpose. But provincial governments have little leeway in adjusting the land price tables to reflect the local market conditions. In contrast, specific land prices are determined on a case-by-case basis after investigation and according to collection of information about land parcels, overall market land prices, and information on land prices in the land database. Specific land prices are currently used for calculation of land use levy (except some cases that use land price tables) or for calculation of land rental or compensation, but not for taxing purposes.

Using the specific price mechanism for the nonagricultural land use tax would therefore give an assessment closer to market value than would using the land price table. Most land price tables are well below the market value. As noted earlier, the land price table in Ho Chi Minh City, Vietnam's largest city, captures only between 30 percent and 50 percent of the market value.

The underestimation of land value has significantly eroded the base of the nonagricultural land use tax. To improve revenue mobilization, the existing land pricing mechanism should be reviewed to bring land assessments closer to market value. This could be done by abolishing the land price frame set in the Law on Land 45/2013/QH13 and giving local authorities more discretion in determining land value, such as by using land value zones. Vietnam should shift incrementally to a data-intensive and more market value–based assessment system. As the real estate market develops, information on land transactions will be more easily collected and analyzed, leading to improved accuracy of estimated land value. However, changes to land valuation for tax purposes must be made through land legislation, not tax legislation. Land valuation, including for tax purposes, is currently under the Ministry of Natural Resources and Environment and the provincial people's committees.

If eventually included in the tax base, buildings should also be assessed under a value-based system. In addition, land and buildings should be taxed together as a single property unit, not separately as in the 2018 proposal of the Ministry of Finance. It is difficult to disaggregate the share of each component in the total value of the property. Using standard construction cost norms as proxy for assessment value of the buildings should be avoided because construction costs do not reflect the market value of buildings. Construction cost norms do not consider the nature of building materials, leading to equity concerns. This approach has drawbacks similar to area-based assessment, because it cannot capture the difference in quality of buildings.

Land valuations (and building valuations) must be kept up to date. The more often the revaluations are carried out, the better the tax base value reflects the current market. Therefore, the five-year assessment cycle should be changed to a three-year cycle. With the five-year period, taxpayers will see a big increase in their tax obligation in the first year of the new stability period. Frequent revaluations are also important to reduce taxpayer resistance to periodic large increases in land value. The development of information technology and advances in collecting and managing the tax cadastre may help reduce the costs of revaluation of lands and buildings.

Property Tax Rate Structure

Design of the tax rate structure should consider whether different types of property (agricultural, residential, or nonresidential) should be taxed uniformly or differentially and whether the tax should have a flat or progressive rate structure. A differential tax rate structure can be justified on theoretical grounds, including benefits received or efficiency, and many jurisdictions use differential tax rates across property classes. A progressive rate structure based on land size provides an incentive for efficient use of land and limits land speculation. However, jurisdictions with a very low statutory tax rate and low assessment ratio have not achieved their objectives. Moreover, the resulting complexities have created difficulties for the implementation. In Vietnam, differentiating the tax rate on the basis of the size of landholding as stipulated in the Law on Nonagricultural Land Use Tax may also lead to low-value land bearing a higher tax burden.

Vietnam should carefully consider the rationale for a tax rate structure in its next property tax reform. Rather than having a system of progressive rates based on land size, Vietnam could apply a uniform rate with respect to the land parcel value to ensure that land parcels of equal value are being taxed equally. Applying a uniform tax rate could also avoid problems for mixed-use properties. Nominal and effective tax rates for both residential and nonresidential land are very low by international standards, and it is critical that Vietnam increase nominal tax rates.

Because the revenue from nonagricultural tax is extremely low, local tax authorities tend to neglect that tax. Rapid urbanization has been a lost opportunity to capture the gains from dramatic increases in land value, especially in large cities, such as Hanoi and Ho Chi Minh City. It has also increased demands on local-government budgets for investments in basic infrastructure and services. Therefore, increasing the tax rate would stimulate revenue mobilization. Higher levels of revenue would also encourage local governments to enforce the tax. In addition, even higher rates on land parcels being used inefficiently, such as vacant lands, would improve land use efficiency. Because existing tax rates are very low, increases should be gradually phased in and follow a well-defined road map. A safety net may be added for people having difficulty paying taxes.

Which level of government should determine the tax rate is another aspect of reform. Property tax rates could be determined by the central government, the local governments, or local governments within limits set by the central government (Bird and Slack 2004). Under Article 70 (4) of the 2013 constitution, the National Assembly determines tax bases and tax rates for all types of taxes; it is vested with the power "to introduce, change, or abolish taxes; to decide on the division of revenues and expenditures between the central and local budgets." Local governments have the autonomy and power to determine only certain types of fees and charges as stipulated in the Law on Fee and Charge.

Giving local governments discretion in deciding the property tax rates has several justifications. First, it could improve efficiency by linking expenditures to revenue decisions. Second, it creates more incentives for local governments to collect revenue. Finally, it strengthens local authority and encourages residents to monitor both revenue income and revenue outgo. However, giving too much autonomy to local governments could also decrease efficiency and equity. The pros outweigh the cons, and provincial governments should have some flexibility in determining the tax rates for their provinces, either as a surtax on the tax rate set by the central government or within a limit set in the tax law. Oversight on tax rates set by the local governments will ensure that revenue, equity, and efficiency objectives are met.

Tax Administration and Collection

Property taxes are difficult to administer and costly to properly administer (Bahl and Martinez-Vazquez 2007). More than other taxes, the success of property tax reform depends crucially on good administration. In Vietnam, property taxes are central taxes, and the central government collects and enforces the tax through the General Department of Taxation. Collection of all types of taxes follows the procedures set in the Law on Tax Administration 38/2019/QH14. Taxpayers are required to calculate, declare, and pay tax on nonagriculture land use in contrast with most international practice, in which the property tax is assessed by the tax authorities. Property tax should be explicitly an officially assessed tax, not a self-assessment tax. This should be explicitly stated in the property tax law by making an exception to self-assessment as required by the tax administration legislation. To ensure a high rate of compliance, property tax assessment and collection must be performed by the local tax authorities or their authorized agencies. The taxpayers may declare the property—for example, provide the owner's name and address and describe the property, such as location, land area, or land use. The local tax authorities then use this information to place a value on the property to calculate the tax liability.

A system for monitoring and recording property transfers will also be needed. Administration of the property tax should be computerized. Computerization will make data and information sharing much easier and more efficient. The required information for implementing property taxation is currently recorded and controlled by three different agencies within the government, including the Ministry of Finance, the Ministry of Construction, and the Ministry of Natural Resources and Environment. An effective property tax requires not only the involvement of local tax authorities but also better collaboration among the related local-government agencies. Some argue that, in addition to taxpayer resistance, poor tax administration and weak enforcement are the main reasons for the low revenue contribution of property tax in developing jurisdictions (Ali, Fjeldstad, and Katera 2017). Therefore, resources should be invested to promote the effective coordination and sharing of data and information required for administering and enforcing the tax among related government agencies and tax authorities at both central and local levels. In addition, it is crucially important to ensure that the sharing of data and information takes place in a timely and efficient manner.

Conditions and Sequence of Reform

Reforming the recurrent property tax requires policy choices, especially on the tax base, tax rate structure, and value assessment. Vietnam's reform faces enormous challenges. The failure of two property tax reform initiatives in the 2010s has shown that many stakeholders do not perceive the need for yet another property tax reform, or they feel that they would be adversely affected by reform. Therefore, reform requires preconditions: (1) political support and commitments to the reform, (2) taxpayer acceptability, and (3) availability of data for assessing property values.

As has been argued in the chapter, a strong tax administration for property identification, assessment, collection, and enforcement is critical to property tax reform. Success also depends on the policy choices made and the approach to reform and implementation. A well-defined road map for effectively informing stakeholders of the objectives, impacts, and sequencing of the reform is critically important.

The property tax is a good local tax. Its development can contribute to sustainability in revenue mobilization, and it can be a major source of revenue at the local-government level. Therefore, awareness of the need for reform must be increased. There should be a mechanism that links property tax revenue to a general improvement in public services at local levels. Taxpayers are more likely to accept tax obligations if they can see the link with specific infrastructure and services they benefit from.

Any policy changes will have winners and losers. Strong leadership and political will to counter opponents of tax reform are crucial. Property tax reform normally burdens higher-income people and invokes resistance from influential interest groups. Given the transition Vietnam is in, property tax reform will face even more difficulties and challenges. Both the central and the local governments will need to agree on the reform. The failure of two initiatives shows that the reason for property tax reform should be communicated as not solely to improve revenue mobilization but to allow local governments to improve public service delivery through improved mobilization and use of the property tax revenue. Public awareness and education campaigns can explain the benefits of having property tax. And the government must follow through and use the property tax revenue to improve public services in an efficient, transparent, and accountable manner.

Gradual economic reform has been used successfully in Vietnam, and tax reform should proceed in the same manner, along an orderly, incremental road map. The reform could address a new tax regime on land for consolidation, rationalization, and modernization of the existing agricultural land and nonagricultural land tax. Buildings, more complex and costly to tax, should be incorporated into the tax base only when the tax authority is able to estimate the market value of buildings with confidence. The existing tax rates are extremely low; hence, there is considerable space for their increase, but it needs to be gradual to avoid large shocks.

Conclusion

The time is right for Vietnam to reform its property tax regime. Property tax is used in developed, developing, and transition economies. In transition jurisdictions like Vietnam, urbanization is a wealth-creating process. If captured in a well-designed property tax regime, local governments will gain a sustainable source of revenue to fund the needed infrastructure and services. However, prerequisites must be met to ensure the success of the reform, including political support and commitment to the reform, taxpayer acceptance, and availability of data required to evaluate the property. A strong tax administration, including a process for property identification, assessment, collection, and enforcement, is also critical to property tax reform.

Notes

1. Throughout this chapter, one-time taxes or levies, such as acquisition or transfer taxes and charges, are distinguished from recurrent taxes, such as the traditional annual property tax.

2. Vietnam is one of a few jurisdictions that have a nested budget system of four levels: central budget and three levels of local budget (World Bank 2015). Budgets of lower government levels are part of the budget of the next higher level. Thus, the provincial budget comprises provincial and district budgets; the district budget comprises district and commune budgets; and the commune budget has no lower levels (Truong 2017).

3. On average, the agricultural land use tax accounted for 3.6% of the total government revenue in the 1990s and nonagricultural land use tax for 0.42%. However, as discussed earlier, the agriculture land use tax was effectively phased out in 2003 by the exemption and reduction program of the National Assembly.

References

Ali, M., O.-H. Fjeldstad, and L. Katera. 2017. "Property Taxation in Developing Countries." *CMI Brief* 16 (1). Bergen, Norway: Chr. Michelsen Institute.

Bahl, R., and J. Martinez-Vazquez. 2007. "The Property Tax in Developing Countries: Current Practice and Prospects." Working paper. Cambridge. MA: Lincoln Institute of Land Policy.

Bird, R., and E. Slack. 2004. "Land and Property Taxation in 25 Countries: A Comparative Review." *CESifo DICE Report* 3 (3): 34–42. https://ideas.repec.org/a/ces/ifodic/v3y2005i03p34-42.html.

General Department of Land Administration. 2019. "Annual Meeting to Review the Operation in 2019 and Developing the Working Plan for 2020 of the General Department of Land Administration." https://chuyentrangsk.monre.gov.vn/hnt ktnmt2019/ket-qua-hoat-dong/linh-vuc-chuyen-nganh/bien-doi-khi-hau .html.

GOV (Government of Vietnam). 2009. "Report to the National Assembly on the Project of the Law on Land and Housing Tax." Text No. 144/TTr-CP. Hanoi.

———. 2015. "Report to the National Assembly on the Project of the Law on the Amendment and Supplement a Number of Articles of the Law on Value Added Tax, the Law on Excise Tax, and the Law on Tax Administration." Text No. 542/TTr-CP. Hanoi.

GSO (General Statistics Office). 2021. *Statistical Year Book 2020*. Hanoi: Statistical Publishing House.

Hanoi Statistics Office. 2019. *Hanoi Statistical Year Book 2107*. Hanoi: Statistical Publishing House.

Ho Chi Minh City Real Estate Association. 2018. "Comments on Land Price Frame for the Period 2019-2024." Text No. 116/2019/CV- HoREA.

Le, T. L. 2018. "A Study on the Development of Property Tax in Vietnam." Ministerial Research Project 2017-02. Ministry of Finance. Hanoi.

MOF (Ministry of Finance). 2018a. "Proposal to the Government on the Draft Law on Property Tax." Text No. 4433/BTC-CST. Hanoi.

———. 2018b. "Report Assessing the Implementation Status of the Tax Regulations on Property." Text No. 4433/BTC-CST. Hanoi.

———. 2019. "Budget Data Publication." Hanoi.

———. 2020. "Proposal to the Government on the Draft Resolution on Agricultural Tax Exemptions and Reductions." Text No. 41/BTC-CST. Hanoi

———. 2021. "Budget Data Publication". Hanoi.

MONRE (Ministry of Natural Resource and Environment). 2021. "Decision 1435/QD-BTNMT dated July 22, 2021 on the Approval of the 2019's Survey on Land Use Status." Hanoi.

Pham, T. H. 2017. "Non-agricultural Land Use Tax in Vietnam: Current Situations and Recommendations." In *Finance and Economic Updates*. Hanoi: Institute for Financial Training, Ministry of Finance / Youth Publishing House.

SCNA (Standing Committee of the National Assembly of Vietnam). 2010. "Report to the National Assembly on the Law on Land and Housing Tax." Report 344/BC-UBTVQH12. Hanoi.

Truong, B. T. 2017. "Fiscal Decentralization and Inclusive Growth in Vietnam." Paper presented at the Roundtable of the Network on Fiscal Relations in Asia, Seoul (December 18–19).

———. 2018. "Theoretical Background and Direction for the Reform of Tax Incentives in Vietnam." Ministerial Research Project 2017-33, Ministry of Finance. Hanoi.

———. 2021. "Results of Tax Reform in Vietnam in 2011-2020 and the Way Forward." *Review of Finance* 746 (1) :17–22.

Truong, B. T., and Dao, M. P. 2018. "Public Finance Restructuring in Vietnam: Key Pillars and Policy Recommendations." Paper presented at Vietnam Finance Forum 2018: Restructuring National Finance towards Rapid, Inclusive and Sustainable Development, Hanoi (September 21).

World Bank. 2015. "Fiscal Decentralization Review in Vietnam: Making the Whole Greater Than the Sum the Parts: Summary Report." Washington, DC: World Bank.

World Bank and Government of Vietnam. 2017. "Vietnam Public Expenditure Review: Fiscal Policies Towards Sustainability, Efficiency, and Equity." Washington, DC: World Bank. https://openknowledge.worldbank.org/handle/10986/28610.

Contributors

Editors

ROY BAHL
Professor Emeritus
Georgia State University

Extraordinary Professor
African Tax Institute
University of Pretoria, South Africa

RIËL FRANZSEN
Director
African Tax Institute

Research Chair in Tax Policy and Governance
University of Pretoria, South Africa

WILLIAM MCCLUSKEY
Extraordinary Professor
African Tax Institute
University of Pretoria, South Africa

Chapter Authors

NIÑO RAYMOND B. ALVINA
Executive Director of the Bureau of Local Government Finance
Department of Finance, the Philippines

RAJUL AWASTHI
Senior Public Sector Specialist
Governance Global Practice
World Bank, Washington, DC

MIMI BROWN
Commissioner (retired)
Rating and Valuation Department
Hong Kong Special Administrative Region

DZURLLKANIAN ZULKARNAIN DAUD
Associate Professor
Faculty of Built Environment and Surveying
Universiti Teknologi Malaysia, Johor, Malaysia

ANDREW DEWIT
Professor
School of Economic Policy Studies
Rikkyo University, Tokyo, Japan

DUANGMANEE LAOVAKUL
Assistant Professor
Faculty of Economics
Thammasat University, Thailand

WENJING LI
Research Associate
Peking University–Lincoln Institute Center for Urban Development
and Land Policy
China

LAY CHENG JASMINE LIM
Senior Lecturer
Belfast School of Architecture and the Built Environment
Ulster University, N. Ireland, UK

TZU-CHIN LIN
Professor
Department of Land Economics
National Chengchi University, Taiwan

ZHI LIU
Senior Research Fellow and China Program Director
Peking University–Lincoln Institute Center for Urban Development and Land Policy
China

OM PRAKASH MATHUR
Senior Fellow and Chair
Institute of Social Sciences
New Delhi, India

RIATU MARIATUL QIBTHIYYAH
Senior Lecturer and Director
Institute for Economic and Social Research
University of Indonesia, Jakarta, Indonesia

YOUNGHOON RO
Senior Economist and Vice President (retired)
Korea Institute of Public Finance, Korea

SALFARINA SAMSUDIN
Senior Lecturer
Faculty of Built Environment and Surveying
Universiti Teknologi Malaysia, Johor, Malaysia

TRUONG BA TUAN
Deputy Director General
Tax Policy Department
Ministry of Finance, Vietnam

NIGEL WOODS
Visiting Professor
Belfast School of Architecture and the Built Environment
Ulster University, N. Ireland, UK

WEN-CHIEH WU
Professor
Department of Public Finance
National Chengchi University, Taiwan

Index

Italicized page numbers refer to tables and figures.

abandoned residences: Japan's incentives for, 256–260; Land and Building Tax Act of Thailand and, 462–464; Malaysia's challenges with, 317; vacant properties refunds in Hong Kong and, 158

acquisition tax, in Korea, 283, 285, 287

Act 828 (National Land Code), in Malaysia, 301, *302*

ad valorem stamp duty, in Hong Kong, 159–161, *161*

adjustment period, for property tax reform in China, 133

administration of property tax: for basic real property tax in Philippines, 359; billing in, 57; collection rates and, 55–56; communication with taxpayers in, 59–60; compliance costs in, 57; decentralization and, 95–96; efficiency in, 55; enforcement and recovery of arrears in, 58–59; for GRET in Korea, 283; in Indonesia, 212–217, *213*, *214*; in Kuala Lumpur, Malaysia, 311–313; in LGUs in Philippines, 366–370; low-income jurisdictions and challenges with, 92; of nonagricultural land use tax in Vietnam, 483–484; in Pakistan, 323–324; payment options in, 57–58; property transfer taxes and, 67; in Punjab, Pakistan, 334; simplification and improvement of, 102; in Singapore, 416–420, *417*; supervision

and control of, 56–57; in Taiwan, 434–438, 440; technology and, 95; Vietnam reform for, 502

Afghanistan, *6*

aggregate land value tax, Korea, 278–279, 294–296

agricultural income tax, Pakistan, 323, 324

agricultural land use tax, in Vietnam, 477–478

agricultural land valuation, in Japan, 245–246

agriculture, urban, Japan incentives for, 260

amnesties, 28–29

annual gross real estate tax, Korea, 25

annual property tax, 5, 17, 60–61; expense of implementing, 91

annual regular income, of LGUs in Philippines, 353, *354*, 380, *383*

annual rental value, 22, 37, 178, 185–186

annual value, in Singapore, 411–412

appeals, valuation: components of, 49–50; in Hong Kong, *51*, 149–151, *152*; by jurisdiction, *51*; LGC of 1991 in Philippines and, 369; Peninsular Malaysia recurrent property taxes and, 310; in Taiwan, 441

Appraisers Act of 1906, Singapore, 416

Aquino, Corazon, 393

area-based systems, value-based systems compared to, 20–22

arrears enforcement and recovery, 59; in Hong Kong, 58, 156, 158, *158*; in Indonesia, *216*, 216–217, *217*, 219, 221; in Japan, 58, 252; in Kuala Lumpur, Malaysia, 313, *314*; of Land and Building Tax Act in Thailand, 463; LGUs in Philippines and, 367–369; Malaysia's inadequate, 316–317. *See also* collections

Article 280, item (3)(c), India, 172, 176

Asia: property tax revenue in North America and Europe compared to, 8, *11*; urbanization in, 3. *See also specific countries*

assessable value (AV), 159

assessment adjustments, in tax relief programs, 28

assessment ratio, 330

assessments. *See* valuation

asset burden adjustments, in Japan, 250–251

auction fee, in Pakistan, *326*, 342

automated mass valuation, 39–43, *41–42*, 131, 153–156, 220. *See also* computer-assisted mass appraisal system; geographic information systems

AV (assessable value), 159

Balochistan, Pakistan, 328, *329*, *330*, 340

Basic Law, Hong Kong, 140

Basic Law to Promote Urban Farming, Japan, 260

basic real property tax, in Philippines, 357–361, *358–360*, 380, *382*

Batangas Port Development Project, in Philippines, 396n22

behavior taxes, in China, *135*

Bhutan, *6*

big data, 48–49

billing: in administration of property tax, 57; automated, 102; digital property, in Singapore, 419–420; in Hong Kong, 156; LGUs in Philippines and, 368; online, 59. *See also* collections

BOT (business office tax), in Japan, 226, 240–241. *See also* Japan

British Columbia Assessment Annual Plan, 418, 421

Budget Procedures Acts of 1959 and 2018, Thailand, 447

building and land tax, Thailand: before 2020, 449, 452–453, *456*; repeal of, 460

building tax, in Taiwan, *428*, 428–429, 431–434, *432–434*

Building Tax Act of 1967, Taiwan, 429, 437

building value, 22; in Taiwan, 437–438

business office tax (BOT), in Japan, 226, 240–241. *See also* Japan

buyer's stamp duty, in Hong Kong, 161

CAMA. *See* computer-assisted mass appraisal system

Cantonment Board Act of 1924, 185

Cantonments Act of 1924, Pakistan, 333

Capital Asset Pricing Model (CAPM), 147

capital gains taxes: on income tax, 70; in India, 70, 192; for Indonesia, 220; in Korea, 296n3; in Malaysia, 70; in Pakistan, 70, *326*, 343; in Philippines, 364; property transfer taxes and, 70–71; in Taiwan, 70; in Vietnam, 66, 70–71

capital value: definition of, 22; GRET in Korea and, 281; in India, 173, 178, 196n6; Pakistan's tax on, *326*, 341–342; Singapore and, 421; in Thailand, 460

CAPM (Capital Asset Pricing Model), 147

case-by-case valuation, 39

central taxes, in China, 110–111, *112*

centralization: of China's political system, 114; in Korea, 288; property tax and, 14. *See also* decentralization

central-to-provincial transfers, in China, 113

China, 3; adjustment period for property tax reform in, 133; automated mass valuation in, *41*; behavior taxes in, *135*; CAMA and, 131; central taxes in, 110–111, *112*; centralized political system in, 114; central-to-provincial transfers in, 113; custom duty in, *135*; deed tax in, 117; environmental tax in, 129; equity and distribution of property tax burden in, *74*; farmland occupancy tax in, 68, 116; farmland preservation in, 122; fiscal policy reform milestones in, 128–130; fiscal system in, 110–117; GIS in, 131; government revenues in, 110, *111*; grandfathering approach for property tax reform in, 133; household income growth in, 122–123; income tax in, 116, 125, *125*, 129; indirect compared to direct taxation in, *125*, 125–126, 128–129; Land Administration Law amendment of 2019 in, 121–122, 124; land appreciation tax in, 68, 116; land concession revenues in, 119, *120*, 122, 130–131; land policy and use in, 79, *80*; land use rights prices in, 122, *123*, 136n8; land-based finance in urban development in, 117–124, *121*; LGFVs in, 119, 123; local government debt problems in, 123–124; local government in, 110; local taxes in, 111, *112*, 114–117, *115*; low tax rate and wide base for, 132; municipalities in, 118, 133–134; owner-occupied residential property preferential treatment in, 29; property tax as percentage of GDP in, 6; property tax implementation barriers in, 130–134; property tax pilot programs in, 126–127, *128*; property tax reform in, 97, 124–130; property transfer taxes in, *62*, 68, 136n6; public land leasing price structure in, 131–132; real estate tax in, 116–117; recurrent property taxes and tax bases in, *23*; resource tax in, 129, *134*; responsibility for valuation and, *53*; revaluation frequency and, *45*; rural land in, 118, 121, 124; shared taxes in, 111, *112*; Sino-British Joint Declaration of 1984 and, 140–141; specific-purpose taxes in, *135*; split-rate tax in, 25; statutory taxation principle in, 129; tax-sharing system in, 110–114, *112*, 125; transitional period in, 103; turnover tax in, *134*; urban and township land use tax in, 114, 116; urbanization projections in, *94*; vacant land determination in, 36; valuation objections and appeals and, *51*. *See also* Hong Kong; Taiwan

Chongqing, property tax experiments in, 126–127, *128*

city planning tax (CPT), in Japan, 226; collections and, 251; coordinated reform for, 263; depreciable assets and, 249; earthquake proofing and, 249; exemptions and tax reductions for structures in, 248–249; municipal tax share of, 227, *227*; overview and characteristics of, 237–238, *240*;

residential land valuation and, 246–247, *247*; tax rates of, by municipal population, 238, *240*; in TMG, 253, *255*. *See also* Japan

classification of properties, for valuation, 54

collections: administration of property tax and rate of, 55–56; deed registration system and, 61; enforcement of, 20; in Hong Kong, 156–158; in Indonesia, 212–217, 219; Indonesia increasing rate of, 220–221; in Japan, 251; of Land and Building Tax Act in Thailand, 463; LGUs in Philippines and, 367–369, *379*, 379–380; of local property tax on land and buildings in Korea, 275, 289–290, *291*; Malaysia's inadequate, 316–317; of nonagricultural land use tax in Vietnam, 483–484; property tax revenue identity and, 21; in Sindh, Pakistan, 337; in Singapore, 419–420; in Taiwan, 438; Vietnam reform for, 502. *See also* administration of property tax; arrears enforcement and recovery

communication with taxpayers, 59–60

comparable sales approach, for market value, 38, 371–372, 417–418

compliance check, during revaluation, 148–149

compliance costs: in administration of property tax, 57; in Indonesia, 215, 218; LGUs in Philippines and, 373–378, *374*, *377*; in Punjab, Pakistan, 334; technology and, 57; voluntary compliance improvements and, 101

Comprehensive Tax Reform Program, Philippines, 391

computer-assisted mass appraisal (CAMA) system, 40, 43; China and, 131; GIS and, 153; in Hong Kong, 153–156; indexation for, 155; integrated property database for, 155–156; in Korea, 277–278; in Malaysia, 318; multiple regression analysis for, 154–155; reference assessment approach to, 154

control of property tax administration, 56–57

cost approach, for market value, 38–39, 372

COVID-19 pandemic: debt and deficit impact of, 3, 30; IMF on impact of, 30; Land and Building Tax Act of Thailand and, 465; tax relief programs and, 30; Thailand and deductions for, 449; Thailand and impact of, 445
CPT. *See* city planning tax, in Japan
creditable withholding tax, in Philippines, 365
current-use value, 37
custom duty, in China, *135*

data: accuracy and quality of, 46–47; on Delhi properties, 191; on India, 173; Indonesia management and accessibility of, 221; intra-agency sharing of, 47; management of, 47–49; new technology for, 48–49; for valuation, 44–49. *See also* computer-assisted mass appraisal system; technology
de Soto, Hernando, 373
dead capital, in Philippines, 373
decentralization: in developing world, 196*n*4; in India, 172–173, 182; Korea and, 288, 295; property taxes and, 95–96; of property transfer taxes, 67; in Thailand, 96, 446, 449; in Vietnam, 488, 494–495. *See also* local government units
Decentralization Plan and Process Act of 1999, Thailand, 449
deductions: GRET in Korea and, 280, 282; integrated real estate transaction tax in Taiwan and, 430; of Land and Building Tax Act in Thailand, 460–462; for rented properties in Hong Kong, 159; in Thailand for COVID-19, 449. *See also* exemptions
deed registration system: collections and, 61; in Hong Kong, 141–142; in Korea, 289
deed tax: in China, 117; in Taiwan, 431
deferrals, 28–29, 370
Delhi, India: annual rental value in, 185–186; data on properties in, 191; governance and economy of, 183–184, *184*; housing and service delivery in, 184–185; politics and public response in, 189; population growth in, 183, *184*; property tax reform in, 185–188; property tax revenue performance in, 189–191, *190*; revenue simulation

exercise in, 188; stamp duties in, *193*, 193–194, *194*; unit-area value system in, 186–188
Delhi Development Authority, 184
Delhi Municipal Corporation Act of 1957, 185, 189
delinquency. *See* arrears enforcement and recovery
depreciable assets, in Japan, 249, 260–261
development charge, in Singapore, 410–411
Devolution of Power Law of 1999, Japan, 228
differential tax rates, single tax rates compared to, 34
digital property billing, in Singapore, 419–420
direct taxation, in China, *125*, 125–126, 128–129
discounts, in tax relief programs, 27–28
DKI Jakarta, Indonesia: arrears enforcement and recovery in, 216–217; compliance costs in, 215; name of, 222*n*1; per capita income in, 206; preferential treatments in, 221–222; property taxes in, *204*; property transfer taxes in, 208; SIMPPEL in, 215; urban and rural property taxes in, 201, 206–207, *207*, 209–210. *See also* Indonesia
documentary stamp tax, in Philippines, 365
Doi Moi program, Vietnam, 472
"Doing Business, 2020," World Bank, 400
donor's tax, in Philippines, 364
double taxation, in Korea, 293–294
Duterte, Rodrigo, 391
dwelling valuations, in Japan, 247–248

earthquake proofing, in Japan, 249
East Delhi Municipal Corporation, 185
Economic Survey, of India, 195
education tax, in Korea, 285
effective tax rates: on land and buildings in Korea, 274, *274*; statutory tax rates compared to, 31; Taiwan and low, 439; on vacant land, 34–35. *See also* tax rates
18th amendment, Pakistan, 321–322
Electronic Local Authority (e-PBT), Malaysia, 318
environmental tax, in China, 129

e-PBT (Electronic Local Authority),
Malaysia, 318
Equalization of Land Rights in Urban
Areas Act, Taiwan, 426
equitable distribution of property tax
burden, 72–73, 74–77, 78, 466
Esri Canada, 126
estate tax: in Hong Kong, 161; in
Philippines, 364; revenue from, xv;
Singapore eliminating, 412
exclusions, in tax relief programs, 26–27
exemptions, 20; of building and land tax
in Thailand, 453; of FAT in Japan,
235, 237; government-owned
property, 29; in Hong Kong, 27, 151,
153; in India, 178–179; in Indonesia,
221–222; in Khyber Pakhtunkhwa,
Pakistan, 338–339; in Kuala Lumpur,
Malaysia, 314, 314; of Land and
Building Tax Act in Thailand,
460–462; from LGUs in Philippines,
365–366; of local development tax in
Thailand, 454; local property tax on
land and buildings in Korea and,
275; in Malaysia, 308, 308; in
nonagricultural land use tax in
Vietnam, 482–483; in Punjab,
Pakistan, 333–334; for recurrent
property taxes in Peninsular
Malaysia, 306, 308, 308; in Singapore,
416; for structures in Japan, 248–249;
in tax relief programs, 26–27; for
UIPT in Sindh, Pakistan, 336;
Vietnam reform options for, 498–499.
See also deductions

farmhouse tax, in Pakistan, 325, 326, 334
farmland occupancy tax, in China, 68,
116
farmland preservation, in China, 122
FAT. See fixed asset tax, in Japan
Federal Board of Revenue (FBR),
Pakistan, 323–324
fiscal space, 17n1
fixed asset tax (FAT), in Japan, 225–226;
abandoned residence incentives and,
256–260; agricultural land valuation
and, 245–246; asset burden adjustments
and, 250–251; collections and, 251;
components of, 235, 236; coordinated
reform for, 263; depreciable assets
and, 249, 260–261; earthquake
proofing and, 249; exemptions and tax
reductions for structures in, 248–249;

exemptions of, 235, 237; industrial
policy and revitalization issues and,
260–262; land registration and, 244;
land types and, 241, 242; municipal
tax share of, 227, 227; overview and
characteristics of, 235, 237, 238; rates
of, by municipal population, 238,
239; residential land valuation and,
246–247, 247; revenues from, 232,
234, 235, 236; simplification of,
262–263; Special Measures for Empty
Residence Law of 2015 and, 256–257;
tax base of, 241–244; in TMG, 253,
254; unclaimed land and, 257–258;
urban agriculture incentives and,
260; valuation of, 242–244. See also
Japan
fixed taxation rate for land and
buildings, Korea, 273–274, 274
Form R1As (rental requisition forms), in
Hong Kong, 162
fractional valuation, 52, 54
freehold of land, Malaysia land tenure
and, 301

GARV (gross annual rental value),
326–327
General Taxation Department,
Vietnam, 484, 502
general taxation rate, Korea: for GRET,
281, 281; for land and buildings,
272–273, 273
geographic information systems (GIS):
benefits of, xvi, 95, 163; CAMA
system and, 153; in China, 131; cost of,
44; in India, 95; in Punjab, Pakistan,
335; use of, 40, 41–42; for valuation,
437; in Vietnam, 103. See also
computer-assisted mass appraisal
system
George, Henry, 79, 84n18, 127, 278,
438–439, 442
GFS (government finance statistics), 8,
9, 10
gift tax, xv
GIS. See geographic information
systems
Global Competitiveness Index, WEF, 399
globalization, xv
goods and services tax (GST), India, 174
government finance statistics (GFS), 8,
9, 10
Government Finance Statistics Manual,
IMF, 5

government-owned property
exemption, 29
grandfathering approach, for property
tax reform in China, 133
GRET. *See* gross real estate tax
gross annual rental value (GARV),
326–327
gross real estate tax (GRET), Korea:
administration of, 283; capital value
and, 281; controversy and, 292;
deductions and, 280, 282; double
taxation and, 293–294; for fewer than
three houses, 281–282, *282*; general
taxation rate of, 281, *281*; history of,
278–279, 293; intergovernmental
arrangements and political economy
implications of, 283, *284*; loopholes
in, 296; for more than three houses,
281–282, *282*; objectives of, 279–280,
295; rate schedule for, *281*, 281–282,
282; reform of, 295; revenue
performance of, 288; special taxation
rate for, 281, *282*; tax base of, 280–282,
281, *282*; valuation of, 283
GST (goods and services tax), India, 174

Hanoi, Vietnam, nonagricultural land
use tax revenue in, 482, *482*
Heritage Foundation, 399–400
HKIS (Hong Kong Institute of
Surveyors), 143
Ho Chi Minh City Real Estate
Association, 481
Hong Kong, 3; ad valorem stamp duty
in, 159–161, *161*; arrears enforcement
and recovery in, 58, 156, 158, *158*;
assessment adjustments in, 28;
automated mass valuation in, 40, *41*;
Basic Law and governance of, 140;
billing in, 156; buyer's stamp duty
in, 161; CAMA techniques in,
153–156; collections in, 156–158;
communication with taxpayers in, 59;
control of property tax administration
in, 56; customer-centric service
delivery in, 157; data management in,
47–48; deed registration system in,
141–142; differential tax rates in, 34;
dollar value in, 170n1; equity and
distribution of property tax burden
in, 74, 78; estate tax in, 161;
exemptions in, 27, 151, 153; Form
R1As in, 162; housing affordability in,
166, 168, 170n6; income tax in, 168;

indexation in, 44; Inland Revenue
Department in, 160; land policy and
use in, 78–79, *80*; Land Registration
Ordinance in, 141; land sales revenue
in, 168, *169*; land tenure based on
leasehold in, 140–141; Land Titles
Ordinance in, 142; Lands Tribunal in,
149, 150; milestones of rating system
in, 144; payment and rates payable
liability in, 145; payment options in,
57; population of, 139; property tax as
percentage of GDP in, 6; property tax
rates in, 142–156; property tax
strategy in, 97; property tax system
challenges in, 161–168; property taxes
on rented properties in, 159; property
transfer taxes in, 62, 68; ratable value
in, 146, 148; rate calculation in,
145–147; rate capping in, 27; rate
concessions in, 145, 163, 165, *165*, *167*,
168, 170, *170*; rate liability in, 144–145;
Rating and Valuation Department in,
126, 142–143; rebates in, 27; recurrent
property taxes and tax bases in, *23*;
reductions in, 27; responsibility for
valuation in, *53*; revaluation efficiency
in, 163, *164*; revaluation frequency in,
43, *45*, 147–149; safeguarding revenue
from rates and government rent in,
162–163; Sino-British Joint
Declaration of 1984 and, 140–141;
Small Claims Tribunal in, 158; special
stamp duty in, 160–161; stamp duties
in, 158, 159–161, *161*; statistical audit,
postrevaluation in, 148; territories of,
139; uniform tax rate in, 32;
urbanization projections in, *94*;
vacancy tax proposal in, 165–166, 168;
vacant properties refunds in, 158;
valuation list in, 148–149, *149*;
valuation methods in, 37–38, 146–147;
valuation objections and appeals in,
51, 149–151, *152*; valuation training in,
143. *See also* China
Hong Kong Institute of Surveyors
(HKIS), 143
housing affordability, in Hong Kong,
166, 168, 170n6

IAAO (International Association of
Assessing Officers), 40, 83n9, 126
identity, property tax revenue, 21
idle land tax, in Philippines, *358*,
361–362, 395n6

IMF. *See* International Monetary Fund
income capitalization approach, for
 market value, 39, 372
income tax, xv; agricultural, in Pakistan,
 323, 324; capital gains, 70; in China,
 116, 125, *125*, 129; in Hong Kong, 166,
 168; in India, 192; in Taiwan, 430–431,
 431; Thailand property transfers
 withholding, 468–469; in Vietnam,
 485
Index of Economic Freedom report,
 Heritage Foundation, 399–400
indexation: for CAMA, 155; valuation
 and, 44
India: Article 280, item (3)(c) in, 172,
 176; automated mass valuation in, *41*;
 capital gains tax in, 70, 192; capital
 value in, 173, 178, 196*n*6; data on, 173;
 decentralization in, 172–173, 182;
 distribution of tax powers in, 174–177,
 176; economic growth in, 181;
 Economic Survey of, 195; equity and
 distribution of property tax burden
 in, 74; exemptions and rebates in,
 178–179; fiscal structure of, 174–177,
 176; GIS in, 95; GST in, 174; income
 tax in, 192; indexation in, 44;
 interstate variation of revenue
 production in, 181, *182*; municipalities
 in, 175–177, *176*; owner-occupied
 residential property preferential
 treatment in, 29; property tax reform
 in, 185–188, 194–195; property tax
 revenue mobilization in, 179–181, *180*,
 181; property taxation general
 framework in, 177–179; property
 transfer taxes in, *62*, 66, 67, 192–194;
 recurrent property taxes and tax bases
 in, *23*; responsibility for valuation in,
 53; revaluation frequency in, *45*;
 74th Amendment in, 172, 174–175;
 stamp duties in, 192–194, *192–194*; tax
 rate structures in, 179; urbanization
 in, *94*, 181–182, 196*n*7; valuation
 methods in, 22, 178; valuation
 objections and appeals in, 50, *51*.
 See also Delhi, India
*Indian Public Finance Statistics and
 Economic Survey*, 173
indirect taxation, in China, *125*, 125–126,
 128–129
Indonesia: administration of property
 taxes in, 212–217, *213*, *214*; arrears
 enforcement and recovery in, *216*,

216–217, *217*, 219, 221; automated
 mass valuation in, *41*, 220; capacity
 constraints in, 218; capital gains tax
 for, 220; collection rate increases in,
 220–221; collections in, 212–217, 219;
 compliance costs in, 215, 218;
 COVID-19 pandemic relief in, 30;
 data management and accessibility in,
 221; decentralization in, 96; equity
 and distribution of property tax
 burden in, 74; exemptions in, 221–222;
 land policy and use in, 79, *80*; narrow
 tax base problems in, 217–218;
 one-time luxury residential property
 tax in, 25; payment options in, 58;
 penalties and enforcement in,
 214–215; politics in, 219; preferential
 treatments in, 211–212, 221–222;
 progressive tax rate structures in, 33;
 property tax as percentage of GDP in,
 6; property tax policy history in,
 199–201, *200*; property tax reform
 options in, 219–222; recurrent
 property taxes and tax bases in, *23*;
 revaluation frequency in, *45*; revenue
 performance in, *202*, 202–208, *203*,
 204; rural land in, 199; simplification
 of taxes in, 222; structure and
 valuation of property taxes in,
 208–212; underdeclaration of sales
 prices in, 47, 213–214; uniform tax
 rate in, 32; urbanization and property
 tax revenue in, 13; urbanization
 projections in, *94*; valuation
 objections and appeals in, *51*;
 valuation problems in, 218; valuation
 responsibility in, *53*; valuation
 upgrades in, 220. *See also* DKI Jakarta;
 natural resource property taxes, in
 Indonesia; property transfer taxes, in
 Indonesia; urban and rural property
 taxes, in Indonesia
information technology. *See*
 technology
Inland Revenue Authority of Singapore,
 416, *417*, 418, 420
Inland Revenue Department, Hong
 Kong, 159
integrated property database, for
 CAMA, 155–156
integrated real estate transaction tax, in
 Taiwan, 429–431, *430*
internal revenue allotment, of LGUs in
 Philippines, 352–354, *353*, *354*

International Association of Assessing Officers (IAAO), 40, 83*n*9, 126
International Monetary Fund (IMF), xviii; on COVID-19 impact on debt, 30; GFS framework of, 8, 9, *10*; *Government Finance Statistics Manual* of, 5; property transfer taxes classified by, 84*n*15; WoRLD dataset and, 8, 9, *10*
International Property Tax Institute (IPTI), 43
intra-agency data sharing, 47
IPTI (International Property Tax Institute), 43
IT. *See* technology

Japan: abandoned residence incentives in, 256–260; agricultural land valuation in, 245–246; arrears enforcement and recovery in, 58, 252; asset burden adjustments in, 250–251; automated mass valuation in, 40, *41*; Basic Law to Promote Urban Farming in, 260; business office tax in, 226, 240–241; collections in, 251; communication with taxpayers in, 59–60; coordinated reform for, 263–264; data management in, 47, 48; depreciable assets in, 249, 260–261; Devolution of Power Law of 1999 in, 228; dwelling valuations in, 247–248; earthquake proofing in, 249; equity and distribution of property tax burden in, 74; exemptions and tax reductions for structures in, 248–249; fiscal system of, 226–232; fractional valuation in, 54; industrial policy and revitalization issues in, 260–262; intergovernmental system in, *230*, 230–232; land policy and use in, 79, *80–81*; land registration in, 244; land types in, 241, *242*; Local Tax Law in, 230–231; municipal fragmentation in, 229, *232*; municipal resident tax in, 227, *227*; municipal tax revenues in, 227, *227*; national and subnational tax revenues in, *226*, 226–227; NSPA in, 257, 259–260; payment options in, 57; population decline in, 228; progressive tax rate structures in, 33; *Property Assessment Information* in, 259; property tax as percentage of GDP in, *6*, 232, *233*; property tax reform in, 229, 256–264; property

taxes overview in, 235–241; property transfer taxes in, *63*, 67, 68–69; rebates in, 28; RECPAS in, 258–259; recurrent property taxes and tax bases in, *23*; residential land valuation in, 246–247, *247*; responsibility for valuation in, *53*; revaluation frequency in, *45*; revenue performance in, 232–235, *233*, *234*; Special Measures for Empty Residence Law of 2015 in, 256–257; split-rate tax in, 25; tax bases in, 241–244; tax deferrals in, 28; TMG property and land taxes in, 252–256, *254*, *255*; topography and population of, 225; Trinity Reform of 2004–2006 in, 228; unclaimed land in, 257–258; urban agriculture incentives in, 260; urbanization projections in, *94*; vacant land determination in, 35–36; valuation in, 242–244; valuation methods in, 37, 39; valuation objections and appeals in, *51*. *See also* city planning tax; fixed asset tax

Khyber Pakhtunkhwa, Pakistan: exemptions and preferential treatments in, 338–339; public services demands in, 337; tax morale issues in, 338; tax rates in, 340; UIPT revenue totals in, 328, *329*, *330*, 338; valuation in, 339
Korea: acquisition tax in, 283, 285, 287; aggregate land value tax in, 278–279, 294–296; annual gross real estate tax, 25; assessment adjustments in, 28; automated mass valuation in, 40, *41*; CAMA system in, 277–278; capital gains taxes in, 296*n*3; centralization in, 288; collection of local property tax on land and buildings in, 275, 289–290, *291*; controversy of taxes in, 292; data management in, 48; decentralization and, 288, 295; deed registration system in, 289; double taxation in, 293–294; education tax in, 285; effective property tax rate on land and buildings in, 274, *274*; equity and distribution of property tax burden in, *75*, 78; exemptions, preferences, and collections on local property tax in, 275; fixed taxation rate for land and buildings in, 273–274, *274*; fractional valuation in, 54; general taxation rate for GRET

in, 281, *281*; general taxation rate for land and buildings in, 272–273, *273*; governance structure in, 269; government-owned property exemption in, 29; gross real estate tax in, 278–283, *280–282*; land policy and use in, 79, *81*; land price inflation in, 279–280, *280*; local property tax on land and buildings in, 272–278, *273–275, 277*; Local Tax Act in, 277; progressive tax rate structures in, 33; property tax as percentage of GDP in, *6*, 288; property tax reform in, 294–296; property tax revenue performance in, 287–290, *289*; property transfer taxes in, *63, 66*, 269, 283, 285–287, *286*, 294; Public Announcement on Real Estate Values Act in, 277; recurrent property taxes and tax bases in, *23*; reductions in, 287; responsibility for valuation in, 52, *53*; revaluation frequency in, *45*; rural development tax in, 285; Seoul local property tax on land and buildings in, 289, *290*; special taxation rate for GRET in, 281, *282*; special taxation rate for land and buildings in, 273, *273*; surtaxes on land and buildings in, 274–275, *275*; tax burden distribution in, 290, 292; urbanization projections in, *94*; valuation for GRET in, 283; valuation for local property tax on land and buildings in, 275–276, *277*; valuation objections and appeals in, *51*; value thresholds in, 27. *See also* gross real estate tax; local property tax on land and buildings, Korea

Korea Appraisal Board, 296*n*1

Kuala Lumpur, Malaysia: administration of property tax in, 311–313; arrears enforcement and recovery in, 313, *314*; exemptions in, 314, *314*; population of, 311; revaluation of 2014 in, 312–313, *313*; revenue performance in post revaluation period in, 313, *313, 314*; tax rates in, 312, *312*; taxable properties in, 311, *311*

Land Administration Law amendment of 2019, China, 121–122, 124

Land and Building Tax Act, Thailand: collection and enforcement of, *463*;

COVID-19 impact on, 465; drafting of, 459; equitable distribution of property tax burden and, 466; exemptions and deductions of, 460–462; implementation challenges of, 464–466; objectives of, 459; potential long-run benefits of, 463–464; property survey for, 465; revenue challenges of, 466; tax base of, 460; tax rate schedule of, 462, *463*; unknown regulatory details of, 465–466; vacant property in, 462–464; valuation and market value shortcomings of, 465

land appreciation tax, in China, 68, 116

land concession revenues, in China, 119, *120*, 122, 130–131

land policy and use, 78–79, *80–82*, 83

land price frame/table, Vietnam, 480, 499–500

land price inflation, in Korea, 279–280, *280*

land reclamation, in Singapore, 400

land registration, in Japan, 244

Land Registration Ordinance, Hong Kong, 141

land rental fee, Vietnam, 487

land sales revenue, in Hong Kong, 166, 168, *169*

land tax. *See* property tax

land tenure, 20; based on leasehold in Hong Kong, 140–141; in Malaysia, 301; in Singapore, 406

Land Titles Ordinance, Hong Kong, 142

land use levy, Vietnam, 486–487, 494

land use right transfer tax, Vietnam, 484–485, *490*, 491

land use rights prices, in China, 122, *123*, 136*n*8

land value, 22

land value increment tax, in Taiwan, *429*, 429–434, *432–434*

land value tax, 25; aggregate, in Korea, 278–279; in Taiwan, 425, *427*, 427–428, 431–434, *432–434*, 440; threshold value in, 427

landed housing, in Singapore, 405, *406*

Lands Tribunal, Hong Kong, 149, 150

Laos, *6*, 445

Law on Land, Vietnam, 473, 476–477, 480, 484, 486–487, 499

Law on State Budget, Vietnam, 488–489, 494

leasehold of land: Hong Kong land tenure and, 140–141; Malaysia land tenure and, 301

LGC. *See* Local Government Code

LGFVs (local-government finance vehicles), in China, 119, 123

LGUs. *See* local government units

local development tax, Thailand: before 2020, 453–455, *457*; repeal of, 460

Local Government Act of 1976, Malaysia, 300, 309, 312

Local Government Code (LGC) of 1991, Philippines, 354; appeals and, 369; basic real property tax under, 357, 359–360; exemptions and, 365; local business tax and, 394*n*2; reforms of, 394; revaluation requirements of, 373; revenue following passage of, 379–380, *381*; special education fund tax and, 361; Tax Watch campaign and, 390; zonal values not allowed by, 363

local government units (LGUs), in Philippines: administration of property tax of, 366–370; annual regular income of, 353, *354*, 380, *383*; appeals and, 369; arrears enforcement and recovery and, 367–369; autonomy of, 391; basic real property tax of, 357–361, *358–360*, 380, *382*; billing and, 368; collections and, 367–369, *379*, 379–380; dead capital in, 373; exemptions from, *365–366*; history of, 393–394, 396*n*28; idle land tax of, *358*, 361–362, 395*n*6; internal revenue allotment of, 352–354, *353*, *354*; market value approaches for, 371–372; property transfer taxes of, *358*, 363; quarry resources tax of, *358*, 363; recentralization and, 392; revaluations and compliance of, 373–378, *374*, *377*; revaluations pilot programs in, 388–390; revenue performance in, 378–384, *381*, *385*; revenue types for, 353, *354*; RPVARA and, 390–391; socialized housing tax of, *358*, 362–363; special education fund tax of, *358*, 361, 380, *382*; special levy on land of, *358*, 362; tax rates imposed by, 352; tax relief programs of, 370; Tax Watch campaign and, 390; taxing powers of, 351–357, *352*; valuation in, 367, 370–372, 388

local property tax on land and buildings, Korea: CAMA system for, 277–278; collection of, 275, 289–290, *291*; controversy and, 292; double taxation and, 293–294; effective property tax rate in, 274, *274*; exemptions, preferences, and collections on, 275; fixed taxation rate in, 273–274, *274*; general taxation rate in, 272–273, *273*; reform of, 295; revenue performance of, 287–290, *289*; for Seoul, 289, *290*; special taxation rate in, 273, *273*; surtaxes in, 274–275, *275*; tax base and rates in, 272–274, *273–274*; tax burden distribution in, 290, 292; unit of taxation and taxpayer in, 272; valuation of, 275–276, 277

Local Tax Act, Korea, 277

Local Tax Law, in Japan, 230–231

local taxes, in China, 111, *112*, 114–117, *115*

local-government finance vehicles (LGFVs), in China, 119, 123

low-income jurisdictions: administration of property tax challenges in, 92; annual property tax implementation expenses for, 91; equitable distribution of property tax burden in, 73; narrow tax bases in, 91; property tax reform challenges in, 92; revenue elasticity in, 91; taxes favored in, 91–92. *See also specific jurisdictions*

luxury house tax, in Pakistan, 325, *326*, 334

luxury residential property taxes, one-time, 25

Malaysia: abandoned residences in, 317; arrears enforcement and recovery in, 58; automated mass valuation in, 40, *42*; CAMA system in, 318; capital gains tax in, 70; communication with taxpayers in, 60; data management in, 48; e-PBT in, 318; equity and distribution of property tax burden in, *75*, 78; exemptions in, 308, *308*; inadequate collection and enforcement in, 316–317; intra-agency data sharing in, 47; Kuala Lumpur, property taxation in, 311–314, *311–314*; land policy and use in, 79, *81*; land tenure and property rights in, 301; Local Government Act of 1976 in, 300, 309, 312; local governments in,

299–300, *300*; National Land Code (Act 828) in, 301, *302*; National Land Code of 1963 in, 301; National Land Code of 1965 in, 304; Peninsular, recurrent property taxes in, 305–310, *306–308*; population of, 299; property tax as percentage of GDP in, *6*; property tax reform challenges in, 314–318; property taxes overview in, *302*, 302–305; property transfer taxes in, *63*; quit rents in, 304, *304*; rate capping in, 27; real property gains tax in, 303, *304*, *315*, 315–316; recurrent property taxes and tax bases in, *24*; reductions in, 308, *308*; responsibility for valuation in, *53*; revaluation frequency in, *45*, 316; Stamp Duty Act of 1949 in, 302; stamp duty in, 302–303, *303*, *315*, 315–316; states and territories of, 299; taxable capacity in, 315; technology adoption challenges in, 317–318; urbanization projections in, *94*; vacant land determination in, 36; valuation methods in, 38; valuation objections and appeals in, *51*. See also Kuala Lumpur, Malaysia; Peninsular Malaysia

Marcos, Ferdinand, 393

market value, 21, 37; comparable sales approach for, 38, 371–372, 417–418; cost approach for, 38–39, 372; income capitalization approach for, 39, 372; Land and Building Tax Act of Thailand shortcomings of, 465

mass valuation, automated, 39–43, *41–42*, 131, 153–156, 220. See also computer-assisted mass appraisal system; geographic information systems

middle-income jurisdictions, equitable distribution of property tax burden in, 73

mining, Indonesian natural resource property taxes from, 203, 205

Mongolia, *6*

multiple regression analysis, for CAMA, 154–155

Municipal Corporation of Delhi, 185, 186, 189–191

municipal resident tax, in Japan, 227, *227*

municipalities: in China, 118, 133–134; in India, 175–177, *176*

Mystery of Capital (de Soto), 373

Naga City, Philippines, revaluation pilot program in, 388–389

National Decentralization Committee, Thailand, 446, 470*n*1

National Internal Revenue Code (NIRC), of Philippines, 376

National Land Code (Act 828), in Malaysia, 301, *302*

National Land Code of 1963, in Malaysia, 301

National Land Code of 1965, in Malaysia, 304

National Spatial Planning Association (NSPA), Japan, 257, 259–260

natural resource property taxes, in Indonesia: from mining, 203, 205; from oil and gas, 203; revenues of, *202–204*, 202–205; sections of, 210; tax rate and base for, 211; valuation in, 211

NAV (net assessable value), 159

nested budget system, in Vietnam, 504*n*2

net assessable value (NAV), 159

New Delhi Municipal Council Act of 1994, 185

NIRC (National Internal Revenue Code), of Philippines, 376

nonagricultural land use tax, Vietnam, 25, 58; administration of, 483–484; collection of, 483–484; exemptions and reductions in, 482–483; Hanoi's revenue from, 482, *482*; historical development of, 478, 495; land price frame/table and, 480, 499–500; tax base of, 479; tax rates of, 480–482, *481*; taxpayers in, 479; valuation in, 479–480, 499

nonlanded housing, in Singapore, 405, *406*

North Delhi Municipal Corporation, 185

NSPA (National Spatial Planning Association), Japan, 257, 259–260

objections, valuation: components of, 49–50; in Hong Kong, *51*, 149–151, *152*; by jurisdiction, *51*; LGC of 1991 in Philippines and, 369; Peninsular Malaysia recurrent property taxes and, 310; in Taiwan, 441

OECD. See Organization for Economic Cooperation and Development

office rentals, in Singapore, 407
oil and gas, Indonesian natural resource property taxes from, 203
one-time luxury residential property taxes, 25
one-time-event revenue, Vietnam, 489, 490, 491
Organization for Economic Cooperation and Development (OECD), 8, 268–269, 296n7; Global Revenue Statistics Database of, 9; property transfer taxes classified by, 84n15
owner-occupancy, in Singapore, 405–406, 406
owner-occupied residential property preferential treatment, 29–30

Pakistan: administration of property tax in, 323–324; agricultural income tax in, 323, 324; assessment adjustments in, 28; auction/tender fee in, 326, 342; automated mass valuation in, 42; Balochistan in, 328, 329, 330, 340; Cantonments Act of 1924 in, 333; capital gains taxes in, 70, 326, 343; capital value tax in, 326, 341–342; discounts in, 28; 18th amendment in, 321–322; equity and distribution of property tax burden in, 75, 78; farmhouse tax in, 325, 326, 334; FBR in, 323–324; fiscal and institutional environment in, 321–324, 322, 323; government structure in, 321–322; indexation in, 44; Khyber Pakhtunkhwa in, 328, 329, 330, 337–340; luxury house tax in, 325, 326, 334; one-time luxury residential property tax in, 25; owner-occupied residential property preferential treatment in, 29; payment options in, 58; property tax as percentage of GDP in, 7; property tax reform problems and options in, 343–347; property tax revenues in, 328–340; property transfer taxes in, 63, 66, 340–343, 341; Punjab in, 325, 326, 328, 329–332, 330, 333–335, 344–345; rebates in, 339; recurrent property taxes and tax bases in, 24; recurrent property taxes in, 325–340, 326; registration fee/town fee in, 326, 342; responsibility for valuation in, 53; revaluation frequency in, 45; rural

land in, 323–324; Sindh in, 328, 329, 330, 335–337, 345–347; split-rate tax in, 25; stamp tax in, 326, 342; urbanization in, 94, 324–325; valuation objections and appeals in, 50, 51; withholding tax in, 326, 342. See also Khyber Pakhtunkhwa; Punjab; Sindh; urban immovable property tax
payment liability, in Hong Kong, 145
payment options, in administration of property tax, 57–58
payment upon purchase of state-owned housing, Vietnam, 487–488
Peninsular Malaysia, recurrent property taxes in: base of, 305–306, 306; calculation of, 309–310; exemptions and reliefs for, 306, 308, 308; objections to, 310; rates of, 306, 307; revaluations for, 310; valuation for, 308–310
phase-in provisions, 27–28
Philippines, 3; administration of LGU property tax in, 366–370; amnesties in, 29; arrears enforcement and recovery in, 59; assessment adjustments in, 28; automated mass valuation in, 40, 42; basic real property tax in, 357–361, 358–360, 380, 382; Batangas Port Development Project in, 396n22; billing in, 57; capital gains tax in, 364; communication with taxpayers in, 60; Comprehensive Tax Reform Program in, 391; control of property tax administration in, 56; COVID-19 pandemic relief in, 30; creditable withholding tax in, 365; dead capital in, 373; discounts in, 28; documentary stamp tax in, 365; donor's tax in, 364; equity and distribution of property tax burden in, 75–76; estate tax in, 364; exemptions from LGUs in, 365–366; fractional valuation in, 54; government-owned property exemption in, 29; idle land tax in, 358, 361–362, 395n6; land policy and use in, 79, 81; national property-related taxes in, 364–365, 384, 386; NIRC of, 376; payment options in, 58; professionalization of property appraisers in, 387–388; progressive tax rate structures in, 34; property tax as percentage of GDP in, 7, 382, 384;

property tax design and structure in, 357–365, *358*; property tax reform in, 384, 387–392; property taxation history in, 392–394; property transfer taxes in, *64*, 66, *358*, 363; quarry resources tax in, *358*, 363; recentralization and, 392; recurrent property taxes and tax bases in, *24*; responsibility for valuation in, *53*; revaluation frequency in, 43, *45*; revaluations in, LGU compliance and, 373–378, *374, 377*; revaluations pilot programs in, 388–390; revenue performance in, 378–384, *381, 385*; RPVARA in, 390–391; self-assessment in, 55; socialized housing tax in, *358*, 362–363; special education fund tax in, *358*, 361, 380, *382*; special levy on land in, *358*, 362; Tax Watch campaign in, 390; taxing powers in, 351–357, *352*; TRAIN Law in, 378; underdeclaration of sales prices in, 47; *urbana* tax in, 392; urbanization and property tax revenue in, 12–13; urbanization projections in, *94*; vacant land determination in, 36; valuation in, 367, 370–372, 388; valuation objections and appeals in, *51*; value-added tax in, 364–365; zonal revaluations in, 376, 378. *See also* Local Government Code; local government units

politics: in Delhi, India, 189; GRET in Korea and, 283, *284*; in Indonesia, 219; property tax reform and, 16, 90; statutory tax rates and, 31; tax relief programs and, 26; in Vietnam, 503

population decline, in Japan, 228

preferential treatments, 20; eliminating unnecessary, 99; in Indonesia, 211–212, 221–222; in Khyber Pakhtunkhwa, Pakistan, 338–339; local property tax on land and buildings in Korea and, 275; of owner-occupied residential property, 29–30; property transfer taxes and, 68–69

private-sector housing, in Singapore, 404–405, *406*

professionalization of property appraisers, in Philippines, 387–388

progressive tax rate, 33–34

Property Assessment Information, Japan, 259

property data. *See* data

property registration fees. *See* registration fees

property size, 22

property survey, for Land and Building Tax Act of Thailand, 465

Property Tax Act, Singapore, 411

property tax reform, 4; adjustment period for, in China, 133; administration simplification and improvement for, 102; in China, 97, 124–130; comprehensive approach to, 97–98; in Delhi, India, 185–188; directions for, 16–17, 96–103; eliminating unnecessary preferential treatments for, 99; grandfathering approach for, in China, 133; in India, 185–188, 194–195; in Indonesia, 219–222; in Japan, 229, 256–264; in Korea, 294–296; low-income jurisdictions and challenges with, 92; Malaysia's challenges with, 314–318; in Pakistan, problems and options for, 343–347; in Philippines, 384, 387–392; politics and, 16, 90; property transfer taxes and, 71, 100; simplification for, 99–100, 222; in Singapore, 421–422; statutory rates and valuation separation for, 98–99; strategy for, 97; Taiwan's prospects for, 441–442; technology in, 102–103; in Thailand, 469–470; valuation improvements for, 100–101; variables in, 20, 21; in Vietnam, 97, 473–476, 492–504; voluntary compliance improvements for, 101

property taxes: administration of, 55–60, 67; annual, 5, 17, 60–61; in Asia compared to North America and Europe, 8, *11*; case studies on, xvii–xviii, 4–5, *6–7*; centralization and, 14; China's barriers to implementing, 130–134; Chinese pilot programs for, 126–127, *128*; constraints on revenue mobilization of, 90–92; decentralization and, 95–96; definition of, 5, 8; Delhi, revenue performance of, 189–191, *190*; in DKI Jakarta, Indonesia, *204*; efficiency of, xv; equitable distribution of burden of, 72–73, *74–77*, 78; Hong Kong challenges with, 161–168; Hong Kong rates of, 142–156; importance of, xv–xvi;

property taxes (*continued*)
India's general framework for,
177–179; India's mobilization of
revenue from, 179–181, *180*, *181*;
Indonesian history of policies on,
199–201, *200*; Indonesian structure
and valuation of, 208–212; Korea and
revenue performance of, 287–290,
289; Korea's system of, overview of,
268–272, *270*, *271*; in Kuala Lumpur,
Malaysia, 311–314, *311–314*; low, for
China, 132; Malaysia overview of,
302, 302–305; modernizing, 3;
Pakistan revenues from, 328–340; in
Philippines, design and structure of,
357–365, *358*; Philippines' history of,
392–394, 396*n*28; regression model
for, 12–17, *13*, *15*; on rented properties
in Hong Kong, 159; revenue from, xv;
revenue identity, 21; rule of law and,
13; rural land and, 13; Singapore's
system of, 407–416, *414*, *415*; strategy
for, 97; Taiwan's system of, 426–431;
taxable capacity and revenue from, 12,
61; taxable effort and revenue from,
12; in Thailand, before 2020 reform
in, 449, 452–455, *456–458*; in
Thailand, in 2020, 455, 459–464, *463*;
total, 5, 12, *15*, 16; urbanization and
revenue from, 12–13, 17, 93. *See also*
recurrent property tax
property transfer taxes, 19;
administration of, 67; advantages and
disadvantages of, 69–70; capital gains
taxes and, 70–71; in China, *62*, 68,
136*n*6; in DKI Jakarta, Indonesia,
208; in India, 192–194; by jurisdiction,
61, *62–65*; in Korea, *63*, 269, 283,
285–287, *286*, 294; land use right
transfer tax in Vietnam, 484–485,
490, 491; OECF and IMF
classification of, 84*n*15; in Pakistan,
340–343, *341*; in Philippines, *64*, *358*,
363; preferential treatments and,
68–69; rationalizing use of, 100;
recurrent property taxes and, 60–61,
71, 97, *98*; reform for, 71, 100;
statutory tax rates and, 66; structure
of, 61, 66; in Thailand, *65*, 466–469,
467; underdeclaration of sales prices
and, 67; valuation of, 67–68; volatility
of, 69
property transfer taxes, in Indonesia, *63*,
68; administration of, 213–214, *214*;

coverage of tax base in, 212;
decentralization of, 67; history of,
200; revenues of, *202–204*, *207*,
207–208; schedule and preferential
rates in, 211–212; underdeclaration of
sales prices and, 213–214
PT-1 form, Punjab, Pakistan, 334
Public Announcement on Real Estate
Values Act, Korea, 277
public housing, in Singapore, 404–405,
406, 414–415, *415*
public land leasing price structure, in
China, 131–132
public response, in Delhi, India, 189
Punjab, Pakistan: administration of
property tax in, 334; assessment ratio
in, 330; compliance costs in, 334;
exemptions in, 333–334; farmhouse
tax in, 325, *326*, 334; GIS in, 335;
luxury house tax in, 325, *326*, 334;
property tax reform options and
problems in, 344–345; PT-1 form in,
334; tax base for UIPT in, 328, 330;
UIPT revenue totals in, 328, *329*,
330, 334–335; valuation for UIPT in,
328, 330, *331*, *332*

quarry resources tax, in Philippines,
358, 363
quit rents, in Malaysia, 304, *304*

ratable value, in Hong Kong, 146, 148
rate calculation, in Hong Kong,
145–147
rate capping, in tax relief programs,
27–28
rate concessions, in Hong Kong, 145,
163, 165, *165*, *167*, 168, 170, *170*
rate liability, in Hong Kong, 144–145
rates. *See* statutory tax rates; tax rates
rates payable liability, in Hong Kong,
145
Rating and Valuation Department,
Hong Kong, 126, 142–143
real estate tax, in China, 116–117
real property gains tax, in Malaysia, 303,
304, *315*, 315–316
Real Property Valuation and Assessment
Reform Act (RPVARA), Philippines,
390–391
rebates: in India, 178–179; in Pakistan,
339; in Taiwan, 436; in tax relief
programs, 27–28
recentralization, Philippines and, 392

RECPAS (Research Center for Property Assessment System), Japan, 258–259

recurrent property taxes: data sources for, 9; by jurisdiction, 23–24; in Pakistan, 325–340, 326; property transfer tax and, 60–61, 71, 97, 98; regression model for, 12, 14, 15, 16; revenue mobilization determinants in, 20, 21; split-rate, 25; statutory tax rates and, 30–34; structures of, 20–36; tax bases and, 20–26, 23–24; tax relief programs for, 26–30; vacant/underused land in, 26, 34–36, 35; value-based compared to area-based systems for, 20–22; in Vietnam, 24, 490, 491–492; in Vietnam, reform of, 492–493; as wealth tax, 25

recurrent property taxes, in Peninsular Malaysia: base of, 305–306, 306; calculation of, 309–310; exemptions and reliefs for, 306, 308, 308; objections and, 310; rates of, 306, 307; revaluations for, 310; valuation for, 308–310

reductions: in Hong Kong, 27; in Korea, 287; in Malaysia, 308, 308; in nonagricultural land use tax in Vietnam, 482–483; for structures in Japan, 248–249. See also exemptions

reference assessment approach, to CAMA, 154

registering land, in Japan, 244

registration fees: in Pakistan, 326, 342; in Thailand, 468; in Vietnam, 485–486

rental information analysis, for revaluations in Hong Kong, 148

rental information collection, for revaluations in Hong Kong, 147

rental requisition forms (Form R1As), in Hong Kong, 162

rented properties, property taxes on, in Hong Kong, 159

Republic of Korea. See Korea

Research Center for Property Assessment System (RECPAS), Japan, 258–259

Reserve Bank of India, 173

residential land valuation, in Japan, 246–247, 247

resource tax, in China, 129, 134

revaluations: compliance check during, 148–149; frequency of, 43–44, 45–46; Hong Kong efficiency of, 163, 164;

Hong Kong frequency of, 43, 45, 147–149; in Kuala Lumpur, Malaysia, 2014, 312–313, 313; LGU compliance in Philippines and, 373–378, 374, 377; Malaysia's frequency of, 45, 316; Philippines' pilot programs for, 388–390; ratable value reviews and updates for, 148; for recurrent property taxes in Peninsular Malaysia, 310; rental information collection for, 147; in Taiwan, 435–436; valuation list for, 148–149, 149; zonal, in Philippines, 376, 378

revenue capping, 27–28

revenue elasticity, in low-income jurisdictions, 91

revenue identity, property tax, 21

revenue simulation exercise, in Delhi, 188

Royal Institution of Chartered Surveyors (RICS), 143

RPVARA (Real Property Valuation and Assessment Reform Act), Philippines, 390–391

rule of law, property tax and, 13

rural development tax, in Korea, 285

rural land: area-based systems for, 22; in China, 118, 121, 124; in Indonesia, 199; in Pakistan, 323–324; property tax and, 13

salable area, 170n3

self-assessments, 54–55, 439–440

Seoul, Korea, local property tax on land and buildings in, 289, 290

74th Amendment, in India, 172, 174–175

Shanghai, property tax experiments in, 126–127, 128

shared taxes, in China, 111, 112

SIMPPEL (Sistem Penyampaian SPPT PBB elektronik), DKI Jakarta, 215

Sindh, Pakistan: collections in, 337; exemptions for UIPT in, 336; property tax reform options and problems in, 345–347; UIPT base and rate in, 335; UIPT revenue totals in, 328, 329, 330, 337; valuation of UIPT in, 335–336

Singapore: administration of property tax in, 416–420, 417; aging population in, 400, 405; annual value in, 411–412; Appraisers Act of 1906 in, 416; automated mass valuation in, 42; capital value proposal for, 421;

Singapore (*continued*)
collection and billing in, 419–420; cultural diversity in, 401; development charge in, 410–411; digital property billing in, 419–420; economic power and stability in, 399–400, 420; educated workforce in, 400–401; equity and distribution of property tax burden in, 76; estate tax eliminated in, 412; exemptions in, 416; government structure in, 401–402; Inland Revenue Authority of, 416, *417*, 418, 420; land administration in, 401–402; land policy and use in, 79, *81*; land reclamation in, 400; land tenure in, 406; landed and nonlanded housing in, 405, *406*; office rentals in, 407; owner-occupancy in, 405–406, *406*; payment options in, 57; population growth in, 400; private-sector housing in, 404–405, *406*; property market in, 404–407, *406*; Property Tax Act in, 411; property tax as percentage of GDP in, 7; property tax reform in, 421–422; property tax strategy in, 97; property tax system in, 407–416, *414*, *415*; property transfer taxes in, *64*, 66, 68; public housing in, 404–405, *406*, 414–415, *415*; real estate laws and statutory boards in, 402, *403*; recurrent property taxes and tax bases in, *24*; responsibility for valuation in, *53*; revaluation frequency in, *45*; stamp duties in, 408–410, *409*, *410*, 422n5; tax base and revenue performance in, 402, *404*; tax rates in, 412–413, *413*; tax yield in, 413–415, *414*, *415*; unemployment in, 399; uniform tax rate in, 32; urbanization projections in, *94*; valuation in, 416–418; valuation objections and appeals in, *51*; value thresholds in, 27
single tax rates, differential tax rates compared to, 34
Sino-British Joint Declaration, 1984, 140–141
Sistem Penyampaian SPPT PBB elektronik (SIMPPEL), DKI Jakarta, 215
Small Claims Tribunal, Hong Kong, 158
socialized housing tax, in Philippines, *358*, 362–363
South Delhi Municipal Corporation, 185

South Korea. *See* Korea
special education fund tax, in Philippines, *358*, 361, 380, *382*
special levy on land, in Philippines, *358*, 362
Special Measures for Empty Residence Law of 2015, Japan, 256–257
special stamp duty, in Hong Kong, 160–161
special taxation rate, Korea: for GRET, 281, *282*; for land and buildings, 273, *273*
specific business tax, Thailand, 468
specific-purpose taxes, in China, *135*
split-rate tax: recurrent property taxes and, 25; in Taiwan, 79, 425, 441–442
stamp duties: documentary, in Philippines, 365; in Hong Kong, 158, 159–161, *161*; in India, 192–194, *192–194*; in Malaysia, 302–303, *303*, *315*, 315–316; in Pakistan, *326*, 342; in Singapore, 408–410, *409*, *410*, 422n5; in Taiwan, 431; in Thailand, 469
Stamp Duty Act of 1949, Malaysia, 302
State Finances (Reserve Bank of India), 173
state-owned housing, payment upon purchase of, in Vietnam, 487–488
statistical audit, postrevaluation, Hong Kong, 148
statutory tax rates, 20, 21; determining, 31; effective tax rates compared to, 31; government setting, 32; politics and, 31; progressive, 33–34; property transfer taxes and, 66; single compared to differential, 34; structure and design of, 32–34; tax relief programs and, 30; uniform, 32–33; valuation separated from, 98–99. *See also* tax rates
statutory taxation principle, in China, 129
Suits, Daniel B., 297n9
Suits index, 293, 297n9
supervision of property tax administration, 56–57
surtaxes on land and buildings, Korea, 274–275, *275*
surveyor fees, in Thailand, 468

Taipei City, Taiwan, revenues in, *433*, 433–434, *434*
Taiwan, 25; administration of property tax in, 434–438, 440; analysis of problems facing, 438–440; arrears

enforcement and recovery in, 59;
automated mass valuation in, *42*;
Building Tax Act of 1967 in, 429, 437;
building tax in, *428*, 428–429,
431–434, *432–434*; building valuation
in, 437–438; capital gains tax in, 70;
collections in, 438; coordination
between government agencies in, 440;
court cases and objections in, 441;
COVID-19 pandemic relief in, 30;
deed tax in, 431; Equalization of Land
Rights in Urban Areas Act in, 426;
equity and distribution of property
tax burden in, 76, 78; government
tiers in, 426; income tax in, 430–431,
431; integrated real estate transaction
tax in, 429–431, *430*; land policy and
use in, 79, *82*; land valuation in,
436–437; land value increment tax in,
429, 429–434, *432–434*; land value tax
in, 425, *427*, 427–428, 431–434,
432–434, 440; low effective tax rates
in, 439; low revenue problems in, 439;
payment options in, 57; progressive
tax rate structures in, 33; property tax
as percentage of GDP in, 7, 432, *432*;
property tax reform prospects in,
441–442; property tax system in,
426–431; property transfer taxes in,
64–65, 66; rebates in, 436; recurrent
property taxes and tax bases in, *24*;
responsibility for valuation in, 52, *53*;
revaluation frequency in, 44, *46*;
revaluations in, 435–436; revenue
performance in, 431–434, *432*, *433*;
self-assessment in, 55, 439–440;
split-rate tax in, 79, 425, 441–442;
stamp duty in, 431; Taipei City
revenues in, *433*, 433–434, *434*;
transparency for, 441–442;
urbanization projections in, *94*;
valuation in, 434–438; valuation
objections and appeals in, *51*. *See also*
China
Taiwan Pay, 438
tambon administrative organizations
(TAOs), Thailand, 447
tax bases: of building and land tax in
Thailand, 452–453; of fixed asset tax
in Japan, 241–244; of GRET in Korea,
280–282, *281*, *282*; Indonesia's
problems with narrow, 217–218; by
jurisdiction, *23–24*; of Land and
Building Tax Act in Thailand, 460; of

local development tax in Thailand,
454–455; of local property tax on land
and buildings in Korea, 272–274,
273–274; low-income jurisdictions
with narrow, 91; natural resource
property taxes in Indonesia and, 211;
of nonagricultural land use tax in
Vietnam, 479; property transfer taxes
in Indonesia and, 211; recurrent
property tax and, 20–26, *23–24*; of
recurrent property taxes in
Peninsular Malaysia, 305–306, *306*; in
Singapore, 402, *404*; for UIPT in
Punjab, Pakistan, 328, 330; urban and
rural property taxes in Indonesia and
coverage of, 209; Vietnam reform and
definition of, 496–498; wide, for
China, 132
tax deferrals, 28–29
tax delinquency. *See* arrears enforcement
and recovery
tax rates: in China, 132; differential
compared to single, 34; effective
compared to statutory, 31; Hong
Kong, concessions and, 145, 163, 165,
165, *167*, 168, 170, *170*; Hong Kong's
property, 142–156; income levels and,
12, *13*; India's structures of, 179; of
Indonesia's natural resource property
taxes, 211; of Japan's CPT, by
municipal population, 238, *240*; in
Khyber Pakhtunkhwa, Pakistan, 340;
Korea's GRET and, *281*, 281–282,
282; Korea's land and building
effective, 274, *274*; Korea's land and
building fixed, 273–274, *274*; in Kuala
Lumpur, Malaysia, 312, *312*; of Land
and Building Tax Act, Thailand, 462,
463; LGUs in Philippines imposing,
352; of nonagricultural land use tax in
Vietnam, 480–482, *481*; progressive,
33–34; rate capping and, 27–28; rate
capping in tax relief programs and,
27–28; in Singapore, 412–413, *413*;
split-rate tax and, 25, 425; statutory,
20, 21, 30–34, 66, 98–99; Taiwan's low
effective, 439; uniform, 32–33; of
urban and rural property taxes in
Indonesia, 208–209; in Vietnam,
500–501. *See also* statutory tax rates
tax reductions. *See* reductions
Tax Reform for Acceleration and
Inclusion (TRAIN) Law, Philippines,
378

Tax Reform Strategy 2011–2020, Vietnam, 474

tax relief programs: COVID-19 pandemic and, 30; exclusions, exemptions, and thresholds in, 26–27; government-owned property exemption and, 29; justifications for, 26; of LGUs in Philippines, 370; owner-occupied residential property preferential treatment and, 29–30; politics and, 26; rate capping, rebates, and discounts in, 27–28; for recurrent property taxes in Peninsular Malaysia, 306, 308, *308*; special cases of, 29–30; statutory tax rates and, 30; tax deferrals and amnesties in, 28–29; valuation and assessment adjustments in, 28

Tax Watch campaign, in Philippines, 390

tax yield, in Singapore, 413–415, *414*, *415*

taxable capacity, 12, 61, 315

taxable effort, property tax revenue and, 12

tax-sharing system, in China, 110–114, *112*, 125

technology: administration of property tax and, 95; automated mass valuation, 39–43, *41–42*, 131, 153–156, 220; compliance costs and, 57; for data, 48–49; digital property billing and, 419–420; e-PBT in Malaysia, 318; Malaysia's challenges adopting, 317–318; for property tax reform, 102–103. *See also* computer-assisted mass appraisal system; data; geographic information systems

tender fee, in Pakistan, *326*, 342

Thailand: arrears enforcement and recovery in, 59; automated mass valuation in, *42*; Budget Procedures Act of 1959 and 2018 in, 447; building and land tax in, before 2020, 449, 452–453, *456*; building and land tax in, repeal of, 460; capital value in, 460; COVID-19 deductions in, 449; COVID-19 pandemic impact in, 445; data management in, 48; decentralization in, 96, 446, 449; Decentralization Plan and Process Act of 1999 in, 449; equity and distribution of property tax burden in, 77; geography of, 445; government

structure and fiscal relations in, 446–449, *447*, *448*; intra-agency data sharing in, 47; Land and Building Tax Act in, 459–466, *463*; land policy and use in, *82*; local development tax in, before 2020, 453–455, *457*; local development tax in, repeal of, 460; local government revenues in, 449, *450*; National Decentralization Committee in, 446, 470n1; owner-occupied residential property preferential treatment in, 30; population density of, 445; property registration fees in, 468; property tax as percentage of GDP in, 7; property tax reform in, 469–470; property taxation before 2020 reform in, 449, 452–455, *456–458*; property taxation in 2020 in, 455, 459–464, *463*; property transfer taxes in, *65*, 66, 466–469, *467*; rate capping in, 27; recurrent property taxes and tax bases in, *24*; responsibility for valuation in, 52, *53*; revaluation frequency in, 43, *46*; revenue performance, before 2020, 455, *458*; self-assessment in, 54–55; specific business tax in, 468; stamp duty in, 469; surveyor fees in, 468; TAOs in, 447; urbanization and property tax revenue in, 13; urbanization projections in, *94*; vacant land determination in, 36; valuation objections and appeals in, *51*; value thresholds in, 27; withholding income tax on property transfers in, 468–469. *See also* Land and Building Tax Act

threshold value, in land value tax, 427

thresholds, in tax relief programs, 26–27

Tokyo Metropolitan Government (TMG), property and land taxes in, 252–256, *254*, *255*

Torrens system, 301

total property tax, 5, 12, *15*, 16

town fee, in Pakistan, *326*, 342

TRAIN (Tax Reform for Acceleration and Inclusion) Law, Philippines, 378

training, valuation, in Hong Kong, 143

transfer tax. *See* property transfer tax

transparency, for Taiwan, 441–442

Trinity Reform of 2004–2006, Japan, 228

turnover tax, in China, *134*

UIPT. *See* urban immovable property tax

unclaimed land, in Japan, 257–258

underdeclaration of sales prices, 46–47, 67, 213–214

underused land, recurrent property taxes and, 26, 34–36, *35*

uniform tax rate, 32–33

unit-area value system, 22, 178, 186–188

urban agriculture incentives, in Japan, 260

urban and rural property taxes, in Indonesia: administration of, 213, *213*; arrears enforcement and recovery in, *216*, 216–217, *217*; compliance costs for, 215; coverage of tax base in, 209; devolution of, 201, 205; in DKI Jakarta, 201, 206–207, *207*, 209–210; penalties and enforcement of, 214–215; reform options for, 219; revenues of, *202–204*, 205–207, *207*; tax rate schedule of, 208–209; valuation in, 209–210

urban and township land use tax, in China, 114, 116

urban immovable property tax (UIPT), in Pakistan, 321; exemptions in Sindh for, 336; legislation for, 325; overview of, *326*; as percentage of GDP, 325; Punjab tax base for, 328, 330; revenue totals by province of, 329, *329*, *330*, 335–336, 337, 338; Sindh tax base for, 335; valuation in Punjab, 328, 330, *331*, *332*; valuation of, 326–328

urban property, value-based systems for, 22

urbana tax, Philippines, 392

urbanization, xv; in Asia, 3; future projections of, 93, *94*; in India, *94*, 181–182, 196n7; in Pakistan, *94*, 324–325; property tax revenue and, 12–13, 17, 93; in Vietnam, *94*, 493

vacancy tax proposal, Hong Kong, 166, 168

vacant land and properties: effective tax rates on, 34–35; idle land tax in Philippines and, *358*, 361–362, 395n6; in Land and Building Tax Act of Thailand, 462–464; recurrent property taxes and, 26, 34–36, *35*; refunds, Hong Kong, 158. *See also* abandoned residences

valuation: agricultural land, in Japan, 245–246; annual rental value for, 22, 37, 178, 185–186; automated mass, 39–43, *41–42*, 153–156, 220; for basic real property tax in Philippines, *359*, 359–360, *360*; building, 22; building, in Taiwan, 437–438; case-by-case, 39; classification of properties for, 54; comparable sales approach for, 38; cost approach for, 38–39; current-use value for, 37; dwelling, in Japan, 247–248; fractional, 52, 54; GIS for, 437; of GRET in Korea, 283; gross annual rental, 326–327; Hong Kong methods of, 37–38, 146–147; improving, 100–101; income capitalization approach for, 39; indexation and, 44; India methods of, 22, 178; Indonesia upgrading, 220; in Indonesian natural resource property taxes, 211; in Indonesian urban and rural property taxes, 209–210; Indonesia's problems with, 218; in Japan, 242–244; in Khyber Pakhtunkhwa, Pakistan, 339; land, in Taiwan, 436–437; Land and Building Tax Act of Thailand shortcomings of, 465; in LGUs in Philippines, 367, 370–372, 388; of local property tax on land and buildings in Korea, 275–276, 277; market value for, 21, 37–39, 371–372, 417–418; methods of, 37–39; nonagricultural land use tax in Vietnam and, 479–480, 499; property data for, 44–49; of property transfer taxes, 67–68; ratable, in Hong Kong, 146; for recurrent property taxes in Peninsular Malaysia, 308–310; residential land, in Japan, 246–247, *247*; responsibility for, 50, 52, *53*; self-assessments and, 54–55, 439–440; in Singapore, 416–418; standards of good, 36–37; statutory tax rates separated from, 98–99; in Taiwan, 434–438; in tax relief programs, 28; training for, in Hong Kong, 143; of UIPT in Pakistan, 326–328; of UIPT in Punjab, Pakistan, 328, 330, *331*, *332*; underdeclaration of sales prices and, 46–47, 67; unit-area value system for, 22, 178, 186–188; Vietnam reform options for, 499–500. *See also* appeals; capital value; computer-assisted mass appraisal system; objections; revaluations valuation list, in Hong Kong, 148–149, *149*

value thresholds, in tax relief programs, 26–27

value zones, *22*

value-added tax, in Philippines, 364–365

value-based systems, area-based systems compared to, 20–22

Vickrey, William, 25

Vietnam: administration reform in, 502; agricultural land use tax in, 477–478; automated mass valuation in, *42*; billing in, 57; capital gains taxes in, 66, 70–71; collections reform in, 502; conditions and sequence for reform in, 503–504; control of property tax administration in, 56–57; decentralization in, 488, 494–495; Doi Moi program in, 472; economic growth in, 472; equity and distribution of property tax burden in, 77, 78; exemptions in, 27; exemptions reform in, 498–499; future reform for, 476; General Taxation Department in, 484, 502; GIS in, 103; government hierarchy in, 472; income tax in, 485; land and real estate taxes and charges in, 476–488; land policy and use in, 79, *82*; land price frame/table in, 480, 499–500; land rental fee in, 487; land use levy in, 486–487, 494; land use right transfer tax in, 484–485, *490*, 491; Law on Land in, 473, 476–477, 480, 484, 486–487, 499; Law on State Budget in, 488–489, 494; nested budget system in, 504*n*2; nonagricultural land use tax in, 25, 58, 478–484, *481*, *482*, 495; one-time-event revenue in, 489, *490*, 491; owner-occupied residential property preferential treatment in, 29; payment options in, 58; payment upon purchase of state-owned housing in, 487–488; politics in, 503; progressive tax rate structures in, 33; property tax as percentage of GDP in, 7; property tax reform in, 97, 473–476, 492–504; property transfer taxes in, *65*, 66; rebates in, 28; recurrent property taxes in, *24*, *490*, 491–492; recurrent property taxes in, reform of, 492–493; reform proposals in, 495–496; registration charge in, 485–486; responsibility for valuation in, *53*; revaluation frequency in, *46*; revenue analysis in, *488*, 488–492, *490*; revenue mobilization and mix in, reform impact on, 474, *475*, 476, 493–494; split-rate tax in, 25; tax bases in, *24*; tax bases in, reform and definition of, 496–498; tax rate structure in, 500–501; Tax Reform Strategy 2011–2020 in, 474; transitional period in, 103; urbanization projections in, *94*, 493; valuation objections and appeals in, 50, *51*; valuation reform options in, 499–500. *See also* nonagricultural land use tax, Vietnam

voluntary compliance, improving, 101

WACC (Weighted Average Cost of Capital), 147

wealth tax, recurrent property taxes as, 25

WEF (World Economic Forum), 399

Weighted Average Cost of Capital (WACC), 147

withholding tax: in Pakistan, *326*, 342; Philippines and creditable, 365; in Thailand, 468–469

World Bank, xviii, 13, 173–174, 194; "Doing Business, 2020," 400; on Pakistan's FBR, 323–324

WoRLD (World Revenue Longitudinal Data) dataset, 8, 9, *10*

World Economic Forum (WEF), 399

World Revenue Longitudinal Data (WoRLD) dataset, 8, 9, *10*

Xiao Jie, 129

Zanzibar, 95

zonal revaluations, in Philippines, 376, 378

About the Lincoln Institute of Land Policy

The Lincoln Institute of Land Policy seeks to improve quality of life through the effective use, taxation, and stewardship of land. A nonprofit, private operating foundation whose origins date to 1946, the Lincoln Institute researches and recommends creative approaches to land as a solution to economic, social, and environmental challenges. Through education, training, publications, and events, we integrate theory and practice to inform public policy decisions worldwide. With locations in Cambridge, Massachusetts, Washington, DC, Phoenix, and Beijing, we organize our work around the achievement of six goals: low-carbon, climate-resilient communities and regions, efficient and equitable tax systems, reduced poverty and spatial inequality, fiscally healthy communities and regions, sustainably managed land and water resources, and functional land markets and reduced informality.

113 Brattle Street
Cambridge, MA 02138-3400 USA
P 1.617.661.3016   1.800.526.3873
F 1.617.661.7235   1.800.526.3944
help@lincolnist.edu
lincolninst.edu